# Habits and Holiness

THOMISTIC RESSOURCEMENT SERIES

Volume 16

# Habits and Holiness

*Ethics, Theology, and Biopsychology*

EZRA SULLIVAN, OP

FOREWORD BY WOJCIECH GIERTYCH, OP

The Catholic University of America Press
*Washington, D.C.*

The paper used in this publication meets the minimum requirements of American National Standards for Information Science—Permanence of Paper for Printed Library Materials, ANSI Z39.48-1984.
∞

Library of Congress Cataloging-in-Publication Data
Names: Sullivan, Ezra, author. | Giertych, Wojciech, 1951– writer of foreword.
Title: Habits and holiness : ethics, theology, and biopsychology / Ezra Sullivan ; foreword by Wojciech Giertych.
Description: Washington, D.C. : The Catholic University of America Press, [2021] | Series: Thomistic ressourcement series; volume 16 | Includes bibliographical references and indexes.
Identifiers: LCCN 2020054776 | ISBN 9780813233291 (paperback) |
Subjects: LCSH: Thomas, Aquinas, Saint, 1225?–1274. | Habit. | Habit (Philosophy) | Will—Religious aspects—Catholic Church. | Psychology—Religious aspects—Catholic Church. | Theological anthropology—Christianity. | Christian ethics. | Psychobiology.
Classification: LCC B765.T54 S798 2021 | DDC 241—dc23
LC record available at https://lccn.loc.gov/2020054776

*Imprimi Potest*:
Very Rev. Ken Letoile, OP
Prior Provincial, Province of St. Joseph

*Nihil Obstat*:
Rev. Basil Cole, OP
Censor Deputatus

*Imprimatur:*
Rev. Daniel B. Carson
Vicar General and Moderator of the Curia

Archdiocese of Washington

January 6, 2020

This work is dedicated to Our Lady, Seat of Wisdom,

offered to her through the hands of Saint Joseph, Saint Dominic,

and Saint Thomas Aquinas,

Doctor Humanitatis

# Contents

## PART 2. HUMAN, INHUMAN, AND DIVINE HABITS



## PART 3. HACKING YOUR HABITS

# Figures and Tables

## FIGURES



## TABLES

# Foreword

*Wojciech Giertych, OP*

The term *habitus* appeared in Aquinas's moral theology as he tried to grasp the workings of grace in the sanctified acting person. The Catholic view, as distinct from the Protestant view, believes that grace really changes the Christian, introducing a fundamental supernatural novelty that is not merely external. We can speak of being in the state of grace, or of not being in it and thus being in the state of mortal sin, because a new divine capacity has been introduced as a result of the gift of grace both in the essential core of the individual and in the operative faculties. Theology has developed various terms that try to articulate this supernatural reality. We speak of justification, deification, the elevation of the soul, transformation, the consequences of Christ's redemption of humanity, charity infused in the soul, participation in the divine life, and the restoration of the divine image in the human person. All these expressions have a rich biblical and theological tradition behind them as they strive to grasp and articulate the fruits of baptism. In his speculative moral theology, Aquinas has opted for one such formula. He focuses on the Aristotelian concept of *hexis,* translated as *habitus* in Latin, so as to describe precisely the new change in man, conducted by grace. The term, deriving from the Latin *se habere,* the having or holding

The author is theologian of the papal household.

of oneself in a specific way that expresses a new psychic reality that manifests personal maturity in which there is a permanent (but not mechanical), creative, well-chosen direction of self in a given way, and so also and above all, in the way that results from the promptings of the Spirit of God.

The translation of the term *habitus* into modern languages comes with difficulty. The proposition that immediately comes to mind and is often currently used, including in this book, *viz.*, "habit" or the French *habitude,* initially suggests a mechanical routine, a customary, automatic way of doing things. Tied with this reading is the application of the term to the clothing worn by religious, which is permanent and leaves no place for the creativity of fashion. This rendering runs contrary to the basic intent of Aquinas, who used the word *habitus* as a generic term that covers virtues, vices, intellectual qualities, and the gifts of the Holy Spirit, all of which by no means express a mechanical routine. In fact they are permanent qualities that incite creative particular action, harnessing various spiritual, psychic, and bodily forces, and engaging them in an inventive way toward such action that can be enticing and joyful in its speedy spontaneity, facility, originality, and moral value, so that people seeing such novel and surprising good actions are inclined to praise not just those who elicit them, but above all the Father in heaven, who in any given moment is working through these virtuous individuals (Mt 5:16).

Likewise it should be noted that the coordination of psychic forces for an evil intent is often also creative. The difference between the one who is truly vicious as distinct from the one who sins out of weakness lies precisely in this capacity for holding oneself in a given way in view of the freely chosen evil intent. It is for this reason that we can enjoy a film about a bank robber. We may not approve of his immoral action, but we may be captivated by his talent, ingeniousness, ability to plan and execute the complicated theft, and also his capacity to creatively change such plans as unpredicted circumstances appear. There is a psychic richness in the one who sins out of conscious malice and it distinguishes such an individual from a lazy weakling, who never bothers to do anything either good or bad. True personalism entails the full creative engaging of the spiritual and psychic powers and it contributes to the development of personal liberty. When a truly vicious person converts, he becomes a great saint!

The *habitus* as a worked-out permanent psychic disposition may be natural, as in an acquired quality, virtue, or vice, and it may be supernatural, as in an infused virtue (whether theological or moral) and as a Gift of the Holy Spirit. As such, some *habits* are subject to empirical observation and study and others are known only within faith, but even their effects may be seen, and furthermore they can be the object of speculative study and precise articulation.

Fr. Ezra Sullivan, OP, has engaged in extensive research to perceive the workings of the *habitus* in the psyche and soul. He not only presents the teaching of Aquinas on the *habitus*, but also correlates this with contemporary neuroscience and biological psychology. This book is an example of the value of a theologically-inspired metaphysical synthesis for modern empirical science. Numerous schools attempting to work out a scientific synthesis often vary among themselves not only as a result of a differing focus on particular empirical phenomena, but also due to divergent organizing theories and even more, at times, due to the lack of carefully thought-out categories. When underlying principles of thought and rationally known truths about the corporeal and spiritual structure of being are totally ignored or accepted only superficially, the end result, even though enriched by multiple empirical data, turns out to be imprecise, vaguely articulated, and even self-contradictory.

The sciences that study man in all his dimensions and actions can profit from the clarity of a well-considered philosophical anthropology. Furthermore, such rational reflection on man can gain enormously from the theological truth about the glorified humanity of Jesus Christ, the only really well-functioning human individual. A clear understanding of Christ's untarnished humanity (united with his divinity), capable of a free gift of self given by his human will in charity, can serve as a rule of thumb for the understanding of man. Thus, speculative theology may courageously offer a clarifying and organizing background for the empirical sciences that study man and they in turn do not need to be ashamed of the fact that they find this useful. Clear theological thought not only about Jesus Christ, but also about moral agency, good habits, and holiness, helps to differentiate between the good and the evil, the sick and the healthy, the free and the unfree addicted or perplexed individual. The human sciences ought not to transfer blindly conclusions about the sick onto the healthy or about animals onto humans. They should understand the truly human, and then they can help those whose humanity in some way is paralyzed.

In this book, Fr. Sullivan grants us with great erudition an overview of the empirical scientific studies of habits, presenting the achievements of neuroscience and its complementary experimental psychology. He shows that such empirical research, while it advances particular knowledge, is limited in its cognitive approach and so it may be invited to expand its viewpoint by turning toward philosophy and theology. He therefore looks into themes that traditionally had been restricted to the field of speculative philosophy and ethics. He studies nonvoluntary and imperfectly voluntary habits in animals, children, and adults. He discusses fully voluntary acquired habits, the natural moral virtues, and dysfunctions and vices. Finally he discusses infused habits, known only in faith, the infused theological and moral virtues, and the Gifts of the Holy Spirit, concluding with a reflection on their practical functioning and development in the spiritual and moral life.

In his conclusion, Fr. Sullivan notes that humans possess a variety of natural instincts and dispositions that are the fruit of the physical and psychic makeup, culture, and experience of the individual. They all influence the mind and the will. Amongst these there are also the consequences of original sin, individual sins, social sins, and compulsive addictions, as well as the positive influences of a virtuous environment in childhood. He observes that often the interpretation of all that is presented by empirical psychology is really philosophy in disguise, offering incomplete, provisional, and inconsistent conclusions. Nevertheless, the relevant results of authentic *a posteriori* research that studies the neurobiological, psychic, and cultural factors that have an impact on moral agency need to be respected and integrated within a comprehensive articulation of the mystery of the acting person. He notes also that engaging a Thomistic theory of action and virtue with empirical research contributes to the refining, corroboration, and even correction of some of Aquinas's positions. All this is an issue that is not only internal to theological reflection as it tries to spell out the consequences of the redemption. This is so because, for example, neuroscience is increasingly being used in contemporary courts so as to prove the innocence or moral culpability that can be justly imputed to a malefactor. The impact of this study is therefore important for numerous sciences that study man, including pedagogics, psychology, law, history, sociology, and economics. And of course this is relevant for ethics and for moral theology as it focuses on the fecundity of grace within action. All of these sciences can profit from such intellectual engagement of philosophical and theological anthropology with their empirical observations.

# Preface

Habit is what makes a human into a saint or a sinner. Just as the body can become stronger through exercise and effort, or weaker through wounds or neglect, so the entire person can acquire a more or less permanent state of goodness or evil through habituation to virtue or vice. As a man, Jesus of Nazareth grew in actual virtue: he "increased in wisdom and in stature, and in favor with God and man."[1] In contrast, Judas grew in vice. He was not wracked with evil in the beginning; it was only through a series of voluntary actions that he eventually "became a traitor."[2] With respect to their souls, Jesus and Judas differed radically differed in the choices they made and the habits they possessed.

Habits also exist on a more mundane level. Research suggests that at least one-third of daily behaviors are caused by habits—including working, social interactions, travel, and relaxation.[3] We commonly say things such as, "I have a bad habit of biting my nails," or we might wonder, "How can I improve my study habits?" Habits are present throughout human life, from the seemingly inconsequential moments to their eternally significant effects.

To show the height, depth, length, and breadth of habits, I will

1. Lk 2:52.

2. Lk 6:16.

3. Wendy Wood, Jeffrey M. Quinn, and Deborah A. Kashy, "Habits in Everyday Life: Thought, Emotion, and Action," *Journal of Personality and Social Psychology* 83, no. 6 (December 2002): 1281–97, at 1286.

work to synthesize the conclusions of biology, philosophy, and theology regarding human habits. Some authors have considered habit primarily from a behaviorist perspective or in terms of neuropsychology or, more rarely, with only philosophy or theology in mind. This text tries to take account of all these perspectives. If this text is riddled with generalities that disappoint readers who prefer technicalities, and if it gives rise to corrections and disputes, the resulting fray will serve to highlight the importance of the material even if it manifests the inadequacy of the author.

## A THOMISTIC PERSPECTIVE ON HABITS

For centuries, St. Thomas Aquinas has been known as "The Angelic Doctor" and "The Common Doctor," indicating respectively the purity and scope his teaching. To these titles, Pope St. John Paul II added another: "Doctor *Humanitatis*," the teacher of humanity. In light of both faith and reason Aquinas teaches human beings the world over, he teaches us *about* human beings, and he teaches us about *being human.*[4] Such teaching is manifested particularly in Aquinas's explanation of human habits, which are intertwined with nearly every part of human life. Following Aristotle, Thomas notes that "habit" in its most general sense indicates "a disposition whereby that which is disposed is disposed well or ill, and either in regard to itself or in regard to another, just as health is a sort of habit."[5] One can speak of habit in many different but analogous ways.[6] This book analyzes the various kinds of human habit as differentiated in relation to the ac-

4. John Paul II, "Inter Munera Academiarum," Apostolic Letter, January 28, 1999, par. 4; available at www.vatican.va. See *Thomas Aquinas: Teacher of Humanity*, ed. John P. Hittinger and Daniel C. Wagner (Newcastle Upon Tyne: Cambridge Scholars Publishing, 2015).

5. *Summa Theologiae* [hereafter *ST*] I-II, q. 49, a. 1; I consulted the English translation, *Summa Theologica*, trans. Fathers of the English Dominican Province (New York: Benziger, 1947). See Aristotle, *Metaphysics* V.20, 1022b10.

6. See Thomas Taylor, *Works of Aristotle Translated from the Greek with Copious Elucidations from the Best of His Greek Commentators* (London: Robert Wilkes, 1812), 1:115–16n9.

tivity of the human will. There are habit-like dispositions of the body (e.g., health); nonvolitional dispositions or habits of emotion (e.g., a tendency toward anger); humanly-volitional habits of character that are acquired virtues or vices (e.g., courage or cowardliness); and supernaturally-volitional habits of the soul that are directly infused by God (e.g., faith).

In this study, I mean to be faithful to the insights and procedure of St. Thomas Aquinas; I consider dispositions and habits from a Thomistic perspective. But this book is more than a mere repetition, explanation, and defense of his thought. In visual representation, a linear perspective provides a viewer with a particular point of view that organizes objects within a picture. For example, from the perspective of a person looking down the center of a railway line, the parallel tracks seem to meet at a distant vanishing point; everything else within that frame can be scaled in reference to those tracks. Within the realm of thought, a theory-perspective considers objects from a particular conceptual point-of-view. This point-of-view organizes the materials under consideration and provides a structure and reference point for understanding everything else. A feminist perspective, for example, might see matters primarily in light of how they relate to women's concerns. This book takes a Thomistic perspective: the philosophical and theological insights of St. Thomas Aquinas serve to unify, order, and clarify the disparate elements of various research on habits. The Thomistic perspective reveals the *unity* underlying various considerations of habit by showing the unity of truth found within them—without pretending that Thomas had articulated every insight possible to man and that later thinkers merely confirm his genius. The Thomistic perspective provides *order,* for its moderate-realist philosophical theology serves as a framework within which to locate and interpret the diverse facts and concepts under consideration. It provides *clarity* as a systematic synthesis of the various understandings of habit, because it discusses points of convergence, divergence, and areas of mutual enrichment. In sum, by situating this study of habits within Thomas's framework of moral theology, I mean to discuss the principles and practices by which we can gain good habits and divest ourselves of bad ones, so as to prepare for eternal life.

Aquinas holds that theology is a science that can incorporate insights from other sciences. As an analogous concept with different levels of meaning, the topic of habit provides a fruitful locus for bringing together and integrating the insights of various sciences in light of theology. This project will be undertaken in light of John Paul II's invitation to Christian thinkers to demonstrate the "close relationship of continuity between contemporary philosophy and the philosophy developed in the Christian tradition."[7] A demonstration of continuity is possible in the realm of philosophy but is more fully realized through the insights of theology, for as the Pope said, "The word of God reveals the final destiny of men and women and provides a unifying explanation of all that they do in the world."[8] Hence, a theological account of the analogous concept of habit can be a source of unity for other sciences. In attempting to harmonize various voices, however, theologians must beware of the danger of eclecticism. John Paul II's warning on this point is germane. *Eclecticism* is the tendency to employ individual ideas from various sources indiscriminately, "without concern for their internal coherence, their place within a system or their historical context."[9] Such a shallow appropriation of facts and concepts risks not penetrating the depth of the material, easily adopting hidden errors, and using elements that are unessential to the task at hand. To avoid this tendency, this book will pay attention to the context and sources of its materials and apply a philosophical analysis to them where appropriate, while respecting the sphere of expertise proper to each field of study.

7. John Paul II, *Fides et Ratio*, Encyclical Letter, September 14, 1988, par. 86; available at www.vatican.va.

8. Ibid., par. 81.

9. Ibid., par. 86.

## STRUCTURE OF THIS BOOK

In order to be coherent, the organization of a thing must be derived from a clear principle that is consistently applied. This book is organized by the distinction among types of habits. There are, of course, a number of different ways to differentiate among the habits. For example, habits can be distinguished according to faculties or powers they qualify. In this case, one would speak of distinct habits of the intellect, memory, will, and so on. Then one would also speak of habits or dispositions among the various parts of the human being, subdividing when necessary. Thus, one would study habits of the nervous system, habits of the brain and parts of the brain, etc. This sort of order is inefficient, though, because it does not differentiate with strict dichotomies: habits divided in this way would overlap categories. Habits of the prefrontal cortex, for instance, involve habits of decisionmaking as well as language and executive function. Again, habits of the will at times engage habits of the memory and imagination. To avoid countless subdivisions among faculties and parts of a human being, and habits they may develop, I do not adopt this approach. Instead, I take a cue directly from Thomas Aquinas, who says that human habits are those which are characteristically perfective of the intellect and will.[10]

I begin with an introduction discussing why habits are necessary for understanding human behavior and for living well, then I consider what I call "subterranean" habits, beneath the level of voluntariness, such as structural dispositions from human nature (chapter 1) as well as individual genes and instinct (chapter 2). After this, I address the issue of habits acquired nonvoluntarily through experience, especially in infancy and childhood, and how they relate to attention and memory (chapter 3). The next chapter discusses the nature of human freedom, especially as it relates to habituation in intentionality and self-determination (chapter 4). The next chapter

10. *ST* I-II, q. 50, a. 5.

treats positive habits acquired by choice, including natural virtues, and how they relate to human flourishing (chapter 5). After this, I delve deeply into negative habits, whether derived from biology, experience, or choice (chapter 6). Then I discuss why grace is necessary for fully human, fully upright habits, especially as seen in light of the various grades of virtue (chapter 7). With grace in mind, I then discuss the infused theological virtues and the Gifts of the Holy Spirit (chapter 8). The final chapters are more practical, outlining how we acquire or eliminate habits (chapter 9), then the foundational habits that form us for life, including the theological virtues, graced merit, and friendship (chapter 10).

For each topic and subtopic considered, I will present Aquinas's philosophical-theological position as well as a representative position offered by neuroscience or biological psychology when possible. The methods and particular data of the various sciences necessitate that earlier parts of this book rely more heavily on the empirical sciences while later parts rely more on the theology of St. Thomas Aquinas. The entire book is leavened with the mutual enrichment of the sciences, helping us see what Aquinas's philosophical-theological account of habit can appropriate from the empirical sciences, and what the empirical sciences may learn from Aquinas.

## *APOLOGIA* FOR PRACTICALITY

Before concluding this preface, I would like to respond to the objection that including practical information seems unscholarly; perhaps un-Thomistic. By his own admission in the *Summa Theologiae*, Thomas is primarily concerned with speculative thought and only secondarily with practical things insofar as they are ordered to God.[11] He acknowledges that, in contrast to what one might call historical or dogmatic theology, "moral science" ought to be more practical, for "the end of this science is not knowledge alone," which

11. See *ST* I, q. 1, a. 4.

can be possessed even by those enslaved by their passions.[12] Rather, the end of moral science is upright human action, so that people follow reason and refrain from acting in accord with disordered passions.[13] Nevertheless, Aquinas discusses what moral action is more than he discusses how to be moral. In the view of Jacques Maritain, Aquinas's treatment of moral affairs—which includes habits—is what one could call "speculatively practical."[14] That is to say, when Aquinas treats human behavior, he does so within a context of a theological approach which, properly speaking, is scientific and therefore treats of matters which are most universal, certain, and explanatory according to causes. In contrast, "practically practical" treatments of human action descend more into particulars and immediately regulate action by offering advice regarding what should be done or avoided.[15] However, such a practically practical approach cannot be scientific precisely because it concerns practical objects in their singularity. The concern of practicality is not to resolve an issue in terms of its principles and reasons, but rather to offer advice to help others prepare for action.[16] J.-P. Torrell affirms that Aquinas rarely offers teaching that is *practically practical.*[17] The great saint was more focused on the eternal and unchangeable truths than on their temporal and contingent applications. Such was the case *even* when Aquinas wrote philosophical ethics or moral

12. *Sententia libri Ethicorum* [hereafter *Sent. Ethic.*], lib. 1, l. 3, n. 40, taken from the *Opera omnia, iussu Leonis XIII P. M. edita* (Rome: Commissio Leonina, 1882–) [hereafter Leon. ed.]. I consulted the English translation, *Commentary on the Nicomachean Ethics,* trans. C. I. Litzinger (Chicago: Henry Regnery, 1964).

13. Ibid., n. 39. See also his discussion of the difference between speculative and practical sciences, the latter of which are for the sake of some work to be done: *Sentencia libri De anima* [hereafter *Sent. de anima*], lib. 1, l. 1, n. 3. I consulted the English translation, *The Soul,* trans. John Patrick Rowan (St. Louis, Mo.: Herder, 1949).

14. Jacques Maritain, *Distinguish to Unite or The Degrees of Knowledge,* trans. Gerald B. Phelan (New York: Charles Scribner's Sons, 1959), 314.

15. Ibid.

16. Ibid., 315.

17. Jean-Pierre Torrell, *Saint Thomas Aquinas,* vol. 2: *Spiritual Master,* trans. Robert Royal (Washington, D.C.: The Catholic University of America Press, 2003), 20.

theology. Nevertheless, he offers us clues as to why a study of habits deserves a treatment that is theoretical and practical.

The "science of the soul," as described by Aristotle in his *De anima*, is among the most useful of subjects to study, Aquinas notes.[18] The theology of habits is, in a way, even more useful. Following the Thomistic commentatorial tradition of Bañez, John of St. Thomas, and Santiago Ramirez, William Wallace explains that moral theology is more helpful, more practical, than moral philosophy and ethics. The reason for this is that theology in this life is derived from the habit of faith which puts us into contact with the truth about living God. The infused virtues incline us to seek and to do the good more effectively than any truth knowable to reason alone.[19] The truths proposed by moral theology are in themselves "more proportioned to move the will towards God, to incite the divine love of charity," which, as we have seen, is decisive for everlasting blessedness.[20] Hence, Wallace states, moral theology can rightly be called the *scientia caritatis* (science of charity).[21] We can develop his insight with the following observations about the study of the greatest habit, namely, charity. The material that moral theology studies is that which *leads to* the act of charity, which in turn further propels a theologian to study; the chief *subject matter* of moral theology is charity, because morality primarily concerns right living, for which virtues are necessary, and charity is the virtue which commands, orders, and vivifies the other virtues; finally, charity and concomitant wisdom are the *goals* of moral theology, for the greatest success of moral theology is that its students and professors contemplate the eternal good and live charity more intensely, in harmony with the other virtues. Put briefly, charity may be understood in some way as the

18. See Aristotle, *De Anima* I.1, 402a5–6: "The knowledge of the soul admittedly contributes greatly to the advance of truth in general, and, above all, to our understanding of Nature." Aquinas, *Sent. de anima*, lib. 1, l. 1, n. 7, explains that metaphysics, philosophical ethics, and even natural science all depend on a knowledge of the soul.

19. Wallace, *The Role of Demonstration in Moral Theology*, 194.

20. Ibid.

21. Ibid.

efficient, formal, and final cause of moral theology. It follows that, while explanations of the nature of various dispositions and habits are worth exploring, what is most useful is an explanation of how to develop faith and the divine love that is charity. Therefore, I also treat practical matters regarding how to acquire and develop habits, with a focus on the habits that matter most.

My hope is that readers will find this book useful for better understanding the theory of habits—the empirical psychology, philosophy, and theology that undergirds what habits are, what purpose they serve, and how they affect our lives—and that readers will be better equipped to develop good habits and escape being trapped by undesirable ones.

# Acknowledgments

Many people have given me much help and support in the genesis of this work; it is a joy to thank them here. Among those who made this work possible were my priors provincial, Frs. Brian Mulcahy, OP, and Ken Letoile, OP, who encouraged my pursuance of studies; my then-regent of studies, John Langlois, for his unfailing support; the priors and Dominican communities of St. Gertrude's, Ohio; San Clemente, Rome; the Angelicum, Rome; Oxford, England; and the Dominican House of Studies in Washington, D.C. Of continual help were staff members at the Angelicum library; Fr. John Martin Ruiz, OP, at the library of Pontifical Faculty of the Immaculate Conception in Washington, D.C.; and Helen Wilton at the Bodleian library in Oxford.

Of particular support were my family, especially my father; and my friends, most notably the Dell'Aira, Gaudinski, Murdock, Ryan, Schindler, and Sheaf families; the Carmelite Monastery of Georgetown, California; and many other helpers and intercessors. John Murdock's friendship in particular has sustained, challenged, and guided me. Special thanks are due to John Martino and Paul Higgins at the Catholic University of America Press and two anonymous readers who helped to improve the text in significant ways. Among those who helped shape the thoughts and content which gave rise to this book, I am particularly indebted to the Most Reverend Augustine DiNoia, OP, especially in getting me started in the right direction; Fr. Nicholas Austin, SJ, for sharing his dissertation; Fr. Nicanor Austriaco, OP, for his invaluable suggestions regarding the approach of this study; Msgr. John Cihak, for his fraternal conversation and editing help; Fr. Basil Cole, OP, for spiritual and brotherly accompaniment, and for offering comments on the whole manuscript; Daniel De Haan, for his friendship and help regarding neuroscientific research; Nicholas Kahm, whose suggestion about a book led to this entire research project; Kenneth W. Kemp, for sharing a crucial portion of his dissertation; Matthew Levering, for his insights and encouragement; Andrew Mullins, for our invaluable conversation and for sharing his research on the neuroscience of virtue; Ivan Colagè and Fr. Lluis Oviedo, OFM, for inviting me to join their Templeton seminars at Antonianum University; Fr. Michael Sherwin, OP, for conversations that proved crucial to my studies; Msgr. Tomas Trafny, for our helpful conversations and the STOQ resources; and Karl Zilles (1944–2020), for showing a neophyte the ropes of neuroscience. Sr. Christine Gautier, OP, provided generous and friendly assistance. Finally, I cannot thank enough Fr. Wojciech Giertych, OP, the papal theologian, for his guidance, good humor and hospitality, and our absorbing conversations.

You are all in my prayers. May the good Lord bless all of you abundantly, now and forever.

# Abbreviations

## TEXTS BY AQUINAS

| | |
|---|---|
| *Compendium theologiae* | *Compendium theologiae ad fratrem Raynaldum* |
| *De decem praeceptis* | *Collationes in decem praeceptis* |
| *De malo* | *Quaestiones disputate de malo* |
| *De motu cordis* | *De motu cordis ad magistrum Philippum de Castro Caeli* |
| *De perfectione* | *De perfectione spiritualis vitae* |
| *De potentia* | *Quaestiones disputate de potentia* |
| *De sortibus* | *Liber de sortibus ad dominum Iacobum de Tonengo* |
| *De veritate* | *Quaestiones disputate de veritate* |
| *De virtutibus* | *Quaestiones disputate de virtutibus* |
| *In De divinis nominibus* | *In librum Beati Dionysii De divinis nominibus expositio* |
| *In Physic.* | *Commentaria in octo libros Physicorum Aristotelis* |
| *In Symbolum Apostolorum* | *In Symbolum Apostolorum, scilicet "Credo in Deum" expositio* |
| *Quodlibet* | *Quaestiones de quolibet* |
| *SCG* | *Summa contra Gentiles* |
| *Sent. De anima* | *Sentencia libri De anima* |
| *Sent. De sensu* | *Sentencia De sensu* |

| | |
|---|---|
| *Sent. Ethic.* | *Sententia libri Ethicorum* |
| *Sent. Meta.* | *In duodecim libros Metaphysicorum Aristotelis expositio* |
| *ST* | *Summa Theologiae* |
| *Super Col.* | *Super Epistolam ad Colossenses lectura* |
| *Super De Trinitate* | *Super Boetium De Trinitate* |
| *Super Eph.* | *Super Epistolam ad Ephesios lectura* |
| *Super Gal.* | *Super Epistolam ad Galatas lectura* |
| *Super Heb.* | *Super Epistolam ad Hebraeos lectura* |
| *Super I, II Cor.* | *Super primam, secundam Epistolam ad Corinthios lectura* |
| *Super Io.* | *Super Evangelium S. Ioannis lectura* |
| *Super Iob* | *Expositio super Iob ad litteram* |
| *Super Is.* | *Expositio super Isaiam ad litteram* |
| *Super Philip.* | *Super Epistolam ad Philipenses lectura* |
| *Super Psalmo* | *In psalmos Davidis expositio* |
| *Super Mt.* | *Super Evangelium S. Matthaei lectura* |
| *Super Rom.* | *Super Epistolam ad Romanos lectura* |
| *Super Sent.* | *Scriptum super libros Sententiarum magistri Petri Lombardi* |

## OTHER ABBREVIATIONS

| | |
|---|---|
| *DSM-5* | *Diagnostic and Statistical Manual of Mental Disorders*, 5th ed. (APA) |
| PL | Patrologia Latina (ed. Migne) |

# Habits and Holiness

INTRODUCTION

# Are Habits Necessary?

In reviewing his life's work as a moral theologian, Stanley Hauerwas lamented his "failure to develop the significance of habit for any account of the virtues."[1] He is not alone in this respect. Throughout the centuries, scholars of ethics and moral theology, and many scientists, have typically discounted the role habits have in human life and morality. Relatively few come to see, as Hauerwas did, that "an account of habit ... is necessary for an adequate account of the virtues."[2]

More and more people, however, are rediscovering the importance of habit, including empirical psychologists, the close followers of Aristotle and Aquinas, and the contemporary reading public.[3] Unlike others who looked to Aristotle primarily for metaphysical insights, or who did not look to Aristotle at all, Aquinas successfully incorporated Aristotle's insights about habits into a larger theological vision of the moral world. Even Aquinas's understanding came rela-

1. Stanley Hauerwas, "Habit Matters: The Bodily Character of the Virtues," in *Habits in Mind: Integrating Theology, Philosophy, and the Cognitive Science of Virtue, Emotion, and Character Formation*, ed. Gregory R. Peterson et al. (Leiden: Brill, 2017), 24–40, at 25.

2. Ibid., 26.

3. See Tom Sparrow and Adam Hutchinson (eds.), *A History of Habit: From Aristotle to Bourdieu* (New York: Lexington Books, 2013); Nicholas Faucher and Magali Roques (eds.), *The Ontology, Psychology, and Axiology of Habits* (Habitus) *in Medieval Philosophy* (New York: Springer, 2018); Bas Verplanken (ed.), *The Psychology of Habit: Theory, Mechanisms, Change, and Contexts* (New York: Springer, 2018).

tively late: only his *Summa Theologiae* treats habits in a thorough and systematic way. There, Aquinas shows that human *habitus* is an essential principle of human action, a part of an action-disposition spiral: it is the result of acts and it is an inclination toward further acts of the same sort. As for the general reader, the importance of habits has been vindicated by the widespread interest in books such as Charles Duhigg's *The Power of Habit* and James Clear's *Atomic Habits*.[4]

This introduction will first discuss the importance of biology and empirical science to the study of habit. Next, I address whether the study of habit is primarily a philosophical concern. After that, Aquinas's theology of habit will be contextualized within his larger project of the *Summa Theologiae*. Finally, I raise a serious concern of Servais Pinckaers regarding the nature of habit and *habitus*, and I resolve the issue by providing a definition and explanation of terms. In doing so, I summarize some of the most important findings of this book as a whole. Ultimately, I mean to show that habits, including some elements of automaticity, are natural and necessary for our perfection. Indeed, through the grace of Christ, infused into us as a habit along with virtues and the Gifts of the Holy Spirit, we can overcome our bad habits and develop good ones through effortful exercise that give us the glorious liberty of an adopted child of God.[5]

## BIOLOGY AND THE SCIENCE(S) OF HABIT

As a Catholic priest, my primary interest in writing is to give glory to God and to help souls reach heaven. This book is ultimately theological, and the thought of St. Thomas Aquinas undergirds every paragraph of this book. However, my approach begins with three principles.[6] First, we can never fully understand dispositions

4. Charles Duhigg, *The Power of Habit: Why We Do What We Do and How to Change* (London: Random House, 2012). James Clear, *Atomic Habits: An Easy and Proven Way to Build Good Habits and Break Bad Ones* (New York: Avery, 2018).

5. See Rom 8:21.

6. I was inspired by Robert Sapolsky, *Behave: The Biology of Humans at Our Best and Worst* (London: The Bodley Head, 2017), 4–5.

and habits if we do not understand their biological and psychological aspects.[7] People primarily interested in the "holiness" aspect of habit-making may think that accounts drawn from empirical science are extraneous to the real work of becoming saints. Too often, such approaches of "spirituality" forget that saints are humans, not angels. Properly speaking, we are not *incarnate spirits*, as if we are some species of angel, a sort of cherub who dons robes of flesh in contrast to the more spiritual members of the celestial hierarchy. Humans are *rational animals*: we are a species of ape—with tired bodies, complicated guts, ranging emotions, and loads of dispositions that shape our natural ability to think and deliberately love, and purposively to shape ourselves through chosen habits.[8] Our physicality is not something optional for us; it is part of who we are. To know ourselves, and our dispositions and habits, recourse to biology and psychology is immensely useful.[9] Second, and perhaps

7. Here I do not mean to enter into the debate as to whether studies of physics (and physical sciences) necessarily precede the study of metaphysics (and theology). On one side, Etienne Gilson, Jacques Maritain, and especially Lawrence Dewan, though disagreeing with each other about many points, seemed to agree that physics does not precede metaphysics in the order of knowledge. See, for example, Dewan, "St. Thomas, Physics, and the Principle of Metaphysics," *The Thomist* 61, no. 4 (1997): 549–66. On the other side, the River Forest school includes James Weisheipl, William A. Wallace, and Benedict Ashley, the latter of whom summarizes the debate in "The River Forest School and the Philosophy of Nature Today," in *Philosophy and the God of Abraham: Essays in Memory of James A. Weisheipl, OP*, ed. R. James Long (Toronto: PIMS, 1991), 1–15. Ashley responded to opponents to the River Forest school in *The Way Toward Wisdom* (Notre Dame, Ind.: University of Notre Dame Press, 2006), 146–63. My claim is more modest than either camp, for I am emphasizing the importance of biology for an understanding of habits and dispositions, which even at the most spiritual levels are related to biological realities.

8. See Aristotle, *Nicomachean Ethics* I.7, 1098a5–15; *De anima* II.3; *Politics* I.2, 1253a8–18, and Aquinas's commentaries on these passages. See also Aquinas, *ST* I, q. 75, a. 3, ad 1; q. 76, a. 3.

9. The object of a given science calls for an account of the thing's proper causes (*Commentaria in octo libros Physicorum Aristotelis* [hereafter *In Physic.*], lib. 1, l. 1, n. 5; *In duodecim libros Metaphysicorum Aristotelis expositio* [hereafter *Sent. Meta.*], lib. 3, l. 4). As qualities of a spiritual soul, human habits are treated in *ST* I-II, qq. 49–54, with little reference to biological science. However, biology remains useful for a broader study of habits. First, although the human soul is "separate" from the body, it has "existence in matter" as its form (*In Physic.*, lib. II, l. 2, l. 4, n. 10). Hence, even spiritual habits, which have a relation to the body, benefit from formal and material explanations. Second, some habits, though qualities of the soul, shape biological-psychological powers (e.g., the habit

more importantly, although biology is not nothing, neither is it everything. Synapses and hormones have a lot to teach us about our inclinations, but they cannot tell the whole story. Any reductive explanation of humans is ultimately unsatisfying, for above material explanations, our rational nature calls for *formal* and *final* explanations of our behavior. Reasons form our thinking and willing, and goals that transcend the entire material universe show our highest reasons for acting. Accounts of formal causality explain the existence of the intellectual soul, its potential for virtue, and its openness to grace. Finally, the various causes that work to make or break habits constitute formally distinct realities that can be understood separately but often operate together, and are almost invariably intertwined. In the lived experience of inclinations and behavior, it is difficult to isolate biological influences from those that are psychological, cultural, or volitional. It is therefore helpful to consider, insofar as it is possible, all of these causes in an ordered way as they contribute to an entire system of dispositions, habits, and behavior.[10]

Insofar as an investigation of habit concerns the human body and behavior, it falls under the domain of the natural sciences. Perhaps most significant in this area is biological psychology, which attempts to understand the biology that underlies human behavior and experience while emphasizing brain functionality.[11] Here one

of fortitude is a quality of the soul that shapes the irascible power: *ST* I-II, q. 56, a. 4; II-II, q. 123, a. 1, ad 3). Third, as will be seen, some habitual dispositions are primarily biological and thereby require a fully biological account. Fourth, because *habitus* is an analogous concept, discussed below, biological accounts of dispositions provide material for reasoning about spiritual habits.

10. See the synthetic work of Dominican Robert Edward Brennan, *General Psychology: A Study of Man Based on St. Thomas Aquinas* (New York: Macmillan, 1952).

11. Here I am assuming that there is no significant difference between biological psychology, biopsychology, and psychobiology, for these seem to be different ways of naming the same discipline. Insofar as biological psychology seems to take account of more biological functions than merely brain functions, it has a wider scope than behavioral neuroscience. See S. Marc Breedlove and Neil V. Watson, *Biological Psychology: An Introduction to Behavioral, Cognitive, and Clinical Neuroscience*, 7th ed. (Sunderland, Mass.: Sinauer Associates, 2013), 3.

can identify different scales of explanation.[12] Brain-functionality: "Paul got angry because neurochemical Y affected his brain." Hormonal-chemical: "Paul got angry because hormone X was secreted in large amounts, thereby increasing the levels of neurochemical Y later on." Cultural: "Paul got angry because he was a victim in his childhood." Genetic and epigenetic: "Paul got angry because he was genetically predisposed toward irascibility." And so on. All of these may indicate something true, but, helpful as they might be, they remain on a surface level.[13] Therefore, I go a level deeper and also take into account what one can call metaphysical psychology, that is, the philosophical study of the soul.

Aristotelian-Thomistic "psychology" entails a study of the *psuchē*, the soul and its proper effects—which encompass spiritual and biological phenomena for humans.[14] Contemporary empirical psychology, influenced by John Locke, David Hume, René Descartes, Wilhelm Wundt, and others, focuses on agent and efficient causes of observable phenomena discovered through the methodical testing of experimental data. Metaphysical psychology, including Gestalt theories and existential-phenomenological forms, focuses more on more explaining common human experience by formal and final causes. These are general tendencies, which can greatly differ from one form of psychology to the next, depending on their grounding

12. The following is an adaptation of Sapolsky, *Behave*, 7.

13. Brian Haig notes a number of methodological inadequacies in present behavioral sciences, and offers notable suggestions for improved investigations: Brian D. Haig, *Investigating the Psychological World: Scientific Method in the Behavioral Sciences* (Cambridge, Mass.: Bradford, 2014). See also Evandro Agazzi, "Some Epistemological Remarks: Unity of the Referent, Diversity of the Attributes, Specificity of the Scientific Approaches," in *Moral Behavior and Free Will: A Neurobiological and Philosophical Approach*, ed. Juan José Sanguineti et al. (Vatican City: IF Press, 2011), 25–46, at 36–38.

14. Kathleen Wilkes argues that Aristotle's *De anima* is a work of "theoretical scientific psychology," whose object of study does not entirely overlap with the modern concepts of "mind" or "psychology": "*Psuchē* versus the Mind," in *Essays on Aristotle's* De Anima, ed. Martha C. Nussbaum and Amélie Oksenberg Rorty (Oxford: Clarendon Press, 1995), 109–27. Aquinas holds that the study of the soul, esp. in *De anima*, is a work of philosophy, natural science, which should undergird biological enquiry (*Sent. De anima*, lib. 1, l. 1, n. 7).

in philosophy. Above and beyond the considerations of these natural sciences, insofar as habit concerns spiritual realities such as infused Gifts of the Holy Spirit, which are known only by revelation, its investigation falls under the domain of theology. Aristotle explains that the science of "theology" investigates a substance that is eternal, immovable, separable from matter, and not formed by nature: the *first* being.[15] What does this say about the human person? How does this understanding relate to a "theology of habit"? Thomas Aquinas provides a thorough and architectonic answer.

## A STUDY OF HABITS: PHILOSOPHICAL, NOT THEOLOGICAL?

There can be little doubt that Aquinas provides a unique and unparalleled contribution to Christian moral thinking with his "Treatise on Habits," which comprises questions 49–54 in the *Prima Secundae* of his *Summa Theologiae*. But the subject of habits is not at first glance obvious in the preaching of Jesus of Nazareth. At best, it is implicit in scripture; at worst, it is a Greek imposition. Furthermore, no thorough, systematic, and sustained analysis of habit as such can be found in the works of John Chrysostom, Augustine of Hippo, Maximus the Confessor, nor in the extant works of any other Church Father; nor in the extensive writings of great medieval thinkers such as Bernard of Clairvaux, Bonaventure, or Duns Scotus. A significant amount of this neglect is likely on account of the fact that the subject of habits and habituation are linchpins to Aristotle's ethical thought—and a minority of Christian scholars have looked to Aristotle's ethical insights to guide their thinking. At most, one finds analyses of habits in relatively minor commentaries on the Stagirite's *Nicomachean Ethics*, or sandwiched in between discussions of matters deemed more important. Even among thinkers who name Aquinas as their master and patron, many fail to

15. See *Metaphysics* VI.1, 1026a10–32.

give prominence to his insights about human habits and their role in moral life.[16] Suárez, for example, treats habit almost entirely as a philosophical matter in order to "avoid repetition" in his theological considerations.[17] Therefore, it could seem that a discussion of habits seems to belong more to a natural ethics derived from Greek philosophy, and less to a theology informed by divine revelation. Servais Pinckaers articulated others' criticism with punch: "St. Thomas's moral teaching ... ought to be called Aristotelian rather than Christian."[18]

In response to this significant objection, we must grasp the nature of Aquinas's overall theological project, and where his discussion of habits fits into that larger endeavor. We can begin by considering moral science in general and then by distinguishing between ethics/moral philosophy and moral theology.[19]

Moral science in general focuses on the moral goodness of the individual, not the family or the *polis*. Its method has three characteristics, according to Aquinas.[20] First, it proceeds in a deductive manner, applying universal principles to singulars. For example, it considers human habits in light of insights about substance, quality, human nature, goodness, and so on. Second, its method has a

16. This trend exists even among Thomists, with notable exceptions, including John of St. Thomas, *Cursus Theologicus, In Iam IIae: De Habitibus*, ed. Armand Mathieu and Hervé Gagné (Québec: Presses universitaires Laval, 1949), and Santiago Jacobus M. Ramirez, *De Habitibus in Communi: In I-II Summae Theologiae Divi Thomae Expositio (QQ. XLIX–LIV)*, ed. Victorino Rodriguez (Madrid: Instituto "Luis Vives" de Filosofia, 1973).

17. Suárez explains in *De Actibus Qui Vocantur Passiones*, disp. II, that he treats habits in *Disputationes Metaphysicae*, disp. XLIV, sec. III.

18. Servais Pinckaers, *The Sources of Christian Ethics*, 3rd ed., trans. Sr. Mary Thomas Noble, OP (Edinburgh: T and T Clark, 1995), 168.

19. Throughout this work, my working premise is that Aquinas's commentaries on Aristotle reflect his authentic philosophical views. See Leo Elders, "S. Thomas D'Aquin et Aristote," *Revue Thomiste* no. 88 (1988): 357–76; Christopher Kaczor, "Thomas Aquinas's *Commentary on the Ethics*: Merely an Interpretation?," *American Catholic Philosophical Quarterly* 78, no. 3 (2004): 353–78. For a contrary view, see Mark D. Jordan, *The Alleged Aristotelianism of Thomas Aquinas* (Toronto: PIMS, 1992).

20. For the three characteristics, see Aquinas, *Sent. Ethic.*, lib. 1, l. 3, n. 4. See William A. Wallace, *The Role of Demonstration in Moral Science* (Washington, D.C.: The Thomist Press, 1962), 99–117.

certitude proportionate to its subject-matter. It does not have mathematical certainty, but moral certainty when its considerations are derived from its proper principles. The variability of certitude is related to the fact that moral science primarily considers *voluntary* actions insofar as they are ordered to each other and to an end.[21] Because the will can aim not only at the good, but also at the apparent good, moral science has to take into consideration human error and fault. Now evil is not something that can be known in itself, but only in relation to the good.[22] Hence, evil will always have a certain lack of intelligibility. Third, moral science speaks of voluntary human actions, etc., as they occur in the majority of cases. As voluntary, human actions do not proceed from compulsion, though they may be greatly influenced by causes exterior to the will. There are individual exceptions to the general trends of human behavior analyzed by moral science, making it impossible to lay out inviolable physics-like laws that govern human behavior. Nevertheless, because the goal or final cause is the "cause of causality," moral philosophy is the "most principal and most architectonic science" among the natural practical sciences, that is, among sciences that consider human behavior and aim at guiding them toward their proper end.[23] Indeed, moral science is the most useful of all sciences, for it helps an individual to form his own habits and positively shape his own character. A psychologist can study the habits of virtue and vice, but always from the perspective of the operations of the soul; or, in the case of modern psychology, from a physiological-behavioral perspective. But a "moral scientist" will delve into the formal and final causes of habits, delineating the various sorts of virtues and vices that exist and pointing toward the proper actions to take in order to acquire good habits and to avoid bad ones.[24] Hence, above biochemistry, neuroscience, and

21. *Sent. Ethic.*, lib. 1, l. 1, n. 2.

22. See Aquinas, *Quaestiones disputate de malo*, q. 1, a. 1 [hereafter *De malo*]. I consulted the English translation, *On Evil*, ed. Brian Davies, trans. Richard Regan (Oxford: Oxford University Press, 2003).

23. *Sent. Ethic.*, lib. 1, l. 2, n. 7.

24. See Wallace, *The Role of Demonstration in Moral Science*, 91.

psychology, while not ignoring them, moral science more powerfully explains human behavior.

What has been said of moral science applies to both ethics, also called moral philosophy, and moral theology. Differences between moral philosophy and moral theology stem from their fundamental principles and from the goal they posit for human life. Moral philosophy considers habits from a human perspective: its principles are derived from human insight, and the end posited in principle can be reached by human power. It takes into consideration common human experience and develops explanations of acts, powers, habits, behaviors, and the like, through metaphysical reasoning. Thomas clarifies that Aristotle investigates natural happiness as the goal for human beings because the human end spoken of the in *Ethics* is not union with God through the beatific vision.[25] Moral philosophy does not consider man's actions in the light of revelation wrought by grace, which tells us that the Trinity is man's ultimate final end. In the words of William Wallace: "The most important thing to note about moral philosophy is that its formal ratio always remains that which is knowable by the light of human reason alone."[26]

In contrast, moral theology is a science that considers human acts and habits in the light of divine revelation and as they lead to supernatural beatitude.[27] Put another way, moral theology considers habits insofar as they come from divine grace and lead to God, the

25. James Doig develops strong arguments for this position in *Aquinas's Philosophical Commentary on the "Ethics": A Historical Perspective* (Dordrecht: Kluwer, 2001). See, for example, *Sent. Ethic.*, lib. 1, l. 14, n. 6: "Ex quo patet, quod felicitas de qua philosophus loquitur non consistit in illa continuatione ad intelligentiam separatam, per quam homo intelligat omnia, ut quidam posuerunt." Despite this explicit statement, J.-P. Torrell argues, "Thomas places himself explicitly in the Christian perspective and arranges things to as to have the Philosopher speak of contemplative finality in which Thomas himself sees the happiness of beatitude" (*Saint Thomas Aquinas: The Person and His Work*, 228). He cites R.-A. Gauthier, editor of the Leonine edition of Aquinas's commentary on the *Ethics*, as support. I am indebted to Nathan Lefler for bringing these details to my attention.

26. Wallace, *The Role of Demonstration in Moral Science*, 153. See his explanation of the difference between moral philosophy and moral theology in ibid., 152–54.

27. See *ST* I, q. 7, a. 2.

object of beatitude—man's supreme ultimate end, the most final of all causes.[28] Here some distinguish between moral theology proper and theological ethics, the latter of which employs theological reasoning but focuses on the human contribution to good action, lacking integration with an understanding of grace, acquired virtue, infused virtues, and the Gifts of the Holy Spirit.[29] As a science, moral theology is distinguished from catechetics, which teaches Catholic doctrines without theological explanations.[30] As we will see, Aquinas's "Treatise on Habits" within his *Summa Theologiae* means to give a "scientific" explanation of habits, contextualized by his understanding of biology, psychology, philosophy, but above all theological anthropology, grace, and man's ultimate end.

Called "a miracle of order and transparency," the *Summa Theologiae* is the fruit of Thomas's mature thought, meant to systematically address the entirety of Christian doctrine.[31] Throughout the *Summa* he consistently accounts for the method and organizational structure of the work, enabling the reader to see how parts of the work fit into the greater whole. Despite these road markers provided by Thomas, there have been debates about the real organizing principles of the *Summa Theologiae*. J.-P. Torrell notes that, despite these disagreements, there is a manifest "organic unity of the work: it is one book that speaks of one and the same subject" throughout its individual parts.[32] M.-D. Chenu influentially proposed that the structure of the entire *Summa* is guided by an *exitus-reditus* pattern; Torrell agrees with this conclusion, noting the many scholarly

28. See *ST* I-II, q. 3, a. 8. Also, Santiago Jacobus M. Ramirez, *De Hominis Beatudine: In I-II Summae Theologiae Divi Commentaria (QQ. I–V)*, ed. Victorino Rodriguez (Madrid: Instituto "Luis Vives" de Filosofia, 1972), 85.

29. See Wojciech Giertych, "Theological Ethics or Moral Theology?," in *Camminare nella Luce: Prospettive della teologia morale a partire da Veritatis splendor*, ed. L. Melina and J. Noriega (Rome: Lateran University Press, 2004), 537–63.

30. See Henricus Benedictus Merkelbach, *Summa theologiae moralis* (Paris: Desclée de Brouwer, 1932), 1:10–11.

31. Rudi Te Velde, *Aquinas on God: The "Divine Science" of the Summa Theologiae* (Burlington, Vt.: Ashgate, 2006), 9.

32. Jean-Pierre Torrell, *Aquinas's "Summa": Background, Structure, and Reception* (Washington, D.C.: The Catholic University of America Press, 2005), 17.

discussions on it.[33] The *prologue* to the treatise on God (qq. 2–43) provides partial justification for Chenu's schema. After all, Thomas states that the "principal intention" of sacred doctrine is to hand on the knowledge of God "not only as He is in Himself, but also as He is the beginning of things and their end."[34] However, the words *exitus* and *reditus* and their equivalent concepts are not employed here, nor in any other structural prologue of the *Summa*.[35] Here is what Thomas says in his prologue to the *Prima Secundae*:

> Since ... it is said that man made in the image of God, insofar as the image signifies "intellectual, free-choice, and self-movement," after having treated of the exemplar, i.e. God, and of those things which came forth from the power of God in accordance with His will; it remains for us to treat of His image, i.e. man, *inasmuch as he too is the principle of his actions,* as having free-choice and power over his actions.[36]

He thereby provides a clear explanation of the *Summa*'s structure up to the prologue:

Part I: God, the exemplar—principle of God's actions
Part II: Man, the image—principle of man's actions

The prologue to the *Tertia Pars* states that, in order to complete the work of theology, we should consider: "Our Savior the Lord Jesus Christ, [who] in order to save his people from their sins, demonstrated to us in himself the way of truth by which we can come to the beatitude of everlasting life by rising [from the dead]."[37] Synthesizing this with his previous prologues, we find that the basic organization of the *Summa* is as follows:

33. See Jean-Pierre Torrell, *Saint Thomas Aquinas: Person and His Work,* rev. ed. (Washington, D.C.: The Catholic University of America Press, 2005), 1:151–53, esp. n22 in the bibliography. See also Torrell, *Aquinas's "Summa"*, 27–29.

34. *ST* I, q. 2, prol.

35. In this first prologue, the language of God as the "principle" and "end" of creatures lends itself more to a monodirectional Christian understanding of history beginning with creation and ending with union with God, rather than to a Neoplatonic circular scheme of emanation and return. For a thorough analysis—and rejection—of the *exitus-reditus* proposal, see Te Velde, *Aquinas on God,* 12–16.

36. *ST* I-II, prol.

37. *ST* III, prol.

Part I: God, the exemplar, and God's acts
Part II: Man, the image, and man's acts
Part III: Christ, the God-Man, and his acts as Savior

Santiago Ramirez, William Wallace, Rudi Te Velde, and Michel Corbin agree that this is the true structure of the *Summa*.[38] Such a structure highlights the centrality of Christ, who is presented in the *Tertia Pars* as a recapitulation of the *Prima* and *Secunda* parts, making the discussion of Christ and his works in the church and her sacraments the pinnacle of the *Summa*.[39]

Importantly for us, the "exemplar-image-agent" structure helps to elucidate Thomas's theology of habit in light of the whole structure of the *Summa*. Each part of the *Summa* is a consideration of free agents and their personal activity: the "Treatise on Habits" is a consideration of how quasi-permanent inclinations come to be present in the human being through the activity of God and man.

The *Prima Pars* teaches that the triune God is the first principle of creation, of which the human being in his complexity is a part. Knowledge of the Trinity is consequently "necessary" to a theology of habits for two reasons.[40] First, to understand creation better, as an effect of God's free love. The heart of creation is God's gift. Hence, we learn about habit by learning about creation, God's love, and the difference between God's triune, uncreated nature and man's created nature in God's image. Second, we learn how to think rightly about salvation. Ultimate human flourishing consists in union with the Father, accomplished by the Son, gift of the Holy Spirit. We consider habit in light of our salvation, which is itself considered in light of the three divine Persons. In other words, with Thomas, we can ex-

38. See Ramirez, *De Hominis Beatudine*, 85; Wallace, *The Role of Demonstration in Moral Science*, 147n13 and 150; Te Velde, *Aquinas on God*, 11–18. The most comprehensive and convincing study of the issue is Michel Corbin's tome, *Le Chemin de la Thèologie chez Thomas D'Aquin* (Paris: Beauchesne, 1974), esp. 792–805. Corbin takes into account previous positions (including Chenu's) and proposes the schema above after comparing Aquinas's method in his *Commentary on the Sentences*, his *Summa contra Gentiles*, his scriptural commentaries, and his *Summa Theologiae*.

39. See Corbin, *Le Chemin de la Thèologie chez Thomas D'Aquin*, 801.

40. See *ST* I, q. 32, a. 1, ad 3.

plain a tertiary reality (habits) through a secondary reality (salvation), which is derived from ultimate reality (Father, Son, and Holy Spirit: one God).[41]

The *Secunda Pars* teaches that habits are principles of free human actions. It is through habits that man is prepared to reach his objective supreme final end, which is God himself, and his subjective supreme final end, which is beatitude. While emphasizing the absolute need for grace, Thomas does not shy away from recognizing man's full responsibility in making his way to salvation. In questions 6–21 of the *Prima Secundae,* he considers the "universal principles" of human action in the abstract, that is, as they exist in the intellect, will, and passions considered separately.[42] The "Treatise on Habits," considered narrowly as questions 49–54, comprises a general consideration of the "intrinsic principles of human acts."[43] His discussion of habits therefore provides the foundation for a more detailed exposition for the remaining part of the *Prima Secundae* and for most of the *Secunda Secundae,* both of which discuss habits in their concrete reality as virtues and vices, along with exterior principles of human actions such as law and grace. Thus, fully voluntary habits are central to explaining human action.[44] Though the subject-matter of a theology of habits is a human reality, we can understand that reality in light of their rootedness in divine causality and their ultimate finality found in God.

Thomas's theology of human habits can be understood as a spiritual exercise, a way of developing one's habits of knowing and loving the truth about the triune God.[45] Thus, the *Tertia Pars* of the *Sum-*

41. See Gilles Emery, *The Trinitarian Theology of St. Thomas Aquinas* (Oxford: Oxford University Press, 2007), 13.

42. *ST* I-II, q. 6, prol.

43. See *ST* I-II, q. 49, prol.

44. See David Decosimo, *Ethics as a Work of Charity: Thomas Aquinas and Pagan Virtue* (Stanford, Calif.: Stanford University Press, 2014), 72.

45. *Liber de veritate catholicae Fidei contra errores infidelium seu Summa contra Gentiles* [hereafter SCG] I, c. 9, n. 54; I consulted the English translation, *On the Truth of the Christian Faith,* trans. Anton C. Pegis, James F. Anderson, Vernon J. Bourke, Charles J. O'Neil (New York: Image, 1955–57). On Trinitarian theology as a spiritual exercise for

*ma* indicates the ultimate goal of a study of habits: union with God, which is only accomplished through the work of Christ in his physical body and in his mystical body, the Church. The Savior's work is above all a product of his wisdom and charity, divinely-infused habits, participations in the substantial divine love that is the Holy Spirit, who unites all persons to the Father in the Son.

For Aquinas, a consideration of habits is not foreign or superfluous to a theological account of morality. Rather, in his view, habits are central: they are the general intrinsic principles of human acts and the foundational principles of many imperfectly-human and superhuman acts. Habits are therefore essential for understanding the Christian theology of virtue, vice, law, grace, and the role of the Holy Spirit in human perfection. Like the golden thread that Theseus laid down in the Minotaur's maze, Aquinas's understanding of habits serves as a lifeline that leads the reader through the complex passages of his works on morality and human behavior in the second part of the *Summa Theologiae* and in many other writings, providing a consistent and more rounded view of this analogical and rich concept.

According to Aquinas, habits as dispositions "are specifically distinct in respect of three things. First, in respect of the active principles of such dispositions; secondly, in respect of nature; thirdly, in respect of specifically different objects."[46] With the schema below, I adapt Reginald Garrigou-Lagrange's explanation of Aquinas's division.[47]

Christians, see Augustine, *De Trinitate* XIII, c. 20, n. 26; c. 15, n. 1. Thomas says that the spiritual exercises include study and teaching wisdom. See *SCG* III, c. 132; *ST* II-II, q. 122, a. 4, ad 3. Also, Gilles Emery, "Trinitarian Theology as Spiritual Exercise in Augustine and Aquinas," in *Aquinas the Augustinian*, ed. Michael Dauphinais, Barry David, and Matthew Levering (Washington, D.C.: The Catholic University of America Press, 2007), 1–40.

46. *ST* I-II, q. 54, a. 2.

47. See Reginald Garrigou-Lagrange, *Beatitude: A Commentary on St. Thomas' Theological Summa Ia IIa, qq. 1–54*, trans. Patrick Cummins (St. Louis, Mo.: Herder, 1956), 375–77.

1. Habits as forms passively received by their proximate principle are either:
   a. Acquired (guided by reason)
   b. Infused (from God as principal agent)
2. Habits as dispositions differentiated with respect to the nature of the subject are either:
   a. Natural
      i. In harmony with nature (good acquired habits)
      ii. Contrary to nature (bad acquired habits)
   b. Supernatural (infused by God)
3. Habits as dispositions directed toward a particular object aim at:
   a. Objects naturally attainable
   b. Objects supernaturally attainable

Garrigou-Lagrange insightfully points out that the three ways of differentiating habits collapse into each other, such that one can distinguish between two sorts of habits with the following characteristics:

Natural – acquired – in harmony with nature – directed toward natural objects

Supernatural – infused – elevating nature – directed toward supernatural objects

This book takes the dichotomy above (between natural-acquired and supernatural-infused) as the primary difference among habits. Drawing from Thomas's detailed treatment of *habitus* in the *Summa Theologiae* and his scattered discussions in many of his other works, I subdivide natural habits according to the role of human agency in producing them, beginning with habit-like qualities that are the most material (dispositions from general nature) and ending with those that are the most spiritual (the Gifts of the Holy Spirit).

### HABITS AND *HABITUS*

Insofar as the topic of habit is clearly subsumed within Aquinas's theology, we are led to a third objection, partly terminological and partly philosophical, to the approach taken in this book. According to this objection—represented by Servais Pinckaers—Aquinas's account of *habitus* was not of automatic "habits" but of free, human qualities of the soul. *Habitus,* the argument runs, enables a person to act at will with great flexibility, creativity, and nondeterminedness. Consequently, any quality possessed by humans that is not rooted in the rational soul is not a *habitus* as Thomas understands it, and ought not to be cultivated or studied as useful for moral improvement. In what follows, I will respond to this contention by proposing an alternate, and I believe more faithful, reading of Thomas.

A number of scholars hold that, though contemporary usages such as the English "habit" and the French "habitude" are historically derived from the Latin *habitus,* the vernacular terms indicate radically different realities than Aquinas's *habitus.* Yves Simon observes that in contemporary English usage, a habit is understood as a stable disposition toward an unconscious, quasi-mechanical, patterned behavior, such as biting one's fingernails or looking both ways before crossing the street.[48] The same is signified by the French *habitude* according to Pinckaers, who notes that *habitude* typically indicates an "automatism" and therefore seems to lie outside of the moral dimension.[49] He rejects the claim that *habitus,* understood in a Thomistic sense, is a "habit" as it is understood in modern parlance. "According to this [erroneous] theory," he writes, "repeated acts develop in the soul a deep-rooted, permanent inclination, called a *habitus,* the na-

48. See Yves Simon, *The Definition of Moral Virtue,* ed. Vukan Kuic (New York: Fordham University Press, 1986), 54.

49. Servais Pinckaers, "La vertu est tout autre chose qu'une habitude," *Nouvelle Revue Theologique* 82 (1960): 387–403, at 389. This was published in English as "Virtue Is Not a Habit," trans. Bernard Gilligan, *Cross Currents* 12 (1962): 65–81.

ture of which is a sort of habit."[50] The term "habit" bears overtones of automaticity and necessity, which run contrary to human freedom, for the term implies "the diminution, if not the total exclusion, of reflective consciousness and voluntary decision right at the very beginning."[51] He continues: "An action performed on the basis of habit does not entail that attentive presence of reason and that personal engagement of free will [*volonté libre*] which give our actions their whole worth and their entire human value. The automatism of habit deprives an action of precisely the thing that gives it its moral dimension."[52] Accordingly, moral theology ought not to study "habits" so much as *habitus*.

Empirical researchers adopt a similar position to Pinckaers when they equate "procedural memory" with habit in general. Two prominent neuroscientists define habit as "that aspect of motor skill learning that refers to acquired, stereotyped, and unconscious behavioral repertoires," such as typing on a keyboard, driving a car, walking, and so on.[53] For them, habituation is learning and remembering "motor programs" that result from repeated "motor performances."[54] Such habits seemingly exclude by definition the higher, rational, and reflective powers of humans and therefore the full voluntariness of human action. Similarly, Coutlee and Huettel describe habits as "highly automated behaviors" that are "overlearned."[55] They point out that rats can learn that they can receive cheese upon pressing a lever. Typically, this sort of habituation is flexible. Rats avoid reward-based actions if the reward has been devalued (e.g., if they

50. Pinckaers, "Virtue Is Not a Habit," 66.

51. Ibid., 67.

52. Ibid.

53. Howard Eichenbaum and Neal J. Cohen, *From Conditioning to Conscious Recollection: Memory Systems of the Brain* (Oxford: Oxford University Press, 2004), 435. The discussion on 439–70 explores the neurological implications of their view.

54. Ibid., 435.

55. Christopher G. Coutlee and Scott A. Huettel, "Rules, Rewards, and Responsibility: A Reinforcement Learning Approach to Action Control," in *Moral Psychology,* vol. 4: *Free Will and Moral Responsibility,* ed. Walter Sinnott-Armstrong (Cambridge, Mass.: MIT Press, 2014), 327–34, at 329 and 332.

have eaten their fill of cheese), but "if the rats are overtrained on the lever-pushing task . . . they cease to demonstrate this flexibility and will continue to press the lever after reward devaluation even though they are unwilling to eat the cheese."[56] This sort of automatic behavior is biologically based, Coutlee and Huettel hold, for when a lesion is made in the brain, preventing the function of the infralimbic medial prefrontal context, the dominance of habitual behavior is reduced and more voluntary behavior appears.[57] Consistent with this finding, people often feel they have strong willpower when they definitively reject undesired habits such as overeating or smoking.[58] It is as if they experience having freedom of choice only when they oppose their habits. Therefore, it seems that there are both philosophical and scientific reasons to hold that habits reduce or even remove voluntariness from human action.

Furthermore, Aquinas understands human *habitus* as something intentional and derived from choice.[59] Such an understanding of *habitus* seems contrary to a mechanical action; as Simon says, "acts done out of habit, insofar as they are done out of habit, are not voluntary acts."[60] Because of this, both Simon and Pinckaers distinguish between habit/habitude and *habitus,* preferring not to translate the Latin term in order to show that the words do not have equivalent meanings. For similar reasons, Anthony Kenny renders *habitus* as "disposition."[61] Kenny's move is reasonable insofar as Aquinas follows Aristotle in defining *habitus* as "a disposition according to

56. Coutlee and Huettel, "Rules, Rewards, and Responsibility," 331.

57. Ibid., 332. See Etienne Coutureau and Simon Killcross, "Inactivation of the Infralimbic Prefrontal Cortex Reinstates Goal-Directed Responding in Overtrained Rats," *Behavioural Brain Research* 146, no. 1–2 (November 30, 2003): 167–74.

58. Daniel M. Wegner, *The Illusion of Conscious Will* (Cambridge, MA: The MIT Press, 2002), 92. Wenger holds that habits are "unconscious action tendencies," "compulsive," and unwilled. See *The Illusion of Conscious Will,* 90–93.

59. *ST* I-II, q. 50, a. 5.

60. Simon, *The Definition of Moral Virtue,* 55.

61. See Kenny's preface in Thomas Aquinas, *Summa Theologiae,* vol. 22: *Dispositions for Human Acts: 1a2ae. 49–54,* ed. and trans. Anthony Kenny (Cambridge: Cambridge University Press, 2006), xix–xxii.

which someone is disposed well or ill," clarifying that the disposition is directed to action.[62] Further analysis shows that, according to Aquinas, one type of *habitus* is also one type of *dispositio* but that the two terms also have non-overlapping meanings. Consequently, the terms should not be equated.[63] Kenny thus translates *dispositio* as "state," as he has already used "disposition" for *habitus*. Where all these scholars agree is that habit does not equal *habitus*, and the two should be conceptually and lexically separated. The underlying motivation of such a move is to maintain that human *habitus* is not reducible to mechanical or robotic realities. In order to evaluate this objection, we will need to examine more deeply the nature and kinds of *habitus*, especially as explained by Aquinas.

In response to these serious objections to drawing a parallel, if not an equation, between "habit" and *habitus*, one can begin with Alexander of Aphrodisias's desire to correct Aristotle. Alexander saw ambiguities in his philosophical master's treatment of the issue, so the student sharply distinguished between nonrational inclinations ("habits/habitude") and inclinations toward rational activity (*habitus*).[64] This position was meant to amend Aristotle's position in his *Physics*, in which "health" and "beauty" are listed as habits analogous to "virtue" and "science."[65] Thomas, with his characteristic synthesizing tendency, worked to harmonize the positions of the two philoso-

62. *ST* I-II, q. 49, a. 2. Here he is referring to Aristotle's discussion of "to have" (*hexein*) in *Metaphysics* V.23, 1023a8–25.

63. Thomas Aquinas, *Sent. Meta.*, lib. 5, l. 20, nn. 1–7. See further discussion in *ST* I-II, q. 49, a. 2, ad 3.

64. In *ST* I-II, q. 50, a. 1, Thomas quotes Simplicius reporting Alexander of Aphrodisias's position that habits are "in no way" in the body but are "only in the soul." See Simplicius's discussion in *Simplicius: On Aristotle, Categories 7–8*, trans. Barrie Fleet (London: Bloomsbury, 2014), 233 (92–93). Moerbeke's translation, used by Thomas: *Simplicius, Commentaire sur les Catégories D'Aristote: Traduction de Guillaume de Moerbeke*, Corpus Latinum Commentariorum in Aristotelem Graecorum, 2 vols., ed. A. Pattin (Louvain: Brill, 1971/1975). For discussion, see Michael Chase, "The Medieval Posterity of Simplicius' Commentary on the Categories: Thomas Aquinas and Al-Farabi," in *Medieval Commentaries on Aristotle's Categories*, ed. L. A. Newton (Leiden: Brill, 2008), 9–29. See also Vivian Boland, "Aquinas and Simplicius on Dispositions—A Question in Fundamental Moral Theory," *New Blackfriars* 82, no. 968 (2001): 467–78.

65. *Physics* VII.3, 246b4–6.

phers. His solution found that habit is an analogous term with great depth, breadth, and flexibility.

When a single term is applied to various things, it can be predicated in three different ways: univocally, equivocally, or analogically.[66] Univocal predication attributes something to different subjects in exactly the same way. Thus, "animal" is predicated of tigers and monkeys because both are living material beings with sensation, movement, and so on. Equivocal predication attributes something to different subjects by name only. For example, a man, a toy, and a fishing tool can share the name "Bob" without essentially sharing anything else. Finally, analogical predication attributes a quality to subjects that differ by nature but share a common quality. The classic example of an analogical term is "health."[67] A physical body, urine, and food can all be called healthy, but the word does not signify entirely the same thing in all three. A person can be called healthy because he is the *proper subject* of health; urine can be called healthy because it is a *sign* of health; food can be called healthy because it is a *cause* of health. Amid this diversity of meanings there is a unity insofar as health is truly and analogously attributed to each of them. Habit is likewise an analogous term.[68]

"Habit" comes from *habitus,* which is derived from *habere,* "to have."[69] *Habitus* in turn translates the Greek ἕξις, *hexis,* is a noun related to the verb *echein,* "to have," "to hold as a possession": *hexis*

66. For the following explanation of analogy, see Thomas Aquinas, *De principiis naturae,* c. 6, n. 46, and *Quaestiones disputatae de potentia* [hereafter *De potentia*], q. 7, a. 7; *Quaestiones disputate de veritate* [hereafter *De veritate*], q. 2, a. 11, co. and ad 6; *SCG,* lib. 1, c. 34; *Sent. Meta.,* lib. 7, l. 4, n. 7 and lib. 11, l. 3, n. 4. For *De veritate,* I consulted the English translation, *Truth,* trans. Robert W. Mulligan, James V. McGlynn, and Robert W. Schmidt (Chicago: Henry Regnery, 1952–54). See also Santiago Jacobus M. Ramirez, *De Analogia,* vol. I, ed. Victorino Rodriguez (Madrid: Instituto "Luis Vives" de Filosofia, 1970), 51–74 and 262–479. See E. J. Ashworth, "Aquinas on Analogy," in *Debates in Medieval Philosophy,* ed. Jeffrey Hause (New York: Routledge, 2014), 232–42.

67. Aristotle, *Metaphysics* IV.2, 1003a33–35.

68. "'Habit' is an analogous term, a term which has a slightly different meaning every time it is used of a different habit. Habit is not a kind of common genus, equally divided among species. Habits in different powers differ." George Klubertanz, *Habit and Virtue* (New York: Meredith, 1965), 97.

69. See *ST* I-II, q. 49, a. 1.

signifies a thing a person possesses in a firm and fixed way, as established by repeated action. These related terms connote the idea of a person having something in addition to his basic properties and essential characteristics. Aquinas insists that nature is the foundation and measure of human habits: "it is of the *ratio* of a habit to signify some relation ordered to a thing's nature, insofar as it is fitting or unfitting [to the nature]."[70] Habit is not a substance; it is not a person's essence, nor one of his powers. Instead, it is a modification of the person, a "quality," Thomas says, for it "qualifies" or forms the powers.[71] Nicholas Kahm explains that a habit is a principle of a stable mode of existing; this principle exists in a substance as an accident in the genus of quality.[72] For example, when we say that a person has a habit of overeating, the habit does not provide the powers of nutrition or movement, or desire for food, or the power to choose one food instead of another. Rather, a habit shapes one's hunger for food by focusing it on particular delightful objects, such as sweets. When one's powers are exercised consistently toward a particular object, they become habituated to respond to that object in predictable ways: habit shapes these powers for good or for ill.[73]

As David Decosimo points out, "The subject [that] habit perfects always has an initial but insufficiently determined direction or inclination, the inchoate, undetermined beginning."[74] Habit specifies nature's general direction. In this way, arising from potential and inclining a person toward action, habit is a midway point between pure potency and pure act.[75] "To have" is stronger than "to borrow" or "to use" but is weaker than "to be."[76] Hence "habit" signifies a modifica-

70. *ST* I-II, q. 49, a. 3.

71. *ST* I-II, q. 49, a. 1. See Klubertanz, *Habit and Virtue*, 98.

72. Nicholas Kahm, *Aquinas on Emotion's Participation in Reason* (Washington, D.C.: The Catholic University of America Press, 2019), 98 and n42.

73. Decosimo, *Ethics as a Work of Charity*, 87.

74. Ibid.

75. *ST* I, q. 87, a. 2.

76. See the discussion of Plato's and Aristotle's distinction between owning and acquiring as it relates to *habitus*: Olivier Boulnois, "The *Habitus* of Choice," in *The Ontology, Psychology, and Axiology of Habits* (ed. Faucher and Roques), 25–45, at 31–34.

tion of a person that is not easily changed.[77] Once attained, a habit exists within the individual, and therefore is present to the individual at least as a form of latent potency. More precisely, from the Aristotelian perspective, human habit at its most basic philosophical level is *a quality that a subject possesses as a per se stable orientation toward act, in being or in operation, for good or ill in relation to one's specific nature.*[78] Aquinas substantially agrees with Aristotle's understanding of *hexis* but develops the insight to cover territory never imagined by the philosopher.[79] Similar to the way that health is an analogous term, Aquinas indicates, so *habitus* is analogous, for there are different ways of considering how a person stably "possesses" a disposition.[80] The analogous nature of *habitus* is shared by the term "habit," which helps us to see why the English word is the best translation of its Latin analogue.

Recent scientific approaches to habit have shown that the term "habit" is used in a number of interlocking ways. Surveying the concept of habit in seventy-seven thinkers across millennia, researchers noticed that there are two main trends in understanding habit: associationism and organicism.[81] The "associationist" trend focuses on exterior behavior: given event-stimulus A, another event-response B will arise when event B has previously and repeatedly followed A.[82] This may be conceived of as a simple stimulus-response mechanism.

77. *ST* I-II, q. 49, a. 2, ad 3. See Roy DeFerrari, "habitus," in *A Latin-English Lexicon of St. Thomas Aquinas* (Washington, D.C.: The Catholic University of America Press, 1949), 477.

78. See Aristotle, *Categories* 15b18–32. Ernst Wolff notes that, according to Aristotle, *hexis* "is characterized 1) as having a hold on something (this is the element of firmness, steadiness or stability), 2) as being possessed, rather than used (it is a potential that could remain hidden), and 3) as a persistent orientation or disposition that could be more passive (in the sense of being mere reaction) or more active (striving to realize an objective)." Ernst Wolff, "Aspects of Technicity in Heidegger's Early Philosophy: Rereading Aristotle's Technè and Hexis," *Research in Phenomenology* 38, no. 3 (2008): 317–57, at 337.

79. *ST* I-II, q. 50, a. 1.

80. See Kahm, *Aquinas on Emotion's Participation in Reason*, 110–11.

81. Xabier E. Barandiaran and Ezequiel A. Di Paolo, "A Genealogical Map of the Concept of Habit," *Frontiers in Human Neuroscience* 8 (2014): 522.

82. Barandiaran and Di Paolo, "A Genealogical Map of the Concept of Habit," 5.

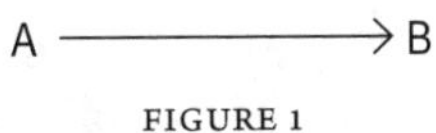


FIGURE 1

Behaviorism defines habits as "memory-based propensities to respond automatically to specific cues, which are acquired by the repetition of cue-specific behaviors in stable contexts."[83] Distinct habitual behavior is an act that a person repeatedly performs as influenced by a corresponding habit.

Behaviorist psychologists who utilize the associationist model do not always explain why B follows A. Often a black box exists between a given stimulus and its normally associated response: identifying such an association suffices for one to measure and modify behavior. If any explanation *is* given, researchers characteristically point to consequence C as a positive consequence-reward.[84] They notice that when antecedent A leads to behavior B, and behavior B leads to positive consequence C, the consequence reinforces the power of antecedent A to produce behavior B. In other words, there are three elements to a simple habit: *antecedents* to the habit-behavior, the *behavior* itself, and the *consequences* from performing the behavior. Because one leads to another, they form a cycle or loop, as illustrated in the following diagram.

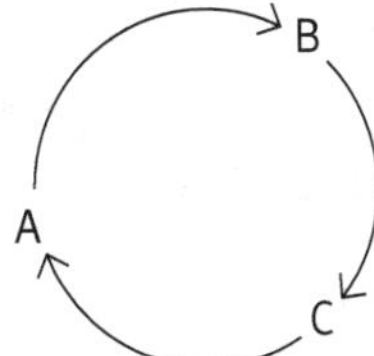


FIGURE 2. SIMPLE HABIT LOOP

83. Bas Verplanken, "Introduction," in *The Psychology of Habit*, 1–12, at 4. Versions of this definition are utilized by various authors throughout the book.

84. B. Gardner and P. Lally, "Modelling Habit Formation and Its Determinates," in *The Psychology of Habit*, ed. B. Verplanken, 207–29, at 208.

This is essentially Charles Duhigg's "habit loop."[85] Here habits are interpreted mechanistically and are considered as deterministic automatisms. This is how the objection from Pinckaers (and others) describes habits.

Contrastingly, the "organicist" view of habits focuses on how humans, like all living things, organize their own behavior through some interior power. Félix Ravaisson in 1838 helped to establish phenomenological and holistic grounds for understanding habits, a trend that continued through Husserl and Merleau-Ponty, and has culminated in a "current sensitivity to the organicist trend" found in areas of neuroscience, embodied-enactive cognitive science, robotics, sensorimotor approaches to cognition, and in other empirical approaches for understanding human habits.[86] Instead of conceiving of habits as forced responses to repeated external circumstances, the organicist view sees habits as tendencies that flower from a creature's natural "self-organizing structures" which exist as a "web of predispositions."[87] Habits in this perspective are not opposed to deliberate and volitional choice. Rather, habits embody the natural dynamism and intelligibility of a creature's potential—including a human's explicit choice, which is a result of an interior movement.

Associationism and organicism may seem to be at odds with each other: the first emphasizes exterior forces and behaviors; the other, interior dynamism. But both find their roots in Aristotle. "Associationism" relates to passages in the Greek thinker's treatise, *De memoria et reminiscentia*, that describe the physical and psychological mechanisms of memory and recollection.[88] Abandoning Aristotle's

85. See Duhigg, *The Power of Habit*, chap. 1, "The Habit Loop." See also B. J. Knowlton, J. A. Mangels, and L. R. Squire, "A Neostriatal Habit Learning System in Humans," *Science* 273, no. 5280 (September 6, 1996): 1399–1402; John G. McHaffie et al., "Subcortical Loops through the Basal Ganglia," *Trends in Neurosciences* 28, no. 8 (August 2005): 401–7; and A. M. Graybiel, "The Basal Ganglia and Chunking of Action Repertoires," *Neurobiology of Learning and Memory* 70, nos. 1–2 (September 1998): 119–36.

86. See references in Barandiaran and Di Paolo, "A Genealogical Map of the Concept of Habit," 6.

87. Ibid., 1.

88. E.g., *De memoria et reminiscentia* 451b11.

debunked physiology, British empiricists drew on his psychological insights, leaving David Hartley in 1746 to attempt the first "associationist" synthesis of both physical and psychological explanations for human habits.[89] Such explanations, focusing on empirical studies, were favored by behaviorists. Meanwhile, "organicism" took hints from Aristotle's broader biological philosophy, holding that "what originates movement is both pre-eminently and primarily the soul."[90]

Habit studies increasingly follow trends of Aristotelian insight and implicitly unite associationism and organicism. Ann Graybiel, for instance, describes the neurological foundations of different kinds of habits.[91] According to Graybiel, reflexes and even instincts can be conceived of as a lower form of habits. Animal behaviors, such as the bowerbird's complex nest building and swan mating rituals, resemble fully human habits insofar as both are learned (related to associationism), both involve self-motivated goal-seeking (related to organicism), and both activate analogous parts of the brain.[92] In 1890, William James laid foundations for brain research into habits by arguing that the foundation of all human habit is to be found in the "plasticity" of organic matter, for the human body (especially the brain) is in "possession of a structure weak enough to yield to an influence, but strong enough not to yield all at once."[93] More recently, Denis Larrivee and Adriana Gini have completed the picture by arguing that Aquinas's definition of virtue as a *habitus operativus bonus* is compatible with empirical explanations of human flourishing through neuroplasticity.[94] Aquinas himself attempts a synthesis of the best scientific explanations of the material and efficient causes (more related to as-

89. See H. W. Buckingham and S. Finger, "David Hartley's Psychobiological Associationism and the Legacy of Aristotle," *Journal of the History of the Neurosciences* 6, no. 1 (April 1997): 21–37.

90. *De anima* I.2, 403b29.

91. Graybiel, "Habits, Rituals, and the Evaluative Brain."

92. Ibid., 372.

93. William James, *The Principles of Psychology* (New York: Henry Holt and Co., 1890), 1:105.

94. Denis Larrivee and Adriana Gini, "Is the Philosophical Construct of 'Habitus Operativus Bonus' Compatible with the Modern Neuroscience Concept of Human Flourishing through Neuroplasticity?," *Frontiers in Human Neuroscience* 8, no. 731 (2014): 1–4.

sociationism), as well as the formal and final causes (more related to organicism) of habit. Indeed, Thomas understands habit as a reality that exists on many different levels of the human person.

One can distinguish among habits according to their "active principles," especially with relation to the will.[95] An "active principle" is an agent that produces a form or quality in a subject.[96] Considering habit as a form, one can distinguish among the movers that cause the habitual qualities to inhere in a subject.[97] Accordingly, I distinguish among habits that arise from an agent's general nature, from one's specific nature, from one's nonvolitional and passive experience, and from one's sensorial and actively-acquired experience. A further type of habit arises from fully voluntary acts of the individual.[98] This sort of quality is different from all the others, for it arises entirely from within the agent. Furthermore, it is proper to the human being, for it arises from the exercise of his intellect and will, the powers that make a human specifically human. In this light, one can make a strict dichotomy between two kinds of habit: (1) habit in its paradigmatic sense—an inclination of the rational soul, primarily of the will—which Thomas at times calls *habitus simpliciter*;[99] and (2) all other inclinations, which arise from any other source. In comparison with *habitus simpliciter,* Thomas calls these other inclinations "dispositions" or "habitual dispositions."[100] A habitual disposition is compared to *habitus* as the imperfect to the perfect.[101]

95. *ST* I-II, q. 54, a. 2.

96. Ibid.

97. Ibid.

98. Looking to the difference between habits existing in the subject *ad formam* or *ad operationem* in *ST* I-II, q. 50, a. 1, later Thomistic writers, represented by Reginald Garrigou-Lagrange, would describe this as the difference between entiative and operative habits, although he does not use the term *habitus entitativus* or its variants. See Reginald Garrigou-Lagrange, *Reality: A Synthesis of Thomistic Thought,* trans. Patrick Cummins (St. Louis, MO: B. Herder, 1950), 285.

99. *ST* I-II, q. 50, a. 1, ad 2.

100. See *ST* I-II, q. 49, a. 3, ad 3: "habitualis dispositio"; ibid., q. 50, a. 1: "habitualis dispositio potest esse in corpore, quod comparatur ad animam sicut subiectum ad formam. Et hoc modo sanitas et pulchritudo, et huiusmodi, habituales dispositiones dicuntur. Non tamen perfecte habent rationem habituum, quia causae eorum ex sua natura de facili transmutabiles sunt."

101. *ST* I-II, q. 49, a. 2, ad 3. "Potest intelligi dispositio proprie dicta condividi contra

When inclinations are rooted in the body, they are more properly called "dispositions" toward action, rather than "habits," for two reasons. First, by their very nature they are "easily lost," as such qualities disappear as soon as the body changes, but habits have staying power.[102] A single sharp blow to the head can immediately change a person's emotional dispositions, and even much of his personality and behavior.[103] Second, a thing's proper operation arises from the specific power of its form. The proper operation for humans as humans is to understand through the mediation of the imagination and senses, and to use one's understanding to perform voluntary acts.[104] Inclinations which arise from the rational soul and its deliberate choice are properly "human" habits: only fully voluntary habits are the same as fully-human habits. Because Thomas's focus is human action, he therefore uses the term *habitus* to indicate "human habits" as such.

While acknowledging Aquinas's clear distinction between dispositions and habits, much of the present study highlights the value in considering Aquinas's broader use of habit as an analogous term. As dispositions, habit in sense (2) include (a) inclinations of the body, sensory powers, and passions as they have been formed by the agent's deliberate choice,[105] and (b) inclinations of the senses as they

habitum, dupliciter. Uno modo, sicut perfectum et imperfectum in eadem specie, ut scilicet dispositio dicatur.... Alio modo possunt distingui ... secundum propriam rationem ut de facili amittantur, quia habent causas transmutabiles, ut aegritudo et sanitas; habitus vero dicuntur illae qualitates quae secundum suam rationem habent quod non de facili transmutentur, quia habent causas immobiles, sicut scientiae et virtutes. Et secundum hoc dispositio non fit habitus. Et hoc videtur magis consonum intentioni Aristotelis."

102. Ibid.; "nomen habitus diuturnitatem quandam importat; non autem nomen dispositionis."

103. The case of Phineas Gage famously illustrates the brain's importance for habituation. In a railroad accident, Gage's prefrontal cortex was pierced by a tamping iron. Though he survived, the injury drastically changed his personality and behavior: Gage's previous reliability and industriousness was replaced with volatility and inconsistency. See the extensive discussion in Anthony Damasio, *Descartes' Error: Emotion, Reason, and the Human Brain* (London: Penguin, 2005), 3–51.

104. See *ST* I, q. 76, a. 1. See also *Quaestiones disputate de anima*, aa. 1 and 3; *De veritate*, q. 13, a. 1.

105. See *ST* I-II, q. 50, aa. 1, 2, and 3 respectively.

have been formed by other agents, as previous sections of this study have shown. By employing an extended sense of habit, Thomas not only helps Aristotle save face. He also highlights the deep unity present amid the complexity of a human being, for this analogous understanding of habit reveals a stepwise gradation of inclinations that point to fully voluntary habits and increasingly share in their *ratio*.

On the lowest categorical level (1), "habit" indicates *a stable disposition toward action that comes from possessing something entirely extrinsic to oneself,* as in the case of clothing. In his commentary on Aristotle's *Physics,* St. Thomas notes that among the predicaments or categories, which include quality, quantity, action, passion, and others that are common to all substances, there is a special predicament for humans only, namely, *habitus.*[106] Animals have a hide or wool or fur as a natural covering that prepares them to tolerate heat and cold; they possess horns or hooves or claws, or the like, as part of their natural readiness for protecting themselves, eating, and performing other actions. In contrast, human beings lack these natural coverings and appendages. Instead, humans are endowed with reason and are thereby able to fashion such things for themselves in order to be prepared for some action. Man *arms* himself as part of his readiness for battle; he *clothes* himself as a preparation to endure foul weather; he puts shoes on his feet and therefore is *shod,* possessing a material disposition for walking long distances, running, or traversing rough terrain. Aquinas explains: "When a man is said to be *armed* or *clothed* or *shod,* he is so named by something extrinsic to him that is neither a cause nor a measure; thus [for this] there is special predicament and it is called 'habit' [*habitus*]."[107]

Catholic religious terminology still employs this sense of "habit" when it refers to the special garments worn by religious persons who have been consecrated to God by special vows of poverty, chastity, and obedience. Accordingly, one speaks of a nun's *habit* as a kind of clothing. At the same time, one can speak of a nun's *habit* of keep-

106. *In Physic.,* lib. 3, l. 5, n. 15.
107. Ibid.

ing her vows. The two meanings are related. Her exterior habit, her clothing, is a *sign* of her spiritual habit, but more than a sign: it facilitates a kind of habitual behavior that characterizes her as a nun. The specialized religious clothing is a *material disposition toward acting like a nun.* Furthermore, when wearing a habit (clothing) is required by religious law, it becomes a part of a nun's habit (religious observance). Therefore, although the habit does not make the nun, it certainly helps. The decisive point is that the English term "habit" contains different levels of interrelated signification. What follows schematizes the other analogous uses of "habit," divided according to the immediate efficient cause, thus setting the stage for a more thorough discussion of each meaning in later chapters.

On a deeper level than clothing, in sense (2) one can speak of "habit" as *a stable disposition derived from "general nature."* These sorts of habitual dispositions perfect the being of the individual, and so have been called "entitative habits." All humans possess them as members of the same species, such that these dispositions are naturally possessed as qualities of "general nature," not as one's individual nature, discussed below. Human-specific dispositions are concomitant with human nature in general and are directed toward particular activities that benefit the person as a member of the human race.[108] Thus, Aquinas and Aristotle speak of health as a habit that one can have at birth and that one can maintain over time: the body's natural habit of health is a disposition to continue performing operations that maintain itself in a dynamic steady state and by metabolism contribute to physical flourishing.[109] Similarly, instincts may be explained as natural dispositions and inclinations.[110]

108. *ST* I-II, q. 51, a. 1: "si loquamur de habitu secundum quod est dispositio subiecti in ordine ad formam vel naturam ... Est enim aliqua dispositio naturalis quae debetur humanae speciei, extra quam nullus homo invenitur."

109. *ST* I-II, q. 49, a. 3, ad 3: "sanitas dicitur habitus, vel habitualis dispositio, in ordine ad naturam ... homo dicitur sanus, vel membrum aliquod, quando potest facere operationem sani."

110. Aquinas argues that everything has a natural "habitude" that makes them tend toward the good of their form; this inclination in nonrational creatures is called their natural appetite. *ST* I, q. 19, a. 1, co.: "Quaelibet autem res ad suam formam naturalem

Next, one can speak of (3) habit as a *stable disposition from individual nature*. In this case, the inclination exists for *this particular person*, on account of that individual's innate personal and unique attributes, such as his genetic structure and epigenetic expression. For example, given that humans in general are born with a "general disposition from nature" toward health, an individual could inherit a genetic structure that opposes such a disposition. General dispositions possessed by members of a species are manifested differently among individuals, for an individual's particular bodily structure itself possesses qualities that further qualify and shape that more general tendency.[111] The individual in such a tragic case would be born with a personalized "disposition" that is a quasi-permanent debility or disease.

After this, one can speak of (4) habit as a stable disposition *acquired in a nonvolitional way*. For example, some children are born with a "drug habit," an addiction to a particular chemical substance that was introduced to them in the womb. Or again, anyone who undergoes a greatly trying event can acquire post-traumatic stress disorder, which is a reactive habit of the body, emotions, memory, and imagination. These would be instances of *passively* acquired nonvolitional habitual dispositions.[112] Then there are dispositions

---

hanc habet habitudinem, ut quando non habet ipsam, tendat in eam; et quando habet ipsam, quiescat in ea. Et idem est de qualibet perfectione naturali, quod est bonum naturae. Et haec habitudo ad bonum, in rebus carentibus cognitione, vocatur appetitus naturalis." Lest one conclude that humans do not have this natural *habitudo*, Aquinas says that our inclination toward happiness in general is not a result of our free choice, but from a natural instinct—the very *habitudo* he described earlier: "liberum arbitrium habemus respectu eorum quae non necessario volumus, vel naturali instinctu. Non enim ad liberum arbitrium pertinet quod volumus esse felices, sed ad naturalem instinctum" (*ST* I, q. 19, a. 10, co.). This inclination is a "natural quality" that exists in his soul: "Ex eo igitur quod homo est aliqualis qualitate naturali quae attenditur secundum intellectivam partem, naturaliter homo appetit ultimum finem, scilicet beatitudinem" (*ST* I, q. 83, a. 1, ad 5). Unlike beasts, humans are not necessarily moved by this natural *habitudo* to some particular end.

111. *ST* I-II, q. 51, a. 1, co.: "talis dispositio quandam latitudinem habet, contingit diversos gradus huiusmodi dispositionis convenire diversis hominibus secundum naturam individui."

112. These sorts of dispositions are implicitly present in Thomas's discussion of

that humans *actively* acquire through nonvolitional or semivolitional behaviors that they themselves perform. These include behaviors that a person performs without full attention, thus making their intention less than fully rational and their volition minimal. For instance, speech accents acquired in early childhood fit this category: language- and region-specific vocal tones are acquired through one's practice and imitation of others, but these sounds are often acquired without one's conscious advertence to the action of acquiring the accent as such and even without advertence to learning one's original language.[113] Culture-wide dispositions, acquired without full and direct choice, can be so powerful and pervasive as to hinder the influence of natural good dispositions—as powerful vicious customs can blot out secondary precepts of the natural law.[114]

Next, we come to (5), habit in its most proper sense: *an acquired and stable disposition of one's soul*, that is, a habit of one's intellect and will that is directed toward a properly human act. These may be named "natural operative habits." St. Thomas notes, "If habit is taken with respect to its operation, then habit is above all found in the soul,"

habits gained by children on account of their upbringing. For example, see *ST* II-II, q. 154, a. 2, where he argues that children are harmed by being raised in a single-parent home. Any kind of customary behaviors, especially from childhood, lead to habits of this sort: "quales operationes assuescimus, et maxime a puero, ad tales habitum habemus" (*SCG* III, c. 85, n. 9). Also, Aquinas also states that celestial bodies can impress a "natural instinct" upon animals that disposes them to respond to subtle changes in nature; see *Liber de sortibus ad dominum Iacobum de Tonengo* [hereafter *De sortibus*], c. 5, co. One way to distinguish between these impressions and species-level instincts is that the impressions are more transitory: "dispositiones autem et passiones, sive corporales sive animales, manent aliquantum post actionem agentis, sed non semper, quia insunt ut in via ad naturam" (*SCG* III, c. 65, n. 7).

113. Aquinas notes that some vocal sounds are naturally formed by all human beings with the same meaning across cultures, such a groans, but other vocal sounds, which signify ideas, are constructs of human institution (*Expositio Peryer.*, lib. 1, l. 2, n. 8). Language-specific sounds are acquired by very young children before their rational faculties fully develop.

114. *ST* I-II, q. 94, a. 6: "Quantum vero ad alia praecepta secundaria, potest lex naturalis deleri de cordibus hominum ... propter pravas consuetudines et habitus corruptos; sicut apud quosdam non reputabantur latrocinia peccata, vel etiam vitia contra naturam." He is referring the Germanic tribesmen in Julius Caesar's day who reputedly did not consider theft immoral: *ST* I-II, q. 94, a. 4.

and he clarifies that "even from the very nature of habit, it is apparent that it is principally related to the will."[115] Here Aquinas indicates the analogous nature of habit, as noted above: habit is *above all* found in the soul and it is *principally* related to the will, but it retains a proper relation to the body and the passions, which in the living person are always united to the soul as their substantial form and mover.[116] From this perspective, one would rightly say that virtue is the truest expression of human habit, for virtue implies the perfection of a power. Virtue necessarily must be good, for evil is a defect and deficiency.[117] Meanwhile, addictions and obsessive-compulsive behaviors may be understood as "extreme habits" and "disorders" of beneficial habits, while vices are clearly bad habits contrary to virtue.[118]

From a theological perspective, one can identify (6) the supernatural entitative habit of grace. Aquinas explains that grace provides a supernatural *esse* in the nature of the soul itself.[119] This *esse* is a sort of *habitus.*[120] Sanctifying grace—as it is typically called in Thomistic tradition—serves as a principle for humans to participate in the divine nature through conformity to Christ.[121] Grace therefore parallels the natural entitative habits, and, more properly speaking, it elevates, perfects, and heals every habit beneath it; it also serves as a root for the other supernatural habits.

115. *ST* I-II, q. 50, aa. 2 and 5.

116. See *ST* I, q. 76, a. 1.

117. *ST* I-II, q. 55, a. 3.

118. Graybiel, "Habits, Rituals, and the Evaluative Brain," 369–70 and 372–75. See also Kent Dunnington, *Addiction and Virtue: Beyond the Models of Disease and Choice* (Downers Grove, Ill.: InterVarsity Press, 2011).

119. *De veritate*, q. 27, a. 1, ad 3: "esse spirituale gratuitum Deus facit in nobis nullo agente mediante, sed tamen mediante aliqua forma creata, quae est gratia."

120. *SCG* III, c. 150, n. 7: "Est autem hic modus proprius hominum, quod ad perfectionem suarum operationum oportet eis inesse, super naturales potentias, quasdam perfectiones et habitus, quibus quasi connaturaliter et faciliter et delectabiliter bonum et bene operentur. Igitur auxilium gratiae, quod homo a Deo consequitur ad perveniendum in ultimum finem, aliquam formam et perfectionem homini inesse designat."

121. *ST* I-II, q. 50, a. 2: "Sed si loquamur de aliqua superiori natura, cuius homo potest esse particeps, secundum illud II Petr. I, ut simus consortes naturae divinae, sic nihil prohibet in anima secundum suam essentiam esse aliquem habitum, scilicet gratiam." See also *ST* I-II, q. 100, a. 4.

Finally, some habits are (7) *non-acquired, stable, supernatural, voluntary dispositions*. These "supernatural operative habits" are infused by God directly, not non-acquired, in harmony with human volition. Some of these habits are caused by God, not human acts, but are put into act by human volition.[122] They exist as theological virtues and infused moral virtues. Others (8) are primarily activated by God moving man freely; these are the Gifts of the Holy Spirit. Here the analogous meanings of "habit" comes full circle, for Aquinas speaks of the Gifts of the Holy Spirit as an infused divine instinct (*instinctum divinum*) in humans.[123]

Among the eight different meanings of habit enumerated above, where can one find the Simon-Pinckaers-Kenny idea of "mechanical habit"? It is unclear, as meanings (2), (3), or (4) could apply: all such habits are "nonvolitional" insofar as their immediate efficient cause is something exterior to the will of the individual who possesses them. Simon, Pinckaers, and Kenny clearly focus on the nonvolitional aspect of "habit" because they want to emphasize that virtue, and thereby *habitus* par excellence, is something nonmechanical. Despite its practical merits, this interpretive move reduces the richness that Aquinas found in the Latin term *habitus*. It is true that a

122. One of the chief characteristics of habit, in Aquinas's view, is that it can be put into action when one wills (*ST* I-II, q. 49, a. 3, s.c.; II-II, q. 171, a. 2, s.c.; III, q. 11, a. 5, ad 2; see also *De malo*, q. 16, a. 11, ad 4); indeed, a habit disposes a person to act: when a person acts according to the inclination of the habit, he chooses to "activate" the habit. *ST* I-II, q. 50, a. 5; *Sent. Ethic.*, lib. 3, l. 6, n. 4: "homo est perfectus secundum intellectum fit homo potens bene operari, non autem bene operans, sicut ille qui habet habitum grammaticae ex hoc ipso est potens loqui congrue; sed ad hoc quod congrue loquatur, requiritur quod hoc velit. Quia habitus est quo quis agit cum voluerit." For this reason, he argues that no power could possess a habit and by that reason be unable to act; see *Quaestiones disputate de virtutibus* [hereafter *De virtutibus*], q. 1, a. 4, arg. 11. Accordingly, Aquinas never bothers to prove that human agents can activate their theological virtues, received by infusion; he takes that possibility as a given. See *De virtutibus*, q. 1, a. 11, co.

123. See *ST* I-II, q. 68, a. 2: "dona sunt quaedam hominis perfectiones, quibus homo disponitur ad hoc quod bene sequatur instinctum divinum. Unde in his in quibus non sufficit instinctus rationis, sed est necessarius spiritus sancti instinctus." See also, *ST* I-II, q. 68, a. 1; II-II, q. 121, a. 1; III, q. 36, a. 5; III, q. 69, a. 5; *Super Evangelium S. Ioannis lectura* [hereafter *Super Io.*], c. 7, l. 5, n. 1090. For *Super Io.*, I consulted the English translation, *Commentary on the Gospel of John*, trans. James A. Weisheipl and Fabian R. Larcher (Albany, N.Y.: Magi Books, 1998).

transliteration does not always equal a good translation. But *habitus* bears a number of related analogous meanings and the transliteration "habit" accurately translates a number of meanings contained in the term *habitus*. By using the word "habit" to name these interrelated realities, as Aquinas himself used the polyvalent word *habitus*, we will be better positioned to understand how mechanical habits are related to acquired virtuous habits and how both are related to habits infused by God. "Habit" thereby proves to be more useful than any other verbal substitution in English. For this reason, I translate *habitus* as "habit."[124] What we will find is that human habits are neither deterministic nor always subject to immediate voluntary control. Rather, as Dunnington explains Aquinas's position, habits occupy a space that mediates between determinism and voluntarism, a space like a "second nature."[125] Habituated dispositions, and the objects to which they become adapted, become *connatural* to us.[126]

124. David Decosimo offers another good reason to translate *habitus* as "habit": several influential social theorists in the past century, including Pierre Bourdieu, have formulated theories using a concept they labeled *habitus*. The extent to which those conceptions overlap with or differ from Aristotle's *hexis* and Thomas's *habitus*, along with that of Pinckaers and Simon, could alone be the subject of a lengthy study. Decosimo, *Ethics as a Work of Charity*, 73–74.

125. Dunnington, *Addiction and Virtue*, 68–69. He cites *ST* I-II, q. 53, a. 2.

126. See *ST* I-II, q. 49, a. 1; q. 78, a. 2; II-II, q. 156, a. 3; *De veritate*, q. 20, a. 2.

# PART 1

# Subterranean Habits

# 1

# Dispositions Derived from Human Nature

While describing his juggling career, Jay Gilligan said that as of 2013 he had practiced with his red plastic rings for at least twenty thousand hours.[1] By his accumulated experience, he said, had become an expert at very specific throws and catches of those rings. That is entirely credible. But what if Gilligan had also said that the red rings themselves were affected by the juggling? What if he claimed that, after being thrown into the air twenty thousand hours, *the rings themselves* had developed a "habit" of shooting up in the air more quickly and easily? Only the gullible would believe him.

Aristotle helps us see why jugglers—not the objects juggled—develop habits: "The stone which by nature moves downwards cannot be habituated to move upwards, not even if one tries to train it by throwing it up ten thousand times."[2] Aquinas develops this insight and points out that humans have the sorts of natures that can be habituated to certain kinds of behaviors. Indeed, we have certain kinds of habits *because of* our natures. He calls innate inclinations "natural habits," for they arise from one's "general" or one's "individual" na-

1. Jay Gilligan, "The Evolution of Juggling," May 20, 2013, YouTube video, 26:02 (at 3:21), https://youtu.be/YB_sfnwbgvk.

2. Aristotle, *Nicomachean Ethics* II.1, 1103a21–22.

ture, but not from one's will.[3] Thomas goes so far as to say that these natural or quasi-natural habits *are caused* by one's nature.[4] Because natural powers precede active volition both ontologically and temporally, natural habits likewise precede fully voluntary habits.

"In the works of Nature," Aquinas observes, "one finds that they proceed in determined ways to determined ends in an orderly and most fitting way ... and for this reason Nature is said to operate wisely."[5] This chapter explores natural habits in their many manifestations and in doing so provides the foundations for assessing the natural causes of human behavior. First, I consider the fact that the natures of nonhumans—from God to molecules to plants—affect their ability to be habituated. Next, I describe what sorts of habits beasts may possess, particularly instincts and inculcated dispositions. Third, I address the habits that humans have by reason of belonging to the species *homo sapiens*. In this regard, I explore instincts and natural dispositions for humans in general, especially as they affect what Aquinas calls the "cogitative power." This sets the stage for a discussion of synderesis and the role of reason with respect to natural instincts. The overall discussion of habitual dispositions possessed by nature sets the stage for the following chapter, in which I treat how particular individuals have innate dispositions and inclinations.

## NONHUMAN DISPOSITIONS

Following Aristotle, Thomas notes that every disposition is bound up with three principles: a subject that underlies the change; the lack of a form (e.g., nonmusical); and the presence of form (e.g., musical).[6] Different subjects have different sorts of dispositions: a human has the disposition to become musical, but while alive she

3. *Sent. Ethic.*, lib. 7, l. 12, n. 4.

4. *ST* I-II, q. 51, a. 1, ad 3.

5. *De operationibus occultis naturae ad quendam militem ultramontanum* (Leon. ed., 179–81).

6. See Aristotle, *Physics* I.7, 190a1–191a20, and the corresponding *lectiones* in Aquinas's *In Physic.*, lib. 1, ll. 12–13, esp. l. 13, nn. 2–3.

cannot become an immovable statue; similarly, a lump of bronze has the "disposition" to be formed into a statue, but it has no disposition to be musical and cannot gain such a disposition. The difference lies in the kind of thing a subject is: the nature of a thing shapes a thing's dispositions and actions. Aristotle says that "in the primary and strict sense," *phusis,* translated as nature, is "a thing's inner principle of movement."[7] Commenting on Aristotle's definition of "nature" in the *Metaphysics,* Aquinas posits that the "form" of a thing is its per se principle of motion and therefore the most important factor of its nature.[8] The nature of a thing—as derived from its form—reveals its dispositions for act.[9]

Some beings by their very nature cannot have habits or dispositions. The first is God, who transcends all categories and so is not a "kind of thing" at all.[10] Thomas notes that change implies the potential to become more or to become less, that is, potential for augmentation and diminishment—and this entails imperfection. But God himself is never in a state whereby he lacks a perfection such that he can gain and then actualize that perfection. There is no unrealized potential within God; he lacks nothing. He is infinite form, absolute perfection, with no limitations.[11] He is pure act. He is *ipsum esse per se subsistens,* "being itself subsisting per se."[12] God is "infinite, comprehending in Himself all the plenitude of perfection of all being, He cannot acquire anything new, nor extend Himself to anything where He did not previously exist."[13] God does not develop over time; he does not become more effective or more truthful. God does

7. Robert Pasnau, *Thomas Aquinas on Human Nature: A Philosophical Study of Summa Theologiae, 1a 75–89* (Cambridge: Cambridge University Press, 2008), 9, referencing Aristotle, *Metaphysics* V.4, 1015a13.

8. *Sent. Meta.,* lib. 5, l. 5, n. 18.

9. See *In Physic.,* lib. 1, l. 15, n. 7.

10. See *Compendium theologiae ad fratrem Raynaldum* [hereafter *Compendium theologiae*], c. 12; I consulted the English translation, *Compendium of Theology,* trans. Cyril Vollert (St. Louis, Mo.: Herder, 1947).

11. See *ST* I, q. 12, a. 1, ad 2.

12. See *ST* I, q. 44, a. 1.

13. *ST* I, q. 9, a. 1.

not change. God's unchangeableness is not on account of being dull and stagnate, as if God stubbornly refuses to change his mind. Rather, God does not change because he exists so perfectly in his substantial goodness—his very being—that he will never deviate from himself. Therefore, God has neither dispositions nor habits, for they indicate an imperfect state between pure potency and act.[14] For example, God does not have a disposition to love; God cannot acquire a greater habit of love; God *is* love.[15]

Looking to the other end of the ladder of being, Thomas argues that material non-organic things such as stones, snowflakes, and molecules have a "natural appetite" and even a "natural love."[16] The foundation for this, he says, is the form of the thing: "every form is followed by some inclination."[17] Inclinations do not come from matter. Consider, for example, the inclination of ice particles to unite together and make a snowflake. One can distinguish between the elements of a body and the form that those elements take (e.g., the hydrogen-oxygen molecules and their structure as a snowflake).[18] One can also distinguish between a material thing and its movement. The term "moving body" indicates two things, the body itself and the modification of the body by which it moves. Movement is a quality that follows upon the form and the nature of the moveable thing. According to Thomas, movement is always directional, which means that it has a goal; consequently, movement is always directed toward a good. In a thing that lacks knowledge, its form determines it to maintain itself in existence and to follow the general laws of nature.[19] Thus, when a stone or a snowflake is moving, its form inclines it to move toward a good proper to itself: its rest in the center of gravity. With this in mind, Thomas can say: "All things strive after

14. See *De virtutibus*, q. 1, a. 1, co.

15. 1 Jn 4:8.

16. See Diana Fritz Cates, *Aquinas on the Emotions: A Religious-Ethical Inquiry* (Washington, D.C.: Georgetown University Press, 2010), 105–8.

17. *ST* I, q. 80, a. 1.

18. See Aristotle, *De anima* II.1, 412a18–22, and Aquinas, *Sent. De anima*, lib. 2, l. 1, n. 10.

19. *ST* I, q. 80, a. 1.

the good, not only those having knowledge, but even those without knowledge."[20] This striving includes a sort of "natural appetite" by which all created things are moved along with an analogous natural love.[21] One can define love in its broadest sense as "the inborn appetite of every power for its act and perfection, a gravitation to completion and rest. It is the foundation of all activity, the underlying principle of every movement, the striving of something imperfect for completion from without."[22] Even stones and snowflakes have a natural love. According to the proper mode of their natures, they strive for the good order of the universe, to which they unknowingly contribute by their existence and in obeying the laws of physics.[23] As for natural appetite, it has a double tendency: (1) to obtain what is suitable and supportive (*amicum*) to the nature of the thing, and (2) to achieve victory over whatever is opposed to it. The first tendency is passive and is achieved by reception (a stone, having been moved, falls toward the center of the earth); the second is active (the weight of a falling stone tends to crush obstacles in its way).[24]

It may seem as if non-organic things have intrinsic powers of self-movement, for scientists speak about instances of "self-assembly" in nature. Snowflakes exemplify how nonliving material things arrange themselves in an orderly way: under the right conditions, water molecules beautifully join together in three-dimensional hexagonal sculptures. Snowflakes illustrate "complex structure formation," which encompasses a unity within a diversity: they "exhibit both repetition (all snowflakes are six-sided, spiky, and branchy) and nearly unlimited variety within this basic pattern."[25] On the nano scale, molecules, atoms, and even smaller particles are in constant motion, creating a "molecular storm," which could seem to indicate

20. *De veritate*, q. 22, a. 1, co.

21. *ST* I-II, q. 26, a. 1.

22. Thomas Gilby, *Poetic Experience* (New York: Sheed and Ward, 1934), 31.

23. *ST* I-II, q. 26, a. 1.

24. *De veritate*, q. 25, a. 2, co.

25. Peter M. Hoffmann, *Life's Ratchet: How Molecular Machines Extract Order from Chaos* (New York: Basic Books, 2012), 100–103, at 103.

self-movement.[26] Once these particles unite, they express new dispositions and behaviors: a snowflake acts differently than individual, free-floating ice crystals.

In response, an Aristotelian-Thomistic perspective would note that, although all things have a natural appetite that is in some way active, they receive their active principle from a prior agent. Though particles may be said to have a sort of proper action (water particles act consistently but differently than helium), they do not act on their own. Rather, "every [physical thing] that is in motion must be moved by something."[27] Water particles that join together must be moved by something else: the molecular storm, supercooled air currents, gravity, etc. Without these external factors, the ice particles would not assemble into the form of a snowflake. As Thomas argues, if that by which something was put into motion is in motion, then there must be a prior mover to them both.[28] Furthermore, "the series [of movers] must come to an end, and there must be a first mover and a first moved."[29] The reason for this is that "no change is infinite; for every change … is a change from something to something."[30] Swirling snowflakes come from moving water molecules, which come from dancing hydrogen and oxygen atoms, which are composed of spinning protons, neutrons, etc. Physical motions are always finite, even when one combination of particles transforms into another, more complex combination. Such changes "cannot go on to infinity, because then there would be no first mover and therefore no other mover."[31] Accordingly, the motions of material things, no matter what complexity they manifest, ultimately come from outside of themselves. Water does not give itself the form of a snowflake any more than water moves on its own: external causes and conditions induce the movement and produce the form. Thus, when a ma-

26. Ibid., 72.
27. Aristotle, *Physics* VII.1, 241b34.
28. *ST* I, q. 1, a. 3.
29. Aristotle, *Physics* VII.1, 242b72.
30. Aristotle, *Physics* VI.10, 241a26.
31. *ST* I, q. 1, a. 3.

terial thing affects something else, it acts only as a derivative agent cause, having been moved by some prior agent cause.

Material things have dispositions to be acted upon, and when they act, it is only through transferred impetus.[32] This applies as much as to water particles as to robots: the first relies on the molecular storm, whereas the second ultimately relies on engineers and software programmers. Much can be done to change the passive disposition of non-organic materials, but nothing can fundamentally make them self-actuating. Thus, purely corporeal things are not self-moving.[33] Their nature does not allow for it.[34] Consequently, stones and snowflakes cannot receive dispositions toward action; they cannot be habituated toward self-movement in any way: "the stone which by nature moves downwards cannot be habituated to move upwards, not even if one tries to train it by throwing it up ten thousand times."[35] As Aristotle and Aquinas say, the principle of self-movement, and therefore of all habituation, is the soul.

Higher than stones, plants also have natural appetites appropriate to their form.[36] Like stones and snowflakes, plants can be affected by exterior causes. Unlike purely material things, plants have an intrinsic principle of life and operation: they have "vegetative souls," which are particular kinds of forms.[37] As animate beings, plants "move themselves to definite kinds of movement."[38] A vegetative soul actuates and organizes a plant's proper material, leading to vegetative activities.[39] The acts in which the vegetative principle manifests itself are self-nutrition and generation.[40] "For anything that

32. Aquinas makes this argument regarding an arrow, which has motion not *per se* but *per accidens*, having received it from the archer. See *De potentia*, q. 3, a. 11, ad 5. He makes a similar argument regarding water flowing from a container and a ball bouncing off a wall. See *In Physic.*, lib. 8, l. 8, n. 7, and *De veritate*, q. 22, a. 1, co.

33. *De veritate*, q. 22, a. 3, co.

34. Ibid.

35. Aristotle, *Nicomachean Ethics* II.1, 1103a21–22.

36. See Cates, *Aquinas on the Emotions*, 108–10.

37. Aristotle, *De anima* 415a1.

38. Aquinas, *De veritate*, q. 22, a. 3, co.

39. See Aquinas, *De potentia*, q. 3, a. 9, co.

40. Aristotle, *De anima* 415a23.

has reached its normal development and which is unmutilated ... the most natural act is the production of another like itself," Aristotle observes.[41] In pursuance of these aims, plants adapt to their environments in creative ways: the roots of a cypress will cling the face of a cliff while its trunk and branches grow downwindward, and a rosebush can be cultivated to cover hundreds of square feet. Over a period of time, vegetal life can receive a modification toward action that is not easily changed. Thus, it can be habituated to some degree. This is what gardeners mean when they speak of "training" a rosebush: even if it had been wild and had previously grown haphazardly according to random circumstances, the plant can analogously be "trained" to grow differently. This training is an analogous form of habituation.

When a rosebush endures external influences, its matter undergoes some kind of change. It may be pruned, for example. Externally-induced change is not the last word, however, for the inner dynamism of the rosebush responds to the change: perhaps it produces more buds. Or perhaps it begins to wither. Habituation can make rose trunks twisted and almost flowerless, or can make them taller, straighter, with more blooms. But roses can only be trained to do something within the limits of their nature. No amount of habituation will teach a rosebush to dance a reel, for that is beyond its natural powers. Nor can a plant be habituated to do something entirely contrary to its nature, such as becoming adapted to bleach as its only nourishment, for then it would die. As Ravaisson recognized: "Life continually suffers external influences; and yet it nevertheless surmounts them and endlessly triumphs over them. In this way it undergoes change through its relation to its inferior form of existence, which is its condition, its matter; it initiates change, it would appear, by the superior virtue which is its very nature."[42]

In other words, the nature of the rosebush includes the power of

41. Ibid., 415a28.

42. Félix Ravaisson, *Of Habit*, trans. Clare Carlisle and Mark Sinclair (London: Continuum, 2008), 31.

adapting to the power of exterior forces such as pruning, but it also has a modicum of power to initiate change on its own: "the life of nature involves self-modification."[43] The more the exterior change is in accordance with its nature, the more the rosebush will flourish. Likewise, the more a rosebush is allowed to live without impediments contrary to its nature, such as bad soil or disastrous pruning, the more it will flourish. The gardener cannot "force" a rosebush to do anything. Instead, he can only "teach" or "train" it. By this kind of habituation, he helps the rosebush to express its inner life more fully. The more the gardener forces his will upon the rosebush without respecting its nature, the closer the rosebush approaches death. "The change that has come to it from the outside becomes more and more foreign to it; the change it has brought upon itself becomes more and more proper to it."[44] In this way, "habit does not simply presuppose nature, but develops in the very direction of nature, and concurs with it."[45] In sum, habits promote flourishing according to a thing's nature.

## NONHUMAN INSTINCTS

A newborn sea turtle ambles toward the water with no help. Within an hour of birth, a blue wildebeest can outrun a predator. Chicks only a few days old are able to demonstrate some basic math skills. Above stones and plants, animals occupy a higher rung on the ladder of being; it is especially by studying them that we can come to an analogous understanding of human behavior and habits.[46] While retaining the perfections held by plants and non-organic matter, animals have a natural spontaneity and flexibility that transcends that of plants. This is because the material of animals is actuated—animated—by a higher sort of life-principle: a "sensitive

43. Editors' commentary, ibid., 84.
44. Ibid., 31.
45. Ibid.
46. See Aquinas, *Compendium theologiae,* c. 80.

soul." Leroi notes the similarities between a soul and a cybernetic system: "It is a set of interacting units (organs) that form an integrated whole (body). It has modules (nutritive, sensitive): and these modules have specialized functions that are hierarchically arranged.... It has a purpose: to regulate the functions of life."[47]

However, unlike a cybernetic system, the animal soul is self-moving and arises from causes found in nature rather than human intervention. By means of this formal principle of life and operation, animals are capable of nutrition and reproduction (like plants) and sensation at the very least. Many animals also have the power of locomotion, for animals naturally possess the power of self-movement more than plants do.[48] Because animals "are born to participate in the divine goodness more eminently than other inferior things," Thomas argues, "they need many operations and helps toward their perfection."[49] This analysis of animal behaviors led Aquinas to designate one animal "higher" than another for one or more of the following reasons: its bodily form is more perfect (and thus more capable of complex behaviors), its generation is more perfect, it is more intelligent, but above all because its body is more subject to its soul.[50] Thus: "land animals, on account of their more perfect life, are like souls mastering bodies."[51] For Aquinas, the more self-mastery an animal has, the higher it is on the hierarchy of being. Plants exhibit a "natural appetite" to pursue their own good and to "gain victory" over obstacles to their flourishing, and these tendencies are found in animals with this difference: animals are better able to adapt their behaviors to pursue good and avoid evil.[52] Consequently, animals are higher on the hierarchy of being, for they initiate operations that promote their own flourishing, and they are

47. Armand Marie Leroi, *The Lagoon: How Aristotle Invented Science* (London: Bloomsbury Circus, 2014), 176.

48. Aquinas, *De veritate*, q. 22, a. 3, co.

49. *De veritate*, q. 22, a. 3, ad 2.

50. See *ST* I, q. 72, a. 1, ad 1.

51. Ibid.

52. See *De veritate*, q. 25, a. 2, co.

thereby more open to gaining new habits: "the higher one goes on the scale of natural beings, the greater is the power of habituation."[53]

Reflexes are the most basic of operations initiated by the animal. As sensory information is correlated, sorted, and ultimately controlled by the central nervous system, which is comprised of the brain and spinal cord, the result may be a reflexive response.[54] All animals have predictable and stereotyped reflexes. Fast reflexes are a sign that the nerves are communicating well with the nervous system. The peripheral nervous system, and specifically the autonomic nervous system and the somatic nervous system, is more immediately responsible for two kinds of reflexes: *unconditioned* (vegetative) reflexes and *conditionable* (somatic) reflexes.[55]

*Unconditioned reflexes* are functions of the autonomic nervous system. They are natural, spontaneous, simple, and determined motor responses to specific stimuli. Identifiable kinds of unconditioned reflexes are present in all healthy members of a given species.[56] These reflexes are unlearned and involuntary, such that animals do not anticipate them and have no direct control over them.[57] As the name "autonomic" implies, unconditioned reflexes are automatic: once a stimulus is presented to a healthy animal, the reflex action ordinarily will take its course until completion. Although Aquinas did not speak of reflexes as such, he discussed the nature of the motion of the heartbeat, which could now be considered as a sort of immanent reflex. In attempting to explain the fundamental cause of the heartbeat, he wrote, "the motion of the heart is a natural result of the soul, the form of the living body and principally of the heart."[58] This conclu-

53. Editors' commentary in Ravaisson, *Of Habit*, 84.

54. John E. Hall, *Guyton and Hall Textbook of Medical Physiology*, 13th ed. (Philadelphia: Saunders, 2015), 600.

55. Ibid., 773.

56. Peter K. Anokhin, *Biology and Neurophysiology of the Conditioned Reflex and Its Role in Adaptive Behavior*, ed. and trans. Samuel A. Corson (New York: Pergamon, 1974), 2.

57. Lauralee Sherwood, Hillar Klandorf, and Paul Yancey, *Animal Physiology: From Genes to Organisms*, 2nd ed. (Belmont, Calif.: Cengage Learning, 2012), 181.

58. Aquinas, *De motu cordis ad magistrum Philippum de Castro Caeli*. See the fascinating study of Marjorie O'Rourke Boyle, "Aquinas's Natural Heart," *Early Science and Medicine* 18, no. 3 (2013): 266–90.

sion can be applied to all such motions: the animal's "sensory soul" acts naturally in the vegetative functions that are essential to the organism's self-maintenance.[59] Notably consonant with this conclusion, some scientists name these functions "vegetative reflexes" because they "regulate those bodily processes that normally transpire without conscious intervention," including sweat secretion, pulse-regulation, pupil dilation/constriction, swallowing, and vomiting.[60]

Ivan Pavlov's experiments famously demonstrated that some natural reflexes are moldable or *conditionable*. The primary functions of conditionable reflexes are protection (e.g., coughing, eyelid closure), health (wiping, scratching), nutrition (sucking), and general self-maintenance (body posture).[61] These reflexes are *natural* insofar as they are in accordance with the flourishing of the animal and ordinarily operate in a stereotyped way according to species. But they are also conditionable. Unconditioned reflexes become *conditioned* or *somatic* reflexes when an animal learns or is trained to counter or inhibit an automatic response and is conditioned to respond to different objects. Indeed, one could rightly say that all habituated powers are adapted to some particular object.[62]

On a higher plane than reflexes, animal *behavior* involves a specific type of activity or operation that is initiated by the animal, such as walking, eating, and playing. Animal behaviors always involve certain types of reflexes, as when eating while standing involves the balancing and swallowing reflexes. But behaviors are more than a chain of reflexes: behaviors have a meaning and goal that provide

59. In *De motu cordis*, Aquinas quotes Aristotle's *On the Motion of Animals* 10, 703a29-ba2, to this effect: "Every part of the animal is naturally established to perform its proper function, such that the function does not require a [distinct] soul to be in every part as a principle of motion, but instead as a kind of principle of the existing body by which the other parts live, that by which they naturally perform their proper function."

60. Hinrich Rahmann and Mathilde Rahmann, *The Neurobiological Basis of Memory and Behavior* (New York: Springer Science and Business Media, 2012), 223.

61. Ibid.

62. Craig Steven Titus, *Resilience and the Virtue of Fortitude: Aquinas in Dialogue with the Psychosocial Sciences* (Washington, D.C.: The Catholic University of America Press, 2006), 126.

unity throughout the complex action. Beyond unconditioned reflexes, then, the *behavior* of an animal indicates the development of its holistic potential. Whereas unconditioned reflexes are generally on the level of muscle control, behaviors incorporate more of the entire individual: muscles, emotions, and what Aquinas calls the "internal powers," including the concupiscible and irascible powers, imagination, memory, and the estimative power.[63] The two basic behaviors of the natural appetite, to pursue good and to avoid evil, are governed by two powers. By the "concupiscible power," which is focused on delightful objects, an animal desires what is suitable and favorable to its flourishing and moves itself toward objects perceived to be good for it.[64] By the "irascible power," which is focused on "arduous" objects, an animal "seeks to gain mastery and victory over things that are contrary to it."[65] Such are powers held by most, if not all, animals. Higher animals also have the "imaginative power," by which the animal retains and combines various forms received from the senses.[66] Some animals also have the "estimative power," by which they "apprehend intentions not received by the senses, such as friendliness or hostility."[67]

Similar to conditionable reflexes, behaviors can be shaped and acquired—with this difference: the acquisition of a new behavior involves engaging the "internal powers" of the animal, especially its "concupiscible power." To change an animal's behavior, to create a new habit, one must appeal to its desires. Citing Aristotle, Thomas notes that animals display aggressive behaviors because they desire to possess the object of their delight without impediments: rams fight with each other in order to reproduce with a ewe, and lions fight over food.[68] Consequently, the irascible power is subordinated

63. *ST* I, q. 81, a. 3, ad 3. See the discussion in Cates, *Aquinas on the Emotions*, 111–17.

64. *De veritate*, q. 25, a. 2, co.

65. Ibid.

66. Ibid.

67. Ibid.

68. See ibid., referencing Aristotle, *De historia animalibus* IX.1, 608b19. In Thomas's edition, the reference was *De animalibus* VIII.1.2.

to the concupiscible, such that positive desire is the motivating force behind animal behavior.[69] The desire for a good is more powerful than an aversion toward an evil.

Having considered some of the basic elements of animal habituation, we can now address their underlying causes more precisely. Some scientists argue that the somatic nervous system (SNS) regulates "voluntary muscle activity,"[70] or that actions controlled by the SNS are "under *voluntary, conscious,* or at least *subconscious control.*"[71] But here the designation "voluntary" is ambiguous. Though conditioned reflexes and behaviors may be subject to variation on account of the animal's appetites, as we have seen, the animal does not freely choose to develop its skills toward a chosen goal. Indeed, the *agent-efficient* cause of animal habituation can be explained without positing free choice on the part of the animal itself. When a sufficient stimulus activates an animal's emotions, imagination, desires, and so on, that stimulus-response system is sufficient to explain the immediate moving force behind the animal's behavior. Animals do not exhibit self-reflexive activity, as if they purposely try to shape their own emotions, reflexes, imagination, knowledge, or behavior and gain habits thereby. Instead, the primary agent of animal habituation apparently exists outside of the animal as a stimulus. Sometimes the primary agent is another animal, as when a mother bird teaches her chicks how to fly.[72] At other times, the agent is a human trainer.[73]

It may seem paradoxical that animal habits and animal behavior in general come partly from the animal itself and partly from anoth-

69. See *De veritate*, q. 25, a. 2, co.

70. Charles R. Noback et al., *The Human Nervous System: Structure and Function* (New York: Springer Science and Business Media, 2005), 142.

71. Hall, *Guyton and Hall Textbook of Medical Physiology*, 815. The SNS may be identified as a *material* cause of animal habituation, an underlying substrate of conditioned reflexes and behaviors (in contrast to the unconditioned, automatic reflexes that are controlled by the autonomic nervous system).

72. *ST* I, q. 101, a. 2, ad 2.

73. *ST* I-II, q. 50, a. 3, ad 2.

er agent. In order to make sense of this, Aquinas developed Aristotle's understanding of instinct. *Instincts* may be initially described as natural dispositions of animal behavioral patterns.[74] William James defines them teleologically: "Instinct is usually defined as the faculty of acting in such a way as to produce certain ends, without foresight of the ends, and without previous education in the performance."[75] Nutcracker birds, for instance, bury hundreds of hoards of pine seeds and, months later, find them beneath the snow.[76] Such instinctual behaviors may be described in terms of the ends at which they aim, such as reproduction, nourishment, defense, care for the young, and so on.[77] These goals are pre-formed for the animal; it did not choose these goals for itself.[78]

Instinctual behavior may be considered rational in one respect and nonrational in another respect. It is rational insofar as it is intelligible, goal-directed, and the result of some kind of knowledge. William James notes, "The performances of animal instinct seem semi-automatic, and the reflex acts of self-preservation certainly are so. Yet they resemble intelligent acts in bringing about the same ends at which the animals' consciousness, on other occasions, deliberately aims."[79] When a dog sees a rabbit that is too far off to catch, Aquinas explains, it makes no movement toward it, feeling no hope for catching it; but if the prey is near, the dog leaps, hoping to catch it.[80] But the rationality is not something that resides in the animal as something to which the animal has direct access. Although high-

74. *ST* II-II, q. 95, a. 7.

75. William James, *The Principles of Psychology* (New York: Henry Holt and Co., 1890), 2:383.

76. Sara J. Shettleworth, *Cognition, Evolution, and Behavior*, 2nd ed. (Oxford: Oxford University Press, 2010), 21.

77. James, *The Principles of Psychology*, 2:383.

78. Although some animals can display remarkable feats of memory (Shettleworth, *Cognition, Evolution, and Behavior*, 230–37), there is little to no evidence that they anticipate days or hours in the future—which makes the very possibility of goal-setting extremely unlikely (ibid., 391).

79. James, *The Principles of Psychology*, 1:5.

80. *ST* I-II, q. 40, a. 3.

er animals such as dolphins have more dominion over their actions than do lower animals such as coral, nonhuman animals are never fully masters of their own actions or appetites.[81]

The goal-directed behaviors of animals are caused by instincts, Thomas insists, not by a command of reason or by free choice. The animal acts according to its senses and feelings, not by making syllogisms or intellectually deciding what to do next. Coordinating with the other interior senses—memory, imagination, the common sense—the "estimative" power guides animal behavior by providing the animal with a practical judgment about a particular object that the animal has perceived as well as an impulse of how to respond to that object.[82] The estimative power operates by giving the animal an estimate as to whether something bears the aspect of being harmful or helpful.[83] Aquinas explains that a sheep runs away from a wolf, not because the wolf's color or shape are ugly, but because the wolf's color and shape suggest that is a "natural enemy"; similarly, a bird collects pieces of straw, not because they are beautiful, but because they appear useful for building a nest.[84] Without knowing what helpfulness or harmfulness is, a sheep correctly but non-intellectually grasps the "intention" that a wolf is harmful to it.[85] The sheep estimates the harmfulness of a wolf, and the woolly creature instinctively runs away from the harm and toward safety. "In

81. *ST* I-II, q. 15, a. 2.

82. *De veritate,* q. 24, a. 2, co. See George Klubertanz, *The Discursive Power: Sources and Doctrine of the Vis Cogitativa According to St. Thomas Aquinas* (St. Louis, Mo.: Modern Schoolman, 1952); also, Miguel Alejandro García Jaramillo, *La cogitativa en Tomás de Aquino y sus fuentes* (Pamplona: Ediciones Universidad de Navarra, 1997).

83. *ST* I, q. 78, a. 4. See *De veritate,* q. 24, a. 2, ad 7.

84. *ST* I, q. 78, a. 4. See John Deely, "Animal Intelligence and Concept-Formation." *The Thomist* 35 (1971): 43–93.

85. This use of intention is distinct from "intention" meaning "the purpose of an agent." Jörg Alejandro Tellkamp notes that "intentio," in the context of perception and knowledge indicates, for Aquinas, "the cognitive content attached to an object, which encompasses what a given object means for a perceiving subject." Tellkamp, "*Vis Aestimativa* and *Vis Cogitativa* in Thomas Aquinas's *Commentary on the Sentences,*" *The Thomist* 76 (2012): 611–40, at 612–13.

this way," Thomas says, "irrational animals intend an end, insofar as they are moved to something by natural instinct."[86]

As soon as an animal is presented with a motivator or end to which its appetite is naturally or habitually inclined, it is moved toward that desirable object, barring obstacles such as satiety.[87] Thus, we can fully define instinct as "an innate arrangement of animal powers which enables its possessor to recognize at once the usefulness and harmfulness of certain objects, to experience emotional excitement as a result of such knowledge, and to act or feel the urge to act in a particular manner according to the biological value of the objects thus perceived."[88] From this perspective, an instinct is the natural habit that inclines an animal to move in response to the impulse of the estimative power. Instinct in animals thus acts analogously to prudence in a human being. The habit of prudence enables humans to deliberate rationally about what they should do, whereas animals do not judge what they ought to through such deliberation, but instead "from some sort of instinct."[89] Their instinct is guided by "a natural estimate about pursing what is fitting and avoiding what is harmful, as a lamb follows its mother and flees from a wolf."[90] "Animal prudence" is a nondeliberative, nonrational judgment about what should be done or avoided for the good of the individual, group, or species.[91]

Ultimately, the source of the rational aspect of animal behavior comes from outside the animal. When *natural instinct* moves the animal, whether from the animal on its own or through the instinctual

86. *ST* I-II, q. 12, a. 5.

87. See *ST* I-II, q. 13, a. 2, ad 2.

88. Brennan, *General Psychology*, 214–15.

89. Aquinas, *Sent. Meta.*, lib. 1, l. 1, n. 11.

90. Ibid. See *De veritate*, q. 24, a. 2: "Bruta autem habent aliquam similitudinem rationis, in quantum participant quamdam prudentiam naturalem ... Sed hoc iudicium est eis ex naturali aestimatione, non ex aliqua collatione, cum rationem sui iudicii ignorent."

91. See Joannes Baptista Dich, "De Comparatione inter Habitum et Instinctum secundum Sanctum Thomam" (STD thesis, Pontifical University of St. Thomas Aquinas, 1959), 64–65.

training from its parent, "the movement of the natural appetite results from the apprehension of the separate Intellect who authored nature."[92] That is, the rationality within instinct derives from God's wisdom. When *habituation as training* underlies animal movement, the rationality of the action is derived from an intentional animal trainer. A trainer shares his or her rationality with the animal by training it to grasp an intention attached to an object or behavior (e.g., a trainer leads a dolphin to estimate "jumping in the air" as a good).[93] Training is something of a science, because properly applied methods often ensure predictable outcomes of animal behavior, but training is also an art, because the individuality of an animal can never be wholly encompassed by general scientific laws.[94] A good trainer realizes that one cannot push an animal beyond the limits of the animal's specific powers and individual characteristics. Thus, animal behavior is *nonrational* insofar as the animal acts without knowing the essence or the final goal of what it is doing; but it is *intentional* insofar as the animal participates in the rationality of another by performing an act that a trainer has intentionally directed toward some object of apprehension.

Motivation is focused on a good, and the heart of animal habituation consists in shaping what the animal perceives as good. Animal behavior can change when a trainer appeals to their desires for different goods and simultaneously habituates their estimative sense regarding an object to be desired. Now Aquinas identifies "end" with "good" insofar as the good is a final cause.[95] We have already seen that rocks and plants have a sort of "natural love" for their proper end. On a higher level, to perceive something as a good for oneself is to desire it, which is the beginning of love. *Desire* is a movement toward an absent good, while *love* is "complacency" in a pres-

92. Ibid.

93. See *ST* I-II, q. 50, a. 3, ad 2, and q. 1, a. 2.

94. Jenifer A. Zeligs, *Animal Training 101: The Complete and Practical Guide to the Art and Science of Behavior Modification* (Minneapolis, Minn.: Mill City Press, 2014), 2.

95. *ST* I, q. 5, a. 4.

ent good, including sensory goods.[96] Animals have this "sensorial love" in addition to the love that they have in common with stones and plants.[97] When directed toward a primary motivator, this sensorial love is consequent on the animal's sensation, imagination, and estimation; habituation plays a role as well when the animal's desires are directed toward a secondary motivator.[98] In sum, another way to characterize animal habituation is as an education in sensorial love.

A simple example may help to illustrate the various concepts explained above. In the wild, a hungry dolphin sees a fish, which activates its unconditioned reflexes: its pupils dilate, it quivers with excitement, it prepares to swim to the food. The dolphin has a sensory love for the food. Following its instinct for nourishing itself, the dolphin engages in natural instinctual food-seeking behavior and swims toward the chow, looking intently and listening all the while. Then the dolphin is captured and brought to an aquarium. Food is highly motivating to a *hungry* animal, whereas food can have a neutral or null effect on an animal that is not hungry. An animal trainer, working with such natural mechanisms of motivation, provides an end or goal for the animal and moves the animal toward that goal by appealing to the animal's desire for food and physical delight. In the following months, the trainer conditions the dolphin's hunger reflexes so that they are activated by a specific stimulus: a bell. The dolphin is trained to perform instinctual food-seeking behaviors in response to the bell's ring. Simultaneously, the trainer is shaping the animal's estimative power to recognize an object or behavior—jumping in response to a bell—as good, insofar as it leads to food. In this way, the trainer directs the animal's desires, instinctual impulses, and estimative judgments toward a specific object or behavior. In time, the dolphin can perform this new behavior easily, quickly, and with delight. The trainer has successfully shaped, directed, and even elicited

96. *ST* I-II, q. 26, a. 2.

97. *ST* I-II, q. 26, a. 1.

98. The perceived value of any particular motivator-stimulus-object largely depends on a wide range of circumstances, including context, time, exposure, physiology, and association. Zeligs, *Animal Training 101*, 152.

the animal's *sensory love.* The dolphin has been habituated to have a sensory love for jumping in the air, and perhaps for the trainer herself. In this way, all animal habituation can be understood as habituation of some kind of desire. Given that the instincts of animals differ according to species, we can now consider the nature, function, and plasticity of human behavior on the sensory level.

## HUMAN INSTINCTS AND NATURAL DISPOSITIONS IN GENERAL

The human being is a "little world," a *microcosm.*[99] As the human being is a body-soul composite, the human soul occupies the lowest place among immaterial substances, but the human body occupies the highest place among material things.[100] On account of our hylomorphic nature, we have the general dispositional and habitual perfections of the lower orders of beings, in addition to properly human perfections of our habits. Every living human being has something in common with every other human, namely, human nature. Aquinas distinguishes between "specific nature" and "individual nature," indicating the difference between what all humans have in common as a species (specific nature) and what is proper to a single person (individual nature).[101] He states that, when considering habit as a disposition of the subject in relation to nature, habit can be natural with respect to "specific nature" or quasi-natural with respect to "individual" nature. In this section, I will discuss whether or not there are some structural dispositions common to all, or nearly all, members of the human race.

99. See Aristotle, *Physics* VIII.2, 252b26 (where he is thought to coin the term μικρῷ κόσμῳ), and Thomas's commentary *In Physic.*, lib. 8, l. 4, n. 3. For a discussion of this concept in general, see William Norris Clarke, "Living on the Edge: The Human Person as 'Frontier Being' and Microcosm," in *The Creative Retrieval of Saint Thomas Aquinas: Essays in Thomistic Philosophy, New and Old* (New York: Fordham University Press, 2009), 132–51.

100. See *ST* I, q. 75, a. 7; also *Quaestiones Disputate de Anima*, a. 7, co.

101. See *ST* I-II, q. 51, a. 1.

On the most fundamental level of being, similar to inanimate matter, a human body follows physical laws of nature such as gravity. Like stones and snowflakes, humans have a "natural love" that expresses itself in striving to maintain the individual in existence and to cooperate with the common good of the universe. On a higher level of being, a healthy human body automatically executes "vegetative" functions, adapting itself to external conditions in order to achieve nourishment, self-maintenance, and reproduction.[102] In this way, one can hold that humans have both reflexes that are unconditioned and those that can be conditioned. What was said about animal reflexes applies *mutatis mutandis* to humans as well. Salivating for food, like Pavlov's dogs, is "just one of several reflexes that humans are biologically prepared to perform: newborns suck when they encounter a nipple (sucking reflex), hold their breath when submerged under water (the diving reflex), and grasp a finger … (the palmar grasp reflex)."[103] Although the so-called primitive reflexes are inhibited by maturity, healthy adults have their own reflexes, such as the knee-jerk reflex, which is produced when a doctor hits the patellar ligament with a rubber mallet.[104] Like those of animals, some human reflexes can be conditioned toward new objects. Humans can also gain new reflex-like motions through training; this will be discussed in the section on acquired habits.

Like the lower animals, we can adapt ourselves to our environment with exterior powers of locomotion; like higher animals, we also possess the interior powers of our passions. We also have a unique and higher way of moving ourselves: we present a chosen end to ourselves before acting. This more perfect mode of self-movement entails that we possess a "more perfect mode of living."[105] Under-

102. In *ST* I-II, q. 17, a. 8, Thomas makes it clear that the "acts of the vegetal soul are not subject to the command of reason."

103. Mark A. Gluck et al., *Learning and Memory: From Brain to Behavior, International Edition*, 2nd ed. (New York: Worth, 2013), 49.

104. See J. M. Schott and M. N. Rossor, "The Grasp and Other Primitive Reflexes," *Journal of Neurology, Neurosurgery and Psychiatry* 74 (2003): 558–60.

105. *ST* I, q. 18, a. 3.

lying our deliberate self-movement, and deeply affected by it, we possess—like other animals—natural physical-emotive-cognitive dispositions called *instincts* that incline us toward nondeliberative self-movement.[106]

Arguments against the existence of human instincts often center on the nature of human intellection. Samuel Malkemus provides an important objection. According to Malkemus, Aquinas's fundamental distinction between animals and humans entails the following: animals have instincts and humans, having rational souls, do not.[107] This objection is paralleled by Robert A. Greene's claim that for Thomas "*instinctus naturae* was, by definition, opposed to reason and free choice."[108] Aquinas, for instance, often contrasts the way animals are constrained by instinct with the freedom that humans have in their choice. He notes that stones and all things without knowledge act without judgment. Above them are animals that act with judgment, but not freedom, as when a sheep flees a wolf: "it judges, not from reasoning, but from natural instinct."[109] Humans contrastingly act from a "free judgment" (*libero iudicio*) which is not determined to a single end: we can move ourselves to various particular ends depending on what reason determines through syllogistic or rhetorical reasoning.[110] Therefore, it could seem as if humans do not have instincts. Additionally, from a biological perspective, Charles Varela, following D. O. Hebb, holds that "the property of *rigidity* identifies *instincts* just as *flexibility* identifies *reflexes*."[111] Consequently, instinc-

106. See ibid.

107. Samuel Arthur Malkemus, "Reclaiming Instinct: Exploring the Phylogenetic Unfolding of Animate Being," *Journal of Humanistic Psychology* (2014): 1–27, at 1.

108. Robert A. Greene, "Instinct of Nature: Natural Law, Synderesis, and the Moral Sense," *Journal of the History of Ideas*, 58, no. 2 (1997): 173–98, at 185. Another of his articles covers a broader historical swath: "The Origin, Definition, Assimilation and Endurance of *Instinctu Natura* in Natural Law Parlance—From Isidore and Ulpian to Hobbes and Locke," *History of European Ideas* 36 (2010): 361–74.

109. *ST* I, q. 83, a. 1.

110. Ibid.

111. Charles R. Varela, "Biological Structure and Embodied Human Agency: The Problem of Instinctivism," *Journal for the Theory of Social Behavior* 33, no. 1 (2003): 95–122, at 109.

tive behavior is invariable, automatic, compulsive, and even "robotic."[112] It follows that humans do not have instinctive actions—that the very idea is "a theoretical self-contradiction"—because "nature" for humans includes intelligence, which always affects and directs sensory reception and behavior.[113]

In what follows, I will argue that these claims do not adequately take Thomas's complete position into account. Thomas affirms that humans have instincts, which incline a person toward various behaviors but they do not create properly human action, nor do they necessitate any action at all. But our instincts are not *opposed* to reason and free choice. On some occasions the impulses of instincts should be affirmed and followed by reasonable free choice.

We may begin by noting that, in his *Commentary on the Sentences* (ca. 1256–57), Thomas flatly denied that humans have instincts and provided an alternative explanation for instinct-like human behavior.[114] There he focused on the cognitive nature of humans, noting that "in things endowed with knowledge," that is, in humans, "the principles of action are knowledge and appetite." For properly human acts, that is, acts "befitting" the human species, there must be natural sources of the act in a person's knowledge and appetite. It would seem that a human's intellect "is imbued with a natural *concept*," and the appetitive power is imbued with a natural *inclination* whereby the individual is directed to act in a proper manner and in turn shapes the appetites. Thomas argued that in other animals, this "natural concept" is called "natural instinct" whereas in humans it is called "the natural law." Therefore, "the natural law is nothing other than *a concept naturally instilled into man,* whereby he is guided to act fittingly in his proper actions," some of which pertain insofar as he is an animal (e.g., eating, reproducing), and some pertain insofar as he is rational (e.g., reasoning).[115] This conclusion marks Thomas's ear-

112. Ibid., 110.

113. Ibid., 114.

114. The following exposition closely follows *Scriptum super libros Sententiarum magistri Petri Lombardi* [hereafter *Super Sent.*], lib. 4, d. 33, q. 1, a. 1, co.

115. Ibid.; emphasis added.

ly attempt to grapple with the issue. A better understanding of habit led him later to refine his position.

In his collection of disputed questions *De veritate* (ca. 1256–59), Thomas again took up the question of natural inclinations toward specific behaviors, this time with a discussion of synderesis.[116] He departs from his earlier work and instead argues that humans have "a natural habit of . . . the universal principles of the natural law" which serves as a foundation of all human action.[117] Likewise, in the *Prima Pars* of his *Summa Theologiae*, Thomas calls synderesis a special habit of understanding certain concepts.[118] By means of this "first natural habit,"[119] without any investigation on the part of reason, a person can know the first principles of action, such as the principle that no one should be harmed.[120] One may define synderesis as *the disposition of the practical intellect by which we understand the actual precepts of the natural law*.[121] Because of synderesis, "by nature each human being has a fundamental awareness of these principles . . . [which] can be used promptly when needed."[122] Because natural law contains the practical principles for the flourishing of created things, the act of synderesis is therefore a natural inclination away from what is harmful for human beings and toward what is naturally good and leads to human flourishing.[123]

Thomas's mature position has a number of advantages over his earlier thought. Firstly, he corrects his earlier position. Instead of

116. See Tobias Hoffman, "Conscience and Synderesis," in *The Oxford Handbook of Aquinas*, 256–62. See also Vernon J. Bourke, "The Background of Aquinas' Synderesis Principle," in *Graceful Reason*, ed. Lloyd Gerson (Toronto: PIMS, 1983), 345–60.

117. *De veritate*, q. 16, a. 1, co.

118. *ST* I, q. 79, a. 12; emphasis added.

119. *ST* I, q. 79, a. 13.

120. *ST* I, q. 79, a. 12; see *Sent. Ethic.*, lib. 6, l. 11, n. 3. See also Jacob W. Wood, *To Stir a Restless Heart: Thomas Aquinas and Henri de Lubac on Nature, Grace, and the Desire for God* (Washington, D.C.: The Catholic University of America Press, 2019), 218–19, for how the agent intellect impresses *ratio seminalis* on the passive intellect as a sort of habit.

121. J. Budziszewski, *Commentary on Thomas Aquinas' Treatise on Law* (Cambridge: Cambridge University Press, 2014), 234. See *ST* I-II, q. 94, a. 1, ad 2.

122. Hoffman, "Conscience and Synderesis," 256.

123. See *De veritate*, q. 16, a. 1, s.c. 4.

positing an indefinite number of innate concepts, which could be multiplied seemingly without end, he observes the harmonious order between the intellect and reality. The practical principles of natural law and our practical reason are naturally fitted for one another: the principles are naturally graspable by reason, while reason has a natural tendency to grasp them. The practical intellect possesses a natural *inclination* toward its proper objects, that is, a stable disposition to grasp the truths about what should be done in general to promote human flourishing.[124] Secondly, he better explains how our lower inclinations are related to our highest activities. Synderesis is a "natural habit as a beginning" that provides "certain principles" of good habits to the appetitive powers, but it is not the "substance of habit" in the soul, for habits of the rational soul are primarily of the intellect and the will, which in turn shape the appetites.[125] The natural and habitual cognition of synderesis is a "nursery" or "seed-bed" of virtue.[126] It tells the practical reason that a person ought to act in accordance with ends of the virtues and avoid behavior contrary to human flourishing.[127] Synderesis always inclines a person toward the good, and men are naturally capable of performing the good acts it suggests.[128] Significantly, Aquinas's account of synderesis helps him to explain why not everyone follows or appears to know the basic principles of moral action. Because these principles are not "innate ideas," it follows that "truth or rectitude is the same for all, but it is not equally known by all."[129] One's mind might be perverted by passion, or synderesis could be weakened by a contrary bad habit, or have a disordered disposition from individual nature, or one might choose not to utilize synderesis.[130]

124. See *ST* I, q. 79, a. 11, ad 2; I-II, q. 51, a. 1; *De veritate,* q. 15, a. 1, co.

125. *ST* I-II, q. 51, a. 1.

126. Ibid.

127. Ana Maria González, "*Depositum Gladius Non Debet Restituiti Furioso*: Precepts, *Synderesis,* and Virtues in Saint Thomas Aquinas," *The Thomist* 63 (1999): 217–40, at 224.

128. *De veritate,* q. 16, a. 1, ad 7 and ad 12.

129. *ST* I-II, q. 94, a. 4.

130. Ibid.

Powerful as it is for our behavior, synderesis alone is insufficient to move us to action. Synderesis provides a juridical formulation of only universal practical precepts to the intellect but cannot establish what must be done in a particular right-here-right-now situation. At best, it indicates the typical ways that flourishing may be obtained, and what general paths lead away from flourishing. This is because synderesis is a habit of understanding by which a man, in virtue of the light of the active intellect, can naturally know indemonstrable principles of right action.[131] These indemonstrable principles are the same always, everywhere, and for each person. Action is more than merely grasping the right principles of action: there must be something else beyond the intellectual habit of synderesis that provides an impulse toward movement in concrete situations. Aquinas holds that it is the *vis cogitativa.*

## THE COGITATIVE POWER AND HUMAN INCLINATIONS

We saw above that the *vis estimativa,* the estimative sense/power, directs animals toward instinctive behaviors. The cogitative power (*vis cogitativa*) plays an analogous role in humans, with crucial differences that stem from human rationality. To understand the cogitative power we must refine our understanding of how the human animal responds to the world. Following the work of Daniel De Haan, we can begin by distinguishing between "sensation" and "perception."[132] Sensation is the operation of the five external senses (touch, sight, hearing, taste, and smell) in response to a *per se* sensi-

131. Aquinas, *Sent. Ethic.*, lib. 6, l. 5, n. 5, and l. 7, n. 20.

132. See Daniel De Haan, "Perception and the *Vis Cogitativa*: A Thomistic Analysis of Aspectual, Actional, and Affectional Percepts," *American Catholic Philosophical Quarterly* 88, no. 3 (2014): 397–437, and "Moral Perception and the Function of the *Vis Cogitativa* in Thomas Aquinas's Doctrine of the Antecedent and Consequent Passions," *Documenti e studi sulla tradizione filosofica medievale* 25 (2014): 289–330. De Haan's account bears a similarity, but also superiority, to Mark J. Barber's article, "Aquinas on Internal Sensory Intentions: Nature and Classification," *International Philosophical Quarterly* 52, no. 2 (June 2012): 199–226.

ble object external to an animal.[133] The operation of the "common sense," an "internal sense," unites the sensations within the person's brain. This unifying work is essential for accurate sensation.[134] The cogitative power operates by perceiving the nonsensible intentions of objects found in the world. De Haan explains: "Perceptibles are real features of real things that, like the essential sensibles we sense, actualize and determine what we perceive."[135] As with animals and their estimative power, humans through the cogitative power grasp a sensed thing's nonsensible "intentions," that is, their perception registers "the cognitive content attached to an object, which encompasses what a given object means for a perceiving subject."[136]

Animal perception greatly contrasts with human perception because the perceived object "means" something different to their vastly different natures as "perceiving subjects." In the case of nonrational beasts, "the estimative power apprehends an individual, not insofar as it is under a common nature, but only insofar as it is the end point or starting point of some action or affection."[137] An ewe does not recognize its newborn as a lamb that belongs to a group of the Shropshire species, but as an *approachable-looking, good-smelling, emotionally-absorbing, thing-that-should-be-nursed-and-protected.* Nonhuman animals are natural nominalists. Because they have no abstract thought, they do not grasp the essence of things—they experience only individuals, even when they intuitively grasp that groups of individuals are "safe."[138] Additionally, through its estima-

133. See Thomas, *Sent. De anima,* lib. 2, l. 13. De Haan notes that "sensation" means both an organic, automatic stimulation of the nerves in response to an object, as well as "a conscious and intentional act of seeing, hearing," etc. He posits that the latter is Thomas's understanding of sensation: "Perception and the *Vis Cogitativa,*" 401n10.

134. *ST* I, q. 78, a. 4, ad 2.

135. De Haan, "Perception and the *Vis Cogitativa,*" 406.

136. Tellkamp, "*Vis Aestimativa* and *Vis Cognitiva,*" 612–13.

137. *Sent. De anima,* lib. 2, l. 13, n. 16.

138. See *ST* I, q. 85, a. 1. Undoubtedly, animal perception and estimation are complex and richly nuanced. See A. Leo White, "Instinct and Custom," *The Thomist* 66 (2002): 577–605, along with the many contemporary studies of these matters, including the works cited above: Shettleworth, *Cognition, Evolution, and Behavior,* and Zeligs, *Animal Training 101.*

tive power, an animal only perceives individuals that bear upon its actions or reactions: "for the natural estimative power is given to animals so that through it they are ordered toward the proper actions or affections that should be pursued or avoided."[139] In other words, nonhuman animal estimation reflects the animal's rather earthly, horizontal interests.[140] Beasts focus on an individual insofar as it has relevance to their appetites such as the desire for food or tactile pleasure, or their aversion and fear of dangers.[141] This helps explain why a human, though he stands frozen in plain sight, can be unperceived by a predator: when a *Tyrannosaurus rex* does not register "intentions" of harmfulness, helpfulness, or tastiness in a khaki-wearing man, the human might as well not exist to the beast.

Natural rationality, in contrast, gives the human cogitative power a much wider cognitive scope. Whereas the perceptual and estimative powers of different nonhuman animals vary greatly—compare the world-awareness of the earthworm versus the elephant—all humans have the cogitative power to perceive three different kinds of percepts. De Haan explains that humans are naturally able to perceive what he calls "aspectual," "actional," and "affective" percepts.[142] On the first level, through the cogitative power, a human can apprehend an individual as an individual on a basic level: "my mother," *this* tree, *this* floating leaf, *this* approaching wolf.[143] "In perception one is able to discern, register, or become acquainted with a superficial identity or aspect determination beyond the raw *per se* sensibles, hence the term *aspectual percept*," De Haan says.[144] In apparent corroboration, a recent study shows that newborns innately detect and prefer an object with biological motion in distinction to

139. Aquinas, *Sent. De anima*, lib. 2, l. 13, n. 16.

140. Tellkamp, "*Vis Aestimativa* and *Vis Cognitiva*," 623.

141. See *Quaestiones Disputate de Anima*, q. 13, co.

142. See De Haan, "Perception and the *Vis Cogitativa*," 412–24. As this issue is rather complex, here I will focus on what is most pertinent to the present study of habit.

143. See Aristotle, *De anima* II.6, 418a20–25.

144. De Haan, "Perception and the *Vis Cogitativa*," 414. See Aquinas, *Super Sent.*, lib. 4, d. 49, q. 2, a. 2.

one with nonbiological motion.[145] On the next level are "actional" or actionable percepts, as when a person perceives not only that one's mother is approaching, but also that she is "confrontable," "ignorable," "flee-able," and so on. Here the cogitative power offers a "judgment about the behavioral orientation of an animal *vis-à-vis* some aspectual percepts concerning things or circumstances perceived here and now."[146] Neither the aspectual nor the actional percept, however, can induce action. By themselves, these perceptions remain on the cognitional level and do not touch the passions. When the mind or imagination considers something as mere object with no relation to the considering subject, it is unconcerned with action and does not consider whether the thing should be fled or pursued.[147] A cognitive perception thus initiates no movement on its own, for the imagination or the sensation of a form "without estimation of fittingness or harmfulness does not move the sensitive appetite."[148] On the final level, therefore, the "affectional" percept informs the practical intellect with estimations of "good," "bad," "fitting," "unfitting," "difficult," or some other impulse toward action. Once the acting subject has registered an actional percept of an object, that is, a quality that amounts to should-be-approached or should-be-shunned, then the cogitative power orients the subject toward one or the other particular behavior. Simply registering that Mom is approachable does not move a person to action. Mom's approachableness must be estimated as *desirable for me, in this moment* before the sensory appetites can be engaged and the perceiver *desires* to approach Mom, such that the perceiver is moved and *actually approaches* Mom. Hence, for human movement to occur on the nondeliberative, nonvoluntary level, the cogitative power must apprehend an affectional percept: a quality that calls forth some movement from the appetite. The affectional

145. Francesca Simion et al., "A Predisposition for Biological Motion in the Newborn Baby," *Proceedings of the National Academy of Sciences of the United States of America* 105, no. 2 (January 15, 2008): 809–13.

146. De Haan, "Perception and the *Vis Cogitativa*," 417.

147. See Aquinas, *Sent. De anima*, lib. 3, l. 14, n. 19.

148. *ST* I-II, q. 9, a. 1, ad 2.

percept provides "the *impulse* to move the sensitive appetites that immediately initiate behavior."[149] When humans do not deliberate or engage their wills, as soon as they apprehend something as fitting or unfitting, their appetite—like that of other animals—is naturally inclined to pursue or avoid the thing.[150] Hence, the cogitative power always involves what Leo White calls "instinctive judgment."[151]

As instinctive judgments are not the result of purely intellectual deliberation, there must be a physical substrate that underlies and guides these estimations and consequent behaviors. Significantly, Thomas's explanation of the cogitative power appears to be supported by the groundbreaking neuroscientific research of Stephen Porges. An expert in how the autonomic nervous system relates to social behavior, Porges developed the "polyvagal theory," which, alongside other matters, explains human behavior denominated as "neuroception."[152] Porges notes that relationships among mammals are contingent upon perceived safety: "the perception of safety determines whether the behavior will be prosocial (i.e., social engagement) or defensive."[153] In order to correctly perceive helpfulness or harmfulness in another thing, humans developed "neuroception," which is the work of neural circuits "that function as a safety-threat detection system capable of distinguishing among situations that are safe, dangerous, or life-threatening."[154] This operation corresponds to the perception of "actional" percepts identified by De Haan (mentioned above); it takes place without cognitive awareness, utilizing subcortical regions of the brain.

149. De Haan, "Perception and the *Vis Cogitativa*," 426.

150. *ST* I-II, q. 17, a. 2, ad 3.

151. White, "Instinct and Custom," 597.

152. Stephen W. Porges, "The Polyvagal Perspective," *Biological Psychology* 74, no. 2 (February 2007): 116–43. See also Porges, "Neuroception: A Subconscious System for Detecting Threat and Safety," *Zero to Three Journal* 24, no. 5 (2004): 9–24, later published as chap. 1 in Stephen W. Porges, *The Polyvagal Theory: Neurophysiological Foundations of Emotions, Attachment, Communication, and Self-Regulation* (New York: Norton, 2011), 11–19.

153. Porges, *The Polyvagal Theory*, 193.

154. Ibid., 194.

An estimated situation may incline one to four basic responses: freeze, fight, flight, or befriending.[155] Porges reasons that the earliest evolutionary adaptive action is freezing—*immobilization* and even loss of consciousness, such as when a deer freezes when seeing the headlights of an oncoming vehicle, or when a mouse feigns death in the presence of a cat. This autonomic function (of the dorsal vagus nerve complex) is to conserve the organism's energy in light of a likely impending harm. The first concern of a thing is to preserve its own existence; self-maintenance has priority. In humans immobilization would probably also involve sympathetic arousal, with activation of the central nervous system. The next stage of adaptation is *mobilization,* as in the flight-or-fight responses to impending danger. This autonomic function (performed mostly through the spinal cord and the sympathetic adrenal system) is meant to activate the animal through increased heart rate and the production of energy. Finally, there is adaptive behavior of befriending—*social engagement and caregiving,* marked by face-to-face contact, prosodic speech patterns, improved listening, and emotional expressivity. Insofar as this function is autonomic (and engages the nucleus ambiguous and the ventral vagal complex), it aims at "neuroprotection," that is, it calms a person down by stabilizing his breathing and heart rate, thus proving physical resources for reciprocal social interactions.

The perception of immediate helpfulness or harmfulness helps a person to estimate which behaviors would be adaptive or maladaptive in the particular situation. Whether a person engages in immobilization, mobilization, or social engagement depends, in part, on how she has perceived the relative risk of her environment and objects within that environment.[156] In a later chapter, I will discuss how free choice can intervene to affirm or negate an impulse toward action. Here it is sufficient to note that the source and directionality of

155. The following is an adaptation of Porges's theory, which he summarizes in Table 19.1 in ibid., 283.

156. By way of example, Porges notes: "the inhibition of defense systems by the social engagement system would be adaptive and appropriate only in a safe environment" (ibid., 194).

those impulses is derived from a natural sensory estimation that has identifiable physiological and emotional components.

The implications of the polyvagal theory and neuroception are enormous. In addition to corroborating and refining a Thomistic theory of the cogitative power, the polyvagal theory helps show how much human behavior, and therefore human habituation, depends on the cogitative power or neuroception as well as synderesis. It also bears upon the nature of human instincts and the extent to which humans can shape their habitual responses to environmental stimuli.

## THE NATURE AND FUNCTION OF HUMAN INSTINCTS

Human behavior provides further evidence that all persons of the human species share some fundamental instincts. As humans are a species of animal, they also possess an analogous natural inclination to nondeliberative behavior patterns.[157] Thomas offers a fundamental explanatory distinction: "some acts of humans are proper to humans, but others are common to humans and animals."[158] Operations common to humans and other animals are called "passions of the soul."[159] Brennan helpfully defines a passion as "the movement of the sensitive appetite, resulting from knowledge, and marked by changes in the regulated functions of the body."[160] Understood in a broad sense, natural passions arise from human-specific estimations of an object in accordance with natural instinct. For Aquinas, instincts are bound up with antecedent inclinations of the passions and even predeliberative inclinations of the intellect and will. He speaks of what we might call a "happiness instinct": "We have free choice with respect to what we will, not by necessity, nor by natural instinct. For *our will to be happy does not pertain to free choice, but*

157. See Dich, "De Comparatione," 111.
158. *ST* I-II, q. 6, prol.
159. Ibid.
160. Brennan, *General Psychology*, 229.

*to natural instinct.*"[161] He also identifies what could be called a "God instinct." He argues that the worship of God is called "religion" because man freely wills to bind (*ligare*) himself to God, but also "because man feels himself *bound by some natural instinct to pay reverence to God,* from whom is the principle of his being and all good."[162] On the plane of the human community, Thomas acknowledges an "altruism instinct." He says that humans naturally love each other, and that "the indication of this is that a *man, by some natural instinct, helps any man in need, even those unknown to him.* For instance, he may call him back from the wrong road, help him up from a fall, and other actions like that: as if every man were naturally the family and friend of every man."[163] Similarly, Thomas argues that there is a sort of "economizing instinct." This includes a natural "gathering instinct": "there is in men a natural desire to gather those things that are necessary for life."[164] It is also directed toward the proper use of exterior things insofar as all humans have a "natural disposition" to preserve their lives individually and communally through the proper use of material goods.[165] Finally, Thomas argues that man has a natural "morality instinct," the scope of which is so broad that it encompasses all of the moral precepts of the Old Law: "Some works of the Law were moral ... man is induced to them by natural instinct and by the natural law."[166] Though Thomas never lists human instincts exhaustively, he unquestionably believes that they incline humans toward a variety of different acts.

How are the various kinds of instincts to be classified? Malkemus

161. *ST* I, q. 19, a. 10; emphasis added. See I-II, q. 17, a. 5.

162. *SCG* III, c. 119, n. 7; emphasis added. See *De regno*, lib. 1, c. 13. See also *De perfectione spiritualis vitae* [hereafter *De perfectione*]; I consulted the English translation, *The Religious State, the Episcopate and the Priestly Office*, trans. John Procter (St. Louis, Mo.: Herder, 1902), c. 13.

163. *SCG* III, c. 117, n. 6; emphasis added.

164. *SCG* III, c. 134, n. 2.

165. See *SCG* III, c. 132, n.3.

166. *Super Epistolam ad Galatas lectura* [hereafter *Super Gal.*], c. 2, l. 4, n. 94; I consulted the English translation, *Commentary on St. Paul's Epistle to the Galatians*, trans. Fabian R. Larcher (Albany, N.Y.: Magi Books, 1966).

notes that attempts to classify the diversity of instinctual behaviors have led to disparate, inconclusive, and even confusing results. The root of the problem is that scientists cannot agree on "a coherent and unified understanding of instinctual life."[167] Meanwhile, Louis Breger's primatology studies identify six affective kinds of instincts: attachment-love, fear, separation anxiety, aggression, sexuality, and play-curiosity-and-exploration.[168] Unfortunately, disagreements about the nature and taxonomy of instincts have contributed to a demise of instinctual theory. Here a Thomistic perspective can prove useful.

Thomas's taxonomy of natural human inclinations can help us grasp how he might distinguish among various instincts. Natural inclinations are ordered to one another in three stages that correspond to the hierarchy of being.[169] First, humans have tendencies in common with all substances, such as to preserve their own being. At this stage, natural law urges people to maintain and defend the basic requirements of life.[170] Second, there are tendencies common to animals and humans; these relate to reproduction, raising offspring, etc.[171] Third, there are tendencies related to actions of the rational nature specifically, such as building the social order and pursuing happiness.[172] It seems that Thomas uses *inclinatio* instead of *instinctus* to speak of the dispositions provided by natural law because *inclinatio* more clearly leaves room for discursive reasoning and free choice, whereas *instinctus* was understood more as an impulse that

167. Malkemus, "Reclaiming Instinct," 10. He quotes Lee Bernard's summary: "Colvin and Bagley list 25 instincts under the following general headlines: Adaptive, individualistic, sex and parental, social, and religious and esthetic. E. A. Kirkpatrick accepts 30 instincts ... Woodworth's 110 instincts are arranged under three general headings of responses to organic needs, responses to other persons, and play instincts." Lee Bernard, *Instinct: A Study in Social Psychology* (1924), 131, quoted in Malkemus, "Reclaiming Instinct," 10.

168. Malkemus, "Reclaiming Instinct," 10.

169. *ST* I-II, q. 94, a. 2.

170. Ibid.

171. Ibid.

172. Ibid.

moved lower passions.[173] One can develop this schema and consider instincts with respect to their formal and final causes.

From a Thomistic perspective, one can posit three categories of human instincts, specified by objects as they relate to the three basic animative functions: substantive-vegetative, sensory, and human. *Substantive-vegetative* instincts are inclinations for behaviors directed toward substantive and organic needs, including instincts of nutrition; self-preservation and the maintenance of an integral unity; and reproduction.[174] Instinctual behaviors on the vegetative level would be initiated by the dorsal vagus nerve complex, which Porges argues "is associated with vegetative function."[175] *Sensory* instincts include parental, social, and emotive. Emotive instincts can be subdivided by passion types: attachment-love, aggression, fear, etc.[176] Instinctual behaviors on the sensory level are associated with both the sympathetic adrenal system and the nucleus ambiguous, which is the "smart vagus" that comprises "an active voluntary motor system associated with the conscious functions of attention, motion, emotion, and communication."[177] This basis for "gut instinct" is arguably verified by studies showing that the enteric nervous system can function independently from the brain.[178] Finally, specifically *human* instincts

173. Greene, "Instinct of Nature," 182.

174. I call these "substantive-vegetative" because Thomas says that even stones have inclinations toward self-preservation. Those inclinations of material substances are not self-actuated, as those kinds of substances do not have souls. Thus, the lowest level of instincts, which derive from the soul of a thing, must be united to the lowest level of animate activity, which is the vegetative level.

175. Porges, *The Polyvagal Theory*, 41.

176. William G. Morrison argues that, although instinctual behaviors may sometimes be inimical to rational decisions, the aggression instinct can be advantageous when it is harnessed by his free choice. "Instincts as Reflex Choice: Does Loss of Temper Have Strategic Value?," *Journal of Economic Behavior and Organization* 31 (1996): 335–56.

177. Porges, *The Polyvagal Theory*, 41.

178. The enteric nervous system includes the vagus nerves connecting brain and bowels, as well as intrinsic microcircuits connecting nerves to each other throughout the bowel system. See Michael D. Gershon and Elyanne M. Ratcliffe, "Developmental Biology of the Enteric Nervous System: Pathogenesis of Hirschsprung's Disease and Other Congenital Dysmotilities," *Seminars in Pediatric Surgery* 13, no. 4 (November 2004): 224–35.

are directed toward specifically human needs; they include a religious instinct, a happiness instinct, and so on. According to Aquinas, these are natural inclinations of the intellect and in the will.

It should be noted that though instincts are distinguished by their objects, they are inclinations of the whole human being because they are all activated by the person's soul and flow from its essence.[179] Wojtyła rightly observes: "Instinct does not consist solely of the somatic dynamism in man.... it is in the psyche that it finds its proper expression."[180] For example, the instinct toward self-preservation is "vegetative": "The human organism is equipped with the necessary mechanisms of self-protection which functions automatically, that is to say, according to the rules of nature without engaging conscious awareness or the person's efficacy."[181] Nevertheless, sensations of bodily health or illness, or of strength or debility, have emotional and social implications: the progress of medical science is rooted in the instinct toward self-preservation and the preservation of the species. Another example makes the point perhaps even more clearly. The "vegetative" instinct toward reproduction has emotional resonances: "the experience itself of this urge, of an incitement or an objectively felt necessity, has a psycho-emotive character while the reaction of the organism only supplies it with the somatic ground."[182] Effects of the reproductive instinct have undeniably enormous consequences for psychological health, interpersonal relationships, and civilization as a whole.

Like all habits, instincts coexist within a person: the different instinctual layers build upon and assume one another. In humans, the instinct toward reproduction is naturally coupled with the parental instinct and the sensory emotive attachment-love instinct on account of the physical and social ramifications of the reproductive act. In order to maintain the species, it is useful for helpless infants

179. See *ST* I, q. 76, a. 4, and q. 77, a. 6.

180. Karol Cardinal Wojtyła, *The Acting Person*, ed. Anna-Teresa Tymieniecka, trans. Andrzej Potocki (Dordrecht: Reidel, 1979), 216.

181. Ibid., 217.

182. Ibid.

to be raised by parents who are emotionally attached to each other. "That towards which nature inclines [a thing] is called 'natural,' although it is completed by means of free choice," Thomas argues.[183] It follows that, "in this way, matrimony is natural ... for nature intends not only the generation of offspring, but also their education and development until they reach the perfect state of man as man, namely, the state of virtue."[184] Although the procreative instinct manifests itself automatically or spontaneously in the body, and to some extent *happens* to a person, bodily reactions to a potential mate "remain sufficiently conscious to be controllable by man. Essentially, this control consists in the adaptation of the body's instinctual dynamism of sex to its proper end."[185] Thus, the procreative instinct forms the natural basis of marriage and, through marriage, the family, and through the family, society.

Wojtyła's observation rings true: instincts are not restricted to the somatic level but constitute dynamic traits of the human being and existence as a whole. The cogitative power of humans cooperates with their synderesis, the natural disposition of the practical intellect by which we understand the actual precepts of the natural law. The cogitative power can have *antecedent* estimative judgments about an object, including judgments that incline the passions to move a person to act. Synderesis presents the precepts of the natural law to the universal practical reason. These are known by natural reason immediately and per se.[186] When these precepts inform the cogitative power's estimative judgments, the human performs an "instinctive practical judgment of the moral act."[187] The product for moral perception is a quasi-moral action.[188] When the cogitative

183. *Scriptum super Sententiis*, lib. 4, d. 26, q. 1, a. 1, co.

184. Ibid.

185. Wojtyła, *The Acting Person*, 217.

186. See *ST* I-II, q. 100, a. 1.

187. See Wojciech Giertych, "Virtue and Addiction," *Nova et Vetera* (English edition) 13, no. 3 (2015): 201–37, at 221.

188. De Haan notes, "Whenever the moral perception exercised by right practical reason flows from the habitual inclination of prudence, then we have a *prudent moral perception*.... And just as with antecedent passions, antecedent cognitive perceptions are

power apprehends an affectional percept in light of synderesis (i.e., is "integrated into the axiological judgments of the universal practical reason"), then natural instincts are activated. In those cases, a person engages in an act that is oriented toward moral behavior but, lacking deliberation and voluntariness, is not moral as such.

These elements can be synthesized and illustrated in the example of an infant seeing his mother. Infants have vegetative instincts to pursue food and sensory instincts to enjoy the company of their parents. Synderesis inclines infants to love their parents; this includes a general judgment that parents are *loveable*. On this occasion, the infant's cogitative power apprehends the percept of *this* woman who radiates aspectual percepts of a unique face and figure, a pleasant smell, familiar sounds, and so on, that the infant grasps as particularly fitting to himself: it is his mother. By synderesis, the infant grasps that his mother is loveable in general; with a parallel movement, his cogitative power grasps the actional percept that his mother can be loved right here and now. Next, through synderesis, the child grasps that his mother *is to be loved*; with his cogitative power, he receives the affectional percept that her *loveableness* calls for immediate action, that is, his passions receive an *impulse* to act. So, when the infant sees his mother's open arms, he naturally and spontaneously runs toward her. He actuates an instinctive behavior. This action is nondeliberative and to that extent nonvolitional. It is oriented to the moral behavior of honoring one's parent, but falls short of it. In ways like this, various human instincts may naturally lead to behaviors when synderesis enlightens the cogitative power in its judgments.

---

only potentially moral, whereas consequent cognitive perceptions—which are integrated into the judgments of practical reason—actually qualify as acts of moral perception." De Haan, "Moral Perception," 317. Likewise, Giertych insists, "for action to be good and contributing to the growth of virtue, the instinctive practical judgment of the moral act has to be in accord with objective truth as it can be known by the speculative reason." Giertych, "Virtue and Addiction," 221.

## HUMAN INSTINCTS AND THE ROLE OF REASON

We can now see how unwarranted it is to claim that humans do not have instincts. Theoretical and experimental evidence suggests that humans indeed have instincts as defined above. A Thomistic viewpoint can affirm with Varela that "unlike reflex behavior, instinctive behavior doesn't constitute predetermined muscular sequences, only a constant and predetermined end," such as to nourish oneself or to protect one's offspring.[189] Additionally, one can affirm that human sensation always involves intelligence to some extent. However, one need not agree with Varela that this intelligence requires *conscious free choice*. Instead, as seen above, instincts involve the lower practical intellect through synderesis and the cogitative power, while instinctual behavior engages both synderesis and the cogitative power without necessarily engaging deliberation or free choice. Furthermore, one may grant that, due to a brain structure in which the association cortex (thinking) dominates the somatosensory and motor cortices (motor control), there is an element of learning in most human behavior.[190] As instincts are *inclinations* or *dispositions to action*, it is likely that purely instinctual behavior is rare or even nonexistent in healthy, fully-aware, and mature humans.[191]

It may seem as if the only way that lower appetites are moved in accordance with reason is when they participate in reason through a command of the will, the intellectual appetite.[192] Aquinas seems to exclude categorically the existence of ordinate movements of the sensory appetite antecedent to reason's judgment. For example, in speaking about the first humans, who were free from all inordinate movements, he says, "In the state of innocence, the lower appetite

189. Varela, "Biological Structure," 113.

190. See D. O. Hebb, *The Organization of Behavior: A Neuropsychological Theory* (Mahwah, N.J.: Lawrence Erlbaum Associates, 2002), 167.

191. The extent to which learning and free choice influence on instincts will be discussed later in the section on acquired habits.

192. See, for example, *ST* I, q. 78, a. 4; q. 83, a. 3; I-II, q. 24, a. 3; *De veritate*, q. 1, a. 11; q. 14, a. 1, ad 9.

was totally subjected to reason; thus there were no 'passions of the soul' except for those consequent upon the judgment of reason."[193] In Richard Mansfield's view, Aquinas's mature position was that antecedent passions necessarily hinder practical reason and thereby diminish the moral quality of subsequent acts.[194] A fuller analysis of Thomas's position, however, reveals that he implicitly distinguishes between *consequent* and *antecedent* cognitive passions.

I have already noted his position on *consequent* passions, that is, movements of the sensory appetite as commanded of reason. There is some evidence for the existence of ordinate antecedent passions—that is, passions that move according to reason but not by the command of reason. Giuseppe Butera notes that Thomas does not deny that the cogitative power can move the sensory appetites ordinately.[195] Indeed, Thomas affirms the opposite: "Sometimes the sensory appetite happens to be suddenly moved by an apprehension of the imagination or sense. And thus such movement is *aside* from the command of reason."[196] When Thomas discusses the distinction between the animal's estimative power and the human's cogitative power, his concern is to lay bare the proper operations of each kind of creature. The sensory appetites of animals are moved by their estimative power, while human sensory appetites *qua* human are moved by reason. Nevertheless, Thomas affirms, "The sensitive appetite is *naturally* moved, not only by the estimative power in other animals, and in man by the cogitative power ... but also by the imagination and sense."[197] Sensation and imagination can present a material object to the cogitative power, prompting it to estimate naturally and spontaneously the benefits or dangers present in the object. This

193. *ST* I, q. 95, a. 2.

194. Richard K. Mansfield, "Antecedent Passion in the Moral Quality of Human Acts According to St. Thomas," *Proceedings of the American Catholic Philosophical Association* 71 (1997): 221–31.

195. Giuseppe Butera, "On Reason's Control of the Passions in Aquinas's Theory of Temperance" (PhD diss., The Catholic University of America, 2001), 439.

196. *ST* I-II, q. 17, a. 7; emphasis added.

197. *ST* I, q. 83, a. 3, ad 2; emphasis added. He makes a similar point in *De veritate*, q. 2, a. 6, ad 6.

operation can be classified as *antecedent cogitative perception*, as it is antecedent to the judgment of practical reason.[198] It leads to an *antecedent movement* of the sensory appetites or passions. Such movements—which are not yet full-blown acts—would be common to prelinguistic humans, to humans incapable of language or operations of higher reason, indeed, to all healthy humans.

If such movements are not *commanded* by reason and are even *aside* from it, they are not necessarily *contrary* to reason.[199] Indeed, there are a few reasons why a healthy person's natural antecedent movements of his sensory appetites are intrinsically in accordance with reason.[200] First, as seen above, the instinctual behavior of animals is in accordance with reason—not because of the deliberate reason of the animal but because instincts are a participation in God's divine wisdom, which providentially orders animals to seek their own natural good. When natural instinct moves the animal, "the movement of the natural appetite results from the apprehension of the separate Intellect who authored nature."[201] The same follows for human instinctual behavior. Secondly, because human instincts are bound up with synderesis, they are directed by the natural law. The human mind possesses a "morality" instinct that inclines it to grasp the first practical truths of morality, and to put them into action. The human will possesses a "God" instinct that inclines it to strive for the ultimate good. Such instincts are clearly in accordance with the natural law, as are all the other human instincts, which means that they are in accordance with reason. This is because the natural law is the good of a creature, ordered by the creature's intrinsic properties, promulgated by God in accordance with and as a participation in his supreme wisdom.[202]

Thomas does not deny that humans have nondeliberative behav-

198. See De Haan, "Moral Perception," 320–21.

199. For a more thorough discussion, see Kahm, *Aquinas on Emotion's Participation in Reason*, 250–55.

200. Here I mean "healthy" in a broad way: healthy in mind and body.

201. *ST* I-II, q. 40, a. 3.

202. See *ST* I-II, q. 91, a. 2.

iors. To the contrary, he acknowledges that humans have behaviors that arise from their natural instincts. These instincts are prerational, nondeliberative, nonvoluntary human inclinations of the appetites and even of the intellect and will. These inclinations stem from antecedent cognitive perception and can naturally unfold into *behaviors antecedent to rational judgment.* While discussing instincts, similar to his discussion of the estimative versus the cogitative powers, Thomas's concern is to show how animals and humans differ in the essential principles of their acts. In this vein, he contrasts nonrational animal instincts with human deliberative choice. As I will discuss in greater detail, animals cannot help but be moved by instinct, whereas mature, healthy humans are not *constrained* by these instincts. Unlike other animals, we are not moved by natural inclinations alone. Mature, healthy humans can repudiate instincts and antecedent movements or affirm them and further them by voluntary choice. For all healthy humans who experience no disorders in their perception or appetites, these movements are naturally ordinate, that is, in accordance with reason *in general* insofar they would be in accordance with the universal principles of natural law laid down by synderesis.

Given that human instincts exist and that they are naturally in accordance with reason, a further question remains: are instincts habits? Charles Varela answers this question affirmatively, distinguishing between "reflex habits," which are learned, and "instinctive habits," which are unlearned, that is, innate.[203] Varela follows D. O. Hebb in holding that instinctive behavior does not have to be learned or acquired through practice. This may seem to exclude instincts from being types of habits, but he defines habits as reactions functionally organized to adapt to an environmental problem.[204] In his view, a habit is preeminently characterized by "the regularity of its order, its automaticity," which is "species-predictable."[205] Thus far, a Thomistic

203. Varela, "Biological Structure," 109. Varela here does not distinguish between unconditioned and conditioned or "learned" reflexes.

204. Ibid.

205. Ibid., 111.

perspective could agree: instincts are ordered, automatic, and predictable according to species-type. But this does not make instincts "robotic" as Verala claims.[206] On the contrary, instincts are habits precisely because they are natural inclinations, not robotic programs.

Robots move by programs, not habits. They have a more or less complex series of instructions or laws that they enact, laws that can take various contingencies into account, but laws that are, of themselves, blind and inexorable. In contrast, an instinct is a dynamic inclination that mediates between the nature of an animal and its perceived environment: this is why it may be considered as a habit. Thomas says: "health is called a habit, or a habitual disposition, in relation to nature."[207] As a dynamic reality, a state of health indicates that the person as a whole is inclined and ready to perform the operations of a healthy organism.[208] Health is an analogous term, because healthy operations for one organism will differ from specific operations of a different species though they have the same general goal: the food-seeking (and health-promoting) behaviors of a healthy *Aplysia* sea slug are analogous to those of a human. Habitual activities necessarily call forth the creativity of an agent according to its capacity, as Ravaisson argued: "habit presents in successive form … the progressive development of the powers of nature."[209] This is easily seen in the case of instinctual behavior, which Varela's theory does not sufficiently take into account. For example, cliff swallows will predictably create nests of a certain type, but the bird must still use its ingenuity to discover and secure the proper materials, select a proper place for the nest, transport the materials, and arrange them according to its ability. Malkemus points to the activity of the sea turtle to prove the same point. The sea turtle must "contend with the continuously modulating environment in which it is embedded.… The sea turtle is thus an autonomous system capable of mak-

206. Ibid., 110.
207. *ST* I-II, q. 49, a. 3, ad 3.
208. Ibid.
209. Ravaisson, *Of Habit*, 65.

ing sense of its environment in important ways. It is not blindly driven by internal mechanisms."[210]

With more precision, a Thomistic perspective could say that the dynamic lifeforce (soul) of the turtle activates its sensory powers and, through an estimative and nondeliberative judgment, moves the turtle toward a goal suitable to its nature. Regularity and order are features of the animal's actions, along with automaticity insofar as the animal naturally enacts the behavior when it is able to do so. But the action is not robotic. Even if the effects appear similar, the causal structure underlying organic behavior is vastly different from that of mechanical operation. Ultimately, the formal cause of a robot's motion is a program that a human has written, whereas the formal cause of an animal's motion is its instinct that follows from its nature.[211] Instincts are habits that lead to an organism's self-actualization according to its proper characteristics.

If nonhuman instincts do not lead to robotic behavior, even less so do human instincts, for a human can always resist his instincts and reshape his inclinations, creatively using intelligence to adapt to a situation.[212] What distinguishes instincts from human habits per se is their cause: instincts are inclinations, dispositions derived from human nature, whereas fully human habits are derived from many acts that arise from deliberate choice. Accordingly, human instincts alone will incline a person to perform acts of a human, whereas human habits incline a person to acts that are human as such, that is, suffused with deliberate volition.

The preceding account of instinct has a number of advantages for our study of habits. First, it harmonizes the various instinct tax-

210. Malkemus, "Reclaiming Instinct," 17.

211. Even more sophisticated programs, and forms of artificial intelligence, find their source in human programmers.

212. Mary Midgley argues that many scientists deny the existence of human instincts because they do not distinguish between "open" and "closed" instincts, that is, instincts that are open to various means of enactment versus instincts that are closer to reflexes and can be enacted only in one or very few ways. *Beast and Man: The Roots of Human Nature* (London: Routledge, 2002), 39.

onomies without rejecting per se what other researchers have identified as instincts. Second, it preserves many theorists' emphasis on the physiological basis of instinct,[213] while allowing room for some instincts that affect nonphysical realities in the person (e.g., the religious and happiness instincts). Third, it clarifies the observation that instinct-driven behavior is "purposeful." The ultimate *ratio* of animal instinctual behavior arises not from some mystic force within the animal or universe, but from God who shaped the instinct according to his wisdom. The same can be said for instinctual human behavior. Fourth, it helps to connect the theory of instinct to the cogitative power insofar as it shows how instinctual behaviors arise from the same physical mechanisms associated with neuroception.[214] Fifth, it incorporates Malkemus's insight that the "traditional" (mechanistic) ethological view of instincts should be replaced by one more in conformity with biological reality. Instead of seeing the baby sea turtle's nocturnal journey toward the ocean as a fixed pattern of behavior in which a definite stimulus (ocean) evokes a stereotyped response (ambulation toward it), a more robust theory would account for "the self-governing dynamics of animate life," for "instinct is not predetermined statically but dynamically."[215] My proposal does this by showing that instinctual behaviors arise from formal and material causes, that is, from the specific nature of a thing. As Wojtyła says: "Instinct with its inherent drive is a form of man's dynamism on account of nature and, so far as man forms part of nature, so far as he remains in intimate union with nature."[216] Because human nature includes the power of free choice (as will be discussed later), human instincts must be in accord with the natural directionality of choice. This view confirms Charles Varela's observation that, "In the case of Homo sapiens especially, the logical of the relationship between state and behavior is one of possibility and not necessity."[217] As Titus

213. See the discussion in Malkemus, "Reclaiming Instinct," 11–12.
214. See Porges, *The Polyvagal Theory*, 48–49.
215. Ibid., 16–17.
216. Wojtyła, *The Acting Person*, 216.
217. Varela, "Biological Structure," 107.

argues, they are a "first step" that helps us to achieve goals that promote human flourishing, such as conserving our health, committing ourselves to procreation and the upbringing of children, worshiping God, pursuing the truth, and so on.[218]

Here, then, we discover a crucial truth regarding our nonvoluntary habits. To act in accordance with our natural instincts—or to act against them—lies within the power of our free choice. For the instinctual movements of the passions to be *fully* human, reason must incorporate them into higher modes of behavior. Properly human acts are those that arise from deliberation and free choice, but they are best when in harmony with our natural instincts in general, which incline us to obey the natural law.[219] As we will see, it is sin or its effects that brings about departure from natural law.[220] As Malkemus observes, each species has an "instinctual core" that cannot be violated without harming the health and continued existence of the individual animal. The instinctual core consists in the most fundamental instincts necessary for survival; it "can only be adapted so far, for its restriction involves a restriction of the lifeforce of the organism."[221] Modern authors who encourage people to "trust" their instincts, etc., implicitly recognize that humans have instincts but are not determined by them. Some of their readers have not acted in accordance with instinct sufficiently and have created habits contrary to those naturally good impulses. In sum, we have instinctual inclinations by natural necessity, but our instincts by themselves do not determine human action.

218. Titus, *Resilience and the Virtue of Fortitude*, 123.

219. Sometimes a particular instinct may have to be overridden for the sake of a good grasped by reason or faith. See *ST* I-II, q. 18, a. 9. See also Giertych, "Virtue and Addiction," 225.

220. See *ST* I, q. 113, a. 1, ad 3, and I-II, q. 85, a. 1, ad 2.

221. Malkemus, "Reclaiming Instinct," 20.

# 2

# Dispositions Derived from Individual Nature

Attempts to explain—or to explain away—negative behavior of a particular individual often end up with this this conclusion: "Well, I am just made that way," or "He can't help it; that's the way he is." Others justify their actions by arguing that in the final analysis "everything in life can be a matter of choice"—and therefore a person can be whatever gender, ethnicity, or identity that he/she/ze/zir personally chooses.[1] Both positions rely on an implicit view of human nature and the fixedness or malleability of the general structure that undergirds human behavior. In chapter 1 we saw that, according to Thomas Aquinas, all human beings have what he calls "natural habits."[2] We all possess habits simply by being human. At the same time, he insists that no "general" human being exists: "humanity" is not a man.[3] Only individual humans exist, and though we possess a common human nature we are each unique. If every snowflake is special and unique, even more so is every human. Each human pos-

1. Renata Salecl, quoted in Patricia Gherovici, *Please Select Your Gender: From the Invention of Hysteria to the Democratizing of Transgenderism* (New York: Routledge, 2010), 7. See Miri Song, *Choosing Ethnic Identity* (Cambridge: Polity, 2003).

2. *Sent. Ethic.*, lib. 7, l. 12, n. 4.

3. See *De ente et essentia*, c. 1, n. 45.

sesses a higher nature than a snowflake or a dog; and each is more individual than any other material creature.[4]

This chapter outlines the dispositions and natural habits that arise from the unique traits of each person, which Aquinas calls "individual nature."[5] A person's individual nature belongs to him alone as that which differentiates him from other humans, whereas all persons share a "specific nature" with each member of the human species, for by our rational souls we are differentiated from other animals.[6] We possess inclinations derived from our form—our rational soul (e.g., our inclination toward happiness)—and inclinations derived from our material, our bodies (e.g., temperament, discussed below).[7] Some inclinations from the body are in accord with what is natural according to the form, that is, some inclinations of the body are in accord with reason: they are not too vehement, observe a moderate mean, and so on. Other bodily inclinations go astray from reason's mean. These will be discussed in chapter 6 on dysfunctional and evil habits. Here we may note that, in Thomas's view, inclinations derived from our soul and those derived from our bodies can be considered "natural" insofar as they are innate. However, our form is "more nature than matter"; insofar as the soul gives life to the body, and differentiates us from beasts, inclinations in accord with the form are "more natural" than those which solely come from our individual bodily quirks.[8]

4. See John Gerard Desilva Finley, "Human Individuation in Aquinas" (PhD diss., University of Dallas, 2010), 185–86, 247, and 247n4. Among other texts, he refers to *SCG* II, c. 68: "Something [composed] of an intellectual substance and a material body is not less one than something [composed] of the form of fire and its matter; rather, it is more so, since the more form transcends matter, the more a thing is one which is made from the form and matter." Also, in *ST* I, q. 29, a. 1, Thomas argues that individuality increases as self-dominion increases. Thus, God is the most individual of all beings (see Finley, "Human Individuation in Aquinas," 270).

5. *ST* I-II, q. 51, a. 1.

6. *ST* I-II, q. 63, a. 1; see also q. 31, a. 7.

7. *De malo*, q. 5, a. 5, co.

8. Ibid. See *ST* I-II, q. 94, a. 3. See also *De malo*, q. 16, a. 2, where Aquinas distinguishes between what is natural according to the higher, rational nature of our intellectual soul, and what is natural according to the lower nature of our bodies.

In what follows, I begin by discussing how the body formed by the soul is the source of the uniqueness that each person possesses from the first moment of his or her existence. Next, I delineate what sorts of dispositions arise from individual nature, including temperament and basic personality type. Finally, I treat how and why divine providence arranges for various individuals to have different, unequal innate habits.

## PHYSICAL FOUNDATIONS OF HUMAN INDIVIDUALITY

There are many unique aspects to a person: facial shape, eye color, fingerprints, musical preferences, dreams, creative expressions, and so on. The heart of uniqueness centers on the principle of individuation, that is, the fundamental source that makes a human being individual. Forms of nominalism hold that each person's individuality is a result of the combination of the various material qualities, accidents, that adhere together like disparate parts of a mosaic that happen to form a greater whole.[9] Others hold that a person's soul is the primary or even the only source of human uniqueness; this is most apparent in Origenism[10] and Mormonism,[11] which argue that human souls preexist their bodies. According to Aquinas, though, the true account of human individuation rests on the hylomorphic principle that body and soul are "proportioned and, as

9. See Eric M. Rubenstein, "Nominalism and the Disappearance of Individuation," *Logical Analysis and History of Philosophy* 5 (2002): 193–204. For a more general discussion, see Jorge J. E. Gracia, *Individuality: An Essay on the Foundations of Metaphysics* (Albany: The State University of New York Press, 1988).

10. For a good summary of Origen's views, see Elizabeth A. Dively Lauro, "Preexistence," in *The Westminster Handbook to Origen*, ed. John Anthony McGuckin (Louisville, Ky.: Westminster John Knox Press, 2004), 178–79; and Peter Martens, "Origen's Doctrine of Pre-Existence and the Opening Chapters of Genesis," in *Zeitschrift für Antikes Christentum* 16 (2013): 516–49.

11. See Terryl L. Givens, *Wrestling the Angel: The Foundations of Mormon Thought: Cosmos, God, Humanity* (New York: Oxford University Press, 2014), 147–75. The same author provides a broader historical perspective in *When Souls Had Wings: Pre-Mortal Existence in Western Thought* (New York: Oxford University Press, 2010).

it were, naturally adapted to one another" in each human being.[12]

The basic definition of "individual" is found in the *Summa Theologiae*: "a distinct and incommunicable substance."[13] Against nominalism, Aquinas holds that humans are not so distinct as to be essentially cut off from each other. Instead, humans are members of a species and therefore each has a formal principle that makes them to be human beings, because "although the human is rightly counted in the same genus as other animals, he differs by species. For specific difference follows from a difference of form."[14] Against monopsychism, wrongly associated with Averroes, Thomas argued that there is not a universal soul in which all men participate.[15] Instead, there exists one soul per body: "the intellectual soul, by its very being, is united to the body as form … and for the same reason, the multiplicity of souls exists according to the multiplicity of bodies."[16] In other words, for however many fully human bodies that exist, there are an equal number of human souls that animate each one individually and give each existence.[17] Furthermore, against any notion of the preexistence of souls, Aquinas insists that a human soul without a body is incomplete.[18] A soul is the most important part of man, but alone it remains only a part of the whole.[19] Souls do not exist before bodies, nor do human bodies exist without souls: "It is contrary to the *ratio* of the perfection of the first arrangement of things that

12. *SCG* II, c. 80, n. 8.

13. *ST* I, q. 29, a. 4, ad 3.

14. *ST* I, q. 75, a. 3, ad 1.

15. See Torrell's discussion in *Saint Thomas Aquinas: Person and His Work*, 1:192–94. See also Richard C. Taylor, "Averroes' Epistemology and its Critique by Aquinas," in *Medieval Masters: Essays in Memory of Msgr. E. A. Synan*, ed. R. E. Houser (Houston, Tex.: University of St. Thomas, 1999), 147–77.

16. *ST* I, q. 76, a. 2, ad 2.

17. *ST* I, q. 76, a. 2, co.

18. See Thomas's stark statement in *Super I ad Cor.* ch. XV, v. 19, lect. 2, no. 924: "But the soul, since it is a part of the human body, is not the entire human, and my soul is not 'I.'" For a discussion of this doctrine, see Stephen Priest, "Aquinas's Claim 'Anima Mea Non Est Ego,'" *Heythrop Journal* 40 (1999): 209–11.

19. See *ST* I, q. 75, a. 4, ad 2. The soul is most important because as the spiritual principle it exists per se and gives being to the body. See *Quaestiones disputatae De anima*, a. 14, and *SCG* II, c. 51.

God would make either the body without the soul, or the soul without the body, since each is a part of human nature."[20] In other words, soul and body are correlative causes that together encompass human nature. Therefore, the soul is not the principle of a person's individuality, nor is a person's essence, nor his existence.[21] Instead, "human souls are created *as* the forms of particular bodies, which bodies do not exist *as such* until the creation of the souls in the properly disposed matters."[22] The creator alone creates each individual soul *ex nihilo* and infuses it into matter that is apt to receive it.[23]

Avoiding the trap of materialism, Aquinas still affirms the indispensable role that physicality plays in rendering our identity. "Individuation depends on the body as its principle," he says, though the soul can exist without the body after death.[24] He explains: "Things in the genus of substance that differ numerically, differ not only by accidents but also by form and matter ... matter subject to dimension is understood to be the principle of this kind of diversity."[25] That is, "signate matter" is the principle of individuation.[26] What "signate matter" means precisely, how "quantity" affects the differentiation of matter, and whether Aquinas identifies a reasonable criterion for individuation, has been the subject of much debate.[27]

20. *ST* I, q. 91, a. 4, ad 3. See also *SCG* II, c. 89, and *ST* I, q. 118, a. 2.

21. See Lawrence Dewan, "The Individual as a Mode of Being According to Thomas Aquinas," *The Thomist* 63 (1999): 403–24.

22. Finley, "Human Individuation in Aquinas," 194.

23. See *SCG* II, c. 87. The much-disputed issue regarding when the body is ensouled lies beyond my topic. For a helpful summary and analysis of positions, especially on Robert Pasnau versus John Haldane/Patrick Lee, see Craig Payne, "Would Aquinas Change His Mind on Hominization Today?," in *Life and Learning XVIII: Proceedings of the Eighteenth University Faculty for Life Conference at Marquette University 2008*, ed. Joseph W. Koterski (Bronx, N.Y.: University Faculty for Life, 2011), 229–48. See also Fabrizio Amerini, *Aquinas on the Beginning and End of Human Life*, trans. Mark Henninger (Cambridge, Mass.: Harvard University Press, 2013).

24. *De ente et essentia*, c. 5, n. 93. See also *Super Sent.*, lib. 1, d. 8, q. 5, a. 2, ad 6.

25. *Super Boetium De Trinitate* [hereafter *Super De Trinitate*], q. 4, a. 2, ad 4.

26. *ST* I, q. 75, a. 4.

27. By no means was this the only proposal for individuation. See Richard Sorabji's account of debates among ancient philosophers regarding individuation: *Self: Ancient and Modern Insights about Individuality, Life, and Death* (Oxford: Clarendon Press, 2006), 137–53. See also Jorge J. E. Gracia, *Individuation in Scholasticism, The Later Middle Ages*

Andrew Payne convincingly argues that, for Aquinas, "matter, when modified by the accidents of quantity and dimension—or dimensive quantity—serves to distinguish one particular composite of form and matter from another individual of the same species."[28] When a thing is material, its parts have a determinate relation to each other, and the thing as a whole has a determinate spatial and temporal relation to all other things. It is precisely that "designate" property that individuates the thing: Peter is *this* substance with *these* parts arranged in *this* way (his living body), that exist in relation to *this* place and *this* time.[29]

Given Aquinas's philosophical theory of human individuation, empirical science would want to see whether or not there is "signate matter" that makes a particular human unique. Here, too, Aquinas is helpful: he provides a clue regarding where to look for this signate matter. While holding that God alone creates a human soul, Aquinas indicates that parents cooperate with God and they contribute to the creation of a human being by generating matter that is properly disposed to receive a rational form.[30] God is the primary efficient cause of human individuality, but the parents are material causes.[31] How

---

*and the Counter-Reformation, 1150–1650* (Albany: The State University of New York Press, 1994); and Stephen A. Hipp, "Existential Relation as Principle of Individuation," *The Thomist* 72 (2008): 67–106, at 68n3.

28. Andrew Payne, "Gracia and Aquinas on the Principle of Individuation," *The Thomist* 68 (2004): 545–75, at 547. He refers to *Super De Trinitate*, pars 2, q. 4, a. 2, co. 6: "For form is not individuated through the fact that it is received in matter, except insofar as it is received in this matter which is distinct and determined to here and now. Matter however is not divisible unless through quantity." Payne also notes that, for Aquinas, matter is distinct from other matter only through "dimensions" and having a specific place. See *Super De Trinitate*, q. 4, a. 3. Lawrence Dewan agrees: "How are the instances of human nature distinct one from the other? The answer lies neither in form just in itself nor in matter just in itself, but in matter as subject to dimensive quantity.... Dimension serves to limit a form which can be in many, so that it still has 'being in,' but has being in one only." Dewan, "The Individual as a Mode of Being," 423.

29. The quantitative aspect of matter entails that individuals will retain their own particular properties after the resurrection, insofar as these are within the range of what human nature allows for a healthy body. See *ST* Suppl., q. 81, a. 2; *Super Sent.*, lib. 4, d. 44, q. 1, a. 3, qc. 2.

30. See *De potentia*, q. 3, a. 9, ad 20.

31. *De potentia*, q. 3, a. 10, co.

do parents provide the material that makes their children unique? Genetics provides much of the answer.

As a branch of biological science, genetics helps explain physical heredity and variations among individuals of a single species. Physical heredity in humans ordinarily begins with the act of natural generation, by which a father's sperm fertilizes a mother's egg in conception which together form a living cell, the beginning of their offspring's body. Within the cell's nucleus is the human genome, a complete set of human chromosomes. Each person has two sets of twenty-three chromosomes, one from each parent; each chromosome contains many DNA molecules, which are arranged in a double helix pattern. The linear sequence of information within DNA is called the genetic code. Because the genetic code is inherited, it serves as a record of our connection with other creatures. Humans and chimpanzees share about a DNA similarity of about ninety-five percent in protein-coding genes,[32] while northern Europeans and some East Asian populations have one to three percent DNA of Neanderthal origin.[33] Scientists are still working to identify which genes are responsible for the uniqueness of the human species, but they agree that each individual has a "DNA fingerprint" that makes him or her genetically unique (identical twins are an exception).[34]

As an embryo develops, its cells will divide and multiply while maintaining a complete copy of the genetic code in each newly formed cell. When different portions of DNA are expressed or unexpressed, cells differentiate, becoming heart tissue, blood, nerves, and so on. The genetic code therefore organizes three different levels of biological organization in the individual, beginning at the *molecular* level, which shapes the *cellular* structural level, which in turn

32. Benjamin A. Pierce, *Genetics: A Conceptual Approach,* 5th ed. (New York: W. H. Freeman, 2013), 153.

33. John Parrington, *The Deeper Genome: Why There Is More to the Human Genome than Meets the Eye* (Oxford: Oxford University Press, 2015), 176.

34. Robert J. Brooker, *Genetics: Analysis and Principles,* 4th ed. (New York: McGraw Hill, 2012), 3; and Leland Hartwell, *Genetics: From Genes to Genomes,* 4th ed. (New York: McGraw Hill, 2011), 98.

affects the level of the entire *organism* as a visible phenotype.[35] Because of its importance for biological development, DNA has been called "the fundamental information molecule of life,"[36] a human "blueprint,"[37] and the genetic code "the language of life."[38]

From a perspective of Thomistic philosophy, Enrico Berti argues that the DNA sequence serves as a quasi-formal cause of the individual person. He says that it is a "formal cause" because it is a principle that serves as a "development plan" or a "program" that gives shape or form to the material of the person.[39] At the same time, he agrees with Aristotle and Aquinas that the absolute formal cause of the human person is the soul which serves as the life-principle that actualizes the material. He points out that "the DNA contained in the nucleus of the zygote . . . already contains all the information necessary for the development of the nervous system, i.e. of matter, by means of which the intellectual soul operates."[40] In his estimation, this means that the fertilized egg constitutes apt matter to receive an intellectual soul at the very moment of conception. From this reasoning it might seem that the DNA sequence is the "signate matter" identified by Aquinas as "the principle of individuation" whereby a human is made a unique individual.[41] However, there are other issues to take into account.

The genome is not simply a static, linear code of information, as it has often been portrayed. Instead, it is "a three-dimensional tangle

35. See Brooker, *Genetics: Analysis and Principles*, 7.

36. Hartwell, *Genetics: From Genes to Genomes*, 1.

37. Brooker, *Genetics: Analysis and Principles*, 4.

38. Fritjof Capra and Pier Luigi Luisi, *The Systems View of Life: A Unifying Vision* (Cambridge: Cambridge University Press, 2014), 195.

39. Enrico Berti, "Is the DNA Sequence a Sufficient Definition of Human Nature? A Comparison between Aristotle, Thomas Aquinas and Jacques Maritain," in *Scripta Varia 109*, ed. M. Sánchez Sorondo (Vatican City: Pontifical Academy for the Sciences, 2007): 79–86, at 80.

40. Ibid., 84.

41. Berti actually goes further than this proposal and says, "Thus it would appear that the question of whether the DNA sequence is a sufficient definition of human nature should be answered affirmatively" (ibid.). This is an exaggeration, as a sequence of chemicals is not a definition in any sense of the term.

of vital string, constantly folding and rearranging itself, responsive to outside input."[42] Some consequences are explored in the growing field of epigenetics, that is, the study of heritable cellular or trait variations that are not caused by changes in DNA but by the environment and other factors.[43] There are at least four different kinds of epigenetic inheritance systems.[44] As the name "inheritance system" indicates, some epigenetic factors can be passed on from generation to generation.[45] These are just as influential on a person as the genome itself.[46] Their power lies in determining whether the information in DNA is activated, silenced, or regulated. Even more, they can modify or mark DNA itself.[47] Epigenetics shows that genes are not a fixed blueprint or mechanism, but rather part of a truly living and adaptable organism. It indicates that we inherit not only physical characteristics of parents from DNA but also certain acquired characteristics, that is, a result of experience or behavior.

Although epigenetic science is still in its embryonic stage, it is now clear that DNA alone does not determine our traits. Our genes can retain their basic structure while experiences or actions of our parents (or even grandparents) can affect how our gene expressions are turned on or off. One study has shown how mice conditioned to dislike a cherry blossom odor passed on the aversion to successive generations—through a physical mechanism that controlled how some genes were activated. Successive generations of mice were born

42. Nathaniel Comfort, "Genetics: We Are the 98%," *Nature* 520, no. 7549 (April 30, 2015): 615–16, at 615.

43. Distinct from epigenetic change are two other kinds of genetic variance: (1) from dominant genetic variance, the process by which certain genes are functionally expressed (dominant genes) and others are not (recessive genes), as originally studied by Mendel; (2) interactive or epistatic genetic variance, which regards how genes interact with each other, determining the process by which some are expressed or suppressed.

44. Eva Jablonka and Marion J. Lamb, *Evolution in Four Dimensions: Genetic, Epigenetic, Behavioral, and Symbolic Variation in the History of Life*, rev. ed. (Cambridge, Mass.: MIT Press, 2014), 117–35.

45. See Jablonka and Lamb, *Evolution in Four Dimensions*, 135–43.

46. David S. Moore, *The Developing Genome: An Introduction to Behavioral Epigenetics* (Oxford: Oxford University Press, 2015), 39.

47. Moore, *The Developing Genome*, 41–42.

with neurons in their noses more sensitive to cherry blossom smell, and with more brain space devoted to smelling cherry blossom.[48] Swedish scientists calculated the effects of food availability on multiple generations and found surprising results. If a boy was undernourished between nine and twelve years old, his future son was less likely to die from cardiovascular disease, and his future grandchildren were less likely to die from diabetes. Meanwhile, overfed boys in the same age range produced grandchildren who were *four times* more likely to die from diabetes-related causes.[49] Effects of tobacco and betel nut use can similarly affect multiple generations.[50]

David Moore insightfully notes, "Our characteristics develop because of the mutual activities of a variety of genetic, epigenetic, and environmental factors *that operate as an integrated system.*"[51] Later, I will discuss how a person's inclinations are influenced by his developmental environment. Here I will conclude the discussion on the physical components of human individuality by noting that epigenetic studies indicate that DNA alone does not satisfy the criteria for "signate matter." An alternate candidate may be the "dene," which is a dynamic gene, that is, a DNA sequence plus regulatory proteins, epigenetic modifications, and so on, by which it interacts with its environment while maintaining its basic structure.[52] The *dene* concept may be precise and yet flexible enough to account for the latest research.

One further issue must be addressed in order to account for the individual human as he or she exists at the moment of conception: the individuality of the soul. Above we saw Aquinas's princi-

48. Brian G. Dias and Kerry J. Ressler, "Parental Olfactory Experience Influences Behavior and Neural Structure in Subsequent Generations," *Nature Neuroscience* 17, no. 1 (January 2014): 89–96.

49. Moore, *The Developing Genome*, 181–83.

50. Ibid., 184.

51. Ibid., 213.

52. Rafel Vicuña, "The Evolving Concept of the Gene," *Acta*, no. 21: *The Scientific Legacy of the 20th Century* (Vatican City: Pontifical Academy for the Sciences, 2011): 197–214, at 210. See the original paper by Evelyn Fox Keller and David Harel, "Beyond the Gene," *PLoS ONE* 2, no. 11 (November 28, 2007): e1231.

ple that an individual's body and soul are "proportioned and, as it were, naturally adapted to one another," and that a particular soul is infused into matter apt to receive it.[53] However, as a study of DNA and epigenetics shows, each human body is unique for each individual member of the species *homo sapiens*. From the principle of body-soul proportionality and the principle of bodily uniqueness Aquinas argues that each soul is unique as well: "The difference of form, which arises only from a different disposition of matter, does not create a specific difference but only a numerical difference, for there are diverse forms of diverse individuals, [differentiated] in accordance with material differences."[54] The consequence may be surprising at first, though Aquinas calls it "manifest": "the better the body's disposition, the better a soul it receives."[55] In the background a fundamental axiom is working: whatever is received, is received according to the mode of the receiver.[56] Thus Thomas says it is clear that souls are variously allotted in the case of different species because "act and form are received in material according the capacity of the material."[57] The plant-like coral possesses a categorically less excellent soul than the human-like chimp, which manifestly has greater capacities of movement, emotion, and so on.

For similar reasons, human souls vary in their capacities: "Since, even among humans, some of the bodies are better disposed, they are allotted souls with greater powers of understanding."[58] Robert Pasnau explains: "Aquinas makes it clear that the mind itself—the soul's immaterial component—is affected by the body's dis-

53. *SCG* II, c. 80, n. 8.

54. *ST* I, q. 85, a. 7, ad 3.

55. *ST* I, q. 85, a. 7, co.

56. "Omne quod recipitur in aliquo, recipitur in eo per modum recipientis" (*ST* I, q. 75, a. 5, co). Thomas employs this principle throughout his thought, with implications for an individual's ability to acquire and develop certain kinds of habits. See *Super Sent.*, lib. 2, d. 32, q. 2, a. 3, ad 4 (regarding whether all human souls are created equal); *ST* I, q. 32, a. 1, ad 2 (the infinite goodness of God communicated variously in diverse creatures); *De veritate*, q. 12, a. 6, ad 4 (how a form, including infused prophetic knowledge, is received into the soul).

57. *ST* I, q. 85, a. 7, co.

58. Ibid.

position."[59] Because the human souls diverge only with respect to non-essential qualities, such as intellectual power, these differences are *accidental*: all humans are definitionally members of the same species and thereby possess the same natural dignity. Differences in non-essential qualities arise from God's design that *this* rational substance is united to *this* particular body as its substantial form. Body and soul are not two complete substances that happen to be united. Rather, *this soul* is the first act, the very life and being of *this body* organized by a unique dynamic gene (DNA plus epigenetic modifications, etc.), so that their union is natural and they are fitted only for each other: "It is the same essential form by which man is a being in act, by which he is a body, by which he is living, by which he is animal, and by which he is man."[60] He corroborates this elsewhere: "Since every perfection is infused in matter in accord with the capacity of that matter, the soul's nature will thus not be infused in different bodies in accord with the same worth and purity. So in each body it will have an existence that is limited by the scope of the body."[61] According to Thomas, a denial of this teaching attacks natural unity of the human person and leads to the Origenist heresy.[62] The affirmation of this teaching, though, helps to explain the difference between dispositions that a person has because he is human and dispositions that he has because of his own unique makeup.

59. Pasnau, *Thomas Aquinas on Human Nature*, 384. In some way, they mutually include each other: "est enim comparatio animae ad corpus sicut est comparatio artis ad artificiatum, ut dicit philosophus. Quidquid autem explicite in artificiato ostenditur, hoc totum implicite et originaliter in ipsa arte continetur; et similiter etiam quidquid in partibus corporis apparet, totum originaliter, et quodammodo implicite, in anima continetur" (*ST* Suppl., q. 80, a. 1; *Super Sent.*, lib. 4, d. 44, q. 1, a. 2, qc. 1, co).

60. *ST* I, q. 76, a. 6, ad 1.

61. *Super Sent.*, lib. 1, d. 8, q. 5, a. 2, ad 6. Cited in Pasnau, *Thomas Aquinas on Human Nature*, 384.

62. See *SCG* II, c. 44, nn. 6–7.

## DISPOSITIONS FROM INDIVIDUAL NATURE

In his *Summa Theologiae* I-II, q. 51, a. 1, Aquinas asks whether humans have any habits by nature. He responds by explaining that human instincts and synderesis may be considered bases of dispositions that follow from human nature. Dispositions derived from human nature in general are "per se and proper accidents" that follow from the *form* of the subject.[63] Some dispositions such as the "religious instinct" have no participation in matter as such. Other dispositions participate in matter, such as the tendency to laugh (a disposition proper to the human species) and the dispositions of the subhuman instincts (analogous to those of nonrational animals, e.g., the hoarding instinct). In the present section, I explore dispositions as accidents that follow from the *material* of the subject, that is, from an individual's given bodily composition. This section focuses on dispositions inseparable from the living individual. Although this would be the place to discuss dispositions that stem from biological sex, I will bypass it entirely: that stupendously important and controversial topic requires much more space than is available here.

Aquinas recognizes that individuals differ widely according to their different inborn constitutions. All created things are "composed" in differing ways, Matthew Rolling explains: the human, in Aquinas's view, is "most perfect in its composition and most balanced in its composition."[64] In levels of increasing complexity, the human body "has three grades of composition: a mixing of elements, a complexion of humors, and the organization of organs or princi-

63. A complete and coherent taxonomy of accidents does not clearly emerge from Aquinas's diverse explanations of them. See *De ente et essentia*, c. 5; *Quaestio disputata De anima*, a. 12; *Expositio Libri Posteriorum*, lib. 1, lec. 10; *Sent. Meta.*, lib. 4, lec. 1 and lib. 10, lec. 11; and *ST* I, q. 77, a. 6.

64. Matthew Rolling, "*Essere Bene Dispositum*: The Factors That Contribute to the Development of Moral Chracter in the Thought of St. Thomas Aquinas" (PhD diss., Pontifical University of St. Thomas Aquinas, 2020), 74, referencing Aquinas, *Q. d. de anima*, q. 8 (Leon. ed., 249–58). Aquinas's phrases are "perfectissimum commixtionis modum ... temperatissimae complexionis."

pal parts."[65] Some inheritances have an indirect influence on human behavior whereas others affect us more directly. Congenital physical dispositions toward physical health or sickness, if they do not develop into acute conditions, can influence behavior generally and indirectly.[66] Inherited aptitude for intelligence seems to influence action more directly, insofar as it affects deliberation. Aquinas writes, "But with respect to individual nature, a habit of knowledge is natural as far as its beginning, such that one man, from the disposition of his [sense] organs, is more apt than another to understand well, since we need sensory powers for the operation of the intellect."[67] In his commentary on Aristotle's *De anima*, he develops the theory that excellence of mind is, other things being equal, proportionate to "sensitivity of touch."[68] He reasons that, because the organ of touch pervades the whole body, the other organs of sense are also organs of touch (e.g., our eyes and tongue can sense touch in addition to sight and taste, respectively). Now the power of touch is preeminent not only extensively, as present throughout the body, but also hierarchically because its presence suffices to indicate that a creature possesses sensory power. Because the sensory powers are intertwined, and touch is somehow preeminent, and a more powerful sensory power indicates a more powerful brain to process received information, Aquinas concludes that one who has a finer sense of touch has more robust sensory powers and consequently possesses more potential intellectual power.[69] Even when he says that "nobility of soul" can account for a greater inherent capacity of intellect, this too is based on "a well-balanced constitution of the body," for "every form is proportionate to its material."[70] Despite disagreement regarding the extent to which purely inherited genetic factors affect intelligence, all

65. Rolling, "*Essere Bene Dispositum*," 74, citing *SCG* II, c. 30; III, c. 22, along with secondary sources in n. 350. See Rolling's discussion in ibid., 74–84.

66. *ST* I-II, q. 51, a. 1.

67. Ibid.

68. *Sent. De anima*, lib. 2, l. 19, n. 5.

69. Ibid., n. 6.

70. Ibid., n. 7.

studies agree with Aquinas that mental potential amounts to more than good education: *a noteworthy portion* comes from inborn biological factors.[71]

In addition to individual differences in natural tendencies of mental functioning, Aquinas also spoke of innate physiological responses and emotional reactivity on account of what he called the *complexio* or temperament of an individual.[72] Aquinas's idea of *complexio* was derived indirectly from Aristotle.[73] More directly, he drew from a multifaceted tradition developed by the Abbey of Monte Cassino in conjunction with the School of Medicine of Salerno, rooted in the thought of Galen, Nemesius, and many others.[74] Galen (ca. 200 A.D.) argued that health is the proper combination (*complexio*, translating the Greek *krasis*) of four qualities: sanguine, choleric, melancholic, phlegmatic.[75] These consist in a mixture of the four basic elements (air, fire, earth, water), and the four basic humors (blood, yellow bile, black bile, phlegm), as represented below in figure 3.[76]

71. The value and meaning of intelligence quotient (IQ) studies is hotly debated, particularly whether tests measure acquired knowledge, basic mental function, or a mixture of both. As people age into adulthood, genetics is the main factor that explains intelligence differences among individuals. See, e.g., Rebecca L. Shiner and Colin G. DeYoung, "The Structure of Temperament and Personality Traits: A Developmental Perspective," in *The Oxford Handbook of Developmental Psychology*, ed. Philip David Zelazo (Oxford: Oxford University Press, 2013), 2:114–41, at 132; Thais S. Rizzi and Danielle Posthuma, "Genes and Intelligence," in *The Oxford Handbook of Cognitive Psychology*, ed. Daniel Reisberg (Oxford: Oxford University Press, 2013), 834.

72. See *Super Sent.*, lib. 2, d. 15, q. 2, a. 1; *ST* I-II, q. 46, a. 5. See also Titus, *Resilience and the Virtue of Fortitude*, 31–35.

73. For a comparison of Aristotle and modern temperament and personality theories, see Daniel E. Lee, "Aristotle's Biophysical Model of Psychology and Conceptualization of Character: Points of Congruence with Modern Models of Psychology" (D. Psych. diss., Adler School of Professional Psychology, 2008), 263–69.

74. See Rolling's extensive research in "*Essere Bene Dispositum*," 1.2, esp. 44–48.

75. Galen's primary works on the topic were *De temperamentis Libri III/De complexionibus* and *De inaequali intemperie/De militia complexionis diversae*. See Faith Wallis, "Medicine, Theoretical," in *Medieval Science, Technology, and Medicine: An Encyclopedia*, ed. Thomas F. Glick, Steven Livesey, and Faith Wallis (New York: Routledge, 2014), 336–40 at 338. Also, Nancy G. Siraisi, *Medieval and Early Renaissance Medicine: An Introduction to Knowledge and Practice* (Chicago: University of Chicago Press, 2009), 84 and 101–4.

76. Adapted from Roy Porter, *The Greatest Benefit to Mankind* (New York: Norton, 1997), 56–57.

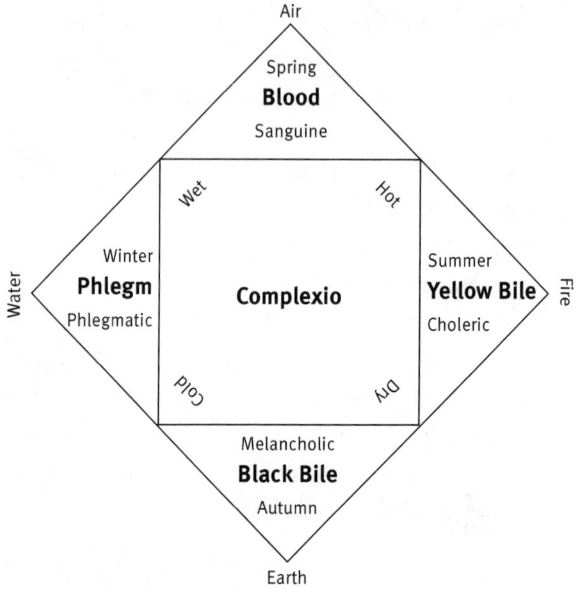


FIGURE 3. *COMPLEXIO*/TEMPERAMENT

*Complexio* structures the whole body and its functions; it is not reducible to the modern idea of complexion, that is, the surface color and quality of the skin, particularly that of the face. The body of a person with a sanguine *complexio,* for example, is dominated by the element of air and the humor of blood, both of which were considered wet and hot. For this reason, each *complexio* corresponds to a temperament, a composition of humors that are tempered according to the nature of the individual: "the balance of humors was held to be responsible for psychological as well as physical disposition, a belief enshrined in the survival of the English adjectives sanguine, phlegmatic, choleric, and melancholy to describe traits of character."[77]

When explaining the different dispositions of individuals, Aqui-

77. Siraisi, *Medieval and Early Renaissance Medicine,* 106.

nas often references an adapted form of Galen's temperament theory.[78] Thomas argues contrary to Galen that the soul cannot be reduced to a mere temperament.[79] Rather, bodily temperament is an emotional-physiological reality affected by the functioning of the heart and diaphragm, but above all by brain size and function.[80] He proposes reasons for why humans, more than other animals, need the largest brains compared their body size. Significantly, both are somewhat upheld by modern studies. First, he argues that a proportionately large brain is necessary to perfect the operations of the interior senses without impediments. A meta-analysis of human brain studies found that a greater brain volume is positively associated with greater intelligence.[81] Hence, some animals have larger sized brains, but our brains have denser tissues dedicated to specific tasks. Individual differences in brain volume, meanwhile, have been correlated to differences in temperament and character.[82] Second, Thomas holds that the brain modifies heart functions and body temperature, and consequently influences all other human actions that stem from the upright posture.[83] This is supported by the finding

78. Much of Galen's thought was mediated through thinkers such as Avicenna in his *Canon on Medicine,* to which Aquinas refers directly and indirectly (e.g., *In Librum Boetii de Trinitate,* q. 5, ad 4; *De veritate* q. 25, a. 2, co.). For Avicenna's influence on Albert the Great and Aquinas, see John McGinnis, *Great Medieval Thinkers: Avicenna* (Oxford: Oxford University Press, 2010), 250–53. For further references to the temperament theory, see notes in Aquinas, *Opera omnia, Tomus 45.2; Sentencia libri De sensu et sensato cuius secundus tractatus est De memoria et reminiscentia,* ed. R.-A. Gauthier (Rome / Paris: Commissio Leonina / Librairie Philosophique J. Vrin, 1985), 131.

79. *SCG* II, c. 63.

80. *ST* I, q. 91, a. 3, ad 1. For Aristotle's position on how the heart, diaphragm, and brain affect an individual's innate inclinations, see Mariska Leunissen, *From Natural Character to Moral Virtue in Aristotle* (New York: Oxford University Press, 2017), 27–31.

81. Jakob Pietschnig et al., "Meta-Analysis of Associations between Human Brain Volume and Intelligence Differences: How Strong Are They and What Do They Mean?," *Neuroscience and Biobehavioral Reviews* 57 (October 2015): 411–32. See also J. Philippe Rushton and C. Davison Ankney, "Whole Brain Size and General Mental Ability: A Review," *The International Journal of Neuroscience* 119, no. 5 (April 2009): 692–732.

82. Peter Van Schuerbeek et al., "Individual Differences in Local Gray and White Matter Volumes Reflect Differences in Temperament and Character: A Voxel-Based Morphometry Study in Healthy Young Females," *Brain Research* 1371 (January 31, 2011): 32–42.

83. *ST* I, q. 91, a. 3, ad 1.

that the brain's hypothalamus helps to regulate cardiovascular and temperature-related functions.[84]

From his understanding of the brain and sensation, Thomas argues that, because of our intellectual powers, the human species possesses "the most balanced temperament" among all the animals.[85] Nevertheless, not all individuals are equally balanced. It is quasi-natural for a person to be prone to health (or sickness) according to his personal temperament.[86] The four temperaments entail various emotional-actional dispositions as they predominate in a person characterized by them, and health is accordingly different for each.[87] Sanguine persons are generally cheerful,[88] joyful,[89] daring,[90] and more loving,[91] but they are also more incontinent in resisting their passions.[92] Cholerics are irascible,[93] can quickly feel the impulse of passion from the velocity and vehemence of their humor,[94] and thereby are more inclined to quick action,[95] and are prone to be more bitter.[96] Phlegmatics tend to have sweeter personalities,[97] to be lazy,[98] softer in resisting impressions,[99] and therefore weaker in continence and fortitude.[100] Finally, melancholics tend to be sad,[101] to have a vehement appetite for delight because of

84. See Noback et al., *The Human Nervous System*, 371–86.

85. *Super Sent.*, lib. 2, d. 15, q. 2, a. 1; *ST* I, q. 91, a. 3, ad 1.

86. *ST* I-II, q. 51, a. 1.

87. *Expositio Posteriorum Analyticorum*, lib. 2, l. 16, n. 5.

88. *Sent. Ethic.*, lib. 3, l. 12, n. 1.

89. *In psalmos Davidis expositio* [hereafter *Super Psalmo*] 29, n. 4.

90. *ST* I-II, q. 45, a. 3.

91. *ST* I-II, q. 48, a. 2, ad 1.

92. *Sent. Ethic.*, lib. 7, l. 7, n. 18.

93. *Sent. Ethic.*, lib. 3, l. 12, n. 1; *SCG* II, c. 63, n. 1; III, c. 85, n. 19.

94. *ST* II-II, q. 156, a. 1, ad 2.

95. *ST* I-II, q. 46, a. 5.

96. *ST* I, q. 75, a. 2; q. 111, a. 4.

97. Such is implied by the material of which "phlegm" is composed. See *Sent. Meta.*, lib. 8, l. 4, n. 1.

98. *Sent. Ethic.*, lib. 3, l. 12, n. 1.

99. *Sent. Ethic.*, lib. 7, l. 7, n. 18.

100. *ST* II-II, q. 156, a. 1, ad 1 and 2.

101. *Super Sent.*, lib. 4, d. 49, q. 3, a. 2, co.; *Sent. Ethic.*, lib. 3, l. 12, n. 1, and many other places.

pain in their bodies,[102] and may be incontinent on that account;[103] they are greatly moved by images,[104] and have strong imaginations,[105] and therefore are difficult to persuade,[106] and tend to be inordinately fearful.[107]

Emotional-actional tendencies of the temperaments are wholly attributable to physical causes: "The impetus of a passion can arise either because of its speed, as in cholerics; or from its vehemence, as in melancholics," or from "the malleability of one's temperament ... as is seen in phlegmatics."[108] Natural temperaments are not passions. Thomas insists that temperaments do not *determine* emotional reaction or personal action: both reaction and action, he says, can be shaped by free choice.[109] Nevertheless, temperaments *incline* a person to respond with typical emotional patterns, for a temperament is a stable, bodily inclination to respond to sensory goods in particular and predictable ways.[110]

Utilizing empirical techniques, scientists in recent decades have extensively studied personality and, to a lesser extent, temperament.[111] Temperament may be seen as the raw material of personality: just as wood or marble may be sculpted into different shapes while retaining basic structural features such as relative hardness, density, and porousness, so temperament retains its own semi-malleable features as the basis of personality. One's innate temperament cannot fully be changed, but it can be shaped by choice and interaction with

102. *Super Sent.*, lib. 4, d. 49, q. 3, a. 5, qc. 1, co.

103. *ST* II-II, q. 156, a. 1, ad 2.

104. *Sentencia De sensu* [hereafter *Sent. De sensu*], tract. 2, l. 8, n. 4.

105. *Super Epistolam ad Hebraeos lectura* [hereafter *Super Heb.*], c. 1, l. 1.

106. *Sent. Ethic.*, lib. 7, l. 9, n. 6.

107. *Sent. De anima*, lib. 1, l. 2, n. 7.

108. *ST* II-II, q. 156, a. 1, ad 2.

109. He specifically mentions that cholerics can resist this impulse: *De veritate*, q. 22, a. 9, ad 2, albeit with difficulty. See also *Sent. Ethic.*, lib. 7, l. 7, n. 18.

110. A passion may be defined as "a motion of the sensory appetite following the sensitive apprehension of a sensory good or evil with a corresponding bodily alteration." See Santiago Ramirez, *De Passionibus animae in I-II Summae Theologiae divi Thomae expositio (QQ. 22–48)* (Madrid: Instituto "Luis Vives" de Filosofía, 1973), 33.

111. See Michael Stock, "Dimensions of Personality," *The Thomist* 33 (1969): 611–66.

one's environment.[112] The lastingness of temperament considerably originates from innate biological factors: an estimated forty to fifty percent of personality is attributable to genetic factors.[113] Twin studies and adoption studies, for instance, show that twins with the same genes tend to have the same personality even more than fraternal twins, and that biological children share more personality traits with their parents than do adopted children.[114]

How to classify temperament and personality traits remains very much a disputed question. In an earlier work, the developmental psychologist Jerome Kagan posited four temperamental types that corresponded with those identified by Galen: timid (phlegmatic), bold (choleric), upbeat (sanguine), and melancholy.[115] Each, he said, was identifiable by particular of brain activity along with typical observable behavioral patterns. More recently, however, he has preferred a fourfold typology: low-reactive, high-reactive, easily aroused, and easily distressed. These do not entirely match with the traditional categories of phlegmatic, choleric, sanguine, and melancholy.[116] C. Robert Cloninger and his associates, meanwhile, developed a model that argued in favor of four temperaments traits: reward dependence, persistence, novelty seeking, and harm avoid-

112. See Paul T. Costa, Jr., and Robert R. McCrae, "A Theoretical Context for Adult Temperament," in *Temperament in Context*, ed. Theodore D. Wachs and Geldolph A. Kohnstamm (Mahwah, N.J.: Lawrence Erlbaum Associates, 2001), 1–19, at 2. Tellegen argues against strict behaviorism and defines "personality trait" with biology in mind: "a psychological (and therefore organismic) structure underlying a relatively enduring behavioral disposition, i.e., a tendency to respond in certain ways under certain circumstances." Auke Tellgen, "The Analysis of Consistency in Personality Assessment," *Journal of Personality* 56 (1988): 621–63, at 622.

113. John Maltby et al., *Personality, Individual Differences and Intelligence*, 4th ed. (London: Pearson, 2013), 200. Nevertheless, up to now, no single gene or group of genes has been shown to be always associated with a particular temperament, mood, or mental illness independent from other factors, such as sex, experiences, and ethnicity. See Jerome Kagan, *The Temperamental Thread: How Genes, Culture, Time and Luck Make Us Who We Are* (New York: Dana Press, 2010), 19.

114. Maltby et al., *Personality, Individual Differences and Intelligence*, 197–200.

115. Jerome Kagan, *Galen's Prophecy: Temperament in Human Nature* (New York: Westview Press, 1997).

116. See Kagan, *The Temperamental Thread*, 31.

ance.[117] A number of studies confirm significant portions of Cloninger's model, including recent analyses of the brain's paralimbic and neocortical regions.[118] The majority of scientists, however, support what has become known as the "Big Five" or the Five-Factor Model (FFM), which has been hailed as initiating a "real progress toward consensus" because of its integrative power.[119] The FFM proposes the following as universal personality traits:

- Openness-to-experience ⇔ intellectual precocity;
- Conscientiousness ⇔ self-control;
- Extraversion ⇔ positive affect;
- Agreeableness; and
- Neuroticism ⇔ negative emotionality.[120]

Proponents point to the many biological studies that have apparently supported the FFM. For example, four out of the five traits were positively associated with the functions of different brain locations.[121] Critics, however, argue that the factors are imprecise, inconsistent, and therefore untenable.[122] On an encouraging note, Jan Strelau's analysis of the theoretical and empirical bases of a great

117. See C. R. Cloninger, "A Unified Biosocial Theory of Personality and Its Role in the Development of Anxiety States," *Psychiatric Developments* 4, no. 3 (1986): 167–226.

118. M. Sugiura et al., "Correlation between Human Personality and Neural Activity in Cerebral Cortex," *NeuroImage* 11, no. 5, part 1 (May 2000): 541–46. Cloninger's model is not without its critics. See Shiner and DeYoung, "The Structure of Temperament and Personality Traits," 120–21.

119. For a summary of the theory and reactions to it, with thorough references, see Christian B. Miller, *Character and Moral Psychology* (Oxford: Oxford University Press, 2014), 129–47.

120. See John P. Oliver et al., "Paradigm Shift to the Integrative Big Five Trait Taxonomy: History, Measurement, and Conceptual Issues," in *Handbook of Personality: Theory and Research*, ed. Oliver P. John et al. (New York: Guilford Press, 2008), 114–58. Here the bidirectional arrow indicates the functional equivalence of terms for experimental purposes.

121. Colin G. DeYoung et al., "Testing Predictions from Personality Neuroscience. Brain Structure and the Big Five," *Psychological Science* 21, no. 6 (June 2010): 820–28.

122. See Jerome Kagan and Nancy C. Snidman, *The Long Shadow of Temperament* (Cambridge, Mass.: Belknap Press, 2004), 56–63. Also, the FFM does not adequately distinguish between inborn temperament and cultivated personality or character.

number of competing temperament theories leads one to conclude that some temperaments indeed exist, that they are biologically based, relatively stable traits that incline people to stimuli differently in intensity, fluctuation, speed, and so on.[123] At this time, though, no single model has completely replaced Galen's.

Developing the Aristotelian-Galenic understanding of human temperament, Thomas considers the moral implications of innate inclinations. Seeing how a temperament disposes a person to have certain kinds of behaviors and emotional reactions, Aquinas argues that different temperaments and bodily characteristics incline various individuals toward corresponding virtues or vices.[124] Some persons, he says, are more dispositionally prudent than others; others more dispositionally temperate.[125] But, because of the oppositional nature of virtues and vices, one can neither be inclined toward every virtue nor toward every vice. For example, he says that some men have a "natural habit" toward anger that arises from their inborn choleric temperament.[126] Now an inclination toward anger entails ease and quickness in raising up things that are contrary and harmful to the good of oneself or one's companions. Thus, a person inclined to anger is thereby also inclined to fortitude, courage, and the like, virtues that involve pursuing what is difficult, including poten-

123. Jan Strelau, *Temperament: A Psychological Perspective* (New York: Kluwer, 2000), 35. This is one of the most thorough, insightful, and objective modern studies on temperament.

124. Animal species have distinct biologically-based temperaments that incline them to analogues of virtue or vice: a likeness of particular prudence inclines lions to "magnanimity" and foxes to "craftiness" (*ST* I, q. 55, a. 3, ad 3); lions possess more physical fortitude than humans (*De veritate*, q. 22, a. 11, co.); dogs have laudable ferocity (*De malo*, q. 3, a. 1, ad 10); horses have a "noble and wonderous" courage in battle (*In Iob*, c. 39, l. 1, v. 39). The diversity and specificity of animal temperaments and behaviors make them apt symbols of human temperaments and behaviors (*ST* I, q. 106, a. 6, ad 1). In addition to temperament, there is evidence that individual animals of the same species can have distinct personalities: Jennifer Vonk and Taryn Eaton, "Personality in Nonhuman Animals: Comparative Perspectives and Applications," in *The SAGE Handbook of Personality and Individual Differences I: The Science of Personality and Individual Differences*, ed. Virgil Zeigler-Hill and Todd K. Shackelford (Los Angeles: SAGE Publications, 2018), 23–31.

125. *ST* II-II, q. 47, a. 15; q. 141, a. 1, ad 2.

126. *ST* I-II, q. 46, a. 5.

tial harms. At the same time, being inclined *toward* one virtue also entails being inclined *away from* the opposite virtue: those naturally brave are also less naturally patient, for patience involves restraining the irascible passions.[127] Melancholics tend to have strong imaginations, which disposes them toward both intellectual virtues and away from physical virtues such as courage.[128] At the same time, melancholics are naturally sadder than others, and they are inclined toward madness if they do not successfully stave off dejection.[129] This is why melancholics have strong drives to seek out pleasure: in order to relieve sadness and retain a balanced mind.[130] More generally, inchoate dispositions for various intellectual and moral virtues can naturally exist in different people in different amounts as aptitudes related to temperament and other bodily conditions.[131]

If it is surprising that Aquinas holds that people are naturally disposed toward acts of virtue, it may be even more surprising that he denominates such dispositions as "wholly imperfect virtues."[132] There are three kinds of virtues, he says: wholly imperfect virtue, partly imperfect virtue, and perfect virtue. The first is virtue without prudence or charity; the second is virtue with prudence, but without charity; the third is virtue with both prudence and charity.[133] Our concern here is with "wholly imperfect" virtues. They include "inclinations which some have from birth toward certain works of virtue."[134] These inclinations are distributed unequally. One person has an inclination toward one virtue, and another toward another virtue. He explains: "An imperfect moral virtue, such as temperance or for-

127. *De virtutibus*, q. 1, a. 8, ad 10.

128. While recognizing melancholy's enhancement of imagination, Thomas argues against the idea that prophecy comes about from it. See *Super Heb.*, c. 1, l. 1, n. 17. He also says that melancholics are often more timid even when no dangers are present. See *Sent. De anima*, lib. 1, l. 2, n. 7.

129. See *ST* I-II, q. 37, a. 4, ad 3.

130. See *ST* I-II, q. 32, a. 7, ad 2.

131. *ST* I-II, q. 63, a. 1.

132. *De virtutibus*, q. 5, a. 2, ad 12.

133. See *De virtutibus*, q. 5, a. 2, co.

134. Ibid.

titude, is nothing other than some inclination in us to do some kind of good deed, whether that inclination exists in us by nature or custom."[135] Thus, "some by natural temperament ... are prompt in works of generosity, but are not prompt in deeds of chastity."[136] None of these inclinations toward virtue have the "perfect *ratio*" of virtue, for two reasons.[137] First, inborn inclinations can be used badly if a person uses them without discernment, similar to the way a blind horse runs faster but more wildly the harder it is beaten. In contrast, no one uses authentic virtue badly, any more than one can use water to make something drier. Second, individual inclinations toward virtue stem from a person's innate physiology. They pressure us independently of prudence. But prudence is the virtue by which a person directs himself and his passions to an authentic good, with his right reason illuminated by acquired knowledge. Prudence provides the *ratio* of virtue. Therefore, these virtue-inclinations are intrinsically imperfect because they are unformed by reason.[138] Through rational habituation, however, our natural inclinations can be taken up and perfected by full virtue.[139]

Individual differences can have enormous behavioral consequences. The ability to develop habits in general is increasingly seen by researchers as a trait in and of itself. Studies indicate that different individuals have varying degrees of "habit propensity."[140] From a Thomistic perspective, it would seem that the propensity is due to a number of factors, and dependent on the nature of the habit in question: raw intelligence may predispose a person to develop habits of syllogistic thinking, whereas physical strength and agility may pre-

135. *ST* I-II, q. 65, a. 1.

136. Ibid.

137. See *De virtutibus* q. 5, a. 2, co.

138. See *Expositio super Isaiam ad litteram*, c. 11, l. 2, n. 361: "Est autem duplex imperfectio virtutis: una per accidens, quae est ex indispositione habentis ... defectus est per se ex parte ipsius habitus."

139. See *ST* I-II, q. 51, a. 1; II-II, q. 108, a. 2; q. 117, a. 1, ad 1.

140. Aukje Verhoeven and Sanne de Wit, "The Role of Habits in Maladaptive Behaviour and Therapeutic Interventions," in *The Psychology of Habit* (ed. Verplanken), 285–303, at 290.

dispose a person to athletic skills. In addition, there seem to be stable character traits that aid a person's habit acquisition, including the willingness to take risks; on the contrary side, perfectionism—the desire to make no mistakes—makes habituation more difficult.[141] One study, for instance, finds that people with more working memory capacity have more consistency in their moral judgments, and are more likely to accept certain kinds of killing.[142] An analysis of grey-matter volumes suggests that individuals with smaller cuneus and precuneus volumes were more prone to pride, whereas those with larger right inferior temporal volumes more readily felt gratitude.[143] Other studies work directly from a temperamental perspective. Kagan's longitudinal studies have shown that the temperaments of infants often manifest themselves in moral behavior later in life. High-reactive children who described themselves as very sensitive to feeling shame if they receive parental criticism displayed more signs of amygdala activity as infants than high-reactives who did not endorse this trait or low-reactives who likewise admitted to similar feelings.[144]

The best studies of personality and temperament account for biology, emotions, and behavioral patterns. Prominent among these is the work of Jaak Panksepp and Lucy Biven, who identified seven basic emotions (seeking, rage, fear, sexual desire, care, panic/grief, and play) and discuss each of their biological underpinnings and behavioral manifestations.[145] The authors note that people can have different innate tendencies, and therefore different morally-tinged behaviors, that stem from differences in the biological systems that

141. Ibid., 293.

142. Adam B. Moore et al., "Who Shalt Not Kill? Individual Differences in Working Memory Capacity, Executive Control, and Moral Judgment," *Psychological Science* 19, no. 6 (June 2008): 549–57.

143. Roland Zahn et al., "Individual Differences in Posterior Cortical Volume Correlate with Proneness to Pride and Gratitude," *Social Cognitive & Affective Neuroscience* 9, no. 11 (November 2014): 1676–83.

144. Kagan and Snidman, *The Long Shadow of Temperament*, 219–20.

145. Jaak Panksepp and Lucy Biven, *The Archaeology of the Mind: Neuroevolutionary Origins of Human Emotions* (New York: Norton, 2012).

underlie the emotions. For example, they have noted that there seems to be a "rage system" within the brain (running from medial areas of the amygdala to the medial hypothalamus and then to areas of the periaqueductal gray). Whenever these brain regions were electrically stimulated, all test animals responded with attack behaviors, and the attacks became more intense when the electricity increased.[146] At the same time, higher testosterone levels makes persons more aggressive.[147] It follows that "sustained arousal of this system leads to chronic irritability and explosive aggressive disorders."[148] People who suffer from these disorders are more likely to harm others when in fits of rage. Similar studies to those of Panksepp and Biven have been collected in the significant *Handbook of Individual Differences in Social Behavior*. Articles in the *Handbook* synthesize biological, cultural/social, and developmental factors to help explain many different kinds of dispositions toward action.[149] Missing from these valuable studies are evaluations of the moral aspects of innate dispositions. Thus, after a thorough discussion of inclinations to anger in almost entirely negative terms, the authors offer a very brief caveat, saying, "it should be remembered that positive functions are also served by hostility, at least in its milder forms. Oppositional behavior is often necessary for the benefit of society, and the absence of hostility and extreme or unmitigated communion is also dysfunctional."[150] With only a sentence, they hint at what Aquinas develops at length, namely, the motives and causes of anger and the relation anger bears to virtues such as courage. In this light, the moral theology of Aquinas offers an invaluable complementary source for comprehensively explaining innate dispositions.

146. Ibid., 150. Likewise, lesions in the ventromedial hypothalamus lead to irritable, even savage, behaviors (156).

147. Ibid., 155.

148. Ibid., 436.

149. Mark R. Leary and Rick H. Hoyle, *Handbook of Individual Differences in Social Behavior* (New York: Guilford Publications, 2013).

150. John C. Barefoot and Stephen H. Boyle, "Hostility and Proneness to Anger," in Leary and Hoyle, *Handbook of Individual Differences in Social Behavior*, 210–26, at 222.

## THE PROVIDENTIAL ORDER IN DIVERSITY

Before ending this chapter, I would like to address the issue of diversity. Rightly understood, Aquinas's views on diversity are essential for understanding the nature of habits, why we possess them, and how to develop or eliminate them. Because political overtones could distort my theme, I will here insist that I am considering diversity only from a philosophical-theological perspective: implications for social action remain implicit. Some of the following exposition anticipates later chapters, but diversity is better addressed here, because natural diversity highlights that not all inequalities are unjust and unwelcome. Rather, as I will show in brief order, naturally diverse human habits are good for the entire universe.

Concerns of equality and diversity are versions of the ancient problem of the "one and the many," or "unity and multiplicity." Aquinas explains: "the *ratio* of 'unity' consists in indivisibility, but the *ratio* of 'multiplicity' contains division,"[151] for "the *ratio* of multiplicity consists in things being divided from each other,"[152] because only things that are separate or divided are actually multiple and diverse. Hence: diversity necessarily entails division and inequality, for "sameness, likeness, and equality follow from unity … but the contraries of these—diversity, dissimilarity, and inequality—pertain to plurality."[153] This holds true for habits.

As we have seen, the more perfect a thing is, the more individual it is, such that humanity admits of more uniqueness than anything else in visible creation.[154] Diversity and inequality abound. Even general inclinations shared by all humans are uniquely shaped according to each individual's dynamic genetic structure and their individual soul. This singular body-soul unity affects bodily structures from head to toe: we see a broad palette of melanin tones and hair

151. *ST* I, q. 11, a. 1, s.c.

152. *Sent. Meta.*, lib. 10, l. 4, n. 2.

153. Ibid., nn. 16, 17. He is speaking here about formal diversity. See *Compendium theologiae*, c. 73. See also *ST* I, q. 47, a. 2.

154. *SCG* II, c. 68.

color; a swath of shapes and sizes of noses, ears, mouths, eyelids; a significant range of heights and raw physical or mental prowess; a novelist's playground of affective-estimative reaction types that we call temperaments: sanguine, choleric, melancholic, and phlegmatic. Individual inclinations, as with all other created forms, do not exist in the abstract. In this life, our personal proclivities are always instantiated in particular matter. Habits exist within a natural habitat: the whole and unique person who lives and moves within a unique, unrepeatable context within the world guided by divine providence. Some innate physical structures and their corresponding inclinations are more advantageous for some activities; others are more advantageous other activities. From this, it may seem as if diversity and equality will always be in tension.

Aquinas would disagree. Although diversity and equality are contraries, Aquinas evidently insists that they need not be incompatible, warring contradictories. Blanchette observes that complementarity supposes difference, but diversity "is not an evil in the universe. It pertains to its perfection in a positive way."[155] Indeed, Aquinas argues that diversity in creation is very good when in accordance with nature. "The lavishness of divine goodness" impelled God to create diversity according to a definite plan.[156] There are a number of reasons why God created a plurality of diversities to exist within nature. The chief divine purpose in creating the universe and all its parts, including each individual with his particular inclinations and abilities, is God's goodness: as perfect and infinite goodness, God himself is the supreme ultimate end of all things as a whole and of each thing individually.[157] Aquinas states: "the entire

155. Oliva Blanchette, *The Perfection of the Universe According to Aquinas* (University Park: The Pennsylvania University Press, 1992), 141.

156. *Compendium theologiae*, c. 73.

157. See *Compendium theologiae*, c. 103; *SCG* III, cc. 17–18; *De veritate*, q. 22, a. 1. In addition to Blanchette's excellent work, see my articles: "Seek First the Kingdom: A Reply to Germain Grisez's Account of Man's Ultimate End," *Nova et Vetera* (English edition) 8, no. 4 (2010): 959–95; "*Non Nisi Te, Domine*: Dietrich von Hildebrand, Germain Grisez, and the Saints on Man's Ultimate End," *Logos Journal* 16, no. 2 (2013): 124–41;

universe, with all its parts, is ordered unto God as its end insofar as the glory of God is represented in it through some imitation of divine goodness."[158] Because humans are made in the image of God, the divine goodness is their end in a special way, because they can move themselves—with the help of divine grace—toward God in loving relationship and thereby manifest God's goodness more perfectly.[159] Diversity also benefits creatures directly, Aquinas states, for finite things are made greater by the addition of other things: "Thus it was better for there to be diversity in created things, and thus for there to be a plurality of goods, than that there should be only one kind of good made by God."[160] Empirical studies of diversity argue for its benefits on similar grounds: "The judicious use of diversity requires moving beyond analogy and metaphor and toward a scientific understanding of the roles that diversity plays. Diversity can drive innovation by creating superadditive effects, it can promote system level robustness and flourishing, and sustain all of those gorgeous particulars that make life worth living."[161] There are also social benefits stemming from ordered diversity (and the graces God dispenses). Aquinas says there are three advantages for the distinction of offices, states, and grades in the Catholic church; these advantages

"Natural Self-Transcending Love According to Thomas Aquinas," *Nova et Vetera* (English edition) 12, no. 3 (2014): 913–46.

158. *ST* I, q. 65, a. 2. See also *Compendium theologiae*, c. 102. The universal work of praising God is manifest in scripture: "Bless the Lord, all his works" (Ps 103:22); "I heard every creature in heaven and on earth and under the earth and in the sea, and all therein, saying, 'To him who sits upon the throne and to the Lamb be blessing and honor and glory and might for ever and ever!'" (Rv 5:13); the *Canticle of the Three Young Men*, etc.

159. See *ST* I, q. 65, a. 2; I, q. 72, ad 3; I-II, q. 1, a. 8; I-II, q. 2, a. 8; I-II, q. 3, aa. 1 and 8. Gerard Manley Hopkins consciously praises diversity in *Pied Beauty*: "Glory be to God for dappled things … Whatever is fickle, freckled (who knows how?) / with swift, slow; sweet, sour; adazzle, dim / He fathers-forth whose beauty is past change: / Praise Him."

160. *Compendium theologiae*, c. 72.

161. Scott E. Page, *Diversity and Complexity* (Princeton, N.J.: Princeton University Press, 2011), 255. See also Page's more recent *The Diversity Bonus: How Great Teams Pay Off in the Knowledge Economy* (Princeton, N.J.: Princeton University Press, 2017), where he emphasizes that *formal* diversity, i.e., diversity of ideas, is the most beneficial sort.

apply *mutatis mutandis* to other diverse organizations.[162] First, just as various bodily organs contribute to the whole person's health, so ordered diversity conduces to the perfection of the community. Second, as different parts of the body have different natural ends and objects that enable the body to perform a variety of acts—the eyes see, the feet walk, etc.—so diverse graces provided to the married, priestly, religious, and episcopal states enable the community to perform a wider variety of spiritual and corporal good works. Third, the diversity in the mystical body of Christ leads to a greater dignity and beauty in the community.[163]

Not all diversity is equally beneficial, however. Page notes: "As should be clear from this book, a scientific and logical approach shows that diversity is no panacea. Too much diversity prevents meaningful structure from emerging; introductions of new species and new products and ideas can destroy as well as create."[164] Aquinas would go further and say that cultural diversity, though often good, does not bring guaranteed benefits, especially because some cultures stray from the principles of natural law that guarantee their flourishing.[165] Apt here are Aquinas's observations regarding four conditions will enable things to coexist harmoniously (*omnium in omnibus … harmoniae cunctae rei*).[166] First, commonality: just as all stones of a house share similar fitting properties, so within a universe all things have something in common with all: higher things participate in the lower, and lower things have a more excellent existence

162. The following exposition follows *ST* II-II, q. 183, a. 2, co.

163. For Thomas's account of beauty, see *ST* I, q. 5, a. 4, ad 1; I-II, q. 27, a. 1, ad 3. For dignity, see Lawrence Dewan, "Some Notes on St. Thomas's Use of 'dignitas,'" *Nova et Vetera* 11, no. 3 (2013): 663–72.

164. Page, *Diversity and Complexity*, 255.

165. See the balanced, Thomas-inspired article by Domènec Melé and Carlos Sánchez-Runde, "Cultural Diversity and Universal Ethics in a Global World," *Journal of Business Ethics* 116, no. 4 (2013): 681–87. For a more robust, non-Thomist refutation of cultural relativism, see John J. Tilley, "Cultural Relativism," *Human Rights Quarterly* 22, no. 2 (2000): 501–47.

166. *In librum Beati Dionysii De divinis nominibus expositio* [hereafter *In De divinis nominibus*], c. 4, l. 6, n. 364. The following exposition follows this passage and Blanchette's exposition closely (*The Perfection of the Universe According to Aquinas*, 12–13).

in the higher. Second, diversified order: because the parts of the universe are diverse, they must adapt to each other, not in a random way but according to some ordering principle, just as the orderly plan of a house ensures that the stones fit together. The first principle of order for unity-in-diversity is the natural law. Third, complementarity: one part should help another without undermining their rightful differences. Just as the roof protects the walls and foundation from above, and the walls and roof are supported by the foundation from below, so higher things should help perfect lower things in the universe, and lower things should support the excellence of superior things. Fourth, proportionality: there should be a certain proportion among the parts so that one single universe is composed from their harmonious unity-in-diversity.[167]

In sum, people have a diversity of habits, and this diversity entails an inequality that is an effect of the merciful working of divine providence, so that various habits in accordance with nature (and grace) conduce to a community's perfection, good works, dignity, and beauty. This leads us to consider next how experience and belonging to a community affects one's habits.

167. For a more thorough discussion, see João César das Neves and Domènec Melé, "Managing Ethically Cultural Diversity: Learning from Thomas Aquinas," *Journal of Business Ethics* 116, no. 4 (2013): 769–80.

# 3

# Experience and Habituation

From Romulus and Remus to Mowgli, classic stories have developed the theme in which children raised by animals gradually come to separate themselves from their beastly upbringing. Modern scientists have turned these tales on their heads and have tried to raise animals in ways that could transform them into civilized creatures. Koko the gorilla was the poster-"child" of these attempts. But more and more, empirical science is recognizing that most inclinations and behaviors—especially those of humans—are neither reducible to biological causes, nor are they entirely produced by environment. Nature and nurture exist in dynamic relation to one another.[1]

Up to this point, I have examined habits only insofar as they relate to nature, discussing natural habits that are derived from "general nature" or "individual nature." In order to explain acquired habits that arise from neither of these sources per se, I begin this chapter by considering the concepts of nature and voluntariness in relation to "nurture." After this, I show that everyone possesses nonvoluntary acquired habits, as seen in the nutrition of preborn infants, as well as parents' treatment of newborns. In the third section, I discuss the concept of imperfectly voluntary acquired habits, that is, disposi-

1. Darcia Narvaez, *Neurobiology and the Development of Human Morality: Evolution, Culture, and Wisdom* (New York: Norton, 2014), 20.

tions developed through sensory engagement without deliberate rationality. The final sections treat, respectively, the meanings and significance of attention, intention, and memory for the development of fully human habits.

## NATURE, NURTURE, AND VOLUNTARINESS

Francis Galton, despite his faulty eugenicist thought, helpfully coined that the phrase "nature and nurture" as two distinct categories for "the innumerable elements of which personality is composed." He wrote:

> Nature is all that a man brings with himself into the world; nurture is every influence from without that affects him after birth. The distinction is clear: the one produces the infant such as he is, including its latent faculties of growth of body and mind; the other affords the environment amid which growth takes place, by which natural tendencies may be strengthened or thwarted, or wholly new ones implanted.[2]

From a Thomistic perspective, the nature/nurture divide denotes two different causes of individual inclinations: innate biology is fundamentally separate from a given environment even if the two are inseparably intertwined in this world. One's body exists within a particular environment, and one's environment affects a person at the boundaries of his body and through his bodily openings. Metaphysically speaking, nature and nurture possess distinct causal structures: the divide between them truly exists and remains ineradicable, for a nature belongs to a particular substance with a unitary form whereas an environment is a non-substance, a circumstantial set of substances, artifacts, and materials that bear an extrinsic relation for some time.

On account of being *an individual substance of a rational nature*, a particular human is distinct from every other substance in the world—including the other persons who surround him, and all oth-

2. Francis Galton, *English Men of Science: Their Nature and Nurture* (London: Macmillan, 1874), 12.

er circumstances in which he exists.[3] In principle, then, it is possible to identify inclinations that arise primarily (or solely) from biology, and others that arise from particular environments and substances within those contexts. Biological causes are easier to identify and measure, for the variables that affect a single body, though vast, are significantly more limited than those of the person's environment. More effort may be necessary to accurately demarcate and measure environmental factors that affect an individual or segments of society. A complete explanation of habits and behavior will take both nature and nurture into consideration, along with how they mutually affect one another through human choice.

When treating human acts, Aquinas begins with a fundamental distinction. On the one hand, there is an "act of a human" (*actus hominis*) that is, an act that a human performs nondeliberatively; for clarity, I will typically refer to these as "movements" or "behaviors." On the other hand, there is a "human act" (*actus humanus*) that proceeds from "deliberate will" (*voluntate deliberate*).[4] He explains: "properly human acts are called 'voluntary,' because the will is the rational appetite, which is proper to humans."[5] I propose that there are at least four types of acts and habits as they relate to voluntariness: involuntary, nonvoluntary, partly voluntary, and fully voluntary.[6] A behavior or habit is *involuntary* when its principle lies outside of the person and it contradicts the person's will in some way.[7] A behavior or habit is *nonvoluntary* when it is "aside" from the will and has nothing to do with the will.[8] Nonvoluntariness proceeds entirely from outside the individual or from total ignorance, as when

3. *ST* I, q. 29, a. 1, quoting Boethius, *De duabus naturis*, in Patrologia Latina, ed. J.-P. Migne (Paris, 1841–55) [hereafter PL], 64:1343.

4. *ST* I-II, q. 1, a. 1.

5. *ST* I-II, prol.

6. The first three correspond to "acts of a human," while the last is a properly "human act."

7. *ST* I-II, q. 6, a. 5, co.: "quod est contra voluntatem, dicitur esse involuntarium."

8. *Sent. Ethic.*, lib. 3, l. 3, n. 1: "Quandoque autem non est contrarium voluntati, sed est praeter voluntatem in quantum est ignoratum et hoc non dicitur involuntarium, sed non voluntarium."

an individual is entirely deprived of the use of reason with respect to the act, for "in things without use of reason, there is neither voluntary nor involuntary."[9] A behavior or habit is *imperfectly voluntary* or partly voluntary when it arises from imperfect knowledge, that is, sensory knowledge and natural estimation alone and without rational deliberation.[10] In this light, I discuss imperfectly voluntary habits, that is, acquired when the individual engages only his sensory knowledge, or when he only partly engages his knowledge and volition as a child or as an adult. Finally, there is the *perfectly voluntary* or fully voluntary act. It proceeds from "perfect knowledge," which consists "not only in apprehending the thing which is the end, but also knowing it under the *ratio* of 'end,' and its proportion to those things which are ordered to the end itself."[11]

In what follows, I explore what I call "nonvoluntary" and "partly voluntary" acquired habits that is, dispositions subsequent to conception that have been acquired aside from the causality of the individual's knowledge and volition. Aquinas calls such dispositions "customary habits," for they are acquired by custom and will develop into a sort of second nature.[12] The term custom (*consuetudo*) bears multiple meanings for Aquinas, including the "custom" of passions that have been shaped by reason (noted above); the "custom" or interior inclinations of trained animals and people whose dispositions were shaped without the use of their reason;[13] and custom as some exterior pattern of behavior established through repetition and bearing the force of law.[14] In other words, the term "custom" is

9. See *ST* I-II, q. 6, a. 7, ad 3, and a. 8, co., where Aquinas equates "involuntary" with "repugnant to the will" and "nonvoluntary" with something done in ignorance. This frequently overlooked topic is admirably discussed in Jeffrey Hause, "Aquinas on Non-voluntary Acts," *International Philosophical Quarterly* 46, no. 4 (December 2006): 459–75.

10. *ST* I-II, q. 6, a. 2: "Imperfectam autem cognitionem finis sequitur voluntarium secundum rationem imperfectam, prout scilicet apprehendens finem non deliberat, sed subito movetur in ipsum."

11. Ibid.

12. *ST* I-II, q. 56, a. 5; *De veritate*, q. 12, a. 1, ad 10. See Cicero, *Rhetorica*, lib. 2, c. 53.

13. *ST* I-II, q. 50, a. 3, ad 2.

14. *ST* I-II, q. 97, a. 3. See Rolling, "*Essere Bene Dispositum*," 128–59. See also Stephen

analogous, indicating both the cause and the effect: custom is the means by which some behavior becomes accustomed, and custom is an interior disposition that inclines one to a customary behavior. Because some customary dispositions arise entirely without the intervention of one's knowledge (and so are nonvoluntary), and others with sensory knowledge (and therefore are partly voluntary), for the sake of clarity in my treatment below I employ the broad term "custom" along with this more precise language.

## NONVOLUNTARY ACQUIRED HABITS

At conception, a rational soul is infused into apt matter; a human person begins to exist and quickly develops the basic physical structure and innate dispositions foundational to all subsequent development. External forces are particularly powerful during an individual's early development and can fashion habits in two ways. First, they can create bodily habits, that is, quasi-permanent and difficult to change physical habitual dispositions that incline the soul to act in a specific way.[15] Second, external forces can change the appetitive powers themselves, imparting a quality that inclines them to respond in one way or another.[16]

Thomas's interest in embryonic development lies chiefly in two areas: how the embryo develops physically in relation to its soul,[17] and what Aristotle called "generation and corruption," which encompasses how organic things, including animals, come to be, how they maintain themselves by nourishment, and the meaning and processes of death and putrefaction.[18] Both embryology and gen-

Paul Grundman, "The Role of *Consuetudo* (Custom) in St. Thomas Aquinas's Philosophy of Law" (PhD diss., The Catholic University of America, 2005).

15. *ST* I-II, q. 50, a. 1.

16. *ST* I-II, q. 50, a. 5, ad 1.

17. More specifically, he is concerned about when the rational soul is infused into the body, that is, the point at which "hominization" takes place. For a thorough list of Thomistic texts on embryology, see Amerini, *Aquinas on the Beginning and End of Human Life*, 10–12.

18. See Thomas's *In librum primum Aristotelis De generatione et corruptione expositio*.

eration/corruption indirectly contribute to an understanding of nonvoluntary dispositions that a person acquires after conception. Below I will construct a framework based on clues in Thomas's writings.

Aristotle said, "It makes no *small* difference [to moral goodness] whether we form habits of one kind or another from our very youth; it makes a very great difference, or rather all the difference."[19] Habit-formation begins perhaps even sooner than he knew. The embryo's state of imperfection entails that it moves from potentiality to actuality, proceeding little by little to greater and greater perfection if unobstructed.[20] Development will naturally proceed through a series of "ages," beginning with *infantia* which lasts from birth to about seven years.[21] Growth ends with full maturity, the stage of greatest personal strength. Aquinas does name the "age" of embryonic life in the womb, but he recognizes that once hominization takes place, the infant's soul and body are distinct from the mother.[22] Even while in her mother's womb, a child has some relation to the world outside. In fact, the womb is like a little universe in which world-events, angels, and God can impart to the embryo what can be called nonvoluntary acquired dispositions. Regarding world-events, Thomas holds that, similar to the way that the moon moves the tides, so "heavenly bodies" can at times move the sense appetites through some "impression" and even "impress" a disposition on the body.[23]

For an overview of Thomas's understanding of generation in general, see Pasnau, *Thomas Aquinas on Human Nature*, 100–103.

19. *Nicomachean Ethics* II.1, 1103b24; emphasis added. For Aristotle on the effects of aging on one's natural character, see Leunissen, *From Natural Character to Moral Virtue in Aristotle*, 36–39.

20. See *ST* I, q. 119, a. 2, and *Sent. De anima*, lib. 2, l. 5, n. 10.

21. See Philip L. Reynolds, "Thomas Aquinas and the Paradigms of Childhood," in *The Vocation of the Child*, ed. Patrick M. Brennan (Grand Rapids, Mich.: Eerdmans, 2008), 154–89, at 156.

22. See *ST* III, q. 68, a. 11, co. and ad 2.

23. *De sortibus*, c. 4, co. (Leon. ed., 129–37): "potest dici, quod ex dispositione caelestium corporum aliqua inclinatio fit in nobis ad haec vel illa facienda, inquantum scilicet ad hoc inducimur per imaginariam apprehensionem, et per appetitus sensitivi passiones, scilicet iram, timorem et alia huiusmodi, ad quae homo est magis vel minus dispositus

Precisely because the heavenly bodies do not move the will, the dispositions are nonvoluntary, though potentially oriented toward the act of a given virtue.[24] As for spiritual powers, Thomas argues that demons can quasi-permanently affect preborn children and make them more prone to sin; to protect them from this demonic power, God provides each child with a guardian angel.[25] As for God's direct influence, in extraordinary circumstances, he has sanctified infants in the womb, as in the case of John the Baptist and the Virgin Mary.[26] Augustine speculated that these saints' reason and will miraculously developed so quickly that, while in the womb, they were able to know, believe, and consent, but Thomas disputes this point.[27] Infants naturally do not have fully activated senses, diminishing their ability to learn, to have complete understanding, and to make acts of the will.[28]

Does Thomas think that humans can impart dispositions to preborn infants? There is good reason to think Thomas would answer affirmatively. He notes that "animated fetuses" share in the life-events of their mother: when a pregnant woman is harmed at the hand of another, her baby can be harmed as well.[29] He also says that because sacraments require a minister to have direct contact with an individual's living body, a preborn infant may not be baptized while remaining in the womb.[30] Thomas likely holds that humans can impart nonvoluntary dispositions to embryos only by affecting the

---

secundum corporalem complexionem, quae subditur dispositioni stellarum." See also *SCG* III, cc. 84–88; *ST* I-II, q. 9, a. 5, ad 2; and *De iudiciis astrorum* (Leon. ed., 28–37).

24. *ST* I-II, q. 9, a. 5, co. See *De virtutibus*, q. 1, a. 8, co.

25. *Super Sent.*, lib. 2, d. 11, q. 1, a. 3, ad 3. In *ST* I, q. 113, a. 5, ad 3, Aquinas modifies his position and says that it is "probable" that the mother's guardian angel watches over the child until birth, when the child's own guardian angel is assigned.

26. *ST* III, q. 27, a. 6.

27. Ibid.

28. See *ST* I, q. 55, a. 2.

29. See *ST* II-II, q. 64, a. 8, ad 2. In this later position, Aquinas says that if the death of the fetus results, the crime is homicide. Earlier he had said that the crime would be less than homicide. See *Super Sent.*, lib. 4, d. 31, q. 2, a. 3, expos.

30. *ST* II-II, q. 64, a. 8.

Table 3-1. Effects of Nutrients on Development

| *Nutrient* | *Positive effect on fetus* |
|---|---|
| Calories | Growth and maintenance of the fetus and the placenta |
| Lysine | Critical for protein synthesis |
| Omega-3 fatty acids | Essential to the development of the brain and central nervous system, as well as new tissues |
| Iron | Assists healthy birth weight and full-term pregnancy |
| Folate | Required for cellular reactions, including DNA and nucleic acid synthesis, and for widespread, sustained cell division |
| Unsaturated fats[1] | Important contributor to a healthy fetal environment; has a beneficial impact on cell membrane physiology |

1. Ryan James Wood-Bradley et al., "Maternal Dietary Intake during Pregnancy Has Longstanding Consequences for the Health of Her Offspring," *Canadian Journal of Physiology & Pharmacology* 91, no. 6 (June 2013): 412–20.

body of the mother or by using means similar to those used by the heavenly bodies and the angels.

An enormous number of empirical studies can confirm many of Thomas's points, and they go beyond his position, definitively showing that humans can acquire nonvoluntary actional dispositions, beginning in utero. Here I can point to only a few of the more salient findings regarding *positive* dispositions, that is, those in accordance with human nature. Because medical practice is more focused on preventing or fixing harms to health, there is much more extensive literature on what causes *negative* dispositions, which will be discussed in chapter 6. The above table lists some essential nutrients for pregnant mothers and their positive effects on the developing infant.[31]

Perhaps more surprisingly, a pregnant mother's diet can also significantly affect her preborn child's everyday choices and social interactions by giving him a penchant for certain kinds of foods.[32]

31. Kathleen Abu-Saad and Drora Fraser, "Maternal Nutrition and Birth Outcomes," *Epidemiologic Reviews* 32, no. 1 (April 1, 2010): 5–25, esp. Table 2. For Aristotle on the influence of diet on one's natural inclinations, see Leunissen, *From Natural Character to Moral Virtue in Aristotle*, 33–36.

32. Amniotic fluid contains molecules originating in the mother's diet, thus allowing the infant to share in the same diet in a microscopic way; this in turn leads to food

Beyond somatic dispositions developed by chemicals, preborn persons can acquire higher-order dispositions of the memory. Studies indicate that children whose pregnant mothers listened to music regularly demonstrated better motor function control and higher performance in regulating their own behavior.[33] More directly, music can be one of many elements that develop a preborn infant's memory and early cognitive functions.[34] Additionally, the brain activity in infants was shown to be directly proportional to their exposure to speech while in the womb: more prebirth talk from mothers meant more postbirth neural firing.[35] In sum, mounds of evidence indicate that infants in the womb develop cognitive, emotional, and behavioral dispositions, with positive benefits lasting after birth.

As a person's sense organs develop, he becomes correspondingly more capable of acquiring habitual dispositions founded on sense-experience and cogitative estimation, that is, imperfectly voluntary habits. After birth a person continues to acquire habits without deliberate volition. Children unquestionably develop dispositions on account of the action of others, notably their parents and caretakers. Breastfeeding, for example, is a well-documented direct source of emotional development for infants; it has a beneficial effect on mothers as well, which creates a positive feedback loop with the infant.[36] Positive touch plays an important role in developing a

---

cravings that last into infancy. For example, mothers who drank carrot juice during pregnancy gave birth to children who enjoyed carrots more than children whose mothers had drunk only water. J. A. Mennella, C. P. Jagnow, and G. K. Beauchamp, "Prenatal and Postnatal Flavor Learning by Human Infants," *Pediatrics* 107, no. 6 (June 2001): E88. See also Kimberly K. Trout and Lisa Wetzel-Effinger, "Flavor Learning in Utero and Its Implications for Future Obesity and Diabetes," *Current Diabetes Reports* 12, no. 1 (February 2012): 60–66, as well as Alison K. Ventura and John Worobey, "Early Influences on the Development of Food Preferences," *Current Biology* 23, no. 9 (May 6, 2013): R401–8.

33. Ravindra Arya et al., "Maternal Music Exposure during Pregnancy Influences Neonatal Behaviour," *International Journal of Pediatrics* (February 2012): 1–6.

34. W. P. Fifer and C. M. Moon, "The Role of Mother's Voice in the Organization of Brain Function in the Newborn," *Acta Paediatrica* Supplement 397 (June 1994): 86–93.

35. Eino Partanen et al., "Learning-Induced Neural Plasticity of Speech Processing before Birth," *Proceedings of the National Academy of Sciences* 110, no. 37 (September 10, 2013): 15145–50.

36. Fatemeh Assarian et al., "The Association of Postpartum Maternal Mental

child's intelligence: preterm babies who receive daily massages gain weight faster and perform better on neonatal behavioral tests,[37] and full-term infants who receive similar massages have improved memory, behavior, and sensory discrimination skills.[38] One study showed that shared pleasure between mothers and infants in face-to-face interaction not only helped the child to develop emotionally, as one might expect; it even provided the infant with a sort of inoculation to a father's mental-health problems up to two years later.[39]

This brief survey shows that we have all developed passive nonvoluntary acquired dispositions. The next section shows that we also gain dispositions by engaging the world more consciously.

## IMPERFECTLY VOLUNTARY ACQUIRED HABITS IN CHILDREN

The plasticity of a child's character is proverbial. Just as a tree that is properly supported and rooted will grow tall and strong in its later years, so a well-raised child will almost certainly become an upstanding adult. In the words of ancient Hebrew wisdom: "Train up a child in the way he should go, and when he is old he will not depart from it."[40] A hackneyed version attributed to the Jesuits states, "Give me the child in his first seven years, and I will give you the man." All of this points to the fact that children are very susceptible to habituation from exterior forces, even when they are not fully capable of acquiring excellent habits on their own.

---

Health with Breastfeeding Status of Mothers: A Case-Control Study," *Iranian Red Crescent Medical Journal* 16, no. 3 (March 2014).

37. Jodi M. Beachy, "Premature Infant Massage in the NICU," *Neonatal Network* 22, no. 3 (June 2003): 39–45.

38. See the series of articles in *Touch and Massage in Early Child Development*, ed. Tiffany Field (San Francisco: Johnson & Johnson Pediatric Institute, 2004).

39. Mirjami Mäntymaa et al., "Shared Pleasure in Early Mother-Infant Interaction: Predicting Lower Levels of Emotional and Behavioral Problems in the Child and Protecting Against the Influence of Parental Psychopathology," *Infant Mental Health Journal* 36, no. 2 (2015): 223–37.

40. Prv 22:6.

The habitability of young children rests on their characteristic imperfectly voluntary acts. There are three sources of an imperfectly voluntary act: (1) sensory information that moves an animal's passions without the intervention of rationality, as is the case of beasts; (2) an organic imperfection that impedes the full functioning of rationality, as is the case for children; and (3) an impediment to a mature rational faculty, as can happen to adults. Imperfectly voluntary acts are the sources of imperfectly voluntary habits. In this section, I introduce Aquinas's view of imperfectly voluntary habits as they exist in animals and I proceed to focus on their existence in children. In the next section, I discuss the ordinary circumstances which induce them in adults.

When explaining the nature of voluntariness in his *Commentary on Aristotle's Ethics,* Thomas states, "whatever animals and even children do, they do according to the passions of their sensitive appetite, but not according to rational appetite, because they lack the use of reason."[41] Given that he defines the will (*voluntas*) as the rational appetite, this description would seem to entail that such behaviors are not voluntary. In reality, Aquinas's position is more nuanced. He argues that an act that proceeds from passions is neither contradictory nor contrary to voluntariness. An act is voluntary when its principle lies within the agent.[42] That is, "agents are said to act voluntarily, not because they operate by the will, but because they act of their own accord by their proper movement in such a way that they are not moved by any external thing."[43] In other words, self-movement is the essence of voluntariness.

All movement stems from an apprehension of a good under the aspect of an end or goal. When the goodness of the end is apprehended merely on an estimative/cogitative level, that is, without deliberate reason, Thomas calls this an "imperfect knowledge" of the end.[44] It is sensory knowledge with a nonrational judgment and an impulse re-

41. *Sent. Ethic.,* lib. 3, l. 4, n. 3.
42. *ST* I-II, q. 6, a. 1, ad 1.
43. *Sent. Ethic.,* lib. 3, l. 4, n. 3.
44. *ST* I-II, q. 11, a. 2.

garding an action here and now.[45] Such imperfect knowledge affects an animal's passions and estimative powers, moving it to act. The appetitive and cogitative powers are so strong that they move a creature "unless there is something to prevent [them]."[46] Actional judgments that proceed from these powers are determined to a particular object that is present to the external senses, memory, or imagination.[47] Unless another judgment intervenes, animals "have the necessity of being moved to flee or pursue something at the very sight of the thing or by an excited passion."[48] As we have seen, an animal is moved by natural instinct toward whatever the animal apprehends as good.[49] The result is what one can call an "imperfectly voluntary" behavior.[50] The classic example is that a sheep flees immediately upon seeing a wolf. I have personally witnessed a puppy afraid to approach a large tusked but taxidermied wild boar. The animal's behavior is *voluntary* insofar as the animal itself initiates the movement; but it is *imperfect* because the animal does not command its appetitive powers freely.

Aquinas's purpose in discussing voluntariness is primarily to explain the human act as such. In that context, he only attributes imperfectly voluntary acts to nonhuman animals. However, his treatment of voluntariness elsewhere demonstrates his recognition that children perform imperfectly voluntary behaviors as a matter of course. In his view, a child in the earliest stages of development entirely lacks the use of reason and therefore cannot perform a fully human act.[51] The material cause of imperfectly voluntary acts in children is not nonrational nature, but rather immaturity, that is, an organic lack of the full flourishing of their rationality.[52] Aquinas at-

45. See *ST* I, q. 84, a. 6.

46. See *De veritate*, q. 24, a. 2, co.

47. Ibid.

48. Ibid.

49. *ST* I-II, q. 11, a. 2.

50. See *ST* I-II, q. 6, a. 2.

51. *Super Sent.*, lib. 4, d. 25, q. 2, a. 1, qc. 2, co.

52. *De veritate*, q. 18, a. 8, s.c. 1. See also *ST* I, q. 99, a. 1, ad 4. See Philip L. Reynolds, "The Infants of Eden: Scholastic Theologians on Early Childhood and Cognitive Development," *Mediaeval Studies* 68 (2006): 89–132.

tributes the weakness of the rational faculty primarily to a developmental immaturity of the brain, specifically an excess of moisture. Because the brain has not fully developed, a child focuses only on sensory information and has difficulty with thinking abstractly and therefore with understanding.[53]

Current studies show that Aquinas was right in general but wrong in particular: brain development is necessary for the activation of rationality, but the key factor is not moisture. Rather, the nervous system, especially the brain, undergoes four stages of development: (1) neurogenesis, the birth of neurons; (2) the "migration" of neurons to their correct location in the body; (3) neuronal maturation and differentiation (e.g., grey brain matter, white brain matter, central and peripheral nervous systems); and (4) synaptic pruning, in which unused neurons are eliminated.[54] Studies suggest that synapses of newborn brains proliferate by about forty thousand *per second*.[55] Brain growth is related to increased intelligence: there are correlations between IQ and grey matter volume, IQ and cortical thickness, performance in vocabulary tests and increased connectivity within the brain, and so on.[56] Brain growth in the prefrontal cortex zone[57] also directly influences "cognitive control," which includes: (1) keeping information in mind, considering it, and acting on it, (2) acting on the basis of choice rather than impulse, exercis-

53. *De veritate*, q. 18, a. 8, s.c. 2.

54. See Bryan Kolb and Bryan D. Fantie, "Development of the Child's Brain and Behavior," in *Handbook of Clinical Child Neuropsychology*, ed. C. R. Reynolds and E. Fletcher-Janzen (New York: Springer Science and Business Media, 2009), 19–46, at 21.

55. Ibid. It should be noted that synaptic growth is highly variable depending on the location in the brain and body. See Tomáš Paus, "Brain Development during Childhood and Adolescence," in *The Oxford Handbook of Social Neuroscience*, ed. Jean Decety and John T. Cacioppo (Oxford: Oxford University Press, 2011), fig. 19.3.

56. For references, see Paus, "Brain Development during Childhood and Adolescence," 302.

57. "Anatomical, neuropsychological, and biobehavioral work with developmental populations have all implicated the unique development and function of the frontal cortex in [cognitive control]." Katherine C. Morasch et al., "The Development of Cognitive Control from Infancy Through Childhood," in *The Oxford Handbook of Cognitive Psychology*, ed. Daniel Reisberg (Oxford: Oxford University Press, 2013), 993.

ing self-control by resisting inappropriate behaviors and responding appropriately, and (3) quickly adapting behavior to fluctuating situations.[58] These activities fall under what a Thomist could call the beginnings of practical rationality. Even though infants have rational powers *in potency*, in seed form, they are unable to exercise them fully.

Developing a suggestion of Aristotle, Thomas posits that there are three different kinds of capacities to understand: some persons have no capacity to understand; some can understand with the help of others; some can understand for themselves.[59] Children are generally in the first two categories. Thomas explains: "Youths can easily understand whatever is included in imagination, but they do not intellectually grasp things exceeding sense and imagination, for their minds are not powerful and trained for such considerations, both because of the lack of time and because of the many changes of their [developing] nature."[60] Here Thomas is saying two things. First, the necessary physical tools for rationality are underdeveloped in children and youths—a "hardware" problem. Human development entails that there is great turbulence or inordinate motions in the body as it grows. Without full rationality to intervene, the passions rule instead.[61] Second, young people do not fully understand abstract concepts, even if they intuitively grasp them—a "software" problem. That is, the young lack habitual deliberative thinking and experience.

Mature understanding emerges from the soil of experience.[62] Through sensing many things, a person builds up phantasms in his

58. See Matthew C. Davidson et al., "Development of Cognitive Control and Executive Functions from 4 to 13 Years: Evidence from Manipulations of Memory, Inhibition, and Task Switching," *Neuropsychologia* 44, no. 11 (2006): 2037–78.

59. See *Sent. Ethic.*, lib. 1, l. 4, n. 12; Aristotle, *Nicomachean Ethics* I.4, 1095b4–13. Aquinas's observation is developed in Reynolds, "Thomas Aquinas and the Paradigms of Childhood," 178–79.

60. *Sent. Ethic.*, lib. 6, l. 7, n. 16.

61. *In Physic.*, lib. 7, l. 6, n. 7.

62. *ST* II-II, q. 95, a. 5, obj. 2. Mark Barker ably shows that *experimentum* here and in similar cases should be understood as "experience," not "experiment" in the modern scientific sense. See Barker, "Experience and Experimentation: The Meaning of *Experimentum* in Aquinas," *The Thomist* 76 (2012): 37–71.

memory and imagination, providing the intellect with a storehouse of information to draw upon for consideration.[63] Thus, "we are unable to acquire perfect knowledge about singular human actions except by experience."[64] Rational operations either do not exist in the immature or are so imperfect that they produce only an imperfect effect.[65] This helps explain the brashness of the young: "on account of inexperience of impediments and [personal] defects, youths easily think something is possible," when in fact it is much more difficult than they imagine.[66] The young by their own power cannot imbue their imperfectly voluntary dispositions with full rationality, for a positive habit implies the perfection of a power.[67] But without full rationality, children and youths are unable by their own power to direct their actions in accordance with understanding, circumspection, and the like.

Nature, it is true, has its own solution to the "hardware" problem. Thomas acknowledges that as the brain and the body as a whole matures, a person is more able to control his actions through the exercise of deliberative judgment, insofar as calmer passions do not obstruct reason.[68] However, the course of nature's development is bound up with the influences of nurture. As we have seen with nonvoluntary habits, "software" ends up influencing "hardware," that is, a person's experiences and deeply-rooted habits end up affecting his body even down to the genetic and epigenetic levels. Thomas repeatedly explains that an impulse can become connatural to a person when it is repeated and stabilized as behavior. During childhood, a person becomes accustomed to doing good or evil. These behaviors shape a person's interior life with deeply-rooted habits, putting

63. See *ST* I, q. 55, a. 2.

64. *ST* I-II, q. 97, a. 2, obj. 3. In his response, Thomas does not deny this premise of the objection.

65. See *ST* I-II, q. 58, a. 3, ad 2.

66. *ST* I-II q. 40, a. 6, co. and ad 2.

67. *ST* I-II, q. 49, a. 2.

68. *In Physic.*, lib. 7, l. 6, n. 7.

him on a course that is increasingly difficult to change.[69] Thomas observes, "what is habitual becomes pleasant insofar as it becomes 'natural,' for habit is like a second nature."[70] Our early experiences are especially engrained in us.[71] As he says, "Custom, especially that which is from childhood, comes to have the force of nature. Consequently, a soul strongly clings to those things in which it was imbued from childhood, as if they were naturally and per se known."[72] The natural process of synaptic pruning and cell death in brain development shows how repeated experiences and behavior can deeply affect us. Brain development is like chipping away at a sculpture. At first, a person has an overabundance of neurons in the brain, like a large, unformed block of marble. In time, neurons that are "chiseled away" through cell death that results largely from disuse or from increased usage in other parts of the brain.[73] Eventually, the brain acquires a certain arrangement, a shape and record of a person's experience that persists through time. A child's innate propensity to seek pleasure vehemently leads to repeated pleasure-seeking activities and pain-avoidance behaviors that develop ever more deeply rooted habits. Unless checked by the guidance of others, childhood experience consists in a self-reinforcing cycle of pleasure (or escape from pain), then behavior, and finally habit.

The huge impact of custom and habituation illustrates the impact that parents, teachers, and cultural environment have on children. These factors "chisel" a child and form him into the kind of person he will be later in life. The plasticity of a young brain, its natural immaturity, and its pleasure-centeredness present nearly insurmountable obstacles for children to develop fully rational habits on their own.[74] But the parental role encompasses more than knowledge off-

69. *Sent. Ethic.*, lib. 2, l. 1, n. 10.

70. *ST* I-II, q. 32, a. 2, ad 3.

71. *Sent. Ethic.*, lib. 2, l. 1, n. 10.

72. *SCG* I, c. 11.1.

73. Kolb and Fantie, "Development of the Child's Brain and Behavior," 28. Also, Paus, "Brain Development during Childhood and Adolescence," 304–5.

74. *SCG* III, c. 122; *ST* I-II, q. 94, a. 2.

loading: parents should form a child to act habitually according to reason.[75] A child's passions become rationalized through imitating good examples and through obeying reasonable commands. The opposite also holds. Probably unsurprisingly, differences in responses to moral transgressions among kindergarteners were related to their mothers' control management and to their siblings' friendly behavior in the preschool period, early understanding of emotions, and verbal ability.[76] On the other hand, a mother's critical comments, intrusive behavior, and rejection of her child predicts his early emotional dysregulation and conduct disorder.[77] Likewise, manipulative and excessive control by a sibling predicts a child's behavioral problems and lower self-confidence even two years after the fact.[78] In the ocean of early experiences, a child is primarily moved by the breeze of his passions and cogitative judgment, thereby developing habits that lack full reasonableness. Learned behaviors stemming from immaturity inculcate imperfectly voluntary habits.

Training a child parallels training one's passions: "As a child must live according to the instructions of his teacher, so the faculty of sensual desire must be in conformity with reason."[79] The shoulders of parents bear the weight of a duty to help their children mature beyond being subject to thoughtless passion to guided by reason.

75. See *De veritate*, q. 18, a. 4.

76. Parents in most animal species tend to remain a unit at least until the offspring is mature. Judy Dunn, Jane R. Brown, and Mary Maguire, "The Development of Children's Moral Sensibility: Individual Differences and Emotion Understanding," *Developmental Psychology* 31, no. 4 (1995): 649–59.

77. Julian Morrell and Lynne Murray, "Parenting and the Development of Conduct Disorder and Hyperactive Symptoms in Childhood: A Prospective Longitudinal Study from 2 Months to 8 Years," *Journal of Child Psychology and Psychiatry, and Allied Disciplines* 44, no. 4 (May 2003): 489–508. The same results did not hold for girls, however.

78. See Brenda L. Volling and Alysia Y. Blandon, "Positive Indicators of Sibling Relationship Quality: The Sibling Inventory of Behavior," in *What Do Children Need to Flourish? Conceptualizing and Measuring Indicators of Positive Development*, ed. Kristin Anderson Moore and Laura H. Lippman (New York: Springer Science and Business Media, 2005), 203–19, at 204. For a good review of sibling studies, see N. Howe and H. E. Recchia, "Siblings and Sibling Rivalry," in *Encyclopedia of Infant and Early Childhood Development*, 154–64.

79. *Sent. Ethic.*, lib. 3, l. 22, n. 13.

For the parental role, "Nature intends not only the begetting of offspring, but also its education and development until it reach the perfect state of man as man," which includes possessing habits in accord with reason.[80] Even children innately inclined toward a particular virtue need formation. "Naturally" kind Suzie or brave Billy or patient Peter still need reason's guidance for character development.[81] Aquinas provides a vivid illustration as proof: "a person can use such [good] inclinations badly and harmfully if he acts without discretion, much as a horse if it lacks vision will run faster the harder it will be beaten."[82] One of the primary ways that leaders help the young to develop rational habits is by accustoming them to perform acts that are good in themselves, even if at first the child does not fully understand the nature of the act. Thus, authorities ought to help children to develop fully voluntary habits in accordance with reason in place of imperfectly voluntary habits focused on pleasure. For Aquinas, obedience to legitimate authorities (especially parents) is a prerequisite for developing the good and fully voluntary habits, whose interior creativity tackles life's complexities with reason.

Thus far, we have looked at nonvoluntary and imperfectly voluntary habits as they relate to what one can call "absolute ignorance," that is, ignorance considered as contradictory to its binary opposite, deliberative knowledge. Human acts cannot be performed in absolute ignorance, for absolute ignorance makes an act to be nonvoluntary. However, there is another kind of ignorance that can be called "partial ignorance." Whereas children and youths develop imperfectly voluntary habits on account of their immaturity, adults develop similar habits on account of partial ignorance that arises from imperfections in their attention, memory, or both, as the following sections discusses.

80. *Super Sent.*, lib. 4, d. 26, q. 1, a. 1, co.
81. See *De virtutibus*, q. 1, a. 8, co.
82. *De virtutibus*, q. 5, a. 2, co.

## INTENTION, ATTENTION, AND HUMAN HABITS

Attention is a valuable commodity for our time-bound, thought-driven life. About half of our waking moments are spent in mind wandering, that is, being occupied with thoughts unrelated to a specific task or external event at hand.[83] Rubbing one's beard while thinking of something else is Aquinas's paradigmatic example of a nondeliberative behavior. In cases like these, the deliberations of the intellect do not intervene because of the mind's lack of attention. As will be discussed below, the guidance of one's attention qualifies the nature of one's actions and the subsequent habits that are developed.

What is attention? This point is debated among psychologists, and Thomists rely on their own lights because he does not give the topic of attention sustained treatment.[84] In what follows, I provide my own definition of attention and consider it in relation to *intention*.[85] I shall argue that a close reading of Aquinas reveals that the acts of attention and intention are formally distinct: they are acts of distinct powers directed to their proper objects.[86] Intention is an act

83. Claire M. Zedelius et al., "Mind Wandering: More than a Bad Habit," in Verplanken, *The Psychology of Habit*, 363–78, at 363.

84. For an overview of psychological theories up to the 1950s, see Brennan, *General Psychology*, 322–24.

85. *De veritate*, q. 22, a. 1, co.: "Cum ergo obiectum huius actus qui est intentio, sit bonum, quod est finis, quod etiam est obiectum voluntatis, oportet intentionem actum voluntatis esse." For an important study on the topic, see Therese Scarpelli Cory, "Attention, Intentionality, and Mind-Reading in Aquinas's *De Malo*, q. 16, a. 8," in *Aquinas's* Disputed Questions on Evil: *A Critical Guide*, ed. M. V. Dougherty (Cambridge: Cambridge University Press, 2015), 164–91.

86. Cory rightly points out that *intentio* is sometimes used to signify the intention to attend to something ("Attention, Intentionality," 165). See, e.g., *ST* I-II, q. 37, a. 1, ad 2 and 3. However, textual evidence does not support the conclusion that *intentio* is equivalent to *attentio*. When Aquinas seems to be switching between synonyms (as Cory claims), he is rather highlighting the hylomorphic nature of the voluntary act that necessarily involves *intentio* and *attentio*. See the masterful treatment of this subject in Lambert Hendriks, *Choosing from Love: The Concept of "Electio" in the Structure of the Human Act According to Thomas Aquinas* (Siena: Edizioni Cantagalli, 2010), 221–322.

of the will that moves a person toward a good object.[87] Attention, in its broadest meaning, is an act of a perceptive faculty directed to an apprehensible object. Different powers of perception entail different kinds of attention: "top-down" intellectual or cognitive attention, and two forms of "bottom-up" attention: estimative attention, and reflexive attention.[88] Each deserves its own treatment.

The noun *attentio* is derived from the verb *attendere* (= *ad* + *tendere*), that is, to stretch oneself (*tendere*) toward a thing (*ad rem*).[89] It goes beyond mere awareness and passive reception of a stimulus.[90] For Aquinas, to "attend" to an object is to bend one's mind to it, to consider it, to perceive it.[91] To be attentive is fix one's mind on something; it is the contrary of being distracted, that is, having a wandering mind that flits from object to object.[92]

Wayne Wu emphasizes the voluntary and actional aspects of attention, defining attention as "the subject's selecting an item for the purpose of guiding action."[93] "Top-down" attention exists when a

87. *ST* I-II, q. 12, a. 1, co.: "intentio proprie est actus voluntatis." Ibid., ad 4: "intentio est actus voluntatis respectu finis."

88. Brennan distinguishes between voluntary/intellectual attention and involuntary/sensory/nondeliberative attention, but omits reflexive attention: *General Psychology*, 316.

89. See entry "tendo" in Nicholas Salmon, *Stemmata Latinitatis: An Etymological Latin Dictionary* (London: W. and C. Spilsbury, 1796), 2:648–49. See also the entry "tendo" in Alfred Ernout and Alfred Meillet, *Dictionnaire Étymologique de la Langue Latine*, 4th ed. (Paris: Klincksieck, 2001), 682–83.

90. Brennan, *General Psychology*, 314.

91. This is how Aquinas employs the term. See *Super Sent.*, lib. 1, q. 1, a. 4, co.: "subjecti cognitio principaliter attenditur in scientia"; *ST* I-II, q. 17, a. 6, co.: "Sed attendendum est quod actus rationis potest considerari dupliciter"; *SCG* III, c. 2, n. 6, etc. See also the entry "attendo" in Roy J. Deferrari, et al. *A Lexicon of St. Thomas Aquinas* (Washington, D.C.: The Catholic University of America Press, 1948), 94.

92. *Super Sent.*, lib. 4, d. 15, qq. 4 and 5; *ST* II-II, q. 83, a. 13; *Super primam Epistolam ad Corinthios lectura* [hereafter *Super I Cor* for the first epistle, "*Super II Cor*" for the second epistle], c. 14, l. 3, n. 840. Aquinas's discussion shows that, for him, attention (in prayer) is an act of the mind directed to intelligible objects: words of prayer, the meaning of the words, and God himself.

93. Wayne Wu, *Attention* (London: Routledge, 2014), 6. This echoes William James's description: "[Attention] is the taking possession of the mind, in a clear and vivid form, of one out of what seem several simultaneously possible objects or trains of thought. Focalization, concentration, of consciousness are of its essence. It implies withdrawal

subject exercises control over his attention by attending to an object for as long as he intends.[94] In other words, voluntary cognitive attention engages "our ability to willfully monitor information at a given location."[95] Top-down, chosen attentiveness is goal-driven; it is the result of a deliberate will. Wu argues that the "empirical sufficient condition for attention" is when a subject selects an object for a particular task.[96] If a subject of an experiment chooses to click a button when seeing a red light, one can infer that the subject had paid attention to the light and to pressing the button. Non-experimental situations confirm this inference, because people clearly choose to pay attention to things for particular reasons: a driver pays attention to the road to remain safe, a chef pays attention to oven temperature to bake a fluffy souffle. The goals of cognitive attention are not always external acts like driving or cooking; sometimes attention facilitates interior activity such as problem-solving and contemplation.[97]

Aquinas also recognizes the role of voluntariness in cognitive attention: when he speaks of "attention," he means intended or intellectual attention. He describes non-attentional acts in as those which "do not arise *from* the intellect ... but *aside* from the order of the intellect."[98] From a Thomistic perspective, then, cognitive attention may be defined as a voluntary cognitive act wherein mind and sense are brought to bear on some particular object, thus detaching it for consideration out of a total background of experiences.[99] He evidently views intellectual attention as *human* attention, because it engages the mind and is "perfectly" voluntary. It thus constitutes

from some things in order to deal effectively with others." James, *Principles of Psychology*, 1:403–4.

94. See Wu, *Attention*, 32.

95. Marisa Carrasco, "Visual Attention: The Past 25 Years," *Vision Research* 51, no. 13 (July 1, 2011): 1484–1525, at 1488.

96. Wu, *Attention*, 39.

97. Wu recognizes this distinction but calls both "action." See ibid., 81.

98. *SCG* III, c. 2, n. 9; emphasis added.

99. Adapted from Brennan, *General Psychology*, 316. Cory states, "for Aquinas ... the intellectual operation just is an act of attending" (Therese Scorpelli Cory, *Aquinas on Human Self-Knowledge* (New York: Cambridge University Press, 2013), 137).

attention *simpliciter,* by which the other kinds of attention can be compared and known. Hence, the act of "paying attention" is willed by the person when one actively moves one's mind to consider an object apprehended by the exterior senses, the interior senses, or the intellect itself.[100] One can call this "intellectual/cognitive attention" because it involves the mind and its cognition, or "intended attention" because it is directed by the will.

Intention and attention are complementary movements in the soul's faculties. When reason attends to something, it does so because the will has moved it to do so, that is, the will has intended the act of attention. Correspondingly, when the soul intends something, it focuses the attention of the reason on that thing as that-which-is-to-be-desired. This is because the soul intends something only insofar as it is informed by reason about that thing. But reason cannot inform the soul about something unless reason has already paid attention to it, that is, unless the will has moved reason to know that thing to some extent. Therefore, intention of the will requires intellectual attention, and intellectual attention is an intended act. Speaking of attention, Aquinas states, "we attend more to those things that delight us. But when attention is more strongly fixed on one thing, it is weakened regarding other things or totally withdrawn from them."[101] Speaking of intention, he says, "When the intention of the soul is strongly drawn towards the operation of one power, it is withdrawn from the operation of another, for the unitary soul can only have one intention."[102] It follows that, "if one thing draws to itself the entire *intention* of the soul, or a great part of it, anything else that requires great *attention* is incompatible with it."[103] To put it another way: "The will and the intellect mutually include one another: for the intellect understands the will, and the will wills the intellect to understand. Therefore, the things that are ordered to the object of

100. See Cory, "Attention, Intentionality," 181–82.
101. *ST* I-II, q. 33, a. 3.
102. *ST* I-II, q. 37, a. 1.
103. Ibid.; emphasis added.

the will are also contained in the intellect, and conversely."[104] Intellectual attention and intention are cognitively conjoined twins: one is never present without the other.

Next, there is a form of "top-down" attention that is nondeliberate but is somewhat activated by the agent, and somewhat elicited by the object or situation. In these cases, a person (or animal) does not deliberately *select an object* as the focus of intellectual attention but instead *utilizes a power* to engage an object sensorially.[105] Insofar as the behavior of attending to an object engages the senses—perhaps including the imagination and estimative powers—but is not intended, this can be called "sensory attention." In experiments, for example, scientists can induce a monkey to shift its attention to various places, objects, or features of objects: the monkey utilizes its sight and hearing, etc., to focus on one thing or another, but it does not manifest deliberation in doing so.[106] Humans display similar behaviors.

As we have seen, rubbing one's beard and shifting one's feet proceed from sensory input, the imagination, and cogitative judgment, but not from intellectual judgment. At the beginning of the *Prima Secundae* of his *Summa Theologiae*, where he is concerned with establishing the principles of acts that proceed from the individual's own powers, Aquinas considers the possibility that humans can act without a goal. It seems that people do things without an end, he notes, for "Man does many things without deliberation, which is the case whenever he thinks of nothing, as when someone intent

104. *ST* I, q. 16, a. 4, ad 1.

105. Alan Allport, "Attention and Control: Have We Been Asking the Wrong Questions? A Critical Review of Twenty-five Years," in *Attention and Performance XIV (Silver Jubilee Volume): Synergies in Experimental Psychology, Artificial Intelligence, and Cognitive Neuroscience*, ed. David E. Meyer and Sylvan Kornblum (Cambridge, Mass.: MIT Press, 1992), 183–218, at 186.

106. Carrasco, "Visual Attention: The Past 25 Years," 1485, 1489, and 1497. See also C. J. McAdams and J. H. Maunsell, "Effects of Attention on the Reliability of Individual Neurons in Monkey Visual Cortex," *Neuron* 23, no. 4 (August 1999): 765–73. These studies denominate such behaviors as a form of "top-down" attention, a phenomenon that seemingly corresponds with behaviors that are voluntary although not deliberate, as discussed above.

on something else moves his feet or hands or scratches his beard."[107] These sorts of nondeliberative behaviors are not done at random, and they should not be categorized as entirely "nonvoluntary," for they proceed from some sort of knowledge. They stem from "some sudden imagination or natural principle, as when a disordered humor that triggers itchiness is the cause of beard scratching—which is done without the attention of the intellect."[108] Non-attentional acts are not contrary to the intellect and will (involuntary), nor are they outside of the knowledge of the person (nonvoluntary). Rather, they have "some imagined end, but not one that is determined by reason."[109] By "imagined end," Thomas does not mean that the end is *illusory*, but that it proceeds from the imagination and the other non-intellectual powers. The knowledge employed by nondeliberative behavior is denominated "imperfect" because it arises only from the exterior and interior senses, and not from "deliberate reason."[110] Hence, inattentive behaviors are *imperfectly* voluntary, for "imperfect knowledge of the end attains the voluntary according to the imperfect *ratio* [of voluntariness], insofar as the agent apprehends the end, but does not deliberate, and is quickly moved to the end."[111] This is why Thomas says that acts performed without attention are not voluntary: he means that they are not "perfectly voluntary."[112] The result of repeated imperfectly voluntary acts are imperfectly voluntary habitual dispositions.

Some complex, mostly-physical behaviors can be explained as engaging imperfectly voluntary, sensory attention. Take commuting for instance. Undoubtedly the complex behavior of driving requires conscious and some sort of attention: a driver must continually ob-

107. *ST* I-II, q. 1, a. 1, obj. 3. Note that his focus is adult behavior; children are naturally beardless. *De veritate*, q. 13, a. 1, co.

108. Ibid.

109. *ST* I-II, q. 1, a. 1, ad 3. See also *De Malo*, q. 2, a. 5, ad 6.

110. *ST* I-II, q. 1, a. 1, ad 3; emphasis added.

111. *ST* I-II, a. 6, a. 2.

112. In the next chapter, I will discuss how an action can be performed with a "virtual" intention, making the act voluntary even though full intellectual attention is not paid during its performance.

serve his surroundings, make a number of judgments about how best to navigate traffic, execute precise physical movements to guide the car, and so on. But if self-reporting is accurate, a driver on a familiar path can do this almost as if in a dream. Commuters often report arriving at work after having driven for some miles, but without any recollection of the commute itself. Some sports play seems to often fit this criterion. Studies show that experienced golfers actually play better when they *do not* deliberate about the precise mechanics of their swing, and instead try to get into the "feel" of it.[113] Similarly, martial artists, marathon runners, and cyclists—along with musicians, artisans, and even chefs—speak of reaching a state of focus in which they no longer need to think about every small movement of their craft, but can let the act flow from them.[114]

Finally turning to "bottom-up" attention, we may note that the mind's act of "paying attention" to something is distinct from the activities of the exterior and interior senses. "Bottom-up" attention "happens without needing the influence of non-perceptual psychological capacities," that is, it is actuated solely by a sensible object, as when "attention is captured by what one perceives, such as a loud bang."[115] This is an involuntary, transient "automatic orienting response to a location where sudden stimulation has occurred."[116] In bottom-up attention, one's attention is not controlled, for the stimulus is powerful enough to attract the focus of the senses, as by a reflex, and without the subject's intention.[117] Robert Pasnau explains: "Cognitive attention … is not an activity that is the responsibility

113. D. F. Gucciardi and J. A. Dimmock, "Choking under Pressure in Sensorimotor Skills: Conscious Processing or Depleted Attentional Resources?," *Psychology of Sport and Exercise* 9 (2008): 45–59. See also Sian Beilock, *Choke: What the Secrets of the Brain Reveal About Getting It Right When You Have to* (New York: Free Press, 2010), esp. 63–89 and 218.

114. For analogous examples, see Beilock, *Choke*, 219–25.

115. Wu, *Attention*, 31. See 91–93 for a discussion of "attentional capture."

116. Carrasco, "Visual Attention: The Past 25 Years," 1488.

117. Wu, *Attention*, 34. In the pages following, Wu suggests that there can also be a form of "top-down, automatic" attention, but he appears to confuse the physical mechanics of attention (e.g., how the eye moves), which might not be controlled, with attention itself.

of the senses but is a state that the senses are put into, either as a result of the will's command or perhaps just as an automatic reaction to a loud noise or a sharp blow."[118] Not infrequently, one's attention is *drawn* by the thing itself, as when one's attention is diverted by something striking.[119] A woman might choose to pay attention to a dog because she is a veterinarian; or a dog's threatening bark might capture her attention and prevent her from focusing on something else.

In sum, one can distinguish among three types of attention: (1) perfectly voluntary attention directed by the deliberate will, (2) imperfectly voluntary attention directed by instincts and cogitative judgment, and (3) reflexive attention directed by the senses alone. Relevant to my argument here is that attention can remain on the sensory level, as indicated by (2). In this case, attention exists without deliberate reason and is not enacted by the will. Such attention named in many ways: "sensory attention" to indicate its source; "imperfectly voluntary attention" to indicate its relation to free choice; "imperfect attentiveness" to note that it lacks the perfection of reason; or "inattentiveness" insofar as the intellectual attention is absent. Whatever it is called, it provides a basis for imperfectly volitional acts and their consequent dispositions.

This assessment of attention may help clarify a much-misunderstood point in moral theology. It was common for manuals of moral theology, even those with a fairly virtue-centered approach, to list "passions" as "impediments to a free act."[120] This assessment is not entirely accurate. The problem is not with passions as such, but in how they interact with reason. Neuroimaging and studies on the electrophysiological and behavioral levels show that we cannot actually sense every present object at the same time, and our neurons have limited response capacities.[121] Furthermore, we cannot consid-

118. Robert Pasnau, *Theories of Cognition in the Later Middle Ages* (Cambridge: Cambridge University Press, 1997), 144.

119. See *De veritate*, q. 13, a. 3, co.

120. See, for example, Merkelbach, *Summa theologiae moralis*, 1:89–92.

121. For references, see Carrasco, "Visual Attention: The Past 25 Years," 1486.

er every thought at the same time.[122] We necessarily give our attention to some things in exclusion of others. Different stimuli vie for our attention, and it is a zero-sum game. In experiments when a subject was presented with two stimuli, only one of which was task relevant, the firing rate of the neuron "corresponded to the stimulus that was the target of attention *as if the second stimulus in the receptive field was ignored*."[123] It was as though the ignored stimulus did not exist. Thus, attention has been compared to a flashlight: "[Attention's] direction, intensity, and scope can be controlled. The way one handles the flashlight—how narrowly one concentrates the beam of light, where one shines it—governs how the illuminated object appears."[124] Some passions, especially those that are vehement, divert the attention of the reason away from higher goods, or exclude the attention of the reason by moving sensory attention toward objects without reason's guidance.[125]

Considerations of attention and passions should consider the phenomenon of emotional "priming," that is, a person being sensorially affected by events and circumstances without deliberate knowledge. Priming can significantly influence a person's emotions and judgment, especially if a person is sensitive to threats.[126] Additionally, the latent problematic effects of antecedent passions are exacerbated with those who suffer from mental illness. For example, negative emotions bias the judgment of individuals diagnosed with schizophrenia, inclining them to avoid rational considerations and instead assess others as untrustworthy.[127] Hence, passions impede

122. See Aquinas, *Quaestiones de quolibet* [hereafter *Quodlibet*] 7, q. 1, a. 2, and *ST* I, q. 85, a. 4, ad 4. See also Cory, *Aquinas on Human Self-Knowledge,* 138–40.

123. Wu, *Attention*, 58.

124. Cory, "Attention, Intentionality," 179.

125. See, e.g., *ST* I-II, q. 37, a. 1, ad 2.

126. Wen Li et al., "Neural and Behavioral Evidence for Affective Priming from Unconsciously Perceived Emotional Facial Expressions and the Influence of Trait Anxiety," *Journal of Cognitive Neuroscience* 20, no. 1 (January 2008): 95–107.

127. See Christine I. Hooker et al., "Can I Trust You? Negative Affective Priming Influences Social Judgments in Schizophrenia," *Journal of Abnormal Psychology* 120, no. 1 (February 2011): 98–107.

reason insofar as they undermine the person's ability to have perfectly voluntary, cognitive attention. However, Thomas insists that, when moderated according to the nature of person and as fitting the circumstances in which they arise, passions aid reason. Moderate pleasure, for instance, helps calm the body so that the mind can think, and a small amount of pain or sorrow can moderate excess pleasure from distracting the mind.[128] This is supported by empirical studies.[129] In sum, we find that attention is a key missing ingredient when passions distract the mind. Indeed, as Titus notes, "attentional processes" shuttle between perceptions, emotions, and thoughts—and the more effectively we can control our attention, the better we develop emotional regulation and experience satisfaction in reasonable behavior.[130]

We have seen that attention is necessary for every fully human act. We can take a step further and note that the more one develops the ability to pay attention, the more perfect a particular act can become. Mental focus channels our energy—which is why we call carefully paying attention to something "concentrating": the action is a concentration of our mental and emotional energy to a particular object. Habits are force-multipliers, expanding the power of nature. It follows that habitual attention to the right things at the right times is crucial for us to optimally perform good behaviors and to develop the most perfect habits. Not just any attention or focus is necessary: at times, we should concentrate on the "interior quality" of our acts.[131] That is, we must attend to not merely to a mechani-

128. *ST* I-II, q. 37, a. 1, ad 2. As for the usefulness of some pleasure, this is implied in Aquinas's comment that "bodily alteration impedes the use of reason because it impedes the act of the imaginative power and the other sensitive powers." Therefore, when these powers are overly disturbed, a moderate amount of pleasure may help to calm them and thereby help the mind to reason. See also *ST* I-II, q. 33, a. 3, ad 3; q. 47, a. 15, ad 2.

129. See Rainer Greifeneder, Herbert Bless, and Michel Tuan Pham, "When Do People Rely on Affective and Cognitive Feelings in Judgment? A Review," *Personality and Social Psychology Review* 15, no. 2 (May 2011): 107–41.

130. See Titus's discussion of managing attention and motivation in *Resilience and the Virtue of Fortitude*, 51–55.

131. Dunnington, *Addiction and Virtue*, 77. See also, Beilock, *Choke*, 184.

cal performance, but even more to our emotion, thoughts, and desires in relation to our behavior. Without this sort of attention, we can at best condition our powers, but we cannot habituate them according to reason.[132] This "interior" attention is necessary not only in the very moment of acting, but in our lives generally. The habit of mental focus, or voluntary attention, is therefore one of the greatest "meta" habits we can cultivate. Indeed, Alexander Bain noted correctly that the power to attend to some things and to ignore others can (and ought) to be acquired. Through habituation, we can learn to focus despite reveries, wandering sensorial attention, and digressions of thought and feeling; we can also learn to ignore sensory inputs and to dismiss some thought from the mind, despite its attractions, with a simple command of the will.[133] To develop this habit of voluntary attention, more is required than the exercise of the will and intellect: reason-infused memory is also necessary, for memory involves the mind's "attention" to the past. As we will see in the next section, habituated memory is crucial to full human flourishing.

## MEMORY AND HUMAN HABITS

Just as a lack of voluntary cognitive attention can lead to partial ignorance and therefore imperfectly voluntary habits, similarly, a memory defect can lead to imperfectly voluntary habits. The power of memory is able to recall events of the past, recognizing them as past.[134] Hence, memory in general may be called the habit of re-

132. Dunnington, *Addiction and Virtue*, 77.

133. Alexander Bain, *Mental and Moral Science: Part First: Psychology and History of Psychology* (London: Longman's, Green, and Co., 1872), 391. Gregory M. Reichberg powerfully argues that the virtue of attention is what Aquinas calls *studiositas*. Much more than bookish "studiousness," this virtue is crucial for every other virtue, as its definition indicates: "vehemens applicatio mentis ad aliquid" (*ST* II-II, q. 166, a. 1). Every virtue is a perfection, and perfect habituation requires an ardent application of one's mind to the object of that habit. Hence, *studiositas* has a particular connection to prudence (*ST* II-II, q. 49, a. 3, ad 2). See Reichberg, "*Studiositas*, The Virtue of Attention," in *The Common Things: Essays on Thomism and Education*, ed. Daniel McInerny (Mishawaka, Ind.: American Maritain Association, 1999), 143–52.

134. Brennan, *General Psychology*, 194.

taining an experience.[135] Thomas proposes the following as a basic definition: "Remembering is nothing other than conserving well what has been previously been received."[136] "Reception" indicates receiving an impression on the soul through the exterior and interior senses, which may be compared to the way a stone receives an etching.[137] Building on Augustine and Aristotle, Thomas argues that memory comes in two basic kinds: sense memory and intellectual memory.[138] Sense memory is sufficient for imperfectly voluntary acts, whereas intellectual memory is necessary for complete human acts and habits. These two types of memory, as I discuss below, are distinguished by two kinds of knowledge and are similar but not equivalent to the contemporary distinction between explicit and implicit memory. The differences highlight the value of Aquinas's theological anthropology.

Humans and the higher nonhuman animals both possess what may be called "sense memory."[139] It is an "interior sense," along with imagination, common sense, and the cogitative power.[140] Aquinas held that the brain is the organ of sense memory, as it is of imagination and the cogitative power.[141] After a person receives a sense impression, the brain retains what was perceived. Sense memory thus is a sort of treasure house that conserves "intentions" received through the senses and perceived by the estimative or cogitative power.[142] Sense memory enables a "quick recall of past things" that have

135. See *ST* I, q. 79, a. 7, co. and ad 1.

136. *Sent. De sensu,* tract. 2, l. 1, n. 5.

137. Ibid.

138. *Quaestiones Disputate de anima,* a. 19, obj. 16 and ad 16. See the discussion in Mary Carruthers, *The Book of Memory* (Cambridge: Cambridge University Press, 2008), 62–68. One study suggests significant parallels between Augustine's concepts of memory and those of contemporary psychology and neuroscience. See Jean-Christophe Cassel et al., "From Augustine of Hippo's Memory Systems to Our Modern Taxonomy in Cognitive Psychology and Neuroscience of Memory: A 16-Century Nap of Intuition before Light of Evidence," *Behavioral Sciences* 3, no. 1 (December 27, 2012): 21–41, esp. 32.

139. *Sent. De sensu,* tract. 1, l. 1, n. 12.

140. See *ST* I, q. 78. a. 4. Also, *Quaestiones Disputate de anima,* a. 8, co., and a. 13.

141. *De veritate,* q. 18, a. 8, ad 5.

142. *ST* I, q, 78, a. 4. See Pasnau, *Thomas Aquinas on Human Nature,* 283.

been impressed on the external senses (what one has seen, what one has heard) and the internal senses (emotional responses, what one has imagined, what one has estimated), as well as actions one has performed, locations one has seen, and so on.[143] Insofar as the object of sense memory is a past sensorial intention as it has been experienced, this sort of memory exists only in the sensitive part of the soul.[144] Aquinas calls sense memory a kind of habit, for we "quasi-habitually" retain whatever we conserve in the memory when do not actually apprehend it.[145] He says "quasi-habitually" because sense memory exists solely on the sensory level; unless contemplated by the intellect, sense memories are not taken up into the rational part of the soul. He explains further: "memory is a habit, that is, a certain habitual preservation of a phantasm, not, indeed in itself (for this pertains to the imaginative power), but insofar as a phantasm is an image of something previously sensed."[146] Through its retention of images and their "intentions," sense memory plays a crucial role in helping humans and animals act according to reason.

Memory perfects the cogitative power by habituating an animal to respond consistently to similar stimuli. Thomas argues, "From the memory of rewards or punishments, nonrational animals apprehend something as friendly and to be pursued and hoped-for, and something else as hostile and to be fled or feared."[147] Memory is thus crucial for achieving long-term or long-distance goals as well as for learning.[148] To catch unseen prey, hunting dogs need a memory of various scents, "for if the anticipated goal by which they are induced to move did not remain in them through memory, they could not

143. *ST* I, q. 78, a. 4.

144. *ST* I, q. 79, a. 6. See *Sent. de anima,* lib. 3, l. 7, n. 16.

145. *Sent. De sensu,* tract. 2, l. 3, n. 3: "passio pertineat ad partem sensitivam, quae est actus organici corporis, huiusmodi passio non pertinet ad solam animam, sed ad coniunctum. Memoriam autem nominat habitum partis huius, quia memoria est in parte sensitiva: et in ea quae in memoria conservamus, quandoque non actu apprehendimus, sed quasi habitualiter tenemus."

146. Ibid., n. 23.

147. *De veritate,* q. 24, a. 2, ad 7.

148. See *Sent. Meta.,* lib. 1, l. 1, n. 13.

continue to move toward the intended goal which they pursue."[149] Dogs can be conditioned to recognize and respond to the scents of deer, duck, particular plants, and even chemicals in drugs or explosives. Through their trained sense memory, coordinated with instinct and estimative judgment, these animals receive a "participated likeness of prudence" which prepares them for future action.[150] In this way, higher animals "seem to share something of experience, although slight."[151] Accordingly, Aquinas follows Aristotle in saying that "the perfect direction of life for animals is through memory together with what has become habitual by training."[152] Humans also need a trained memory to guide their behavior, especially for moments when distraction diverts them.

For animals to flourish, they need instinct and estimative judgment to be coordinated with sense memory: together these internal senses will for the most part direct them rightly. Humans, in contrast, have greater intellectual capacity. To flourish, humans need to think accurately, to remember what they have learned, and apply those lessons to new circumstances. We need the kind of memory that would help us to apply deliberative thought to our actions.[153] Above sense memory, therefore, humans have intellectual memory, "for memory is not only of sensible things for instance, when someone remembers that he has sensed; but it also of intelligible things, for instance, when someone remembers that he understood."[154] After someone perceives through his senses, the intelligible species or the forms of the sensed things enter the imagination and can remain in the memory.[155] The agent intellect abstracts intelligibility from these species, presenting the species to the possible intellect, which

149. *Sent. Meta.*, lib. 1, l. 1, n. 10.

150. *Sent. De sensu*, tract. 2, l. 1, n. 1. See also *Sent. Meta.*, lib. 1, l. 1, n. 11.

151. *Sent. Meta.*, lib. 1, l. 1, n. 15.

152. *Sent. Meta.*, lib. 1, l. 1, n. 16.

153. See *ST* II-II, q. 47, a. 1, ad 3; a. 3; a. 15, ad 3.

154. *Sent. De sensu*, tract. 2, l. 2, n. 10.

155. For a summary and critique of Thomas's explanation, see Jeffrey E. Brower and Susan Brower-Toland, "Aquinas on Mental Representation: Concepts and Intentionality," *Philosophical Review* 117, no. 2 (2008): 193–218.

the person can engage at will. Within this system, memory operates in the intellective part of the soul as the receptacle of intelligible species.[156] Put more strongly, intellectual memory is not a power distinct from the intellect.[157] Because intellectual memory is bound up with the act of abstractive cognition, it belongs to humans alone.[158] Through it, humans are able to perfect their intellects on the natural level and thereby develop fully human habits.

Given the two main types of memory in the Thomistic system—sense memory, which we have in common with higher nonhuman animals, and intellectual memory, which is unique to humans—it would be useful at this point to consider some contributions of modern science on the matter. We can begin by noting that Maine de Biran, in his treatise *The Influence of Habit on the Faculty of Thinking* (1802), identified three basic kinds of memory: mechanical, sensory, and representative.[159] Like Aquinas, he distinguishes types of memory by faculty and formal objects and their corresponding behaviors.[160] Mechanical memory—what would later be called "muscle memory"—results from objects that are sensible to the five exterior sense faculties: touch, taste, sight, smell, and hearing. Sensory memory relates to the interior senses of the imagination, as well as the passions. Representative memory results from objects that have been understood by the mind. Significantly, de Biran's taxonomy of memory resembles the distinction between "sense memory" and "intellectual memory" that we discovered in Aquinas.

Since Maine de Biran, scientists have worked to distinguish among memory systems, forms or kinds of memory, processes and tasks of memory, and expressions of memory. Endel Tulving, for in-

156. *ST* I, q. 79, a. 6.

157. *ST* I, q. 79, a. 7.

158. See *ST* I, q. 79, a. 6, ad 1.

159. Maine de Biran, *Influence de l'habitude sur la faculté de penser* (Paris: Chez Henrichs, 1802). Translated by Margaret Donaldson Boehm as *The Influence of Habit on the Faculty of Thinking* (Baltimore, Md.: Williams and Wilkins Company, 1929).

160. See Daniel L. Schacter and Endel Tulving, "What Are the Memory Systems of 1994?," in *Memory Systems 1994*, ed. Daniel L. Schacter and Endel Tulving (Cambridge, Mass.: MIT Press, 1994), 5.

stance, developed the concept of *memory systems* and distinguished them by cerebral mechanisms, the kind of information they process, and their specific operations.[161] Many contemporary scientists and philosophers of memory follow suit and differentiate memory in the following ways: by material object (e.g., visual memory, olfactory memory), by formal object (e.g., episodic memory [life events], semantic memory [facts]), by task (e.g., procedural memory, perceptual memory), by relation to time (e.g., long-term, short-term), and so on.[162] Scientists also distinguish memory by its various modes of retrieval: *explicit* or declarative memory is the intentional recollection of past episodes, whereas *implicit* or nondeclarative memory is the unintentional use of acquired information.[163] Typically scientists argue that different brain locations activate different kinds of human memory.[164]

Despite the widespread use of these categories, it must be noted that serious conceptual problems exist for much contemporary brain and memory research. One of the chief issues is that their fundamental concepts of memory are founded on the cardinal sin against taxonomy, for they employing overlapping criteria differentiate among kinds. For instance, the distinction between "explicit" and "implicit" expressions of memory appears conceptually vacuous. "Explicit" memory, according to Tulving and Schacter, in-

161. Schacter and Tulving, "What Are the Memory Systems of 1994?," 13. See Endel Tulving, "How Many Memory Systems Are There?," *American Psychologist* 40, no. 4 (1985): 385–98, at 386.

162. Schacter and Tulving, "What Are the Memory Systems of 1994?," 12.

163. Ibid.

164. For references, see Howard Eichenbaum, "The Hippocampal System and Declarative Memory in Humans and Animals: Experimental Analysis and Historical Origins," in *Memory Systems 1994* (ed. Schacter and Tulving), 147–201, at 148–49. See also F. Gregory Ashby and Shawn W. Ell, "Single versus Multiple Systems of Learning and Memory," *Stevens' Handbook of Experimental Psychology*, 3rd ed., ed. Hal Pasher and John Wixted (New York: Wiley, 2002), 4:655–91, at 677. Nevertheless, after a review of the literature, two researchers argue, "For any single set of data that purportedly supports the existence of multiple [memory] systems ... it is highly likely that a clever researcher will be able to construct a single system model that can account for these data." Ashby and Ell, "Single versus Multiple Systems of Learning and Memory," 657.

volves "conscious or intentional recollection" of previously learned information, such as of autobiographical events, whereas "implicit" memory denotes "unintentional, nonconscious use of previously acquired information," such as of motor skills or visual forms.[165] At first glance, the idea seems plausible. Explicit memory would include looking at a postcard and remembering how you smiled when you stood on the Ponte Sant'Angelo in Rome as you recalled playing outside with a childhood friend; implicit memory would include the procedure of walking to the familiar bridge. A deeper look, however, manifests the unserviceability of this distinction. Tulving et al. suggest that the act of remembering standing on the bridge is "explicit"—an intentional, conscious thought—only if one chooses to call up the memory. But perhaps a photo of a bridge is like Proust's madeleine: a physical stimulus that summons an unbidden memory, or even one's entire childhood. In that case, would one's unbidden memory be "implicit" because it was unintended? Or would it be "explicit" because it was autobiographical? As for walking to the bridge: that counts as "implicit" because the mechanics of walking were not chosen at the time; but is not walking part of one's overall choice, and part of one's autobiography? Again, some scientists hold that "semantic" memory refers to the *intentional* recollection of facts decontextualized from events, while others hold that it is the *unintentional* recollection of the same.[166] Similarly, some scientists hold that there is a procedural component to every kind of recall, including episodic remembering, while others deny this.[167] These significant disagreements illustrate how psychologists regularly take fac-

165. Schacter and Tulving, "What Are the Memory Systems of 1994?," 12.

166. Thus, Schacter and Tulving place semantic memory under "implicit" retrieval, while Baddeley et al. hold that it is "explicit" memory. See Schacter and Tulving, "What Are the Memory Systems of 1994?," 26 (Table 1). Compare table 1 with figure 1.6 in Alan Baddeley, Michael W. Eysenck, and Michael C. Anderson, *Memory*, 2nd ed. (London: Psychology Press, 2014), 13.

167. See P. A. Kolers and H. L. Roediger, "Procedures of Mind," *Journal of Verbal Learning and Verbal Behavior* 23 (1984): 425–49. See also H. L. Roediger, E. J. Marsh, and S. C. Lee, "Varieties of Memory," in *Stevens' Handbook* (ed. Pasher and Medin), 1–41, at 6–7.

ile definitions as the basis of their experiments and writings about memory, to the greater detriment of their research.

The root of many conceptual difficulties is that scientists search for purely empirical grounds to distinguish between the voluntary and the involuntary, when the ground actually rests on the difference between intellectual knowledge of universals through abstraction versus sense knowledge of particulars through apprehension.[168] As a result, empirical psychology and neuroscience, despite great advances in describing various functions of memory, have trouble explaining how memory relates to full human flourishing and moral action. Aquinas's account is more explanatory in this regard, as manifested in his position that experience is a crucial link between memory and right action. For him, experience spans sense memory and intellectual memory. Sense experience begins when a person comes to know individual things through his senses.[169] Next, the exterior senses inform one's inner senses—including the imagination and the cogitative power—with intelligible species, which are then retained by memory.[170] From many memories, which include the sense impressions along with the cogitative judgments associated with them, experience arises. This experiential knowledge then enables a person to act "easily and rightly" in situations in which his experience is relevant.[171] Human experience covers far vaster conceptual territory than that of nonhuman animals, for humans can have memories of considering causality at work, memories of having had an insight, memories of deliberating, and so on; experience can even discover the secondary principles of right action.[172] A physician's experience with many patients and many treatments teaches him that a medicine is beneficial to Socrates, Plato, and to others with simi-

168. See Houston Smit, "Aquinas's Abstractionism," *Medieval Philosophy and Theology* 10 (2001): 85–118.

169. *ST* I, q. 54, a. 5.

170. See *In Physic.*, lib. 7, l. 6, n. 9.

171. *Sent. Meta.*, lib. 1, l. 1, nn. 17 and 18.

172. *ST* II-II, q. 47, a. 15.

lar diseases.[173] Sense experience for humans is therefore bound up with cogitative judgment. More purely intellectual experience helps a person recall intellectual effort and its products.[174] The "possible" intellect retains intelligible species of a thing whose essence a person has grasped; these species remain in the soul habitually so that the person can "attend to" the object in the future.[175]

Sense experience is of singulars, and does not involve knowledge of universal causes as such, but only of particular causes: experience helps a person know *that* something is true, but not *why* something is true.[176] "Above experience," therefore, "humans have universal reason by which they live, as through what is principal in them."[177] Universal reason utilizes experience in order to know the formal and final causes of things.[178] Prudence then applies universal knowledge to particulars that are known by experience, which is the result of many memories.[179] As is detailed more in a later chapter, prudence is necessary for making fully human habits because it perfects and directs human thought and action.[180]

Right action requires prudence, prudence relies on experience, and experience is composed of memories.[181] The work of the sense memory is named "simple recall" from a Thomistic point of view, which is common to humans and animals, and occurs without deliberate choice.[182] When a person deliberately controls his memory with his intellect and will, he performs the operation of "reminiscence," which is crucial for prudence.[183] Because this higher act of

173. See *Sent. Meta.*, lib. 1, l. 1, n. 19.

174. Hence Aquinas says that an analogous form of experience can be attributed to angels, who have intellectual memory. *ST* I, q. 54, a. 5; see also q. 64, a. 1, ad 5. Because humans have intellectual (spiritual) memories, they too have this kind of experience.

175. Hamid Taieb, "Intellection in Aquinas: From Habit to Operation," in *The Ontology, Psychology, and Axiology of Habits* (ed. Faucher and Roques), 127–41, at 132.

176. *Sent. Meta.*, lib. 1, l. 1, n. 24.

177. *Sent. Meta.*, lib. 1, l. 1, n. 15.

178. *In Physic.*, lib. 7, l. 6, n. 5.

179. *ST* II-II, q. 49, a. 1, ad 2.

180. See *ST* I-II, q. 65, a. 1.

181. See *ST* II-II, q. 49, a. 1.

182. Brennan, *General Psychology*, 197.

183. Ibid. Through reminiscence, we purposely exercise memory and put learned

memory is a part of prudence, and prudence is necessary for fully human habits, memory is also bound up with one's ability to develop fully human habits.[184] At times voluntariness depends on one's recollection of a key circumstance of one's act. Thomas offers the example of a person who reveals a secret. Such a person might excuse himself after the fact by saying that it "escaped from his memory" that the secret was indeed a secret, that is, something he should not have spoken.[185] One who speaks such things "is ignorant of what he does, because he does not know that this [act] is an uncovering of secrets."[186] Insofar as a defect in memory is a defect in deliberate knowledge, the loss of memory can efface voluntariness. With the ignorance caused by a defect in memory, such as forgetting a key circumstance of one's act, a person can be ignorant of what he does in the immediate moment and so act involuntarily. This principle extends more generally to the human act. Aquinas says that forgetfulness can "impede" prudence by removing the knowledge upon which prudence depends for its right judgment.[187] A serious loss of memory can make a person's experience so inaccessible that it gravely enfeebles his ability to make prudent judgments.[188] This can happen regarding particular things, such as the way Clive Wearing's loss of short-term memory leaves him unable to make long-term plans though he retains episodic memories of the distant past.[189] It can

knowledge to work. Hence, "Aquinas compares [reminiscence] to inference, because of its resemblance to those mental procedures by which we pass from what is already known to what is unknown."

184. See *ST* I-II, q. 56, a. 5, ad 3.

185. *Sent. Ethic.*, lib. 3, l. 3, n. 12.

186. Ibid.

187. *ST* II-II, q. 47, a. 16.

188. Nevertheless, Thomas insists that insofar as the principal act of prudence is to direct the appetite, "prudence is not directly taken away by forgetfulness, but rather is corrupted by the passions," which corrupt one's right estimation of one's proper end. *ST* II-II, q. 47, a. 16. See *Sent. Ethic.*, lib. 6, l. 4, nn. 9–10.

189. Clive Wearing is an expert in the music of Orlando de Lassus, a musician who contracted a virus that left him with the inability to establish new short-term memories; his consciousness lasts only about thirty seconds, though he remembers his wife and how to play and conduct classical music. See Oliver Sacks, *Musicophilia* (New York: Random House, 2008), 201–31.

also happen more globally, for amnesia of related practical experiences removes the knowledge of those things upon which prudence relies. Because an act can be nonvoluntary due to a defect of memory, it follows that one can develop involuntary, nonvoluntary, or imperfectly voluntary habits on account of the same defect.

At this point, it should be clear that memory is crucial for building habits, for sense memory trains the cogitative judgment and the passions, and, when combined with cognitive memory, it gives a person the experience by which he can guide his actions according to reason. But memory is even more closely associated with habit than this. Through custom, a habit is "like a second nature," and custom is passively acquired by experiences that are fixed into one's memory. "Things we frequently saw or heard are more firmly in the imagination after the mode of some kind of nature," Aquinas notes, and what is in the imagination can be retained by the memory as an experience.[190] Similarly, on account of the inclination of custom we easily recollect things we have experienced or considered many times.[191] We also more easily remember something that was striking, which can be due to uniqueness, newness, intensity, or a combination of the three.[192] The young can remember some things more firmly because they experience them as new, although in general their developing body and cognitive skills can make memory weaker.[193] Because sense experience can be built up without the intervention of the will, "that which a person acquires by custom in his memory, and in his other powers of sensory apprehension, is not a habit *per se,* but something annexed to the habits of the intellective part [of the soul]."[194] Repeated experiences in this way are a result of a person's habituated imagination, cogitative judgment, and memory. When coordinated, these interior senses produce a connatural affective response to something as if it were good (or bad) in itself.

190. *Sent. De sensu,* tract. 2, l. 6, n. 11.

191. Ibid., n. 10.

192. See ibid., tract. 2, l. 3, n. 6.

193. Ibid.

194. *ST* I-II, q. 56, a. 5.

When fully voluntary choices cause such habituation, these connatural affective responses can be attributed to the person.[195]

Memory is so closely tied to habit that acquired habits are equivalent or at least inextricably tied to different kinds of memory; habit has even been called "memory incarnate."[196] There are deep connections, then, between memory, experience, learning, and habit.[197] In this way, every acquired habit corresponds to acquired memories that have an analogous level of voluntariness. As noted above, a person develops nonvoluntary acquired habits when external forces affect his bodily disposition, appetitive dispositions, or both. That is to say, experience of certain events or forces shapes interior dispositions; by shaping the memories and experience, the external forces also form a habit. One could call nonvoluntary acquired habits "bodily memories" of one's experience. When a person develops imperfectly voluntary habits, he also develops imperfectly voluntary memories, or, more precisely, sensory memories. Finally, fully (or perfectly) voluntary habits are tied to intellectual memories. Considering intelligence as the habit of grasping the essences of things, Aquinas goes so far as to say, "Intelligence arises from memory, as act from habit, and in this way it is even equal to it."[198] Mary Carruthers reminds us that, for Thomas, "memory, like thought and imagination, is also a *vis*, an agent, a power, not just a receptacle."[199] In modern parlance, memory is creative: we can use memory to make new habits, especially those most typical to humans. Ethical theory could argue that such a use is morally necessary. Prior to the modern period, "training the memory was much more than a matter of providing oneself with the means to compose and converse intelligently when books were not readily at hand, for it was in trained memory that

195. *Sent. Ethic.*, lib. 3, l. 13, n. 6.

196. See Marion Joan Francoz, "Habit as Memory Incarnate," *College English* 62, no. 1 (September 1999): 11–29.

197. See Brennan, *General Psychology*, 209–10.

198. *ST* I, q. 79, a. 7, ad 3.

199. Carruthers, *The Book of Memory*, 68.

one built character, judgment, citizenship, and piety."[200] This does not mean that a good memory makes a person good, only that the right use of memory is a *sine qua non* of virtue.[201] Good people develop their memories well, that is, they constantly remember good things and thereby facilitate developing a better character. This leads us to consider fully voluntary acquired human habits, which include both skills and virtues.

200. Ibid., 9.

201. Aquinas names habituated memory as a "quasi-integral" part of prudence, because virtue is fostered by experience (*ST* II-II, q. 49, a. 1).

# PART 2

# Human, Inhuman, and Divine Habits

# 4

# Freedom and Habituation

Lifeless statues, once formed, are fixed: gesture, posture, scowl, or smile remain on the frozen face. Only an exterior force can change them. We are different. We are incredibly adaptive creatures. We can shape our interior selves, and the shape can become like second nature. Plants can twist to capture more of the sun; they deepen roots, thicken branches, and endure as best they can. As for us, we can learn to like the cold; or we can walk to better climates. Beasts have passions, imaginings, memories, and urges that are shaped by the mundane goods that capture their downward glance. But we gaze at the stars—and with ingenuity and courage, we can reach them. We can look up; we can also look within. Our interior gaze enables us to see the world with freedom, and knowingly to shape the world and our inclinations so as to reap a bountiful future.

Part 1 of this book looked at how we have been shaped by "subterranean habits" derived from our human nature and our particular individual nature; and how experience nurtures within us certain nonvoluntary and partly voluntary habits. For some thinkers, the territory we have thus explored comprises the totality of human nature and nurture. But we have only just begun to see the horizon of our potential. Part 2 of this book explores why we are not shackled by our inheritances or environment, and how we can freely engage in shaping our capacities with right deliberative action.

This chapter focuses on how freedom relates to habituation. My argument counters the presupposition held by Pinckaers and Kant alike: that automaticity in action is contrary to voluntariness and freedom. Pinckaers states:

> The difficulty: habit creates an automatism which diminishes the moral tone of an action. The notion of habit ... implies the diminution, if not the total exclusion, of reflective consciousness and voluntary decision right at the very beginning.... The automatism of habit deprives an action precisely of that thing that give it its moral dimension, namely, the fact that it proceeds from a reflective decision and a freely considered commitment.[1]

Kant, meanwhile, holds that a habit is "a physical inner necessitation to continue behaving in the same way we have behaved thus far."[2] For Kant, a habit necessarily "deprives even good actions of their moral value because it detracts from our freedom of mind; moreover it leads to the thoughtless repetition of the same action (mechanical uniformity) and so becomes ridiculous."[3] Accordingly, Kant proposes that human dignity is obtainable only by "personality," which he defined as "freedom and independence from the mechanism of the whole of nature," and the rejection of all inclinations.[4]

In contrast to these views, I show that habits, even habits with automatic elements, are not necessarily contrary to human freedom. One of the chief consequences of our rational nature is that with some effort we can freely act to modify, destroy, or create our habits.[5] Consequently, we can cultivate some forms of automaticity so as to enable our freedom to stretch itself toward the highest goods.

1. See Pinckaers's early essay, "Virtue Is Not a Habit," 65–66.

2. Immanuel Kant, *Anthropology from a Pragmatic Point of View*, trans. Mary Gregor (The Hague: Martinus Nijhoff, 1974), 148–49.

3. Ibid. See *The Metaphysics of Morals*, trans. Mary Gregor (Cambridge: Cambridge University Press, 1996), 407 and 409.

4. Immanuel Kant, *Critique of Practical Reason*, in *Practical Philosophy*, trans. Mary J. Gregor (Cambridge: Cambridge University Press, 1996), 209–10.

5. For a more detailed argument in favor of free choice, see my article, "Objections and Responses to the Existence of Free Choice," *Nova et Vetera* (English edition) 3, no. 17 (2019): 901–30.

In the first section, I discuss the problem of "behavioral momentum" and its relation to the habit loop. Next, I treat how behavioral momentum relates to human freedom. These early sections ground the third section, in which I argue that behavioral momentum and habitual automaticity does not undermine the nature of the human act. Fourth, I show that some automaticity is compatible with intentionality. Fifth, I discuss Aquinas's position that some inclinations can be both necessary and voluntary through acts of deliberate will. Sixth, I show that some automaticity can be quasi-necessary and yet voluntary to a high degree. Finally, I discuss Aquinas's view of "determining" oneself through voluntary habituation—a process of repeatedly acting in favor of particular objects of choice, which may entail "necessary" results that nevertheless remain voluntary.

## BEHAVIORAL MOMENTUM AND THE HABIT LOOP

According to William James, "the philosophy of habit" is first of all "a chapter in physics rather than in physiology or psychology."[6] This section tests James's claim. We will find that, even when detached from quantitative analysis and mathematical equations, some basic concepts from Newtonian physics can illuminate certain fundamental causal structures of habits.[7]

Thomas says that just as an arrow takes a straight movement to hit a target, so the will has a rectilinear motion toward the good presented to it by the intellect.[8] An arrow thus provides an initial mod-

6. James, *The Principles of Psychology*, 1:105.

7. See John A. Nevin and Timothy A. Shahan, "Behavioral Momentum Theory: Equations and Applications," *Journal of Applied Behavior Analysis* 44, no. 4 (2011): 877–95, and Timothy L. Hubbard, "Forms of Momentum across Time: Behavioral and Psychological," *Journal of Mind and Behavior* 36, nos. 1–2 (2015): 47–82.

8. *ST* I-II, q. 4, a. 4, ad 2. Here he speaks about the "rectitude" of the will toward the end of beatitude, but one can speak of a "straight" movement toward any end. *In Physic.*, lib. 8, l. 20, n. 1: "Quia in recto determinatur principium, medium et finis, et omnia haec tria est assignare in ipsa linea recta: et ideo est in ipsa linea unde incipiat motus, et ubi finiatur; quia omnis motus quiescit apud terminos, scilicet vel a quo vel ad quem."

el to describe the human act. The beginning represents early stages of apprehension, the line represents the continuity of one's sub-acts of cognition and volition, and the point refers to the end of the act and fruition. Because an arrow is a moving object, a projectile, one can see human behavior as distantly analogous to the movement of physical bodies as described in Newton's first law of motion, which states: "Every body perseveres in its state of being at rest or of moving uniformly straight forward, except insofar as it is compelled to change its state by forces impressed."[9] Bodies maintain their own status quo of motion: if at rest, inertia will keep the body at rest; if in motion, the direction and velocity will remain. Change in motion, in both cases, arises only when a new cause intervenes. Human behavior and action have their own sort of inertia or staying power. Just as a body tends to move in the same direction through time when unobstructed, our behavior in undisturbed conditions tends to repeat itself in response to given stimuli and to resist change. E. L. Thorndike encapsulated this phenomenon with his "first law of behavior," which states: "the same situation will, in the same animal, produce the same response, — and … if the same situation produces on two occasions two different responses, the animal must have changed."[10]

According to Thorndike, there are a few corollaries to the law of behavioral inertia. First, behavior is, for the most part, predictable: given that animals tend to repeat their behaviors in the same situations, and to resist doing differently, we can predict their future behavior if we know the conditions that caused their earlier behavior.[11]

---

Dionysius also speaks of a soul's "straight movement" when it proceeds from itself to something outside of itself—which, for him and Aquinas, also has a mystical meaning (see *De veritate*, q. 8, a. 15, ad 3). Aquinas explains that for Dionysius, an intellect possesses straight motion when it grasps the principle, the end, the means in between them, as well as the order that unites their manifoldness (*In De divinis nominibus*, c. 4, l. 7, nn. 372 and 378).

9. Isaac Newton, *The Principia: Mathematical Principles of Natural Philosophy: A New Translation*, trans. I. Bernard Cohen and Anne Whitman (Berkeley: University of California Press, 1999), 416.

10. Edward L. Thorndike, "Laws and Hypotheses of Behavior," in his *Animal Intelligence: Experimental Studies* (New York: MacMillan, 1911), 241–81, at 241.

11. Ibid.

Second is what he calls the "law of instinct," which can be described in Thomistic habit-language in the following way: to any situation, a person will, apart from learning or conscious choice, respond by virtue of his inherited nature as influenced by his habits, whether nonvoluntary, partly voluntary, or fully voluntary.[12] We can depict Thorndike's law in the following way, with B representing behavior and E the end of the behavior:

B ——————→ E

FIGURE 4. BEHAVIORAL ARROW

Later psychologists would describe this phenomenon as "behavioral momentum,"[13] defined as the persistence of behaviors despite various kinds of disruption.[14] Note that the notion of behavioral momentum is implicitly teleological: it is identifiable and consistent because of its end. More will be said about end-directedness later.

The concept of inertia, as it is now understood, is central to Newtonian physics. A moving object (projectile) continues its motion along a particular trajectory because of inertia: a power of resisting change, such that the projectile "perseveres in its state either of resting or of moving uniformly straight forward."[15] Classical physics held that this intrinsic change-resisting power was attributable to the object's mass. On the psychological level, one might speak of "thought-mass," that is, a thought's power to resist change; on the behavioral level, there also seems to be "behavioral mass," that is, a behavior's power to resist change.[16] We may also speak about the

12. See ibid., 243.

13. See, for instance, the extensive discussion of the analogy in John A. Nevin and Randolph Grace, "Behavioral Momentum and the Law of Effect," *The Behavioral and Brain Sciences* 23 (March 1, 2000): 73–90; discussion 90–130.

14. See Peter R. Killeen, "A Passel of Metaphors: 'Some old, some new, some borrowed . . .,'" *The Behavioral and Brain Sciences* 23 (March 1, 2000): 102–3, at 103.

15. Newton, *The Principia*, Definition 3 (404). See commentary on this concept by I. Bernard Cohen, "A Guide to Newton's *Principia*," in ibid., 4.7–4.8 (96–101).

16. Hubbard describes the many similarities between behavioral and psychological momentum in his article, "Forms of Momentum Across Time," esp. 69 (Table 1). How-

"mass" of a person's character, constituted by the qualities that all together set him in a particular direction of life and which make it difficult for him to change any particular thought or behavior here and now. This character "mass," a bundle of predispositions and inclinations, exists because of habits of experience, thought, desire, and so on. With our character mass, we have preferential inclinations toward what we perceive as good for us in the moment, and resistance to what is opposed to that good. Hence, we tend to continue behavior that we perceive as beneficial, and we tend to resist changing such behavior. Because dispositions and habits possess natural behavioral momentum, some have described habits as possessing a "ballistic route to completion."[17]

Mass is distinct from the object's velocity, that is, its speed in a specific direction. One can also speak of an individual's "velocity" in life, that is, how quickly he responds to various situations he encounters: the young and those with character agility generally "move" faster, are quicker to adapt, whereas the old, fragile, or sluggish possess lesser actional "velocity."[18] Similar characterizations may be made about the velocity of thoughts and behaviors. Like mass, some aspects of psychological-behavioral velocity are derived from habit, whereas others are derived from more immediate forces: one basketball player may quickly respond to his coach's directions on account of his habitual obedience, whereas another may respond more slowly because of sadness from the recent death of a loved one. Therefore, two persons may be acting from similar habits and choices, but the results may differ widely on account of the complex interactions of the various predispositions and inclinations they possess.

---

ever, Hubbard only shows possible relationships (75), and omits causal relations—which is precisely what Aquinas's habit theory provides.

17. Hans Marien et al., "Understanding the Formation of Human Habits: An Analysis of Mechanisms of Habitual Behavior," in *The Psychology of Habit* (ed. Verplanken), 51–69, at 52.

18. See Aristotle, *Rhetoric* II.12, 1389a6–8 (description of youthful quickness to change) and II.13, 1389b13–1390a23 (description of the elderly). See also Adam Woodcox, "Aristotle's Theory of Aging," *Cahiers des études anciennes* 55 (April 28, 2018): 65–78.

The concept represented by a straight line—behavior continued toward its natural end—gains more nuance when we consider not only the behavior and its end in light of the forces that put it into motion. Here we encounter the three curved lines of what Charles Duhigg calls the habit loop, which is composed of three parts: a cue/trigger/stimulus/antecedent, a routine/behavior, and a reward/positive consequence.[19] These elements may be summarized as A-B-C: antecedents to the habit-behavior, the behavior itself, and the consequences from performing the behavior. In the discussion of animal training, we saw that agents tend to repeat action for which they are rewarded in some way. In other words, in the absence of intervening forces, antecedent A tends to produce behavior B; and when the consequent reward C follows, behavior B tends to reinforce the power of antecedent A and thereby to restart the cycle (see figure 2, above).

A *cue* is a trigger that initiates the habit. Often a cue is something exterior to the agent, like a "click" sound that made Pavlov's dogs salivate, or that leads mice to run on a treadmill. Cues can also be interior, such as a person's imagination of success, or positive self-talk such as, "You can do it!" A *routine* is a stereotyped form of behavior that is the chief manifestation of the habit. Duhigg says that a routine can be "physical or mental or emotional."[20] It can include salivating, walking, playing football, feeling calmer, and praying. Finally, a reward is the effect of the habit "that helps your brain figure out if this particular loop is worth remembering for the future."[21] The reward is a good that causes some kind of *fruition*, the experience of satisfaction and joy upon the completion—or attempted completion—of the act that aims at some good.[22] After salivating, dogs experience

19. See Duhigg, *The Power of Habit*, chap. 1, "The Habit Loop." See also Knowlton et al., "A Neostriatal Habit Learning System in Humans"; McHaffie et al., "Subcortical Loops through the Basal Ganglia"; and Graybiel, "The Basal Ganglia and Chunking of Action Repertoires," 119–36.

20. Duhigg, *The Power of Habit*, 19.

21. Ibid.

22. See the discussion of fruition below.

delight after eating the anticipated food; after praying, a virtuous person might experience spiritual joy, the satisfaction of the will in being united with the ultimate good. In sum, because the human action tends to be repeated it can be depicted as a loop. The habit loop exists along the line of human action, and the line of human action tends to become a habit loop.[23]

Three practical consequences follow from the reality of the habit loop. First, behavior possesses a momentum such that a person's character and certain triggers operate together to incline a person to respond similarly in similar situations. We can call these "interior antecedents," comprised of all interior inclinations toward a particular end; and "exterior antecedents," comprised of events and objects outside of a person that incline him toward a particular end. A person will tend to repeat behaviors when he is inclined to do so—especially when interior antecedents such as genetics, childhood experience, character, and custom are combined with at least one consonant and powerful exterior antecedent. The seeming inevitability of habits led John Dewey to argue that a "truer psychology" takes into account the "inertness of established habit": "No matter how accidental and irrational the circumstances of its origin, no matter how different the conditions which now exist to those under which the habit was formed, the latter [established habit] persists until the environment obstinately rejects it. Habits once formed perpetuate themselves, by acting unremittingly upon the native stock of activities. They stimulate, inhibit, intensify, weaken, select, concentrate and organize the latter into their own likeness."[24] Dewey is correct about the power of habits as *inclinations,* but he erroneously sees these inclinations as leading to inevitable acts: he supposes that free choice does not exist, or is helpless to intervene. Nevertheless, we may posit if a person's interior world (his thinking, desires) and his

23. In a very different context, Aquinas points out that a straight line is not the contrary of a circular line (*In De caelo,* lib. 1, l. 8, n. 5).

24. John Dewey, *Human Nature and Conduct: An Introduction to Social Psychology* (New York: Modern Library, 1922), 125.

exterior world (circumstances, experience) remain fairly constant, his behavior will also tend to remain constant. Consequently, much habitual behavior can be predicted and often it takes some exterior drama to divert a person out of a long-engrained routine.

Second, the habit loop helps us identify signs that a person possesses a habit. When a person continually acts similarly in similar situations, he is not acting at random. Rather, he is manifesting that there is some underlying cause, a stable quality that inclines him to seek some kind of benefit from that behavior. A repeated behavior in response to similar antecedents is typically caused by a habit, or many habits operating simultaneously. Indeed, a habit's strength is indicated by the speed with which a person reacts to a given cue for a habitual behavior.[25] Depending on the origin of the quality, a habit may be voluntary, imperfectly voluntary, nonvoluntary, or involuntary. No matter what is the underlying cause, patterned, stereotyped, repeated behavior consequently serves as a diagnostic for the existence of habits.

Third, Aquinas's thought, interpreted in light of contemporary studies on habit formation, indicates that there are particular techniques that a person can employ in order to help his knowledge and desire to be realized. In order to utilize the techniques effectively, however, we must address the habit loop's absence of goal-directedness, that is, its failure to address the object of choice as well as the end of the habit-behavior itself.

## BEHAVIORAL MOMENTUM AND FREEDOM

In terms of inertia, we can say that the momentum that habits provide is so great that they seem to entail automatic behavior. Presaging behaviorist psychology, and with Newton in mind, Kant argued that the more habits one possesses, "the less he is free and indepen-

25. Asaf Mazar and Wendy Wood, "Defining Habit in Psychology," in *The Psychology of Habit* (ed. Verplanken), 13–29, at 24.

dent."[26] For him, animals and humans possess habits in the same way: "they always retain a certain propensity for that to which they were accustomed early. The child must therefore be prevented from getting accustomed to anything; he must not be allowed to develop any habits."[27] Contemporary behaviorists likewise associate habits with automated behaviors.[28] One could conceptualize such views as positing an unstoppable behavioral momentum that exists on account of habits.

Servais Pinckaers has a similar understanding, as we have seen: for him, habits are in tension with human freedom, in contrast to what he identifies as freedom-enhancing *habitus*. As an initial response, I grant that modeling habits as arrows and loops may too easily lead to mechanistic and functionalist, pragmatic interpretations. Someone who desires to develop a habit could reduce habit-making to utilizing whatever techniques are sufficient to produce the desired behavior. Indeed, it may seem that a person can develop habits without being concerned about his motives or the further end of the looked-for habit. Simply choose a powerful enough trigger and a sufficiently satisfying reward, and a selected behavior will inevitably result. This has been the view of many people who have engaged in brainwashing, torture, advertising, and gamification techniques. Many of these practices treat humans as if they were merely animals or machines. To induce a desired behavior, the habit-constructors bypass a subject's deliberation and rationality, and instead habituate him without engaging his freedom to cooperate (or reject) such exterior influences. Such has been depicted in terrifying sharpness by George Orwell's *1984* and Anthony Burgess's *A Clockwork Orange*.

As a more proper response to the objection above, I will detail why not all habits are contrary to *habitus*, and momentum—even automaticity—is not by itself opposed to freedom. My argument

26. *Lectures on Pedagogy*, trans. Robert Louden, in *Anthropology, History, and Education*, ed. Robert Louden and Günter Zöller (Cambridge: Cambridge University Press, 2007), 9:463.

27. Ibid.

28. Coutlee and Huettel, "Rules, Rewards, and Responsibility," 329 and 332.

begins by differentiating among different kinds of human freedom; then I evaluate how these relate to habituation and the human act.

Human freedom exists in three forms, according to Aquinas.[29] First, we possess *freedom from necessity or restraint*. Thomas says plainly, "the will is free insofar as it is not necessitated."[30] This does not mean free from all necessity whatsoever. Rather, the will is not bound by any necessity in the performance of its own act, although it is necessarily moved toward the universal good.[31] Second, we possess *freedom of choice*, that is, the freedom to choose this object or that object and pick among alternatives, or at least to will or not will an apprehended good. Natural or acquired inclinations toward particular objects, whether helpful or harmful, only serve to enhance or to weaken voluntariness. They cannot eradicate it.[32] Third, we possess *freedom for good or evil*, moral freedom: a freedom to order this or that object toward a good or evil end. These three forms of human freedom, and especially the last two, express themselves in fully voluntary actions and are the foundation for fully-human habits.

Free choice (*liberum arbitrium*) proceeds from the deliberate will.[33] Aquinas sees the will (*voluntas*) as a power that possesses active and passive characteristics. It is passive insofar as a person can move himself by his will only after he apprehends a particular thing as good with his reason. In other words, the "rational appetite" must be formed by reason in order to move itself toward what his reason apprehends as good and suitable for him.[34] Particular objects at times can move the will through the passions, for a particular good's attractiveness can sway the reason to see only its good side and thus move the will toward it.[35] However, in principle the will is active

29. The following exposition follows the structure of Thomas's exposition in *De veritate*, q. 22, a. 6.

30. Ibid.

31. See *ST* I-II, q. 13, a. 6. *De malo*, q. 6: "Ex parte exercitii actus, non ex necessitate movetur."

32. See *ST* I-II, q. 49, a. 2, ad 3.

33. See *ST* I-II, q. 1, a. 1.

34. *ST* I-II, q. 9, a. 1, ad 3.

35. *ST* I-II, q. 9, a. 2.

and free, for, as we have seen, it moves itself toward the good. The will can also command the reason. Animals cannot help but desire things they apprehend as good for themselves.[36] But humans can direct their reason to consider what is lacking in a particular good, why it may be inappropriate in one's concrete circumstances, and how it may be undesirable from different perspectives.[37] Therefore, the will is free to choose particular goods or not. This is why Aquinas says that "humans necessarily have free choice from the very fact that they are rational."[38] Reason frees the will from necessarily and always pursuing particular goods and it thereby keeps the will open to the universal and complete good. Therefore, "the root of all freedom is established in reason."[39]

Reason is the root of all freedom because it is the power by which a person can come to know and understand universal truths, and thereby obtain reasons for acting. The power of the rational appetite does not consist in choosing among present options—even dogs have a sort of facility to do this.[40] In common with all higher animals, humans receive impressions of the world through their exterior senses, which in turn affects their interior sensory powers. Unlike animals, though, humans are able to extract or abstract the "essences" of impressions received through their senses, imagination, memory, or cogitative judgment.[41] Understanding is the proper operation of a human as human; it distinguishes him from all other animals.[42] The intellect is able "to consider the nature of the [intelligible] species apart from its individual qualities represented by the phantasms [in the imagination or memory]."[43] The process of ab-

36. *De veritate*, q. 22, a. 4.

37. *ST* I-II, q. 10, a. 2.

38. *ST* I, q. 83, a. 1.

39. *De veritate*, q. 24, a. 2.

40. See *ST* I-II, q. 13, a. 3, ad 3.

41. For a general overview, see Norman Kretzmann, "Philosophy of Mind," in *The Cambridge Companion to Aquinas*, ed. Norman Kretzmann and Eleonore Stump (Cambridge: Cambridge University Press, 1993), 128–59. See also Chad Ripperger, *Introduction to the Science of Mental Health* (Denton, Neb.: Sensus Traditionis Press, 2007), 51–71.

42. *ST* I, q. 79, a. 6.

43. *ST* I, q. 85, a. 1.

straction is performed by the "agent" or active intellect.[44] The "possible" or passive intellect, in turn, receives the essences or intelligible species of things.[45] This is the highest cognitive power in humans, an immaterial power by which a person understands, judges, and reasons.[46] Although the active intellect is determined in its activity, the passive intellect can be directed by the will and is therefore susceptible to habituation.[47]

On account of his intellectual power, a person is able to act not only by feelings or imagination, but also by reason. Insofar as the intellect considers actions to be performed, it can be called "practical reason."[48] An action is fully voluntary (or perfectly voluntary) when it proceeds from a person's knowledge of his end, whether ultimate or proximate, "under the *ratio* of 'end,' and its proportion to those things which are ordered to the end itself."[49] The end is the good sought by the agent as suitable for himself; it is the "principle" of a human act because it provides a reason for acting.[50] Hence, Pinckaers rightly argues, "free will is not a faculty distinct from reason and the will. It is a prolongation of each.... Freedom is the outcome of the mind's inclination to truth and the will's inclination to goodness."[51] Because happiness is the fulfillment of the human person in all of his capacities, deliberately willed action is the necessary way for a person to achieve ultimate happiness.[52]

Here we encounter the third type of freedom listed above. Humans have the freedom not only to will or not-will something, and

44. Ibid., aa. 3–4.

45. See *SCG* II, c. 73.

46. See *SCG* II, c. 62, n. 7. Thomas lists the acts of understanding (basic apprehension), judgment, and reasoning in *ST* I, q. 79, a. 8, and q. 85, a. 5.

47. See *ST* I, q. 79, a. 6.

48. See *ST* I, q. 79, a. 11. See also Thomas Osborne, "Practical Reasoning," in *The Oxford Handbook of Aquinas*, ed. Brian Davies and Eleonore Stump (Oxford: Oxford University Press, 2014), 276–83.

49. *ST* I-II, q. 6, a. 2.

50. *ST* I-II, q. 14, a. 2.

51. Pinckaers, *The Sources of Christian Ethics*, 381. Altered to make the verbs present tense.

52. See *ST* I-II, q. 6, prol.

the freedom not only to choose one thing or another. We also have the freedom to transform ourselves through our choices. This is *freedom for good or evil,* the freedom to order this or that chosen object toward a good or evil end.[53] This can also be called "moral freedom." It is close to what Pinckaers meant by "freedom for excellence."[54] As a foundation for explaining moral freedom, Aquinas makes a crucial distinction between "making" (*facere*) and "acting" (*agere*). "'Making,'" he says, "is an action passing into outward matter, such as building, sawing, and the like; whereas 'acting' is an action abiding in the agent, such as seeing, willing and the like."[55] *Making* is primarily a transitive action: it involves acting upon a thing exterior to oneself. *Acting,* in contrast, is primarily a self-reflexive action: though exterior actions may be involved, acting above all shapes the interior person. Eliminative materialists see the human being as an *object* of concern and something-to-be-acted-upon exteriorly. Whether on the macro- or microscopic level, for them, the human is purely material, a lump of clay that is shaped by material and efficient forces. In contrast, Aquinas argues that the human is a proper self-moving agent, an acting person who shapes himself through his fully voluntary acts. Because habits are the imprint of previous acts, habits by their nature share in the teleology of the acts from which they were made. Because nature is teleological, natural and nonvoluntary habits also bear a teleology even when such teleology exists beneath the surface of consciousness. The teleology of a habit is illustrated in the following figure:

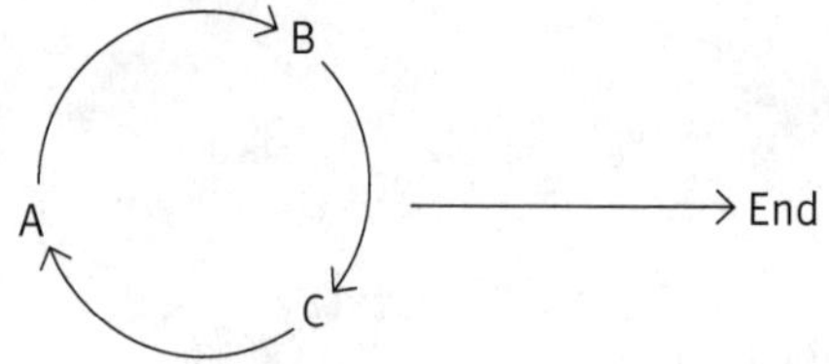


FIGURE 5. HABIT LOOP AND END

53. *De veritate,* q. 22, a. 6.
54. See Pinckaers, *The Sources of Christian Ethics,* 354–78.
55. *ST* I-II, q. 57, a. 4.

Table 4-1. Elements of a Human Act

| | *Affirmation* | *Intention* | *[Deliberation]* |
|---|---|---|---|
| *Cognition* + → *Volition* | Apprehension + → Simple wishing | Ordination + → Intention | [Counsel + → Consent] |

| | *Decision* | *Execution* | *Fruition* |
|---|---|---|---|
| *Cognition* + → *Volition* | Judgment + → Choice | Command + —— Use | Enjoyment (*frui*) |

To see how freedom relates more specifically to behavioral momentum, we must examine the nature of the human act as a whole.

## HUMAN ACTION, MOMENTUM, AND DIRECTIONALITY

Thomas explains the structure of the human act in questions 1–7 of the *Prima Secundae* of his *Summa Theologiae*. Subsequent commentaries on this portion of the *Summa* have often misinterpreted this crucial, but complex, portion of the Angelic Doctor's moral theology. Here I follow Lambert Hendriks's development of Pinckaers's insight. Hendriks argues that Thomas presents twelve "elements" of a complete human act.[56] One can schematize the elements as in Table 4-1.[57]

These are not discrete and linear stages that careen back and forth between intellect and will, as some think. The bold arrow indicates a single movement of the united intellect and will (cognition and volition) coursing through every point of a human act. The "partial acts" of affirmation, intention, etc., together comprise an intrinsically uni-

56. Hendriks, *Choosing from Love*, 279. See the seminal article by Servais Pinckaers, "La structure de l'acte humain suivant S. Thomas," *Revue Thomiste* 55 (1955): 393–412.

57. See Hendriks, *Choosing from Love*, 283. See also Michael S. Sherwin, *By Knowledge & By Love: Charity and Knowledge in the Moral Theology of St. Thomas Aquinas* (Washington, D.C.: The Catholic University of America Press, 2005), 84 (fig. 1).

fied and fully voluntary act. Just as the soul as formal cause enlivens and actualizes the body, so the intellectual motivation for an act, that is, the goodness of the object apprehended by the reason, serves as the formal cause of an act that is efficiently caused by the will: "the intellect proposes to the will its object, and the will causes the external action."[58] The will tends only toward something that is intellectually apprehended as good for the agent here and now.[59] William Wallace explains that both intellect and will are united principles of a single human act: "the intellect is primary in the order of final and formal causality, while the will is primary in the order of efficient causality, although a certain efficiency is also attributed to the intellect insofar as it is the faculty through which the will comes to exercise its causality."[60] Lambert Hendricks speaks of a "mutual causality" of the intellect and will: "Both reason and will can equally move the other and itself. Reason moves itself by knowing its principle and it moves the will by the reason's object, which is an end for the will. The will moves itself by willing the end and it moves reason by the exercise of the act. What moves the agent actually, is hence reason and will together."[61]

When the human act is interrupted, the elements of the act can resemble chronological stages but they are never complete in themselves, for as Thomas says, "the will and the intellect mutually include one another: for the intellect understands the will, and the will wills the intellect to understand."[62] On account of the substantial unity of the soul, Thomas insists on this principle in many places.[63] It follows that the partial acts of the reason or will, or elements of a single act schematized above, cannot be hermetically sealed off from each other as if they exist exclusively in one part or another.[64]

58. *ST* I-II, q. 13, a. 5, ad 1.

59. See *ST* I-II, q. 8, a. 1.

60. Wallace, *The Role of Demonstration in Moral Theology*, 111.

61. Hendricks, *Choosing from Love*, 322. See *ST* I, q. 82, a. 4; I-II, q. 9, a. 3; q. 17, a. 1; q. 19, a. 1.

62. *ST* I, q. 16, a. 4, ad 1.

63. See *Sent. de anima*, lib. III, l. 14, n. 8: "in rationabili enim est voluntas." See also *ST* I-II, q. 82, a. 5, s.c.; q. 87, a. 4; I-II, q. 15, a. 1, ad 1; q. 15, a. 4.

64. See Hendriks, *Choosing from Love*, 287.

This is why choice is a movement of the will that *also belongs to reason,* and why counsel belongs to reason but also belongs to the will.[65] To consider partial acts entirely on their own, as separate from the organic unity of human action that includes a unified reason and will, is a work of dissection. Like every act of dissection, it destroys the organic substance considered even as it organizes its parts.

The intellect-will unity present in human choice highlights the fundamental unity of the human agent and his actions. A human's appetites belong to the entire person; through reason, he links them together by understanding their relation to a particular end. Hence, in a chosen act, there is a continuity between the sensory and rational appetite: reason can share rightness with the whole of a person's affectivity by directing it toward the good. Here we may notice that there are similarities between the chart of the human act above, and the simple diagram that described "associationist" mechanisms in which stimulus A leads to behavior B in Newtonian-like rectilinear movement (in figure 1, p. 23). Aside from rare exceptions like Hendricks, many Thomistic explanations of the human act do not consider the beginning (left-hand side) of the human act: the antecedent stimulus/trigger/cue A that leads to the response/routine behavior B. Typically they omit such an analysis because the antecedent constitutes a circumstance that does not affect the essential voluntariness of the act. Provided an agent concurs or acquiesces with a behavior "in motion," the movement counts as voluntary no matter what antecedents initiated it. What begins as a nonvoluntary movement will be transformed into a voluntary act when the will affirms that movement. For example, in response to an explosion, a soldier could inadvertently lurch forward: in a particular instance, the lurch could become a willing lunge to save a buddy; or it could become the slightest flinch when he tries to squelch his reflex. Again: a person may feel initial fear when seeing a violent protest; he can confirm that fear by running away, or disconfirm the fear

65. Ibid. Hendricks refers to *ST* I-II, q. 14, a. 1, ad 1.

through a courageous act. The only way to evaluate the voluntariness of the exterior act is to account for the agent's intellectual, volitional, affective, and reflexive dispositions toward the good.[66] These shape the fully voluntary act and *are shaped by* the fully voluntary act.

Acts that are fully voluntary will, through repetition, develop fully voluntary habits. Recall that habits in general are summarized by behaviorism-associationism with the habit loop diagram (in figure 2, above). Again, we recall that *antecedents* lead to the *behavior* itself, and positive *consequences* from the behavior incline a person to perform a similar behavior when faced with the same stimulus.

One problem with linear accounts of habits—whether represented as a straight line or a cycle—is that they erroneously depict each repetition as if it were precisely like the one before it. They thereby "imply that each repetition—whether the fourth or the 444th—strengthens habit equally."[67] But habits do not develop in this precise way. Evidence suggests that habits follow an asymptotic development: the contribution of each repetition differs along an upward trajectory until a plateau is reached.[68]

From a Thomistic perspective, fully voluntary habits must be more than mere acquired physical dispositions to respond unthinkingly to some stimulus. They are qualities developed in the rational soul, such that the person comes to engage knowingly with an apprehended and chosen object. Through his practical intellect, the person may then direct the object toward an intended end, as when a soldier with a habit of courage purposely directs his acquired battlefield prowess toward the safety of his comrades, even at his own risk. Deliberate choice is, in this way, the "heart" of a voluntary act as well as a fully voluntary habit. The presence of intentionality, however, does not necessarily disrupt the operation of the habit loop on the cogitative-reflexive level. Indeed, the object of one's choice

66. See Hendriks, *Choosing from Love*, 184.

67. Gardner and Lally, "Modelling Habit Formation and Its Determinates," 210.

68. Ibid. Without strong evidence, James Clear depicts habit development as a continually asymptotic, potentially limitless increase: *Atomic Habits*, 13–23.

can be one's own bodily movements, one's exterior action, including a complex routine. The object can also be one's habits, or an act-as-influenced-by-habits. Instincts and cogitative estimations can coexist with voluntary habits, and can even operate together, as a brave solider chooses to turn his lurch into a helpful lunge; or a voluntary habit can influence the agent to reject the reflexive-cogitative movements, as when a hardened soldier keeps performing his duty amidst falling bombs. These different possibilities can be schematized in the following way:

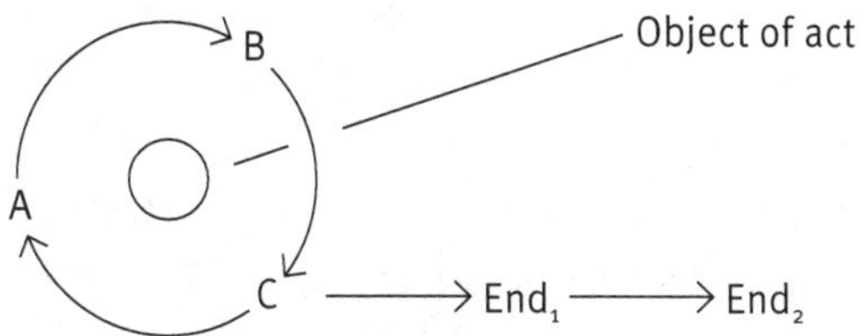


FIGURE 6. HABIT LOOP WITH END AND OBJECT

When a movement possesses the core of intentionality, that is, when an agent chooses an object and directs it toward an end, the movement is no mere movement: it constitutes a human act, even when the movement is part of a habit loop. The primary question for voluntariness is not what constitutes the immediate trigger for some behavior, but what intended end (if any) informs the chosen action.[69] Intentions are "assumed" within the act as a whole. Because the core of an intention is the intellect's apprehension of the practical good to be performed, an intention can be considered as an accidental form that exists in the soul and "spills over" into the internal and external behavior. Hence intentions inform the act as a whole.[70] Insofar as the intended object is directed to some chosen end, then the

69. *ST* I-II, q. 6, a. 1: "cum homo maxime cognoscat finem sui operis et moveat seipsum, in eius actibus maxime voluntarium invenitur."

70. *ST* I-II, q. 12, a. 5, co.: "hoc nomen intentio nominat actum voluntatis, praesupposita ordinatione rationis ordinantis aliquid in finem." See also ibid., a. 1, ad 3: "hoc nomen intentio nominat actum voluntatis, praesupposita ordinatione rationis ordinantis aliquid in finem."

end itself—the primary good to which the person directs the object—in turn informs the act. A movement of lunging can be transformed into an act of bravery when it is intentionally directed toward saving a person in danger; or it can be transformed into an act of vainglory when it is directed toward a soldier's worldly honor.

While discussing behavioral momentum theory, A. Charles Catania notes a significant drawback of a purely physical analogy to describe consistent, repeated behavior: it is not historical. The circle is an adequate model to describe the regular movements of material objects such as planets or comets, for their orbits are fairly fixed over time and the circle is more perfect and eternal.[71] In contrast, Catania cogently argues, human behavior exists within history: our previous choices and experiences affect our future behaviors with a deepening effect on our thoughts, feelings, and character. Consequently, human behavior has more in common with biology than with physics, not least because the biology of individuals—like their particular behaviors—"depends on the particulars (the history) of the organism under study."[72] Insofar as a cause predisposes a person to be moved by a stimulus, that cause may be understood as "historical." In previous chapters, I have discussed many of these causes, including those that arise from biology; these "historical" causes are represented by the arrow on the left, which may be seen as a sort of force inclining a person to react to a behavioral antecedent/trigger/stimulus.

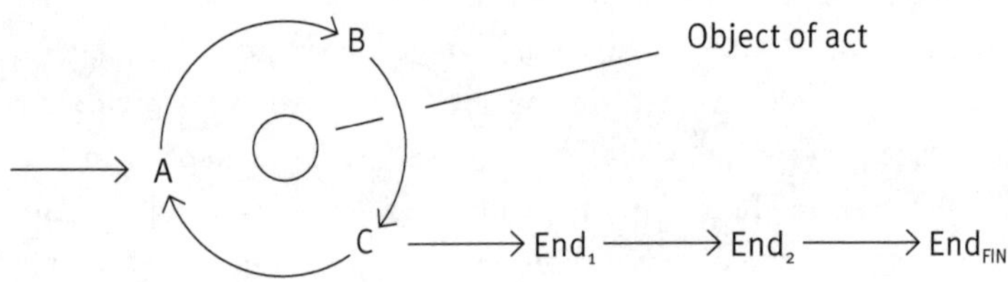


FIGURE 7. HABIT LOOP WITH END, OBJECT, AND CHARITY

71. *In De divinis nominibus*, c. 4, l. 7, nn. 371 and 375. See *De veritate*, q. 8, a. 15, ad 3. See also, *In Physic.*, lib. 8 l. 19, n. 3.

72. A. Charles Catania, "Metaphors, Models, and Mathematics in the Science of Behavior," *The Behavioral and Brain Sciences* 23 (March 1, 2000): 94–95, at 95.

A habit therefore may be seen as the historical footprint of previous causes as they affect one's present state.[73] This raises questions about how the "imprint" of previous choices continues to affect unfolding behavior.

## PERSISTENT INTENTIONALITY

Exterior antecedent cues seem to initiate habitual behaviors even without the direct choice of an agent, leading theologians like Pinckaers, philosophers such as Kant, and contemporary psychologists to suggest that automaticity and nonintentionality are the chief qualities of a habit.[74] They even define automatic processes as those which "can function in the absence of, or even contrary to, intentions."[75] These conclusions may be true to the extent that habitual behaviors do not always depend on immediate choices or intentions conceived in the present moment. However, intentionality can persist over time, and automation can be an expression of previous free choices. Indeed, Aquinas states that one of the functions of moral habits is to help man judge rightly, connaturally regarding the end.[76]

Intentions and chosen ends inform acts and fully voluntary habits—the result of many acts—can extend actional intentions through time. A human act has an intentional-teleological nature: it is naturally directed to an intended end. Likewise, a habit possesses a teleological (and therefore intentional-historical) nature that ex-

73. To this extent, we may agree with Casey's presentation of Merleau-Ponty, that habit serves "to anchor our temporal being," mediating past and future, not merely as a recollection of historic experience, but as an experience that pushes one into the future as an inclination. See Edward S. Casey, "Habitual Body and Memory in Merleau-Ponty," in *A History of Habit* (ed. Sparrow and Hutchinson), 209–25, at 213.

74. See Mazar and Wendy Wood, "Defining Habit in Psychology," 17–18.

75. Ibid., 17.

76. *ST* I-II, q. 58, a. 5. See Rolf Darge, "'As One Is Disposed, so the Goal Appears to Him': On the Function of Moral Habits (*habitus*) According to Thomas Aquinas," in *The Ontology, Psychology, and Axiology of Habits* (ed. Faucher and Roques), 143–65; references at 153n47, discussion 158–63.

presses some of the intentionality that shaped it. Psychologists note that habituated behaviors may be the residual side effects of repeated choice. A librarian might be demure throughout her day, even when outside, as an effect of her goal of providing quiet help while at work.[77] Chosen goals can also elicit a series of repeatedly selected means, as when shopping for groceries initiates driving in a car and all of the apparently automated, semiconscious skills learned through driving. Once activated, the means tend to continue until completion; they are "controlled by an internal model that monitors progress" and aims at the goal until the desired outcome has been obtained.[78] As stable forms implanted within the soul by voluntary repetition, fully voluntary habits remain in the soul and extend through time the intention that gave them birth. How habits affect action through time is best explained by the classic distinctions among "actual intention," "virtual intention," and "habitual intention."[79] These distinctions also help to explain the long-term effects of fully voluntary habits on character as a whole.[80]

An *actual intention* is the intention whereby one performs an act in the present moment.[81] As we have seen, the intention of the will is informed by the intellect's apprehension of an object as good and directed toward one's end. When a person has an actual intention, he directs his intellect to his present chosen act and forms the act according to his desired end. In the case of multiple ends, willing a proximate end as part of a remote end makes the remote end formal with respect to the present act and its proximate end because the re-

77. Marien et al., "Understanding the Formation of Human Habits," 59.

78. Ibid.

79. See Thomas Osborne, "The Threefold Referral of Acts to the Ultimate End in Thomas Aquinas and His Commentators," *Angelicum* 85, no. 3 (2008): 715–36.

80. For the following exposition, I rely on Edmund Robert Skrzypczak, "Actual, Virtual, and Habitual Intention in St. Thomas Aquinas" (Master's thesis, Loyola University Chicago, 1958). See Steven J. Jensen, "Venial Sin and the Ultimate End," in *Aquinas's* Disputed Questions on Evil (ed. Dougherty), 75–100, at 77–86, revised in Jensen's *Sin: A Thomistic Psychology* (Washington, D.C.: The Catholic University of America Press, 2018), 17–23.

81. See *ST* I, q. 93, a. 7, a. 3.

mote end provides the inner *ratio* of the present act.[82] For example, when a doctor gives his patient medicine, "healing" is both the goal of giving medicine and its *ratio*.[83] An agent is therefore actually able to intend many things at once, provided his reason grasps a formal unity among them, such that proximate ends become like means to more remote ends.[84] This is only possible when one is intellectually attentive to their inner relationships. Hence, actual intention is inseparable from perfectly voluntary attention given to one's act, end, motives, and the means to that end.

A "virtual" intention is a previous intention whose power continues through one's present act. Edmund Skrzypczak notes that, "strictly speaking, one does not *make* a virtual intention, as one might correctly be said to make an actual intention. One *acts with* a virtual intention, or one *has* a virtual intention in his action."[85] After one has made an actual intention, that intention retains its force through a number of secondary acts which are subordinated to it—even when the agent does not actually think about the end. The force (*virtus*) of the earlier intention leads the agent to perform further acts.[86] In other words, actual intention to the end is not required for an act that is virtually intended. When we take a walk, for instance, it is unnecessary to think of the goal at every step to make progress.[87] Employing the example of the physician above, Thomas says: "a physician, while actually gathering herbs, intends to prepare a medicine, while perhaps not thinking about health. Nevertheless, he *virtually* intends health, for the sake of which he administers medicine."[88] It follows that, "whoever actually intends some secondary end virtually intends the primary end," for there is an ontological continuity that remains intact unless a person wills something con-

82. See *ST* I-II, q. 8, a. 3.
83. *ST* I-II, q. 12, a. 4. See also *ST* I-II, q. 12, a. 3.
84. See *ST* I-II, q. 12, a. 3, ad 2, and *SCG* III, c. 17, nn. 4 and 9.
85. Skrzypczak, "Actual, Virtual, and Habitual Intention in St. Thomas Aquinas," 48.
86. *ST* I-II, q. 1, a. 6, ad 3.
87. Ibid.
88. *De virtutibus*, q. 2, a. 11, ad 2; emphasis added.

trary to the original intention.[89] The persistence of intention in its virtual form helps to explain why we often continue to perform habitual behaviors even when the behavior no longer serves its original purpose.[90] The power of the original choice persists so long as we have not chosen to stop the behavior, or to pursue some goal incompatible with the behavior.

A "habitual" intention exists insofar as an agent's intention remains *habitually* as a form in his soul. Whereas virtually intending something entails action, habitually intending something entails no action at all. The difference between the two is illustrated in the difference between what happens in a nun's soul that causes her to pray, and what happens when she sleeps. She prays in choir because her previous intention to be in union with God provides an impulse that flowers into prayer. The same intention remains while she sleeps, but she does not actually make the intention nor does she act upon it: it exists in an habitual manner.[91] As the bride in the *Song of Songs* says, "I was sleeping, but my heart kept vigil."[92] In this way, habitually *intending* something is parallel to habitually *knowing* something.[93] When the intelligible species of an object resides in the mind between potency and act, Aquinas says, then it resides in the intellect habitually.[94] Thus, if a person is not actually considering what he knows, his knowledge remains habitually within his memory as intelligible species that he can recall whenever he wills.[95] Likewise, because he can remember that he has previously intended certain ends, the act of his will can habitually reside in his memory as well.[96]

Habitual intention does not necessarily result in activity: the ac-

89. Ibid. See Skrzypczak, "Actual, Virtual, and Habitual Intention in St. Thomas Aquinas," 69.

90. Gardner and Lally, "Modelling Habit Formation and Its Determinates," 208.

91. See *De virtutibus*, q. 2, a. 11, ad 3.

92. Song 5:2.

93. See *Sent. Ethic.*, lib. 7, l. 3, n. 11.

94. *ST* I, q. 79, a. 6, ad 3. See also *De veritate*, q. 10, a. 2, ad 4.

95. See *ST* I-II, q. 53, a. 1.

96. See *ST* I, q. 93, a. 7, ad 3.

tualization of one's knowledge, intentions, or impulses toward an end is not inevitable. Though habits are oriented toward action, nevertheless they can be impeded. Unconsciousness, for example, impedes a person from actualizing habitual knowledge. When napping, Einstein knows physics in a habitual manner, but he cannot put his genius into action while he remains asleep. Similarly, immaturity or mental deficiency can prevent a person from using his knowledge of moral principles, or even the natural law, which remains in him habitually.[97] Children can often accurately repeat memorized rules, such as not talking in class, while being unable to act upon them consistently. Nevertheless, when a person retains knowledge and intentions habitually, he has a "preparedness of soul," a definite orientation of his person toward particular behaviors that have identifiable ends.[98] This is because a habitual intention is a disposition to produce a particular intention to act in accordance with the will's last deliberate choice.[99] Hence, the goodness or evil of an actual intention is retained through habit, provided a contrary act is not produced and the habit is not greatly diminished or wholly destroyed by one's cessation from acting.[100] This is why, for instance, a sacrament remains valid even though a priest's mind may wander during the ceremony: his original intention to do what the church does remains at least habitually.[101]

After intention as an element of a human act, there follows con-

97. *ST* I-II, q. 94, a. 1, ad 3.

98. Thus, though a person with charity in the present life cannot always actually refer everything to God, nor actually intend good toward each of his neighbors, his goodwill toward each nevertheless remains habitually. See *ST* II-II, q. 184, a. 2, ad 3. In many places, Aquinas discusses the importance of "preparing the soul" for grace, often working from Prv 16:1, 9: "It is the part of man to prepare the soul: and of the Lord to govern the tongue.... The heart of man disposes the way: but the Lord must direct the steps" (translated from the Vulgate). He insists that we can freely cooperate with prevenient grace so that our soul operates as an instrumental agent under God, the principal agent, who moves our soul to prepare itself for further graces. See, e.g., *SCG* II, c. 149, n. 2; *ST* I-II, q. 108, a. 4, ad 4; q. 109, a. 4, ad 4; q. 112, a. 2; II-II, q. 25, a. 8; etc.

99. See *ST* I-II, q. 52, a. 3.

100. See *ST* I-II, q. 53, a. 3.

101. See *ST* III, q. 64, a. 8, ad 3.

sent to counsel's recommendation for a means that leads to an end. Aquinas explains that one applies one's intentional and appetitive movement to something that is to be done.[102] It is the human subject's way of moving himself by directing his desires toward an action. Thomas explains: "In nonrational animals, the determination of the appetite toward something is found to be only passive. But consent indicates a determination of the appetite that is not passive alone, but is more active."[103] Thus, through acts freely performed with deliberate will, a person "determines" his act by consenting to direct his powers to a particular end.

Once a person's reason commands him to put into act what he has decided upon and chosen, that command springs forth into *usus* and enters the world outside of the agent to become act. The agent then reacts both to the sought-after object and to his action itself. Both reactions are manifestations of "fruition" (*frui*).[104] In Thomas's view, the human act does not consist in an exterior movement alone, nor is it completed solely through the execution of one's intentions. Rather, human action always has a reflexive character, for a person either finds fruitful pleasure (*fruitio*) or displeasure upon having achieved the good object he desired. Thus, the power of the act extends beyond mere exterior completion of the physical movement.

102. *ST* I-II, q. 15, a. 2.

103. *ST* I-II, q. 15, a. 2, ad 1.

104. I am indebted to Fr. John Corbett, OP, for suggesting this insight. Perfect fruition exists only upon union with the highest good, God himself, in heaven—for it is a participation in the fruition of the Trinity. See I *Sent.*, d. 1, q. 2, a. 2, quoted in Gilles Emery's discussion of fruition in *The Trinitarian Theology of St. Thomas Aquinas*, 375, 384, and 391. However, imperfect fruition is experienced while we are still here on earth: *ST* I-II, q. 11, a. 3. Aquinas speaks of some analogous but lower form of fruition or enjoyment even with respect to lesser goods: in *ST* I-II, q. 28, he states that the love of concupiscence is unsatisfied with mere *fruitione amati* (a. 2); and that with the love of concupiscence, a person seeks *frui* in some good outside of himself (a. 3). He essentially equates fruition with a "quiet attainment of that which one loves" (a. 4), and with *delectatio* (a. 5). See Ramirez: "Fruition properly and simply speaking is only in the ultimate final end simply; but fruition *secundum quid* is even in a non-ultimate end; but merely useful goods or means are not fruition in any way." Jacobus M. Ramirez, *De Actibus Humanis: In I-II Summa Theologiae Divi Thomae Expositio (QQ. VI–XXI)*, ed. Victorino Rodriguez (Madrid: Instituto "Luis Vives" de Filosofia, 1972), 276.

It has an interior effect upon the soul when the will affirms and enjoys—or disavows and hates—the choice made. Thomas compares the exterior aspect of one's act to the production and eating of fruit, and he compares the interior experience of fruition to the sweetness enjoyed by tasting the fruit.[105] Put more precisely, "*Fruition* signifies the pleasure that results from the will resting in the good [that it sought and achieved]."[106] An agent does not experience fruition upon every movement of the will, but only upon those volitions that achieve the good that he has sought. If an agent does not achieve the good, he experiences sorrow, not fruition.[107] One experiences pleasure in a complete act only as an object-achieving-act. That is, one's acting is sought as a secondary end that is effectively a means ordered to the final end (the object in itself). Thus fruition arises primarily from the object itself and secondarily from having completed an act that achieved the desired object. One could call this secondary pleasure fruition-from-use.[108]

Fruition is crucial for habituation for the will's response to the object affirms and confirms the effect of the action that sought that object. The more fruition a person feels upon completing an act, the more he will be inclined to perform that act again. In this regard, we may turn to E. L. Thorndike's contribution to the notion of behavior momentum. His "Law of Effect" captures the much of the same reality as Aquinas's insight into fruition:

> Of several responses made to the same situation, those that are accompanied or closely followed by satisfaction to the animal will, other things being equal, be more firmly connected with the situation, so that, when the situation recurs, those responses will be more likely to recur. Conversely, responses that are accompanied or closely followed by discomfort to the animal will, other things being equal, have their connections with that sit-

105. *ST* I-II, q. 11, a. 1.

106. Daniel De Haan, "*Delectatio, gaudium, fruitio*: Three Kinds of Pleasure for Three Kinds of Knowledge in Thomas Aquinas," *Quaestio* 15 (2015): 543–52, at 544. See Hendriks, *Choosing from Love*, 307, and Daniel Westberg, *Right Practical Reason: Aristotle, Action, and Prudence in Aquinas* (Oxford: Clarendon Press, 1994), 132.

107. See *ST* I-II, q. 35, a. 1, ad 3.

108. Sherwin, *By Knowledge and By Love*, 186–87.

uation weakened, so that, when the situation recurs, those responses will be less likely to recur. In sum, *the greater the satisfaction or discomfort, the greater the respective strengthening or weakening of the bond.*[109]

This "law" has been verified by countless psychological experiments, and helps to explain Pavlov's successful conditioning of canine instincts.[110]

Aside from practical implications for habit development, which will be discussed later, here we can note that Thomas agrees: when a person feels displeasure with the object he obtains, or at having performed an act, or both, he is less likely to perform it in the future. But when a person feels pleasure in the object, or in having performed an act that achieves a desired object, or both, he is more likely to repeat the action and thereby to form an enduring inclination toward a behavior pattern. The object forms us by "rewarding" us with a positive experience of achieving it, and we conform ourselves to the object by affirming the good it offers. So, as Thorndike says, the impulse with positive effects comes to be "stamped in," such that we are inclined to respond similarly when a similar situation arises.[111] When the act is a merely that of a human, then the effect of the positive consequent reinforces a nonvoluntary or only partly voluntary habit—thereby validating the observations of Kant, Pinckaers, et al., that habits can be merely automatic. But if the act is voluntary, or if the agent acquiesces to the positive consequent, then the habit that is formed becomes voluntary even if its proper act entails some automation. This is more than blind habituation to a stimulus. As Aquinas argues, fruition is part of a deliberate human act and develops voluntary habits. In this way, the habit loop helps to illustrate the process by which habits are developed—not only on the subrational level, but also on the rational, reflective level.

109. Thorndike, "Laws and Hypotheses of Behavior," 244. Slightly adapted for clarity.

110. See S. R. Coleman and I. Gormezano, "Classical Condition and the 'Law of Effect': Historical and Empirical Assessment," *Behaviorism* 7, no. 2 (1979): 1–33.

111. Edward L. Thorndike, *Animal Intelligence: An Experimental Study of the Associative Processes in Animals* (New York: MacMillan, 1898), 45 and 103.

## NONCHOSEN HABITS AND VOLUNTARINESS

To anyone who has experienced the powerful urges consequent upon deeply-rooted habits, or who has known others who struggle to overcome long-held habits, it may seem that nonchosen habits can so overwhelm the soul as to preclude voluntariness. Aquinas was familiar with this concern. When discussing free choice, he considers the following objection.[112] Human behavior follows deliberation and judgment. But, as Aristotle says, "as each person is, so does the end seem to him."[113] And it is not within our power to be an entirely different person, for we are individual persons from the first moment of our existence. From birth, our individual includes inclinations derived from general nature, individual nature, and from exterior influences.[114] It therefore seems that "automatic" behaviors proceeding from these sorts of habitual inclinations are incompatible with full voluntariness.

In response, Aquinas agrees that people have many different inclinations that are nonvoluntary. For instance, he holds that by nature we all possess "a necessary appetite for the ultimate end, that is, happiness."[115] But our "necessary" hunger for happiness is not contrary to free choice. Rather, Aquinas explains that in some cases, "something can be necessary and nevertheless voluntary."[116] As noted above, the will naturally and necessarily desires the universal good. Also, "the will necessarily abhors misery, and this is because of a natural inclination, which is similar to the inclination of a

112. *De veritate*, q. 24, a. 1, obj. 19. Following Daniel Westberg's account, and contrary to Lottin, Lonergan, et al., I hold that Aquinas did not change his position on the will from the *De veritate* (ca. 1256–59) to the *De malo* (ca. 1270). The account below shows that one can find a consistency in Thomas's thought on the will throughout his various works. See Daniel Westberg, "Did Aquinas Change His Mind about the Will?," *The Thomist* 58 (1994): 41–60.

113. *Nicomachean Ethics* III.5, 1114a31.

114. *De veritate*, q. 24, a. 1, obj. 19.

115. *De veritate*, q. 24, a. 1, ad 19.

116. *De veritate*, q. 24, a. 12, ad 10, s.c.

habit."[117] In addition, there are bodily dispositions that are acquired from various sources, such as environment ("the power of the heavenly bodies"), parents, and one's particular bodily structure.[118] Previous sections in this book have shown how these dispositions can be considered as nonvoluntary habitual dispositions that arise from general nature, individual nature, and from extrinsic causes.

Habitual dispositions that arise from human nature have a twofold relation to morality. First, from the perspective of their inner nature, Thomas says that such habits "do not *yet* have the *ratio* of good, because they precede even the habit itself, which is the first perfection [of a power]."[119] As such habits are not commanded by reason and determined by the will, Aquinas holds that they are only *habits of a human*, not properly *human habits*. The "not yet" (*nondum*) indicates that these inclinations do indeed have inherent directionality. They can and ought to become human habits with the help of rational choice, and so can be qualified as "natural cognitive habits according to their beginning."[120] Second, considered as movements belonging to a rational person, they always have a relation to human nature as "rational animal," which is the natural source and the measure of their goodness.[121] They are therefore ordered to the human good and participate in it as their formal cause: "by reason of being ordered to this good, they have the *ratio* of the good and the pleasurable."[122] But the human good is nothing other than moral good. Absolutely speaking, the moral good is man's good for himself as such. Because we are rational, we are also moral: "moral habits have the *ratio* of virtue insofar as they are in conformity to reason."[123] Such a view is corroborated by comparisons between the rational capacities

117. Ibid.
118. *De veritate*, q. 24, a. 1, ad 19.
119. *Sent. Ethic.*, lib. 7, l. 12, n. 4; emphasis added.
120. *ST* I-II, q. 51, a. 1.
121. See *ST* I-II, q. 49, a. 3.
122. *Sent. Ethic.*, lib. 7, l. 12, n. 4.
123. *ST* I-II, q. 58, a. 2.

of humans and the mere estimative capacities of other animals.[124] It follows that habits arising from partly voluntary causes, that is, from one's sensory experience and cogitative judgment, are not *wholly nonrational*. Nevertheless, they have an order to reason, and are measured by it, even if the principle of their reason comes from outside of themselves.[125] If they are contrary to a person's rational nature, they are harmful; likewise, if they are harmonious with reason, they are in principle beneficial.[126]

The considerations above indicate that, although nonvoluntary habits arising from human nature could be called "premoral" insofar as they are not directly chosen by the will, they possess a real orientation to morality insofar as they belong to a person who can affirm or reject them. For Aquinas, bodily and emotional inclinations exist within the context of the "great dignity" of the entire human person, who is a body-soul unity, a single subsistence of a rational nature.[127] Thus, he could agree with the insight of John Paul II: "The person, by the light of reason and the support of virtue, discovers in the body the anticipatory signs, the expression and the promise of the gift of self, in conformity with the wise plan of the Creator. It is in the light of the dignity of the human person . . . that reason grasps the specific moral value of certain goods towards which the person is naturally inclined."[128] The will of a person always chooses within a context of inclinations of powers and an environment which provides the horizon within which those inclinations may be actualized. In concrete

124. See Francisco J. Ayala, "The Difference of Being Human: Morality," *Proceedings of the National Academy of Sciences* 107, Supplement 2 (May 11, 2010): 9015–22. See also Mortimer J. Adler, *The Difference of Man and the Difference It Makes* (New York: Fordham University Press, 1993).

125. Thomas says that animals trained by humans have habits in some way, though the habits are incomplete. *ST* I-II, q. 50, a. 3, ad 2.

126. See *ST* I-II, q. 31, a. 7; q. 85, a. 6.

127. See *ST* I, q. 29, a. 3, ad 2. See Gilles Emery, "The Dignity of Being a Substance: Person, Subsistence, and Nature," *Nova et Vetera* (English edition) 9, no. 4 (2011): 991–1001.

128. *Veritatis Splendor*, Encyclical Letter, August 6, 1993, par. 48; available at www.vatican.va.

reality, a habit is a quality of the whole person insofar as the lower powers point toward moral choice, and the lower powers can share in rationality through being directed to a chosen end.

By nonchosen habitual dispositions, "the soul in some way is made prone to choose something, insofar as the rational soul's choice is inclined by the passions, which are in the sensitive appetite, which is a bodily power that follows the dispositions of the body."[129] The reason for this is that, "just as natural appetite or inclination follows the naturally inherent form," as when water congeals because of the structure of its molecules, "so the appetite of the animal follows the apprehended form" that it has estimated as helpful or harmful.[130] This is also the case for humans. Deeply rooted habits—whether arising from chosen or nonchosen sources—"always deliver a similar act."[131] This "always" is predictive, not per se determinative. Habits predict action: "While the habit remains, the person cannot long remain without acting according to the habit."[132] Nevertheless, "free choice is able to make use of a habit or not."[133] Therefore, "one who has a habit is able to issue an act contrary to the habit, for it is not necessary for him always to make use of the habit."[134] In sum, a person can sometimes act contrary to a habit, at least by rejecting its inclination, "although with difficulty."[135]

Habits by themselves cannot generate fully voluntary action. They may impel actions of a human, but they do not cause action that is human as such. Habits do not cause the rational soul to choose one particular thing over another as those things exist in con-

129. *De veritate*, q. 24, a. 1, ad 19.

130. *Sent. Ethic.*, lib. 3, l. 13, n. 1.

131. *De veritate*, q. 24, a. 12, ad 19.

132. *De veritate*, q. 24, a. 12, ad 13.

133. Ibid.

134. *De veritate*, q. 24, a. 12, ad 19. See also *De malo*, q. 6: "Si autem sit talis dispositio quae non sit naturalis, sed subiacens voluntati, puta, cum aliquid disponitur per habitum vel passionem ad hoc quod sibi videatur aliquid vel bonum vel malum in hoc particulari, non ex necessitate movetur voluntas; quia poterit hanc dispositionem removere, ut sibi non videatur aliquid sic, ut scilicet cum aliquis quietat in se iram, ut non iudicet de aliquo tamquam iratus. Facilius tamen removetur passio quam habitus."

135. *De veritate*, q. 24, a. 12, ad 13. See *ST* I-II, q. 49, a. 2, ad 3.

crete reality.[136] For example, an eating habit might incline a person consistently to choose cake over steak, but habits are always dispositions toward general goods; no habit inclines a person to *this particular cake right here, right now*. Likewise, a habit of exercise might strongly incline a person to run every morning at five o'clock, but such a habit does not necessarily and inescapably compel a person to run the morning after Thanksgiving. The runner still has choices: he could choose to sleep in, to wake up earlier, or to have a leisurely turkey sandwich for breakfast. Even nonvoluntary habits do not impede free choice as such, for a person retains the freedom to chose diverse ways to attain one's end.[137] Furthermore, humans can choose contrary to their habits at times, with a freedom beyond that of instinctual animal action.[138] The rational soul is always free to act or not to act, and therefore it has the power to reject the inclinations and movements of his passions at least some of the time.[139]

Behavior manipulation on its own will be effective only in producing behavioral responses. When an act is emptied of its intentional core, deprived of intellect's understanding and the will's free choice, it cannot be directed toward a chosen end. In such a case, the trigger-induced behavior would remain only an act of a human, and not a human act. The habits that produce these subhuman behaviors are themselves subhuman qualities. Thus, as soon as a person becomes free from the triggers and rewards of incarcerated life, he will often relapse into his previous behavior. In contrast, a free person who possesses habits that stem from his free choice, that emanate outwardly from the core of his self-possession, understanding, and conviction, will strive to perform a habitual behavior even in the

136. Ibid.

137. *De veritate*, q. 24, a. 1, ad 19.

138. See *SCG* III, c. 85, n. 7.

139. See *ST* I-II, q. 13, a. 6, and *De veritate*, q. 24, a. 2. Thomas argues that the passions at times can move the will by presenting it an object that seems good and suitable in the moment: *ST* I-II, q. 9, a. 2. Nevertheless, the will remains free in its act. *De malo*, q. 6: "Quantum ad aliqua voluntas ex necessitate movetur ex parte obiecti, non autem quantum ad omnia; sed ex parte exercitii actus, non ex necessitate movetur."

absence of adequate antecedents and rewards. Hence, when evaluating seemingly automatic behavior, one must consider its source. If it arises from involuntary causes, that is, those which are directly opposed to one's will, then it could result in habits that undermine free choice. But if automatic behavior is caused by nonvoluntary or partly voluntary habits, such as instincts and cogitative powers that have been developed in accordance with nature, then it is compatible with full voluntariness. However, as we will see in the chapter on negative habits and vice, if some disordered automatic behavior that arises from habits of one's individual nature, or from some unwanted acquired habituated disposition, then it is contrary to one's human inclinations and it works against one's natural inclination toward the good.

My findings thus far confirm Dunnington's observation that habits have a dual relation to voluntariness in Aquinas's view. On the one hand, if we consider voluntariness as an expression of one's true character—an act is "voluntary" because it is congruent with one's deepest and most consistent desires—then habit-driven action is the most voluntary. After all, human habits develop only on account of many deliberate choices and their byproduct which is the spiritual inertia we call character. On the other hand, if we understand voluntariness to mean the ability to choose or reject any behavior one may desire at a single moment in time, with no reference to context or previous choices, then habits are most involuntary. After all, a fleeting desire and present deliberation may not be able to turn the flooding tide of habit that inundates our mind and emotions before we make a choice to act.[140] In order to elucidate the relation between chosen habitual behavior more clearly, I now turn to the seeming-paradox of "chosen automaticity."

140. See Dunnington, *Addiction and Virtue*, 71.

## CHOSEN AUTOMATICITY, BEHAVIORISM, AND HUMAN PERFECTION

It is one thing to have strong inclinations that one has not chosen; it is quite another to have those inclinations as a result of one's many choices. A similar difference exists for seemingly-automatic behavior: it can be the result of nonvoluntary forces or the result of deliberate choice. But automaticity is not always contradictory to deliberateness: in a single human action they can coexist and mutually benefit one another.[141] When such mechanical behavior stems from one's free choices, it does not introduce necessity nor remove freedom of choice.[142] Indeed, if one of the characteristics of habit is that one can use it when one wills,[143] then certain kinds of automaticity are habits, for experience and evidence show that one can harness automaticity for the sake of some further end. Craig Steven Titus recognizes that "a very great diversity of almost automatic habits surrounds our more conscious efforts and what I would like to call voluntary *habitus* or dispositions."[144] Noë goes further, arguing that "you *need* habits of thought and behavior in order to be decisive and deliberate," meaning "habits" as automatic routines.[145] As psychological studies have found, "automatic processes are efficient and rigid, whereas controlled ones are costly (i.e., in terms of effortful

141. The contradictory of voluntary is involuntary. But "automatic" and "determined" are not always "involuntary." As I discuss, even nonvoluntary is not the contradictory of voluntary, because both can qualify the same movement in different respects (e.g., nonvoluntary in beginning, voluntary in completion; nonvoluntary as nondeliberative movement, voluntary as virtually caused by a previous act). Some present too rigid a dichotomy between the voluntary and the determined: "Like ruts in Roman roads, habits are viewed as determining us to one fixed course. For Aquinas and the ancients, however, *habitus* was exactly the opposite of diminishment and restriction." Michael Sherwin, "Virtue as Creative Freedom and Emotional Wisdom," *Edification* 6, no. 1 (2012): 32–35, at 32–33.

142. *De veritate*, q. 24, a. 1, ad 19.

143. *ST* I-II, q. 49, a. 3, s.c.

144. Craig Steven Titus, "The Christian Difference of *Habitus* in Virtuous Acts, Dispositions, and Norms," *Edification* 6, no. 1 (2012): 38–42 at 39.

145. Alva Noë, *Out of Our Heads* (New York: Hill and Wang, 2000), 118; emphasis added.

consumption of resources) and flexible."[146] When an operative power has a habit, its efficiency is increased.[147] Neuroscientific research supports this philosophical claim. Studies discuss a long-term potentiation effect, such that "coincident, repetitive neural activity" leads to "a wholesale restructuring of synaptic contacts" and a "stabilization and proliferation, of coordinated synaptic activity" that is routed through select pathways.[148] Habitual activity enhances synaptic strength, makes behavioral performance more easily operative, and disposes the person to operate similarly in the future.[149] Only after we have achieved a "basic level of skillful expertise" are we "able to pause, and deliberate, and wonder."[150] Consider a pianist's thought processes while playing. Only after the musician no longer has to think about where to put his fingers, how to sit, when to press the foot pedals, and so on, can he transform a clumsy, mechanical performance of Mozart's *Rondo alla Turca* into one of true artistry. Similarly, although driving a car may be a fully-human act, only after a person develops the skills required for driving well can he free his mind from the present particularities of driving and consider abstract matters such as why he wants to travel to Nuremberg or what is the nature of justice. Noë observes, "Trying something new is always risky; by relying on what has been tested [through habit], we save energy for the excursions that count the most."[151] In sum, developing certain types of automaticity allows one to pay attention to higher matters instead of spending time and effort on step-by-step discursive issues.

George Klubertanz offers a threefold classification of composite habits, which helpfully illustrates how the intellect can relate to an-

146. Muraven and Baumeister, "Self-Regulation and Depletion of Limited Resources," 247.

147. See Klubertanz, *Habit and Virtue*, 99.

148. Larrivee and Gini, "Philosophical Construct." See Fabio Benfenati, "Synaptic Plasticity and the Neurobiology of Learning and Memory," *Acta Bio-Medica: Atenei Parmensis* 78, Supplement 1 (2007): 58–66.

149. Larrivee and Gini, "Philosophical Construct," 2.

150. Noë, *Out of Our Heads*, 120.

151. Ibid., 123.

other power in a habitual action.[152] First, in the case of actions that are substantially cognitive, a "form-matter" relation obtains: the intellect ("form") shapes the "material" provided by the imagination and memory and infuses them with its own insight.[153] To perform its operations, the intellect needs images and experience supplied by the imagination and memory. Mathematicians and physicists, for example, rely on symbols and figures such as numbers, Greek letters, and graphs in order to apply discursive thinking to them. Richard Feynman-levels of expertise and charismatic explanations of complex physics involve an operation that has two aspects: (1) easily, quickly, and reliably recalling the symbols stored in one's imagination and memory, without the delays and difficulties of slow and imperfect retrieval; (2) easily, quickly, and reliably grasping the meaning represented by the symbols to as to make use of them creatively. Here, recall and insight into what is recalled are not separate acts, but two aspects of a single act of mastery. A mnemonic showman might be able to recall the symbols, but only a true physicist can explain their meaning. Consequently, expertise-level cognitive operations are predicated on a single habit of the intellectually-formed imagination. The intellect relies on the results of the harmoniously operating imagination and memory that have been habitually formed by insight and strengthened by time, experience, and purposeful exercise.[154]

Next, there are composite habits that bear an "accident-substance" relationship with the intellect. In these cases, the intellect provides an accidental modification of a habit that is substantially non-cognitive.[155] Such habits reside predominantly in the lower powers, shaping reflexes, passions, and the imagination and memory as directed toward bodily performance. Previously-chosen acts enable such a skilled physical performance, making it intentional ei-

152. Klubertanz, *Habit and Virtue*, 109–14.

153. See ibid., 110–12.

154. This is why Thomas names "memory" as the first quasi-integral part of prudence. See *ST* II-II, q. 49, a. 1.

155. See Klubertanz, *Habit and Virtue*, 113–14.

ther virtually or habitually. For example, when playing basketball, Michael Jordan activated his body's trained reflexes, tactile sense, imagination, memory, and passions, which had been habituated to respond promptly, easily, etc., to the "accidental form" of his practical intellect's judgments about best performance. His basketball habits were predominately or "substantially" physical-sensorial, and they were secondarily or "accidentally" imbued with intellectual insight. Even if his intellect did not command each individual movement, it commanded the overall performance virtually. Hence, playing basketball was a *human* act; it was informed by rational cognition and choice; it was possible only with fully voluntary habits in place. But the habit was not substantially intellectual, for sports performance is primarily an act of the body and senses. A times, a great player will engage in higher-order intellectual reflections, but these typically happen during breaks in the action. These reflections can help them adjust their performance to the performance of their teammates, to their opponents' behavior, and so on. Consequently, bodily "mechanisms" are present and necessary in these cases for the sake of higher-order considerations—either the perfection of the work through more skillful refinement, or a contemplation of the work itself or other things. As Noë poetically expresses it, "To 'boldly go where no man has gone before,' we must first travel to the limits of the known world. We must master the skills and habits that form the groundwork of all animal life."[156]

Finally, there is a "principal-instrument" relationship in which the intellect-will ("principal agent") acts as an efficient cause that uses the instrumentality of its imagination or cogitative power.[157] Here, the intellect and will harmoniously function in concert, though "what is produced is a new image in the imagination, a new formal structure on the sensory level."[158] This relationship is most obvious in the highest levels of creativity. Low-level creativity is diffi-

156. Noë, *Out of Our Heads*, 124.
157. Klubertanz, *Habit and Virtue*, 114.
158. Ibid.

cult, ponderous: a blogger painstakingly searches for a pointed word, a jingle composer hums flat melodies and rejects one after another. True creative geniuses, in contrast, work with an automaticity that is a result of many previous choices. Studies show that when one task has become habitual, a master is able to perform another task simultaneously with relatively little interference.[159] Such virtually- or habitually-intellectual automaticity enables a huge amount of output. Consider the astonishing number and depth of the works of Augustine, Aquinas, Bach, Mozart, and similar geniuses. Through the repetitive work of learning, memorizing, and in general automating the lesser skills necessary for a deep understanding and appreciation for their realm of expertise, they developed a "fingertip feel" for the materials necessary for their compositions, and they were able to marshal that material, shape it into a new form, and organize it according to their profound insight.[160] Hence, habits help agents to allocate their attention and energy to crucial situations "without recruiting additional resources and effort."[161]

These considerations help explain why fully voluntary habits—including those suffused with certain kinds of automaticity—can make subsequent actions *more* voluntary, not less. Fully-voluntary habits are principally related to the will, for they are primarily inclinations of the will toward particular objects.[162] Recent studies support both points I have been making: (1) agents can choose

159. Marien et al., "Understanding the Formation of Human Habits," 53.

160. Such immediate, physical-estimative-rational intuition develops in practically every human habit. Military studies have noted how great generals often develop a highly-refined intuition for war, which enables them to quickly apprehend, judge, and act upon information as a battle situation develops. This is variously described as *fingerspitzengefühl*, "gut intuition," the power of a *coup d'oeil*, and so on. For quotations from Sun Tzu, Jomini, and von Clausewitz, see Michael I. Handel, *Masters of War: Classical Strategic Thought*, 3rd ed. (Portland, Ore.: Frank Cass, 2001), 267–71. See also John Boyd, "Strategic Game of ? and ?," quoted in Frans P. B. Osinga, *Science, Strategy, and War: The Strategic Theory of John Boyd* (London: Routledge, 2007), 212. For a summary of the issue, see Robert Greene, *The 33 Strategies of War* (New York: Viking Penguin, 2006), 38–39.

161. Marien et al., "Understanding the Formation of Human Habits," 53.

162. *ST* I-II, q. 50, a. 5, co. and ad 1.

among various habits and put them into action in an appropriate situation;[163] likewise, (2) a habitual goal or intention helps a person choose among lesser, subordinate goals.[164] In both cases, the automaticity endemic on some forms of habit may reduce the need for immediate control, as particular decisions were made earlier, as when a skilled pianist foregoes rethinking how to move his fingers. A possible tradeoff is that some kinds of habituation may impede fine-tuned acts that are appropriate to the situation, as when advanced skill in basketball impedes high-level performance in baseball, or when habits of logic-chopping find rhetorical theology opaque to syllogisms. However, the gain is that, in no longer thinking of subordinate goals, the master may be freed up to contemplate and experience higher things, as Glenn Gould's expertise helped him enter more deeply into Bach's world, and Aquinas penetrated the insights the Church Fathers through his mastery of metaphysics. The result of expertly harnessing certain kinds of automaticity is that the power of one's original intention in gaining the habit retains its force, and even grows stronger through subsequent affirmations and actions. Gould's achievement of the subordinate goal of finger-control allowed him to achieve the higher goal of musical contemplation; and Aquinas's prowess in logic and metaphysics enabled him more tremendously to contemplate God. Once again, we find that fully voluntary habits form a self-reinforcing spiral. In order to increase the intensity of one's will toward a particular object, it is necessary for an agent to have habits already in place. Just as a fire can grow hotter only if something is already burning, an agent can increase the intensity of his will only if *he has already turned his will toward a particular object.* But once a person turns himself toward an object, and experiences a positive fruition upon completing the act, he be-

163. Amir Dezfouli and Bernard W. Balleine, "Actions, Action Sequences and Habits: Evidence That Goal-Directed and Habitual Action Control Are Hierarchically Organized," *PLOS Computational Biology* 9, no. 12 (December 5, 2013): e1003364.

164. Fiery Cushman and Adam Morris, "Habitual Control of Goal Selection in Humans," *Proceedings of the National Academy of Sciences of the United States of America* 112, no. 45 (November 10, 2015): 13817–22.

Table 4-2. Aristotle and Behaviorism

| *Aristotle* | *Behaviorism* |
|---|---|
| Objects that elicit natural love/hate ≅ | Unconditioned stimuli |
| Natural love-attraction ≅ | Unconditioned approach |
| Habituation by associating object with pleasure ≅ | Conditioned pairing of stimulus and response |

comes more likely to will it again and with more intensity. Now we come an extraordinary conclusion: contrary to a rejection of inclinations, dispositions, and even certain kinds of automaticity, these can be subordinated to fully voluntary habits and even enhance excellence. Only by harmoniously uniting the panoply of habits can a human being come to act *in a fully human mode.*[165] Only by the right habits can someone be an excellent person.

## HOW HABITUATION TECHNIQUES WORK

The very possibility of chosen automaticity helps to explain why behaviorism provides a helpful, albeit incomplete, model for habit development. Daniel E. Lee's research suggests many points of congruence between Aristotelian thought and behaviorism—which has clear applicability to Thomism as well—seen in Table 4-2.[166]

Furthermore, granted that no technique is sufficient completely to develop a human habit, nevertheless, action is necessary. We cannot develop skills and moral habits just by reading and thinking about them. Ordered action, whose stages are verified through experimental controls and corroborated by Thomistic anthropology, is better than action performed without any deliberate order.

As noted above, Ivan Pavlov showed that, through training, one can mold or condition some basic reflexes so that one more or less

165. See *De virtutibus,* q. 1, a. 10, co.

166. Lee, *Aristotle's Biophysical Model,* 271–77. My schema is a modified version of Table 5.6 (274).

automatically responds to a chosen cue or trigger with a particular behavior. This habituation is established in the following way. Specific qualities in sensible objects (stimuli) activate the exterior senses of an animal's corporeal organs, such as the powers of touch, sight, hearing, and taste.[167] After activating one or more exterior senses, the stimulus then provokes a motor reflex: the food that is seen and smelled induces a dog to salivate. The salivation reflex naturally activates when a hungry or non-satiated dog is presented with food. A trainer can alter the salivating reflex so that it is activated by a ringing bell instead of by food.[168] The training process entails that an animal gains a new, particularized disposition toward action. Thus, a conditioned reflex may be considered as an acquired physiological habit. One author writes, "Acquiredness ... characterizes the principal peculiarity in the adaptive behavior of the animal," and the fact that a reflex may be altered according to physical, social, or ecological circumstances indicates that an animal can acquire new ways of responding with reflexes.[169]

A key characteristic of conditioned-habituated reflexes is that they signal an anticipated activity. In other words, such reflexes are activities "which anticipate the course of sequentially developing external events."[170] Salivation is a signal that a dog bodily anticipates eating food. When salivation is activated in response to a bell instead to food, it is a sign that the dog's bodily anticipation of food has adapted itself to new circumstances. This illustrates how the conditioned reflex is a "mechanism which permits the anticipation of the course of future events for the purpose of achieving the best adaptation to the environment" for the sake of surviving and flourishing.[171] Upon the ringing of a bell, the habituated somatic nervous system induces salivation; there is no longer a need for the extra step of pre-

167. See Shettleworth, *Cognition, Evolution, and Behavior*, 65. See also *ST* I, q. 78, a. 3.

168. See Ivan P. Pavlov, *Conditioned Reflexes: An Investigation of the Physiological Activity of the Cerebral Cortex*, trans. G. V. Anrep (Mineola, N.Y.: Dover, 2003).

169. Anokhin, *Biology and Neurophysiology of the Conditioned Reflex*, 2.

170. Ibid., 3.

171. Ibid.

senting food. Of course, quasi-automated responses on account of habituation are not restricted to conditioned reflexes. One can induce a habituated reflex-like response for many actions or series of actions. Thomas notes that when a person is habituated to perform actions that exist as an ordered series, "On account of practice, one movement follows another. Upon the upsurge of the first movement, the second follows, even if man does not intend it."[172] On a neurological level, this means that "the brain can immediately reproduce the entire chain of chemical reactions previously fixed by these slowly proceeding events of reality, provided the same sequence of events has recurred many times."[173] Whether habituation took ten days or ten years to acquire, the nervous system is imprinted by time and training and makes them present in the compressed form of a specific reflex-like movement that is provoked by a specific stimulus.

There is more. Habituation not only makes action more efficient; it also makes subconscious judgments more precise and actionable by retraining our cogitative power. Recall that the cogitative power provides us with estimations of things and situations, indicating what is beneficial or harmful, pleasant or painful, desirable or avoidable, to be pursued or to be shunned.[174] These estimations arise without the operation of our intellect; they are not the product of the mind's deliberation. Cogitative estimations can be considered judgment-like impulses that result from neuroception, that is, a sensory perception of present helpfulness or harmfulness that helps a person estimate which behaviors would be immediately adaptive or maladaptive. Aristotle's dictum holds true even on the non-intellectual level: according to the character of an individual, so does the end seem to him.[175] Inclinations from instincts of a specific nature influence our estimation. So do inclinations from our individual nature, such as those that arise from our temperament: "natural character traits" mediate

172. *Sent. De sensu*, tract. 2, l. 5, n. 10.

173. Anokhin, *Biology and Neurophysiology of the Conditioned Reflex*, 15.

174. See Aquinas, *Sent. De anima*, lib. 2, l. 13, n. 16.

175. *Nicomachean Ethics* IV.5, 1114a32-b1. In Aquinas's edition, the reference is found in III.7.

perceptions and feelings of pain, and emotional responses to these perceptions by modifying them, minimizing, aggrandizing, or otherwise coloring them.[176] In addition to these, there are inclinations that arise from habituated memory, imagination, and the passions. When a person's interior senses and faculties have been shaped by habit, they in turn shape one's perception of things and situations, and this perception in turn shapes one's estimations of them. This is why Dunnington rightly calls the cogitative power "the paradigmatic locus of habit as *embodied knowledge*."[177] Aquinas notes that the impulse of passion can make one judge something to be good here and now, but "the judgment by which man judges something to be good in itself and simply proceeds from the inclination of habit."[178] Repeated action leads the form of the thing received or acted upon to become more fully impressed on our memory and imagination: the thing forms us. As this process of formation occurs, we are more conformed to the thing, so that its properties seem more like our own—this is the process of acquiring a "second nature" of habit.[179] Indeed, a habit can become so integrated with our way of perceiving the world and our very selves that we can act from a habit without being fully aware of it.[180] We then seek more and more what conforms us to the thing that has habituated us, and we find satisfaction in union with these sorts of things, for they seem fitted to our nature. Consequently, when the cogitative power estimates the quality of something we sense, it compares the thing with our habituated nature and its inclinations. When the thing is conformable to our habituated inclinations, it is estimated to be beneficial and worth pursuing.

Because cogitative estimations can operate below the level of our intellectual attention, Dunnington argues that they can be the

176. See *Sent. Ethic.*, lib. 3, l. 13, n. 9, and Leunissen, *From Natural Character to Moral Virtue in Aristotle*, 134.

177. *Addiction and Virtue*, 74.

178. *Sent. Ethic.*, lib. 3, l. 13, n. 6.

179. See *Sent. De sensu*, tract. 2, l. 6, n. 11.

180. See ibid., l. 7, n. 11.

source of intuitions.[181] Without being able to articulate exactly why, we can often intuit that a person is hostile toward us, that the weather is getting worse, or that food may be safe to eat. Such intuitions can be accurate because they are "a reserve of learned wisdom that has become interwoven with the objects of our experience."[182] Because our estimations arise from our new quasi-nature, they give us inclinations that, if unimpeded, will lead us to act in a way that seems automatic. In reality, if the inclinations arise from previous choices, the behavior that arises from the inclinations is voluntary.[183] On account of the power of free choice, we can override these inclinations in the moment, provided we pay enough attention to them. But slamming the brakes on these initial "automatic" movements exacts a rather high cost: "this does violence to agency and depletes the limited power of the embodied will."[184] Even after the decision not to act is made, this does not change the basic orientation of the preestablished habit. In fact, as we have all experienced, overriding habits with a brute act of will can intensify our desire for the forbidden object. We cannot with a single decision change our habits or their inclinations: the only way to move our sensory appetites is gradually to modify the judgments of our cogitative estimations by repeated acts.[185] Nor can we despotically rule our passions and make them feel a certain way in response to some stimulus.[186] Consequently, even when deliberate reason tells us to perform a certain behavior, we might feel that the behavior is somehow *unfitting*; likewise, when reason commands us to avoid some habitual bad behavior, we might feel that doing the right thing is somehow *wrong for us*. These cogitative estimations, and our consequent emotional feelings, are based less on our specific nature as human beings and more

181. *Addiction and Virtue,* 75.

182. Ibid.xz

183. *Nicomachean Ethics* IV.5, 1114b15–1115a4.

184. Dunnington, *Addiction and Virtue,* 87.

185. Ibid.

186. Recall Aquinas's observation that the passions act somewhat freely, like persons living under a royal and political sovereign: *ST* I-II, q. 9, a. 2, ad 3; q. 17, a. 7.

on our second nature, which is acquired through habituation. Dunnington observes: "It is the nature of habit in general to be recalcitrant, to a greater or lesser degree, to the immediate and fleeing deliverances of deliberate reason, but this is especially true of the cogitative estimation. For habits of the cogitative estimation generally operate as automatism habits, and thus they can operate quite independently of those conscious mental efforts of an agent—and often in spite of those efforts."[187] Undoubtedly, the fixity of cogitative estimations can spell disaster in a person's life, as when they lead to a seemingly-unbreakable addiction. But when the cogitative estimations are in accord with reality and strengthen a person's attachment to what is truly good, their fixity becomes a crucial element to personal flourishing.

Full or perfect virtue—which includes the personal ability to direct and shape oneself—is possible only when the sensory parts of the soul are suffused with reason and thereby subordinated to reason. The formation of reason ensures that our lower powers exist in a "proportionate relation" to one another and respond to sensible things according to reason, working harmoniously under the guidance of reason's wisdom.[188] A truly virtuous person, in contrast to the merely continent person, possesses "all the character virtues as one unified psychological disposition," and knowingly acts upon his virtuous inclinations, which are stable, integrated, and mutually enriching.[189] Consequently, the seemingly-automatic estimations of the cogitative power are key for a person acting according to reason.

One of the chief advantages of behaviorist-inspired methods is that they focus on a person performing repeated actions in light of a deliberate plan. Through this method, the intellect deliberately shapes his lower powers, especially his cogitative power. He gradually comes to estimate that his behavioral performance is good and desirable: at first, because of its association with the reward that is its

187. *Addiction and Virtue*, 164.

188. Leunissen, *From Natural Character to Moral Virtue in Aristotle*, 137.

189. Ibid., 128.

result; later, good in itself insofar as it seems to be fitting for himself. The fact that a person acts seemingly-automatically in response to a cue or trigger is not necessarily negative. Rather, the behavior that follows quickly and easily in response to the trigger helps a person to more easily override his cogitative estimates, and emotions, that would incline him to do the contrary. In this respect, William James correctly observed,

> The great thing, then, in all education, is to *make our nervous system our ally instead of our enemy.... For this, we must make automatic and habitual, as early as possible, as many useful actions as we can,* and guard against the growing into ways that are likely to be disadvantageous to us.... The more details of our daily life we can hand over to the effortless custody of automatism, the more our higher powers of mind will be set free for their own proper work.[190]

In sum, when utilized properly, the behaviorist method can help a person to judge and act according to reason more easily than if he simply applied his will to some goal without an ordered method.

## SELF-DETERMINATION AND THE ENDS AND OBJECTS OF CHOICE

Thus far, I have often referred to human excellence to illustrate how habituation can coexist with automaticity. This perspective may give rise to an objection, namely, that habits may be useful but they are ultimately unnecessary because human nature is good as such.[191] After all, a thing is good insofar as it has being,[192] and a human soul with its various powers, as the natural form of the body, is the intrinsic source of human being.[193] Therefore, additional forms provided by habits are only additional perfections that aid top-level performance. As such, they are unnecessary for a person's goodness.

190. James, *The Principles of Psychology*, 1:122.
191. See *ST* I-II, q. 49, a. 4, obj. 1.
192. See *ST* I, q. 5, a. 1, ad 1.
193. See *ST* I, q. 75, a. 5, ad 1.

In response, Thomas agrees that the *nature* of a thing is perfected by its form, but he points out that all creaturely and organic forms are ordered toward operations.[194] Plants are ordered toward growth and the generation of their species; animals are ordered toward movement, growth, generation, and so on. The natural forms of these sorts of things are sufficient for their perfection: whatever additional forms such creatures gain do not conduce to their perfection as such. Cultivating an orange tree may make it more fruitful, but the change is only accidental, for unless it is impeded an orange tree will bear fruit by its own power, as its form makes it tend toward that determined end.[195] Likewise, animals have no capacity for rational self-reflexive action.[196] A dog cannot decide among various ends; they are selected by its nature or by training. How it seeks them is not a matter of directing itself voluntarily, but of following its appetite as it has been shaped by nature and circumstances.[197] This is only somewhat the case for humans. In previous chapters, we have seen that humans have a bundle of inclinations that were not derived from fully voluntary choice. Dispositions from human nature in general, such as synderesis and instincts, incline a person to enact behaviors that are generally beneficial for the individual and species. Dispositions from individual nature particularize general inclinations and sometimes provide a force of their own, as temperament inclines a person toward some virtues and not others. Finally, dispositions acquired by experience, whether in the womb or later in life, can even entail behaviors that are nonvoluntary or only partly voluntary. But none of these lower-level habits guarantees personal goodness.

As rational, our soul is open and indeterminate with respect to proximate ends and the way in which we reach our ultimate end.

194. *ST* I-II, q. 49, a. 4, ad 1.

195. Ibid.

196. The greatest good they naturally seek is the good of the species. See *Sent. De anima* II, l. 7.

197. See *ST* I-II, q. 12, a. 5, ad 3; Decosimo, *Ethics as a Work of Charity*, 98; and Klubertanz, *Habit and Virtue*, 104–9.

Precisely because we can misunderstand our ultimate end, we often choose inappropriate means to reach it.[198] Inclinations from our individual physiology, from childhood experience, or from choices for erroneous ends or unsuitable means can habituate us to desire objects that do not lead to our ultimate flourishing. Therefore, we need stable dispositions in our intellect and will, and all of our lower powers in harmony with them, that turn us to the appropriate means for reaching our true ultimate end.[199] In order to be rightly-ordered, that is, to live human life well, we must habituate our intellect and will. Habits of the soul shape the entire person: "when we act repeatedly according to reason, a modification is impressed in the appetite by the power of reason."[200] In sum, plants and nonhuman animals do not have the power of *usus* or self-determination, but humans perfection calls for the right habituation of all our powers and indeed our bodily nature, so that they may be guided in accordance with reason to our true good.

Right habituation means being habituated to respond rightly to the right objects that we apprehend. Put another way, we cannot be good unless we "determine" ourselves to the good through the right habits. In this regard, Aquinas speaks about the first moral act that a child makes, which is either for the ultimate good or against it, either opening him to grace or closing his soul in mortal sin.[201] As Steven Jensen has helped untie many of the knots surrounding Aquinas's understanding of the first moral act[202] and its implication for one's life-choices, here I focus on the interplay between self-determination and being determined by goods we choose as more proximate ends.

Freedom of choice does not quarantine us from the world's influence, as if we were Olympian gods untouched by lower realms. Instead, the objects of our choice can greatly change the state of our soul. Nicholas Austin explains that an object has a "crucial role" in

198. See *ST* I-II, q. 2.
199. See *ST* I-II, q. 49, a. 4, ad 1.
200. *Sent. Ethic.*, lib. 2, l. 1, n. 5.
201. *ST* I-II, q. 89, a. 6, co. and ad 3.
202. See Jensen, *Sin: A Thomistic Psychology*, 84–102.

human acts: it specifies powers, habits, and acts.[203] An object is that to which something is directed: the object of the power of sight is whatever is visible; the object of the habit of study is knowledge and understanding of the truth; the object of the act of eating is nourishment.[204] Austin follows John of St. Thomas in holding that an object is most properly understood as a kind of "extrinsic formal cause" that can also be a final cause.[205] Aquinas says that intending an end "determines" the agent toward that end.[206] An object of an act is a particular kind of end, that is, the proximate end of an act. It is both the "matter" of the exteriorly performed act as well as the proximate end of the interior choice.[207] This is because an object is "something external to which the power, habit, or act is ... intrinsically referred."[208] As the end grasped by the intellect that forms the appetite, the object of an act specifies that act and gives it its fundamental moral character.[209] The object serves to "formalize" the act of the will by presenting to the appetite something desirable: the desirability quality of the object shapes and "informs" the appetite.[210] It follows that when an act that is by itself and per se directed to an object that is gravely wrong, the act is, by that reason and independently from circumstances or intention, "intrinsically evil."[211] That is, the object "determines" the act, and the act in turn "determines" moral outcomes: acts that are "irremediably evil," such as murder, blasphemy, greed, and so on, are "per se and in themselves they are not capable of being ordered to ... the good of the person."[212] Hence, these sorts of objects have a necessary effect on the person's moral life;

203. Nicolas Austin, *Aquinas on Virtue: A Causal Reading* (Washington, D.C.: Georgetown University Press, 2017), 79.

204. "An object has a formal aspect insofar as it is related per se to an active principle." Osborne, *Human Action in Aquinas, Scotus, and Ockham*, 158.

205. See Austin, *Aquinas on Virtue*, 83–88.

206. *ST* I-II, q. 1, a. 2.

207. See Osborne, *Human Action in Aquinas, Scotus, and Ockham*, 163–65.

208. Austin, *Aquinas on Virtue*, 83.

209. *Veritatis Splendor*, par. 78. See *ST* I-II, q. 19, a. 2.

210. Ibid., 85. See *ST* I-II, q. 18, a. 5.

211. John Paul II, *Reconciliatio et Paenitentia*, par. 17; *Veritatis Splendor*, par. 80.

212. *Veritatis Splendor*, par. 81.

they point him toward what is evil and not to his authentic good. Indeed, all objects of a human act root the chosen object more deeply in the soul of the one who performed it. The person, in deliberately choosing an object, takes its form into himself, thereby shaping his soul with the object: performed habitually, such acts conform the soul more and more to the object, until choices in favor of the object become like second nature.

Fully-voluntary actions have a spiraling effect, for self-determination, in the words of Hendriks, "constructs the agent's identity according to the choices he or she makes. And this remains so, until the human agent decides to make contrary choices."[213] Aquinas explains that subsequent to nonvoluntary and partly voluntary habits, "man is made 'this person' through a particular acquired habit, of which we are the cause, or by an infused [habit], which is not given without our consent though we are not its cause."[214] Here Thomas conceives of the human person as moldable and somewhat non-individualized without fully voluntary habits. A person can knowingly shape himself, and as a matter of course, his self-shaping becomes behavior. Chosen habits arise directly from an agent's rational deliberation about how to reach his end. Vernon Bourke notes that the rational soul, as a self-mover, is the sort of the thing that controls its own operations "within well-defined limits."[215] When the rational power moves itself, what results "is not merely a passion but a quality, of the nature of a form, which remains after the period of actuation has ceased."[216] Understood in this way, fully-human habits, which shape the appetites, are not given by nature at birth but instead are produced by man in accordance with the full exercise of his nature.[217] Thus, fully voluntary habits are the result of repeated

213. Hendriks, *Choosing from Love,* 270.

214. *De veritate,* q. 24, a. 1, ad 19.

215. Vernon Bourke, "The Role of Habitus in the Thomistic Metaphysics of Potency and Act," in *Essays in Thomism,* ed. R. E. Brennan (New York: Sheed and Ward, 1942), 103–9, at 104.

216. Ibid.

217. See *ST* I-II, q. 51, a. 1.

acts of self-dominion and self-determination, that is, acts by which a person's deliberate choices end up shaping his intellect, will, interior senses, and passions.[218] The imagination, for example, is not directly under human control, nor are the passions or cogitative power; but these are shaped by many choices, which habituates them to apprehend something as good and suitable (or not).[219] One might say that objects have a determining factor on one's interior senses, and in turn on one's thoughts, emotions, and desires. Character develops as a result of choosing similar objects with similar acts repeatedly. As Aristotle observed, a man's character shapes his judgment, such that when a person has been changed by "a particular disposition," something seems good to him that did not seem good prior to having that disposition.[220] Chosen ends specify one's actions toward a particular good, and, because a human comes to resemble what he desires, intended ends also shape the agent.[221]

Observing the reflexive nature of our voluntary action, Daniel De Haan writes, "Through the efficacy of the will, the person transcends the natural determinations of the physical order and *becomes* the sort of person who chooses and performs certain axiologically specified activities."[222] By constantly acting in preference for honor over suffering, for instance, a person can habituate his passions and cogitative power to judge that death is not an absolute evil, but only relatively so. He can then encounter dangers with delight, or at least without sadness. Such a person would be brave.[223] Because fully voluntary habits arise from fully voluntary acts, they tend to produce the same, for "like actions produce like habits."[224] In other words,

218. See ibid., a. 2.

219. *Sent. Ethic.*, lib. 3, l. 13, n. 6.

220. *ST* I-II, q. 9, a. 2. See Aristotle, *Nicomachean Ethics* III.5, 1114a31.

221. See *ST* I-II, q. 26, a. 2; q. 62, a. 3. Recognizing love as the foundation of all action, Hendriks puts it this way: "the agent becomes what he loves" (*Choosing from Love*, 270).

222. Daniel De Haan, "Thomistic Hylomorphism, Self-Determination, Neuroplasticity, and Grace: The Case of Addiction," *Proceedings of the American Catholic Philosophical Association* 85 (2012): 99–120 at 100.

223. *Sent. Ethic.*, lib. 2, l. 3, n. 2. On the judgments of the brave, see Aristotle, *Nicomachean Ethics* III.7, 1115b7.

224. Aristotle, *Nicomachean Ethics* II.1, 1103b22.

character-forming habit tends to generate the same actions that produced it.[225] A brave person performs brave deeds. Once a person has acquired or obtained fully voluntary habits, "it results that man efficaciously desires the end consonant with those habits."[226] A brave person wants to perform brave deeds; he revels in bravery, and acts of bravery become quasi-natural to him. Even more, he can perform brave deeds at will, for a human habit is a stable quality by which a person can perform a human act whenever he wills to do so; it is "a principle of operation."[227] This operative power of habit exists because habits are ordered to nature, and "operation is the end of nature or leads to that end."[228] Habits are teleological by nature. Well-ordered acquired habits direct a person toward the act which is the end of his nature, and to the smaller acts that lead to his final end. Those acts therefore both shape character and are reinforced by character. Our "self-forming actions," Can Laurens Löwe notes, are acts by which we generate the sort of agent we will be (or will continue to be): "an agent determines who she wants to be *whenever* she acts according to her character, inasmuch as she always freely chooses … to let her character influence what she does."[229]

A human act is enfleshed by the person who performs it, within a highly individual physiognomy, experience, and circumstances provide what Porter calls "a subjective orientation" for the individual.[230] Previous sections of this study have shown the great variety of nonvoluntary and partly voluntary habits that a person has through his genetic heritage, the place and time he was born, how he was raised, the cultures which formed him in youth, and so on. Such tendencies incline a person one way or another—perhaps toward cour-

225. *Sent. Ethic.*, lib. 2, l. 3, n. 12.

226. Ibid.

227. *ST* I-II, q. 49, a. 3, ad 1.

228. *ST* I-II, q. 49, a. 3.

229. Can Laurens Löwe, "Thomas Aquinas on Our Freedom to Use Our *Habitus*," in Faucher and Roques, *The Ontology, Psychology, and Axiology of Habits*, 167–84, at 182.

230. Jean Porter, "Why Are the Habits Necessary? An Inquiry into Aquinas's Moral Psychology." in *Oxford Studies in Medieval Philosophy*, ed. Robert Pasnau (Oxford, Oxford University Press, 2013) 1:113–35 at 122.

age, perhaps patience. But innate inclinations cannot orient an individual to the right choice in every situation, and by themselves they will not lead a person to the ultimate good: "the pre-rational activities of the human agent are not, in themselves, sufficient to sustain rational action."[231] A person inclined toward courage needs habits of patience to counterbalance his natural passions, helping him consistently choose the good despite the rumbles of anger in its beginnings. Without rightly ordered habits, an irascible person cannot consistently act toward his true good. Without balanced habits, he will more often than not choose objects of his predilections, and those objects will in turn shape him, creating a spiral that reinforces the power of his untutored inclinations.

By directing a person to an end grasped by reason, fully voluntary and rightly ordered habits enable a person to respond to life reasonably, even when nonvoluntary habits and circumstances pressure him to act like a brute. When a sheep sees a wolf, he will run away, consistent with his instinct. When a shepherd sees a wolf, he might be conquered by his fear and run away. Or he might follow his reason, which tells him that protecting sheep is good, and choose to fight the wolf. In the long run, the shepherd's cogitative judgments will come to be shaped by his choices. After a series of victories over wolves, he will gradually experience less and less fear in future confrontations. This will result in a positive upward spiral in which he becomes more and more brave. Peter Hampson observes, "*habitus* moves us closer to attaining or actualizing (making real) the goods we value, desire, and seek, until we cohere with them ... our actions become more attuned to their goals as they approach them."[232] Fully-voluntary acts do not simply come and go, leaving no trace behind like a foot stepping through a flowing stream. Rather, they change the agent who performs them by producing fully voluntary habits. Furthermore, habits themselves can either perfect a per-

231. Ibid.

232. Peter Hampson, "'By knowledge and by love': The Integrative Role of *Habitus* in Christian Psychology," *Edification* 6, no. 1 (2012): 5–18, at 7.

son's nature or tend to destroy it; they can incline an agent toward acts that are either perfective or destructive of the person.[233] Gavin Lawrence explains, "To do something successfully is at least to do it in accord with (*kata*) the excellences, or virtues, (*aretai*) proper to it (and to do it unsuccessfully, or badly, is to do it in accord with its proper defects (*kakiai*))."[234] In sum, fully voluntary habits cannot be morally neutral: they are necessary for perfect human action; they incline a person toward good or evil; and they shape a person to have an intuitive feel for good or evil. The Greek word for habituation, *ethismos,* makes this clear: to develop a fully-human habit is to develop an *ethic.*[235] According to Aquinas, the habits that have perfected a person and his powers by ordering him to the rational good are the same as virtues.[236] In this way, the insight is proved true: "Habit both shows and makes the man, for it is at once historic and prophetic, the mirror of the man as he is and the mold of the man as he is to be."[237]

233. See *ST* I-II, q. 54, a. 3.

234. Gavin Lawrence, "Human Excellence in Character and Intellect," in *A Companion to Aristotle,* ed. George Anagnostopoulos (Oxford: Wiley-Blackwell, 2009), 419–41, at 421. See Aristotle, *Nicomachean Ethics* I.8, 1098a8–12.

235. See Lawrence, "Human Excellence in Character and Intellect," 422.

236. See *ST* I-II, q. 55, a. 1.

237. Arthur T. Pierson, *George Muller of Bristol* (Eugene, Ore.: Wipf and Stock, 1999), 137.

# 5

# Positive Habits and Virtues

When Thomas Aquinas decided to teach about the morality of human behavior, ecclesiastical law-oriented works dominated the scene. Peter Cantor's "Of Sacraments and Councils for the Soul" (ca. 1190) begins with long discussions of penance and other sacraments then discusses how to resolve difficult moral cases.[1] Most books about morals follow the same path and focus on avoiding the seven deadly sins and receiving the sacraments worthily. Even Thomas's saintly Dominican brother, Raymond of Peñafort, in 1221 organized his *Summa de paenitentia* according to sins against God, sins against neighbor, and duties for various states of life.[2] Helpful as these various books were, they often did not penetrate into the fundamental causes of moral goodness or evil; their emphasis on law and avoidance of sin tended to obscure the need for a positive approach to human nature and an explanation of interior transformation through time.

Aquinas recognized that moral theology must do more than

1. Peter the Chanter, *Summa de Sacramentis et Animae Consiliis,* 5 vols., ed. Jean-Albert Dugauquier, Analecta Medievalia Namurcensa 4, 7, 11, 16, and 21 (Paris, 1954–67). See the discussion in Emily Corran, *Lying and Perjury in Medieval Practical Thought: A Study in the History of Casuistry* (Oxford: Oxford University Press, 2018), 68–73.

2. Raymond of Peñafort, *Summa de paenitentia,* ed. Xaverio Ochoa et Aloisio Díez (Rome: Commentarium pro religiosis, 1976).

enumerate which behaviors to avoid. Penetrating more deeply than case-law perspectives of human behavior, Aquinas decided to organize his moral theology in his *Summa Theologiae* primarily around the virtues.[3] Accordingly, he set himself to explain the principles of positive activity, that is, to elucidate the virtues which shape the soul. The result was a magnificent synthesis which explained how God created human nature to be perfectible through time, effort, and, ultimately, grace. Aquinas's exposition of the virtues constituted more than an extension of Aristotle, reworked to be reconciled with scriptural and Augustinian texts. It re-envisioned moral life. With his account of the cardinal and theological virtues, Aquinas set "the multiplicity of known authors in their proper pedagogical relation—the relation that proves most instructive for the Christian believer en route to a supernatural end."[4] In this chapter, I first address the issue of whether habituation like strengthening a "willpower" muscle. Next, I delineate the nature of virtue as the perfection of our faculties. Then I consider what constitutes the material of virtue in general. After that, I discuss each cardinal virtue—prudence, justice, fortitude, and temperance—in light of biological psychology. I round out the chapter by discussing human virtue and flourishing in this life and the next.

## IS HABIT GROWTH LIKE STRENGTH TRAINING?

Many psychological studies argue in favor of a "strength training" model of habitual willpower. Like physical strength, one's willpower, also called "self-control" and "self-regulatory strength," has limit-

3. See Reginald Garrigou-Lagrange, "Du charactère métaphysique de la Théologie moral de saint Thomas, en particulier dans ses rapports avec la prudence et la conscience," *Revue Thomiste* no. 34 (1925): 341–56, at 342. This is not to claim that Aquinas was antinomian: Aquinas incorporated the Ten Commandments into his virtue-centered organization.

4. Robert Miner's observation, though focused on the treatise on prudence, applies to Aquinas's work on virtue as a whole in his *Summa Theologiae*. "Non-Aristotelian Prudence in the *Prima Secundae*," *The Thomist* 64, no. 3 (2000): 401–2.

ed resources: "initial acts of self-control tend to impair subsequent acts."[5] After a person has exercised self-control in a meaningful way, he experiences what is called "ego depletion." One's "depletion" makes resisting future temptations much more difficult, despite the desire to do so. This is manifest in spending behavior, sexual behavior, alcohol consumption, persisting in difficult challenges, sustaining physical stamina, regulating emotions, and controlling thoughts.[6] Subjects who had to suppress particular thoughts found it more difficult to inhibit their laughter when shown a humorous video.[7] People who were trained for two months of physical exercise found that they gained self-regulatory power in other areas, such alcohol consumption and studying.[8] These findings purport to show that one can build up the strength of his will, that is, a habit of making discrete choices, through exercising the will in a moderate way. But this model has serious flaws.

As with previously-discussed models of habits, the "willpower-strength" analogy contains elements of truth. Following Aristotle, Aquinas notes that fully voluntary habits function like physical strength insofar as habits are strengthened by moderate exercise and weakened through non-use and excessive use.[9] But there are at least two deficiencies of the "willpower as muscle power" model of habits. First, it could inaccurately imply that the will is a blind or nonintentional, indifferent power.[10] Muscles are invariably blind—they grow stronger no matter what weights are used as resistance. But one does not gain a stronger will by choosing anything

5. M. Muraven and R. F. Baumeister, "Self-Regulation and Depletion of Limited Resources: Does Self-Control Resemble a Muscle?," *Psychological Bulletin* 126, no. 2 (March 2000): 247–59, at 256.

6. Isabelle M. Bauer and Roy F. Baumeister, "Self-Regulatory Strength," in *Handbook of Self-Regulation: Research, Theory, and Applications*, 2nd ed., ed. Kathleen D. Vohs and Roy F. Baumeister (London: The Guilford Press, 2013), 64–82, at 70.

7. Ibid., 71.

8. Ibid., 76.

9. See Aristotle, *Nicomachean Ethics* II.2, 1104a11–b2, and Aquinas, *Sent. Ethic.*, lib. 2, l. 2, nn. 7–8.

10. See Klubertanz, *Habit and Virtue*, 67.

whatsoever. Rather, the will is naturally directed toward the perceived good. The will is a rational appetite; it acts only in conjunction with the intellect, which informs the will by presenting goods to it as worthy of choice.[11] As we saw in the last chapter, the will is deeply affected by the objects of its choice. When the will consistently chooses a disordered good, it grows weaker and is more enslaved to what it has chosen.[12] In other words, one's will is oriented by one's habits, habits are specified by their objects, and objects are shaped by one's mode of willing.[13] By making choices, one enters into a habit-volition cycle that either spirals upward toward virtue and strengthens the soul, or that spirals downward toward vice and weakens the soul.

Second, muscle power has a very limited scope: it can only provide resistance to physical weight in material objects. However, the will is naturally "open" to all objects, for the intellect can consider all things under some aspect of goodness. Though the will is directed toward outward goods such as family or political life, "it is not innately oriented towards right relations in all these contexts."[14] The will must be directed properly toward the truly good end, and the right means to reach it.[15] Specification is the role of habits, for they "give a more determinate direction and shape to capacities that are not disposed in sufficiently narrow ways."[16] It follows that "men do not build up 'will power in general.'"[17] Rather, they build up an inclination to will one thing or another, to desire some things and not others. One does not learn music in general. One learns individual pieces of music—Bach's *Goldberg Variations,* for example—and one learns these as played on the piano or harpsichord; and these one plays in a particular way. We not only choose the object of our

11. See *ST* I-II, q. 8, a. 1.
12. See *ST* III, q. 87, a. 2, ad 3.
13. See *ST* I-II, q. 54, a. 2, ad 1.
14. Porter, "Why Are the Habits Necessary?," 134.
15. See *ST* I-II, q. 49, a. 4, ad 2.
16. Decosimo, *Ethics as a Work of Charity,* 74.
17. Klubertanz, *Habit and Virtue,* 68.

action, we also develop our own style of appropriating the object to ourselves through our action, as every musician knows.

Here we discover a significant reason why humans have habits: "a life without habits would be robotic."[18] In contrast, human action and habits are quite unrobotic. Human action is not simply choosing this or that in a single instance, with no effect on the agent, the way turning a light on or off does not affect the bulb except to wear it down. Habituated acts that are truly human cannot be reduced to a series of discrete and disconnected behaviors commanded by a bodiless, detached observer. Robotic acts only bear the appearance of continuity, naturalness, and wholeness. In contrast, human acts exist within the organic life-situation of the person as a whole—with all the inheritances and inclinations provided by one's habits and exterior environment. Our lives do not resemble those of robots at all: "we are always already in full stream," that is, we live in a stream of life whose pressure on us comes from the events of past and orients us toward a future over which we have some control.[19] Consequently, habituation involves the perfection of our various faculties as they engage particular objects and are directed to chosen ends appropriate for the agent.

## HUMAN HABITS AS "EXCELLENCES" AND "PERFECTIONS"

The word "virtue" in contemporary English connotes some kind of moral goodness, especially unselfishness and doing good for others. According to this understanding, a virtuous person is one who works at a soup kitchen or cleans a polluted stream in her neighborhood. Others see "virtue" more generally as a disposition to follow a rule well.[20] But the ancient roots of the word dig deeper. Aristotle

18. Noë, *Out of Our Heads*, 119.

19. Ibid.

20. According to Walter E. Schaller, this is the "standard view" of virtue-theory. See Schaller, "Are Virtues No More than Dispositions to Obey Moral Rules?," *Philosophia* 20, nos. 1–2 (July 1990): 195–207. Steven J. Jensen notes that, according to Thomas, the

notes that *hexis* (habit) exists in two basic forms: *technai* (skills) and *aretai* (excellences/perfections).[21] Skills make a person good at performing some exterior action; the second make a person good simply speaking. The Greek word that has often been translated as "virtue" is ἀρετή, *arete*. In the ancient context, it meant "prowess" or "excellence," as in the way young men preparing for Olympic games were exhorted to employ their bodies in a display of prowess, or in the way someone who had cultivated his political skill was said to have developed an "excellence" for ruling.[22] Virtue is consequently something deeply related to practice and skill, but in this case, it is a "skill" of doing what is most natural to humans, that is, being authentically human. Hence Aristotle wrote, "The excellence we must study is human excellence; for the good we are seeking is human good and the happiness human happiness. By human excellence we mean not that of the body [primarily] but that of the soul."[23] There is a similar view in divine revelation as reflected in Aquinas.

Aquinas stated that, at its most fundamental level, "virtue designates the completion of a power."[24] In Aquinas's Vulgate, the word *virtus* is translated in English as "power," indicating the strength that comes from God's nature and is directed toward good actions. The author of the Book of Wisdom praises God, saying, "Your power is

---

first cause of moral wrongdoing is one's failure to consider the moral rule: a person who commits moral evil does not pay attention to the moral rule that he already knows. *Sin: A Thomistic Psychology*, 3, citing *De malo*, q. 1, a. 3, and *SCG* III, c. 10, n. 14. It should be noted that Aquinas did not consider morality to consist in adherence to an external rule arbitrarily promulgated, but to the natural law, which interiorly directs a person toward what is good for human nature (*ST* I-II, q. 94, a. 4), and to the perfecting law of grace, the "New Law" of the Gospel, inscribed on the human heart (*ST* I-II, q. 106, a. 1). However, as we shall see, moral perfection in Aquinas is not obeying a rule through justice, but conforming one's will to God's through charity (*ST* II-II, q. 23, a. 7).

21. See Aristotle, *Nicomachean Ethics* II.1, 1103b6–25.

22. See the illuminating articles that discuss these terms as used by Homer, Plato, Aristotle, Thucydides, and others: Margalit Finkelberg, "Virtue and Circumstances: On the City-State Concept of Arete," *The American Journal of Philology* 123, no. 1 (Spring 2002): 35–49; and Debra Hawhee, "Agonism and Aretê," *Philosophy & Rhetoric* 35, no. 3 (2002): 185–207.

23. *Nicomachean Ethics* I.13, 1102a15.

24. *De virtutibus*, q. 1, a. 1.

the source of righteousness"; the Gospel of Luke records that when Christ walked among the people, "all the crowd sought to touch him, for power came forth from them and healed them all."[25] Humans have *virtus* as well, in accordance with our nature. Aquinas states that the perfection of fully-human habits is that same perfection called "virtue" by the Latin tradition.[26] A virtue perfects one's power and thereby makes one more powerful. With that perfection, that quality, one rules and directs one's appetites so that one can perform a good act more quickly, easily, skillfully, and so on. Accordingly, the word *virtuoso* designates an artist who has so mastered his passions and body that he is able to produce a expert work of art with a seemingly-natural effort.[27] Virtue is also a particular kind of habit, a good habit. It is good because it is directed toward the right end, good because it perfects the agent who has it by directing him to that right end; and it is a habit because it is a semi-permanent quality stamped into a person's soul.[28] Because human virtue is the product of human choice, it is necessarily the result of self-cultivation and mastering the art of being human; it is integral to the full flourishing of the individual, and it conduces to that end.

Robert Merrihew Adams shows the excellence of virtue by noting its objectively fulfilling property: "Excellence is the objective and non-instrumental goodness of that which is worthy to be honored, loved, admired, or (in the extreme case) worshipped for its own sake."[29] Virtue is somehow "intrinsic" to the person because it is a perfection of the person; its value does not depend on any consequences: "what is excellent is good as an end in itself and not merely

25. Wis 12:16: "Virtus enim tua justitiæ initium est, et ob hoc quod Dominus es, omnibus te parcere facis" (see an echo in *Super Psalmo* 8, n. 1). Lk 6:19: "Et omnis turba quærebat eum tangere: quia virtus de illo exibat, et sanabat omnes" (cited in *ST* III, q. 43, a. 4).

26. *ST* I-II, q. 61, a. 1.

27. See Nicola Monaco, *Le Passioni e I Carrateri: Origini, Natura, Rimedi* (Rome: Societá Apostolato Stampa, 1944), 70.

28. See *De virtutibus*, q. 1, a. 1. See also *ST* I-II, q. 55, a. 3.

29. Robert Merrihew Adams, *A Theory of Virtue: Excellence in Being for the Good* (Oxford: Oxford University Press, 2009), 24.

as a means to some ulterior end," which means that "it is good objectively and independently of our actually valuing or prizing it."[30] Julia Annas argues that virtuous action is performed for its own sake, for we deny virtue to people who do good things for ulterior motives other than the goodness itself.[31] Aquinas agrees: "the choice of a virtuous action should not be done for anything else, as when a person does virtuous actions for the sake of money or vainglory, but for the sake of the virtuous action itself."[32] But the Dominican friar does not endorse a morality which sees perfection in divesting oneself of self-love and pursuing good without benefit to oneself.[33] Rather, Aquinas argues that a truly virtuous is one who acts from right habits of virtue, and consequently finds virtuous action to be pleasing on its own, whether or not benefits accrue to self. The reason for this is rooted in human nature.

Aquinas argues that the mode in which virtue operates is an activity of unimpeded good habits; this sort of activity is per se pleasurable.[34] This conclusion is supported by the insightful work of Mihaly Csikszentmihalyi, who investigated the psychology of "op-

30. Ibid., 25.

31. Julia Annas, *Intelligent Virtue* (Oxford: Oxford University Press, 2011), 110.

32. *Sent. Ethic.*, lib. 2, l. 4, n. 4.

33. The "problem of self-love" has been a source of significant debate among theologians. Pierre Rousselot established terms of the debate in his work, *Pour l'histoire du problem de l'amour au moyen age,* Beiträge zur Geschichte der Philosophie des Mittelaiters 6.6 (Münster: Aschendorffsche Buchhandlung, 1908). Reginald Garrigou-Lagrange weighed in: *L'amour de Dieu et la Croix de Jésus* (Paris: Editions du Cerf, 1929). Chap. 2 of that work treats "Le Problème de l'Amour pur." Two years later, a more historical study was made in H.-D. Simonin, "Autour de la solution thomiste du problème de l'amour," *Archives d'Histoire doctrinale et littéraire du Moyen Age* 6 (1931): 174–275. Rousselot's was rejected in a series of publications: Louis-B. Geiger, *Le problème de l'amour chez saint Thomas d'Aquin* (Montreal: Institut d'Etudes Médiévales, 1952); Jean-Hervé Nicolas, "Amour de soi, amour de Dieu, amour des autres," *Revue Thomiste* 56 (1956): 5–42; Avital Wohlmann, "Amour du bien proper et amour de soi dans la doctrine Thomiste de l'amour," *Revue Thomiste* 81 (1981): 204–34. See also David Gallagher, "Thomas Aquinas on Self-Love as the Basis of Love of Others," *Acta Philosophica* 8 (1999): 23–44. More recently, see Christopher J. Malloy, *Aquinas on Beatific Charity and the Problem of Love* (Steubenville, Ohio: Emmaus Academic, 2019).

34. *Sent. Ethic.*, lib. 7, l. 13, n. 8.

timal performance."[35] His work shows that one crucial aspect to feelings of fulfillment is that people engage in *activity*—not passivity, such as merely watching a movie—in a particular mode, which he calls a state of "flow." A person enters "flow" when he avoids discursive reasoning and gives sustained and focused attention to a goal "for as long at it takes to achieve a goal, and not longer."[36] Flow involves intuitively ordering and harmonizing one's various goals and adapting to the immediate situation in the present act in order to achieve one's purposes.[37] A musician playing in the state of flow can creatively improvise in the moment—think of a jazz band, or Irish instrumentalists at a pub session. Such musicality is very enjoyable for the performer, and it facilitates his emotional-intellectual integration and a deeper connection with others.[38] What many thinkers fail to emphasize, if they note it at all, is the fundamental reason why this mode of action brings pleasure. Aquinas explains that no matter the *kind* of action it is, whether playing music, engaging in sports, writing, etc. (so long as the action is not self-destructive), a habitual *mode* of action brings pleasure because such an activity results from a conatural quality in the soul, "which, since it exists in the mode of a kind of nature, renders its activity quasi-natural and consequently enjoyable."[39] In fact, he defines pleasure in terms of its relation to habit: "pleasure is the connatural activity of a previously-existing habit."[40] Pleasure results most from habituation, and habit becomes more established through pleasure. The pleasure-habit connection exists because of nature: "habit exists in the mode of some kind of nature, and something is enjoyable which befits a thing according to nature."[41] From a Thomistic perspective, one could argue that

35. Mihaly Csikszentmihalyi, *Flow: The Psychology of Optimal Experience* (New York: Harper and Row, 1990).

36. Ibid., 31.

37. See Annas, *Intelligent Virtue*, 70.

38. See Andrew T. Landau and Charles J. Limb, "The Neuroscience of Improvisation," *Music Educators Journal* 103, no. 3 (March 1, 2017): 27–33.

39. *De virtutibus*, q. 1, a. 1.

40. *Sent. Ethic.*, lib. 7, l. 12, n. 10.

41. *Sent. Ethic.*, lib. 2, l. 3, n. 1.

virtuous activity results in *frui*, which makes the good action pleasurable because it "flows" from the person, feeling connatural to the agent—and whatever feels natural is pleasant, at least for a time.

The notion of nature shows that a virtue is more than a *way of doing things* that brings pleasure. Rather, as noted, it is a perfection of one's powers—and such perfection is inherently satisfying, particularly when directed toward the right object.[42] The presence of a habit indicates that the person has acquired a sort of "second nature," which is the result of the individual's choice put into action over time, with effort, toward a definite end-good.[43] Through conscious efforts in repeated choice and action, one shapes one's desires, emotions, and even one's own powers of choosing and thinking. Insofar as these desires and behaviors are the results of one's free choice, they are new and they transcend the inclinations and limitations of instincts and reflexes—indeed, they transform those lower movements into something qualitatively different: personal character. But the result of this self-shaping is not something entirely new. Thomas maintains that "habit is *similar* to nature, but falls short of it."[44] Whereas the nature of a thing cannot in any way be taken away from a thing, a habit may be removed, though with difficulty. As Shakespeare said, "Use *almost* can change the stamp of nature."[45] Indeed, the presence of a "second nature" assumes the existence of a prior and more fundamental "first nature" characterized by a bounded plasticity.

If one attempts to transcend "first nature" completely, or if one ignores its fundamental laws, the person will not survive. A human body can never be adapted to assimilate sulfuric acid as its only nourishment: any attempt would lead to physical death. The mind cannot be adapted to live only in lies: that way leads to madness. To the extent that the "first nature" of a thing is respected, that far

42. See James W. Grice, "*Habitus*: A Perfecting Quality of the Soul," *Edification* 6, no. 1 (2012): 23–25.

43. See *De veritate*, q. 20, a. 2.

44. *ST* I-II, q. 53, a. 1, ad 1; emphasis added. See also ibid., q. 50, a. 1.

45. *Hamlet*, act 3, sc. 1, l. 170.

will the person flourish with a "second nature." Aquinas puts it this way: "a good habit is one that disposes to an act fitting to the nature of the agent, whereas a habit is evil that disposes to an act unfitting to nature."[46] This is because a thing is most natural or "according to nature" (*secundum naturam*) "when it has the virtue [power] of its nature, for the virtue of a nature is the sign of a completion of nature, and when a nature has its nature completely it is said to be perfect."[47] And what is most natural? The perfection of one's proper form, which makes a thing what it is.[48] The figure of a circle is best when it is drawn with the greatest circularity, that is, with evenness in its radius traced equally to all edges from its center. Likewise, an apple tree is most perfect when it flourishes according to its nature as an apple tree—by growing straight and strong, flowering, bearing fruit in due season, and so on.

We have seen that a person's individual nature also has its own inclinations toward virtue, based in the body. In this way, a person can have a natural aptitude for intellectual and moral virtues—and an aptitude away from some of them.[49] These inclinations are like forms added to the more primary and fundamental form, and must be made in harmony with reason in order to conduce truly to the individual's excellence. A habit adds a quality, an accidental form to the human person. To the extent that the new, accidental form is in harmony with the natural, substantial form of the person—the rational soul—that far will the habit be good, and that far will the person be in harmony with himself.[50] But to the extent that the two forms clash, and, even worse, the self-imposed form becomes a sort of "second nature" in tension to the first—to that extent a person will be out of harmony with himself. It follows that "habit does not simply presuppose nature, but develops in the very direction of nature, and

46. *ST* I-II, q. 54, a. 3.

47. *In Physic.*, lib. 7, l. 6, n. 2.

48. Ibid. See also lib. 2, l. 2, n. 6: "Ergo forma rei naturalis est natura"; and *Sent. Meta.*, lib. 5, l. 5, n. 13.

49. See *ST* I-II, q. 63, a. 1.

50. See *ST* I-II, q. 49, aa. 2 and 3.

concurs with it."[51] Hence, the "first nature" we are speaking of here is man's rational nature, or what Aquinas calls man's specific or general nature. Every "determination" of the self is always measured in relation to reason, which is "right" insofar as it enacts "first nature's" laws of authentic human flourishing. Consequently, perfection for a human—the excellence of virtue—is to be in accord with what is specific to humans, namely, the rational soul. The human agent acts within a freedom for excellence and fully living engages himself by developing the best habits in accordance with his nature. Nature is therefore the source, the measure, and the goal of the acquired virtues.[52] This is the case both for the human person as a whole and for the individual parts of the human, which Aquinas calls the "subjects" of virtue.

## THE MATERIAL OF VIRTUE IN GENERAL

Humans are born without claws, hooves, tough skin, and other animal appendages, but we possess more potential to reach a greater perfection.[53] McGuiness argues that, "because the sensory powers are virtually contained in the rational form of man which determines his essence, all of man's passions and actions possess an el-

51. Ravaisson, *Of Habit*, 31.

52. *In Physic.*, lib. 2, l. 2, n. 7. See *ST* I-II, q. 71, a. 2, ad 1; q. 58, a. 1; q. 56, a. 5. Fergus Kerr argues that the concept of "nature" is central to Aquinas's ethics and is the key to his entire theological project: "The clue to uncovering the internal coherence of Thomas's *Summa Theologiae* ... lie[s] in the effects of the concept of 'nature.' ... If there is a single concept that runs all the way through, underpinning one consideration after another, it is surely the notion of 'nature.' If Thomas's doctrine of God has any internal link with his ethics, natural theology and natural law might seem to be the connection." *After Aquinas: Versions of Thomism* (Oxford: Blackwell, 2002), 120. Kerr's claim gains more plausibility if by "nature" he includes the nature of God, the nature of creatures on account of creation, and the new nature provided by grace. Aquinas states that the acquired virtues do not aim at beatitude, but natural happiness: "per virtutes acquisitas non pervenitur ad felicitatem caelestem, sed ad quamdam felicitatem quam homo natus est acquirere per propria naturalia in hac vita secundum actum perfectae virtutis, de qua Aristoteles tractat in X *Meta.*" (*De virtutibus*, q. 1, a. 9, ad 6).

53. See Cyrinus Scharff, *L'Habitus Principe de Simplicité et D'Unité dans la Vie Spirituelle* (Utrecht: N.V. Dekker and Van de Vegt, 1950), 87.

ement superior to that found in the brute animal."[54] The body's union with the self-moving soul entails that human development depends largely on his individually-directed activity. Habits are the chief means for regulating one's activity, and habits are distinguished by the powers and the objects to which they are directed: "habit is a kind of disposition that determines a power in reference to something. When the determination is fitting to the nature of the thing, there will be a good habit disposing an agent to do something well. Otherwise there will be an evil habit according to which something will be done evilly."[55] As noted above, human excellence is called "virtue": such excellence is the perfection of habits in the soul. This section discusses the "subject" of virtue, that is, the "matter in which virtue exists"—the human powers.[56] When a person's powers are perfected together, he develops virtue and thereby naturally flourishes.

Not all human powers are susceptible to virtue. Aquinas recalls that self-dominion is the foundation or properly human, that is, fully voluntary acts.[57] Virtues cannot exist in powers over which a person has no dominion, for if a person cannot direct their operations by his will, he cannot come to perfect them according to his reason. Hence, there are no virtues in the "vegetal" powers such as growth, digestion, bodily self-maintenance, and so on. But man can exercise dominion over himself in three ways. (1) As *moving and commanding*: by reason and will the agent moves himself to act.[58] Above I discussed how the agent moves himself by his rational appetite; he can even be said to "cause" himself by his will.[59] (2) As *moved*

54. Raymond McGuiness, *The Wisdom of Love: A Study in the Psycho-Metaphysics of Love According to the Principles of St Thomas* (Rome: Officium Libri Catholici, 1951), 32. He refers to *ST* I, q. 76, a. 1.

55. *Sent. Ethic.*, lib. 2, l. 5, n. 10.

56. *ST* I-II, q. 55, a. 4.

57. *De virtutibus*, q. 1, a. 4.

58. Ibid.

59. *Sent. Meta.*, lib. 1, l. 3, n. 7. See *SCG* I, c. 72, n. 8: "Liberum est quod sui causa est: et sic liberum habet rationem eius quod est per se," as well as *ST* I, q. 104, a. 1; I-II, q. 108, a. 1, ad 2; II-II, q. 19, a. 4; q. 162, a. 4.

*mover,* the sense appetite "is moved by the higher appetite insofar as it obeys it, and then it moves the exterior members by its command."[60] (3) As *moved only,* the external members can be moved by the will or by the lower appetites, or by the will through the lower appetites.[61]

The first way of exercising dominion over oneself, with reason and will moving and commanding one's operations, is the actional mode in which virtue properly resides, for "the act of virtue is nothing other than the good use of free choice."[62] Fully-voluntary habits, we may recall, are principally related to the will as inclinations toward particular objects.[63] In light of his strong emphasis on the unity of the intellect and will, Aquinas follows Augustine in defining virtue as "a good habit of the mind by which we live rightly, which is used wrongly by no one."[64] He points out that virtue has an interior and an exterior dimension: "virtue itself is an ordered disposition of the soul, according to which the powers of the soul are ordered to one another and to that which is exterior [to the person]."[65] As Pinckaers explains, there are "two dimensions of a human act: its inwardness and its outwardness," which stand in relation to each other as soul to body.[66] "The interior act is paramount," Pinckaers continues, "because it directly emanates from the will, from the person. It takes place at the source of human morality. Virtues are likewise interior principles of action as contrasted with law, which, by its origin, is an external principle."[67] In sum, the rational soul is the prin-

60. *De virtutibus,* q. 1, a. 4. See Aristotle, *De anima* III.10, 433b16, and *Metaphysics* XII.7, 1072a26.

61. *De virtutibus,* q. 1, a. 4.

62. *ST* I-II, q. 55, a. 1, ad 2.

63. *ST* I-II, q. 50, a. 5.

64. *ST* I-II, q. 55, a. 4. Augustine said virtue is a "qualitas" of mind, but Thomas goes out of his way to say that "habitus" is more suitable for the definition than the more generic term.

65. *ST* I-II, q. 55, a. 2, ad 1.

66. Servais Pinckaers, "The Role of Virtue in Moral Theology," in *The Pinckaers Reader: Renewing Thomistic Moral Theology,* ed. John Berkman and Craig Steven Titus (Washington, D.C.: The Catholic University of America Press, 2005), 288–303, at 291.

67. Ibid., 292. See *ST* I-II, q. 20, a. 4, ad 3.

cipal seat of virtue because by it a person moves himself—including his lower powers—toward the good.

The second source of self-dominion—one's lower appetitive powers—are also seats of virtue insofar as they can participate in reason.[68] Thomas divides the appetitive powers into the irascible and the concupiscible; both can participate in reason, as can the appetitive power as a whole.[69] Reason rules—or ought to rule—over the lower appetites as a king rules over a city, for the inner dynamism of the appetites remains even when they become habituated to the direction of reason toward the good.[70] In humans, the sensory is ordered to the rational element, and the intellect naturally exercises a supereminent power that integrates and harmonizes with the functions of the lower powers. When awake and attentive, the mind takes account of bodily sensations and emotions as they occur and relates them to a chosen end. Pinckaers notes: "The emotions are thus good if they contribute to a good action, and bad in the opposite case."[71] As seen above, the right emotional dispositions are essential for human action for the human act in its fullness employs the emotions in directing them toward one's good. In addition, we are often faced with "objects of sense appetite," that is, things that arouse our sensory passions. However, our passions "do not obey reason blindly, but have their own proper movements."[72] In an analogous sense, "they have a will of their own," because they are guided by the partly voluntary habits of instinct and estimative judgment.[73] Here is a simplified scenario: Hank senses an object, and his cogitative power estimates the object's benefit or danger—an estimation colored by Hank's natural, individual, and acquired habits. In response, Hank's nerves and muscles affect his imagination and emotions, inclining

68. *ST* I-II, q. 55, a. 4, ad 3.

69. *ST* I-II, q. 56, a. 6, ad 2.

70. See *De virtutibus*, q. 1, a. 4, ad 7.

71. Pinckaers, "Reappropriating Aquinas's Account of the Passions," in *The Pinckaers Reader*, 273–87, at 275.

72. *ST* I-II, q. 56, a. 4, ad 3.

73. Ibid.

him to instinctively accept or reject the object. Such an unbidden quasi-natural movement, arising from Hank's complex habit-world, tends toward satisfaction. If he voluntarily accedes to his partly voluntary movement, he will feel a physiological pleasure; if he rejects it, he will feel the pain of loss to some extent—even if he experiences some rational joy in knowing that he rejected something that was *evil for him* according to his reasonable judgment. A person will experience holistic joy only when his reason accords with his estimative judgment. In that case, his spirit will not work against his body; rather, they will function together with a delightful harmony.

Just as each string on a piano ought to be tuned and tempered to allow the notes to harmonize with each other, so a person's passions need to be habituated to act promptly, easily, and joyfully according to reason in order to achieve interior harmony. Although one's instinct is naturally directed toward the good in general, it can be led astray in particular situations when one's estimative judgment is inaccurate.[74] Hence, "the good of the operation requires that there be in the sense appetite some disposition or perfection by which the appetite easily obeys reason. This is what we call a virtue."[75] Nicholas Austin explains that the good habits of the appetites can be principles of right choice in three ways simultaneously: "*indirectly* (by removing a negative influence on the will), *participatively* (by participating in being a principle of right choice), and *concurrently* (by disposing a person together with a well-disposed will)."[76] According to Austin, this threefold work of virtue is summed up in Bernard Lonergan's notion of "sublation," in which "what sublates goes beyond what is sublated, introduces something new and distinct, puts every-

74. See the illuminating discussion of the morality of the passions in Robert Miner, *Thomas Aquinas on the Passions* (New York: Cambridge University Press, 2009), 88–108.

75. *De virtutibus*, q. 1, a. 4.

76. Nicholas Owen Austin, "Thomas Aquinas on the Four Causes of Temperance" (PhD diss., Boston College, 2010), 132. References for *indirectly* (*ST* I-II, q. 10, a. 3; q. 56, a. 4, ad 4); *participatively* (*De virtutibus*, q. 1, a. 4, ad 1; *ST* I-II, q. 55, a. 4, ad 3; *De veritate*, q. 16, a. 1); and *concurrently* (*ST* I-II, q. 56, a. 6, ad 3). See also Austin, *Aquinas on Virtue*, 138–39.

thing on a new basis, yet so far from interfering with the sublated or destroying it, on the contrary needs it, includes it, preserves all its proper features and properties, and carries them toward a fuller realization in a richer context."[77] It follows that the intellect and will "sublate" the sensory appetites, elevating them to a new level without replacing them. In this way, the appetites, and the passions that follow them, become virtuous.

The third category of self-dominion—the mind moving parts of the self that have no self-movement—includes external members of the body, such as one's hands and feet, as well as exterior and interior senses such as the sense of taste and the memory, respectively. These powers can be habituated to some extent.[78] As we have seen above, some animal reflexes can be conditioned; humans can condition their reflexes and instinctual movements to a much greater degree. One can practice an art or sport to directly habituate the movements of one's limbs, as in ballet or baseball. One can perfect one's use of the powers of taste and smell by acquiring the proficiency of a sommelier, and one can perfect one's memory through the mastery of mnemonics. In all such cases, Thomas argues that physical skills and mastery over these powers is not equivalent to virtue, because "the soul has domain over the body by despotic rule."[79] Except in cases of poor health, bodily weakness, or lack of skill, one's limbs obey one's choice. Accordingly, the perfection of one's body and bodily skill does not perfect the soul any more than a hard-working, efficient slave makes his master a better man.

Practice makes the body more docile to decisions of the will, but the value of an art or skill resides primarily in the soul, not in the body.[80] Improving one's locomotive and sensory powers does

77. Bernard Lonergan, *Method in Theology* (Toronto: University of Toronto Press, 1990), 241, quoted in Austin, "Thomas Aquinas on the Four Causes of Temperance," 133.

78. See *ST* I-II, q. 56, a. 6.

79. *De virtutibus*, q. 1, a. 4.

80. David Decosimo explains this with the example of an experienced skier returning to the slopes: "We *know* what we need to do and how to do it, but we find our bodies slow to comply, strangely disobedient. What has faded is not the habit, but the body's

not affect one's whole person; it perfects only one aspect of the person.[81] Unlike the virtues, which are pointed only toward the good, these skills can be used for good or evil: one's kung fu can help save an innocent bystander from an evil warlord, or it can be employed by the evil warlord for mercenary purposes.[82] The potential toward good or evil does not reside in the skills, but in the soul of the one who wields them. Pius XII noted, "Just as the physical heart is the principle of bodily movements, so the will is the principle of all spiritual movements, because it is the will that moves the intellect, the interior faculties and the passions, and the exterior powers toward the operation grasped by the intellect and by the internal and external senses."[83] To perfect the whole person, therefore, arts and skills must be put into the service of one's will that one habitually directs by reason to one's authentic good. In other words, one's organs, limbs, and senses must be subordinated to one's reason, directed by one's good will, and transformed within one's virtues. In considering the various human faculties, which include the intellect and the appetites, Aquinas distinguishes between "intellectual" virtues and "moral" virtues, arguing that only the latter perfect the person as an integral whole, as we will see below.

### ACQUIRED VIRTUES OF THE INTELLECT

"No desire carries one to such heights as the desire to understand the truth," Aquinas observes.[84] The habits that perfect the intellect so that it knows and understand the truth, whether speculative or practical, are called intellectual virtues.[85] The intellect is the hu-

prompt disposition to comply. After a few days we do not say, 'So *that's* how to ski,' but, 'I'm getting my ski-legs back.'" *Ethics as a Work of Charity*, 76. See *ST* I-II, q. 50, a. 1.

81. See Klubertanz, *Habit and Virtue*, 178–79.

82. See *ST* I-II, q. 56, a. 6.

83. *Discourse* (November 12, 1941), quoted in Monaco, *Le Passioni e I Carrateri*, 65.

84. *SCG* III, c. 50, n. 9.

85. *ST* I-II, q. 56, a. 3, ad 2. For a summary of the intellectual virtues, see *Sent. Meta.*, lib. 1, l. 1, n. 34. See also Gregory M. Reichberg, "The Intellectual Virtues (Ia IIae, qq. 57–58)," in *The Ethics of Aquinas*, ed. Stephen J. Pope (Washington, D.C.: Georgetown

man person's spiritual power which rises above sensation's grasp of particulars, and above the imagination's ability to store and combine images, and above the memory's storage of intentions and images. The intellect is open to the reality of things as they are; it is open to unlimited truth in itself.[86] Put simply, the "proper object" of the intellect is "the true."[87] Truth is the good of the intellect; it is the "end" for the sake of which the intellect exists; it perfects the intellect to apprehend, understand, and judge all things in light of the truth.[88] Ignorance and believing falsehood, in contrast, are evils for humans. Augustine insightfully noted: "I ask all whether they would rather rejoice in truth or in falsehood. They will no more hesitate to answer, 'In truth,' than to say that they wish to be happy. For a happy life is joy arising from the truth.... I have met many who wished to deceive, but not one who wished to be deceived."[89] Obtaining the truth therefore perfects the intellect. Habits of the speculative intellect may thus be called virtues insofar as they perfect the good activity of considering the truth.[90]

There are five principal intellectual virtues.[91] (1) *Wisdom* perfects one's knowledge of reality in light of the highest causes. (2) *Understanding* perfects one's capacity for grasping things knowable in themselves—the "principles" of knowledge. (3) *Science* perfects

University Press, 2002), 131–50; Tobias Hoffman, "The Intellectual Virtues," in *The Oxford Handook of Aquinas,* ed. Brian Davies and Eleonore Stump (Oxford: Oxford University Press, 2012), 328–34.

86. See *Sent. De anima,* lib. 1, l. 3, n. 9.

87. *De virtutibus,* q. 1, a. 7, s.c. 2. See also *ST* I, q. 54, a. 2.

88. *De virtutibus,* q. 1, a. 7. Also *ST* I-II, q. 57, a. 2, ad 3: "Bonum autem intellectus est verum, malum autem eius est falsum."

89. Augustine of Hippo, *Confessions,* trans. Vernon J. Bourke (Washington, D.C.: The Catholic University of America Press, 1953), lib. 10, c. 23, n. 33 (293). Translation slightly changed for clarity.

90. *ST* I-II, q. 57, a. 1. See Sr. Mary William, "The Relationships of the Intellectual Virtue of Science and Moral Virtue," *The New Scholasticism* 35 (1962): 475–505; Richard Sorabji, "Aristotle on the Role of the Intellect in Virtue," *Proceedings of the Aristotelian Society* 74 (1973–74): 107–29.

91. Although Aquinas lists only wisdom, understanding, and science as intellectual virtues in *ST* I-II, q. 57, a. 2, he speaks of art as a virtue in a. 3, and prudence in aa. 4–6; q. 58, aa. 2–5; etc.

one's knowledge of a particular subject matter through systematic demonstration of its proper causes. (4) *Skill* perfects one's practical knowledge of an art, craft, or profession. Then there is *prudence* (5). The first four intellectual virtues are virtues only in a qualified sense. They do not count as virtues simply because they do not make the person good as a whole, and they do not incline the person to perform good works, for they do not perfect human desires: they perfect the intellect without touching the will per se.[92] Many professors live immoral lives, even professors of ethics. Such persons could be said to find joy in the *knowing* the truth, if indeed they know it on the notional level, but not in *living* the truth and realizing it in their actions. The problem is that their will moves their intellect toward the truth so that it may be known, but not so that they may will the good once it is known as true. In this way acquired wisdom, understanding, and science are similar to skills, for on their own they do not perfect the person in his entirety.

A virtue perfects the whole person because it is aligned with a good will that is directed to the right end. It follows that "habits that are in the speculative or practical intellect insofar as the intellect follows the will more truly have the *ratio* of virtue, for through them the person is made not only *capable* or *knowledgeable*, but *actually willing* to act rightly."[93] Augustine rightly observed, "When they love the happy life, which is none other than joy arising from truth, they certainly love truth, also.... Wherever I found truth, there did I find my God, Truth Itself."[94] Hence, speculative virtues are always incomplete when one grasps the *truth of words* whereby a proposition is true, but does not attain the *truth of life* whereby one lives according to the proper rule and measure delineated by divine law.[95] The-

92. *ST* I-II, q. 57, a. 1. See *De virtutibus*, q. 1, a. 6, ad 1, and Klubertanz, *Habit and Virtue*, 180–86.

93. *De virtutibus*, q. 1, a. 7; emphasis added.

94. Augustine, *Confessions*, lib. 10, c. 23, n. 33 (294); c. 24, n. 35 (295).

95. See *ST* II-II, q. 109, a 2, ad 3. See also Gilles Emery, "Trinity and Truth," in his *Trinity, Church, and the Human Person: Thomistic Essays* (Naples, Fla.: Ave Maria University, 2007), 111; and Thomas Hibbs, *Virtue's Splendor: Wisdom, Prudence, and the Human Good* (New York: Fordham University Press, 2001), 222–27.

oretical reasoning therefore is focused on ensuring that one makes true assertions and avoids false assertions. Contrastingly, practical reasoning focuses on achieving one's good goal and avoiding evils; this is the work of prudence.

Within Thomas's moral theology, prudence plays an architectonic role.[96] The Common Doctor underlines the primacy of this virtue among acquired habits, and thereby avoids moralities of conscience that place the discernment of conscience above every other factor in moral goodness, and above systems of "moral empiricism" that aim for watertight ethical rules to fit every concrete situation.[97] According to Garrigou-Lagrange, Aquinas teaches that "the upright and certain conscience is nothing other than an act of prudence which counsels, which judges practically, which commands."[98] Garrigou-Lagrange quotes Merkelbach, who says that Aquinas's "Treatise on Prudence" could be entitled "On Prudence and its annexed virtues, in relation to forming the conscience."[99] The virtue of prudence rules and guides the act of conscience.[100] Pieper goes so far as to say that conscience and prudence are "well-nigh

96. John of St. Thomas says that moral theology is a kind of prudence "not proximately and formally, but directively and architectonically," because it directs prudence through the light of faith to the end proposed by charity. *Cursus Theologicus* I, disp. 2, a. 10, n. 17, quoted in Wallace, *The Role of Demonstration in Moral Theology*, 202. See also William A. Gerhard, "The Intellectual Virtue of Prudence," *The Thomist* 8, no. 4 (1945): 413–56.

97. See Garrigou-Lagrange, "Du charactère métaphysique," 344. In the *Secunda Secundae*, Aquinas treats the cardinal virtues in the order of their function and object: prudence, justice, fortitude, temperance. Contrastingly, in the *Nicomachean Ethics* Aristotle begins his discussion of particular virtues with fortitude and temperance in Book III to show their relation to voluntariness; in Book V he addresses justice, and in Book VI the intellectual virtues including prudence. See Miner, "Non-Aristotelian Prudence in the *Prima Secundae*," 408–9.

98. Garrigou-Lagrange, "Du charactère métaphysique," 346.

99. Ibid.

100. In *ST* I, q. 79, a. 13, Aquinas argues that conscience is a cognitive act by which the intellect applies general moral knowledge to a particular situation. In *ST* I-II, q. 19, aa. 5 and 6, he treats the questions respectively, "whether an erring conscience binds" and "whether an erring conscience excuses." He does not explicitly discuss conscience in his treatise on prudence in *ST* II-II, qq. 47–56. His lengthiest discussion of conscience is in all five articles of *De veritate*, q. 17.

interchangeable."[101] However, Ralph McInerny more persuasively argues that conscience remains in the realm of intellectual assessment whereas prudence shapes one's acts.[102] In a moral act, there are three different realities in play: (1) antecedent conscience as the rational act of assessment before one acts; (2) prudence as the virtue that rightly reasons about things to be done in the present moment—and prudence moves one to perform the good act; (3) consequent conscience as the cognitive appraisal of one's acts in light of general principles. Everyone at least implicitly performs an act of antecedent conscience whenever they perform a human act; but does not implicitly employ prudence or post-factum self-reflection. Our focus here is on the virtue of prudence.

In Aquinas's view, prudence is a perfection of the intellect whereby a person engages his rational faculties to make the best decision about how to reach his goals. Put more pithily, prudence is "right reason applied to action."[103] A prudent person *takes counsel* about how to achieve and preserve the good end he wills; he *judges* among various things that lead to that end; and he *chooses* those means in a concrete act.[104] Finally, a person applies the choice in the concrete act. Thus, "The perfection of practical reasoning, as opposed to practical knowledge, consists not merely in any one of these three actions—deliberating well, judging rightly, or commanding—but in all three proceeding harmoniously from the first to the last."[105]

Human perfection is impossible without the habit of prudence, Aquinas argues, for morality concerns not only *what* a person does, but *how* he does it.[106] Nonhuman animals, as we have seen, act in a

101. *The Four Cardinal Virtues: Prudence, Justice, Fortitude, Temperance,* trans. Richard and Clara Winston et al. (New York: Harcourt, Brace and World, 1965), 11.

102. "Prudence and Conscience," *The Thomist* 38, no. 2 (1974): 291–305, at 305. See *De veritate* q. 17, a. 1, arg. 10.

103. *ST* II-II, q. 47, a. 2, s.c.

104. The three cognitive acts of prudence, *concilium, iudicium,* and *praeceptum,* form a whole as elements leading to a human act. See *De virtutibus,* q. 1, a. 7; *ST* II-II, q. 47, a. 8.

105. Brian Kemple, "The Preeminent Necessity of Prudence" (unpublished manuscript), 1–22, at 5. Cited with the author's permission.

106. *ST* I-II, q. 57, a. 5; see also q. 55, a. 2, ad 1.

partly voluntary way from instinct and estimative judgment or what Aquinas calls "natural virtues."[107] This sort of behavior is limited in scope: all American cliff swallows build their mud nests the same way, and the same species of spiders spin similar webs.[108] But for rational animals, good human action proceeds not merely from impulse, instinct, or passion, but from deliberate choice. When a person perfects his habit of thinking rightly about things to be done, he thereby develops the virtue of prudence as a principle of living rightly.[109] A person acts prudently when he applies the primary precepts of the natural law, as grasped by synderesis, to concrete situations.[110] This happens when the agent employs a practical syllogism in his reasoning, with its major premise focusing on what is natural as an indication of the good end to be attained.[111]

The conclusion of the practical syllogism is the prudent act itself. Tobias Hoffman explains: "Prudence guides the stages of human action from the good intention to the actual performance of the deed."[112] Because reason is "the first principle of all human acts," and prudence is the virtue of reasoning about acting rightly, prudence is therefore unlimited in scope.[113] It extends to a person's ultimate end and to all actions possible to human creativity throughout a person's lifespan.[114] All other principles of human action are related to prudence, which, through its direction, makes them directly participate in reason.[115] Even if the appetites are directed toward one's proper good and the intellect grasps speculative truth correctly,

107. *De virtutibus*, q. 1, a. 6.

108. Ibid.

109. *ST* I-II, q. 57, a. 5; see II-II, q. 47, a. 4.

110. See Thomas M. Osborne, Jr., *Human Action in Thomas Aquinas, John Duns Scotus, and William of Ockham* (Washington, D.C.: The Catholic University of America Press, 2014), 69–72. He would also apply the secondary and tertiary precepts when appropriate.

111. See *ST* I-II, q. 47, a. 7, ad 3, and *Sent. De anima*, lib. 3, l. 16, n. 7.

112. Hoffman, "The Intellectual Virtues," 333.

113. *ST* I-II, q. 58, a. 2.

114. *ST* I-II, q. 57, a. 4, ad 3.

115. *ST* I-II, q. 58, a. 2, ad 1. See *De virtutibus*, q. 1, a. 6: "Ab ipsa est rectitudo et complementum bonitatis in omnibus aliis virtutibus."

without prudence there would be no integration of the person's understanding and desire. It follows that there can be no moral virtue without prudence: to act rightly, in a truly human manner, a person needs a habit whereby he is always inclined to receive counsel, judge accurately, and command rightly a good action.[116] Hence, prudence is necessary for all of the moral virtues. Indeed, Thomas insists that prudence "is the virtue most necessary to human life."[117]

The expansiveness of prudence gives the virtue an almost bewildering series of related "parts": integral, subjective, potential.[118] These broad groupings, and their subgroupings, are derived from Aquinas's synthesized reading of Cicero, Macrobius, Plotinus, Aristotle, and Andronicus.[119] Thomas compares the integral, or "quasi-integral," parts of prudence to the parts of a house. Just as a house is composed of its various parts—a wall, roof, foundation, etc.—so an act of the virtue of prudence at least virtually requires the concurrent acts of its integral parts. Conversely, the quasi-integral parts can function on their own, but not as virtues. A wall can provide shelter, that is, it can possess a "quasi-integral" existence on its own; but properly speaking it is not a wall *of a house* unless it exists in an actual integration with the other parts which exist together as a unified whole house.[120] Likewise, one can possess good memory and shrewdness on their own, but only as they pertain to prudence are they parts of a virtue.

The "subjective" parts of prudence concern the virtue insofar as it is applied to different subjects capable of being governed and commanded.[121] Indeed, prudence is the virtue of commanding well.[122] Above all, prudence is the virtue whereby man governs himself to act rightly: "the proper act of prudence, according to Aquinas, is to

116. See *ST* I-II, q. 58, a. 4; q. 65, a. 1.
117. *ST* I-II, q. 57, a. 5; see II-II, q. 47, a. 2, ad 1.
118. *ST* II-II, q. 48, a. 1.
119. Ibid., obj. 1.
120. See Kemple, "The Preeminent Necessity of Prudence," 8.
121. *ST* II-II, q. 50, a. 1.
122. *ST* II-II, q. 51, a. 2.

'command' oneself to put the decision into practice."[123] The practice of "self-regulation" is closely related to prudence, as recognized by some empirical psychological literature, although just as often psychologists typically employ a more voluntarist model and consider self-regulation as a form of "will-power."[124] But prudence is not solely about the self. It exists in various forms insofar as an individual has responsibility for the command of other persons. As the virtue that governs and directs a city or kingdom, ordering things to the common good, it exists as "regnative prudence"—the most universal and therefore the most perfect species of prudence.[125] There also exists forms of prudence as it applies to the realms of politics, the military, and the home. Given the natural economic instincts of humans, there may also be a "business prudence" by which a person directs the production and trade of goods.[126] One can infer connections of these various types of prudence with the neuroscience of leadership, which explores brain mechanisms, processes, and functions that underlie making good decisions and directing others toward desired goals.[127] Significantly, personal acquired habits parallel the habits one can inculcate within a group: the shape of a leader's new neural pathways, carved through conscious repetition, can

123. Hoffman, "The Intellectual Virtues," 333.

124. For implicit connections between intellectual virtue, especially prudence, and self-regulation, see Kateri McRae et al., "The Reason in Passion: A Social Cognitive Neuroscience Approach to Emotion Regulation," in *The Handbook of Self-Regulation*, 2nd ed., ed. Kathleen D. Vohs and Roy F. Baumeister (New York: The Guilford Press, 2011), 186–203. See also, in the same volume, M. Rosario Rueda et al., "Attentional Control and Self-Regulation," 284–99; Daniel Cervone et al., "Self-Efficacy Beliefs and the Architecture of Personality: On Knowledge, Appraisal, and Self-Regulation," 461–84. For a more voluntarist view of self-regulation, see Christopher Peterson and Martin Seligman, *Character Strengths and Virtues: A Handbook and Classification* (New York: Oxford University Press, 2004), chap. 22, "Self Regulation," which they subtitle "Self-Control."

125. *ST* II-II, q. 50, a. 1. For a contemporary application of this idea, see Alasdair Marshall et al., "Can an Ethical Revival of Prudence Within Prudential Regulation Tackle Corporate Psychopathy?," *Journal of Business Ethics* 117 (2013): 559–68.

126. See *SCG* III, c. 134, n. 2, and c. 132, n. 3.

127. See, e.g., Nikolaos Dimitriadis and Alexandros Psychogios, *Neuroscience for Leaders: A Brain Adaptive Leadership Approach* (London: Kogan Page, 2016).

shape those of his followers.[128] Through the acquisition and practice of personal prudence, therefore, a person develops his ability to govern others and to help them become prudent as well.

Prudence bears a significant relation to every other virtue. Unlike perfections such as wisdom, science, and art, prudence is the linchpin of moral virtue.[129] It is necessary for every virtuous act, for a person cannot act virtuously as a complete human person unless his practical intellect has, as an expression of interior ordered state, commanded him to act reasonably.[130] From a neurobiological perspective, one can note the crucial role prudence plays in the integration of one's body (especially the passions) and one's mind (intellect and will). Such personal integration is assisted by the habitual perfection of the practical intellect which regulates the passions and behaviors of the person. The physical growth of the brain is an imperfect image of the development of cognitive control through prudence. Put in a greatly simplified way: large bodily organs (especially the heart and surrounding muscles) are among the first to develop; they are primarily regulated by the brain stem and nervous systems (with a flight, fight, freeze, or befriend response to estimated benefit or danger), which in turn are regulated by the higher and more central limbic area of the brain (emotion, motivation, attachment, memory); this area is regulated by the right and left sides of the outer cortex, the last portion of the brain to develop.[131] The cortex is a complex and adaptive "neural system" that is shaped throughout life by one's behaviors and choices.[132] Although neural pruning takes

128. See ibid., 144–45.

129. See *ST* I-II, q. 58, a. 4, co.; *De virtutibus*, q. 5, a. 2; *Sent. Ethic.*, lib. 6, l. 11, n. 10, "virtus moralis est habitus cum ratione recta, quae quidem est prudentia"; and ibid., n. 13, "quando prudentia quae est una virtus inerit, omnes simul inerunt cum ea, quarum nulla erit prudentia non existente."

130. *ST* I-II, q. 57, a. 4, ad 2.

131. See Daniel J. Siegel, *Pocket Guide to Interpersonal Neurobiology* (New York: Norton, 2012), chap. 14. See also Morasch et al., "The Development of Cognitive Control," 989–99.

132. Siegel, *Pocket Guide to Interpersonal Neurobiology*, chap. 14–4.

place in childhood, the brain retains some plasticity that enables lifelong learning even in late adulthood.[133] Similarly, prudence is slowly acquired though the various stages of life. For prudence to operate well, the agent "needs to be perfected by certain habits according to which it becomes natural [to him] to judge about the end."[134] Therefore, Aquinas says that the young cannot possess acquired prudence, "neither in habit nor in act."[135] Prudence is in the old because their long experience of commanding well.[136]

Researchers have found empirical evidence that decisionmaking processes are benefitted by emotional regulation. For making moral decisions, the cortex is involved in evaluating emotional consequences of an act; and for avoiding immoral decisions, the full functioning of the emotional brain (limbic system) is crucial, because negative emotions often signal the immorality of one's choice.[137] Integration in the brain contributes to a balance and coordination in the nervous system, which in turn affects the entire person's choices and behaviors in relation to others and the context in which an agent lives.[138] In Thomistic language, for habitually reasonable decisions, a person needs well-ordered passions.

Disordered passions typically draw reason astray, as when a craving for junk food can overwhelm the reason even of a diabetic. William Wallace explains, "Each appetite is ... said to be 'right,' or rectified, insofar as it is in conformity with reason, and reason itself is said to be 'right,' insofar as it, in turn, is in conformity with the right appetite."[139] Now a person enjoys well-ordered appetites when he

133. Yan Gu, Stephen Janoschka, and Shaoyu Ge, "Neurogenesis and Hippocampal Plasticity in Adult Brain," *Current Topics in Behavioral Neurosciences* 15 (2013): 31–48.

134. *ST* I-II, q. 58, a. 5.

135. *ST* II-II, q. 47, a. 14, ad 3.

136. See *ST* II-II, q. 47, a. 15, ad 2; ibid., a. 16, ad 2.

137. See Nasir Naqvi, Baba Shiv, and Antoine Bechara, "The Role of Emotion in Decision Making: A Cognitive Neuroscience Perspective," *Current Directions in Psychological Science* 15, no. 5 (October 1, 2006): 260–64.

138. Siegel, *Pocket Guide to Interpersonal Neurobiology*, chap. 3–3. See also Dimitriadis and Psychogios, *Neuroscience for Leaders*, 116–23.

139. Wallace, *The Role of Demonstration in Moral Theology*, 111. He refers to *ST* I-II, q. 57, a. 5, ad 3.

possesses the moral virtues, for, as Aristotle noted, a person judges things according to his character: as a man is, so does the end seem to him.[140] Prudence's operation therefore requires the moral virtues so that a person can habitually and properly reason about things to be done without impediment.[141] Reciprocally, prudence integrates a person's passions and reason, and he thereby becomes *integrated with his own nature* and *integrated with reality*, and he learns to live in harmony with others, for his practical judgments and his emotions properly come to reflect what is truly good in his concrete circumstances.[142] Nicholas Kahm explains it well: "Virtue is a kind of mirror-image of hylomorphism, reason and passion working together harmoniously as matter and form."[143] Consequently, prudence and the other moral virtues—justice, fortitude, and temperance—mutually depend on each other.[144]

Whereas the perfection of art lies chiefly in the thing *made*, through prudence the perfection lies chiefly resides in the acting person.[145] With prudence, in the words of Josef Pieper, man draws upon his experience of reality and "acts in and upon reality, thus realizing himself in decision and in act."[146] It does so by shaping and directing the appetites, which constitute the primary "matter" of moral virtue. Virtue, we may recall, is a "quasi-natural inclination toward some [good] activity," and such operative inclinations belong to the appetitive powers.[147] By itself, the speculative intellect cannot move a person: in order for a person to be moved, he must not only see the truth; he must see the truth as good and desirable for himself. That

140. *Nicomachean Ethics* III.5, 1114a32.

141. *ST* I-II, q. 58, a. 5.

142. *ST* I-II, q. 65, a. 1, co.: "tota materia moralium virtutum sub una ratione prudentiae cadit." See also *ST* I-II, q. 58, a. 2, ad 4: "recta ratio, quae est secundum prudentiam, ponitur in definitione virtutis moralis, non tanquam pars essentiae eius, sed sicut quiddam participatum in omnibus virtutibus moralibus, inquantum prudentia dirigit omnes virtutes morales"; ibid., a. 4.

143. Kahm, *Aquinas on Emotion's Participation in Reason*, 241.

144. *ST* I-II, q. 65, a. 1.

145. See Kemple, "The Preeminent Necessity of Prudence," 19.

146. Pieper, *The Four Cardinal Virtues*, 22.

147. *ST* I-II, q. 58, a. 1.

is, a person's desires move him toward an end-object apprehended as good in the present moment but with reference to the past.[148] In this way, decisionmaking links one's learned judgments regarding desired objects and one's choice: it bridges memory of fulfilled appetite (fruition) and behavior.[149] There is, then, a mutual influence between reason and appetite: the appetite moves the reason by desire, and the reason moves the appetite by command.[150] Aquinas acknowledges that appetites have something of their own movements, but in principle they can be commanded by reason. Just as an army's progress in battle depends on the command of the general, so humans progress in the good when the appetites depend upon the command of right reason.[151] An act of deliberation need not intervene at each choice; it is sufficient that prudence retains at least a virtual command over the appetites. The appetites become virtuous when they are habitually informed by prudence, so that their obedience to reason occurs quasi-naturally, that is, easily, quickly, and stably.[152]

We should be careful to note that the mutually reinforcing relationship among the moral virtues is not equivalent to their self-sufficiency. A broader look at Thomas's teaching on virtue reveals that the general end provided by synderesis, and the particular ends proposed by prudence, remain within a field accessible to human power: they aim at natural goods. Thus, as will be discussed later, a person needs infused prudence to direct himself according the measure known only by faith, as will be discussed in a later chapter. Similarly, because one's appetites can be thrown into disarray by original and personal sin, which can coexist with acquired virtue, perfect prudence relies upon charity, which, as we will see, orders

148. See *ST* I-II, q. 9, a. 1, ad 2.

149. See Lesley K. Fellows, "The Neuroscience of Human Decision-Making Through the Lens of Learning and Memory," in *Current Topics in Behavioral Neurosciences*, ed. Mark Geyer et al. (Berlin: Springer, 2016), 1–21.

150. See *ST* I-II, q. 65, a. 1, ad 3.

151. *De veritate*, q. 25, a. 4.

152. See *ST* I-II, q. 58, a. 1, ad 3.

one's appetites by directing the entire person to his supreme ultimate end, the Trinity. Prudence, in sum, is a *sine qua non* for every other virtue, but it is not the greatest of the habits. With this in mind, we can look to the moral virtues as implicitly guided by prudence.

## JUSTICE AND RELATED VIRTUES OF THE WILL

We have just learned that the perfection of the intellect by prudence is necessary for virtue and man's moral goodness. Not all accounts of ethics agree with this assessment. Indeed, moralities that give supremacy to the will's goodness are prevalent throughout the world. We can call these versions of voluntarism. According to a voluntarist morality, good human behavior is for the most part a matter of controlling one's "free will" and directing it to obey a moral law. For voluntarists, the two proper foci of ethics are free will and obligations to a superior's will, typically expressed as law. Everything else orbits around these two centers of gravity and the consequent system of obligation.

Whether or not William of Ockham deserves the "voluntarist" epithet, he certainly holds that the will precedes reason and is the measure of morality.[153] Because God is wholly omnipotent and possesses a "freedom of indifference" with respect to the Good, he is wholly free to command whatever he wills; and what he wills is good

153. Ockham's theory of the will and morality is certainly more nuanced than is often recognized. David W. Clark argues that Ockham should not be called a "voluntarist" because the friar's insistence on the role of "right reason" in moral decisions "balances out" his insistence on the will's freedom of indifference with respect to the true good. Clark, "Voluntarism and Rationalism in the Ethics of Ockham," *Franciscan Studies* 31 (1971): 72–87. Quibbles about monikers aside, Ockham holds that the goodness of exterior acts is a nominal reality (with the labels supplied by God), the interior act of the will determines moral value, and reason's rightness is derived from a priori moral principles, experience, or commands. See Marilyn McCord Adams, "The Structure of Ockham's Moral Theory," *Franciscan Studies* 46 (1986): 1–35. See also Osborne, *Human Action in Thomas Aquinas, John Duns Scotus and William of Ockham*, esp. 175–84; Peter King, "Ockham's Ethical Theory," in *The Cambridge Companion to Ockham*, ed. Paul Vincent Spade (Cambridge: Cambridge University Press, 1999), 227–44.

because he wills it. The divine will can command humans to perform acts that must be obeyed, even acts now deemed intrinsically evil, such as to hate God. Human goodness therefore ultimately consists in moving one's will toward what is commanded by God and in shunning what is prohibited by God. Irrelevant to moral goodness are considerations of divine nature, human nature, inclinations, intellectual virtues, and habits. Only the will possesses virtue; and the only virtue is to love because God commands it. As Terence Irwin sums it up: "Ockham asserts the independence of the will from reason and makes reason simply the servant of the will."[154]

Voluntarist trends also appear in the thought of Roy F. Baumeister, one of the world's leading researchers on "will-power" and "self-regulation." Baumeister claims, "Morality is a set of rules ... and virtue involves internalizing those rules. Insofar as virtue depends on overcomes selfish or antisocial impulses ... self-control can be said to be the master virtue."[155] Baumeister also stated that willpower or self-control failure is the cause of "most major problems, personal and social," including compulsive spending, violent outbursts, academic mediocrity, drug abuse, chronic anxiety, and overeating.[156] For him, delayed gratification is one of the primary markers of self-control: beyond techniques for producing desired results, there is little positive content that he attributes to a strong will.[157] As discussed above, this view reductively sees the will as a

154. Irwin, *The Development of Ethics: A Historical and Critical Study*, vol. 1: *From Socrates to the Reformation* (Oxford: Oxford University Press, 2007), 704.

155. Roy F. Baumeister and Julie Juola Exline, "Virtue, Personality, and Social Relations: Self-Control as the Moral Muscle," *Journal of Personality* 67, no. 6 (1999): 1165–94, at 1165.

156. Roy F. Baumeister and John Tierney, *Willpower: Rediscovering the Greatest Human Strength* (New York: Penguin, 2011), 2 and 11. See also R. F. Baumeister et al., *Losing Control: How and Why People Fail at Self-Regulation* (San Diego, Calif.: Academic Press, 1994).

157. See the studies that Baumeister cites as demonstrating the importance of self-control in Baumeister and Tierney, *Willpower*, 264. These include the famous "marshmallow experiment," which tested the resolve of children to avoid eating the treat. A follow-up study noticed that years later those with the most "no"-power were more successful in life: W. Mischel et al., "The Nature of Adolescent Competencies Predicted

blind moral muscle that is trained to choose what is good and avoid what is bad as delineated by choice. Habituation, then, is presented as a strengthening of the will to achieve its chosen goals, which have little explicit relation to apprehended truth or the object to which one is being habituated.[158] There no concern here for prudence and shaping oneself in accordance with right tendencies of nature and the authentic good.[159]

Where would Thomas stand on the will's role in moral perfection? In David Gallagher's view, Thomas would define the will as "that power or faculty of the soul by which a human agent is in control of his actions."[160] Granted that the will moves itself, reducing the will's role to "self-control" without a notion of its teleological nature leans toward versions of voluntarism seen above. Fuller definitions of the will are available, and more in accordance with Aquinas's expressed thought. The will may be described as "the appetite for a rationally apprehended good end," or, as Deferrari notes, *voluntas* in the broad sense of the term connotes every appetitive faculty, but in the narrower and proper sense, *voluntas* is the rational appetite.[161] Aquinas explains that humans possess a higher appetite and a lower appetite.[162] He clearly states that "the will is the rational appetite"; it is a higher form of appetite, for it desires goods as apprehended by

by Preschool Delay of Gratification," *Journal of Personality and Social Psychology* 54 (1988): 687–96.

158. Baumeister, for example, recognizes the importance of goal-setting, but is seemingly indifferent to the content of the goal itself, were as if all are equally choiceworthy (see Baumeister and Tierney, *Willpower*, 62–71).

159. Although we are told that "self-control is a vital strength and key to success in life," it is also said that "much of self-control operates unconsciously" (Baumeister and Tierney, *Willpower*, 13 and 15). No definition of willpower is offered, nor how it engages critical thinking about the good; at best, there are hints that it relates to memory and pattern-matching (see ibid., 16).

160. "The Will and Its Acts (Ia IIae, qq. 6–17)," in *The Ethics of Aquinas* (ed. Pope), 69–89, at 70.

161. "Voluntas – Liberum Arbitrium," in Nuntio Signoriello, *Lexicon Peripateticum Philosophico-Theologicum* (Rome: Federicus Pustet, 1931), 430. Also, "voluntas" in Deferrari, *A Lexicon of St. Thomas Aquinas* (previously cited on p. 133), 1179–82.

162. See *ST* I, q. 80, a. 2; *Sent. De anima* lib. 3, l. 14, n. 8.

the intellect.[163] The sensory appetite is lower, for it desires goods as apprehended by the senses. Our appetites naturally desire apprehended goods; through the will, we are able to rationally desire what we apprehend, and it therefore more properly constitutes the principle of human acts than the sensory appetite.[164]

For Aquinas, to be morally good, one's will does not merely need more *power* or efficient forcefulness; it needs to be *better formed* so that it is more in harmony with the good and thereby is more inclined toward the good: to be morally upright, a person and his actions must be in conformity with the natural and divine law.[165] But morality is more than following some exterior set of rules: it is a perfection of the individual, an interiorization of the law, such that the goodness aimed at by the law flows from the heart outward. The appetite is naturally ordered toward the good in general, but in order for it to be inclined *easily* to respond to reason, and to the right objects, it must be habituated to do so, for voluntary habituation involves shaping one's powers in light of one's reasons for acting toward an end.[166] In acts that consist principally in choice and will, it is easy to perform them in *some way*, but, Aquinas states, "it is not easy to do them in the proper mode, that is, unimpededly, consistently, and joyfully."[167] Thus the will requires a habit of being docile to reason so that it easily obeys the immediate command of reason in every situation.[168] That virtue is justice.

Justice may be defined as the habit "according to which a person gives each his due with a constant and perpetual will," in harmony with the divine and natural law.[169] When we habitually will and act

163. *ST* I-II, q. 8, a. 1. See *Super Sent.*, lib. 2, d. 24, q. 3, a. 1, co.; *SCG* III, lib. 2, c. 47, n. 2.

164. *ST* I, q. 80, a. 1. See also, *ST* I-II, q. 73, a. 1.

165. For a balanced view of Aquinas and later thinkers on the will's goodness, see Bonnie Kent, *Virtues of the Will: The Transformation of Ethics in the Late Thirteenth Century* (Washington, D.C.: The Catholic University of America Press, 1995).

166. See *De virtutibus*, q. 1, a. 12, ad 19.

167. *De virtutibus*, q. 1, a. 1, ad 13.

168. Ibid.

169. *ST* II-II, q. 58, a. 1.

to render good to God and created persons, we develop the virtue of justice.[170] Through justice, a person is directed outside of himself, for by it, an agent seeks an equality between what he can give and what a recipient ought to have. Hence, justice "links the subjective side of the virtuous actor with the objective domain of the recipient of the virtuous act, and articulates justice a relational or a societal virtue"; it concerns "an internal act of the moral agent's will but also comprises an external effect directed to another."[171]

Attempts to discover the physiological roots of justice have led to observations that several animal species, including macaque monkeys and ravens, manifest "inequity aversion and respond negatively to receiving less reward than a social partner."[172] Scientists were led to the conclusion that "evolution favors the independent emergence of inequity aversion in any species that engages in repeated cooperative interaction and possesses sufficiently complex cognitive abilities."[173] As for humans, many studies have been conducted on infants to discover the emergence and sources of justice-related thinking and behavior. There is widespread evidence of a preverbal sense of fairness, but sensitivity to perceived fairness and consequent "prosocial" behavior varies widely among people.[174] Significantly, genetics seem to affect prosocial behavior—perhaps related to temperamental factors recognized by Aquinas as natural inclina-

170. See ibid., ad 3; a. 8. For an overview of the virtue in its complexity, see Jean Porter, "The Virtue of Justice," and Martin Rhonheimer, "Sins Against Justice," in *The Ethics of Aquinas* (ed. Pope), 272–86 and 287–303 respectively.

171. Claus Dierksmeier and Anthony Celano, "Thomas Aquinas on Justice as a Global Virtue," *Humanistic Management* (n.d.): 11. Available at humanisticmanagement.org/cms/knowledge_center/research_papers/downloads/Thomas_Aquinas_on_Justice_as_a_Global_Virtue.pdf.

172. Among many studies, see S. F. Brosnan, "Justice- and Fairness-Related Behaviors in Nonhuman Primates," *Proceedings of the National Academy of Sciences of the United States of America* 110 (2013): 10416–23. See also C. A. F. Wascher and T. Bugnyar, "Behavioral Responses to Inequity in Reward Distribution and Working Effort in Crows And Ravens," *PLoS One* 8 (2013): e56885.

173. Jean Decety and Keith J. Yoder, "The Emerging Social Neuroscience of Justice Motivation," *Trends in Cognitive Sciences* 21, no. 1 (January 1, 2017): 6–14, at 8.

174. Ibid.

tions toward virtue.[175] Additionally, justice-related values that parents have communicated are detectable in infants as young as twelve months old.[176] Nevertheless, even adults retain a subvoluntary inclination to estimate justice variably. A number of studies of "morality salience" exposed people to subliminal signs of threat and, perhaps unsurprisingly, found that we are typically kinder to people who are more similar to us, and we are more hostile to the "other."[177]

Considered from a Thomistic perspective, the empirical findings above suggest that we are inclined by biology and early learning to perform behaviors allied with or supportive of justice. These inclinations call for reason's regulation in order to consistently benefit society. Some prosocial inclinations are derived from the combination of activated genes, individual differences, parenting, societal education, and so on—even apart from a person's deliberate cognitive engagement with the world. Unless a person mentally considers these habitual dispositions, they remain subrational. The full-fledged act and the virtue of justice proceed from a deliberate will, which is the *rational appetite*. Thomas says, "justice is sometimes called 'truth,'" for, "since the will is the rational appetite, when the rectitude of reason, which is called 'truth,' is imprinted on the will on account of its close relationship with reason, retains the name 'truth.'"[178] In other words, one's act of will does not proceed from mere sensory information and an estimation about the nature of things. It is informed by reason itself.

A will that relies solely on a subrational estimation to make its choice cannot be consistently just. One's natural inclination to treat strangers with caution, or even antagonism, easily goes astray. Although this pattern may lead to greater group survival, it does not al-

175. See T. J. C. Polderman et al., "Meta-analysis of the Heritability of Human Traits Based on Fifty Years of Twin Studies," *Nature Genetics* 47 (2015): 702–9.

176. See also J. M. Cowell and J. Decety, "Precursors to Morality in Development as a Complex Interplay between Neural, Socioenvironmental, and Behavioral Facets," *Proceedings of the National Academy of Sciences of the United States of America* 112 (2015): 12657–62.

177. Siegel, *Pocket Guide to Interpersonal Neurobiology*, chap. 42–5.

178. *ST* II-II, q. 58, a. 4, ad 1.

ways lead to justice, which is a good that transcends relations based on mere physical necessity. Hence, one's subrational inclinations need to be incorporated into a rational life: they need to be brought into one's awareness, considered, checked if necessary, and responded to according the demands of virtue as contextualized by the common good. When the will is informed or imprinted with the truth received from right reason then a willed act participates in the truth insofar as an agent desires what is true under the aspect of the good. The will habitually participates in the truth when, through the virtue of prudence, the practical intellect habitually grasps and directs the person toward the truth of life and thereby desires to render to others what is truly due to them. In the words of Martin Rhonheimer, "Like any moral virtue, only more emphatically, justice can only exist when joined to prudence."[179]

An act of the virtue of justice, which is a commanded movement of the will, is founded on reason that accurately judges the existence of disproportionality among persons and commands a person to rectify the relationship in some way. Distributive justice, among other kinds of justice, achieves the *geometrical* mean of virtue, that is, not absolutely but considered in proportion to what an individual deserves and to the good in consideration. For example, a hospital distributes health benefits to patients differently based on criteria of need, availability of physicians, and so on. In order that justice be ensured, whether particular or general, lawful public authority must pronounce judgment to those subject to the community.[180] To apportion adequate rewards and punishments, a judge must ascertain the responsibility and intention of the agents. Consequently, much of the neuroscience related to public justice focuses on the contours of legal responsibility, even though these matters more properly belong to more general discussions of human freedom as previously discussed in this chapter.[181]

179. Rhonheimer, "Sins Against Justice," 297.

180. *ST* II-II, q. 60, a. 6.

181. See, for instance, the essays arguing in favor of moral culpability (and therefore

Centuries of moral manuals concerned themselves primarily with exterior behavior and therefore devoted vastly more space to justice than to any other virtue. Although Aquinas's discussion of justice is, in Jean Porter's estimation, "the longest, the most complex, and arguably the most difficult treatment of a particular virtue in the *Summa Theologiae*,"[182] Aquinas did not obscure the primacy of prudence and the ways that other virtues contribute to moral goodness. Justice is superior to fortitude and temperance because it is a perfection of the will, the highest human appetite, and because its object is the good of another person, whereas fortitude and temperance perfect lower appetites and focus only on the individual.[183] However, the virtues of prudence, temperance, and fortitude sufficiently and directly perfect one's self-reflexive actions. Only metaphorically can a person be "just" toward himself.[184] The primary object of justice concerns external behaviors and things, whereas its secondary object concerns the passions and everything that can assist or obstruct its act. Hence, when public opinion threatens to obstruct a judge's duty to render justice to a legal defendant, the virtue of justice may call upon the virtue of fortitude to overcome the fear of public shaming. There should be no doubt that the virtue of justice never undermines the other virtues.

The virtue of justice is so reasonable that, at times, it must do the good contrary to concepts of justice defined by civil law. Following positive human law punctiliously can, at times, lead to injustice. Aside from cases of evil law, even good civil law cannot account for all circumstances that make for just action. Therefore, the virtue of *epikeia* moderates the observance of the letter of the law in

---

the possibility of public justice) in Nicole A. Vincent (ed.), *Neuroscience and Legal Responsibility* (New York: Oxford University Press, 2013). For concerns about neuroscience possibly usurping the jury's proper role in making judgments, see Bernice B. Donald, "On the Brain: Neuroscience and Its Implications for the Criminal Justice System," *Criminal Justice* 30, no. 3 (2015): 1 and 47–48.

182. Jean Porter, "The Virtue of Justice," 272.

183. See *ST* II-II, q. 58, a. 12.

184. See ibid., a. 2.

favor of the *ratio* of justice and the common good.[185] But this virtue is not an alternative to the strict observance of the law. If the law is not followed strictly when it should be followed, injustice results.[186] *Epikeia* upholds what is just in itself; it only sets aside the letter of the law in a particular circumstance unforeseen by the law, as "to follow the letter of the law when it ought not to be followed is vicious."[187]

The potential parts of justice, or virtues adjoined to it, are many and varied.[188] Among these, the virtue of religion is chief. We have noted that justice extends beyond humans, for people have the natural obligation to honor God above all things, and to direct all things to him. Perfect justice therefore commands all the moral virtues through religion by ordering them to their final end, which is the honor of God.[189] It is true that a person can never, on his own power, render to God all that is his due.[190] Nevertheless, the chief value of a virtue is derived from the good will that it engenders, not upon its effects per se.[191] Hence, the virtue of religion clarifies what it means for the will to be perfected.[192] For Aquinas, "virtue and rectitude of the human will consist chiefly in conformity with God's will and obedience to His command."[193] Obedience, for Aquinas, is not blind, ignorant, and infantile. Truly human obedience is formed by one's knowledge and understanding of the good. Religion, then, perfects the highest power of a person—the will in union with the intellect—by directing the person to his proper and highest end, namely, the one true God known by reason (whether enlightened by faith or

185. *ST* II-II, q. 120, a. 1.

186. Ibid., ad 1.

187. Ibid.

188. See *ST* II-II, q. 80, aa. 1–2.

189. *ST* II-II, q. 81, a. 1, ad 1 and a. 4, ad 1.

190. *ST* II-II, a. 80, a. 1.

191. *ST* II-II, q. 81, a. 6, ad 1.

192. For an excellent account, see Robert Jared Staudt, "Religion as a Virtue: Thomas Aquinas on Worship through Justice, Law, and Charity" (STD diss., Ave Maria University, 2008).

193. *ST* II-II, q. 104, a. 4, ad 2.

not). By doing so, religion perfects the individual as a whole by leading the parts of the person to participate in right reason.

The will is not a ghost in a machine. As an intrinsic principle of motion embedded within the reality of the entire person, "Will is that whereby the soul uses itself and any of its powers that can be subject to reason's command. And the will alone, among the powers, is able to *use* itself—having its own use in its power."[194] In a human act, only the agent's will can efficiently move habit-bearing powers and thereby lead them to obey reason's command.[195] By fully voluntary habits, the will's influence over the other powers increases through time, extending reason's command and imparting a character that is attributable to the person as a whole: "the effects echo through the whole person," Decosimo observes.[196] The right-ordering of the will thus contributes to the perfection of all the powers that it employs. When the will is habituated to choose all things for the highest end through the virtue of religion, the entire person is perfected along with it. The virtue of religion therefore excels the moral virtues because acts of religion more directly and immediately order things to the one true God.[197] With the formation of charity, acquired justice is able to reach its natural end and to direct those natural ends to the supernatural end of beatitude. Only the infused virtue of justice, however, directly aims to render others their due as understood in the light of faith and as measured by a supernatural rule.

## FORTITUDE AND RELATED VIRTUES

Turning to the perfections of the lower appetites, we notice two basic kinds of movements. At times, an object is perceived as good to the senses simply because it garners pleasure. Pleasures call forth

194. Decosimo, *Ethics as a Work of Charity*, 95.
195. See ibid., 85.
196. Ibid.
197. *ST* II-II, q. 81, a. 6.

one's "concupiscible" or "desiring" appetite for simple sensory delight.[198] Other objects seem good because they are a means by which one can freely enjoy sensory delight or some other good. These call forth one's "irascible" or "aggressive" appetite, whose proper object is the difficult good.[199] The aggressive appetite acts to obtain victory over what is opposed to the agent. It is a sort of "fighter" that is moved on behalf of the desiring appetite for the sake of a good difficult to acquire. For example, when an animal is hungry or in heat, it will fight for the pleasures of food or intercourse.[200] Corresponding to the twofold division in the lower appetite, there are two sorts of virtues that perfect those lower powers: virtues of temperance are habitual excellences of one's desire for pleasures, whereas virtues of fortitude are habitual excellences of one's desire to combat dangers and achieve the difficult good.[201] I turn now to examine these virtues in turn.

Lower than prudence and justice, fortitude moderates the irascible, aggressive appetite, so that a person may pursue the good even in the face of difficulty. Accordingly, the object of the irascible appetite is the sensible good or evil apprehended as difficult to obtain or avoid.[202] The appetite can relate to its objects with a passion in five ways: (1) tending toward the difficult good object through *hope*; (2) turning away from the difficult good object through *despair* of reaching it; (3) avoiding the difficult evil through *fear* of its harm; (4) attempting to evade being subject to the arduous evil through *audacity* or daring; (5) attacking a present hurtful evil through *anger*.[203] The list above indicates the passions' order of generation, such that anger is the final effect of the series of passions.[204] The irascible

198. *Sent. De anima*, lib. 3, l. 14, n. 10.

199. *Sent. De anima*, lib. 3, l. 14, n. 11.

200. Ibid.

201. See *ST* I-II, q. 60, aa. 4–5; q. 61, aa. 2–3.

202. *ST* I-II, q. 23, a. 2; q. 25, a. 3, ad 3.

203. For the first four, see *ST* I-II, q. 23, a. 2; qq. 40–45; for anger, see *ST* I-II, q. 23, a. 3; qq. 46–48.

204. *ST* I-II, q. 25, a. 3.

appetite takes its name from anger, *ira*, because the passion of anger is more manifest the passions that precede it.[205] Nevertheless, it is not fortitude that moderates an ill-temper, but temperance through meekness.[206] Instead of reducing one's forceful energy, the virtue of fortitude channels it and directs it toward a fitting end.

Fortitude's proper role is to "firmly preserve the will in the good of reason against the greatest evil" by regulating one's fears, lest one turn away from what reason dictates.[207] Philosophical analysis and neuroscientific explanations help to clarify the causes and nature of fear. Neurological studies suggest that the amygdala is central to feelings of fear.[208] But no portion of the body is solely dedicated to feelings of fear.[209] Fear involves brain activity in response to a perceived threat that makes the heart pound and the palms sweat, and which boosts adrenaline, engaging the nervous system and preparing a person to fight, freeze, or flee. These material causes point to the deeper formal cause: fear is the emotion of avoidance toward a severe impending evil that one cannot overcome.[210] Fear may be thus distinguished from similar behaviors: "being startled" is an immediate avoidance toward a present but slight evil, and "dread" could mean despairing of overcoming an impending and severe evil. Fear, especially the fear of death, combined with the desire of self-preservation, tends to make a person flee difficult goods. One's imagination is engaged in fear, for "fear may be defined as a pain or disturbance due to imagining some destructive or painful evil in the

205. Ibid., ad 1.

206. *ST* II-II, q. 157, a. 1, ad 3.

207. *ST* II-II, q. 123, a. 4. See also *ST* I-II, q. 62, a. 2. One of the best contemporary books on fortitude in print is Titus, *Resilience and the Virtue of Fortitude*.

208. Roger Marek et al., "The Amygdala and Medial Prefrontal Cortex: Partners in the Fear Circuit," *The Journal of Physiology* 591, no. 10 (May 15, 2013): 2381–91. The following example parallels an example in Eysenck and Keane, *Cognitive Psychology*, 21–22.

209. Many different parts of the brain are activated during a single activity or behavior, indicating that "fear" is not located in the amygdala alone. Jane Neumann et al., "Meta-Analysis of Functional Imaging Data Using Replicator Dynamics," *Human Brain Mapping* 25, no. 1 (May 1, 2005): 165–73.

210. See *ST* I-II, q. 41, a. 2.

future [that is near at hand]."[211] Memory is characteristically a factor as well, for those who have suffered, or remember evils suffered, often fear that something similar will happen again. Reason, however, does not always play a role in one's fears, which can be baseless, irrational, exaggerated, or otherwise disengaged from good judgment.[212] When fear begins to rule a person's life, pathologies (including various phobias) may be at work. Faced with daily dangers and one's own vulnerability, a person therefore needs the habitual interior strength to combat evils or to endure them in a reasonable way; he needs the virtue of fortitude.[213]

Choleric temperaments are more apt to erupt into passions of hope, daring, and, of course, anger; persons with greater physical power and skill can be more confident when faced with physical dangers; the foolish can be brash because of their ignorance of danger; but the virtue of fortitude cannot reduced to any of these tendencies. Fortitude exists within every virtuous person who habitually moderates his irascible appetite according to reason, and whose mind is habitually strengthened against any disordered passions whatsoever.[214] The two acts of fortitude are, in the translation of Craig Steven Titus, initiative-taking (*aggredi*) and endurance (*sustinere*).[215] The principal act is *sustinere*, to endure, which Aquinas argues is more excellent than taking initiative insofar as a person experiences more difficulties in enduring evil over time than in quickly attacking an onslaught

211. Aristotle, *Rhetoric* II.5, 1382a22; quoted in *ST* I-II, q. 42, a. 2.

212. Here, clinical applications of the polyvagal theory appear promising. Central to this therapy are exercises that calm the autonomic nervous system help a person feel safe. Only an experience of safety can open a person to therapeutic intervention by quelling estimations that cause fear and anxiety. See especially Bessel van der Kolk, "Safety and Reciprocity: Polyvagal Theory as a Framework for Understanding and Treating Developmental Trauma," and Pat Ogden, "Polyvagal Theory and Sensorimotor Psychotherapy," in *Clinical Applications of the Polyvagal Theory*, ed. Stephen W. Porges and Deb Dana (London: W. W. Norton and Company, 2018), 27–33 and 34–49 respectively.

213. *ST* II-II, q. 123, a. 6. See Rebecca Konyndyk De Young, "Power Made Perfect in Weakness: Aquinas's Transformation of the Virtue of Courage," *Medieval Philosophy and Theology* 11, no. 2 (September 2003): 147–80.

214. *ST* I-II, q. 61, a. 3.

215. *ST* II-II, q. 123, a. 6. See Titus, *Resilience and the Virtue of Fortitude*, 147.

of evil.[216] We should note that endurance in this sense is not a passive lack of action seen in the sluggish who refuse to expend energy to survive or thrive, nor is it the mask of niceness worn by weak personalities who resentfully remain silent when they are insulted. Virtuous endurance, rather, is the soul's firm adherence to the good, clinging so strongly that it remains unswayed by bodily passion in its fixed attachment to what reason apprehends and the will desires.[217] The psychological strengths of resilience and grit are closely tied to the virtue of fortitude.[218] Virtuous endurance can be called bravery in enduring the weaknesses of one's own flesh when in the presence of evil.[219] As for the initiative-taking, it employs the energy supplied by the passion of anger, but it bears none of the negative moral overtones of the term "aggression." In contemporary speech, an aggressive person characteristically is belligerent and overbearing, immoderately giving free play to his inclination to attack others. Contrastingly, a person with the virtue of fortitude powerfully takes initiative *according to the judgment of right reason,* in union with prudence and justice. If courage calls for moderate anger on the battlefield or in some combat, a virtuous person deploys that explosive passion in order to more quickly and powerfully accomplish the good end.[220]

As a rationally directed movement of a passion, the act of courage possesses three distinct levels of intention: an external goal, an internal goal, and a "countergoal," an objectionable result.[221] The ob-

216. *ST* II-II, q. 123, a. 6, ad 1.

217. Ibid., ad 2.

218. See Titus, *Resilience and the Virtue of Fortitude,* esp. chaps. 4–6, and Angela Duckworth, *Grit: The Power of Passion and Perseverance* (New York: Scribner, 2016).

219. *ST* II-II, q. 123, a. 1, ad 1. Psychological "exposure therapy" facilitates the exercise of fortitude by having a patient engage with a feared but benign stimulus. Through exposure, the patient gradually develops desensitization toward the object, altering his estimation of its danger and enabling a more rational response. See Kristen G. Benito and Michael Walther, "Therapeutic Process during Exposure: Habituation Model," *Journal of Obsessive-Compulsive and Related Disorders* 6 (July 1, 2015): 147–57. See also J. S. Abramowitz et al., *Exposure Therapy for Anxiety: Principles and Practice,* 2nd ed. (New York: Guilford Press, 2019).

220. *ST* II-II, q. 123, a. 10.

221. This threefold analysis comes from Patrick Clark, *Perfection in Death: The Christological Dimension of Courage in Aquinas* (Washington, D.C.: The Catholic University of

ject of the external goal is some change in circumstances, or at least one's own behavioral response to fear. The object of an internal goal consists in "the axiological quality" of one's behavior, that is, one's maintenance of reason despite present fears.[222] The objectionable result regards the cost of one's courage, for all acts of courage necessarily involve suffering and sacrificing some good in the course of pursuing a higher good: taking initiative includes sacrificing the pleasure of the status quo, and endurance means not fully enjoying whatever good that is precluded by a present evil. However, to the degree that a person's health and character is excellent, he will in turn sense the pain embedded in courageous acts—for a person naturally enjoys the goods of life, and a virtuous person especially finds life worth living.[223] Consequently, "the very excellence of character that makes courage possible is also what make it painful."[224] Instead of dampening the ardor of bravery, the presence of difficulty could increase it, because the courageous person chooses excellence of the soul over more mundane goods. The quasi-virtue of confidence is one's sure hope in initiating great and honorable undertakings. It prepares one for magnificence, which pertains to giving away great expenses, and magnanimity, which pertains to performing great deeds.[225] When magnanimity and magnificence are restricted to the proper matter of fortitude, namely, dangers of death, they will be quasi-integral to the virtue—as when English recusant Catholics supported the church even though their generosity made them targets of state-sanctioned persecution. When magnificence and magnanimity regard a matter that is not an issue of life or death, they exist as virtues specifically distinct from fortitude but joined to it. In sum, acts of fortitude re-

America Press, 2015), 166–68; he depends on Lee Yearley's formulation in *Mencius and Aquinas: Theories of Virtue and Conceptions of Courage* (Albany: State University of New York Press, 1990), 113–18.

222. Clark, *Perfection in Death*, 167.

223. See *Nicomachean Ethics* III.9, 1117b11–13.

224. Clark, *Perfection in Death*, 167. See *Nicomachean Ethics* III.9, 1117b14–16.

225. On magnificence, see *ST* II-II, q. 134; on magnanimity and confidence, see *ST* II-II, q. 129, a. 6.

quire that a person pay a price for his virtue. At the same time, virtue is, in a way, its own reward. A person with advanced virtue can experience spiritual joys even while he suffers in his passions—as did Christ on the cross.[226]

The scope of fortitude extends to nearly all walks in life, for one encounters obstacles to right habituation at every turn: martial courage is necessary on the battlefield, intellectual courage in the classroom, political courage among legislators, and so on.[227] Here we may recall Aristotle's vivid example of how a single virtuous act can affect a group pattern: "a rout in battle [can be] stopped by first one man making a stand, and then another, until the original formation has been restored."[228] The rout begins with a single act of courage; others follow him; in time, these brave acts, lauded and rewarded after the battle, and later remembered in song and history, can develop into personal and communitarian habits that characterize a society and become incorporated into its overall virtue-culture. In a culture immersed in lies, one needs courage to speak the truth; in a culture of death, one needs courage to support life; in a culture of irreligion, one needs courage to worship the one true God. Fortitude is necessary for all the virtues, for it helps a person and his community to develop and practice good habits despite any evil whatsoever.

In order to be perfect, the acquired habit of fortitude needs to be formed by the infused virtue of charity so that one's endurance and initiative can reach their natural ends and be directed to their supreme ultimate end. The infused virtue of fortitude measures one's good in light of faith as formed by charity; it enables a person to perform courageous acts for the sake of supernatural goods. The Holy Spirit's Gift of fortitude makes a person endure evils in a Christ-like way, so that all fear is expelled from his mind and he experiences confidence in all matters even in the face of martyrdom.[229]

226. *ST* III, q. 46, a. 8.

227. See Richard Avramenko, *Courage: The Politics of Life and Limb* (Notre Dame, Ind.: University of Notre Dame Press, 2011).

228. *Posterior Analytics* II.19, 100a11.

229. *ST* II-II, q. 139, a. 1, co. and ad 1. See Clark, *Perfection in Death*, 181–244.

## TEMPERANCE AND RELATED VIRTUES

On account of its importance in correcting predominant vices of the day, and on account of renewed scholarly interest, temperance can rightly be called "a virtue for our time."[230] Considered objectively, temperance may be accounted as the lowest of the moral virtues because it moderates the concupiscible-sensory appetite, which is the most material of the internal powers.[231] The concupiscible appetite relates to reality in six ways:[232] (1) apprehending an object as good for oneself with the passion of *love*; (2) drawing near to the beloved but absent object with *desire*; (3) finding repose in the present beloved object with sensory *pleasure* or *joy*. Each of these positive passions is opposed by negative shadow passions: (4) apprehending an object as evil for oneself with *hatred*; (5) tending away from an absent evil with *avoidance* or *aversion*; (6) feeling the pain of a present evil with *sorrow*. Love is the fundamental and first movement a person experiences, so one can say that every virtue is a moderation of love in some way.[233] The particular object of temperance is the effect of sensory love, that is, sensory pleasures, particularly pleasures of touch.

Pleasure is good and natural, Aquinas insists, for no one can live without some sensible and bodily pleasure.[234] Nevertheless, pleasure should not be sought for its own sake; it should rather be experienced as "the enjoyment of the good," a well-ordered fruition consequent on a virtuous act.[235] In other words, God created us to find pleasure in doing good, so that we might be more firmly attached to

230. See Austin's superb study, "Thomas Aquinas on the Four Causes of Temperance," chap. 1.1.

231. *ST* II-II, q. 141, a. 4.

232. For a summary, see *ST* I-II, q. 25, aa. 1–2; these are treated individually in *ST* I-II, qq. 26–39.

233. See *ST* I-II, q. 23, a. 4.

234. *ST* I-II, q. 34, a. 1.

235. *ST* I-II, q. 25, a. 2; q. 34, a. 2, ad 2. See Kevin White, "Pleasure, A Supervenient End," in *Aquinas and the Nicomachean Ethics*, ed. Tobias Hoffmann et al. (New York: Cambridge University Press, 2013), 220–38.

the good on every level of our being. Consequently, humans naturally desire pleasures that are fitting to them and are ordered to virtue.[236] Because we are rational animals, the pleasures that befit us are those that exist in accordance with reason, that is, pleasures that are not contrary to natural inclinations or obstacles to them, but befit the habitual dispositions that flow from our specific nature.[237] On account of our individual nature, with our unique inclinations, strengths, and weaknesses, different people find pleasure in different things. Each temperament modifies one's passions with respect to both their objects and their function. It directs the passions toward objects that are particularly suitable for oneself. This in turn affects the functioning of the passions, because when one recognizes that an object is particularly good for oneself, one naturally takes pleasure in that thing more than in others.[238] For example, a melancholic person typically desires physical pleasures to ward off sadness, whereas a sanguine person might desire intellectual pleasures to develop thoughtfulness. But because habituation to pleasure can go awry, the virtue of temperance is needed to moderate one's desire for pleasing objects.[239] In sum, "the temperate man does not flee from all pleasures, but only those that are immoderate and not in accord with reason."[240]

Given Thomas's positive account of pleasure, it might seem as if temperance primarily regards learning how to find pleasure in the right objects, namely, those in accord with reason. However, the Angelic Doctor does not depict temperance as the virtue of enjoying life well.[241] He argues that temperance operates primarily through moderation, retraction, or restraint.[242] In fact, one definition of temper-

236. *ST* I-II, q. 141, a. 1, ad 1.

237. Ibid.

238. See *Sent. Ethic.*, lib. 3, l. 20, n. 9, and lib. 7, l. 5, n. 2.

239. *ST* I-II, q. 34, a. 2.

240. *ST* I-II, q. 34, a. 1, ad 2.

241. The following exposition relies heavily on Austin, "Thomas Aquinas on the Four Causes of Temperance," chap. 2.4.

242. See, respectively, *ST* II-II, q. 141, a. 7; *De virtutibus*, q. 1, a. 12, co.; *ST* II-II, q. 57, a. 3.

ance reads, "a certain disposition of the soul that imposes a measure [*modum*] on any passions or operations, lest they be carried beyond the due."[243] Hence, in an extended sense, "any virtue that curbs [*cohibet*] and quiets [*deprimit*] the passions is called 'temperance.'"[244] Thomas thus argues that temperance has a primarily negative function. This is no crypto-Manichean position; there is no hatred for the body or bodily goods here. In the next chapter I will discuss how original and personal sin tend to subordinate reason to the passions and thereby incline an individual to seek pleasure unduly. Below, I will explain how pleasure and positive experiences have certain addictive qualities, demanding a virtuous moderation for the sake of freeing us to acquire any good habits, and for our overall well-being.

Everyone, especially the young, craves pleasure. Thomas notes that "the desire for pleasure is insatiable. Indeed, because pleasure as such is desirable, the more pleasure is tasted, the more it is desired."[245] Pleasure, we may recall, is the enjoyable effect of reaching a desired good. Habituation undoubtedly shapes our attraction to different things, and makes certain objects feel connatural and pleasurable for us. Ordinarily, feeling pleasure as a reward and fruition of one's choice increases one's craving for an object. But the pleasure-reward cycle can fail. Every created object of desire is good only in some respect, which means that we can consider it under the aspect of its imperfection. It is fairly common for us to experience a good (or at least a disordered good) as repulsive once we obtain it after some difficulty—as when a thief comes to hate the jewels he took such pains to steal. Therefore, we can tire of created goods and feel intellectual disgust even while sensory pleasure is present.

The addiction research of Kent Berridge indicates that one should distinguish among: (1) wanting as "a cognitive desire with a declarative goal," which in Aquinas's language is a movement of the intellectual appetite; and (2) "incentive salience 'wanting,'" which is

243. *ST* I-II, q. 61, a. 4.
244. *ST* I-II, q. 61, a. 3.
245. *Sent. Ethic.*, lib. 3, l. 22, n. 12.

"triggered in pulses by reward-related cues or by vivid imagery about the reward," and therefore remains on the level of the sensory appetite.[246] Berridge confirms that the second kind of "wanting" can coexist with a certain kind of *dislike* of the object. Heroin addicts often come to feel disgust with injecting the drug, even while performing this behavior. Thus, Berridge concludes, "Addicts weren't people who happened to *like* the drugs they were taking—they were people who *wanted* those drugs very badly even while they grew to dislike them for destroying their lives."[247] In this case, "dislike" indicates experiencing some lack of pleasure in a thing that one nevertheless pursues. The bifurcation between "wanting" and "liking" occurs not only for concrete things such as drugs. It also exists for behaviors, which is why psychological research now recognizes "behavioral addictions." Adam Alter reports: "A number of current and former behavior addicts," for example, those with extreme gambling or video game addictions, "told me the same thing: that consummating their addictions is always bittersweet. It is impossible to forget that they're compromising their well-being even as they enjoy that first rush of gratification."[248] Aquinas's conclusion seems to be upheld: people come to be addicted to pleasure itself, the emotional gratification, and not so much the object.

Considering the development of our desiring appetite, Aquinas astutely notes that people are habituated toward pleasure early in life: "Pleasure itself is fostered within all people from childhood, for a newborn delights in milk."[249] Moderate, health-promoting pleasures do not lead to addiction.[250] Children do not become addicted to nurs-

246. Kent C. Berridge and Terry E. Robinson, "Liking, Wanting, and the Incentive-Sensitization Theory of Addiction," *American Psychologist* 71, no. 8 (2016): 670–79, at 671.

247. Quoted in Adam Alter, *Irresistible: The Rise of Addictive Technology and the Business of Keeping Us Hooked* (New York: Penguin Press, 2017), 87.

248. Alter, *Irresistible*, 80.

249. *Sent. Ethic.*, lib. 2, l. 3, n. 12. Actually, as we saw above, epigenetic studies indicate that children can become habituated to food preferences in the womb on account of their mother's food choices.

250. See Alter, *Irresistible*, 73–79.

ing or to milk any more than healthy adults are addicted to breathing or eating. Rather, an addiction arises on account of a disordered emotional attachment to a particular physical pleasure: "the substance or behavior itself isn't addictive until we learn to use it as a salve for our psychological troubles."[251] The difficulty, in Aquinas's view, is that we often indulge our desire for comfort, even if we are motivated by good reasons such as nourishment. We therefore develop, early on, a deeply-rooted disposition to pursue pleasure at the whim of our appetites. Consequently, "it is difficult for a person to rule this passion [for pleasure] acquired with life, for it starts in man at the beginning of life."[252] In other words, we are all more or less prone to addiction because we are typically habituated to intemperance. Nonscholastic psychologists seem to echo Aquinas's basic understanding of the concupiscible appetite by arguing that "addiction is a sort of misguided love. It's love with the obsession but not the emotional support."[253] Aquinas would add that such love is disordered insofar as it remains without the guidance of right reason. When sensory love is habitually misdirected toward a particular harmful object, when it is not tempered by prudence, and when a person does not courageously endure the sting of hardship, addiction is formed.[254] Addiction can be characterized as an extreme form of habitual intemperance.

There is another reason why youths greatly desire pleasure: they suffer "disturbances of spirits and humors," that is, they experience growing pains.[255] These pains may be physiological, psychological, or some mixture of the two. When a person is in pain, he will ordinarily seek pleasure as a relief. Thus, while undergoing the labor of maturation, the young "above all live according to concupiscence, for they desire pleasure above all."[256] It follows that "if a child and

251. Ibid., 73.

252. *Sent. Ethic.*, lib. 2, l. 3, n. 12.

253. Alter, *Irresistible*, 75.

254. See Helen Fisher, "Love is Like Cocaine," *Nautilus* (February 4, 2016), available at nautil.us/issue/33/attraction/love-is-like-cocaine.

255. *Sent. Ethic.*, lib. 7, l. 14, n. 16.

256. *Sent. Ethic.*, lib. 3, l. 22, n. 11.

[his] concupiscence are not adequately influenced by reason, they come to rule and increase so that the appetite for pleasure, that is, concupiscence, will be master."[257] A disordered attachment to pleasure leads them down a vicious downward spiral, in which a person becomes so habituated to pursuing pleasure that his reason is impeded, making it simultaneously easier for him to pursue pleasure and more difficult for him to act reasonably.[258] Empirical studies confirm that addiction occurs more frequently in the young (teens to early twenties).[259] Factors include insufficient brain development and being ruled by the appetite for pleasure. "Children are especially vulnerable to addiction," Alter argues, "because they lack the self-control that prevents many adults from developing addictive habits."[260] Thomas acknowledges that in principle people can sin with regard to pleasure either by an excessive attachment to it or by an insensible disregard for it. In practice, most people from childhood forward tend to love pleasure too much rather than too little. Consequently, temperance is more a matter of curbing and restraining one's desire for gratification rather than searching for the right object in which to find pleasure—a pleasure-treasure hunt could easily lead to addiction. However, if we acquire temperance, our capacity for enjoying higher goods is immeasurably expanded.

Temperance is the beautiful virtue that renders us truly beautiful.[261] Its attractiveness revealed in its "integral parts." First, the virtue *verecundia* turns away from disgraceful and immodest things,

257. Ibid.

258. See *Sent. Ethic.*, lib. 3, l. 22, n. 12.

259. See Nicole L. Schramm-Sapyta et al., "Are Adolescents More Vulnerable to Drug Addiction than Adults? Evidence from Animal Models," *Psychopharmacology* 206, no. 1 (September 2009): 1–21.

260. Alter, *Irresistible*, 240.

261. See *ST* II-II, q. 145, a. 2. This point is emphasized by many contemporary authors. See Pieper, *The Four Cardinal Virtues*, 203; Shawn Floyd, "Aquinas on Temperance," *The Modern Schoolman* 77, no. 1 (1999): 35–48; Giuseppe Butera, "On Reason's Control of the Passions in Aquinas's Theory of Temperance," *Mediaeval Studies* 68 (2006): 133–60; and Lucy Smith, "Temperance and the Modern Temper: Aristotle and Aquinas Revisited," in *Temperance Revisited: A Call for Restraint in Contemporary Australia*, ed. Phillip Elias (Sydney: Warrange College, 2009), 65–79 and 81–83.

both revealing and engendering beauty in its possessor—as the blush of a modest woman is a visible blossom of her interior resplendence.[262] We may call this habitual reaction "healthy shame,"[263] in contrast to negative forms of shame that crush a person's confidence. Considered positively, shame is a praiseworthy habitual passion whereby a person without perfect virtue recoils from evil deeds—specifically from the disgrace that accrues to deeds contrary to temperance.[264] Healthy shame therefore disposes a person to be temperate and lays the first foundation of the virtue.[265] The second integral part of temperance is *honestas*. Thomas Ryan notes that *honestas* is often rendered as "honor," but in Aquinas's view honor is properly earned; a person who has *honestas* is worthy of receiving honor and respect from others.[266] In this way, *honestas* is the same thing as virtue, for it denotes one's acquired moral excellence that deserves to be recognized as such.[267] In itself, virtue or moral excellence is spiritually beautiful, for "spiritual beauty consists in a man's way of life or action being well proportioned to the spiritual clarity of reason."[268] Consequently, the winsome beauty of *honestas* is an integral part of temperance, for it draws a person to desire virtue for himself and to avoid the ugliness of bestial lust.[269]

Seen in its widest scope, the desiring appetite aims at receiving whatever is capable of preserving a thing's nature.[270] By regulat-

262. *ST* II-II, q. 144, a. 2.

263. See Markus van Alphen, "Shame as a Functional and Adaptive Emotion: A Biopsychological Perspective," and Thomas Ryan, "The Positive Function of Shame: Moral and Spiritual Perspectives," in *The Value of Shame: Exploring a Health Resource in Cultural Contexts*, ed. Elisabeth Vanderheiden and Claude-Hélène Mayer (New York: Springer International, 2017), 61–86 and 87–108 respectively. See also Thomas Ryan, "Aquinas on Shame: A Contemporary Interchange," in *Aquinas, Education and the East: Sophia Studies in Cross-cultural Philosophy of Traditions and Cultures*, ed. T. Mooney and M. Nowacki (Dordrecht: Springer Science and Business Media, 2013), 4:73–101.

264. See *ST* II-II, q. 143, a. 1.

265. *ST* II-II, q. 144, a. 4, ad 4.

266. Ryan, "Aquinas on Shame: A Contemporary Interchange," 85.

267. *ST* II-II, q. 145, a. 1.

268. Ibid., a. 2.

269. Ibid., a. 4.

270. *De veritate*, q. 25, a. 2.

ing one's desire for pleasure according to right reason, temperance facilitates fruition in a good act and thereby aids the development of every other good habit. The restraints of temperance help us achieve goods that are higher than temporary sensory delights. In this way, temperance is intertwined with every virtue, for "pleasure is the principal end of all the moral virtues. For what is required in all moral virtues is that a person delights and sorrows in the right things."[271] In effect, temperance modulates one's sensory appetite through a higher desire, namely, the desire for a right relationship to oneself, others, God, and even creation.[272] Politeness, for instance, teaches people to cough away from others, to maintain an upright posture, to eat in a measured way, and so on. Even as one of the "lesser" virtues associated with modesty and temperance, etiquette is a matter of controlling one's natural, conditionable, reflexes in order to preserve an atmosphere of rational dignity within the context of one's culture.[273] Together, temperance and the other virtues help prepare humans for the delights to which their nature inclines them: the contemplation of the highest truth, namely, God.[274] With the infused virtue of temperance, one moderates one's sensory appetite through a rule measured by faith and the supernatural good, as I will discuss in more detail in a later chapter. Through formation in charity, one's temperance is able to be free from defects and to moderate one's appetites directly for the sake of union with Christ. In sum, the virtues in their fullest development organically grow together and mutually support each other. Unfortunately, the perfecting work of human virtues often fails, and humans then experience the devastating effects of nature gone awry. The following chapter explores dysfunctions of human flourishing in detail, that is, negative acquired habits on the physical, psychological, and volitional levels.

271. *Sent. Ethic.*, lib. 2, l. 3, n. 3.
272. See Austin, "Thomas Aquinas on the Four Causes of Temperance," 323.
273. See *ST* II-II, q. 168, a. 1.
274. See *Sent. Ethic.*, lib. 7, l. 13, n. 14.

# 6

## Negative Habits and Vices

Aaron Kushner was only fourteen when he died from the premature aging disease progeria. In response to this tragic situation, his father wrote a book that touched millions, *Why Do Bad Things Happen to Good People?* Rabbi Harold Kushner's answer to his own question led to some controversy, as he seemed to undermine God's omnipotence with respect to evil.[1] Here, considering tragedies created by humans, I would like to ask: *Why do good people happen to do bad things?*

Most people recognize that nature's good inclinations and people's good desires are insufficient to ward away wickedness. Some might be surprised to hear that a the prime source of vicious behavior is a bad habit. In contemporary English, the notion of "bad habits" conjures up ideas of compulsions toward negative but superficially benign behaviors such as biting one's nails, wasting time on Facebook, or rudeness toward colleagues. These do not seem to cause murder, grand theft, and other great evils. Instead, biology or environment are proposed as root causes of truly evil actions. A closer look at the issue shows that the idea of bad habits somehow encapsulates every disposition and inclination toward evil, whether

1. See Rabbi Yitzchok Kirzner and Yonason Rosenblum, *Making Sense of Suffering: A Jewish Approach* (Rahway, N.J.: Mesorah Publications, 2002), 18–22.

great or small, on a sliding scale of voluntariness. Such habits are influenced by biological dysfunction and environmental harms along with disordered free choice.

This chapter begins by considering the nature of evil in general. After this, I analyze—in successive sections—influences on negative habits, including physical dysfunction, biological factors, environmental-biological factors, and original sin. In a later section, I treat acquired negative dispositions, that is, vice. Then I discuss how acquired vice is, in a meaningful way, voluntary. I then address how good intentions relate to bad habits. Finally, I lay out Aquinas's understanding of the steps that lead to a downward spiral of evil.

## DEFINING AND DESCRIBING EVIL FOR HUMANS

In order to understand where habit goes wrong, we must first understand what "wrong" means in a human context. From a Thomistic perspective, this means considering defining evil and then describing its basic features.

Sam Harris compares evil to the good of well-being. He argues that scientific terms are more adequate than those of theology for understanding good and evil, because science concerns "facts" about thoughts and behaviors.[2] Harris admits to professing a version of "moral realism" and "consequentialism" when it comes to good and evil, saying, "Moral view A is truer than moral view B if A entails a more accurate understanding of the connections between human thoughts/intentions/behavior and human well-being."[3] Fair enough. But where may we find an adequate understanding of well-being in relation to evil? Herbert McCabe helps:

2. Sam Harris, *The Moral Landscape: How Science Can Determine Human Values* (New York: Free Press, 2010), 62.

3. Ibid., 65.

> Since evil is a deprivation of good, in order to understand what an evil is we need to know of what good it is the deprivation; and this means that we must know the nature of the thing that is said to be evil. From this it follows that whatever is evil must at least have a nature; it must have its essence, even if all its properties are lacking to it.[4]

Evil for human acts—like all evil—is measured by what Colleen McCluskey calls "metaphysical goodness."[5] But moral goodness and flourishing ultimately comes from God and is measured by its relation to the goodness of one's natural form. Therefore, evil is the contrary to natural and supernatural goodness.

Evil in itself is contrary to good as darkness is contrary to light, and bitter to sweet.[6] From a metaphysical perspective, Aquinas says, "the term 'good' signifies perfect being" from the perspective of a substance's nature, "whereas the term 'evil' is nothing other than the privation of perfect being."[7] Not all privation is evil, however. At this moment, I am not wearing boots. But there is nothing wrong with having bootless feet. This sort of privation is one of *mere absence*. One could endlessly multiply examples of mere absences: raindrops are not purple, rocks cannot photosynthesize, plants cannot talk, and so on. These are simple states of affairs (or non-affairs as it were). There is another sort of privation, namely, the privation of something that should be naturally possessed at a natural *time*, and in a natural *way*.[8] This privation is a definite lack, as in a dog's sightlessness.[9] Mere absence is featureless, a pure negation.[10] But a definite lack is evil: a deficiency entails lacking a perfection a thing

4. Herbert McCabe, *God and Evil: In the Theology of St Thomas Aquinas*, ed. Brian Davies (London: Bloomsbury Academic, 2010), 66.

5. Colleen McCluskey, *Thomas Aquinas on Moral Wrongdoing* (Cambridge: Cambridge University Press, 2017), 36.

6. See *ST* I, q. 48, a. 1; *Compendium theologiae*, c. 116; *De malo*, q. 1, a. 1: "malum simpliciter."

7. *Compendium theologiae*, c. 114.

8. See ibid., c. 114: "Privatio proprie accepta, est eius quod natum est, et quando natum est, et quomodo natum est haberi."

9. *Sent. Meta.*, lib. 10, l. 6, n. 8. See Aristotle, *Metaphysics* X.4, 1055a32.

10. See *ST* I, q. 48, a. 5, ad 1.

should naturally have. In Charles Journet's formulation, evil is "the privation of some good which should be present."[11]

Evil manifestly is not a *thing* contrary to the good. It has no being, no nature, no form, no quality in itself: it is the absence of form that presupposes a subject.[12] As a privation, evil in itself has no per se causal power. It has no efficient causality: "No dynamic force emanates from it, no power of action, since all special qualities, dynamic forces, and powers of action, are different forms of the expansion of the being itself."[13] Nor is evil a formal cause: "Formal causality consists in the form giving itself, communicating itself to another being to complete that other being, to perfect it," as when a sculptor shapes bronze, giving it the form of a statue that he had first in his imagination.[14] Evil entails a subtraction, not an addition: properly speaking, evil's corruption of a thing is not the communication of a form but a privation or corruption of one.[15] Neither is evil a material cause in any way, for matter is a positive principle enacted by form, whereas evil is a privation and not a principle from which something comes to be.[16] Finally, evil is not a final cause. As noted, something exerts final causality on another through attraction: it draws actual things to their completion and potential things into being. Attraction occurs because goodness has the *ratio* of an "end" and is pleasing in itself.[17] Thus, as the contrary of good, evil is repulsive in itself and it corrupts what is good.[18]

Evil corrupts in two ways: through non-action or through accidental change. In the first case, something that is evil in itself (evil

11. Charles Journet, *The Meaning of Evil*, trans. Michael Barry (London: Geoffrey Chapman, 1963), 28.

12. *Sent. Meta.*, lib. 10, l. 6, n. 16. See *De malo*, q. 1, a. 1; *ST* I, q. 5, a. 3, ad 2; q. 48, a. 1.

13. Paul Siwek, *The Philosophy of Evil* (New York: The Ronald Press, 1950), 107. See *De malo*, q. 1, a. 3; *ST* I, q. 49, a. 1.

14. Siwek, *The Philosophy of Evil*, 108.

15. *De malo*, q. 1, a. 1, ad 8.

16. Hence, Aquinas says that prime matter, though a nonbeing because of a privation of form, nevertheless "participates in some good" because it has a relation and an aptitude for goodness. See *ST* I, q. 5, a 2, ad 3.

17. *ST* I, q. 5, a. 2, ad 2.

18. See *De malo*, q. 1, a. 1.

*simpliciter*), brings about corruption in act and effect, not by acting but by a lack of action. Blindness prevents seeing. In the second case, what is not evil in itself—that is, something good—brings about an evil effect not *simpliciter* but by something else.[19] For example, the brain contributes to sin by storing harmful images that it has received. Evil therefore has a paradoxical character: "it both 'is' and 'is not.' It exists, not as a positive thing, but as a privation."[20] Evil is not a substance, but one can truly say that something is "really evil"—not because it has an extra quality of "evilness" added to it, but because it lacks a good that it ought to have.[21] A habit is a sort of form or quality existing in a subject as the subject's perfection (e.g., intelligence as an excellence of mind) leading to more perfect action. The ultimate cause of a thing's goodness is its form, which gives it being and therefore actual goodness. But evil is not a substantial form; in the "terrible reality of its privative existence," it is the privation of a due accidental form.[22] Evil is therefore in a subject as bad habit—or, more, precisely, an anti-habit, a the corruption or privation of what should naturally exist, leading to deformed character and evil action.[23]

Although for animals it may be otherwise, *all* evil for humans exists in one of two categories: *malum poenae* or *malum culpae*.[24] McCabe translates these concepts as "evil suffered" and "evil committed."[25] Alone, reason might not discover this distinction. Thomas derived it from divine revelation. He insists that "according to the teaching of the Catholic faith" when humans suffer evil, whether of

19. *De malo*, q. 1, a. 1, ad 8.

20. Journet, *The Meaning of Evil*, 46.

21. *De malo*, q. 1, a. 1, ad 20. See McCabe, *God and Evil*, 61–65.

22. Journet, *The Meaning of Evil*, 47.

23. See *De malo*, q. 1, a. 1, ad 2: "Bonum et malum proprie opponuntur ut privatio et habitus." For a defense of Aquinas against objections to his "privation theory," see McCluskey, *Thomas Aquinas on Moral Wrongdoing*, 45–51.

24. *De malo*, q. 1, a. 4, co. and ad 10. See *ST* I, q. 48, a. 6.

25. Herbert McCabe, *God Matters* (London: Continuum, 2005), 30–36. Brian Davies provides helpful expositions of these concepts in his *The Thought of Thomas Aquinas* (Oxford: Clarendon Press, 1992), 89–97, and *Thomas Aquinas's Summa Theologiae: A Guide and Commentary* (Oxford: Oxford University Press, 2014), 114–18.

the body or the soul that does not proceed from their will, "it must be called 'punishment' [*poena*]."[26] He goes on to say, "the Tradition of faith" teaches that rational creatures would not have been able to incur any harm "unless sin preceded it, either in the person or at least in [human] nature."[27] His argument is based on a series of scriptural texts: "The wages of sin are death"; God promised that he would punish Adam and Eve if they sinned by disobedience, "On whatever day you shall eat it you shall die the death"; this punishment affects all humans, who are their offspring, "By one man sin entered into this world, and by sin death"; consequently, "The body is dead because of sin."[28]

Augustine and Isidore provide authoritative interpretations: the first holds that death and other defects in this life come from the condemnation of sin; the second, "If man had not sinned, water would not have drowned him, nor fire burned him, nor any other similar harm come upon him."[29] In this light, Thomas says, "Without any doubt, it must be held by Catholic faith that death and all such defects of the present life are punishment for original sin."[30] He explains that the body, as material, will naturally disintegrate, but the soul is naturally immortal because it is rational.[31] Humans therefore possessed a "natural disposition" for organic nondisintegration and homeostatic maintenance, that is, "impassibility" and bodily immortality, which was completed by God's supernatural grace.[32] This grace was "original justice," which ordered the body to the soul, and the soul to God as the supreme ultimate end.[33] That gift was withdrawn justly by God only as a punishment for the orig-

26. *De malo*, q. 1, a. 4.

27. Ibid.

28. Rom 6:23, Gn 2:17, Rom 5:12, and Rom 8:10 (respectively). See *De malo*, q. 5, a. 4, s.c. 1–2; *ST* I, q. 97, a. 1, s.c.; I-II, q. 85, a. 5, s.c.

29. *De malo*, q. 5, a. 4, s.c. 2.

30. *De malo*, q. 5, a. 4.

31. See *De malo*, q. 5, a. 5.

32. Ibid.

33. See *ST* I, q. 97, a. 1.

inal sin of Adam and Eve.[34] Holding fast to the deep union of all persons with our "original parents," Aquinas concludes that all bodily defects, ills, and pains are consequences of the punishment they incurred. Hence, *malum poenae* is evil suffered as something that befalls the will from outside of the will, from the bodily and emotional part of man, and therefore is experienced *as punishment.* This is not to be understood as a arbitrary juridical decision applying some external law, but as the natural consequence of violating nature's order.

*Malum culpae,* "evil committed," is simpler at first. Committing evil means *doing* evil, that is, performing an act that is evil in some way. Contrasted with evil suffered, evil voluntarily committed *causes* moral fault.[35] By willingly doing evil, an agent causes himself to be deprived of a due good absolutely, for he chooses to act for a good that is not ordered to a due end.[36] No agent chooses evil in itself, but by seeking a disordered good one incurs an evil that he does not choose.[37] By eating the dessert that we want, we gain weight that we do not want. Here the center of the evil lies less in the suffering and more in the action itself, for by *doing* evil things a person becomes an evildoer; through a bad will an agent becomes a bad person.[38] Clearly evil committed opposes the good more directly than evil suffered, not least because evil acts develop evil habits.[39] Evil committed is contrary to the nature of God, who is goodness itself and the source of all goodness.[40] All creaturely goodness comes from him and continues to exist by participation in his goodness.[41] Evil committed results in a separation from God and from

34. See *ST* I-II, q. 85, a. 5.

35. See *De malo,* q. 1, a. 1, ad 4.

36. *De malo,* q. 5, a. 4. See *ST* I, q. 48, a. 5, and a. 6, ad 3.

37. *De malo,* q. 1, a. 4, ad 1 and ad 2.

38. *ST* I, q. 48, a. 5, ad 4. See also a. 6: "Ex bona voluntate, qua homo bene utitur rebus habitis, dicitur homo bonus; et ex mala, malus."

39. See *De malo,* q. 1, a. 1, ad 4.

40. *ST* I, q. 48, a. 6.

41. See John F. Wippel, "Metaphysical Themes in *De Malo,*" in *Aquinas's Disputed Questions on Evil* (ed. Dougherty), 12–33, at 15–16.

one's God-given nature. Such separation leads to suffering, which is evil absolutely, though good in a certain respect—for it is just that a person should suffer for doing evil even when suffering is contrary to his will and painful to his emotions and senses.[42]

Habit's close connection to desire leads Aquinas to note that human evil experienced within the person, whether as *suffered* (*malum poenae*) or as *committed* (*malum culpae*), is tied to unnatural pleasures. Corresponding habits arise from these unnatural pleasures, and are experienced as connatural, even though they are unnatural simply speaking.[43] Aquinas implies that there are two sources of connatural but unnatural pleasures: pathology and habituation.[44] Although Aquinas does not explicitly say so, one can subdivide habituation into that which arises nonvoluntarily—including customs derived from childhood experience and one's environment—and that which arises voluntarily. Accordingly, below I discuss negative habit in light of physical dysfunction and environmental causes, respectively. After that, I treat evil as committed voluntarily in different degrees and with different levels of weakness present.

## PHYSICAL DYSFUNCTION AND NEGATIVE HABITS

A large number of mental disorders, that is, habitual defects of the practical and speculative intellect, are characterized by deficient rationality. Signs include impaired working memory, attention, cognitive flexibility, and control of inhibitions.[45] What causes these "evils" for people?

Previous chapters described how individual differences in genes and epigenetics, along with temperament and personality, can induce habitual inclinations toward different positive behaviors. Simi-

42. *De malo*, q. 1, a. 1, ad 1. See Wippel, "Metaphysical Themes in *De malo*," 20.
43. *Sent. Ethic.*, lib. 7, l. 5, n. 4.
44. See *Sent. Ethic.*, lib. 7, l. 5, n. 7.
45. Verhoeven and de Wit, "The Role of Habits," 291.

larly, inborn physical factors can have long-lasting negative effects on inclinations and behaviors. I use term "negative" to describe nonvoluntary or involuntary inclinations, which therefore exist outside of the realm of fault; they are *malum poenae*. The adjectives "bad" and "evil" could misleadingly imply that these inclinations are the result of the agent's action (*malum culpae*). The following analysis helps explain the extent to which a person can be inclined from birth toward disordered behavior, while recalling that such factors can never force a person to commit evil. This section necessarily builds upon and strengthens my previous account of human flourishing, for, as Bacon says, "He who knows the ways of nature will also more easily recognize the deviations. And conversely he who recognizes the deviations will more accurately describe the ways."[46] A study of human dysfunction in its physical and spiritual dimensions will help us better understand human habit even on a supernatural level.

Aquinas and many present empirical scientists agree on the general principles of diagnosing and understanding biological dysfunction. They recognize that a proper diagnosis of physical malady depends above all on the observation of a person's physical condition and his actions. Empirical scientists describe physical diseases in terms of exterior symptoms or signs, some of which can be known directly through observation and others aided by the self-reporting of the sufferer.[47] Similarly, psychological wellness or illness is examined in terms of patterns of exterior behaviors and self-reporting.[48] The data collected by observations are judged to be signs of flourishing or dysfunction by comparison to a norm. Teratology, the study of abnormal fetal development, is successful only insofar as it measures death, disease, growth delays, malformations, etc., as deviations from *normal and natural* flourishing.[49] Just as not all pri-

46. Francis Bacon, *New Organon*, ed. Lisa Jardine and Michael Silverthorne (Cambridge: Cambridge University Press, 2003), 148.

47. See David Linden, *The Biology of Psychological Disorders* (New York: Palgrave Macmillan, 2011), xxi.

48. See Maltby et al., *Personality, Individual Differences and Intelligence*, 590.

49. See Douglas Wilson et al., "Principles of Human Teratology: Drug, Chemical,

vations are evil, so not all deviations from the norm are diseases. Genetic mutations are not categorized as diseases or nondiseases, but are considered on the functional level as either "loss-of-function" or "gain-of-function."[50] Practice thus suggests that empirical science and even evolutionary theory measure diseases by their relation to the good as specified by a thing's proper ends, such as the health and self-maintenance of the individual and the continuance of the species. Thus, empirical science implicitly recognizes that both flourishing and dysfunction are measured by their relation to the goodness of a thing's nature, as manifested in the exterior arrangement of the body as well as behavior and self-reported feelings. This leads us to consider the nature of "monsters."[51]

As a biologist, Aristotle painstakingly researched the nature of human development through his own observations along with claims from authorities deemed trustworthy. With the mind of a physician, he tried to diagnose causes of problematic conception, including irregular musculature, excesses or absences of semen or menstrual fluid, and so on.[52] He held that, absolutely speaking, "nature makes nothing contrary to nature," for the form and the material of a being are naturally adapted to each other for the good of the individual and the overall benefit of the species and cosmos.[53] Thus, humans are born wingless, for wings would impede walking upright, which is natural to us. At times, though, "in the realm of nature occurrences take place which are even contrary to nature or

---

and Infectious Exposure," *Journal of Obstetrics and Gynaecology Canada* 199 (2007): 911–17. See also Harold Kalter, *Teratology in the Twentieth Century Plus Ten* (New York: Springer Science and Media, 2010), 4–5 and 8–15.

50. Armand Marie Leroi, *Mutants: On the Form, Varieties and Errors of the Human Body* (London: Harper Perennial, 2005), 14. Evolutionary theory sees a mutation as beneficial if it confers a greater likelihood of reproductive success (gain-of-function); otherwise, it is considered harmful (loss-of-function) (ibid., 17).

51. See Stephen T. Asma, *On Monsters: An Unnatural History of Our Worst Fears* (Oxford: Oxford University Press, 2011).

52. See *History of Animals* X.1–5, 633b10–637b7.

53. *Progression of Animals* XI, 711a6.

fortuitous,"[54] as when a human is born with teeth.[55] Infant-teeth are neither contrary to the form nor to the matter of a person, but short circuit the body's natural, gradual development. For Aristotle, an "error" of nature in the development of a human being was a τέρας, a surprising and extraordinary event. *Teras* was translated into Latin as *monstrum*. Thus, the study of monsters was called *teratology*. Considered biologically-medically, a monster is something negative, "for a monstrosity is actually a kind of deformity."[56]

Augustine saw more deeply into the providential ordering of things. He argued that *monstrum* comes from *monere*—related to *demonstrare*—which means to instruct, to warn, and to foretell.[57] In this Christian view, a "monster" instructs us about nature, warns us about the effects of impeded nature, and foretells God's plans for the human body at the end of time. Because monsters are aberrations from nature, their unnaturalness teaches us indirectly about the state of nature and the importance of the supernatural. They have an important role to play in coming to recognize the state of life in which we live, and the life to which we are all called.

With Aristotle and Augustine in sight, Aquinas explains monsters by considering the ultimate cause of all things. He notes that God is the only being in whom no defect can arise.[58] When God generates, he does so perfectly, following the principle *omne agens agit sibi simile*: every agent produces things similar to itself.[59] This

54. *On Memory* II, 452b1.

55. *Generation of Animals* II.6, 745b10–13.

56. Ibid., IV.3, 769b30.

57. See *De Civitate Dei* XXI.8.

58. *Compendium theologiae*, c. 123: "Deus est in quem nullus defectus cadere potest."

59. *SCG* II, c. 6, n. 5; c. 30, n. 5. Thomas employs this principle, in variations, throughout his works. It is derived from Aristotle, *De anima* II.4, 415a27: "For any living thing that has reached its normal development and which is unmutilated, and whose mode of generation is not spontaneous, the most natural act is the production of another like itself, an animal producing an animal, a plant a plant, in order that, as far as nature allows, it may partake in the eternal and divine." See *Sent. De anima*, lib. 2, l. 7, nn. 7–9; Philipp W. Rosemann, *Omne Agens Agit Sibi Simile: A "Repetition" of Scholastic Metaphysics* (Leuven: Leuven University Press, 1996); and John F. Wippel, "Thomas Aquinas on Our Knowledge of God and the Axiom That Every Agent Produces Something Like

applies to acting, to making, and, analogously, to generating.[60] Some things generate others that are like them in one respect but different in another—not as contrary to nature, but simply different, as when God the Father generates God the Son, who is like the Father in all things except personhood. Similarly, a human father can generate a daughter, who is like him in humanity but different in sex. But when a generator produces something that is so unlike itself that it is contrary to the generator's nature, it brings forth a "monster" or a monstrosity.[61] That is, when nature deviates from the rational mean, it produces monstrosities.[62] This does not mean that "Nature" chooses an error or deliberately makes a mistake, only that there is something wrong when a thing is born without its natural panoply of parts, powers, inclinations, and so on.

Material things naturally undergo "natural corruption," that is, they sustain accidental changes that entail the dissolution of some structures and the formation of new ones.[63] Such changes are not always harmful: most genetic variations—in contrast to mutations—have little effect.[64] However, when a thing undergoes a change that entails "the kind of privation that removes what is due to the generated thing, this will be by chance and simply evil, as when monstrous offspring are born."[65] Contemporary science similarly maintains a distinction between serious congenital malformations and trivial physical variants that have little or no effect on the health of the person.[66] Major malformations disrupt the basic function-

Itself," in *Metaphysical Themes in Thomas Aquinas II* (Washington, D.C.: The Catholic University of America Press, 2007), 152–71.

60. Thomas applies this to creaturely generation, e.g., in *SCG* II, c. 30, n. 5. See also *SCG* II, c. 98, n. 16; III, c. 71, n. 5; etc. It can be analogously applied to the eternal generation of the Son: God the Father generates the Son by communicating the "form" of divinity. See *SCG* III, c. 52, n. 3, and *ST* I, q. 27, a. 4.

61. See *Sent. Meta.*, lib. 7, l. 8, n. 23.

62. *In Physic.*, lib. 2, l. 14, n. 3. See also *SCG* III, c. 2, n. 7; *De potentia*, q. 3, a. 6, ad 5. For a discussion of this use of "peccata," see *Super Sent.*, lib. 2, d. 37, q. 1, a. 1; *ST* I-II, q. 21, a. 1, ad 1.

63. See *SCG* III, c. 5, n. 9.

64. See Jablonka and Lamb, *Evolution in Four Dimensions*, 269.

65. *SCG* III, c. 5, n. 9.

66. See Kalter, *Teratology in the Twentieth Century Plus Ten*, 4–5.

ing of the person, leading to premature death or serious deficiencies in skeletal, organ, and muscular formation, metabolism, breathing, sensing, and so on. Because of the serious handicaps that they produce, malformations often call for many surgical interventions.

How can monsters exist if nature is so orderly? Aristotle explains that "monsters" are indeed generated aside from the order of nature, but not entirely so: "The monstrosity belongs to the class of things contrary to nature, not any and every kind of nature, but nature taken as what holds for the most part; nothing can happen contrary considered as eternal and necessary, but only those cases where things generally happen in a certain way but may also happen in another way."[67] Aquinas summarizes this position by saying, "Monsters are a result that is contrary to a particular nature, but not to universal nature."[68] Deviations from specific nature, that is, the rational nature a person has as a human, are not contrary to "universal nature," that is, nature as a whole, because the deviations such as cancer and neurodegeneration still follow physical laws in general. Congenital defects are nevertheless evil for the individual who is born with them, and "entirely apart from the intention of nature,"[69] and "accidental to the nature"[70] of the individual, even while they somewhat manifest the orderly working of nature as a whole.[71] The generative power is good, and the laws of nature are good; but an "altering principle" is introduced which is consonant with the laws of nature but dissonant with the end of the generative power.[72] With this understood, Aristotle makes a further point: "Even in the case of monstrosities, whenever things occur contrary indeed to the established order but still always in a certain way and not at random, the result seems to be less of a monstrosity because even that which is contrary to nature is

67. *Generation of Animals* IV.4, 770b9–13.

68. *De potentia*, q. 6, a. 2, ad 8.

69. *SCG* III, c. 5, n. 15.

70. *Compendium theologiae*, c. 112.

71. *In Physic.*, lib. 2, l. 14, n. 3.

72. *De malo*, q. 1, a. 3, co. See McCluskey, *Thomas Aquinas on Moral Wrongdoing*, 43–44.

in a certain sense according to nature, whenever, that is, the formal nature has not mastered the material nature."[73] Here we may recall Thomas's observation that "natural" can mean two things. Some things are called natural according to their form (e.g., it is natural for humans to be intelligent), and others are called natural according to their matter (e.g., it is natural for people to have two hands). Utilizing this distinction, Thomas sees physical dysfunctions in two ways: first, insofar as they result from the body's adaptation to the soul; second, as they stem from some necessity of the material alone.[74]

Consider a person born with polydactyly (too many fingers).[75] His hand as a whole exists because the large majority of his material is adapted to his form, which naturally produces hands. But the extra finger exists "according to the necessity of matter," that is, the extra finger grew as a determined result of the physical causes at work. Some might be tempted to call the extra finger "natural" because it was produced according to the laws of nature in general and it clearly belongs to the person from birth, but Aquinas makes a further distinction here. "Since form is more the nature than matter," Aquinas says, "what is natural according to the form is more natural than what is natural according to the matter."[76] Because the form of a human naturally produces five fingers, it is more natural to have five. The extra finger is *less natural*; it is a deviation from general human nature. In this vein, Aquinas says, "Things that pertain to the nature of the species are transmitted from parents to children unless there be a defect of nature."[77] Hence, simply speaking, when someone lacks something that pertains to the human form, including the natural shape, strength, function, etc., then he suffers from a defect of

73. *Generation of Animals* IV.4, 770b13–18.

74. *De malo*, q. 5, a. 5.

75. This example is employed by Albert the Great. See his *Quaestiones super de animalibus*, lib. 19, qq. 5–6. Translated as *Questions Concerning Aristotle's* On Animals, trans. Irven M. Resnick and Kenneth F. Kitchell, Fathers of the Church: Medieval Continuation 9 (Washington, D.C.: The Catholic University of America Press, 2011), 538–40.

76. *De malo*, q. 5, a. 5.

77. *ST* I-II, q. 81, a. 2.

nature. If a physical defect inclines an individual away from his proper end—as when a tumor prevents a person from thinking—to that extent it is *contrary to nature* and must be dealt with accordingly.[78] A person may thus possess innate dispositions that are contrary to nature, even though they are accidentally like a second nature to him—quasi-natural unnatural inclinations.[79] They are directed not to the good of the individual as a composite whole, but only toward apparent goods of a part (e.g., the survival of a tumor).[80]

Thomas would agree that the body and behavior, understood rightly, provide signs of both flourishing and dysfunction. As noted, people flourish when they use their powers in accordance with reason and direct themselves to objects that are properly ordered to their ultimate end. Human flourishing is always in accordance with human nature; it entails the perfection of a person's nature and powers. Because a human is a body-soul composite, a dysfunction is primarily either of the body or of the soul. Dysfunctions of the body fall below the level of fully voluntary; they are contrary to the specific nature of a person (i.e., the rational form) and therefore are better considered as "errors" of nature and evil that is suffered (*malum poenae*). Dysfunctions of the soul, as we will see, are in some way voluntary (*malum culpae*). Because voluntary dysfunctions are contrary to nature as such, Aquinas calls people who commit them "monsters," for "sins have made them similar to beasts in their affections."[81] In other words, physical abnormalities can be congenital, but moral monstrosities are chosen and moral monsters are self-made. Hence, we must investigate the extent to which biology can influence bad moral choices.

78. *ST* I-II, q. 31, a. 7. For a thorough discussion of Aquinas's understanding of innate but unnatural inclinations, see Sean B. Cunningham, "Natural Inclination in Aquinas" (PhD diss., The Catholic University of America, 2013), 265–99.

79. See *De veritate*, q. 24, a. 10, ad 5.

80. See *ST* I-II, q. 8, a. 1.

81. *Super De Trinitate*, pars 1, pr. 4.

## BIOLOGICAL INFLUENCES ON EMOTIONAL AND BEHAVIORAL DISORDERS

In chapter 2, we explored dispositions that arise from one's individual nature, that is, from one's bodily composition. We saw that a Thomistic account can agree with the general conclusions of empirical studies showing that individual differences in intelligence and temperament/personality are measurably influenced by congenital factors such as genes and physical factors (e.g., brain size and emotional-reactivity). While focusing on the virtuous dispositions that can result from biology, I also noted how Aquinas holds that people have natural inclinations toward vice. Below I will consider a standard empirical model of how biology influences emotional behavioral disorders and objections to this model. After this, we will see how Aquinas's position helps to resolve some of the controversies raised by the standard model.

When considering the negative behavior of humans, one can distinguish between biological influences from those of the intellect and will, for these constitute metaphysically distinct causes even though they interact. Nonvoluntary causes of behavioral abnormality include chemical imbalances: excess dopamine is linked to schizophrenic sorts of disorders, and serotonin deficiencies are associated with wild mood swings and similar pathologies. Some findings are clear: specific personality disorders can be caused primarily by *chemical* disorders.[82]

Working in tandem with chemical explanations, psychiatric genetics attempts to explain how human psychology is influenced by genetic and epigenetic factors.[83] Often this field of study is tied with evolutionary psychiatry, which provides tentative and speculative evolutionary explanations for physical causes

82. See L. J. Siever and K. L. Davis, "The Pathogenesis of Mood Disorders," in *Foundations of Psychiatry*, ed. K. L. Davis and H. Klar (Philadelphia: Saunders and Company, 1991), 254–62.

83. See Linden, *The Biology of Psychological Disorders*, 80–82.

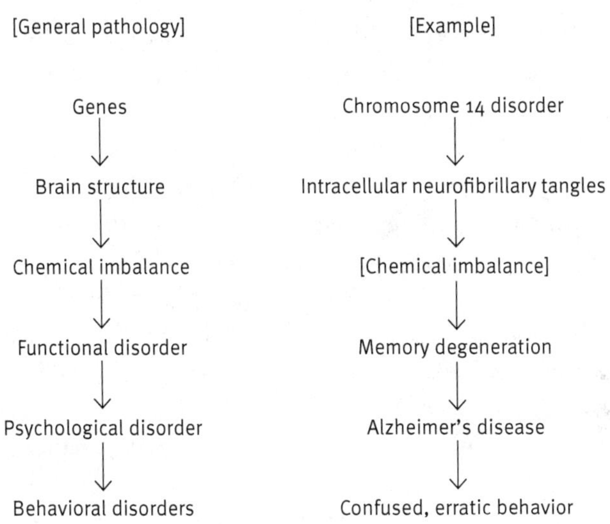


FIGURE 8. PHYSICAL CAUSES OF NEGATIVE BEHAVIOR

of psychologically-based behaviors such as dominance or submission.[84] When accurate, these studies demonstrate a strict connection between physical cause and external display—what is sometimes called a "genetic predisposition" to a psychological or behavioral manifestation such as violence.[85] Genetic predispositions are notoriously difficult to establish because of the great number of factors involved, including sample collection, eliminating false-positives due to shared environment, and so on. Because genetic explanations are concerned only with physical mechanisms, they do not consider whether there are nonphysical causes of psychological (and behavioral) disorders. The efficient causality model omits formal and final causal explanations.

84. See ibid., 204–5.

85. See James Tabery, *Beyond Versus: The Struggle to Understand the Interaction of Nature and Nurture* (Cambridge, Mass.: MIT Press, 2014), esp. chap. 7, "Disarming the 'Genetic Predisposition to Violence.'"

There are two basic objections to this standard model of explaining disordered behavior. The first argues that most diagnoses are illusory: current classifications of disordered behavior and psychological maladies are inadequate, vague, and misleading. The second argues that there is insufficient empirical evidence for most if not all diagnoses of psychological maladies. The following paragraphs will consider each objection before turning to Aquinas's position on the matter.

The first objection to the standard model is what Richard Bentall provocatively calls the "Myth of Diagnosis."[86] This position holds that psychiatric diagnoses are practically meaningless. The American Psychology Association, for instance, defines a mental disorder as "a dysfunction in the psychological, biological, *or* developmental processes underlying mental functioning."[87] The conjunction "or" suggests that the *DSM-5* acknowledges that *not all* diagnosable disorders have an identifiable biological cause. Some therefore distinguish between "mental illness" and "mental disease."[88] Mental *illness* is meant to denote a person's subjective experience of their disease, for example, feeling unwell, whereas mental *disease* denotes the physical problem itself. Some psychologists further try to match up these disorders with their opposites, arguing that the first is the contrary of "subjective" or "hedonic" well-being, whereas the second is contrary to "psychological" or "eudaimonic" well-being.[89] Within a materialistic framework, however, these are distinctions without essential differences, for all disorders are reduced to biological problems.

In addition, the definitions of mental illnesses are often too imprecise to identify truly distinct phenomena.[90] The *DSM-5* recognizes the problem, but instead of making the definitions more precise,

86. See Richard P. Bentall, *Doctoring the Mind* (New York: Penguin, 2010), 89–112.

87. American Psychiatric Association, *Diagnostic and Statistical Manual of Mental Disorders*, 5th ed. [hereafter *DSM-5*] (Washington, D.C.: American Psychiatric Association, 2013), 20; emphasis added.

88. Linden, *The Biology of Psychological Disorders*, xxii.

89. See Maltby et al., *Personality, Individual Differences and Intelligence*, 584–87.

90. "Surely the real reason why patients meet the criteria for more than one diagnosis is that diagnoses do not pick out discrete diseases after all." Bentall, *Doctoring the Mind*, 101.

it introduces a "multidimensional" approach—which makes it more difficult to distinguish one illness from another and to care for illnesses separately.[91] Its broad and loose categories have led to "diagnostic hyperinflation" and the unnecessary medication of countless patients.[92] As the editor of the fourth edition of the *DSM* laments, "During the past two decades, child psychiatry has already provoked three fads—a tripling of Attention Deficit Disorder, a more than twenty-times increase in Autistic Disorder, and a forty-times increase in childhood Bipolar Disorder."[93] The criteria in the *DSM*-5 are so vague that, in a recent field trial, in which clinicians from major medical centers around the United States interviewed patients, less than thirty percent agreed on whether a person was depressed, and less than fifty percent agreed on who was schizophrenic or not, whereas around eighty percent could agree on who suffered from major neurocognitive disorders such as Alzheimer's disease.[94] These findings demonstrate that the term "mental disorder" is imprecise and subject to much confusion.

The second objection to the standard causal model for behavior aberrations involves the "myth of genetics."[95] Bentall argues that "the fundamental error of psychiatry" is the claim that "psychiatric disorders are genetic diseases."[96] The extent of genetic influence for *any disease* may be far less than many people assume. Although virtually all diseases are thought to have some genetic component, many studies suggest that less than two percent are due to single genes; these include cystic fibrosis, albinism (albino traits), and sickle-cell anemia (common among people with African heritage). The remain-

91. American Psychiatric Association, *DSM*-5, 5.

92. Allen J. Frances, "DSM 5 Is Guide Not Bible—Ignore Its Ten Worst Changes," *Psychology Today* (December 2, 2012), available at www.psychologytoday.com/blog/dsm5-in-distress/201212/dsm–5-is-guide-not-bible-ignore-its-ten-worst-changes.

93. Ibid.

94. Darrel A. Regier et al., "DSM-5 Field Trials in the United States and Canada, Part II: Test-Retest Reliability of Selected Categorical Diagnoses," *American Journal of Psychiatry* 170, no. 1 (January 1, 2013): 59–70.

95. See Bentall, *Doctoring the Mind*, 113–47.

96. Ibid., 113.

ing ninety-eight percent of "genetic" disorders are activated or not, in different levels of severity, by many genes while they are affected by various environmental factors.[97] A further study shows that genes alone may be even less influential on human health than the modest studies mentioned above.[98] As for mental diseases, aside from a few—such as Huntington's or rare forms of Alzheimer's—genetic causes have not been discovered. Schizophrenia and bipolar disease are said to have "strong associations of inheritance," up to seventy percent,[99] but no culprit genes have been discovered.[100] Even for alcohol or cocaine dependence, estimated to be inheritable at rates of up to fifty percent and seventy percent respectively, no specific genetic causes have been identified.[101] A thorough and rigorous critique of gene studies has been performed by Jay Joseph, and his results run contrary to mantras in the popular science community.[102] Perhaps most salient are Joseph's claims: "There is little evidence pointing to the existence of specific genes for psychiatric disorders or human psychological trait variation. There is little evidence that socially undesirable behaviors such as criminality have a genetic basis."[103] It should be noted that Joseph's studies are compatible with the previous objection, namely, that definitions of psychological phenomena such as "schizophrenia," "intelligence," "personality," and "criminality" are so poorly conceived that they do not serve as

97. Jablonka and Lamb, *Evolution in Four Dimensions*, 57.

98. Replication in research regarding genetic associations with disease is needed. For example, out of 166 reported associations between gene variants and specific diseases, only six were replicated consistently by repeated studies. See Joel N. Hirschhorn et al., "A Comprehensive Review of Genetic Association Studies," *Genetics in Medicine* 4, no. 2 (March 2002): 45–61; and Lon R. Cardon and John I. Bell, "Association Study Designs for Complex Diseases," *Nature Reviews Genetics* 2, no. 2 (February 2001): 91–99.

99. Linden, *The Biology of Psychological Disorders*, 157 and 231.

100. Ibid., 204.

101. Ibid., 246 and 255.

102. See Jay Joseph, *The Trouble with Twin Studies: A Reassessment of Twin Research in the Social and Behavioral Sciences* (New York: Routledge, 2015), and *The Missing Gene: Psychiatry, Heredity, and the Fruitless Search for Genes* (New York: Algora, 2006).

103. Jay Joseph, *The Gene Illusion: Genetic Research in Psychiatry and Psychology Under the Microscope* (New York: Algora, 2004), 336.

an adequate basis for empirical research.[104] Joseph concludes that a large body of the research is seriously flawed.[105] Although there may be a high correlation between genetic research predictions and what they conclude (after they collect and analyze their data), there are often multiple valid explanations of the data available.[106] A fully biological explanation for most psychological disorders rests on shifting and uncertain grounds.

Despite the serious objections above, a Thomist need not reject the possibility that at least some psychological and behavioral disorders arise from strictly biological causes.[107] Aquinas was well aware that things can go wrong at the level of individual nature. In a number of places, he discusses how one's biology can incline a person toward emotional and behavioral disorders. For him, disordered biology, emotions, and behavior are all a perversion or corruption of a natural disposition.[108] That is, they involve an inclination *contra naturam.*

An inclination can be *contra naturam* in two basic ways: contrary to the good of reason or contrary to the preservation of the body.[109] These disordered inclinations can exist in different "subjects"—in a particular part of the body or in the temperament as a whole—as anti-virtuous dispositions that corrupt the human person instead of perfecting him.[110] For example, Thomas says that, for some people, reason is perverted because of an evil habit of nature (*male habitudine naturae*).[111] Likewise, he holds that persons can have an "innate habit" (*habitus innatus*) that inclines them "toward evil."[112] Even more strongly, he says that "pernicious natures" (*perniciosas*

104. Ibid., 337.

105. Ibid., 339.

106. See ibid., 341–42.

107. For Aristotle on how disease can affect our natural behavioral dispositions, see Leunissen, *From Natural Character to Moral Virtue in Aristotle*, 39–42.

108. *Sent. Ethic.*, lib. 7, l. 1, n. 4.

109. *ST* I-II, q. 31, a. 7; see q. 94, a. 3, ad 2.

110. *ST* I-II, q. 31, a. 7.

111. *ST* I-II, q. 94, a. 4.

112. *De veritate*, q. 16, a. 1, ad 11.

*naturas*) are a source of disordered temperaments, which give dispositions toward enjoying unnatural pleasures.[113] Thomas explains that a biological disorder is contrary to a person's general or specific nature, that is, contrary to the person as a human, because it entails a corruption of the principles of human goodness.[114] Seen from the other end of causality, innate pleasures are caused by one's individual nature, as a person finds pleasure only in what is adapted to him in some way. Thus "if one takes pleasure in a particular action or passion, this is a sign that he is naturally inclined to it."[115] And if one is naturally inclined to one passion or another, such as shyness, he must have by nature the temperament that corresponds to shyness.[116]

A primary effect of a "pernicious nature" is that a person finds pleasure in disordered behavior. For Aristotle, this inborn perverse delight was exemplified in the man who enjoyed slitting the wombs of pregnant women to devour their fetuses, and in the cruel tyrant Phalaris who found glee in torturing people.[117] Others are inclined toward pleasures because they are born "soft."[118] Still others have an inborn, pathological anxiety, so that they "fear everything, even the squeak of a mouse" on account of a "bestial timidity."[119] Seen more generally, pernicious natures and inclinations make people "like beasts."[120] Whereas sickness can cause unnatural inclinations in the body (discussed in the next section), a pernicious nature causes "corrupt and perverse bodily temperaments" that render "most perverse" (*perversissima*) one's sensory appetite and the apprehensions of one's imagination and the judgments of the cogitative power.[121] This "wickedness of temperament" oppresses reason, so that

113. *Sent. Ethic.*, lib. 7, l. 5, n. 3; see also lib. 3, l. 20, n. 9.
114. *ST* I-II, q. 31, a. 7.
115. *Sent. Ethic.*, lib. 2, l. 11, n. 7.
116. Ibid., lib. 4, l. 10, n. 24.
117. Ibid., n. 5.
118. *ST* II-II, q. 138, a. 1, ad 1.
119. *Sent. Ethic.*, lib. 7, l. 5, n. 13.
120. Ibid., n. 5.
121. Ibid., n. 3.

people who suffer from this condition have "some universal apprehension, although greatly limited."[122] It does not reach the level of vice itself, for such inclinations cannot touch the will: "it is evident that moral virtues are neither in us by nature nor in us contrary to nature" (*contra naturam*).[123] A person cannot possess a full *habitus* of sin by nature.[124] However, Thomas recognizes that a brain lesion in a frenetic person can impede the act of the imaginative power, or a similar lesion could impede an act of the memorative power in a person with lethargy (which might now be called Chronic Fatigue Syndrome)—and that both of these conditions can impede the actual use of reason.[125] People with these innate conditions, he argues, may be called "naturally irrational, not because that have no reason, but [because it is] greatly limited and centered on particular things that they perceive by their senses, so that they live solely according the senses."[126] Seeing how lower animals pursue pleasures of the flesh directed to natural goods, Aquinas says such persons are "quasi-bestial by nature."[127] They possess natural human dignity as members of the human species, but by their individual natures they are inclined toward goods that are contrary to good on both the human and animal levels. If a person acts on these inclinations *contra naturam*, he corrupts himself below the level of beasts.[128]

Significantly, Thomas holds that the passions that arise from a person's pernicious nature can somehow cause disordered behavior that may be partly voluntary or even involuntary. Although in principle a person can choose to see how a good before him is not-good in some respect, or he can ignore the good, "Sometimes it happens

122. Ibid., n. 8.

123. *Sent. Ethic.*, lib. 2, l. 1, n. 5.

124. *Super Sent.*, lib. 2, d. 42, q. 2, a. 1, co.: "habitus peccati neque sit naturalis neque infusus, oportet quod per actum peccati sit acquisitus. Restat ergo ut radix peccati dicatur in nobis vel passio aliqua vel pronitas ad passionem, quae ex corruptione originalis peccati consequitur."

125. *ST* I, q. 84, a. 7.

126. *Sent. Ethic.*, lib. 7, l. 5, n. 14.

127. Ibid.

128. See *Super Epistolam ad Romanos lectura* [hereafter *Super Rom.*], c. 1, l. 8, n. 147.

that a man not only has these [unnatural] desires, but even is overcome by them."[129] This is because a person vehemently tends toward objects of his innate inclination,[130] even to the point where the pleasure or pain he experiences corrupts the judgment of his reason.[131] Toward such people, Aquinas says, we should have compassion. We should not blame or mock people born in this condition, any more than we would reproach or ridicule a person born with a disease or a physical disfiguration.[132] At the same time, instead of arguing that an innately disordered temperament *excuses* a person from perverse behavior, Aquinas argues that this demonstrates our need to draw ourselves as much as we can toward inclinations and behaviors contrary to our innate inclinations—that is, toward the virtues most difficult to us.[133] When we zealously devote ourselves to receding from the sins to which we are prone, we will just barely and with difficulty arrive at the mean.[134] Adapting the Aristotelian image developed by Thomas, we can say that the presence of innate disordered inclinations shows that, in order to flourish truly, we must cultivate ourselves the way gardeners straighten crooked saplings. To make a crooked sapling stand upright, they bend it in the direction opposite to its native inclination; likewise, we develop our own virtue only by striving against our disordered dispositions, whether innate or acquired.[135]

My exposition above shows how Aquinas's thought both in-

129. *Sent. Ethic.*, lib. 7, l. 5, n. 15.

130. Ibid., lib. 2, l. 11, n. 7.

131. Ibid., lib. 6, l. 4, n. 10.

132. Ibid., lib. 3, l. 12, n. 8.

133. Thomas's late text *De malo*, q. 3, a. 10, argues that the will can even rebuff evil inclinations of the passions by redirecting the attention of disordered reason. The source of the will's rebuff is the intellect's recognition that doing so would be good. See McCluskey's account of sin arising from the passions, as well as "weakness of the will" in *Thomas Aquinas on Moral Wrongdoing*, 100–115.

134. *Sent. Ethic.*, lib. 2, l. 11, n. 7. In *ST* I-II, q. 64, a. 1, s.c., Aquinas follows Aristotle's definition in *Nicomachean Ethics* II.6, 1106b36: "virtus moralis est habitus electivus in medietate existens." See also *Sent. Ethic.*, lib. 2, l. 7. The virtuous mean is less measured by the thing which is ruled by reason than by the rule of right reason itself, which takes account of relevant circumstances (*SCG* III, lib. 3, c. 136, n. 12; *De malo*, q. 14, a. 1, ad 6).

135. See Aristotle, *Nicomachean Ethics* II.9, 1109b5; *Sent. Ethic.*, lib. 2, l. 11, n. 7.

cludes and develops a standard model of how biology affects certain psychological and behavioral disorders. Although he lacked knowledge of particular biological causes, Thomas admitted that, in principle, physiological disorders can so impede rational functioning, and at times can lead to such vehement passions that a person performs actions that are no longer "human acts" but remain on an animal level. Such innate negative inclinations do not make a human less of a person, for they do not diminish the individual's essential rational nature. Nevertheless, these negative inclinations impede human action for individuals afflicted by them, and highlight the need for grace and virtue. Thomas's more theoretical stance omits speculations regarding how frequently purely biological disorders arise, but his many references to them suggest that he knows they are not uncommon. Because a disorder caused by innate biology is ontologically distinct from a disorder caused by the environment, he distinguishes the two, although he would likely recognize their mutual interaction. In the following section I highlight that interaction.

## ENVIRONMENTAL-BIOLOGICAL INFLUENCES ON NEGATIVE HABITS

Bad behavior cannot always be chalked up to biology, as not everyone with brain damage or disability becomes morally bad, and not every bad person has physical brain damage. Environment, or nurture, plays an important role in forming inclinations toward behavior.[136] We saw above that, as embryos, humans can acquire positive nonvoluntary actional dispositions through proper nutrition and experiences such as being exposed to beautiful music and their mother's voice. Below I will discuss how negative habits are influenced by sickness, post-traumatic stress disorder, and detrimental upbringing and culture.

136. For examples of people who suffered similar brain damage but ended with very different behavior, see Adrian Raine, *The Anatomy of Violence: The Biological Roots of Crime* (New York: Vintage, 2014), 156–57.

Table 6-1. Effects of Pathogens on Behavior

| *Agent/pathogen* | *Risk to fetus* |
|---|---|
| Excessive alcohol | Central nervous system damage, mental dysfunction |
| Smoking | Low birthweight, cognitive defects |
| Thalidomide | Extreme physiological deformation |
| Cytomegalovirus (herpes) | Epilepsy, deafness, retardation |
| Syphilis | Severe damage to the brain, eyes, skin, bones |
| Oral contraceptives[1] | Female masculinization |

1. High doses of progestin hormones—often used in lower doses in contraceptive compounds, with traces in a pregnant mother—can make females develop masculine traits, including hirsutism and genital abnormalities. See Bertis B. Little, *Drugs and Pregnancy: A Handbook* (Boca Raton, Fla.: CRC Press, 2006), 93–98.

Just as people can develop positive dispositions from balanced nutrition and a generally healthy womb environment, so they develop negative dispositions from the very first stages of life due to similar biological factors.[137] The table above provides a representative sample of chemical agents and pathogens proven to harm a fetus.[138]

Many of these pathogens have been proven to have not only negative biological effects; they can also induce long-lasting negative dispositions toward violence, emotional dysregulation, and other emotional and behavioral disorders. Children with any prenatal alcohol exposure were found to be more likely to have more difficulties in controlling dispositions toward aggressiveness and disobedience, along with suffering from greater anxiety and social with-

137. Medicine conventionally distinguished between congenital and acquired defects, that is, inherited and not inherited, for one can in principle distinguish between the individual (genetic causes) and his environment (nongenetic causes). However, present investigatory techniques often cannot identify the precise causes of a malformation. Thus, for Kalter and others, "congenital" means "present from birth." *Teratology in the Twentieth Century Plus Ten*, 3 and 7.

138. See Wilson et al., "Principles of Human Teratology: Drug, Chemical, and Infectious Exposure," 913–15 (Tables 1–2); and Lise Eliot, *What's Going on in There: How the Brain and Mind Develop in the First Five Years of Life* (New York: Bantam, 2000), 40–80 and 93.

drawal symptoms.[139] Smoking also has been shown to have a small but measurable negative impact on externalizing behavioral problems,[140] which may be on account of the way it harms brain function.[141] In addition to being harmed by agents and pathogens, a preborn infant's long-term cognitive functions and overall health can also be greatly injured by the mother's malnutrition.[142] During the Dutch "Hungerwinter" of 1944, many pregnant mothers were effectively starved by a Nazi siege. In the spring of 1945, the Allies abruptly rescued Holland and food levels returned to normal. Studies have shown that the short period of starvation permanently harmed some fetuses. Even many years later, persons who as fetuses were affected by this first trimester of malnourishment were much more likely to develop obesity, schizophrenia, and antisocial behavior.[143] Other studies bear out that malnutrition is persistently associated with poor cognitive performance and antisocial behavior.[144]

Aquinas recognizes many of the aforementioned causes as possible sources of nonvoluntary acquired dispositions. He identifies climate: "On account of intemperate climate even the bodies [of the inhabitants] have a bad disposition by which their use of reason is

139. See B. Sood et al., "Prenatal Alcohol Exposure and Childhood Behavior at Age 6 to 7 Years: I. Dose-Response Effect," *Pediatrics* 108, no. 2 (August 2001): E34; and Balapal S. Basavarajappa, "Fetal Alcohol Spectrum Disorder: Potential Role of Endocannabinoids Signaling," *Brain Sciences* 5, no. 4 (2015): 456–93.

140. Among the many studies, see C. V. Dolan et al., "Testing Causal Effects of Maternal Smoking During Pregnancy on Offspring's Externalizing and Internalizing Behavior," *Behavior Genetics* 46 (2016): 378–88.

141. See Nathalie E. Holz et al., "Effect of Prenatal Exposure to Tobacco Smoke on Inhibitory Control: Neuroimaging Results from a 25-Year Prospective Study," *JAMA Psychiatry* 71, no. 7 (July 1, 2014): 786–96.

142. An excess of metals that are beneficial at small doses is also associated with behavioral disorders. For discussion and references, see Raine, *The Anatomy of Violence*, 223–30.

143. Many human and rat studies show how nutrition affects "fetal programming," with long-term effects for the person in the womb. The basic idea is that the fetal body develops dispositions adapted to a harsh environment that it does not encounter later on. For examples and references see Moore, *The Developing Genome*, 125–27.

144. For discussion and references, see Raine, *The Anatomy of Violence*, 209–11 and 218–19.

impeded."[145] Another culprit is sickness, explained as a disequilibrium of the humors,[146] or more generally as "an inordinate disposition of the body"[147] combined with a privation of the equilibrium of health,[148] which could arise from one's environment, birth defects, or other causes.[149] Thomas reasons that some people "are made irrational from sicknesses such as epilepsy or mania. These [people] are thoughtless by disease."[150] Sickness can impede "contemplative happiness" in this life because it causes forgetfulness,[151] destroying the habit of science by corrupting the phantasms in the memory,[152] as when Alzheimer's disease limits a scholar's ability to find pleasure in the academic subjects he once enjoyed teaching.

Some illnesses, Aquinas affirms, can be so powerful that they lead to desires that are gravely harmful to human dignity and good behavior: "Some things *contra naturam* are made delectable, on account of particular illnesses, such as mania or madness or something like that."[153] He references Aristotle's retelling of a man who, going insane, killed his mother and ate her, and then killed his fellow servant and ate his liver.[154] Similarly, because a person desires what he lacks, sickness can incline a person to misunderstand the true nature of happiness, for an ill person sometimes thinks that happiness consists in being healthy.[155] It seems, then, that for Aquinas, while health of the body is ordered to the good of the soul,[156] sickness of the body can incline the soul toward evil, because "natural causes sometimes serve to facilitate or impede things that are done by free

145. *Sent. Ethic.*, lib. 7, l. 5, n. 14.
146. See *ST* II-II, q. 6, a. 2.
147. *ST* I-II, q. 82, a. 1.
148. See ibid., ad 1.
149. See *ST* I-II, q. 82, a. 2.
150. *Sent. Ethic.*, lib. 7, l. 5, n. 14.
151. *ST* I-II, q. 5, a. 4.
152. See *ST* I-II, q. 67, a. 2, ad 2.
153. *Sent. Ethic.*, lib. 7, l. 5, n. 6.
154. *Nicomachean Ethics* VII.5, 1148b25–27.
155. *Sent. Ethic.*, lib. 1, l. 4, n. 6. See *Nicomachean Ethics* I.4, 1095a23.
156. *ST* I-II, q. 13, a. 3.

choice."[157] Hence, sickness—whether temporary or chronic—can "entirely snatch away a person's happiness by entirely impeding the operation of virtue," as when "by sickness a person incurs mania, madness, or any other mental incapacity."[158] In sum, Aquinas was willing to admit that sickness at times can so affect the mind and the rest of the person that it can incline the sick person away from natural happiness and toward the opposite extreme, toward evil behaviors such as murder and cannibalism.

Beyond the realm of sickness and nutrition, a mother's experiences can also imprint certain dispositions on a preborn infant. After terrorists attacked on 9/11, about one out of five persons who lived closest to the World Trade Center developed post-traumatic stress disorder (PTSD). PTSD is a well-documented syndrome that affects some people who have experienced traumatic stress from events such as combat, sexual assault, terrorism, natural and manmade disasters, and life-threatening accidents.[159] Symptoms of PTSD include (1) re-experiencing the event in varying sensory forms (e.g., flashbacks), (2) avoiding triggers or reminders of the trauma, and (3) chronic hyperarousal in the autonomic nervous system.[160] PTSD is primarily marked by somatic disturbance, and therefore can be classified as an acquired bodily-emotional habit. The condition can be considered a *nonvoluntary* habit to the extent that the person did not know about the event, or did not and could not have predicted the event (e.g., a commuter awakens to discover that he was in a car wreck; a civilian steps on a land mine and dies); it can be considered *involuntary* to the extent that the traumatic event was contrary to or against person's will (e.g., assault). Pregnant women with PTSD have chronically depleted levels of cortisol, the hormone that helps moderates stress. This directly affects their

157. *De veritate*, q. 12, a. 3, ad 6.

158. *Sent. Ethic.*, lib. 1, l. 16, n. 11.

159. Babette Rothschild, *The Body Remembers: The Psychophysiology of Trauma and Trauma Treatment* (New York: Norton, 2000), 6.

160. Ibid., 7.

preborn children. A mother's stress can have long-term negative effects on her child's heartrate; repeated maternal mood patterns (including depression) affect fetal neurobehavioral development; and anywhere from ten to twenty percent of cortisol in a mother's blood passes to the fetus, which, if continued over time, affects the blossoming brain.[161] This helps explain why infants born to mothers who developed PTSD after witnessing the events of 9/11 had abnormally low cortisol—and more difficulty moderating stress—compared to infants whose mothers did not develop the syndrome. As one researcher put it, the children of PTSD sufferers bore "the scar without the wound."[162]

The symptoms of PTSD help one to analyze the disorder, and others like it, from a Thomistic perspective. Re-experiencing a traumatic event pertains to the sensory memory; avoiding triggers pertains to the cogitative judgment; chronic hyperarousal pertains to the somatic system as a whole. Considered together, PTSD is a negative habit of the lower apprehensive powers combined with a negative bodily habit. PTSD can arise from a single traumatic incident, whereas habits are ordinarily generated by repetition. Hence, the question arises as to how Aquinas would account for PTSD. Aquinas's position is largely contained in the *Summa Theologiae* I-II, question 51, article 3, "Can a habit be generated by one act?" Here and in auxiliary texts Aquinas compares the development of habits to quasi-permanent changes that occur naturally. Just as many drops can hollow out a stone, so habits are ordinarily established by repetition.[163] Just as fire gradually consumes a combustible, such as wood,

161. Michael T. Kinsella and Catherine Monk, "Impact of Maternal Stress, Depression & Anxiety on Fetal Neurobehavioral Development," *Clinical Obstetrics and Gynecology* 52, no. 3 (September 2009): 425–40. See Janet A. DiPietro, "Maternal Influences on the Developing Fetus," in *Maternal Influences on Fetal Neurodevelopment: Clinical and Research Aspect*, ed. A. W. Zimmerman and S. L. Connors (New York: Springer Science and Business Media, 2010), 19–32.

162. Rachel Yehuda et al., "Transgenerational Effects of Posttraumatic Stress Disorder in Babies of Mothers Exposed to the World Trade Center Attacks during Pregnancy," *The Journal of Clinical Endocrinology and Metabolism* 90, no. 7 (July 2005): 4115–18.

163. See *De virtutibus*, q. 1, a. 9, ad 11; *Super Sent.*, lib. 1, d. 17, q. 2, a. 3, ad 4.

so habits develop gradually by time and effort.[164] This is particularly salient for intentionally developing appetitive habits—discussed in the final chapter—for the will is fully conformed to a good object only by choosing it many times. The intellect, by contrast, can immediately recognize the truth of a proposition when it is presented with a sufficiently convincing proof. However, for the intellect to develop a true opinion, lower than full knowledge, it must be presented with many probable arguments so that it can consider the data from different angles. As for the lower apprehensive powers, Aquinas held that an agent needs to repeat an act many times in order for anything to be actively habituated on this level. For all these reasons, Aquinas says that human habits cannot be corrupted by a single act or event.[165] Finally, Aquinas considers habits on the somatic level, saying that bodily habits (*habitus corporales*) can be caused in a single act if the agent is powerful enough.[166] In sum, Aquinas does not directly discuss *passively*-received habits on the sensory level, which pertain to PTSD, but he provides a principle sufficient to explain the disorder: "the more the action of an agent is efficacious, the more quickly it induces a form."[167] The empirical research into PTSD indicates that traumatic events can be sufficiently strong enough to firmly imprint suffering onto one's memory and thereby to affect one's cogitative judgment.

## ORIGINAL SIN: OUR FIRST BAD HABIT

Considering the "disappointments of life, the defeat of good, the success of evil … the prevalence and intensity of sin, the pervad-

164. See *ST* I-II, q. 51, a. 3. The rest of this paragraph closely follows this article.

165. *ST* I-II, q. 51, a. 3, co. See *ST* I-II, q. 63, a. 2, ad 2; ibid., q. 71, a. 4; II-II, q. 24, a. 12; *De virtutibus*, q. 1, a. 1, ad 5.

166. *ST* I-II, q. 51, a. 3. Memory is typically developed through repetition, but a striking image or event can remain with the soul because of the deep impression it has made: "quia ea quae sunt inconsueta magis miramur, et sic in eis animus magis et vehementius detinetur; ex quo fit quod eorum quae in pueritia vidimus magis memoremur" (*ST* II-II, q. 49, a. 1, co.).

167. *De virtutibus*, q. 1, a. 9, ad 11.

ing idolatries, the corruptions, the dreary hopeless irreligion," John Henry Newman concluded that man's disorientation from his creator "is a fact, a fact as true as the fact of its existence."[168] For him, the doctrine of original sin was "almost as certain as that the world exists, and as the existence of God."[169] Aquinas, in contrast, invokes the Catholic faith to warrant belief in original sin.[170] Evils are indeed all around us, but only from divine revelation can we have certainty that their underlying source is original sin. Scripture teaches that God created human beings "very good" but that Adam and Eve sinned and that the effects of their sin reaches down to every other human being through the process of generation.[171]

Reflecting on the vital force of original sin, Thomas reaches a conclusion most germane to the present study: original sin is a habit.[172] It is a nonvoluntary habit by which our nature "holds itself" (*se habet*) ill toward something; it is a "a disposition has been changed almost into nature, as is manifest in health or sickness."[173] Health and sickness are often nonvoluntary, quasi-permanent dispositions: according to one's innate bodily disposition, one can said to be "naturally" healthy or sickly. In both cases, the disposition is an accident of the person. A sort of soul sickness, original sin is a personal, quasi-permanent deprivation of an accidental form, a disposition that entails a privation and a positive disorder: a privation of original justice, and a positive inordinate disposition of the soul.[174]

168. John Henry Newman, *Apologia Pro Vita Sua* (London: Longmans, Green, and Co., 1908), 242–43.

169. Ibid.

170. *De malo*, q. 5, a. 4.

171. See *ST* I-II, q. 81, aa. 1 and 3.

172. *ST* I-II, q. 82, a. 1, s.c. For a historical overview of original sin, emphasizing the role of Bernard Lonergan, not wholly in conformity with Aquinas, see Tatha Wiley, *Original Sin: Origins, Developments, Contemporary Meanings* (Mahwah, N.J.: Paulist Press, 2002). For a view that more closely follows St. Thomas, see Mark Johnson, "Augustine and Aquinas on Original Sin: Doctrine, Authority, and Pedagogy," in *Aquinas the Augustinian*, ed. Michael Dauphinais et al. (Washington, D.C.: The Catholic University of America Press, 2007), 147–58.

173. *ST* I-II, q. 82, a. 1.

174. See ibid., ad 1.

The body, as material, will naturally disintegrate, but the rational soul is inherently immortal.[175] Humans originally possessed a "natural disposition" for organic nondisintegration, that is, a habitual grace of "impassibility" and bodily immortality.[176] This grace was the infused habit of "original justice," which ordered the body to the soul, and the soul to God.[177] As a punishment for their original sin, God justly withdrew that grace from Adam and Eve and from all humans, their descendants.[178] Aquinas concludes that bodily defects, ills, and pains are consequences of the punishment they incurred.

The privation of justice constitutes the quasi-formal element of original sin, whereby the will is deprived of its ordination toward God; the inordinate desire for creaturely goods constitutes the quasi-material element.[179] Because desire is the engine that pulls the other powers, original sin is attributed to concupiscence, which is "the more principal [passion], in which all the other passions are in some way included."[180] Hence, "original sin, materially speaking, is habitual concupiscence."[181] It may be called a "sin" because it is a disordered inclination to sin and it is an effect of sin. But we must insist: original sin is not derived from human nature; it is not *actual* sin, for it is not the individual's sin in act; it is not *infused* sin, for it is not a positive form added to the soul by God; nor is it a *positive habit* that is the result of the individual's efforts; nor is it an *acquired habit* resulting from one's personal acts. Original sin is, rather, a negative "innate" deprivation of right habit incumbent on one's origin,[182] a "weakness of nature," a transmitted disease of the soul.[183]

With original sin in the background, we can now consider how

175. See *De malo*, q. 5, a. 5.

176. Ibid.

177. See *ST* I, q. 97, a. 1.

178. See *ST* I-II, q. 85, a. 5.

179. See *ST* I-II, q. 82, a. 3. In *De malo*, q. 4, a. 2, Aquinas adds the qualifier "quasi" to clarify that original sin is not, properly speaking, a form that exists within the soul.

180. *ST* I-II, q. 82, a. 3, ad 2.

181. *De malo*, q. 4, a. 2, ad 7.

182. *ST* I-II, q. 82, a. 1, ad 3. See *De malo*, q. 4, a. 2, ad 8.

183. See Augustine, *In Psalm.* 188, serm. 3; quoted in *ST* I-II, q. 82, a. 1.

sin relates to nature in general, especially as it relates to habit formation. Thomas explains that sin, on the broadest level, harms the threefold "good of nature": (1) the essence, essential properties, and powers of the soul; (2) original justice; and (3) a virtuous inclination.[184] Here I will only discuss the first and the third.

Regarding the first, he insists that no sin, whether original or personal, destroys or diminishes what he calls the "principles of nature by which nature is constituted," such as the very essence of the rational soul; nor can sin destroy the soul's essential properties, such as risibility, or its powers, such as the intellect and will.[185] After sin, nature remains intact—the very nature which can be habituated to the natural good by acquired virtue, and habituated to the supernatural good by infused virtue. Accordingly, the wound of original sin instead "infects" the essence of the soul and its powers.[186] Aside from the act of existence itself, the chief power of the soul is its inclination to perform acts, located in the power of the will. Therefore, original sin infects this power first, inclining a person to sin.[187]

Aquinas argues that, because the essence of the soul remains intact after original and personal sin, some inclination toward virtue survives as well. The good inclination remains because man retains his general and specific nature.[188] The good inclination is weakened, for an increase of one inclination entails the decrease of its contrary: the inclination toward sin diminishes the natural inclination toward virtue.[189] Insofar as original sin directs a person away from God, the final end of all things and the principle of all order, the result of original sin is that "all the powers of the soul remain in some way destitute of their proper order, by which they are naturally directed toward virtue."[190] Each power, like man as a whole, is "wounded":

184. *ST* I-II, q. 85, a. 1. Here I reorder the list for the sake of clarity.
185. Ibid.
186. *ST* I-II, q. 83, a. 3.
187. Ibid.
188. See *ST* I-II, q. 85, a. 2.
189. *ST* I-II, q. 85, a. 1.
190. *ST* I-II, q. 85, a. 3.

Insofar as the reason is deprived of its order to the true, there is the wound of ignorance; insofar as the will is deprived of its order to the good, there is the wound of malice; insofar as the irascible appetite is deprived of its order to the arduous, there is the wound of weakness; and insofar as the concupiscible appetite is deprived of its order to the delightful as moderated by reason, there is the wound of concupiscence.[191]

The powers retain their natural objects, but not their supernatural object, for an obstacle is placed before each power, preventing it from attaining its terminus.[192] After original sin, reason remains oriented toward some natural truth but not toward the supernatural truth of God; the will remains oriented toward some natural good, but not the ultimate good of beatitude; etc. Accordingly, original sin makes us live outside of the proper order of the universe.[193] The habit of original sin also deprives us of the proper mode of acting: because of the habit of original sin, the intellect no longer works supernaturally, the emotions do not perfectly harmonize with reason, and so on. Original sin, in sum, is a habit that inclines us to selfishness, egoism, pettiness. Turning us away from our ultimate end, it darkens the mind and inclines us to think that sensory pleasures are always choiceworthy.[194] This disordered inclination excludes the infused habit of charity, for it is "an habitual aversion from the unchangeable good."[195]

## ACQUIRED NEGATIVE DISPOSITIONS

When a disposition arises from actively-acquired sensory knowledge, we may consider it imperfectly voluntary insofar as its acquisition requires a person's sensory attention. Above we saw how parental interaction and various circumstances can affect a child's rational abilities and cogitative judgment. We also saw how adults can devel-

191. Ibid.
192. *ST* I-II, q. 85, a. 2.
193. See *ST* I-II, q. 85, a. 4.
194. See *De veritate*, q. 24, a. 12.
195. Ibid., ad 2.

op imperfectly voluntary habits when their intellectual attention is not directed to their actions. To illustrate the principle at work on the negative side, I will now consider how biology and culture can influence criminally violent behaviors.

We may recall that innate sensory sensitivity, particularly that of touch, is a predictor of future intelligence, and that early positive experiences of touch can help a child's intelligence blossom. Research also shows what can happen in negative conditions. A mother's postpartum depression, the "baby blues," which typically includes fewer smiles and positive interactions, predicts that her child will have worse biological stress reactivity in adulthood.[196] Likewise, a father's disengaged and remote interactions predict his child's behavioral problems one year later.[197] Extreme neglect has worse consequences. A well-known and distressing study followed over one hundred children who were raised as orphans in Communist Romania. These poor victims were not cuddled and loved. Instead, they were abandoned to lie in their own excrement, fed like gerbils from bottles affixed to their cots, and washed by being hosed down with cold water.[198] Even if they were adopted at the young age of two, the orphans who spent more than six months in the institution did not develop normally. After a decade, their brains were still smaller compared those of their peers.[199] Furthermore, they more frequently displayed behavioral disorders such as disinhibited attachment, cognitive impairment, and quasi-autism.[200]

196. Tom J. Barry et al., "Maternal Postnatal Depression Predicts Altered Offspring Biological Stress Reactivity in Adulthood," *Psychoneuroendocrinology* 52 (February 2015): 251–60.

197. Paul G. Ramchandani et al., "Do Early Father-Infant Interactions Predict the Onset of Externalising Behaviours in Young Children?," *Journal of Child Psychology and Psychiatry, and Allied Disciplines* 54, no. 1 (January 2013): 56–64.

198. Michael Rutter et al., "Effects of Profound Early Institutional Deprivation," *European Journal of Developmental Psychology* 4, no. 3 (2007): 332–50, at 335.

199. Mitul A. Mehta et al., "Amygdala, Hippocampal and Corpus Callosum Size Following Severe Early Institutional Deprivation: The English and Romanian Adoptees Study Pilot," *Journal of Child Psychology and Psychiatry, and Allied Disciplines* 50, no. 8 (August 2009): 943–51.

200. Rutter et al., "Effects of Profound Early Institutional Deprivation," 347.

The early experiences of the Romanian orphans strongly resemble trauma that causes PTSD. If their mothers had been affected by PTSD during pregnancy, and the children were subsequently traumatized, the children were doubly victims. These studies have been corroborated many times. A series of studies has found that children who underwent birth complications, or experienced negative biological influences such as malnutrition or secondhand smoke, *and* who experienced early maternal rejection such as being reared in a public-care institution for more than four months during their first year after birth, or surviving an attempted abortion, were much more likely to manifest violence.[201]

All this evidence points to a multidimensional understanding of behavior—a "biosocial" explanation. At times, a genetic defect, or biological malformation due to chemical exposure, creates conditions for criminal behavior. At other times, causal factors include malnutrition, inadequate education, and harmful parenting. Most likely, however, it is a combination of many different biological and social elements—biosocial factors—working together.[202] The causal lines are sometimes surprising. Criminals who come from good families more often have biological dysfunction, such as loss of brain mass, whereas criminals from bad families often have good brains put to bad use.[203] In sum, "We can get to bad brains through bad genes or bad environments—or ... through the combination of

201. Raine, *The Anatomy of Violence*, 188 (Figure 6.1). The two studies referenced in the figure are, first, A. Raine, P. Brennan, and S. A. Mednick, "Birth Complications Combined with Early Maternal Rejection at Age 1 Year Predispose to Violent Crime at Age 18 Years," *Archives of General Psychiatry* 51, no. 12 (December 1994): 984–88; second, A. Piquero and S. Tibbetts, "The Impact of Pre/perinatal Disturbances and Disadvantaged Familial Environment in Predicting Criminal Offending," *Studies on Crime & Crime Prevention* 8 (1999): 52–70. See also Jianghong Liu, "Early Health Risk Factors for Violence," *Aggression and Violent Behavior* 16, no. 1 (2011): 63–73.

202. See Cesar J. Rebellon, J. C. Barnes, and Robert Agnew, "A Unified Theory of Crime and Delinquency: Foundation for a Biosocial Criminology," in *The Routledge International Handbook of Biosocial Criminology*, ed. Matt DeLisi and Michael G. Vaughn (Oxford: Routledge, 2014), 3–21.

203. For references, see Raine, *The Anatomy of Violence*, 254–55. See also Adrian Raine, "Biosocial Studies of Antisocial and Violent Behavior in Children and Adults," *Journal of Abnormal Child Psychology* 30, no. 4 (August 2002): 311–26.

both."[204] In other words, some people have an "interactive predisposition" or a "differential susceptibility" to certain negative psychological states and behavioral manifestations: a genetic factor interacting with the environmental condition may "predispose" someone and make him more "susceptible" to particular disorders.[205] This conclusion should be acceptable to sociologists and neuroscientists[206]—and perhaps to Aquinas.

In his analysis of the natural law, Aquinas notably took account of cultural influences toward evil by considering the case of German thievery.[207] According to Julius Caesar, the ancient Germans encouraged young men to maraud their enemies in order to diminish sloth and enrich their tribes.[208] Aquinas saw this as an example for how natural law in its general principles are known to all, but in some cases can "fail" (*deficere*) because people have "depraved reason from passion, or from evil custom, or from an evil habit of nature."[209] Thus, although theft "is expressly contrary to the natural law," the ancient Germans no longer grasped that theft was evil: their minds, and consequently their habits and behaviors, had been corrupted by their culture.[210] Human law serves as a corrective in this cultural situation, when "natural law was corrupted in the hearts of some [people] regarding certain things, such that they estimated to

204. Raine, *The Anatomy of Violence*, 270.

205. Tabery, *Beyond Versus*, 179.

206. See Anna S. Rudo-Hutt et al., "Biosocial Criminology as a Paradigm Shift," in *The Routledge International Handbook of Biosocial Criminology* (ed. DeLisi and Vaughn), 22–31.

207. For a good overview of the complex issues involved, see Gregory Doolan, "The Relation of Culture and Ignorance to Culpability in Thomas Aquinas," *The Thomist* 63, no. 1 (1999): 105–24.

208. Julius Caesar, *The Gallic War*, trans. Carolyn Hammond (Oxford: Oxford University Press, 1999), 161.

209. *ST* I-II, q. 94, a. 4.

210. Ibid. See María Elton, "The Darkening of Natural Reason and the Force of Law and Custom," in *Natural Law: Historical, Systematic and Juridical Approaches*, ed. Alejandro Néstor García Martínez et al. (Newcastle upon Tyne: Cambridge Scholars, 2008), 65–84. For a fascinating and thorough empirical study of the effects of intra-group and inter-group dynamics on individual moral behavior, see Naomi Ellemers, *Morality and the Regelation of Social Behaviors: Groups as Moral Anchors* (London: Routledge, 2017).

be good things that are naturally evil."[211] With even stronger language, Aquinas says, "the secondary precepts of the natural law can be removed from the hearts of men … on account of depraved customs and corrupt habits."[212] Whereas human habits are the result of repeated individual action, customs are the result of a united group's repeated communal actions: as habits are to an individual, so customs are to a group. Aquinas says that a culture is barbaric, properly speaking, "when there is no rule according to nature" (*secundum naturam*).[213] When nature, or some aspect of nature, is abandoned in society, the customs become unnatural, and the result, Aquinas says with surprisingly forceful language, is that "men are rendered irrational and almost beastly."[214]

In addition to the issue of ancient Germanic theft culture, Aquinas raises another example of evil societal customs that corrupt individuals, namely, "vices *contra naturam*."[215] He takes his cue from St. Paul's discussion of unnatural vice in the first chapter of the Epistle to the Romans, where he argues that God's "invisible nature," his "eternal power and deity," can be "clearly perceived in the things that have been made," but some "became futile in their thinking and their senseless minds were darkened."[216] They became idolatrous and so "God gave them up to dishonorable passions," namely, "their women exchanged natural relations for unnatural, and the men likewise gave up natural relations with women and were consumed with passion for one another, men committing shameless acts with men and receiving in their own persons the due penalty for their error."[217] Aquinas notes that, strictly speaking, vices of lust are primarily harmful to the individuals who practice them, as they are not per se directed to harming one's neighbor.[218] Nevertheless, they have

211. *ST* I-II, q. 94, a. 5, ad 1.
212. *ST* I-II, q. 94, a. 6.
213. *Sent. Politic.*, lib. 1, l. 1, n. 16.
214. *ST* I-II, q. 97, a. 3, ad 3.
215. *ST* I-II, q. 94, a. 6.
216. Rom 1:20–21.
217. Rom 1:26–27.
218. Lust primarily regards an inordinate desire for venereal pleasures that accrue

huge social consequences and can lead to societal customs, for they are often intertwined with sins directed against one's neighbor due to "malignity, which signifies an evil fire, that is, an evil affect in the heart."[219]

Culture can also undermine the *supernatural* good. In the religious sphere, Aquinas says, heretics and false Catholics desire "a fellowship of peace" with Catholics in order to draw virtuous Catholics away from grace and toward "infamous deeds depraved doctrine."[220] In general, therefore, Aquinas follows St. Paul in arguing that "bad company ruins good morals,"[221] which he interprets to mean: "Do not be seduced, for the bad speech of those who deny the resurrection corrupts good morals."[222] For Thomas, this is not binary advice to avoid all non-Catholics or non-Christians. In commenting on this very passage, Aquinas follows St. Jerome in holding that St. Paul's advice comes from Menander, a pagan philosopher.[223] There is something of a paradox here: a pagan author's advice cautions a Christian community about pagan company thereby manifesting the utility of pagan wisdom.[224] According to Aquinas, the benefit of non-Christian insight provides justification for scripture to utilize

to the self; Aquinas discusses violent lust (*ST* II-II, q. 154, a. 7), and the vice of brutality, delight in torturing others, as both are contrary to temperance (*ST* II-II, q. 159, a. 2). Indirectly, sins of lust undermine the sacrament of marriage, and, when fruitful, harm children born from an illicit union (see *ST* Suppl., q. 41, a. 1 = *Super Sent.*, lib. 4, d. 26, q. 1, a. 1).

219. *Super Rom.*, c. 1, l. 8, n. 150.

220. *Contra impugnantes*, pars 2, c. 4, arg. 1. This is a quotation of the gloss on Neh 6:2.

221. 1 Cor 15:33.

222. *Super I Cor.*, c. 15, l. 4, n. 931.

223. It is a word-for-word quotation from Menander's play *Thais*: W. A. Oldfather and L. W. Daly, "A Quotation from Menander in the Pastoral Epistles?," *Classical Philology* 38, no. 3 (1943): 202–4. See also Hans Conzelmann, *1 Corinthians* (Hermeneia Series), trans. James W. Leitch (Philadelphia: Fortress Press, 1975), 278.

224. William O. Walker argues that the presence of quotation from a pagan suggests that the passage was not written by St. Paul: see Walker, "1 Corinthians 15:29–34 as a Non-Pauline Interpolation," *The Catholic Biblical Quarterly* 69, no. 1 (2007): 84–103. Kenneth E. Bailey, noting that the quotation from Menander is immediately preceded by a quotation of Is 22:13, more persuasively argues that Paul's references mean to persuade both Jews and Gentiles of his point: see Bailey, *Paul Through Mediterranean Eyes: Cultural Studies in 1 Corinthians* (Downers Grove, Ill.: IVP Academic, 2011), 453.

Gentile authorities, and more generally for Christians to learn from and keep company with good pagans.[225]

The above exposition shows that Aquinas considers causes of bad inclinations as ontologically distinct, but he often lists together nonvoluntary and partly voluntary influences toward evil. However, the medieval theologian does not discuss how these different causes may be mutually influencing: he presents biological and social factors as discrete factors. The accumulation of scientific knowledge, possible only through massive data analysis, now presents a more holistic understanding of the nonvoluntary sources of vicious inclinations. Because the *Doctor Humanitatis* accepts the individual causal lines of biology and environment, it would seem that in principle he could accept the "vulnerability-stress model," which proposes that people can have an innate or acquired biological vulnerability to a disorder that is only activated by certain environmental stressors.[226] Here, then, we find a place where empirical science clearly enriches Aquinas's position on the levels of theory and particularized knowledge. Reciprocally, he enriches empirical science through his understanding of the human intellect and will as the primary co-causes of moral evil, as the following section discusses.

## GOOD INTENTIONS AND FULLY VOLUNTARY EVIL HABITS

With insight gleaned from experience, Oscar Wilde developed the chief character in *The Picture of Dorian Gray*, a half-image of himself. Dorian Gray's handsome appearance remained unchanged while his interior state became increasingly corrupt, exemplifying how voluntary evil primarily corrupts the soul. When describing such deviation, contemporary discourse favors the term "wrongdoing" to "wickedness." Although the average person would admit that others commit faults sometimes, people increasingly deny that evil

225. *Super I Cor.*, c. 15, l. 4, n. 931.
226. See Linden, *The Biology of Psychological Disorders*, xxi.

habits are fully voluntary. Many find it difficult to acknowledge that anyone is wholly responsible when he deviates from the good, especially when that deviation is consistent and feels "natural" to the deviant agent. Thomas articulates one version of this argument: if an impulse arises from nature, then it cannot be sinful, as "whatever is natural cannot be the cause of sin, for sin is *contra naturam*."[227] But we experience all sorts of impulses that can draw us astray, though they are ultimately rooted in nature, such as impulses toward food and reproduction. Therefore, it seems that evil choices are not fully voluntary or they are extremely rare.

A weaker form of this argument centers around the claim that people generally have good intentions. Even Aquinas argues that people never choose evil in itself; it would be impossible to do so, because evil constitutes something to be avoided and, as such, is repugnant to the appetite and will.[228] Thus, the root of all human choice is a desire for good and people always will something they apprehend as good, even if their choice has evil effects.[229] It seems to follow that the development of vice is a case of double-effect, for Thomas says: "Nothing prohibits one act from having two effects, of which only one is intended, while the other is beside the intention. But moral acts receive their species according to what is intended, and not from that which is beside the intention, since this is *per accidens*."[230] What a person primarily wants is the good associated with his choices—such as the sensual pleasure in adultery—not to have a vicious character.[231] Another version of this argument is to say that a person does not *intend* to become vicious—he just wants a little fun; he *means well* in the end, perhaps having made a fundamental option for the good; he just cannot help himself.

227. *ST* I-II, q. 75, a. 2, obj. 3.

228. See *ST* I-II, q. 8, a. 1, ad 1.

229. *ST* I-II, q. 8, a. 1.

230. *ST* II-II, q. 64, a. 7. For a standard summary of double effect reasoning, see Joseph Mangan, "An Historical Analysis of the Principle of Double Effect," *Theological Studies* 10 (1949): 41–61.

231. This is the example given in *De malo*, q. 3, a. 12, co.

Aquinas addresses the supposed inevitability of sin and sees in that claim a version of Manichean pessimism, which holds that man necessarily sins and in no way can avoid sin.[232] One response to this claim is to note that "all necessity is either that of constraint or of natural inclination. But the necessity of sinning is not a natural inclination, because then our nature would be evil insofar as it would incline us to evil."[233] However, sinning cannot be forced, because then the act would not be a sin, as it would not be voluntary, and "free choice is a power established under reason and over the executive motive power."[234]

Regarding supposed good intentions, Aquinas addresses whether or not a person can sin from certain knowledge of his action (*certa scientia*), which he equates with "malice" (*malitia*).[235] He reasons that to pursue evil action knowingly is possible; to do so repeatedly is nothing other than to develop habits of voluntary evil, that is, vices.[236]

When discussing evil we commit (as distinguished from evil we suffer), Aquinas follows his broad definition of *sin* as a defect in the due order, form, or measure of an agent's action.[237] He considers sin as an analogous reality and distinguishes between (1) evil that is committed involuntarily, which he calls a general kind of dysfunction or sin-defect (*peccatum*), and (2) evil that is committed voluntarily, which is a *voluntary sin* (*peccatum voluntarium*) and therefore

232. See *De veritate*, q. 24, a. 12, co.: "Manichaei dixerunt quod homo necessario peccat, nec aliquo modo peccatum vitare potest."

233. Ibid., s.c., 9.

234. Ibid., co.: "liberum arbitrium sit quaedam potentia constituta infra rationem, et supra motivam exequentem."

235. See Carl N. Still and Darren E. Dahl, "Evil and Moral Failure in *De malo*," in *Aquinas's Disputed Questions on Evil: A Critical Guide* (ed. Dougherty), 146–63.

236. Gregory M. Reichberg, "Beyond Privation: Moral Evil in Aquinas's 'De Malo,'" *Review of Metaphysics* 55 (2002): 751–84, argues that this possibility undermines Aquinas's conception of evil as a privation. A closer analysis suggests otherwise: "Insofar as a vice is a habit, the habit itself qua habit is not what is bad about a vice. Rather, what is bad is the fact that the habit moves the agent away from the all-things-considered good, depriving her of that good" (McCluskey, *Thomas Aquinas on Moral Wrongdoing*, 71).

237. *De malo*, q. 2, a. 2. See *De veritate*, q. 24, a. 7.

also a fault (*culpa*).[238] When Thomas speaks about "sin" he usually means voluntary sin and fault, for he describes sin as an act that is opposed to an act of virtue, that is, it is a fully voluntary act that proceeds from a good fully voluntary habit.[239] By definition, "the first cause of sin is in the will, which commands all voluntary acts, in which alone sin is found."[240] Sin in this sense is not only the privation of a good act, nor merely a disordered exterior act, but primarily a disordered interior act.[241] Sin is a particular evil *act*, whereas vice is an evil *habit*, a disposition to perform a sin easily, quickly, skillfully, and with pleasure.[242]

A person can firmly desire to commit evil before a vice is developed.[243] Aquinas argues that when a disordered will knowingly chooses a temporal good such as adulterous pleasure knowing that it excludes a higher spiritual good, such as the order of reason and natural law, or divine law, or divine charity, he willingly makes a tradeoff.[244] He chooses to relinquish the spiritual good because he prefers a lower good. But choosing to relinquish a spiritual good constitutes willing a spiritual evil, and deforms the soul. Here we can recall that moral evil is not a mere absence of good, but a privation of a *due form*, for Aquinas argues that moral evil is also "a form contrary to a thing's due perfection."[245] Some accidental form (a principle of disorder) substitutes for the proper form of a thing, similar to the case of "monsters" when a mutation of a healthy gene induces a deformity in a person.[246] When an exerciser decides to walk in Georgia during a summer afternoon, she necessarily wills to appropriate

238. *De malo*, q. 2, a. 2.

239. See, for example, *ST* I-II, q. 71, a. 1; q. 72, a. 1, ad 2.

240. *ST* I-II, q. 71, a. 6.

241. *De malo*, q. 2, a. 2.

242. See *De malo*, q. 2, a. 1, ad s.c. 9; *ST* I-II, q. 71, aa. 3–4.

243. See the discussion in Jensen, *Sin: A Thomistic Psychology*, 177–82. He cites *ST* I-II, q. 78, a. 3, as a chief text supporting his position.

244. *ST* I-II, q. 78, a. 1. McCluskey defends this position against objectors in *Thomas Aquinas on Moral Wrongdoing*, 140–47.

245. Still and Dahl, "Evil and Moral Failure in *De malo*," 150.

246. See *De malo*, q. 1, a. 3.

to herself the quality or form of "having-walked," that is, she wills to be a-person-who-has-walked-in-a-hot-and-humid-environment, and when a sick person takes medicine, he wills to be one-who-has-received-medicine. Similarly, a person who has intercourse with another person's spouse necessarily wills appropriate the negative "form" or quality of a-person-who-has-committed-adultery. Persons in such cases secondarily and consequently choose a deformity they knows to be inseparable from the good they desires.[247] In cases where a person does not make such an explicit tradeoff, she may more simply choose to reject those helps and circumstances that would help her avoid committing what he knows to be evil.[248] It is otherwise if the agent is ignorant that such an effect follows from such a cause, as when a hunter—believing that he is killing a deer—unintentionally kills his enemy,[249] or as when Jacob had intercourse with Leah while thinking that she was his wife Rachel.[250] But when a person knows that he is committing adultery, and he knows that adultery is disordered behavior, then by performing adultery he knowingly chooses disorder for himself. In doing so, he shapes himself into a person who has voluntarily performed evil and is more prone to becoming wicked. When a person becomes an evildoer, he does not become a victim of an unfortunate side-effect of repeatedly doing evil—he experiences the invariable result of his voluntary actions.

One might object that the adulterer does not really want vice (the effect); what he wants is a different effect (pleasure).[251] As an initial response, Aquinas argues that the sign that one does not want the disorder is when he gives up the good to which the disorder is

247. *De malo*, q. 3, a. 12, co. and ad 10.

248. *De malo*, q. 2, a. 8, ad 4.

249. See *ST* I-II, q. 6, a. 8.

250. See Gn 29:17–26. Aquinas discusses a similar case in *De Malo*, q. 3, a. 8. However, a person can sin through malice and ignorance when he knows in general that a particular act is sinful, but his passion stops him from considering in the moment that the particular temptation is not worth trading off for the loss of a spiritual good (*ST* I-II, q. 78, a. 1, ad 1).

251. *De malo*, q. 1, a. 3.

united: such would be the case if a person were to flee adultery and so reject the pleasure as well.[252] When he chooses a disordered pleasure repeatedly, he thereby desires it more than he wishes to avoid its consequent vice. Aquinas bases his argument on a general principle: "If someone wills a cause from which he knows a particular effect results, it follows that he wills that effect."[253] In the case of knowingly-disordered actions, a person who wills a good that is always conjoined with evil unavoidably wills the evil too. Furthermore, we can acknowledge that a single sin may not cause a habit of sin.[254] Single acts of sin are temporary and passing, but their effects can last through time, especially on the person who committed them. When a person commits a single mortal sin, he does not ordinarily acquire the corresponding habit of a vice in that moment.[255] One evening of drunkenness does not create a drunk. Nevertheless, by choosing a single mortal sin, a person places himself in the *state of attachment to sin.* Because his will "has forsaken the unchangeable good [and] has attached itself to a changeable as its end, and the power and inclination of this attachment remains in it until it once again attaches itself to the unchangeable good."[256] Once the person has turned his back on the end established by the path of virtue, he is habitually attached to sin because he has directed himself toward the end established by the path of vice. When someone willingly performs the act of adultery as a cause of pleasure, that person seeks pleasure through a gravely disordered act. The foreseen pleasure does not move his will, for he can resist it. Rather, the person moves himself toward the foreseen pleasure despite its disorder.[257] Therefore, "although perhaps he does not will that effect in itself, never-

252. *De malo*, q. 3, a. 12, ad 3.

253. *Sent. Ethic.*, lib. 3, l. 12, n. 6. This is different than saying that to will the end is to will the efficacious means thereto: *ST* I-II, q. 8, a. 2, s.c. Here Aquinas is not considering an ends-means relation, but rather a cause-effect relation.

254. See *ST* I-II, q. 71, a. 4.

255. See *ST* I-II, q. 68, a. 2; q. 71, a. 4: "sicut enim non generatur habitus per unum actum, ita nec per unum actum corrumpitur."

256. *De veritate*, q. 12, a. 12.

257. See *De malo*, q. 1, a. 3.

theless he prefers that the effect exist more than that the cause not exist."[258] Consequently, the person is disposed to choose another mortal sin in conformity with that previous choice—and, when presented with the possibility, he will indeed choose it quickly "unless he restrains himself with much deliberation."[259] When adulterous pleasure is repeatedly sought, the acts of adultery necessarily cause the vice of adulterous lust—which is nothing other than a habitual delight in pleasures per se disordered, as they are obtained in sexual union with another person's spouse.[260] By committing the same sort of mortal sin many times, whether it is an act of grave drunkenness, gluttony, lust, or any other, a person will gradually become enslaved to the corresponding vice. The scriptural proverb vividly captures this wretched reality: "As the dog returns to his vomit, so the fool repeats his folly."[261]

Vice is undesirable in itself; sweat is uncomfortable; bitter tastes are repugnant—these are not ordinarily chosen for their own sake. Nevertheless, if the actions of virtue are voluntary, so are those of vice, for just as virtue is the product of free choices, so is vice.[262] Thomas explains, "Nothing prohibits something being not-voluntary in itself that nevertheless *is* voluntary on account of something else, as a bitter medicine [is taken] for the sake of health."[263] A person who knows that certain evils are inextricably bound up with a good that he desires may be said to choose them when he chooses their conjoined good. More properly speaking, because the apparent good is bound up with evil, the person "chooses something that is good in some respect but evil absolutely."[264] A person is presented with an apparent good (sexual pleasure), and he then "pre-considers" a

258. *Sent. Ethic.*, lib. 3, l. 12, n. 6.

259. Ibid.

260. See *ST* II-II, q. 154, a. 8.

261. Prv 26:11 (see usage in *Super Psalmo* 17, n. 14).

262. *Sent. Ethic.*, lib. 3, l. 12, n. 6: "Si enim verum est quod actiones virtutum et vitiorum sint voluntariae, et per consequens virtus et malitia." See also ibid., n. 8.

263. *Sent. Ethic.*, lib. 3, l. 12, n. 6.; emphasis added.

264. *De malo*, q. 1, a. 3.

moral defect in the good (it comes from adultery) but chooses to go ahead with his decision despite the disorder. The result is that the agent voluntarily chooses an act that is lust-making, that is, by its nature it tends to produce the vice of lust. Vice naturally follows repeated voluntary evil acts: by knowingly doing evil, a person habituates himself and shapes his will, intellect, desires, imagination, and so on, to find pleasure in doing evil. Aquinas summarizes his argument this way: "It is manifest that men who commit injustice become unjust, and seducers become incontinent. Therefore, it is irrational that someone desires to commit injustice but does not desire to be unjust, or desires to seduce but does not desire to be incontinent. Thus, it is manifest that, if not ignorant, a person voluntarily does things from which it follows that he becomes unjust, he will be voluntarily unjust."[265] As he says in another place, "virtues are voluntary because we are the causes of the habits by which we are disposed toward that in which we establish our end," that is, virtue is voluntary because we voluntarily habituate ourselves to be disposed to seek and delight in proximate ends and goods that we desire; "for similar reasons, it follows that evils also are voluntary."[266]

Continued disordered choices create vice, for repeated voluntary sin results in a voluntary evil habit—a persistently twisted will.[267] Over time, a person might cultivate vice through different choices in different circumstances, slowing shaping himself into a person of disordered desires rather than a virtuous person. Because of this dynamic, sin is an active principle of chosen evil, opposed to virtue which is an active principle of chosen good.[268] Properly speaking, vice is opposed to the *ratio* of virtue, for vice consists in a voluntary disposition contrary to one's nature.[269] As inverted mirror images of virtuous actions and virtues in themselves, sins and vices are spe-

265. *Sent. Ethic.*, lib. 3, l. 12, n. 6.
266. Ibid., l. 13, n. 11.
267. See *De malo*, q. 1, a. 1, ad 4.
268. *ST* I-II, q. 71, a. 1, ad 1.
269. *ST* I-II, q. 71, aa. 1–2.

cifically distinguished by their matter or object.[270] Because the will commands voluntary acts and thereby moves or restrains a person's powers, all those powers are potentially subjects of good or evil habits, for act and habit belong to the same subject.[271] Accordingly, in the *Secunda Secundae* of the *Summa Theologiae,* Aquinas considers vices after the virtues to which they are opposed.

Just as good acts tend to develop into virtue, so voluntary evil has its own sort of corruptive dynamism that develops into vice. Thomas highlights the interior "life" of sin in his discussion of the distinctions among sins. After pride, some sins are the "heads" and directors of other particular sins, and therefore are called "capital" vices.[272] To the extent that they deploy other sins to obtain their objectives, they are also "commanders" and the sins directed by them like an "army."[273] Seeing how actual sins are specified according to their objects,[274] Aquinas, following Gregory the Great, enumerates seven capital vices as follows: *vainglory* is the disordered desire for honor and glory;[275] *envy* is the destructive sorrow over another's good;[276] *acedia* is a deadening sorrow that leads one away from spiritual goods;[277] *wrath* is the excessive anger against a good that prevents one from achieving one's goal;[278] *avarice* is the excessive desire for material goods;[279] *gluttony* is the excessive desire for the pleasures of food and drink;[280] *lust* is excessive desire for pleasures associated with procreation.[281] In his *De malo* (Disputed Questions on Evil), Thomas goes to great lengths to

270. See *ST* II-II, prol.
271. See *ST* I-II, q. 74, a. 2.
272. *De malo,* q. 8, a. 1.
273. Ibid.
274. See *ST* I-II, q. 72, a. 1.
275. *ST* II-II, q. 132; *De malo,* q. 9.
276. *ST* II-II, q. 36; *De malo,* q. 10.
277. *ST* II-II, q. 35; *De malo,* q. 11.
278. *ST* II-II, q. 158; *De malo,* q. 12. For anger as a passion, see *ST* I-II, qq. 46–48, and my discussion of the irascible appetite with respect to fortitude in chapter 5 above.
279. *ST* II-II, q. 118; *De malo,* q. 13.
280. *ST* II-II, q. 148; *De malo,* q. 14.
281. *ST* II-II, q. 153; *De malo,* q. 15.

show how each capital vice leads to other vices, which he calls their "daughters."[282] Aquinas's exposition provides a "forensic and therapeutic"[283] analysis of the spiritual and psychological effects that habitual sin has upon a person, showing how the weight of sin can lead a person down in a spiral of ever-greater corruption. He illustrates how each capital sin contains within itself seeds of other sins, just as a mother conceives offspring within herself.[284] This entails naming realities as they stand.

Vice is the anti-virtue: whereas virtue perfects a power—especially the will—along with the person who has the virtue, vice instead corrupts the will and the entire person.[285] Voluntary habits—whether good or evil—give rise to distinctive desires and actions that shape a person's character. Through habitual mortal sin, one's mind, will, and emotions become fixed on a temporal good, or against a good, and through one's attachment to self, one's character is transformed in a quasi-permanent manner. One could rightly call this habitual attachment a sort of slavery, for "evil habits are not subject to the will after they have been generated."[286] For example, "although one voluntarily becomes unjust, it does not follow that he can cease to be unjust and to become just whenever he wills," similar to the way a person cannot choose to be instantaneously healthy after a lifetime of a lack of exercise, eating poorly, and not following his doctor's advice.[287] After becoming habituated to a particular mortal sin, a person is justly called an "adulterer" or a "thief" or whatnot, for "a person is designated [as such], not from an act or an emotion, but from a habit."[288] Thus, we designate people by their vices, nam-

282. See M. V. Dougherty, "Moral Luck and the Capital Vices in *De malo*: Glutty and Lust," in *Aquinas's Disputed Questions on Evil: A Critical Guide* (ed. Dougherty), 222–34.

283. Eileen C. Sweeney, "Aquinas on the Seven Deadly Sins: Tradition and Innovation," in *Sin in Medieval and Early Modern Culture: The Tradition of the Seven Deadly Sins*, ed. Richard G. Newhauser and Susan Janet Ridyard (Rochester, N.Y.: Boydell and Brewer, 2012), 85–106, at 99.

284. *De malo*, q. 9, a. 3.

285. See *ST* I-II, q. 71, a. 1, ad 2.

286. *Sent. Ethic.*, lib. 3, l. 12, n. 7.

287. Ibid.

288. *De malo*, q. 8, a. 1, ad 15.

ing persons thieves or adulterers from their characteristic evil voluntary habits.[289]

Above we saw that "malice" is a voluntarily evil act; when performed repeatedly, it becomes "a habit of vice opposed to virtue" such that "a person who sins from habit is said to sin from malice."[290] Aquinas notes that a thing can be inclined to something "through its proper form" and precisely in this way "the will is inclined to a mutable good to which the deformity of sin is conjoined."[291] This can happen through weakness and passion or "through habit, when by custom the inclination to a particular good is now turned into habit and [second] nature. At that point, [the will] is inclined by its own proper movement without some passion; and this is to sin from choice, whether by effort, or by certain knowledge, or even from malice."[292]

A person who voluntarily and habitually chooses evil thereby acts from malice and develops vice within himself. This claim does not violate the principle of double-effect for at least two reasons. First, one can apply double-effect reasoning only when the effect is *not* inextricably tied to the cause. Regarding morally evil effects that necessarily result from one's act, Thomas says: "The consequences of an action are either foreseen or not. If they are foreseen, it is clear that they increase goodness or evil. For when someone knows that many evils may follow from his action, and does not desist on account of this, it is clear that his will is even more disordered."[293] Unless the foresight in this argument refers to knowledge of an evil effect that is inseparably bound up with his action, then it would contradict his observation that a person can not-will an evil effect that results from his action.[294] Hence, Thomas applies the princi-

289. See *De malo*, q. 8, a. 1, ad 15.

290. *Super Rom.*, c. 1, l. 8, n. 158.

291. *De malo*, q. 3, a. 12.

292. Ibid.

293. *ST* I-II, q. 20, a. 5.

294. *ST* II-II, q. 64, a. 7. He calls the will's rejection of evil "nolition" (*ST* I-II, q. 8, a. 1, ad 1).

ple of double-effect regarding consequences that are only *accidentally* and *probably* resultant from one's action. Elizabeth Anscombe agrees, saying that double-effect reasoning becomes "absurd" when it chooses "a description under which the action is intentional, and [gives] the action under that description as *the* intentional act.... This is as if one could say 'I am merely moving a knife through such-and-such a region of space' regardless of the fact that the space is manifestly occupied by a human neck, or a by a rope supporting a climber."[295] Hence, in the judgment of Denis Sullivan, one has grounds to say that an agent is not responsible for an evil effect of his action only "when one is dealing with effects that are probable, but ... these grounds disappear when one is dealing with those effects that are certain."[296]

Second, one can apply the "tests of intentionality" to the development of vice.[297] There are three such tests. (1) The countermeasures test: *does the agent take steps to avoid the bad effect?* In the case of vice, evildoers do not take steps to avoid vice. Rather, they prefer to commit an evil deed rather than to avoid developing vice. (2) The non-realization test: *what if only the good effect results?* For vicious acts, it is impossible for only good effects to result. A person cannot repeatedly experience sexual pleasure with another person's spouse and thereby commit adultery, without developing the vice of lust. (3) The counterfactual test: *what would the agent have done if he had had the means of attaining the good effect only?* For vice, it is impossible to find means for performing the good alone, as the choice is to

295. Elizabeth Anscombe, "Action, Intention, and 'Double Effect,'" *Proceedings of the American Catholic Philosophical Association* 56 (1982): 12–25, at 23.

296. Denis F. Sullivan, "The Doctrine of Double Effect and the Domains of Moral Responsibility," *The Thomist* 64 (2000): 423–48, at 448. A similar conclusion is drawn by Thomas A. Cavanaugh in his article, "Aquinas's Account of Double Effect," *The Thomist* 61 (1997): 107–21.

297. See Kenneth W. Kemp, "Lecture #7: St. Thomas Aquinas, *Summa Theologiae*. Thomistic Ethics: The Principle of Double Effect" (n.d.), slide 12; available at courseweb.stthomas.edu/kwkemp/ethics/L/Pt1/L07PDE.pdf. See also Kemp, "Just-War Theory and the Casuistry of Prima Facie Duties" (PhD diss., University of Notre Dame, 1984), 194–212.

do evil. Either one will experience a disordered pleasure that leads to vice or one will not experience the pleasure and therefore not reach the good that he desires. These tests help show that vice is a fully voluntary evil habit, and that vice exists in people who purposely, effectively, and repeatedly perform morally disordered actions with resulting pleasure.

Through personal sin, a person further deepens the wounds he received from original sin: "reason is dulled, especially regarding actions to take; the will is hardened to the good; great difficulties are added to doing good; and concupiscence blazes more powerfully."[298] One effect specific to personal sin is the "stain" that the soul receives from clinging to created things inordinately.[299] This spiritual stain, defilement, and shadow lessens the splendor of truth that shines upon the mind and the consequent loveliness that comes from a will that chooses good.[300] The darkness of the stain deepens with every voluntary evil act. We have seen that habits create a connatural instinct within a person: "things seem natural, good and pleasant to each habit that are proper to it, that is, those things that are fitting to it."[301] At the same time, things that are contrary to the habit slowly become less poignant to the soul: in the case of vice, this leads to a desensitization toward the good, similar to the way wine is gradually diluted by the addition of water.[302] Bad habits, therefore, are focused on creaturely ends in a disordered way. Vices make things contrary to nature—perverted things—seem delightful to the person mired in them.[303] Thus, vices pervert persons, for "the perversion of a thing happens because its necessary interior harmony is corrupted."[304] Now the highest good is naturally the most de-

298. *ST* I-II, q. 85, a. 3.

299. The stain from disordered free choice is not attributable to original sin, for, Aquinas makes clear, it comes from the action of the soul itself. See *ST* I-II, q. 86, a. 1, ad 1.

300. See *ST* I-II, q. 86, a. 1.

301. *Sent. Ethic.*, lib. 3, l. 10, n. 7.

302. For a general explanation of the dilution of natural virtue, see *ST* I, q. 119, a. 1, ad 4.

303. See *Sent. Ethic.*, lib. 7, l. 5, n. 7.

304. *Sent. Ethic.*, lib. 7, l. 1, n. 4.

lightful thing. The general effect of every bad habit is therefore the increase of self-love and the contempt of God, for pride is primarily harbored in the will, which ought to love God above all things.[305] In this way, everyone who sins because of a habit "necessarily sins through a certain malice."[306] That is, the sinner through his own power and "industry" wills to suffer the loss of a spiritual good so that he can obtain a disordered temporal good.[307]

Venial sin, for its part, does not affect the character in such a deep way, though its corrosive effects include disposing a person to commit mortal sin, and developing habitual dispositions that prevent full personal flourishing. Starting with Ecclesiasticus 19:1, "He who spurns small things shall fall little by little," Aquinas argues that venial sin, especially the habit of venial sins, causes a "lust for sinning" to increase, and it thereby strengthens one's disposition or habit for sin.[308] In addition, venial sin generally can undermine one's bulwarks against mortal sin. This is not to say that many venial sins can be transformed into a mortal sin, for this is impossible.[309] Rather, intentional venial sin habituates the will to be averse to subjecting itself to due order in small things. Purposeful venial sins thereby incline a person to commit mortal sin, and dispose him to avoid subjecting his will even to the order of the ultimate end.[310] The reason for this is that, as Jensen says, venial sin arises from a confusion about a person's actual state of affairs; it is not actually ordered to God: "the ultimate end to which venial sin is virtually ordered is broader—or less determinate—than either the divine good or any good to be found in creatures."[311] Aquinas compares this process to the way that overwork disposes a person to develop a fever: overwork will not always and necessarily lead to a fever, but it certainly can do

305. See *De malo*, q. 8, a. 3.
306. *ST* I-II, q. 78, a. 2. See also *Super Rom.*, c. 1, l. 8, n. 158.
307. See *ST* I-II, q. 78, a. 1.
308. *ST* I-II, q. 88, a. 3.
309. See *ST* I-II, q. 88, a. 4.
310. See *ST* I-II, q. 88, a. 3.
311. Jensen, "Venial Sin and the Ultimate End," 99.

so.[312] Garrigou-Lagrange says souls habituated to venial sin are like infantilized persons "who do not happily pass through the crisis of adolescence and who, though they do not remain children, never reach the full development of maturity."[313] The long-term results of habitual venial sin include: a cooling of one's fervor for virtue, a dulling of one's delight in doing good, a blunting of one's understanding of truth, a slowing of one's spiritual growth, a hindrance of certain graces, a growth of one's indifference to evil, and an increase of one's attachment to creaturely goods and things that harm the soul.[314] Repeated voluntary sin has a definite trajectory: a downward spiral that drags one from his ultimate good and makes his soul ugly, as happened with Dorian Gray.

### THE DOWNWARD SPIRAL OF EVIL

On account of original and personal sin, and their devastating effects in this good world, man experiences disorders at every turn. Physical dysfunctions, psychological and emotional dysfunction, and mortal and venial sin threaten to turn man away from his true good, away from God, the ultimate good. Humans experience devastating, widespread, and ever-increasing disorder, for one sin causes other sins: sin is its own punishment.

Although evil is a privation, chosen evil moves along a fairly regular, destructive trajectory. Everyone who suffers from original sin and its effects, along with personal defects from individual nature and nurture, experiences some form of disordered passions. We are not merely passive with respect to evil. The prophet Hosea said to iniquitous Israel: "You have plowed iniquity, you have reaped injustice, you have eaten the fruit of lies."[315] St. Paul developed this

312. See *ST* I-II, q. 89, a. 6, ad 1.

313. Ibid., 461. Reginald Garrigou-Lagrange, *The Three Ages of the Interior Life*, Vol. 1, trans. M. Timothea Doyle (St. Louis, MO: B. Herder, 1947).

314. See Jordan Aumann, "The Theology of Venial Sin," *Proceedings of the Catholic Theological Society of America* 10 (1955): 75–94, at 93–94.

315. Hos 10:13.

theme, saying, "Do not be deceived; God is not mocked, for whatever a man sows, that he will also reap. For he who sows to his own flesh will from the flesh reap corruption."[316] Aquinas explains that, for the most part, seed bears fruit according to the condition of the soil in which it is planted.[317] Hence, for the one who "sows in the flesh," that is, "is fervent and places his work [in the flesh], it is necessary that that work should corrupt and go to waste."[318]

By synthesizing Aquinas's various statements and sources, we can establish a stepwise pattern by which evil corrupts the soul. According to Jerome, sins can be divided into sins of thought, word, or deed.[319] With his characteristic insight, Thomas accepts and develops this division. Insofar as one's thoughts, words, and deeds are united by a single motive, Aquinas says, these constitute degrees of a single sin or stages in the generation of sin: it begins in thought, expresses itself in words, and is consummated in deeds.[320] For example, when a person is angry and wants revenge, he is first disturbed in his thoughts; second, he erupts into abusive language; finally, he goes to the point of harmful actions.[321] Once deeds are repeated to some extent, they create a disposition of incontinence, as noted above. In this case, a person is weakly inclined to perform some evil action, typically in a limited number of circumstances; when he commits the evil, he might do so unskillfully, and he feel some disgust at it. Gregory the Great helps Aquinas to add two more stages to this picture.[322] After committing evil deeds, a person develops evil customs or habits, that is, vices, and these tend to develop into presumption of God's mercy or despair.[323] Combining the insights

316. Gal 6:7–8.

317. *Super Gal.*, c. 6, l. 2, n. 359.

318. Ibid.

319. *ST* I-II, q. 72, a. 7, s.c. See Jerome, *Super Ezechiel*, lib. 13, on Ezek 44:23 (PL 25:427).

320. See *ST* I-II, q. 72, a. 7.

321. Ibid.

322. Ibid., obj 2. See Gregorius Magnus, *Moralia in Job*, lib. 4, c. 27 (PL 75:662).

323. *ST* I-II, q. 72, a. 7, obj. 2. In his response to this objection, Thomas notes that Gregory's second stage (performing sin openly) corresponds to Jerome's second and third stages: expressing evil in words and acting upon evil in deed.

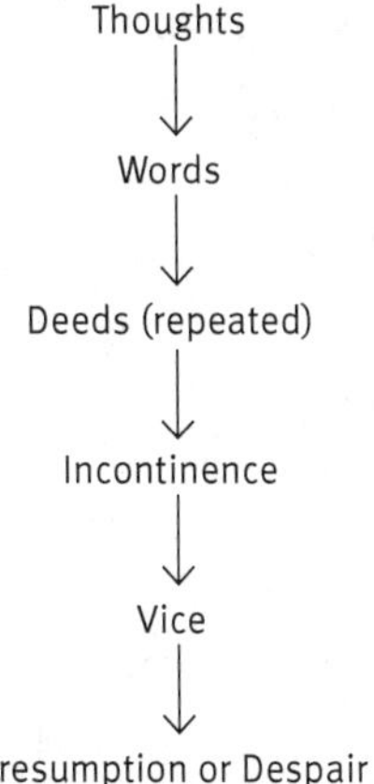


FIGURE 9. STAGES OF VOLUNTARY EVIL

of Jerome, Aristotle, and Gregory, we can see a six-stage process in the development of sin:

1. A person has voluntary disordered thoughts and/or desires.
2. The person voluntarily expresses his disordered thoughts.
3. The person acts upon his disordered thoughts.
4. The person repeatedly and voluntarily commits the same evil act, and so develops incontinence.
5. The incontinent person repeatedly sins and so develops vice.
6. After being confirmed in vice, a person presumes on God's mercy or despairs of it.

These stages can be depicted in a causal schema, as depicted in Figure 9 above.

It is important to note that although a previous stage *can* cause a later stage, one stage does not necessarily lead to the next. A person can have evil thoughts without speaking about them; he can threaten to do evil without going through with it; he can perform one evil deed but not develop a vice; and he can have vice without falling into despair. Each stage naturally leads to the other, just as a person naturally develops from the embryonic stage to childhood and then to adolescence.[324] But just as a person's maturation can be arrested by some rare exterior cause, so in principle a person can stop on any given stage without descending to further evil. Aquinas insists that the decisive factor in the development of personal evil is one's fully voluntary habit.

Nonvoluntary and involuntary influences do not affect the will directly, or at least not in the majority of cases. Negative influences combine with the effects of one's personal choices, so that the nonvoluntariness of movements caused by these influences largely depends on how one has voluntarily responded to the object and one's own movements. Some behaviors arise from within us "quasi-unexpectedly on account of the inclination of habit."[325] In these situations, the less an action comes from premeditation, the more it comes from habit. A person can choose by reason and deliberation without habit something he foresees, but when an event occurs suddenly, a person typically chooses according to habit.[326] For example, when a knife-wielding thug approaches in daylight, a kung fu master has time to consider what he will do; but when the expert is ambushed, he will react according to the skills he has developed. Similarly, when a person considers that he will enter a place where liquor flows freely, he can prepare himself to respond with temperance; but if he is suddenly offered alcohol, he will respond with whatever sobriety or indulgence that he has previously developed. Responding from habit does not equal responding involuntarily; Aquinas points out that the fully voluntary habits were developed through free choices for particular goods that served as goals for the person: the kung fu master voluntarily cultivated ways to repulse physical threats and the drinker shaped his temperance by choosing or rejecting drinks in the past. Habits such as these entail

324. *ST* I-II, q. 72, a. 7, ad 2.
325. *De veritate*, q. 24, a. 12.
326. Ibid.

that an agent will easily, quickly, and skillfully choose whatever accorded with his previously-chosen goal, unless he impedes his inclination with greater and more attentive deliberation.[327]

Like a powerful cancer that devastates every organ it touches, evil has a sort of inertia that will continue until something potent eliminates it. Because evil is precisely that which corrupts nature, the goodness of natural power is insufficient to save man from this death spiral. When Dorian Gray realized this truth, he began to question things seriously:

> Was it really true that one could never change? He felt a wild longing for the unstained purity of his boyhood—his rose-white boyhood, as Lord Henry had once called it. He knew that he had tarnished himself, filled his mind with corruption and given horror to his fancy; that he had been an evil influence to others, and had experienced a terrible joy in being so; and that of the lives that had crossed his own, it had been the fairest and the most full of promise that he had brought to shame. But was it all irretrievable? Was there no hope for him?[328]

The answer to Dorian Gray's question is treated in the next chapter. There we will see what Oscar Wilde discovered on his deathbed: we are continually in need of a supernatural power to overcome the effects of evil habits.[329] We are ever in need of grace.

327. Ibid.

328. Oscar Wilde, *The Picture of Dorian Gray: An Annotated, Uncensored Edition*, ed. Nicholas Frankel (Cambridge, Mass.: The Belknap Press of Harvard University Press, 2011), 248.

329. See *ST* I-II, q. 87, a. 2.

# 7

# Grace, Flourishing, and the Grades of Virtue

In the film *The African Queen,* Humphrey Bogart plays the character Charlie Allnut, a rough boat captain with a penchant for gin. Looking at the prim and disapproving Methodist missionary Rose Sayer, played by Katherine Hepburn, Charlie attempts to justify his drunkenness, saying, "A man takes a drop too much once in a while, it's only human nature." Rose replies, "*Nature,* Mr. Allnut, is what we are put into this world to rise above." With this remark, we enter into questions regarding sin, nature, and grace. Working with nature alone, we can achieve at best only mundane results. If we were able to develop full virtue in accordance with reason on our own, the goal, power, and final fruit of our perfected habits would extend only as far as our own strength can reach. This natural happiness, though, is not a real possibility. Charlie Allnut's vicious habit is one example of many that illustrate how our world is fraught with evils and obstacles to happiness. On account of original sin, we live under the "law of sin and death," and we can feel its effects in our bones.[1] On account of the faults of others, we have received harmful dispositions. Worst of all, by our own faults and sins we have shaped ourselves

1. Rom 8:2. *Super Rom.*, c. 8, l. 1, n. 596: "Illis vero qui non sunt in Christo Iesu, damnatio debetur."

with bad habits: evil feels natural to us, and rising above it is beyond our strength. To turn toward our ultimate true good, we need a higher principle of action, one that transcends our natural powers. We need God himself to give us the right habits and dispositions that help us to achieve union with him. This chapter therefore explores, in the first section, why grace is necessary for good habits. The second section treats the nature of grace as a source of supernatural being, acts, and habits. The final section proposes a schema with which to understand false virtue and the three grades of virtue.

## WHY GRACE IS NECESSARY FOR GOOD HABITS

There are manifest difficulties with a solely Aristotelian understanding of human flourishing and happiness and a purely "eudaimonistic" account of morality. Perhaps the most salient problem is that virtue, as conceived of by Aristotle, does not seem to lead to complete human flourishing. The following sections explore, first, the limits of naturally acquired habits in our current condition; subsequently I discuss the nature and necessity of grace for developing perfect habits and reaching true happiness.

An objection of Christine Swanton highlights the inadequacy of Aristotelian virtue; her critique creates space for considering other principles of human happiness. Swanton defines eudaimonism as the thesis that "it is a necessary condition of being a virtue that its exercise characteristically brings in its wake personal satisfaction and flourishing."[2] If virtue is human flourishing, the eudaemonist says, then a virtuous person necessarily flourishes. Virtue may not entail all kinds of success or create a "meaningful" life, but "virtue is constitutive of goodness qua human being," which is practically equivalent to human flourishing and happiness.[3] That said, Swanton provides

2. Christine Swanton, *Virtue Ethics: A Pluralistic View* (Oxford: Oxford University Press, 2005), 81.

3. Ibid., 80 and 84.

three examples that purportedly illustrate virtue's inability to guarantee flourishing and happiness. First, a woman performs exhausting and joyless, though important, work in helping jungle tribes; she suffers from malaria and dysentery until a virus kills her.[4] Second, an artist with manic depression struggles to express her creative goals, but fails to receive recognition before death. Third, a Cassandra-like figure tries to warn people of the world's impending environmental doom, but his charisma fails to ignite interest and deep political change; in despair, he dies from a heart attack. Swanton says that these are not simply cases of persons lacking the necessary luck or positive circumstances to allow their virtue to come to its full fruition. Rather, she claims, these tragedies—and others like them—show that virtue is disconnected from human flourishing or happiness, that some virtues are nonteleological and others are not directed toward human good.[5]

In response to Swanton, one could argue that her examples are not illustrations of virtue, because the individuals lacked some essential aspect of virtue, such as contemplation of the highest good; or that the individuals in her examples somewhat flourished because they were partly virtuous but their suffering and despair shows that they lacked full virtue. For our purposes, though, we can concede that there are irrefutable examples showing that natural virtue does not lead to full flourishing *properly understood*. This need not precipitate a necessary and irremediable divorce between acquired virtue and flourishing because of irreconcilable differences. Rather, as I will show, natural virtue in the concrete circumstances of this present state of life *cannot* lead to full flourishing.

The doctrine of original sin helps us to see that man, despite his best efforts, cannot achieve the perfection of natural virtue in this life, for he is now habitually turned away from his highest good. Swanton recognizes real problems: they are endemic to the world problematized by sin. Original sin causes imperfections in the world

4. See ibid., 82–83.
5. See ibid., 93–94.

that prevent or at least mitigate man's full flourishing: thorns and thistles make Adam's work difficult and are a sign that the world itself groans for redemption.[6] Aquinas says that before original sin, in the "state of integral nature," when human nature was untouched by corruption, "man through his natural choice and action could do the good proportionate to his nature, such as the good of acquired virtue."[7] But paradise has been lost: the state of corrupt nature hobbles man, disabling his attempts to "fulfill good through his natural powers."[8] Personal sin compounds negative interest in achieving the good. Presently, man "is impeded by weakness of reason, which is easily brought into error, ... and by passions of his sensory parts, and by affections by which he is drawn to sensory and inferior things—for the more he is attached to these, the further he is from his ultimate end ... and by many bodily infirmities, he is impeded from the execution of virtuous acts, by which he tends toward beatitude."[9]

Even worse, the human mind grew accustomed to sin and thereby practical reason was befogged, even to the point where faulty judgment rejoices in a transvaluation of values, calling evil good, and good evil.[10] Not fully corrupt, however, human nature retains some ability to achieve particular goods, such as cultivating farmland or developing architecture and technology.[11] Furthermore, a person suffering from sin can still develop virtues of some sort: "although without grace a man is not able to avoid mortal sin, so that he never sins mortally; nevertheless, he is not impeded from acquiring a habit of virtue, through which he abstains from evil in most cases, especially in things that are clearly contrary to reason."[12] Our minimal virtue ability arises from "certain seeds or principles of acquired vir-

6. See Gn 3:18–20 and Rom 8:19–22. See *Super Rom.*, c. 8, l. 7, n. 723.
7. *ST* I-II, q. 109, a. 2.
8. Ibid.
9. *SCG* III, c. 147, n. 7.
10. *ST* I-II, q. 99, a. 2, ad 2.
11. See *ST* I-II, q. 109, a. 2.
12. *ST* I-II, q. 63, a. 2, ad 2.

tues pre-exist in us by nature," such that "human acts, insofar as they proceed from [these] higher principles are able to cause acquired human virtues."[13] Thus, a person can do good deeds proportionate to his nature, such as giving alms out of a certain natural love or generosity.[14] Nevertheless, his inherited sickness of soul, original sin, prevents man from achieving his full flourishing, which is union with God, the highest good.[15] In the state of integral nature, man could have naturally and habitually loved God above all things and referred all things to him, but in the state of corrupt nature, man needs the help of grace for this.[16] A person can with difficulty fulfill the substance of a given commandment, but he cannot completely fulfill all of the commandments, nor can he entirely avoid sin in the long run.[17] Purely human virtue in this life cannot realize full human flourishing. For these reasons, every virtue theory—whether that of Aristotle, Swanton, or others—that does not consider the effects of original sin will be unable to fully explain virtue's present qualities or failures.[18] We need supernatural help both to *understand* and to *practice* human virtue in its fullness.

A second, and related, reason why we need grace is that only through the direct and supernatural help of God can we escape sin and its debilitating effects. Because original sin is but indirectly evidenced through human experience, and mortal sin is a theological concept, empirical science cannot directly verify its own inadequacy for completely healing the effects of sin. At best, an empirical approach can support the view that supernatural help is necessary for

13. Ibid., ad 3.

14. *De veritate*, q. 24, a. 14.

15. *ST* I-II, q. 85, a. 5, ad 2: "peccato originali non debetur poena aeterna ratione suae gravitatis, sed ratione conditionis subiecti, scilicet hominis qui sine gratia invenitur, per quam solam fit remissio poenae." See also *De malo*, q. 5, a. 1, co.: "conveniens poena peccati originalis est subtractio gratiae, et per consequens visionis divinae, ad quam homo per gratiam ordinatur."

16. *ST* I-II, q. 109, a. 3.

17. See *De veritate*, q. 24, a. 14, ad 7; *ST* I-II, q. 109, a. 4.

18. For a cogent argument that bolsters this claim, see Steven A. Long, "Speculative Foundations of Moral Theology and the Causality of Grace," *Studies in Christian Ethics* 23, no. 4 (2010): 397–414.

complete human virtue and happiness. For example, to help illustrate the destructive nature of original sin, especially as it turns us away from our supreme, ultimate good, we can turn to a philosophical understanding of habit's central organizing role in our life. Some empirical studies have conceptualized habit as a "holon," that is, as "a kind of 'middleman' which organizes action and thoughts of a lower order into autonomous gestalts which are, in turn, organized into a larger system."[19] The concept of a holon, as explained by its originator, Arthur Koestler, is based on the principle that "hierarchical organization [is] a fundamental principle of life."[20] In Aristotelian language, a habit exists between potentiality and actuality, providing a principle by which ordered action may be performed. The habit of emotional regulation, for instance, is a quasi-permanent inclination to respond well to emotionally-trying situations; it is a "holon" that serves as a state between chaotic emotions (less ordered) and actually responding well to a particular event (higher-order in act). In a wider sphere, a habit can provide a higher-order structural principle of organizational habit for other, lesser habits and skills: "Habits reflect how a person organizes the totality of his life space, his tasks, his free time, and so forth."[21] One's overarching habit of familial prudence can order one's justice regarding provision for one's family; this can in turn order a skill required for one's labor.[22] Empirical studies indicate that as one's habits become more fixed, and one's life becomes more ordered to particular chosen ends, it seems that one's brain activity becomes more efficient, which is a sign of greater order.[23] In contrast, the effect of original and personal sin is in-

19. Gary Kielhofner, Roann Barris, and Janet Hawkins Watts, "Habits and Habit Dysfunction," *Occupational Therapy in Mental Health* 2, no. 2 (1982): 1–21, at 5.

20. Arthur Koestler, "Beyond Atomism and Holism: The Concept of the Holon," *Perspectives in Biology and Medicine* 13, no. 2 (Winter 1970): 131–54, at 132. This article was a reprint of a chapter of the same title in *Beyond Reductionism: New Perspectives in the Life Sciences*, ed. A. Koestler and J. Smythies (London: Hutchinson, 1968), 192–232.

21. Kielhofner et al., "Habits and Habit Dysfunction," 6.

22. Ibid.

23. An increase of habit shifts primary brain activity from the frontal lobes (used for retrieving memories of images) to the parietal-occipital areas (used for memories

creased disorder on the levels of the intellect-will, the passions, and even the body, arguably including the neurological level. The habit of original (and personal) sin acts as a holon that mediates disorder: as a habit that turns man from being ordered to God as his ultimate end, it occasions disorder on every other level. Consequently, although man can perform occasional acts that are ordered to God as he is known by reason alone, "in the state of corrupt nature, man needs habitual grace to heal [his] nature, so that he can entirely abstain from sin."[24] Although man in the state of sin can, if he applies himself diligently, avoid particular sins,[25] he cannot for long avoid acting according to a negative habit he possesses.[26] Thus, without supernatural help, a person will always fall short of an "unfailing inclination toward the good."[27]

The power of unaided free choice cannot rise from the state of sin to the state of grace, any more than a dead person can bring himself back to life.[28] Man needs a habitual supernatural gift to remove the stain of sin, to free him from the debt of punishment due to sin, and he needs to be moved to actually turn himself toward God.[29]

---

of events), suggesting that as habit develops fewer resources are needed for the memory of specific images of something that happened as one gains a "feel" for situations. Thus, brain adaptation to habituation is a process of a more highly-ordered and therefore efficient use of brain resources. See Beat Meier et al., "From Episodic to Habitual Prospective Memory: ERP-Evidence for a Linear Transition," *Frontiers in Human Neuroscience* 8 (2014): 489; and Stéphane Lehéricy et al., "Distinct Basal Ganglia Territories Are Engaged in Early and Advanced Motor Sequence Learning," *Proceedings of the National Academy of Sciences of the United States of America* 102, no. 35 (2005): 12566–71.

24. *ST* I-II, q. 109, a. 8.

25. See *ST* I-II, q. 74, a. 3, ad 2; *De veritate*, q. 24, a. 1, ad 10 and 12. In these places, Thomas argues that a person in the state of sin necessarily *has* a sinful inclination, but does not necessarily *use* his sinful inclination in every instance, for a person can use his reason to avoid evil on particular occasions.

26. *De veritate*, q. 24, a. 12, ad 13; see also ad 19 and ad s.c. 1–3.

27. *De veritate*, q. 22, a. 5, ad 7.

28. *De veritate*, q. 24, a. 12, ad s.c. 4. See also, *Super Io.*, c. 11, l. 4, n. 1516: "Christus autem est tota causa resurrectionis nostrae, tam animarum quam corporum, et ideo hoc quod dicit ego sum resurrectio, est causalis locutio, quasi dicat: totum hoc quod resurgent in animabus et in corporibus, per me erit." See J. A. Di Noia, "Christ Brings Freedom from Sin and Death: The Commentary of St. Thomas Aquinas on Romans 5:12–21," *The Thomist* 73, no. 3 (2009): 381–89.

29. See *ST* I-II, q. 109, a. 7.

In turning toward God, a person must turn away from sin. One must will not to sin (*aversio*), but this is not sufficient in itself: a positive motion toward God, and union with him, is necessary (*conversio*).[30] In the empirical language used above, a new habit acting as a "holon" is required to order all the lower habits to itself. Now moving oneself toward God involves two things, namely, "a free choice cooperating with the act of rising [from sin], and the grace itself. But it is certain," Aquinas insists, "that one has this free choice itself from a prevenient grace."[31] If a person loses the power of sight, his "habitual" blindness cannot be healed unless that power is restored—and that power cannot be restored by the eyes themselves; likewise, the soul's habitual aversion to God cannot be healed without grace and infused charity in the soul.[32] Contrary to Pelagianism, we cannot move ourselves so that we gain divine help, which is above us; instead, we are moved by God's to gain it.[33] Only grace, which transcends nature, can interrupt the cycle of habitual evil and direct one's powers habitually to their proper end.

A third reason why grace is necessary is that humans cannot perform supernatural acts, nor have supernatural habits, nor reach beatitude without it. The capacities of nature exist solely within the sphere of nature. Consequently, man cannot on his own power—or with a merely natural aid, such as technology or the help of other creatures—perform an act that transcends his natural powers.[34] Man needs the supernatural help of grace to perform works that are not in proportion to human power, namely works of supernatural

30. See *De veritate*, q. 28, a. 2.

31. *Super Epistolam ad Ephesios lectura* [hereafter Super Eph.], c. 5, l. 5, n. 300; I consulted the English translation, *Commentary on St. Paul's Epistle to the Ephesians*, trans. Matthew L. Lamb (Albany, N.Y.: Magi Books, 1966). See *ST* I-II, q. 109, a. 7, ad 1. See also Thomas's use of Lam 5:21: "Convert us, O Lord, to thee, and we shall be converted," to illustrate the work of prevenient grace: *SCG* III, c. 149, n. 6; *ST* I, q. 23, a. 5, co.; q. 62, a. 2, ad 3.

32. *De veritate*, q. 28, a. 2. Thomas recalls Augustine's mystical interpretation of Christ's healing of the man born blind, that it signifies one's need for the enlightenment of baptism in order to receive spiritual sight (*Super Io.*, c. 9, l. 1, n. 1311).

33. *SCG* III, c. 149, n. 1.

34. *ST* I-II, q. 109, a. 3, ad 2.

virtue, which are per se meritorious of everlasting life.[35] Above all, this means loving God as a friend with charity: "We cannot acquire grace by ourselves, but through Christ alone.... But the right use of grace is through the work of charity."[36] Acts of charity are supernatural, for they are directed toward a supernatural object, namely, God who reveals himself to be our friend and the object of our beatitude, and they are the fruit of grace. Aquinas makes this clear in an important passage from the *Summa Theologiae*:

> Charity loves God above all things more eminently than nature. For nature loves God above all things insofar as He is the principle and end of natural good, but charity [loves Him] as He is the object of beatitude and as man has a kind of spiritual fellowship with God. Charity even adds above the natural love of God a sort of quickness and delight, just as every habit of virtue adds to a good act which is performed solely by the natural [powers] of man who does not have the habit of virtue.[37]

With grace and infused charity, man can love the triune God more than himself and above all created things. This may include performing actions such as giving alms with the motive and the impelling power of friendship with God.[38] In contrast, in the current state of corrupt nature, "the rational will ... follows its private good unless it is healed by the grace of God."[39] That is not to say that all love without grace is selfish, that is, turned toward the individual. As Decosimo argues, Thomas recognizes that a person with civic virtue can sacrifice his property and even his life for the sake of his country, because creatures naturally love the common good more than themselves.[40] Nevertheless, even this love for a created common good remains "private" in a certain respect, for it is not directed toward God "who is the common good of all ... for beatitude is

35. See *ST* I-II, q. 109, a. 2.

36. *ST* I-II, q. 108, a. 2.

37. *ST* I-II, q. 109, a. 3, ad 1.

38. *De veritate*, q. 24, a. 14.

39. *ST* I-II, q. 109, a. 3.

40. Decosimo, *Ethics as a Work of Charity*, 241–42. He references *ST* II-II, q. 26, a. 3. It should be noted that this "common good" is personal, something in which the individual participates: Blanchette, *The Perfection of the Universe*, 282.

in God as in the common and fontal principle of all who are able to participate in beatitude."[41] It follows that *every* act tending to beatific life is disproportionate to human power and all acquired habits. To perform salvific acts, a higher habit is needed, namely, "the power of grace."[42] In order to better grasp the transcendent heights of the power of grace existing habitually in the soul, we turn to examine its nature.

## GRACE IN ITSELF: THE SOURCE OF SUPERNATURAL *ESSE*, ACTS, AND HABITS

The topic of grace has been a continual source of theological discussion, and controversies regarding even the most atomized issues of grace proliferate, commanding some of the lengthiest and most polemical works of a great variety of thinkers.[43] Here I will provide a brief and necessarily incomplete sketch of grace from the perspective of St. Thomas, focusing especially on how it relates to the topic of habit.[44]

My study up to this point has illustrated that the perfection of things entails not only that they perform acts that are good in themselves, but that these acts proceed from an individual dynamism, an interior principle, a form, whereby the act is made connatural to the agent. In other words, living things act according a sort of "law of

41. *ST* II-II, q. 26, a. 3.

42. *ST* I-II, q. 109, a. 5. Beatitude, understood as union with the divine essence in the beatific vision, surpasses man's natural knowledge and powers. See *ST* I-II, q. 5, a. 5.

43. For an excellent historical survey of thinkers and issues in the time of Thomas (with a final chapter on Henri de Lubac), see Wood, *To Stir a Restless Heart*. For works of a wider historical scope, see Henri Rondet, *Gratia Christi: essai d'histoire du dogme et théologie dogmatique* (Paris: Beauchesne et ses fils, 1948); Donald Fairbairn, *Grace and Christology in the Early Church* (Oxford: Oxford University Press, 2003). Matthias J. Scheeben provides two superb synthetic works: *Nature and Grace,* trans. Cyril Vollert (St. Louis, Mo.: Herder, 1954); and *The Glories of Divine Grace,* trans. Patrick O'Shaughnessy (Rockford, Ill.: TAN Books, 2000).

44. To see how grace fits within Aquinas's broader thought, see Thomas F. O'Meara, "Grace as a Theological Structure in the *Summa theologiae* of Thomas Aquinas," *Recherches de théologie ancienne et médiévale* 55 (1988): 130–53.

habit" whereby natural or acquired habits ensure that their acts proceed from the agent himself by way of inclination. Instinct is a law for animals; acting in accordance with reason is a law for humans; and the results of original sin are now a law for humans as well.[45] This "law of habit" exists analogously in the supernatural realm, for God not only establishes the possibility of supernaturally good acts with the habit of sanctifying grace; he also gives us the interior principle whereby *they can move themselves* to those acts.[46] Hence, sanctifying grace comprises part of the "New Law" implanted in our hearts.[47] Grace as a habit is an interior inclination of a new nature given through union with Christ.[48]

To understand the essence of grace, we may compare it to the mode of union between the divine and human natures in the incarnation.[49] While discussing Christ's possession of divine and human nature, Aquinas provides a historical etymology of the term "nature."[50] With the help of Boethius, Thomas argues that the concept of "nature" signifies the "essence," the "what-it-is" or the "quiddity" of a species.[51] Unlike creatures, God does not *have* a nature; he is identical with his nature or essence, which is "to be."[52] In the incarnation, the divine Person of the Word joined human nature to himself by assuming it neither accidentally nor essentially, but substantially and hypostatically, that is, personally—not as a soul is the form of a body, but as a body is the instrument of the soul; not as extrinsic and foreign to human nature, but as proper and conjoined.[53]

45. See *ST* I-II, q. 91, a. 6.

46. See *ST* I-II, q. 110, a. 2.

47. *ST* I-II, q. 106, a. 1.

48. See Daria Spezzano, *The Glory of God's Grace: Deification According to St. Thomas Aquinas* (Ave Maria, Fla.: Sapientia Press, 2015), 116–19.

49. See Walter H. Principe, "St. Thomas on the Habitus-Theory of the Incarnation," in *St. Thomas Aquinas 1274–1974: Commemorative Studies*, ed. Etienne Gilson (Toronto: Pontifical Institute for Medieval Studies, 1974), 381–418.

50. See *ST* III, q. 2, a. 1; *De unione Verbi*, a. 1.

51. *ST* III, q. 2, a. 1. See Boethius, *Liber de Persona et Duabus Naturis Contra Eutychen Et Nestorium*, c. 1 (PL 64:1342).

52. *ST* I, q. 3, aa. 1–3; q. 4, a. 2. See *De potentia*, q. 7, a. 2, ad 1.

53. *De unione Verbi*, a. 1.

Therefore, the divine and human natures are "unchangeably and inalterably united in Christ."[54] The hypostatic union of the divine and human nature is unparalleled in all the universe: "this is a certain singular union above every mode of union known to us."[55]

To highlight the uniqueness of this mode or way of being united to God, Thomas compares it to how grace works in the saints. He explains that human nature is "elevated unto God" in two ways: first, by "operation," by which the saints know and love God.[56] Second, by "personal being," which is "a mode singular to Christ, in whom human nature was assumed so as to be of the person of the Son of God."[57] Then Thomas shows that the first mode of union, the way saints are united to God, is directly related to habit. "It is manifest," he says, "that for the perfection of operation it is required that a power be perfected through a habit."[58] As we have seen, no human act can be perfect without a habit, for a habit is the perfection of a power. Thus, for a person to be united to God by way of knowledge and love, he must have within himself supernatural habits in the intellect and will. Action follows being[59] and operation follows nature,[60] because "the operation that belongs to thing by reason of its form is proper to it."[61] The possession of supernatural habits that perfect the intellect and will is a state which requires that the essence of the soul be united to God. This is precisely the work of sanctifying grace: "as it is prior to virtue, it has a subject prior to the powers of the soul, so that it is in the essence of the soul."[62] By sanctifying grace, humans participate in the divine nature through a sort of "re-

54. Ibid., ad 3.

55. Ibid., a. 1.

56. *ST* III, q. 2, a. 10.

57. Ibid.

58. Ibid.

59. See *SCG* III, c. 69, n. 20; *ST* III, q. 34, a. 2, ad 1.

60. *ST* III, q. 19, a. 2, s.c.: "operatio sequitur naturam." Aquinas appropriates this principle from John Damascene, *De fide orthodoxa* III, c. 1. See also, "propria operatio rei sequitur formam substantialem eius" (*ST* III, q. 75, a. 6, obj. 3); "agere sequitur ad esse in actu" (*SCG* III, c. 69, n. 10).

61. *ST* III, q. 19, a. 1.

62. *ST* I-II, q. 100, a. 4.

generation" or "re-creation" that elevates their souls and deifies their very nature.[63] Such transformation on the level of nature is analogous to, but far exceeds, the way that habit perfects particular powers.[64] It follows that the grace given to humans is a "created *habitus* that is a participation in the divine nature."[65] Thus we see that the doctrine of grace is inextricably bound up with Thomas's developed understanding of habit.[66]

We can better fathom grace by comparing nature with the supernatural character of grace.[67] It may be thought that the supernatural is the opposite of the natural, as if the two were opposed or one excluded the other. Matthias Scheeben points out that although one may describe the supernatural as that which is not natural, this is inadequate: what is *unnatural* is per se opposed to nature and excludes it. But the supernatural has a positive character that is not antagonistic to nature. Thus, a better expression is this: "The natural is that which belongs to nature, proceeds from nature, or corresponds to nature. Similarly, the supernatural is that which belongs to supernature, proceeds from it, and corresponds to it."[68] Nature and supernature therefore are distinct spheres. They are not wholly

63. Ibid.

64. Scheeben notes, "A transformation of our nature does not mean that our natural substance is destroyed or is absorbed into the Divine Substance . . . You would, however, esteem this change entirely too little, if you supposed that grace makes us new men only in the sense in which a change of disposition or the acquiring of new habits makes us new men. The change wrought by grace come from God, not from the will or power of the creature; it is a miracle of Divine Omnipotence, which lifts us out of the limits of nature . . . and so elevates and transforms us, that we are not only made other men, but more than men, that we appear as beings of a Divine nature and kind." *Glories of Divine Grace*, 41–42.

65. Spezzano, *The Glory of God's Grace*, 138.

66. In *De veritate*, q. 27, a. 2, ad 7, Aquinas argues that sanctifying grace cannot "properly" be called a habit, insofar as "habit" is a philosophical concept borrowed from the Greeks, who had no concept of an accidental quality that could proportion the soul to a supernatural measure. Aquinas seems to have abandoned this concern in his later writings by employing the term "habit" analogously, such that it bears a meaning on natural and supernatural levels, as this present study shows.

67. In the following two paragraphs, I rely greatly on Scheeben, *Nature and Grace*, 33–35.

68. Ibid., 33.

independent of each other like two air bubbles floating separately in water; nor are nature and supernature merely adjacent to one another, influencing each other exteriorly like billiard balls bouncing off one another. Rather, nature and supernature are related to one another similar to the way that the terrestrial and celestial spheres are related to one another in medieval cosmology, ingeniously treated in Dante's *Divine Comedy*. Just as the celestial sphere surrounds the terrestrial and includes it, so supernature encompasses the lower sphere of nature and presupposes it. Thus, Thomas says that the supernatural is "higher" than nature, and that its capacities "exceed" those of nature.[69]

Supernature, understood in the strict sense, exceeds nature sweetly: it transcends the laws of nature without contradicting them. We may recall that, according to Aristotle, nature in the primary and strict sense is "the substance of things which have in themselves, as such, a source of motion."[70] Aquinas explains that this interior principle of movement is a thing's proper form, for "the form is the principle of motion in those which exist according to nature, whether in act or in potency."[71]

Habits acquired by our own power can be called "second nature," as we have seen, for they operate in a manner similar to that of nature, that is, quickly, easily, accurately, and resulting in joy. However, acquired habits are manifestations and perfections of human power—they may extend the reach of one's previous power, but they do not produce a power whose object or moving force is outside of nature as a whole. Consequently, even new powers given to man by technology—bionic eyesight, for instance, or enhanced genes—do not count as "supernatural" in the strict sense. Even when they affect the expression of the genetic code, techniques are developed by humans whose powers extend only to the sphere of previously-existing,

69. See *ST* I-II, q. 91, a. 4, co. and ad 1.

70. Aristotle, *Metaphysics* V.4, 1015a13; see *Physics* II.1, 192b14.

71. *Sent. Meta.*, lib. 5, l. 5, n. 19. See also *SCG* II, c. 49, n. 5; *De potentia*, q. 1, a. 1, co. The form is also the principle of being (*SCG* III, c. 68, n. 3) and subsistence (*ST* I, q. 29, a. 2, ad 5).

created being and not beyond it. As Scheeben says, "the most notable feature of the elevation of nature I call supernature is that it imparts to nature *new* capacities and powers, and hence opens up a new and permanent field of activity in a higher sphere."[72] This follows Thomas's teaching:

> Grace is a certain perfection elevating the soul to a certain supernatural *esse*: and no supernatural effect can come to be by any creature, for two reasons. First, because to elevate a thing beyond the state of its nature belongs solely to the one whose it is to establish the grade and limit of nature; and that this is God alone is plain. Second, because no created power works without presupposing the potency of material or something else in place of material. But natural created potency does not extend itself beyond natural perfections. Thus no creature can effect any supernatural work.[73]

The good ushered into the soul by grace exists on an unimaginably higher plane than the natural good: it is "greater than the good of nature in the entire universe," Thomas insists.[74] Grace, as we have seen, effects a regeneration or re-creation in the person, making him an adopted child of God.[75] Grace is God's creation of something—a new quality—from nothing. Nevertheless, supernature does not confer an entirely new essence to a creature: a graced human remains a rational animal. Supernature grows from nature as an engrafted shoot grows from its host plant: it "is adapted to and received by" nature.[76] Therefore, the *esse* of grace does not cancel out, destroy, or replace the *esse* of nature. Rather, just as "perfection" presupposes the prior existence of something that can be perfected, so grace heals, elevates, and perfects the *esse* of nature.[77] Hence, Thomas says, "the infusion of grace is a sort of creation," as it requires a new *esse*: "For [created] *esse* is double, namely, the *esse* of nature and

72. *Nature and Grace*, 34.

73. *De veritate*, q. 27, a. 3.

74. *ST* I-II, q. 113, a. 9, ad 2.

75. *ST* I-II, q. 110, a. 4. Aquinas's language of "re-creation" stems from that of St. Paul, who said, for instance, "If anyone is in Christ, he is a new creation: the old has passed away, behold, the new has come" (2 Cor 5:17).

76. Scheeben, *Nature and Grace*, 35.

77. See *ST* I, q. 1, a. 8, ad 2; q. 2, a. 2, ad 1.

the *esse* of grace."[78] The first creation was produced out of nothing by God in the *esse* of nature; but this grew "old" because of original sin. Therefore, a new creation was necessary which would be produced in the *esse* of grace, which is a sharing in the very nature of God, a creation capable of development through cooperation with God.[79] The fundamental power of grace stems from the fact that, by it, God "draws the rational creature above the condition of nature to a participation in the divine good."[80] This leads us to consider the nature of participation, especially as it pertains to grace.

The metaphysics of participation has proved fertile ground for Thomistic discussions, for its concerns range far beyond pure philosophy.[81] According to Thomas, one thing participates in another when it receives in particular fashion a quality or perfection that belongs to another in universal or total fashion.[82] Within the relationship of participation, the *participating* thing relates to the thing *participated-in* as potency to act, for participating means being actualized in a certain way by a thing participated-in.[83] To explain participation, Aquinas likes to use the example of fire, which we can adapt. A person standing near a fire participates in the fire's heat, not by becoming a new substance (a person does not become fire), nor by sharing in its substance (a person does not become a human-fire hybrid), but by sharing a quality or perfection that belongs properly to the fire as a hot thing: a person is heated (i.e., gains the quality of "heat") through the heat that continues to exist in and from the fire.[84] This example contains two principles of participation ar-

78. *Super II Cor.*, c. 5, l. 4, n. 192.

79. Ibid.: "Et sic patet, quod infusio gratiae est quaedam creatio."

80. *ST* I-II, q. 110, a. 1.

81. For a discussion of this issue, including a summary of important twentieth-century interlocutors, see Wippel, "Participation and the Problem of the One and the Many," in *The Metaphysical Thought of Thomas Aquinas*, 94–131. For a more sustained study, see Rudi A. Te Velde, *Participation and Substantiality in Thomas Aquinas* (Leiden: Brill, 1995).

82. *Expositio libri Boetii De ebdomadibus*, l. 2. See also *Sent. Meta.*, lib. 1, l. 10, n. 4.

83. *SCG* II, c. 53, n. 4.

84. See *SCG* II, c. 52, n. 8.

ticulated by Daniel Keating: "(1) that which participates is necessarily distinct (and distinct in kind) from that which is participated in; (2) that which participates possesses the quality it receives only in part."[85] John Wippel points to a third principle: participation "is a way of accounting for the fact that a given kind of characteristic or perfection can be shared in by many different subjects."[86]

On the natural level, one can compare a creature's participation in God to hypothermic persons who become warm by standing around a fire: creatures participate in *esse* because they do not have *esse* in and of themselves; only God is *esse* in itself.[87] In Wippel's words, to avoid a pantheistic interpretation, Thomas makes it clear that "the divine essence itself remains uncommunicated . . . or unparticipated; but its likeness, through those things which it communicates to creatures, is propagated and multiplied in creatures."[88]

On the supernatural level, humans become "partakers in the Divine nature," in the words of St. Peter,[89] and have "a certain participation in the divinity"[90] by grace, without appropriating to themselves the divine essence. Just as flaming wood participates in the nature of fire, so humans similarly become participators in the divine nature and are "deified" by God "by communicating a *consortium* of the divine nature through a certain participated likeness."[91] Now this likeness is due to a "likeness in quality," which is a source

85. Daniel A. Keating, *Deification and Grace* (Ave Maria, Fla.: Sapientia Press, 2007), 98; quoted in R. Jared Staudt, "Substantial Union with God in Matthias Scheeben," *Nova et Vetera* (English edition) 11, no. 2 (2013): 515–36, at 532.

86. Wippel, *The Metaphysical Thought of Thomas Aquinas*, 97.

87. See *ST* I, q. 44, a. 1. The image limps, of course, because hypothermic people naturally possess heat apart from the fire, whereas we have no being apart from God.

88. Wippel, *The Metaphysical Thought of Thomas Aquinas*, 120. See *SCG* II, c. 35, n. 8; *In De divinis nominibus*, c. 2, l. 3. Aquinas speaks of participation in divinity by way of a created similitude in many places: *Super Sent.*, lib. 1, d. 8, q. 3, a. 1, ad 1; *SCG* I, c. 96, n. 3; *ST* I, q. 38, a. 1, co., and so on.

89. 2 Pt 1:4: "He has granted to us his precious and very great promises, that through these you may escape from the corruption that is in the world because of passion, and become partakers of the divine nature."

90. *ST* I-II, q. 62, a. 1. See also, *ST* I-II, q. 58, a. 3, ad 3.

91. *ST* I-II, q. 112, a. 1; q. 62, a. 1, ad 1.

of union between God and creature.[92] The quality is a sort of habit, which is like "a living fire which absorbs and assimilates all the powers of the soul."[93] According to Aquinas, habitual grace is a quality that acts upon the soul "in the mode of a formal cause," making it like God in graciousness.[94] Through a participation in the divine nature by grace, Aquinas says, our life is ordered and guided unto divine "fruition."[95]

Congruent with our discussion of grace in general, habitual grace is not a substantial form; it is an "accidental form of the soul itself," directly infused by God, such that "what is substantially in God, is created accidentally in the soul participating in divine goodness."[96] Through habitual grace, the soul is "ordered to the divine nature"; the form involves a "reception" of the divine nature so that we are said to be "reborn as children of God."[97] Insofar as habitual grace is the perfection of the essence of the soul, and not the perfection of a power, it is "as" (*sicut*) "an interior habit infused into us inclining us toward acting rightly, it makes us freely do things that are fitting to grace, and to avoid things that are repugnant to grace."[98] It follows that sanctifying grace is not the same as an infused virtue, which is the perfection of a power; rather, it is "a certain habitude" (*quaedam habitudo*) "which is presupposed in the infused virtues as their principle and root."[99] As a quality added to the soul, grace is accidental to the person;[100] as inhering in the essence of the soul, it is "intrinsic" and "transforms the creature to be the proper principle of its own supernatural activities";[101] as a gift from God that unites

92. *ST* I, q. 93, a. 9.

93. Joseph Wilhelm and Thomas B. Scannell, *A Manual of Catholic Theology: Based on Scheeben's "Dogmatik"* (New York: Benzinger, 1909), 1:478.

94. *ST* I-II, q. 110, a. 2, ad 1.

95. *ST* II-II, q. 19, a. 7, co.

96. *ST* I-II, q. 110, a. 2, ad 2.

97. *ST* I-II, q. 110, a. 3.

98. *ST* I-II, q. 108, a. 1, ad 2.

99. Ibid., ad 3.

100. See Spezzano, *The Glory of God's Grace*, 141.

101. Ibid.

the creature immediately to God,[102] and therefore remains distinct from the divine substance, grace is created.[103]

Habit is the foundation for God's presence in his holy ones. Thomas clarifies: "God is said to dwell spiritually in the saints as in a family home, whose mind is capable of God through knowledge and love, even if they are not actually knowing and loving Him, provided that they possess the habit of faith and charity through grace, as is clear for baptized children."[104] The divine indwelling is continuous and uninterrupted, so long as the "habitude" of grace along with the supernatural habits of faith and charity remain in the soul.

Francis Cunningham explains the continuance of the indwelling by noting that "habits are specified by their objects, and like all powers involve a real relation to their objects."[105] He continues: "A habit or power is not a simple non-repugnance toward some act and object, nor a naked and indeterminate susceptibility of receiving something; it is a vital tending toward some object ... in virtue of its very form."[106] Consider two great friends, Basil and Gregory. On account of their many interactions and deep communication, they bear a real relation to one another; they have been "shaped" by the other as the object of each other's knowledge and love. Gregory's mind is directed to the reality that his friend Basil encompasses. He grasps Basil's reality, at least in part, and retains it within itself, while his activity reflects his desire to extend and deepen this real relation—and the same applies to Basil's relation to him. Thus, Cunningham reminds us, "the one possessing a habit or potency is weighted in this direction toward this object, which becomes connatural to the subject in virtue of the habit and draws the subject to it.... And this real inclination precedes actual operation ... [and] is already there in first act

102. *ST* I-II, q. 111, a. 2.

103. See the discussion in Spezzano, *The Glory of God's Grace*, 359–66.

104. *Super I Cor.*, c. 3, l. 3, n. 173.

105. Francis L. B. Cunningham, *The Indwelling of the Trinity: A Historico-Doctrinal Study of the Theory of St. Thomas Aquinas* (Dubuque, Iowa: The Priory Press, 1955), 209.

106. Ibid.

and remains when the subject ceases to act."[107] When a person habitually knows and intends something or someone, his soul maintains a definite orientation toward particular acts with identifiable ends.[108] Thus, Aquinas says that "the grace of the Holy Spirit is as an interior habit infused into us inclining us toward acting rightly."[109] The soul in the state of grace has real inclinations and a real ability to know and love God because it has a *real relation* to the divine Persons of the Trinity, who are really present to the soul as abiding objects of knowledge and love.

When a human has a habitual relation to the Trinity, he is thereby "assimilated" by gifts of grace to the divine missions of the Son and the Spirit, which are reflections of the divine processions.[110] Only God performs this work, for he alone is the initiator of the graced relationship. Scheeben beautifully summarizes the doctrine of grace in the following words: "the infusion of grace, as a quality affecting the very being of the soul, represents also the entrance of the Holy Ghost into the soul. By virtue of this grace, He takes root in the soul's innermost depths, and establishes there His throne, from which He pours out the Divine gifts on the sanctified soul."[111] The infusion of grace, virtues, the Gifts of the Holy Spirit, and the presence of the Trinity are simultaneous, so that the indwelling is ontologically but not temporally prior to all other graces and effects in the soul. The greatness of the effects of grace are directly related to the quality of one's charity and the acts that are performed out of the habits of one's other virtues.[112]

107. Ibid., 209–10.

108. See *ST* II-II, q. 184, a. 2, ad 3.

109. *ST* I-II, q. 108, a. 1, ad 2.

110. *ST* I-II, q. 43, a. 5, ad 2.

111. Wilhelm and Scannell, *A Manual of Catholic Theology: Based on Scheeben's "Dogmatik,"* 478.

112. See *ST* I-II, q. 57, a. 1; q. 114, a. 4.

## GRACE, VIRTUE, AND HUMAN FLOURISHING

Grace, as we have seen, works to heal, elevate, and perfect human nature. Grace, therefore, may be seen as an essential element for the full flourishing of humans and our habits. But what is human flourishing in itself? Martin Seligman, a vocal proponent of what he calls "human flourishing and well-being," provides a psychological answer.[113] He began to study flourishing, in part, as a reaction to the psychological establishment's lack of a full account of mental health.[114] Seligman identified five core features that are always present in human flourishing: positive emotion, engagement in life, relationships, meaning, and accomplishment.[115]

Because personal flourishing includes flourishing of the body, it makes sense that Seligman's position seems to be supported by biological studies of human health: participants who practiced his version of resiliency had fewer symptoms of physical illness and fewer doctor visits.[116] One of the most complete empirical reviews indicates that "dispositional optimism" predicts variations in physical flourishing: greater optimism is associated with better health even when various risk factors and psychosocial factors are accounted for.[117] Likewise, a number of studies show that stress and depres-

113. The results of his studies are summarized in Martin E. P. Seligman, *Flourish: A Visionary New Understanding of Happiness and Well-Being* (New York: Atria Books, 2012). For another take, see Tyler J. VanderWeele, "On the Promotion of Human Flourishing," *Proceedings of the National Academy of Sciences* 31 (2017): 8148–56.

114. The same motivation produced Peterson and Seligman, *Character Strengths and Virtues: A Handbook of Classification*, which they say was written as a "manual of the sanities" meant to highlight qualities that lead to real fulfillment (3 and 17). Christian Smith provides a comparison of many different accounts of basic human goods and motivations, which are the basis of his theory of flourishing in his *To Flourish or Destruct: A Personalist Theory of Human Goods, Motivations, Failure, and Evil* (Chicago: University of Chicago Press, 2011), 160–222. For a more classically-minded account, see Kristján Kristjánsson, *Flourishing as the Aim of Education: A Neo-Aristotelian View* (London: Routledge, 2020).

115. See Seligman, *Flourish*, 16–29.

116. Ibid., 82–83.

117. Heather N. Rasmussen, Michael F. Scheier, and Joel B. Greenhouse, "Optimism and Physical Health: A Meta-Analytic Review," *Annals of Behavioral Medicine* 37, no. 3 (May 2009): 239–56.

sion jeopardize immune functioning, whereas social support, intentional relaxation, and trusting relationships can strengthen it.[118] Perhaps more significantly, positive affect in most cases improves problem solving, decisionmaking, and makes thinking more flexible, creative, thorough, and efficient.[119] In other words, the flourishing of the emotions is intertwined with a flourishing of the brain's neural networks, which removes impediments to the mind's flourishing. This in turn has behavioral effects. For these reasons, when Seligman was tasked with defining a biological understanding of health, he found it necessary to include behavioral and even moral elements. He said that "health," a necessary element of physical flourishing, includes biological assets (e.g., the hormone oxytocin, longer DNA telomeres), subjective assets (e.g., optimism, vitality), and functional assets (good marriage, rich friendships, engaging work).[120]

Along similar lines, Aristotle argues that happiness is something in accord with human excellence. His description matches with the five characteristics identified by Seligman. Happiness is accompanied by pleasure (positive emotion), is achieved through action (engagement),[121] is impossible without friendship (relationships),[122] has significant content grasped through contemplation (meaning),[123] and seems to need some sort of prosperity or success (achievement).[124]

118. See Christopher Peterson, *A Primer in Positive Psychology* (New York: Oxford University Press, 2006), 231.

119. Alice M. Isen, "An Influence of Positive Affect on Decision Making in Complex Situations: Theoretical Issues with Practical Implications," *Journal of Consumer Psychology* 11, no. 2 (2001): 75–85; "A Role for Neuropsychology in Understanding the Facilitating Influence of Positive Affect on Social Behavior and Cognitive Processes," in *Handbook of Positive Psychology*, ed. C. R. Snyder and Shane J. Lopez (Oxford: Oxford University Press, 2002), 528–40.

120. Seligman, *Flourish*, 209.

121. "Excellent actions must be in themselves pleasant." *Nicomachean Ethics* I.8, 1099a21.

122. "Even the happy man lives with others; for he has the things that are by nature good" (ibid., IX.9, 1169b19); "Without friends no one would choose to live, though he had all other goods" (ibid., VIII.1, 1155a5).

123. "The activity of wisdom is admittedly the pleasantest of excellent activities" (ibid., X.7, 1177a26).

124. "Yet evidently, as we said, it [happiness] needs the external goods as well; for it is impossible, or not easy, to do noble acts without the proper equipment.... happiness

Unfortunately, by themselves these features do not capture the essence of human flourishing. Considered in isolation, they are broad enough to coincide with great evil. If Stalin reported predominately positive emotions, was fully "engaged" in life, had significant supportive relationships, felt meaning and purpose in his life, and could revel in personal achievements, then—according to Seligman's criteria—his totalitarian and murderous life was a great example of human flourishing. To avoid this misunderstanding of human flourishing, some thinkers have preferred to focus on what they call "character strengths."[125] Excellence of character is necessary for us to flourish: the two realities depend on each other, for the greatest human excellence must be an exercise of what is highest and characteristically human; it must be an activity of the intellectual soul. As Aristotle said, "Happiness must be some form of contemplation" in accordance with virtue.[126] Hence, flourishing indeed manifests itself in right behavior—and its "assets" are defined and guided by virtue, which is defined and guided by nature. We are adapted by nature to gain virtue through the perfection of our powers by habit.[127]

Taking stock of what the human sciences tell us about human flourishing, we are left with a number of unresolved but crucial issues related to habit. Psychologists note that analogies with musical and mathematical prodigies imply that "character prodigies" *ought* to exist, but few if can be readily identified from the experimental, sociological perspective.[128] With a similar tone, Aristotle observes that the life of complete happiness "would be too high for man; for it is not in so far as *man* that he will live so, but in so far as something divine is present in him."[129] From a human perspective, complete

seems to need this sort of prosperity in addition" (ibid., I.8, 1198a32–33, 1199b6). See also X.8, 1178b33–1179a117. These, however, are instrumental goods: "Success or failure in life does not depend on [good of fortune], but human life, as we said, needs these as well, while excellent activities or their opposites are what determine happiness or the reverse" (I.10, 1100b7–10).

125. Peterson and Seligman, *Character Strengths and Virtues*, 18.

126. *Nicomachean Ethics* X.8, 1178b32. See also X.7, 1177a11.

127. See ibid., II.1, 1103a23–25.

128. Peterson and Seligman, *Character Strengths and Virtues*, 26.

129. *Nicomachean Ethics* X.7, 1177b27–28; emphasis added. The Greek text here differs

happiness and virtue are difficult if not impossible to achieve.[130] The philosopher gropes for a concept like grace. Here Aquinas's theological anthropology proves essential. His account of human flourishing helps explain paragons of virtue and "character prodigies," how the habits of virtue can be more stably implanted in man, what unites the virtues, how "something divine" could be in humans to help them achieve complete happiness, and what is the essence of ultimate happiness.[131]

Thomas's discussions of "flourishing" cover all the elements of his theology of habit. For him, flourishing is first of all an image derived from nature that helps to elucidate the nature and effects of the Trinity. Just as a tree produces flowers as the natural effect that proceeds from its form, so the Father and the Son love each other by their essence.[132] Likewise, speaking notionally, just as flourishing is to produce flowers, so the Father and the Son love each other and humankind by the Holy Spirit, that is, by love proceeding from them both.[133] In other words, the substantial love of God is the "flourishing" of God's essence, and the love of the Holy Spirit is the "flourishing" of the Father and the Son in relation to each other. By his mission to the world, the Spirit is also the "flourishing" of God's relation to creatures. The situation is analogous for us. According to Aquinas, human flourishing can only be understood as an effect of union with the Trinity. In his commentary on Isaiah 11:1 ("There shall come forth a rod out of the root of Jesse, and a flower shall rise up"), he notes that "Christ wished to flourish by his holy way

significantly from Aquinas's Latin translation. Aquinas reads the text as saying that the contemplative person does not live merely as a body-soul composite, but insofar as he "participates in an image of the divine intellect" (*Sent. Ethic.*, lib. 10, l. 11, n. 9). The Greek is more ambiguous and hints at man's need for divine assistance in order to be perfectly happy. This is implied in *Metaphysics* I.2, 982b29: "The possession of [the highest wisdom] might be justly regarded as beyond human power."

130. See *Nicomachean Ethics* I.10, 1100a10–21.

131. For an overview of how the views of Aquinas and psychosocial sciences on human flourishing can be mutually enriching, see Titus, *Resilience and the Virtue of Fortitude*, 105–9.

132. *ST* I, q. 37, a. 2.

133. Ibid. See also *De potentia*, q. 10, a. 4, ad 1.

life," and "the flesh of Christ flourished with the flowers of integrity and incorruption."[134] The flesh of the first man, Adam, flourished through innocence of life; in Christ human flesh "reflourished" in the resurrection because he had been conceived without sin by the Holy Spirit.[135] Christ, then, is the ultimate moral prodigy—both a model and a causal source of the goodness of others.[136] Following this model, and with his help, Christians flourish in holiness through their habituation to goodness through good action. Just as a flower is a sign of hoped-for fruit, so the works of virtue are the hope of eternity and beatitude.[137] This is only possible through grace and virtues that are not acquired but are infused directly by God. Virtue, then, is the flourishing of the individual insofar as the acts of virtue are directed toward one's supernatural end, namely, blessed union with the Trinity: "Just as a flower is a fruit in its beginning, so the work of virtue is the beginning of the beatitude that will exist when understanding and charity are perfected."[138] Even more, the acts of virtue lead to the full fruition of the human, which is to enjoy the fruit of union with God.[139]

134. *ST* III, q. 35, a. 7; see *Super Psalmo* 27, n. 7. See also *Super Isaiam*, c. 11: "Judaei dicunt, quod flos et virga refertur ad Christum; et dicitur virga propter potestatem et flagellationem malorum, et flos propter honestatem et consolationem bonorum."

135. *Super Psalmo* 27, n. 7.

136. See Nicholas Crotty, "The Redemptive Role of Christ's Resurrection," *The Thomist* 25, no. 1 (1962): 54–106, at 59–62; Ulrich Horst, "Christ, exemplar ordinis fratrum praedicantium, according to Saint Thomas Aquinas," in *Christ among the Medieval Dominicans*, ed. Kent Emery and Joseph Wawrykow (Notre Dame, Ind.: University of Notre Dame Press, 1998), 256–70. Linda Trinkaus Zagzebski offers valuable insights as one of the foremost contemporary proponents of exemplarism as a central pillar of moral theory. See "Exemplarist Moral Theory," *Metaphilosophy* 41, nos. 1–2 (January 2010): 41–57; *Exemplarist Moral Theory* (Oxford: Oxford University Press, 2017). But her work could benefit from greater metaphysical rigor (Clark, *Perfection in Death*, 246–51, 261–66, and 281–85). For a general understanding how exemplars operate, see John Meinert, "In Duobus Modis: Is Exemplar Causality Instrumental According to Aquinas?," *New Blackfriars* 95, no. 1055 (2014): 57–70.

137. *Super Gal.*, c. 5, l. 6, n. 328. Here Thomas is commenting on Rom 6:22: "Habetis fructum vestrum in sanctificationem."

138. Ibid.

139. *ST* I-II, q. 11, a. 3, ad 3.

### LEVELS OF VIRTUE AND VICE

We have seen that man is perfected by virtue, by which he is directed to some good, which is directed toward the ultimate good of happiness in union with God, but that in our current state of affairs natural virtues are insufficient for this end. We have also seen that by grace man can escape the effects of sin and death, for it serves as a supernatural principle in man's soul whereby he produces acts that merit eternal life. Insofar as grace is a perfection of the essence of human nature rooted in the soul, it extends itself to the powers of man and thereby produces principles of virtues. Two questions confront us when we aim to see how grace relates to virtue. The first is whether a person without habitual grace can have acquired virtue. In other words, can "pagan virtue" exist?[140] Next, can a person in the state of grace possess acquired virtue? Although distinct, the issues are clearly related, for if the first question is answered affirmatively, and a person without habitual grace can indeed acquire virtue through his own acts, then there are only two possible answers to the second question. Either grace coexists with natural virtues or it does not.

Thomas Osborne claims that for any Thomist, there can be no doubt that pagan virtue exists: "To interpret Thomas as saying that there is no acquired virtue or acquired prudence without grace is nonsense. I do not know who might have held this view."[141] The issue then arises: if there can be acquired virtue without grace, can acquired virtue coexist with infused cardinal virtues and grace in the same person? Four years later, William Mattison boldly replied: "Christians cannot possess acquired cardinal virtues."[142] All Thomis-

140. In his *Ethics as a Work of Charity: Thomas Aquinas and Pagan Virtue,* David Decosimo provides a thorough and convincing explanation of the extent to which humans can have virtue without grace. See esp. chaps. 4–5 and 9–10, which have significantly influenced the discussion in the following sections. See also Brian Shanley, "Aquinas on Pagan Virtue," *The Thomist* 63 (1999): 553–77.

141. Thomas M. Osborne, Jr., "Perfect and Imperfect Virtues in Aquinas," *The Thomist* 71 (2007): 39–64.

142. William C. Mattison, "Can Christians Possess the Acquired Cardinal Virtues?," *Theological Studies* 72 (2011): 558–85, at 559.

tic scholars, Mattison notes, agree on the principle that *grace perfects nature* and conclude that there is some sort of continuity in the person and his virtuous activity before and after the infusion of grace. The sticking point lies in the nature and name of that continuity. In his evaluation, many Thomists affirm the simultaneous presence of infused and acquired moral virtues but provide no positive argument as to why that may be the case: "this position is too often simply assumed rather than proved."[143] Such an assumption cannot be made in the present study. It is of the utmost importance to know whether or not fully voluntary, perfective habits in the absence of grace can be acquired, and, if so, whether they persist in the presence of grace. A proper account of these two issues will give us a more profound understanding of how man's natural ability to acquire good habits relates to how God works within man and in cooperation with man.[144]

In order to be as clear as possible about the relation between grace and virtue, I will provide a schema of different virtue and seeming-virtue states, noting Osborne's observation that Thomas's view is complex enough that no single schema will satisfy every thinker and resolve every dispute.[145] In what follows, I will provide a synthesis of Thomas's various schemata. This includes the fourfold schema of temperance (and other virtues) that he adapts from Aristotle, organized according to how a person habitually responds

143. Ibid., 559. He does not name which scholars, but on 559n2, he notes—among others—the work of Gabriel Bullet and Angela McKay Knobel. Further, on 567n29, Mattison notes the works of Romanus Cessario, Bonnie Kent, Michael Sherwin, Denis J. M. Bradley, and Andrew J. Dell'Olio. One could reasonably conclude that Mattison thinks that most if not all of these Thomistic scholars assume rather than prove the coexistence of acquired and infused virtues.

144. In *ST* I-II, q. 111, a. 2, Aquinas says that in graced acts commanded by man's will "God helps us in that act, both by interiorly confirming the will so as to come to action, and exteriorly by providing the faculty of operation." Quoting Augustine: "When we will, he cooperates that we may be perfected." See also in ibid., ad 2: "presupposing the end" provided by habitual grace, "grace cooperates with us."

145. Osborne, "Perfect and Imperfect Virtues in Aquinas," 51. Osborne notes that Cardinal Cajetan, the Carmelites of Salamanca, and Reginald Garrigou-Lagrange provide lists that slightly differ.

to pleasure, especially his experience upon performing moral good or evil. This schema is compatible with another schema of grades of virtue, organized according to the principle that causes the habit as it exists in the soul. I therefore propose that the state of "false virtue" corresponds to the states of vice and incontinence; and that the state of continence corresponds to entirely imperfect virtue as well as true but imperfect virtue. Finally, the state of "virtue" in general relates to perfect virtue, which itself has various grades.[146]

It might seem that all virtue that does not proceed from grace is false virtue. In an objection to his position, Aquinas quotes Romans 14:23, "whatever does not proceed from faith is sin," and the gloss to this effect.[147] This position has been attributed to Augustine.[148] Characteristically, in his reply, Thomas sees a distinction that makes all the difference. For him, virtue's promise is happiness. As a perfection of man, virtue is that interior stable inclination whereby man acts well in accordance with his ultimate end. Whatever does not conduce to one's ultimate end is not a virtue. Because in this life the only virtues that tend toward our ultimate end are virtues infused directly by God, all the others may be considered false. However, some inclinations are directly *contrary* to our ultimate end—and these are more accurately called "false," for they impede one's beatitude. This is any inclination that proceeds from one's *lack* of faith and charity, such as every inclination an idolater derives from his "religiosity."[149]

146. Thomas makes a threefold division of virtue in *De virtutibus*, q. 5, a. 2. Not seeing this text as programmatic, Osborne argues in favor of "true but imperfect acquired virtue," which he considers as virtues that are "unconnected" because they survive without prudence. In his opinion, these exist for most pagans, that is, people who continually live without grace. See Osborne, "Perfect and Imperfect Virtues in Aquinas," 53 and 54. Similarly, Stump's position, that only infused virtues are *real* virtues, is difficult to reconcile with a broader reading of Aquinas. Eleonore Stump, "The Non-Aristotelian Character of Aquinas's Ethics: Aquinas on the Passions," *Faith and Philosophy* 28, no. 1 (2011): 29–43, at 33.

147. *ST* I-II, q. 63, a. 2, obj. 1.

148. Shawn Floyd, "How to Cure Self-Deception: An Augustinian Remedy," *Logos* 7, no. 3 (2004): 60–86, at 72, quoting Augustine's *City of God*, lib. 19, c. 25: "the virtues that [the soul] seems to possess ... are rather vices than virtues so long as there is no reference to God in the matter."

149. See *ST* II-II, q. 23, a. 7, ad 1. Aquinas explains this verse in detail, saying that

When there is a stable habit whereby a person directs himself to an apparent good, and not a true good, he does not have "true virtue" but "a false imitation of virtue."[150] Aquinas provides the example of "avaricious prudence" in achieving riches. It is not chosen at random.[151] For him, false virtue is often "prudence of the flesh," that is, an inclination to direct one's actions toward bodily goods as his ultimate end.[152] Insofar as a disordered inclination is directed toward any created good as one's ultimate end, every false prudence is equivalent to false virtue.

The state of false virtue includes the Aristotelian states of viciousness and incontinence. Following Aristotle, Aquinas notes that a fourfold schema helpfully categorizes how people respond to pleasure and pain as it relates to virtuous action: Vicious—Incontinent—Continent—Virtuous.[153] Properly speaking, incontinence and continence concern objects that appeal to the concupiscible appetite, that is, objects of self-indulgence or temperance, such as food, drink, and sex.[154] As Robert Pasnau points out, Aquinas's exposition in the *Summa Theologiae* makes it clear that incontinent actions, understood in the strict sense, are a very small subset of actions contrary to reason.[155] However, insofar as morality requires moderating the vehemence of evil desires, and given that persons can moderate their desires for any appetible objects (including intellectual goods, such as justice), "incontinence" and "continence" are categories that apply to *any virtue* in an extended sense.[156] Habituated character

an unbeliever does not sin when he performs a good deed in accordance with reason, and avoids referring it to an evil end. But such an act does not merit eternal life, as it is without grace. But when an unbeliever does an act that stems from his unbelief, he sins thereby (*Super Rom.*, c. 14, l. 3, n. 1141).

150. *ST* II-II, q. 23, a. 7.

151. See ibid.

152. *ST* II-II, q. 55, a. 1.

153. See Aristotle, *Nicomachean Ethics* VII.4, 1147b21: "Both continent persons and persons of endurance, and incontinent and soft persons, are concerned with pleasures and pains."

154. See *ST* II-II, q. 141, aa. 3–4; q. 155, a. 2; I-II, q. 81, a. 2.

155. Pasnau, *Thomas Aquinas on Human Nature*, 247–48.

156. *Nicomachean Ethics* VII.5, 1149a21. See *ST* II-II, q. 155, a. 4; *Sent. Ethic.*, lib. 7, l. 11, n. 3: "virtus et malitia moralis sunt circa delectationes et tristitias."

in general consequently exists in a sliding scale, measured by how much pleasure (fruition) a person experiences upon performing acts of virtue or vice.

The vicious and intemperate person feels pleasure upon doing evil; he is led by choice and judges that he should always pursue pleasure—and therefore what is objectively evil.[157] The incontinent person pursues excesses of disgraceful pleasure "contrary to his choice and judgment," for he knows that not all pleasures are to be pursued but still he pursues them because he is becoming habituated to doing so.[158] The incontinent person typically follows his passions, not his reason, albeit with some admixture of sadness. Aristotle says that he is similar to persons who are asleep, mad, or drunk: his reason is actually deficient but may remain intact more or less habitually.[159] Every habitually incontinent behavior may be understood as an abdication from reason and "moral weakness" from following one's voluntarily disordered passions that arise from "weakness of the will" as a dispositive cause and indirectly as a final cause.[160] A person who is incontinent by habit, or incontinent simply speaking, is blameable for his emotional responses, including his mixed feelings of pleasure in doing wrong and shame after doing it.[161] In contrast, a person who is born feeling pleasure at disordered goods may be said to have an "innate" incontinence.[162] Such a person is not culpable for possessing inborn disordered desires, but he ought not

157. See Aristotle, *Nicomachean Ethics* VII.3, 1146b15.

158. Ibid., VII.4, 1148b10.

159. Ibid., VII.3, 1147a18. See *Sent. Ethic.*, lib. 7, l. 3, n. 7: "Et sic manifestum est quod incontinentes similiter disponuntur dormientibus, aut maniacis aut ebriosis, quod scilicet habent habitum scientiae practicae in singularibus ligatum."

160. Bonnie Kent exposes errors in arguments that a "weak" will can be an efficient cause of evil despite itself in "Aquinas and Weakness of the Will," *Philosophy and Phenomenological Research* 75, no. 1 (July 2007): 70–91. Steven Jensen goes further and explains that the will's desires can debilitate a person indirectly as a dispositive cause and as an indirect final cause of moral evil (*Sin: A Thomistic Psychology*, 142–57).

161. Aristotle, *Nicomachean Ethics* VII.5, 1148b30. See Aquinas, *Sent. Ethic.*, lib. 7, l. 5, n. 8.

162. See Aristotle, *Nicomachean Ethics* V.10, 1152a30; Aquinas, *Sent. Ethic.*, lib. 7, l. 10, n. 13. For an illuminating discussion about incontinence and habit, see Daniel P. Thero, *Understanding Moral Weakness* (New York: Rodopi, 2006), 115–21.

to follow them. An incontinent person does not yet cultivate vice. The wicked person, in contrast, having practiced evil often, lives a fullness of vice and is creative in his wrongdoing. A vicious person is one who finds it easy and pleasurable to invent new ways to pursue what is evil.[163] For the completely intemperate person, moral wrongdoing is intuitive and feels natural, for his cogitative power on the prerational level has been habituated to perceive a disordered situation as good for himself, his intellect has come to believe this estimation of things corresponds to reality, his will desires these things and moves him to act for them, and he has developed a sort of skill through frequent disordered activity.

In *De virtutibus*, q. 5, a. 2, Aquinas argues that, above the level of sin and false virtue, there is a threefold grade of what counts as virtue in some way.[164] On the lowest level is virtue that is entirely imperfect (*omnino imperfecta*). This exists "without prudence, not attaining right reason."[165] Such is what Aquinas calls an "imperfect moral virtue" that is "nothing other than some inclination to do something generically good existing in us, whether the inclination is in us by nature or by custom."[166] As we have seen, by genetic heritage, some people are more inclined to temperance, others to fortitude, and so on.[167] Furthermore, from conception to adulthood, people can develop good inclinations that range from nonvoluntary to imperfectly voluntary—inclinations that could exist without having engaged a person's full reason and will. Insofar as they are directed to a good end, they are morally good in a generic sense. But being habituated to doing good within a narrow field of life is not the same as virtue in the specific sense.

Imperfect virtue extends only to some matters, some occa-

163. See *ST* II-II, q. 156, a. 3.

164. *De virtutibus*, q. 5, a. 2.

165. Ibid. See *ST* I-II, q. 61, a. 1, co.: "Sed secundum imperfectam rationem virtutis dicitur virtus quae non requirit rectitudinem appetitus, quia solum facit facultatem bene agendi, non autem causat boni operis usum."

166. *ST* I-II, q. 65, a. 1. See also, *ST* II-II, q. 141, a. 1, ad 2.

167. See also *ST* I-II, q. 63, a. 1, which addresses innate inclinations directly.

sions, and some circumstances, whereas perfect virtue extends to all things at all times in all circumstances. When a person performs good deeds in all matters that pertain to his life, he will acquire the good habits of all the moral virtues.[168] For example, when a person keeps his anger in check but not his lust, "he will indeed acquire a certain habit of restraining his anger, but this habit will not have the *ratio* of virtue," for his lack of self-control in matters of lust is a sign that he lacks prudence.[169] And without prudence, the "perfect *ratio* of virtue" does not exist.[170] But just as reason provides the light whereby one's mind can grasp many things under one formal object, as when a person recognizes various individuals as members of a family, so the light of prudence provides unity to one's good inclinations. Without prudence, good inclinations remain unconnected from each other. They can be used badly, as when a person uses his inclinations toward bravery for the sake of his own vainglory. Without reason's guidance, inborn inclinations rely on the dynamism of imagination, memory, and estimation. They do not rise to the level of fully human habits and thus "do not have the perfect character of virtue."[171] Without prudence, even an acquired virtuous disposition does not have *ratio* of virtue.[172] The disposition could be pointed toward the good in general and without contradicting prudence, and therefore have the character of imperfect virtue.

Here we find the continent person, for Aquinas states that "continence is compared to temperance as imperfect to the perfect."[173] In contrast to vicious and incontinent persons, a continent person acts according to reason at times. Indeed, in comparison with the majority of people, the continent person does well, for he "abides by

168. Ibid.

169. *ST* I-II, q. 65, a. 1, ad 1.

170. Ibid.

171. *De virtutibus*, q. 5, a. 2.

172. Ibid., co. and ad 9. For an extended defense of the necessary role of prudence in every moral virtue, see Andrew Kim, "Progress in the Good: A Defense of the Thomistic Unity Thesis," *Journal of Moral Theology* 3, no. 1 (2014): 147–74.

173. *ST* II-II, q. 155, a. 4.

right reason more than many people can, for he overcomes the desires which overcome many people."[174] His uprightness remains despite a strong emotional inclination in the other direction—unlike the temperate person, who acts according to his well-formed choice and judgment.[175] The continent person lacks the integrating character of complete virtue. When he chooses the good—and sometimes he may fail in it—he acts primarily out of willpower and does not experience right action as consistently easy or pleasurable. In moments of sudden temptation, he can often do the right thing, but he is not at peace, for evil still entices him. Worse, he may not feel satisfaction in performing virtuous acts. Or he enjoys them for their ancillary rewards. His cogitative power has not yet acquired the intuitive recognition that the rightly-ordered good is good *for him*. He may waver on the intellectual level in grasping the full reality of the situation, for his emotions may tend to draw his judgment in an imbalanced way. At times, the continent person's passions do not obey the command of reason, to his consternation.[176]

The second grade of virtues "attain right reason but nevertheless do not attain God through charity."[177] In the *Summa Theologiae,* q. 61, a. 1, Thomas states that "when we speak of virtue simply, we are understood to speak of human virtue," and he references his prior explanation of how people can acquire habits.[178] In that earlier discussion, Aquinas distinguished between habits that consist in a power for a particular good act and habits that make the right use of that power.[179] He states that the second kind of habits "are called virtues simply, for they render a work good in act, and simply make the person who has them good."[180] Clearly, Thomas means acquired virtues, for he compares the light of prudence regarding the right things

174. *Sent. Ethic.*, lib. 7, l. 10, n. 11.
175. Aristotle, *Nicomachean Ethics* VII.9, 1152a1–5.
176. *De virtutibus*, q. 1, a. 4.
177. Ibid., q. 5, a. 2.
178. *ST* I-II, q. 61, a. 1.
179. See *ST* I-II, q. 56, a. 3.
180. Ibid.

to be done with "the natural light of the active intellect" that disposes a person to the principles of speculative truth.[181] For example, a person might be temperate because of his calm temperament, or because he comes from a well-mannered and introverted culture, but this will not reach the level of virtue unless he actively chooses the good as such. He might be the proverbial Victorian gentleman who was polite at court but wicked at home. Contrastingly, "the perfect moral virtue is a habit that inclines one to do a good deed well."[182] Because it stems from the united intellect and will that are directed toward the right end for man, perfect moral virtue perfects the human form: it leads to good deeds and makes the person who does them good. In this case, "the whole matter of moral virtues falls under the one *ratio* of prudence," which unifies the virtues by informing them with reason's judgment and command.[183]

Aquinas clarifies that up to q. 61, a. 5, he had been speaking about virtues "insofar as they are in man according to the condition of his nature," that is, his nature as a political animal.[184] Brian Shanley takes such reasoning to mean that "pagan" virtues, that is, those regulated by human reason alone, are ordered to the common good of the *polis*.[185] Augustine seems to hold such a view when he states that God allowed pagan Rome to acquire an immense empire as a reward for their natural virtue.[186] Thomas appears to be more optimistic than Augustine regarding the scope of natural virtue. Aquinas ar-

181. Ibid.

182. *ST* I-II, q. 61, a. 1; see q. 55, a. 3; q. 56, a. 3.

183. *ST* I-II, q. 61, a. 1, ad 3; see q. 57, a. 5.

184. *ST* I-II, q. 61, a. 5.

185. Shanley, "Aquinas on Pagan Virtue," 573–75. For a helpful clarification of these issues, see Justin M. Anderson, "Aquinas on the Graceless Unbeliever," *Freiburger Zeitschrift für Philosophie Und Theologie* 59, no. 1 (2012): 5–25, which argues that without grace an unbeliever can possess virtue but, practically speaking, cannot consistently live a virtuous life. Various authors offer a similar reading. See Kim, "Progress in the Good," 165; Romanus Cessario, *The Moral Virtues and Theological Ethics: Second Edition* (Notre Dame, Ind.: University of Notre Dame Press, 2009), 144; Clare Carlisle, "The Question of Habit in Theology and Philosophy: From Hexis to Plasticity," *Body and Society* 19 (2013): 30–57, at 37.

186. *De civitas Dei*, lib. 5, c. 15.

gues: "Through human deeds, it is possible to acquire moral virtues as they produce good deeds ordered to an end that does not exceed natural human ability."[187] This is because the human will is able to reach a good object that proportionate to its power.[188] Consequently, when the will desires a good that comes under the power and rule of natural reason, the human acts that follow can cause what Aquinas calls "human virtue."[189] The temperate person—that is, one with full human virtue—acts according to reason joyfully, quickly, easily, and creatively. A virtuous person's appetites, intellect, will, and performance have been voluntarily habituated to the reasonable mean, so that his whole person has been rooted in the good as something connatural to him. A virtuous person, when doing good, experiences at least spiritual pleasure in the highest parts of his soul.[190]

In Aquinas's conception, good habits that dispose a person to an act fitting to "lower nature" are human virtues.[191] These are the same as acquired virtues.[192] They are regulated by true but imperfect prudence. It is true because it makes a person good and regulates the other virtues toward a good end, but is imperfect because it is not directed to the supreme ultimate end of human life.[193] He also notes: "If, however, we take virtue as being ordered to some particular end, then virtue can be said to exist without charity, insofar as it is ordered to some particular good."[194] Natural virtue contributes to the individual's good character, a particular good, even if it does not necessarily attain heaven. In contrast with false virtue, if the particular good to which man is habitually inclined is truly good, "there will indeed be true virtue, but imperfect, unless it is referred to the final and perfect good."[195] An act from this sort of virtuous inclination

187. *ST* I-II, q. 65, a. 2.

188. *ST* I-II, q. 56, a. 6.

189. *ST* I-II, q. 63, a. 2. This is the topic of Decosimo's entire work, *Ethics as a Work of Charity*; see esp. 131–36.

190. *ST* III, q. 46, a. 8.

191. *ST* I-II, q. 54, a. 3.

192. See *ST* I-II, q. 55, a. 4.

193. *ST* II-II, q. 47, a. 13.

194. *ST* II-II, q. 23, a. 7.

195. Ibid. He makes a similar claim in *ST* I-II, q. 65, a. 2.

would proceed "not according to his lack of charity, but according to his possession of some other gift of God, either faith or hope, or even a natural good, which is not totally removed by sin."[196] In sum, imperfect virtue is directed to imperfect happiness, which can be acquired in this life through the operations of such virtue.[197]

Even after sin, humans maintain their nature and its powers, including the power to move themselves toward particular goods such as self-perfecting habits. Because "effects must be proportionate to their cause," and a person's natural powers remain as causes of his own actions,[198] it follows that some virtues are generated in us by our own action: "Insofar as moral virtues perform good that is ordered to an end that does not exceed the natural power of man, they can be acquired by human action. And thus acquired, they can exist without charity, as they were in many gentiles."[199] Both moral and intellectual virtues can be acquired when we act according to the natural light of our reason.[200] Thomas affirms: "Human virtue ordered to a good that is measured by the rule of human reason can be caused by human acts, insofar as these acts proceed from reason, under whose power and rule such a good falls."[201] This gives us a clue as to why acquired virtue is not ordered to one's supreme ultimate end—not simply because it exists without grace, for that is only a lack of a cause—but because it is formed by natural prudence, which provides a created measure and rule that perfects one's appetites and intellect.[202] Thomas leaves little doubt that individuals can acquire natural prudence by their own efforts: "Acquired prudence," he explains, "is caused by the exercise of acts, so that 'time and experience are necessary for its generation.'"[203] Lacking both years and experience, youths cannot possess acquired prudence, although they can

196. *ST* II-II, q. 23, a. 7, ad 1.
197. *ST* I-II, q. 5, a. 5.
198. See *ST* I-II, q. 63, a. 3.
199. *ST* I-II, q. 65, a. 2.
200. See *ST* I-II, q. 63, a. 3, ad 1.
201. *ST* I-II, q. 63, a. 2.
202. See *ST* I-II, q. 64, a. 4, ad 2.
203. *ST* II-II, q. 47, a. 14, ad 3.

have the infused virtue through baptism.[204] Acquired prudence directs an agent's powers and appetites toward a natural good end, and therefore serves as the formator for the other acquired virtues.[205] These sorts of virtues are virtues *secundum quid,* not virtues *simpliciter.*[206] They exist as a sort of "beginning" of virtue simply speaking, because they are directed to real good and remove obstacles to the working of such virtue.[207]

Thomas explains that acquired virtues "are indeed in a way perfect in regard to human good, though they are nevertheless not simply perfect, for they do not attain to the first rule, which is the ultimate end."[208] To the extent that acquired virtues "fall short of the true *ratio* of virtue," Thomas says they exhibit the following analogous relationship—entirely imperfect virtues : acquired virtues :: acquired virtues : perfect virtues.[209] In this way, Aquinas makes it clear that acquired virtues that proceed from principles of natural reason are of an entirely different kind than those that proceed from grace. They are analogous to one another because they perfect the same subject, but they differ by formal, final, and efficient causality. It will be helpful to recall that in our present state, perfect natural virtue cannot fully exist in the absence of grace, for the perfect operation of prudence is affected by sin and the wayward tendency of the passions. Angela Knobel helpfully compares the situation of pagan virtues to a pre-Copernican scientist.[210] To the extent that he has some true knowledge about the world, he can explain reality and engage in

204. See ibid.

205. Aquinas argues that a man who moderates his anger but not his concupiscence "will indeed acquire a certain habit of restraining his anger, but this habit will lack the nature of virtue, through the absence of prudence, which is corrupted in things regarding concupiscence. Thus natural inclinations do not have the perfect *ratio* of virtue if prudence is lacking." *ST* I-II, q. 65, a. 1, ad 1. For a discussion of this point, see Kim, "Progress in the Good," 162, and Cessario, *The Moral Virtues,* 141.

206. *ST* I-II, q. 65, a. 2.

207. *ST* I-II, q. 65, a. 4.

208. *De virtutibus,* q. 5, a. 2.

209. Ibid.

210. See Angela Knobel, "Ends and Virtues," *Journal of Moral Theology* 3, no. 1 (2014): 105–17, at 117.

authentic scientific endeavors. But to the extent that his geocentric theory excludes heliocentrism, his endeavors will be flawed. Similarly, to the extent that natural reasoning functions well, a person can acquire virtue through practice.

Next, we come to the "third grade" of virtues, namely, perfect virtues simply speaking.[211] Because a person's ends are his principles for acting, the perfection of a virtue depends on its teleological direction.[212] It follows that "only the infused virtues are perfect and should be called virtues simply speaking, for they order man to his ultimate end simply speaking."[213] These sorts of virtues, both infused cardinal virtues and the theological virtues, "perfectly and truly have the *ratio* of virtue, and cannot be acquired by human acts but are infused by God."[214] Now the only way for infused virtues to have this order and *ratio* is to be formed by charity, for it is the supernatural love that directs all things to God as one's supreme ultimate end. By rightly ordering the will, charity orders the other movements within man.[215] The last grade of virtue is called "perfect" not because it exists perfectly in every person who has arrived at this grade, or because every person who possesses it has achieved perfection. Rather, virtues on this level are perfect according to their formal and final causes, even if they are not yet perfected according to their mode of existence in a particular man. No virtue is lacking on this level—they all exist together here—and virtues that have been formed by charity lack nothing essential to their nature; they are consequently ordered to man's perfect ultimate end, and they perfect man most readily.

The threefold division of grades of virtue above, considered in light of their causes, is compatible with Aquinas's explanation of the kinds of virtues.[216] He suggestes the following:

211. *De virtutibus*, q. 5, a. 2.
212. See ibid.
213. *ST* I-II, q. 65, a. 2.
214. Ibid.
215. See *ST* I-II, q. 65, a. 4.
216. *ST* I-II, q. 61, a. 5.

- "Social" virtues, which are in man "according to the condition of his nature," that is as ruled by reason alone, which checks the passions according to a relative mean.[217] Because these virtues exist solely on the natural level, with prudence but without charity, they are equivalent to what Aquinas above calls "true but imperfect."
- Purifying virtues (*virtutes purgatoriae*), which are possessed by persons who are on their way to perfection in the divine likeness. Because these are formed by charity, these would be included under the rubric of "perfect" virtue above.
- Purified virtues (*virtutes purgati*), which are possessed by those "who have already attained the Divine likeness," including the blessed in heaven and those who are most perfect in this life.[218] These also would be considered instances of "perfect" virtue.
- Exemplar virtues, which are possessed solely by God, in whose nature the *ratios* of all things preexist.[219]

Aquinas's division of states of virtue, and his two ways of distinguishing among virtues have notable overlap, although each contains elements absent in the other. Summarizing the different relations, grades, and kinds of virtues, we get Table 7-1 below.

Seeing how the virtues relate to each other altogether helps us to better grasp the true nature of flourishing. For Thomas, full flourishing is practically equivalent to "excellence" in act, which is "happiness" or *beatitudo*.[220] Titus notes: "Imperfect flourishing is

217. *ST* I-II, q. 61, a. 5, co. and ad 2.

218. *ST* I-II, q. 61, a. 5, co.

219. See *ST* I, q. 15, aa. 1–3.

220. Craig Steven Titus notes that in the *Summa Theologiae*, "Aquinas used *beatitudo* to cover the notions of both complete and incomplete flourishing." Thus, Titus translates *beatitudo* as "flourishing" throughout his text "to safeguard the unity and correlation between incomplete and complete states of *beatitudo*." Titus, *Resilience and the Virtue of Fortitude*, 100 and 100n93. In this study, I use qualifiers such as "complete/incomplete," "perfect/imperfect," and so on, to distinguish between the two states of *beatitudo*-flourishing-happiness.

Table 7-1. Relations, Grades, and Kinds of Virtue

| *Relation to pleasure in virtuous acts,* Sent. Ethic., *lib. 7, l. 10* | *Grades of virtue,* De virtutibus, *q. 5, a. 2* | *Kinds of virtue,* ST *I-II, q. 61, a. 5* |
|---|---|---|
| Vicious<br>Incontinent | False virtue | |
| Continent | Entirely imperfect virtue (good inclinations; natural virtues without habitual prudence) | |
| Virtuous | True but imperfect virtue (with acquired prudence, but not charity) | "Social" virtue (regulated by natural reason): checks inordinate emotions |
| | Perfect virtue (formed by charity) | Perfecting<br>Perfect |
| | | Exemplar (existing in God) |

inadequate or conflictive unless ordered to complete and perfect flourishing."[221] A good habitual inclination is perfect, however, and truly has the *ratio* of virtue when it produces good works ordered to the ultimate supernatural end.[222] Hence, Aquinas says, "Virtues are nothing other than those perfections by which reason is ordered to God and the inferior powers are disposed according to the rule of reason."[223] These virtues follow the counsels, judgments, and commands of "true and perfect" prudence, which acts with regard to the supreme ultimate end of life.[224] This end is perfect human happiness, that is, union with the Trinity, which consists in seeing and loving the Trinity.[225] Such virtue cannot be acquired by a person. It is given to us through the gift of grace, and cannot exist without divine

221. Titus, *Resilience and the Virtue of Fortitude*, 104.
222. *ST* I-II, q. 65, a. 2.
223. *ST* I, q. 95, a. 3.
224. *ST* II-II, q. 47, a. 13.
225. *ST* I-II, q. 5, a. 5.

charity.[226] Because charity is directed toward a good higher than the limits of human nature, it can only be given by God.[227] Considered individually, Aquinas calls these virtues "infused" insofar as they are directly placed in the soul by God; "divine" because by them, God makes a person virtuous and directs persons to himself; and "heroic" because they are principles of acts that transcend the ordinary good acts of people.[228] They are also called "theological" because their object is God himself, ὁ Θεός (*ho Theos*), because they rightly order a person to God, and because they are known only by divine revelation.[229]

A plant can be sickly for many reasons, but to flourish it must have all the right elements in place simultaneously: light, nourishment, water, oxygen, and so on. Analogously, there are three ways that virtue can be imperfect, but it can be perfect in only one way.[230] If virtue lacks the proper mode, extent, or order to the supreme ultimate end, it is imperfect. It is perfect only when it has all three together. When the excellence of virtue is fully present, one's strengths and capacities are wholly perfected. In fact, the nature of infused virtue ensures the connection of the virtues and it makes a person good (mode), it extends to all parts of human life (extent), and it is ordered to God himself as seen in the beatific vision (order). Hence, ultimate human flourishing only takes place when grace and all the infused virtues are operative in a person's life. Romanus Cessario expresses it well:

> Although one cannot simply develop a natural clone of a complete virtuous life by scraping off what appears distinctively Christian, it is still possible to recognize a "thick" version of human flourishing even in the

226. See *ST* I-II, q. 65, a. 2; q. 63, a. 2, ad 2.

227. *ST* I-II, q. 65, a. 2; q. 56, a. 6.

228. See *ST* I-II, q. 54, a. 3: "Virtus humana, quae disponit ad actum convenientem naturae humanae, distinguitur a divina virtute vel heroica, quae disponit ad actum convenientem cuidam superiori naturae." See also *ST* I-II, q. 62, a. 1, ad 2; and *Sent. Ethic.*, lib. 7, l. 1, nn. 7 and 9.

229. *ST* I-II, q. 62, a. 1.

230. This is because of the Dionysian principle: "bonum causatur ex integra causa, malum autem ex singularibus defectibus." See *ST* I-II, q. 18, a. 4, ad 3; q. 19, a. 6, ad 1; etc.

> acquired moral virtues.... In fact, Aquinas lists scores of specific virtues which shape the human person toward the attainment of human flourishing; in the order of grace these virtues find perfection in charity which, according to Saint Paul (see 1 Cor 13:13), forms the permanent heart of *beatitudo*.[231]

This position holds a middle ground between saying there is *no* human flourishing without grace and saying that there can be *full* human flourishing by human power alone. Here the analogy between human flourishing and human health comes to the fore. Just as a healthy person has all of his fingers that grow proportionately, so a person who is fully flourishing has all the virtues existing in a harmonious unity and growing proportionately to one another.[232] The ultimate end to which an individual is directed by acquired habits is achievable in principle, provided his natural faculties are working properly and without impediment. That end is natural happiness.[233] Unfortunately, full human flourishing does not always take place. Humans currently live in a state of corrupted nature. In this state, humans fall short of what they could ordinarily do by their natural powers.[234] Even in the state of innocence, grace was necessary for a complete relationship with God. Nevertheless, human nature is not completely corrupt: a person is still capable of some imperfect good, just as a sick person on his own strength is able to move somewhat, though he is not able to do the things that a perfectly healthy person could do.[235] However, at every level where human virtue is possible, therefore, "infused habitual forms" are necessary to serve as the principles of action directed to beatitude.[236] Chronologically, grace and all the virtues are infused simultaneously.[237] In a single act, God infuses into the soul all gifts necessary for the in-

231. Romanus Cessario, *Introduction to Moral Theology*, rev. ed. (Washington, D.C.: The Catholic University of America Press, 2001), 38.

232. *De virtutibus*, q. 5, a. 3, ad 1.

233. See *ST* I-II, q. 3, a. 6; q. 4, aa. 5–6; q. 62, a. 1; q. 63, a. 3.

234. *ST* I-II, q. 109, a. 2.

235. Ibid.

236. *De virtutibus*, q. 5, a. 2.

237. See *ST* I-II, q. 65, a. 3.

dividual to achieve eternal beatitude through his own acts: grace, "through which the soul has as sort of spiritual *esse*"; the theological virtues, so that soul can know, desire, and will the supernatural good; finally, all the infused moral virtues, which order man's powers to the supreme ultimate end.[238] It is to the theological virtues and the infused Gifts of the Holy Spirit that we now turn.

238. See *De virtutibus*, q. 1, a. 10.

# 8

# Theological Virtues and the Gifts of the Holy Spirit

The difference between nature and grace, Fulton Sheen observed, is exemplified in the difference between making and begetting. When you make something, it does not share your nature; but when you beget someone, he or she does. You make a chair: the chair does not share your nature. When parents beget a child, the child is like themselves, another person. As creator, God made all things; but when he begets us as children through grace, he does so as Father.[1] This reality is expressed by Christ through the image of the vine and the branches: "I am the true vine, and my Father is the vinedresser.... I am the vine, you are the branches. He who abides in me, and I in him, he it is that bears much fruit."[2] The same sap, the same life-giving principle runs through the vine to all of its branches. Thus does the grace of Christ, planted in our souls by the Father, run through us, so that we might participate in the Father's divine fruitfulness. Our share in God's life by grace offers us new potencies that correspond to the supernatural end set before us. These new powers are the infused virtues and Gifts of the Holy Spirit, which

1. Fulton J. Sheen, *Your Life Is Worth Living: The Christian Philosophy of Life* (Schnecksville, Penn.: St. Andrew's Press, 2001), 172.

2. Jn 15:1, 5. See *Super Io.*, c. 15, l. 1, nn. 1993 and 1996.

enable us able to act habitually as deified persons and even as cooperative instruments of the Spirit of God.[3] That is the topic of this chapter. Here I treat the theological virtues successively in relation to some natural habit: infused faith compared with natural belief; infused hope with natural behaviors of "seeking" and confidence; infused charity with natural affection and love. The final section discusses the nature and role of the gifts of the Spirit.

## THE INFUSED VIRTUE OF FAITH

In our time, we are told to be tolerant toward all faiths and simultaneously to beware of "fundamentalisms." Why this mandate? There is a widespread conviction that every faith is mostly tolerable, but none too defensible, because all are equally wrong. Nietzsche cynically expresses this spirit, saying, "We 'men of knowledge' have gradually come to mistrust believers of all kinds; our mistrust has gradually brought us to make inferences the reverse of former days: wherever the strength of a faith is very prominently displayed, we infer a certain weakness of demonstrability, even the *improbability* of what is believed."[4] To speak about the infused virtue of faith, we must begin with a natural faith in the truth. We must take some truths as indemonstrable starting-points of our inquiry, not least the starting presupposition that truth exists and it can be known by us. With that as a foundation, we can next compare infused, theological faith with analogous habits and acts of natural faith.

Aquinas distinguishes between three aspects of a single act of theological faith, and these distinctions apply equally to natural faith.[5] These are (1) the material object of faith, the content believed; (2) the formal object of faith, belief in a speaker who proposes con-

3. See Juan Arintero, *The Mystical Evolution in the Development and Vitality of the Church*, trans. Jordan Aumann (Rockford, Ill.: TAN Books, 1978), 1:198.

4. Friedrich Nietzsche, *The Genealogy of Morals*, §24, in *Basic Writings of Nietzsche*, ed. and trans. Walter Kaufmann (New York: Modern Library, 1992), 584.

5. See *ST* II-II, q. 2, a. 2. His source for this triple distinction is Augustine, e.g., *Sermones ad populos* 144.2 (PL 38:788).

tent to believe; and (3) the goal of faith, the end toward which the faith tends.[6] To illustrate: suppose a peasant, relying on the testimony of his mother, declares that a king is his father and for that reason decides to lead an army into battle for the glory of king and country.[7] Prior to genetic testing, paternity could not be proved with absolute certainty; it was a belief based on the claims of others, supported by exterior signs that bolstered their claim, such as the similarity between one's face and that of the purported father. Consider Don Juan of Austria's purported filial relation to Holy Roman Emperor Charles V. The material object or content of Don Juan's belief was the claim that the king was his father: he believed *that* something was true. The formal object of his belief was the credibility of his mother: Don Juan believed *in* a claimant (his mother) as a reliable witness to her claim, although later Charles V acknowledged his paternity. Finally, the goal or end of his belief was manifested in some way: he believed *unto* patriotic gallantry for the sake of king and country. This is what one might call fidelity or faithfulness, in which the believer actualizes his love for the truth he believes by directing his energy toward the particular end in which his belief terminates.

Is natural faith or fidelity a virtue? It may seem so, insofar as being faithful to another indicates trustworthiness, which involves living in accordance one's truth-claims. An "attitudinal faith," Robert Audi points out, invites and can even engender a relationship of trust because it affirms another's value and good qualities.[8] But this

6. For an examination of Catholic faith organized along similar lines, see Mattias Joseph Scheeben, *Handbook of Catholic Dogmatics: Book One, Theological Epistemology; Part Two, Theological Knowledge Considered in Itself*, trans. Michael J. Miller (Steubenville, Ohio: Emmaus Academic, 2019), I, §40 (formal object of faith); I, §41 (material object of faith; I, §46 (irrefutable certainty of faith because of its origin and end).

7. Aquinas specifically mentions a paternity-claim as an instance in which natural faith operates; it is analogous to Christ's claim, calling for supernatural faith, that God is his Father. See *In Symbolum Apostolorum, scilicet "Credo in Deum" expositio* [hereafter *In Symbolum Apostolorum*], prol.

8. See Robert Audi, "Faith as Attitude, Trait, and Virtue," in *Virtues and Their Vices*, ed. Kevin Tempe and Craig A. Boyd (New York: Oxford University Press, 2015), 342. Audi quotes Aquinas, but he uses his own unique vocabulary and argumentation that would take some work to square with a Thomistic stance.

position requires more nuance, for credulousness or fidelity does not constitute moral uprightness: trust increases among gang members after perpetrating violence cooperatively.[9] They are faithful to each other while being faithless to society. Thus, the virtuousness of attitudinal faith should be measured by what a person is faithful to—by its goal along with its material and formal objects. If a thief bears allegiance to his mafia boss, that is not virtuous. Even when fidelity indicates adherence to the good, it ought to be described an act of the virtue of perseverance and not one of "faith" per se. Natural faith is more than a behavior; it is a disposition of the intellect. It may involve some action, but an action that stems from a belief of a truth-claim, based on the authority of the claimant. Faith regards identifiable, understandable content, and its apprehension of that content is more than opinion, but less than full knowledge. Unlike science, in which a person grasps the essence of a matter, natural faith relies on the authority of a fallible person and his claims. Thus, Thomas says, natural faith falls short of the *ratio* of a virtue, for it always remains on the level of probability and never reaches the absolute certainty of truth.[10]

Whereas natural faith is imperfect, every infused habit is a perfection of a natural inclination, power, faculty, or appetite, and faith is no exception—it is a certain perfection of the intellect. Thomas calls it a "knowing habit" (*cognoscitivi habitus*).[11] Prior to the infusion of faith, some virtues can exist in the soul accidentally insofar as they remove obstacles to belief.[12] This is especially the case with intellectual virtues. By nature, the intellect is ordered to God inasmuch as he is the principle and end of nature, and the ground of all truth; but the intellect is not naturally and "sufficiently" ordered to God as the object of supernatural beatitude.[13] To the extent that a

9. Paolo Campana and Federico Varese, "Cooperation in Criminal Organizations: Kinship and Violence as Credible Commitments," *Rationality and Society* 25, no. 3 (August 1, 2013): 263–89.

10. *ST* I-II, q. 63, a. 3, ad 2.

11. *ST* II-II, q. 1, a. 1.

12. *ST* II-II, q. 4, a. 7.

13. *ST* I-II, q. 62, a. 1, ad 3.

person grasps truth—especially the truth about God—with the natural light of reason, albeit with difficulty, after much time, and with the admixture of error,[14] his intellect is better disposed to receive divine revelation.

Recent studies of the cognitive science of religion (CSR) significantly develop our understanding of human openness to the infused virtue of faith. By examining stable features of human cognition, seen in infants and young children, CSR aims at explaining the "enduring intuitive appeal of natural theological arguments."[15] In other words, cognitive scientists have noted that, despite inroads of atheism and the sort of skepticism celebrated by Nietzsche, religion remains a nearly-universal phenomenon even in technology-developed countries. Some scientists propose that this is because the human mind is naturally open to belief in God or gods of some sort. Empirical psychologists have shown that infants as young as four months possess an intuitive physics, in which they expect certain features to be consistent in material reality; children at fifteen months have an intuitive psychology or theory of mind; and youngsters also have an intuitive biology, and even intuitive engineering.[16] Aristotle's developed theory of substance and accidents apparently finds a foundation in a "psychological essentialism" found in young children: they say that surgically modifying a dog to resemble a raccoon does not actually change a dog into a raccoon.[17] There is also widespread and persistent intuitive teleology.[18] Three-year-olds, for instance, manifested a sense of teleology (goal-directedness) by correctly inferring the food of a bird based on its beak shape, and by predicting that an unknown mammal must be aquatic because of its webbed feet.[19] One result of these quasi-natural intuitions is our "design stance," that is,

14. See *ST* I, q. 1., a. 1.

15. Helen De Cruz and Johan De Smedt, *A Natural History of Natural Theology: The Cognitive Science of Theology and Philosophy of Religion* (Cambridge, Mass.: MIT Press, 2014), 5.

16. See De Cruz and De Smedt, *A Natural History of Natural Theology*, 26–30.

17. Ibid., 29.

18. See ibid., 68–70.

19. Ibid., 29.

our innate tendency to infer evidence of design wherever we look.[20] Such ways of nondeliberate estimating, or crudely-deliberative thinking, do not prove the inadequacy of St. Thomas's fifth way of proving the existence of God (which focuses on teleology), and they do not debunk natural theology in general.[21] Rather, this "implicit philosophy," these theological intuitions of children, may serve to strengthen belief.[22] Such intuitions may be evidence of a "*sensus divinitatis*, a robust, innate propensity to believe in God," similar to an "innate propensity to believe in the existence of the external world."[23] Perhaps this explains Aquinas's comment that "man feels himself bound by some natural instinct to pay reverence to God."[24] A natural habit or instinct like this, when followed without obstruction, would open a person's mind and heart to receive an infused, theological virtue.

Natural faith, then, remains on the created plane, whereas the transcendent God is the fundamental focus and cause of supernatural faith. Aquinas explains:

> It is one thing to say, "I believe in God" [*credo Deum*], for this designates the [material] object. It is another thing to say, "I believe God" [*credo Deo*], for this designates the one who testifies [formal object]. And it is yet another thing to say, "I believe unto God" [*credo in Deum*], for this designates the end [of belief]. Thus, God can be regarded as the object of faith, as the one who testifies, and as the end [of belief].[25]

Regarding the material object of faith, God reveals the things that are to be believed; he can do this directly or through those who

20. See ibid., 65–68.

21. See *ST* I, q. 2, a. 3.

22. De Cruz and De Smedt, *A Natural History of Natural Theology*, 195. For a discussion of implicit philosophy, see John Paul II, *Fides et Ratio*, pars. 4, 70–71, and 75.

23. De Cruz and De Smedt, *A Natural History of Natural Theology*, 195. They refer to Kelly James Clark and Justin L. Barrett, "Reidian Religious Epistemology and the Cognitive Science of Religion," *Journal of the American Academy of Religion* 79, no. 3 (September 1, 2011): 639–75. Clark and Barrett in turn refer to Thomas Reid's understanding of John Calvin's claim about man's innate *sensus divinitatis*. A similar concept seems to be present in Aquinas as well.

24. *SCG* III, c. 119, n. 7; emphasis added. See *De regno*, lib. 1, c. 13; *De perfectione*, c. 13.

25. *Super Io.*, cap. 6, l. 3, n. 901.

preach the faith.[26] The primary material object known through the infused virtue of faith is the first truth, God, as he reveals himself to us.[27] Only God can be the ultimate source of revelation, for only he can reveal his interior life, and this supernatural knowledge exceeds man's natural powers.[28] Supernatural faith is therefore based on the infallible authority of God as its formal object, making it the most certain grasp of truth and the strongest of claims on the mind.[29] The primary object of supernatural faith—God—reveals the subject of faith, that is, man's intellect.[30] Regarding the assent of faith, God supplies the "supernatural interior moving principle" by which a person makes the act of faith.[31] This is because the act of supernatural faith can be defined as "the will of believing things of the faith on divine authority alone."[32] In other words, although "the intellect is moved to the act of faith by the command of the will,"[33] grace must be given to the will so that the individual is *inclined* to believe and indeed *chooses* to believe what is above the capacity of his nature to believe.[34] This moving grace cannot be charity, which presupposes faith; it must therefore be prevenient actual grace.[35] It follows that faith, rooted in grace, perfects the faculty of the intellect by illuminating it with divine truth; it also thereby perfects previous intellectual habits.

A theological virtue in general is "a virtue that orders man to the good as measured by divine law, and is produced in us by the divine operation alone."[36] Hence, faith is the theological virtue that

26. See *ST* II-II, q. 6, a. 1.
27. *ST* II-II, q. 1, a. 1.
28. See *SCG* III, c. 149, n. 5.
29. See *ST* I, q. 1, a. 8, ad 2.
30. The fact that faith is an imperfect way of seeing God now in this life points to the fact that faith is primarily a seeing of the intellect. See *ST* II-II, q. 4, a. 2, s.c.
31. *ST* II-II, q. 6, a. 1.
32. *ST* II-II, q. 2, a. 10, a. 1.
33. *Super Heb*., c. 11, l. 1, n. 553.
34. See *ST* II-II, q. 6, a. 1, ad 3.
35. See *ST* II-II, q. 4, a. 7, ad 5.
36. *ST* I-II, q. 63, a. 2.

directs us toward the supernatural good[37] by disposing our minds to know the divine law and the divine giver of law, who is our beatitude in his full truth and goodness. Faith is infused in the soul through baptism, and remains there as a habitual principle until it is put into act. Infused faith as such may thus be defined as "a habit of mind in which eternal life is begun in us, making the intellect assent to non-apparent [truths],"[38] especially the truth that "the blessed will see and enjoy God" forever in heaven.[39] As an infused habit, faith is a theological virtue that can exist in two modes: living and lifeless, or formed and unformed. In order for faith to be a life-giving and fully-formed habit, the intellect must "infallibly tend to its good, which is truth," otherwise it would tend to something false, which is contrary to the perfection of the intellect.[40] In addition, the intellect must be "infallibly ordered to its ultimate end, on account of which the will assents to the truth," so that one's belief makes one good.[41] Charity provides this infallible order to all the virtues by directing them all to the end of the will, that is, to God who is loved by charity. Hence, the act of living faith is formed, enlivened, and perfected by charity.[42] Living faith is pointed toward the truth that charity loves. Dead faith, in contrast, is an intellectual assent to truths proposed by God or his ministers, that exists without charity.[43] Without its life-giving form and direction, dead faith is only the beginning of virtue; an imperfect virtue, properly speaking, and thus not a virtue.[44] Nevertheless, because unformed and lifeless faith still apprehends supernatural truth, it is numerically the same habit as living faith.[45]

37. See *ST* I-II, q. 63, a. 3.
38. *ST* II-II, q. 4, a. 1.
39. *Super Heb.*, c. 11, l. 1, n. 557.
40. *ST* II-II, q. 4, a. 5.
41. Ibid.
42. See *ST* II-II, q. 4, a. 3.
43. For the terminology of dead faith, see Jas 2:26 and Council of Trent, session 6, "Justification."
44. *ST* I-II, q. 65, a. 4.
45. See *ST* II-II, q. 4, a. 4.

The reason for this is that "when formed faith becomes unformed, faith itself is not changed, but the subject of faith, which is the soul," which no longer possesses charity, grace, and a teleological orientation toward supernatural life in heaven.[46]

Living faith is an *absolute* assent to what God has said, and a *firm* adherence to it. There are no higher truths than those that God reveals; there is no science higher than that of the faith.[47] Nevertheless, faith is "obscure" to us, for "every creature is darkness compared to the immensity of divine light."[48] Faith's obscurity is not a consequence of error or sin, but of the natural defect of the human intellect as it exists in this present state of life.[49] Truths that are in themselves luminous and piercing hide under words and figures that are more suited to our human mode of understanding.[50] Thus, faith's absoluteness and firmness arises not because our natural reason can fathom the truths grasped by faith, but because God has spoken. The absolute firmness of faith is far greater than the assent one gives to natural knowledge, even scientific knowledge, for it rests on the infallible authority of God.[51] One's choice to believe rests on divine authority "so that it firmly adheres to the things of faith and assents to them with the greatest certitude."[52] Faith therefore is not a disposition of doubt that wavers between belief and unbelief, as a person wavers if he does not have reasons to believe or if there is an apparent equality between reasons to believe and reasons to doubt. One who doubts withholds assent, because he does not adhere to one thing more than another.[53] Assent is an act whereby the intellect gives absolute adherence to what is assented-to as true.[54] Thus,

46. Ibid.
47. *ST* II-II, q. 4, a. 8.
48. *ST* II-II, q. 5, a. 1, ad 2.
49. *ST* II-II, q. 7, a. 2, ad 3.
50. See *ST* II-II, q. 8, a. 1.
51. See *De veritate*, q. 14, a. 1, ad 7.
52. *Super Heb.*, c. 11, l. 1, n. 558.
53. See *De veritate*, q. 14, a. 1.
54. Ibid. and ad 3.

when a person assents with faith to truths proposed by God or his ministers, he gives absolute assent in that he does not doubt any of them and he accepts them unconditionally.

There are at least seven effects of living faith.

1. The soul is "espoused" to God: "through faith the Christian soul enters into a sort of marriage with God."[55]
2. Eternal life is begun in us, "for eternal life is nothing other than knowing God."[56]
3. We learn "everything necessary for living rightly."[57]
4. We possess the principle for overcoming temptations.[58]
5. We gain fear of the Lord: servile fear for dead faith, filial fear for living faith.[59]
6. The purification of the heart becomes possible.[60]
7. All of the other virtues and gifts become available to us, for "faith per se precedes all other virtues."[61]

According to the order of perfection or dignity, charity precedes the other virtues, for—as we have seen—charity forms the theological virtues, and all virtues are virtually or actually commanded by it.[62] However, according to the order of generation, "according to which matter is prior to form, and the imperfect to the perfect," faith comes first, providing the "matter" for the rest of the infused virtues.[63] Thus, Thomas says, "faith is ordered to things to be hoped-for as a sort of beginning, in which the whole is somehow essentially contained, as conclusions [are contained] in principles."[64] It follows

55. *In Symbolum Apostolorum*, prol.
56. Ibid. See also *ST* II-II, q. 4, a. 1; *De veritate*, q. 14, a. 2.
57. *In Symbolum Apostolorum*, prol.
58. Ibid.
59. See *ST* II-II, q. 7, a. 1.
60. *In Symbolum Apostolorum*, prol.
61. *ST* II-II, q. 4, a. 7. See *De veritate*, q. 14, a. 2, ad 3.
62. See *ST* I-II, q. 62, a. 4.
63. Ibid.
64. *Super Heb.*, c. 11, l. 1, n. 557.

that the act of faith, stemming from the habit of faith which is rooted in grace, is a prerequisite for all the other supernatural acts.

## THE INFUSED VIRTUE OF HOPE

Like many a middle child, the virtue of hope often receives far less attention than its siblings, faith and charity. In the *Summa Theologiae*, Aquinas treated hope as a theological virtue in only two questions (*ST* II-II, qq. 17–18), whereas he allotted seven to faith (qq. 1–7) and five to charity (qq. 23–27). Neither the beginning of eternal life nor the union of the soul with God, hope's forward-facing energy is nevertheless so attractive that a thoughtful poet could even say that "hope springs eternal,"[65] though, strictly speaking, the virtue exists only in this life.[66] Hope, then, wonderfully helps us move forward today so that we can reach the tomorrow of eternal life, and while with us it remains a gift: "What future bliss, [God] gives not thee to know / but gives that Hope to be thy blessing now."[67]

Like faith, theological hope has natural analogues that help to reveal its inner character. In this way, hope exists on three different levels.[68] First, there is the passion of hope, a natural movement of the irascible appetite that stems from a prior movement of the concupiscible appetite.[69] Next, there is intellectual hope, which "follows cognition and exists in the rational will" as a confidence of future natural goods.[70] Finally, there is the theological virtue of hope, which elevates the will in light of faith. Each level can be evaluated according the good for which one hopes (the material object), and the help by which that good becomes possible (the formal object).[71]

65. Alexander Pope, *An Essay on Man*, Epistle I, 91.

66. *ST* II-II, q. 18, a. 2.

67. Pope, *An Essay on Man*, Epistle I, 89–90.

68. See Mary Michael Glenn, "A Comparison of the Thomistic and Scotistic Concepts of Hope," *The Thomist* 20 (1957): 27–74, at 32.

69. See *ST* II-II, q. 17, a. 8, ad 2.

70. Glenn, "A Comparison of the Thomistic and Scotistic Concepts of Hope," 32.

71. These can also be called the object *quod* and the object *quo* (ibid., 43).

Aquinas's account of the passion of hope can be fruitfully compared with Panksepp's and Biven's (hereafter referred to as "Panksepp's") account of the neurobiology of emotions, especially what they call the SEEKING and RAGE systems.[72] Diverging starting points exist, of course: Aquinas considers hope as an appetite in relation to the soul, distinguished by its formal object; he is less concerned about hope's bodily substrate. Panksepp, in contrast, focuses on the physical system that underlies observable behavior, and therefore works to avoid formal distinctions that are not upheld by experimental results. Despite these differences, their accounts are largely compatible, for they seem to be more or less treating the same human phenomenon.

Where Aquinas distinguishes among the passions of love, desire, and hope, Panskepp describes SEEKING-EXPECTANCY; and what Aquinas attributes to the concupiscible and the irascible appetite, Panksepp fits under the more general SEEKING system, but in relation to the RAGE system. In Aquinas's view, when an animal senses an object, it begins to estimate whether the object is suitable or unsuitable to its needs: if suitable, love is awakened; if unsuitable, repugnance and "hatred."[73] If the good thing is absent, love leads to the movement of desire to be united with it. Aquinas calls such desire "cupidity" because it arises from the "concupiscible" appetite, that is, the faculty of the soul which regards the future good-to-be-obtained absolutely.[74] When the desire is fulfilled, and the object obtained, one's love is realized more perfectly and so the emotional movement comes full circle.[75] Panskepp's description of SEEKING is remarkably congruent. Significantly, he argues that SEEKING is a specifi-

72. Panksepp and Biven use all-capital letters to indicate seven basic affective systems that can be empirically shown to have "real physical and distinct networks" that exist "in mammalian beings." Panksepp and Biven, *Archaeology of the Mind*, 2.

73. See *ST* I-II, q. 26, a. 1; q. 29, a. 1. In modern parlance, hatred has a cognitive component and seems to be mixed with anger. For Aquinas, however, hatred is simply an emotional reaction of movement away from what is perceived as harmful.

74. *ST* I-II, q. 26, a. 1; q. 40, a. 1.

75. *ST* I-II, q. 26, a. 2. See Aristotle, *De anima* III.10, 433b22–27; Aquinas, *Sent. De anima*, lib. III, l. 15, nn. 831–35.

cally "appetitive" behavior, an "expectant euphoria that prompts people and animals to search for resources they need."[76] The emotion is an urge to extend oneself toward "appealing stimuli"—a movement Aquinas would call "ecstasy"[77]—and also to evade "those stimuli that are threatening."[78] The positive feeling is aroused in rats, for instance, when they sniff for rewards such as food when they are hungry, or extra-sweet sugar water when they feel satiated. More generally, it moves a person to satisfy unfulfilled needs and to look for resources, or, as Aquinas would say, suitable goods. It is activated in *anticipation* of the good, not in the enjoyment as such[79]—a difference which leads Aquinas to distinguish between desire/cupidity and joy/fruition.[80] Similar to how Aquinas sees love and desire as the foundation for all emotion,[81] so Panksepp argues that because every emotion begins with some "appetitive phase," SEEKING may be considered as "the 'granddaddy' of all the emotional systems."[82] Dopamine is the chief neurotransmitter that serves as a chemical fuel for the SEEKING system of the brain; it activates a greater portion of the cortex in humans than other animals, indicating the analogous nature of the feeling for different species.[83]

Following a tradition stemming from Plato, Aquinas argues for a distinction between simple desire and "spirited," combative desire, a distinction requiring concupiscible and irascible parts of the soul.[84] Aquinas thus distinguishes between desire and hope by arguing that hope arises when an animal apprehends a desired object as obtained only with difficulty.[85] This natural, sensory hope is

76. Panksepp and Biven, *Archaeology of the Mind*, 86 and 98.

77. *ST* I-II, q. 28, a. 3.

78. Panksepp and Biven, *Archaeology of the Mind*, 127.

79. Ibid., 122.

80. *ST* I-II, q. 26, a. 2.

81. *ST* I-II, q. 27, a. 4.

82. Panksepp and Biven, *Archaeology of the Mind*, 86, 98, and 105.

83. Ibid., 104–5.

84. *ST* I, q. 81, a. 2; I-II, q. 23, a. 1. See the discussion in Robert Miner, *Aquinas on the Passions* (previously cited on p. 227), 46–53.

85. *ST* I-II, q. 40, a. 1.

a "passion" or emotional reaction to a future and possible but difficult good. The object lies in the future in the sense that the animal must move itself in order to obtain it. The object is apprehended as "possible" and "difficult" insofar as the animal estimates that it can obtain the thing, albeit with concerted effort. Hope therefore is a desire of the "irascible appetite," a sort of energy that pushes the animal to strive more intensely and to struggle to overcome obstacles to the good it desires.[86] Panksepp, for his part, confidently asserts that a RAGE system exists in all mammalian brains,[87] but there remain questions about how to classify aggressive behaviors, such as the difference between affective and predatory violence.[88] Affective RAGE is invariably aroused when something disrupts the desires of the SEEKING system.[89] RAGE tries to prevail over these disruptions; it is positively correlated with many chemicals, including testosterone, which often inclines a person toward higher levels of aggression and social dominance.[90] Panksepp writes: "Even though the SEEKING system is still in a state of arousal and even though SEEKING arousal can produce positive enthused results, the RAGE system may also concurrently become aroused due to frustration and the two passions can synergize."[91] This fits well with Aquinas's observation that hopeful struggle will be experienced as painful to the extent that the desired object is distant; but the struggle is simultaneously experienced as a good to the extent that the object is brought closer by hope and estimated as a real possibility.[92] This observation has a provenance that includes the imagination and even ratio-

86. See *ST* I-II, q. 40, a. 8.

87. Panksepp and Biven, *Archaeology of the Mind*, 148.

88. Joseph E. McEllistrem, "Affective and Predatory Violence," *Aggression and Violent Behavior* 10, no. 1 (November 1, 2004): 1–30. See also Christopher J. Patrick, "Psychophysiological Correlates of Aggression and Violence: An Integrative Review," *Philosophical Transactions of the Royal Society B: Biological Sciences* 363, no. 1503 (August 12, 2008): 2543–55.

89. Panksepp and Biven, *Archaeology of the Mind*, 149.

90. Ibid., 154–55 and 168–70.

91. Ibid.

92. See *ST* I-II, q. 32, a. 3.

nal judgment, but it contains a physiological element as well. Studies have shown that as intense physical exertion toward a desired object releases pleasurable chemicals including endorphins and endocannabinoids—a process that brings the temporary euphoria called "runner's high" and helps a person overcome feelings of despair and hopelessness.[93] Like Aquinas's description of anger as a complex reality,[94] Panksepp recognizes that the RAGE system, although a "basic" system, is more complex than SEEKING.[95] In sum, although Panksepp does not recognize the two basic functions of the sensory appetite (concupiscible and irascible), his research indicates that one can meaningfully distinguish between sensorial desire and hope even on a physiological level.

On a higher, cognitive level Diana Fritz Cates identifies "intellectual hope" as that which incorporates one's passion of hope into one's thoughts and willing desire.[96] Related is what is now called optimism or positive thinking. Originally, Voltaire used the word *optimism* to mock the philosophical view that everything in the world is "optimal," the best it can be.[97] In time, optimism came to signify an unreflective positive estimation about one's future, namely, that everything somehow *will turn out* optimally for the optimist.[98] This sort of naïve optimism or belief in the "power of positive thinking," which persists despite the lack of evidence, or even when confronted with evidence to the contrary, lies in contrast with what psychologist Martin Seligman calls "learned optimism."[99] According to him, learned

93. See Johannes Fuss et al., "A Runner's High Depends on Cannabinoid Receptors in Mice," *Proceedings of the National Academy of Sciences* 112, no. 42 (October 20, 2015): 13105–8; Ross Balchin et al., "Sweating Away Depression? The Impact of Intensive Exercise on Depression," *Journal of Affective Disorders* 200 (August 2016): 218–21; and Panksepp and Biven, *Archaeology of the Mind*, 163.

94. *ST* I-II, q. 46, a. 1.

95. Panksepp and Biven, *Archaeology of the Mind*, 154.

96. See Cates, *Aquinas on the Emotions*, 196.

97. Such is the subject of his satire, *Candide ou l'Optimisme* (Paris: Marc-Michel Rey, 1759).

98. See the discussion in Ayşe Sibel Türküm, "Optimism: Its Benefits and Deficits on Individuals' Behaviors," in *The Psychology of Optimism*, ed. Phyllis R. Brandt (New York: Nova Science, 2011), 103–22, at 104–6.

99. Martin Seligman, *Learned Optimism* (New York: Viking, 2006), 221.

optimism is a skill of managing one's fear and despair through rational thinking about real possibilities. Aquinas goes further and asserts that hope is more than an optimist outlook: as a passion it moves an agent into action to reach the desired, difficult good.[100]

The intellectual hope described above is not a virtue in Aquinas's view. Even if it is learned and developed over time as a skill, even if it is not plagued by error or false estimates, even if it helps us achieve many goods, including physical and psychological well-being,[101] it does not necessarily make a person better, because it is only a probable expectation of gaining created goods.[102] Natural hope's nonvirtuousness persists even if we have learned optimism and self-efficacy and adopt Fritz-Cates's definition of intellectual hope: "a habit of the intellectual appetite, a stable disposition of the will that causes one to desire rightly what pertains to one's highest end."[103] If one's highest end is understood as natural happiness, or God understood by natural reason, then that would be the material object of the natural virtue of hope. But Thomas explicitly says that having natural hope—like natural faith—falls short of the *ratio* of virtue.[104] Like natural faith, the value of hope is relative to its material and formal objects. A person can *wish* that his friend might help him, and if he knows his friend well enough, he may have grounds to *hope* and even *trust* in his friend's help. But such trust does not constitute a virtue.[105] The virtuous quality of the hope is contingent on the trustworthiness of the

100. *ST* I-II, q. 40, aa. 2 and 8. Peterson and Seligman come close to this definition when they recognize that hope is more "emotional" than optimism, and is more of a *wish* and a *motive* than a mere belief that remains on the cognitive level. See *Character Strengths and Virtues*, 570 and 572.

101. Türküm, "Optimism," 110–13. See also the essays in *Handbook of Hope: Theory, Measures, and Applications*, ed. C. R. Snyder (San Diego, Calif.: Academic Press, 2000), especially Scott T. Michael, "Hope Conquers Fear: Overcoming Anxiety and Panic Attacks," 301–19.

102. Glenn remarks: "since hope pertains to things not possessed and human power can be frustrated, reliance on it cannot be sufficiently firm to establish natural hope as a virtue" ("A Comparison of the Thomistic and Scotistic Concepts of Hope," 32).

103. Cates, *Aquinas on the Emotions*, 196.

104. *ST* I-II, q. 63, a. 3, ad 2.

105. Intellectual hope is opposed to mistrust and hesitation (*ST* I-II, q. 67, a. 4, ad 3).

friend: the more a friend is good and trustworthy, the more hoping in him is sensible. However, human friends fail; and they can never fully help us reach our ultimate good. Considering the formal object or motive of hope, hope is only reasonable to the extent that the object of hope is worthy of our trust. But only one being is absolutely trustworthy, is completely good, and never fails, nor can fail: this is God. By natural knowledge, one can know that God is completely good, that he is immutable, and that he orders all things according to his unchanging wisdom. One also knows that God is absolutely just and punishes the evildoer. But on account of evil, we cannot reasonably hope to reach God with our own power, and God has not promised that we can reach him by our own power. Only by faith in God as Savior who overcomes evil can one hope in God's help to reach our ultimate good. Hence, the principal material and formal objects of the virtue of hope are *God as believed-in by faith.*[106]

Once again, considering the material object of hope, in order for a person to have a reasonable hope, the hoped-for good must be "possible," that is, obtainable. But only by faith can one know that supreme beatitude is truly obtainable through our power (in cooperation with divine grace). Hence, "the act of hope presupposes faith."[107] Using language that compares hope to a baptismal garment or religious habit, Thomas says, "This hope has been placed on us by Christ."[108] In addition, "through faith in Christ, hope for eternal life and entrance into heaven is given to us."[109] In other words, only through Christ's saving power can one hope to live eternally as an adopted child of God.[110] In comparison, merely natural hopes may be more or less reasonable, but they always remain contingent and uncertain—and therefore they are not necessarily perfective. One can have an absolutely sure hope only in God the Father, who demonstrates his never-failing love for us through his Son,

106. See *ST* II-II, q. 17, a. 5.
107. *ST* II-II, q. 17, a. 6, ad 2.
108. Ibid.
109. *Super Heb.*, c. 10, l. 2, n. 508.
110. *Super Rom.*, c. 5, l. 1, n. 385.

Jesus Christ, who together send the Spirit of love upon the world. "A distinguishing mark of Christians [is] the fact that they have a future," Benedict XVI says, and that future is union with the Trinity.[111] Thomas therefore avoids discussing the possibility of a natural virtue of hope and instead consistently discusses it as a theological virtue.

"Hope is a virtue," Thomas says, "because it causes a human act to be good and to attain its due rule."[112] The "due rule" is the good end measured by faith, which tells us that the triune God is our end. Hence, the act of hope attains God—not as possessed, which is proper to love—but as he-who-can-be-possessed.[113] Because supernatural hope attains God, this virtue cannot be used wrongly, for one cannot hope *for* God or *in* God too much.[114] In contrast, natural hopes can be used wrongly. Accordingly, the primary material object of virtuous hope is God himself: "For we should hope from Him nothing less than Himself, for His essence is nothing less than His goodness by which He communicates goods to creatures."[115] Because God himself is obtained perfectly through the beatific vision, the beatific vision is included in the supreme ultimate object of hope in an ancillary way.[116] As for any other created goods, we should only hope for them as they are the means to union with God. They are suitable objects insofar as they are secondary means to obtain the supreme ultimate good. The goodness of created things will never entirely make us happy, so we never hope to obtain them except insofar as they can lead us to what will actually make us happy, that is, God himself. Hence, supernatural hope looks for them "secondarily as ordered to eternal beatitude."[117]

The primary formal object, or motive, of hope, is present when one believes by faith that God's almighty power to save is directed

111. *Spe Salvi*, par. 2.
112. *ST* II-II, q. 17, a. 1.
113. Ibid.
114. Ibid., ad 1.
115. *ST* II-II, q. 17, a. 2.
116. See *ST* I-II, q. 3, a. 1.
117. See ibid., ad 2.

toward us unfailingly. As noted, this is best manifested in Christ our precursor. He has fixed our hope like an anchor in heaven, where he has gone before us.[118] Thus, God's intrinsic goodness encourages us and is the reason why we adhere to him with hope.[119] The secondary formal object of our hope is the goodness of God working through creatures. We only place hope in creatures insofar as they are secondary and instrumental agents that help us to obtain goods that are ordered to beatitude.[120] In other words, nothing other than God has the intrinsic power to make us happy, so we should not place our hope in creatures as we do in God. From this it is clear that we can place great hope in the saints, who are proven instruments of God's goodness and desire to save man.

One might think that the "subject" of hope, or place in the person where hope resides, would be the irascible appetite, as that is where the passion of hope resides. The subject of a virtue is proportionate to its object: as perfections of the irascible appetite, acquired and infused fortitude are both directed toward objects that are difficult but possible to obtain—and these objects are in some way sensory. Hence, the virtue of fortitude perfects the irascible appetites, and the infused virtue of fortitude orders the irascible appetite to God through charity. However, the object of hope is "an arduous intelligible," even something above the senses and the intellect, that is, God himself.[121] Thomas concludes that hope resides not in the sensory powers of man, but in the spiritual faculty of the will, which has an intellectual desire for a good not obtained.[122]

If hope is a perfection of the will, how is it distinguished from love?[123] Thomas says that, in a certain way, hope is a form of love.

118. See *Super Heb.*, c. 6, l. 4, n. 325.

119. See *ST* II-II, q. 17, a. 6.

120. See *ST* II-II, q. 17, a. 4.

121. See *ST* II-II, q. 18, a. 1, co. and ad 1.

122. See *ST* II-II, q. 18, a. 1.

123. For an analysis of hope in terms of the *amor concupiscentiae* and *amor benevolentiae*, discussed below, see Roman Cessario, "The Theological Virtue of Hope (IIa IIae, qq. 17–22)," in *The Ethics of Aquinas* (ed. Pope), 232–43, at 236–38.

> Some love is perfect, another imperfect. Perfect love is that by which someone is loved in himself, as one wills good only for another, as when a man loves his friend. Imperfect love is that by which someone loves something not for itself, but so that the good might come to himself, as when a man loves a thing that he desires. The first love of God pertains to charity, which clings to God for His own sake, whereas hope pertains to the second love, because he who hopes intends to obtain something for himself.[124]

In another place, Thomas insists: "Hope directly looks for one's proper good, and not that which pertains to another."[125] It might sound as if Aquinas is saying that hope is self-centered, whereas charity is other-centered, but this is only the case for *dead* hope. Like faith, hope can be living or dead, formed or unformed. Living hope is formed and commanded by charity, such that "man hopes for good from God as from a friend."[126] Living hope not only exists within a loving relationship with God; it ultimately is focused on God as a friend for whom one wills the good. In contrast, hope unformed by charity exists insofar as a person can hope for good things from God, even beatitude, but in a self-centered way. Without charity, one's hope would no longer be commanded by love, although one could still hope to obtain heaven, and to avoid hell, for one's own private good. One's longing for heaven apart from God and the transformative work of grace seems to be a form of presumption and inordinate self-love.[127] Thus, Aquinas underlines the distinction between charity and hope by explaining that both hope and charity are focused on God, but under different aspects: "Hope makes us tend unto God as unto the good to be obtained in the end, and as the efficacious helper for arriving there. But charity properly makes us tend unto God by uniting the affection of man to God, so that man lives not for himself but for God."[128] Living hope sees God

124. *ST* II-II, q. 17, a. 8.
125. *ST* II-II, q. 18, a. 3.
126. *ST* II-II, q. 17, a. 8, ad 2.
127. See *ST* II-II, q. 21, a. 1, ad 2.
128. *ST* II-II, q. 17, a. 6, ad 3.

as a distant good in himself and therefore as the supreme object of desire. Charity is united to God—and all who are loved for God's sake—actually or potentially in a single fellowship that makes other persons the objects of one's divine affection. Loving hope is an efficacious desire for the union of love in God. Living hope and charity are therefore mutually reinforcing: "because one considers that he can obtain a good from someone, he begins to love him, and from the fact that he loves him, he thereby hopes for him all the more."[129] This, then, is how one can hope for something good for another, particularly another's salvation: through the union of charity.[130]

Thomas names three qualities of living hope: it is great, vehement, and firm. The *greatness* of a hope, as noted above, can be seen by the greatness of what is hoped-for, that is, by its material object.[131] Supernatural hope longs for God in himself, perfect beatitude, and everything related to it, such as the perfection of the virtues and a glorified body. Hope is directed toward the "inheritance" of the children of God, which is "the glory that God has in Himself."[132] The *vehemence* of living hope is measured by what it impels him to endure. One who vehemently hopes for something will gladly endure difficult and bitter trials to gain it, similar to how a thirsty man will continue trekking through a desert in order to find an oasis, or how a sick person will gladly take a bitter medicine in the hopes of being cured by it.[133] Thus, the magnitude of evils we are willing to suffer serve to measure one's vehemence in hoping for union with Christ in heaven. Finally, the *firmness* of one's hope, as noted, is measured by the formal object or reason for hoping. The better reason one has for hoping, the firmer is one's hope. Because infused hope is founded in the goodness of God, it does not fail us unless we fail it.[134] There are two unimpeachable reasons to hope: the Holy Spirit has poured

129. *ST* I-II, q. 62, a. 4, ad 3.
130. See *ST* II-II, q. 18, a. 3.
131. *Super Rom.*, c. 5, l. 1, n. 385.
132. Ibid.
133. Ibid.
134. Ibid.

charity into our hearts, and charity never fails; and because Christ died for us, showing us that God could have no greater love for us, for he gave his own Son for us. Theological hope is therefore divinely certain; as certain as God is omnipotent and merciful.[135] Hope is as certain as God is a keeper of his promise to save mankind.[136] Thus hope is "certain" and "most firm" because it is impossible for God, who is truth, to lie.[137] Despair is a sin because it undermines the certitude and firmness of hope. Anything less than firm confidence in God's saving help indicates one's deficient faith or charity.[138]

There are at least eight beneficial effects of theological hope:

1. Hope gives us a most certain confidence in God and everything that leads to eternal union with him.
2. Hope withdraws us from evil by moving us to desire the true good.[139]
3. Hope inclines us to pursue good.[140]
4. Hope for eternal happiness makes every burden seem light.[141]
5. Hope leads to confessing by word and deed our confidence in Christ.[142]
6. Hope leads to endurance of trials and great sufferings: "the saints, on account of hope for the ultimate end of eternal happiness, chose afflictions and poverty over riches and pleasures, for by them they would have been impeded from obtained the hoped-for end."[143]

135. See *ST* II-II, q. 18, a. 4, ad 2. Glenn notes: "Hope does not *merely desire* the Good; it *expects* it through divine Mercy and relies on Infinite Power to obtain it" ("A Comparison of the Thomistic and Scotistic Concepts of Hope," 47).

136. See *Super Heb.*, c. 6, l. 4, n. 318.

137. Ibid.

138. *ST* II-II, q. 20, aa. 2–3.

139. *ST* II-II, q. 20, a. 3.

140. Ibid.

141. See *ST* II-II, q. 18, a. 2, ad 3, and *Super Rom.*, c. 5, l. 1, n. 389.

142. See *Super Heb.*, c. 10, l. 2, n. 508.

143. *Super Heb.*, c. 11, l. 5, n. 616.

7. Because hope is focused on a future eternal good, it can help heal memories of past indulgence in sensible goods.[144]
8. Hope leads to charity and is thus a preparation for eternal union with God.[145]

## THE INFUSED VIRTUE OF CHARITY

Although thought of as too intellectual, it was Aquinas who articulated the broadest ontological argument for love's centrality in the universe. According to the *Doctor Angelicus*, love is the principle for all that an intelligent being does; indeed, it is the principle of all that any agent does.[146] The topics of love and charity have arisen many times so far in this book; here I will address charity directly.[147] In order to understand how humans have charity, we must see how charity relates to human love. Just as the theological virtue of faith perfects natural belief, and the theological virtue of hope perfects man's desires, so charity perfects natural love. Here I would like to note that although, as Benedict XVI rightly states, the love called *eros* can be purified, elevated, and incorporated into charity, I cannot address *eros* here.[148] The complexities of *eros* on its own and in relation to *caritas* deserve their own extensive treatment.[149] Instead, I will focus on love primarily understood as friendship as it unfolds in natural and supernatural ways.

We have seen that love exists analogously in all things according to the levels of being. Love (*amor*) in a broad sense is the first act of the appetite, the principle of motion for tending toward a good that

144. See *Super Heb.*, c. 6, l. 4, n. 324.

145. See *ST* I-II, q. 40, a. 7; q. 62, a. 4, ad 3.

146. McGuiness, *The Wisdom of Love*, 38. See *ST* I-II, q. 28, a. 6.

147. For a sage contemporary Thomistic treatise, see Giorgio Maria Carbone, *Ma la più grande di tutte è la carità* (Bologna: Edizioni Studio Domenicano, 2010). A creative discussion of the centrality of the topic can be found in Gérard Gilleman, *The Primacy of Charity in Moral Theology* (London: Burns & Oates, 1959).

148. See Benedict XVI, *Deus Caritas Est*, pars. 3–11.

149. See *Confessions of Love: The Ambiguities of Greek* Eros *and Latin* Caritas, ed. Craig J. N. de Paulo et al. (New York: Peter Lang, 2011).

is loved.[150] The different kinds of appetite entail different kinds of love. On the lowest level of being, as we have seen, even rocks manifest a sort of mineral love insofar as by a "natural appetite" they move toward their connatural end, overcome obstacles to their movement, and rest in their end when they achieve it.[151] Thus, the gravity of a rock, the principle by which it moves toward its proper end, is its "natural love."[152] Love, then, is the principle of dynamism for all beings according the proper mode of their natures.[153]

The complex nature of humans, composed of both body and soul, entails a love with both biological and spiritual elements. That is, humans possess both sensory and voluntary love. The examination of hope above showed that the neurochemical SEEKING system seems to be a foundation for sensory love and desire as it relates to objects in general. Here we can notice that, even before SEEKING for a specific object begins, an animal must deactivate its fear response. As Stephen Porges says, an animal must have the "neuroception," or in Aquinas's terms, a sensory "estimation" that the object is safe.[154] In the absence of perceived safety, the animal's dorsal vagal complex may induce protective and defensive responses such as nausea, vomiting, and preparations for fighting, fleeing, or freezing.[155] Once the animal perceives relative safety, however, those negative responses are modulated by the chemical oxytocin in favor of positive affect.[156] With this in mind, researcher Barbara Fredrickson says that the first precondition for love is the perception of safety with respect to the other.[157] Oxytocin has received much attention in psychological literature lately; it is sometimes called the

150. *ST* I, q. 20, a. 1; I-II, q. 26, a. 1.

151. See *ST* I-II, q. 26, a. 1.

152. Ibid., a. 2.

153. See Arkadiusz Gudaniec, "Love as the Principle of the Dynamism of Beings," *Studia Gilsoniana* 3 (2014): 301–19.

154. See Porges, *The Polyvagal Theory*, 172, 181, and 194–96.

155. Ibid., 173.

156. Ibid., 174–79.

157. Barbara L. Fredrickson, *Love 2.0: Creating Happiness and Health in Moments of Connection* (New York: Plume, 2013), 19.

"cuddle" hormone,[158] and the calm-and-connect chemical, for has been positively correlated with calmer emotions in groomed rat pups, and biochemical synchrony in general.[159] However, oxytocin can also intensify negative and antisocial behaviors such as gloating, mistrust, and even aggression.[160] Perhaps, then, we should consider oxytocin less as the "love" chemical, and more as that which softens fear and enhances assertiveness by moderating "vagal tone," the physical foundation of the estimative/cogitative sense.[161] With the help of oxytocin, (good) vagal tone helps a person more easily adapt to different circumstances, have positive emotions, and be more open to encountering others. Thus, Frederickson calls high vagal tone a "biological capacity for love."[162] By this, we can take her to mean what Aquinas speaks of as the passion of love, which resides primarily on the sensorial level.

When a subject apprehends something as good-for-himself, Aquinas says, the subject develops sensorial love, the act of its concupiscible appetite. In Aquinas's view, the passion of love has a three-stage movement: love → desire → joy.[163] From our understanding of apprehension and cogitative estimation, we can add preparatory stages to this schema: [estimation of object as safe and good-for-me] → [assertive feelings] → love → desire → joy. Once the object is estimated as safe and good in the concrete circumstances, it can be loved. It then moves the appetite of the subject, adapting the subject to itself by existing in the animal's intention as a form. This change is sensorial love. It is closely allied with what Aquinas calls

158. Peterson, *A Primer in Positive Psychology*, 249.

159. Fredrickson, *Love 2.0*, 51–53. See C. S. Carter, "Neuroendocrine Perspectives on Social Attachment and Love," *Psychoneuroendocrinology* 23, no. 8 (November 1998): 779–818.

160. Panksepp and Biven, *Archaeology of the Mind*, 39. See also Helen Shen, "Neuroscience: The Hard Science of Oxytocin," *Nature* 522, no. 7557 (June 25, 2015): 410–12.

161. Panksepp and Biven, *Archaeology of the Mind*, 42. See also, Richard A. I. Bethlehem et al., "The Oxytocin Paradox," *Frontiers in Behavioral Neuroscience* 8, no. 48 (February 17, 2014): 1–5.

162. Fredrickson, *Love 2.0*, 57.

163. See *ST* I-II, q. 26, a. 2.

*complacentia,* which Cates defines as "the interior motion of resonating with pleasure at the apprehension of an apt connection."[164] Peter Kwasniewski notes the subtlety and complexity of this "basic appetitive stance" that a lover takes toward a beloved thing, for Thomas uses many different words to express the idea: *aptitudo, connaturalitas, convenientia, proportio,* indicating that the object "fits" with the one who loves it; *coaptatio,* the adaptation of lover to the beloved; *consonantia,* a consonance, resonance, or harmony between the two.[165] Kwasniewski argues that the idea of "liking" something approximates *complacentia*: "if we did not already feel that a certain object was 'right' for us, we would not want to possess it or be in its presence. I have to *like* caviar before I can *want* a plate of it, and *a fortiori* before I can *eat* a plate of it and *enjoy* the eating."[166] Additionally, the word "like" is useful, because it indicates Aquinas's insight that the thing we love is "liked" by us because we are somehow "alike,"[167] and that by loving things we become more like them.[168] This bears similarities to Aron and Aron's understanding of love as "expansion of the self" and Fredrickson's findings that positive emotions broaden one's attention beyond a narrow focus on a single individual while increasing feelings of self-other overlap.[169] Whichever term we want to use for it, this *complacentia* leads the lover to move himself toward the beloved object. The movement itself is the second stage of love, namely, desire.[170] The last stage is "joy," which is

164. Diana Fritz Cates, "Love: A Thomistic Analysis," *Journal of Moral Theology* 1, no. 2 (2012): 1–30, at 12.

165. Peter A. Kwasniewski, "The Ecstasy of Love in Thomas Aquinas" (PhD diss., The Catholic University of America, 2002), 120.

166. Ibid., 120n4.

167. See *ST* I-II, q. 27, a. 3.

168. See *ST* I-II, q. 26, a. 2, ad 2.

169. Arthur and Elaine Aron, *Love as Expansion of the Self: Understanding Attraction and Satisfaction* (New York: Harper and Row, 1986). Christian E. Waugh and Barbara L. Fredrickson, "Nice to Know You: Positive Emotions, Self–other Overlap, and Complex Understanding in the Formation of a New Relationship," *The Journal of Positive Psychology* 1, no. 2 (April 1, 2006): 93–106. See also John F. Dovidio et al., "Group Representations and Intergroup Bias: Positive Affect, Similarity, and Group Size," *Personality and Social Psychology Bulletin* 21, no. 8 (1995): 856–65.

170. *ST* I-II, q. 26, a. 2.

the appetite's rest in and enjoyment of the good it has obtained.[171]

In addition to the sensory appetite's passion of love, the intellectual appetite, the will, has a love of its own. "Intellectual" or "rational" love, as Thomas calls it, is in a certain way common to men, angels, and God insofar as it is an inclination of the will toward the good.[172] Thomas names intellectual love in humans *dilectio*, noting that "*dilectio* adds above *amor* a preceding choice [*electionem*], as the very name indicates."[173] Because choice is a purely spiritual act, Aquinas maintains that "*dilectio* is not in the concupiscible [power], but solely in the will, and only in a rational nature."[174] Whereas sensory love stems from an estimation of a thing's fitting goodness, intellectual love stems from the mind's judgment that a thing's goodness is somehow fitting to oneself.[175] Based on this judgment, the person through his will can direct his appetite to find complacency in an object or not.[176] Because the will has a natural inclination or habit of love for the good in general, and the sensory appetites are naturally inclined to the particular fitting good through love (*amor*), it is the role of the reason to determine how to direct these tendencies in the concrete situation; if the will affirms the good, it exercises *dilectio*.[177] In this light, Christopher Malloy defines rational love as "the freely chosen complacency of the appetite in a concrete good, based upon the natural tendency of the will to the last end, beatitude."[178]

Rational love exists in two modes: love of desire (*concupiscentia*) and love of benevolence (*benevolentia*), which Aquinas equates with

171. See ibid. and q. 23, a. 3.

172. For a discussion of intellectual love in angels, see *ST* I, q. 60, a. 1; in God, see *ST* I, q. 20, a. 1, ad 1. For both together, see *ST* I-II, q. 22, a. 3, ad 3.

173. *ST* I-II, q. 26, a. 3.

174. Ibid.

175. See *ST* I-II, q. 27, a. 2; I, q. 82, a. 3.

176. See David Gallagher, "Thomas Aquinas on the Will as Rational Appetite," *Journal of the History of Philosophy* 29 (1991): 559–84.

177. *Super Io.*, c. 21, l. 3, n. 2622.

178. Christopher Malloy, "Love of God for His own Sake and Love of Beatitude: Heavenly Charity According to Thomas Aquinas" (PhD diss., The Catholic University of America, 2001), 123.

love of friendship.[179] Love of desire is that whereby one wills a good for someone; love of friendship is that whereby one loves the person for whom he wills something good.[180] These are not two different types of love so much as two *modes* of a single act of love. Thomas clearly explains this twofold tendency of love:

> Love, therefore, tends to something doubly: in one way, as toward a substantial good that indeed happened when we thus love something so as to wish it good, as we love a man, willing his good. In another mode, love tends to something as towards an accidental good, as we love virtue, not indeed for the reason that we will it to be good, but for the reason that by it we may be good. Now some call the first mode of love the "love of friendship," but the second, the "love of concupiscence."[181]

Love of concupiscence is the love *of an object*; it is acquisitive, the desire to receive. In contrast, the love of friendship is love *of a person*, the desire to give to another. These two modes of love include each other within a single act: "An act of love always tends to two [things]: to the good that one wills toward another, and to the person for whom one wills the good."[182] On the one hand, the love of friendship implies love of concupiscence—if we love someone, we will something good for him. To will a good toward another does not mean having an ongoing stable relationship of friendship (*amicitia*), only that one bears good will toward the other with a love of friendship (*amor amicitiae*), "For this is properly 'to love another': to will him good."[183] On the other hand, love of concupiscence implies love of friendship—for when we love a thing, we love it *for someone*. We do not love wine or mere things primarily in themselves, for "we have no friendship with wine and those sorts of things."[184]

179. The following paragraph is indebted to Malloy's book (a revised version of his dissertation), *Aquinas on Beatific Charity and the Problem of Love*, esp. chaps. 2 and 3.

180. See *ST* I-II, q. 26, a. 4.

181. *In De divinis nominibus*, c. 4, l. 10.

182. *ST* I, q. 20, a. 1, ad 3. For a helpful outline of the differences and subtypes of acquisitive versus benevolent love, see Robert G. Hazo, *The Idea of Love* (New York: Frederick A. Praeger, 1967), 15–28.

183. *ST* I, q. 20, a. 1, ad 3.

184. *ST* I-II, q. 26, a. 4, s.c.

Rather, we love things primarily because they are goods for a person we love, and only secondarily for the thing's good qualities: one loves wine for oneself, because one enjoys its taste, or one loves it because someone else can enjoy it.[185] Thus, love of concupiscence is love of a thing for the sake of a person. It follows that the love of concupiscence is ordered to the love of friendship: "What is loved with the love of friendship is loved simply and for itself; whereas what is loved with the love of concupiscence, is loved, not simply and for itself, but for another."[186] Consequently, love of friendship is love *simpliciter*, whereas love of concupiscence is love *secundum quid*.[187] In sum, according to Aquinas love is person-centered: the love of something in an abstract, impersonal way is ordered to love of persons, who are the ends of all human actions.[188] Natural love is the foundation of all movements of the passions, voluntary love is the foundation of all voluntary movements of the soul, and the love of friendship is the perfection of voluntary love.

Seeing that the love of friendship is a principle of union among rational beings, Thomas's understanding of created charity as a stable principle of union with the Trinity led him to see charity as friendship with God.[189] As Guy Mansini shows, Aquinas understands charity to be friendship, understood strictly but analogically, despite any objections to the contrary.[190] Aquinas's insight into the charity-friendship nexus is one of his unique contributions to moral theology.[191] Aristotle held that men cannot be friends with God, or,

185. See *In De divinis nominibus*, c. 4, l. 10.

186. *ST* I-II, q. 26, a. 4.

187. Ibid.

188. *ST* I-II, q. 73, a. 9. See David Gallagher, "Person and Ethics in Thomas Aquinas," *Acta Philosophica* 4 (1995): 51–71, at 62.

189. One of the most thorough treatments of this theme may be found in H.-D. Noble, *L'Amitié avec Dieu: essais sur la vie spirituelle d'après saint Thomas d'Aquin* (Paris: Desclée de Brouwer, 1932).

190. See Guy Mansini, "Aristotle and Aquinas's Theology of Charity in the *Summa Theologiae*," in *Aristotle in Aquinas's Theology*, ed. Gilles Emery and Matthew Levering (New York: Oxford University Press, 2015), 121–38, at 125 and 125n26. Mansini helpfully answers the objections to charity as Aristotelian friendship in ibid., 127–28.

191. Aquinas developed Augustine's understanding of *caritas* as the love of God (see,

if they are friends with God, they cannot remain so, because the distance between the divine and creation is too great.[192] He was correct regarding the current state of the world: sin prevents us from loving God above all things. We can neither perform an act of charity, nor acquire the virtue, by our own power. However, one can love God with the help that God has given him; this helping gift perfects and elevates man's freedom. The gift is an interior active principle, an infused habit whereby God empowers us to love him as our supreme ultimate end.[193] Aquinas explains that by sanctifying grace the soul participates in divinity and becomes capable of friendship with the Trinity.[194] Through the grace that comes from Christ, friendship is established between God and man, for as in the Son of God's incarnation human nature is hypostatically joined to the divine nature, so by sanctifying grace a person participates in the divine nature, making one capable of loving God as a friend.[195] Charity is thus the divine gift of the stable disposition, inclination, and desire to love God in himself and above all things. Because love connotes some sort of union with the beloved as the object of one's love, charity reaches God himself.[196] Thus, through charity we love God primarily with the love of friendship, that is, we love God for himself.[197] Secondarily, we love those whom God loves, and all creatures, as ordered to him.[198] Thomas says, "Although all gifts are from the Father of lights, still, this gift, that of charity, greatly surpasses all other gifts. For all others can be possessed without charity and the Holy Spirit,

e.g., *De doctrina christiana* 3.10) and insightfully equated it with the highest form of *amicitia* (*philia* in Greek).

192. *Nicomachean Ethics* VIII.7, 1158b36–1159a1.

193. See *ST* II-II, q. 23, a. 4 and ad 2.

194. Noble notes, "L'amitié, tout au moins l'amitié d'excellence, ne suppose pas l'égalité absolue. L'ami riche aime son ami pauvre et met en partage, avec lui, sa richesse d'argent, de vérité ou de vertu. L'amour de Dieu pour nous doit nécessairement condescendre.... Par sa grâce et la destinée qu'il nous prépare, il tend à nous élever à son niveau, à nous faire participer à son vie divine" (*L'Amitié avec Dieu*, 34–35).

195. See *SCG* IV, c. 54, n. 6.

196. See *ST* II-II, q. 23, a. 6, ad 1 and 3.

197. *ST* II-II, q. 27, a. 3.

198. See *ST* II-II, q. 23, a. 5, ad 2.

but with charity it is necessary to possess the Holy Spirit."[199] As it exists in creatures, charity is not the Holy Spirit.[200] Rather, charity is "poured into our hearts."[201] It resides in us "through the infusion of the Holy Spirit, who is the love of the Father and Son, whose participation in us is created charity itself."[202] Just as supernatural faith is a participation in the Word proceeding from the Father, and grace is a participation in the divine nature, so charity is a participation in the Holy Spirit proceeding from the Father and Son.

As if to underline that charity is located in the spiritual faculties and is not a passion that moves with every wind of sensory experience, Thomas discusses the order of charity at length, showing how love of God prefers what is more spiritual, more morally perfect, more godly, to what is more temporal, more earthly, more sensory. He points out that "wherever there is a principle, there must needs be also order of some kind."[203] Therefore, even love has a certain order to it, and this is based on the nature of things.[204] Thomas's discussion of the order of charity is rather intricate, but the foundation of the order is rather simple: we love God with our whole heart, mind, soul, and strength "if there is nothing in us that lacks divine love, that we do not actually or habitually refer to God."[205] Indeed, this sort of love is obligatory by divine precept, for Christ commands us to love God in this fourfold way.[206] Thomas explains each aspect of this order. First, we love God with all our *heart* by referring all things to God as his supreme ultimate end, that is, by do-

199. *Collationes in decem praeceptis*, prol. [hereafter *De decem praeceptis*]. Text taken from J.-P. Torrell, "Les 'Collationes in decem praeceptis' de saint Thomas d'Aquin. Édition critique avec introduction et notes," in Torrell, *Researches Thomasiennes: Études revues et augmentées*, Bibliothèque Thomiste 52 (Paris: J. Vrin, 2000), 65–117.

200. See *ST* II-II, q. 23, a. 2; a. 3, ad 3.

201. Rom 5:5.

202. *ST* II-II, q. 24, a. 2.

203. *ST* II-II, q. 26, a. 1.

204. *ST* II-II, q. 26, a. 13, s.c.

205. *De perfectione*, c. 5.

206. Mk 12:30: "You shall love the Lord your God with all your heart, and with all your soul, and with all your mind, and with all your strength."

ing all things for his sake, "virtually ordering everything to God."[207] Second, we love God with all our *mind* by subjecting our intellect to Him, "believing what has been divinely handed on in tradition."[208] Third, we love God with all our *soul* by "loving everything in God, and by universally referring all one's affections to the love of God."[209] Fourth, we love God with all our *strength* "when all our exterior words and deeds are derived from divine charity."[210] The order of charity therefore flows from the nature of things and this fourfold precept of loving God, so that the nearer something is to God, the more we love it absolutely speaking, because it is nearer to us according to our participation in the divine nature by grace; however, we may accidentally love a thing more intensely because it is nearer to our nature as a human being.[211]

I can now recapitulate my earlier discussion of charity as the form of the virtues. In my comparison of acquired and infused virtues, it became clear that acquired virtues can be true virtues insofar as they are directed toward man's natural happiness, but they will fail to help man reach that happiness if they do not exist in a soul infused with grace. We saw that charity is the form of all virtues, whether acquired or infused, insofar as it directly or indirectly orders them to God. To the extent that virtue is "the disposition of the perfect for the best," no virtue *simpliciter* is possible without charity, for only charity directs man's will to the best and perfect good, man's final end, which is God, and the will in turn directs all the other powers of man.[212] Not intrinsic to any of the other virtues, charity is neither their substantial nor their accidental form.[213] Rather, it is their exemplar form, for the form of an act follows the form of the agent, which is the agent's intended

207. *De perfectione*, c. 5.

208. Ibid.

209. Ibid.

210. Ibid.

211. See *ST* II-II, q. 26, a. 7.

212. See *ST* II-II, q. 23, a. 7.

213. Thomas says this about faith, but it applies to all the virtues that are not per se part of charity. See *De veritate*, q. 14, a. 5, ad 4.

end.[214] Charity therefore serves as the efficient and exemplar-formal cause of all virtuous acts by commanding them; it serves as the "foundation or root" of all virtues by uniting them to God, the source of all life; it is the "mother" of all virtue because, through the power of God, "charity conceives the acts of the virtues within itself."[215] Along with faith and hope, charity admits of degrees. Increasing the intensity of charity will be discussed in the final chapter, which concerns developing good habits. Here we can note that Thomas lists at least fifteen effects of charity.[216]

1. Charity makes man a friend of God.[217]
2. Charity makes all who are friends of God to be friends with each other.[218]
3. Charity effects real union between God and man.[219]
4. Charity effects a "mutual indwelling" between God and man which "makes the beloved to be in the lover, and vice versa."[220]

214. See *ST* II-II, q. 23, a. 8.

215. For these titles and descriptions of charity, see *ST* II-II, q. 23, a. 8, ad 1–3 respectively. See Noble, *L'Amitié avec Dieu*, chap. 20, "La charité, mère de toutes les vertus," 339–54.

216. A number of these effects are listed as effects of natural love. They apply to charity *a fortiori*, for divine love is a perfection of natural love and includes all of its perfections. Such a comparison works because Thomas sees charity as virtue that is analogous to the acquired virtues. See Sherwin, *By Knowledge and By Love*, 229–30. For an extended discussion of the interior effects, see Kwasniewski, "The Ecstasy of Love in Thomas Aquinas," chap. 3, sections 3–8. For a broader overview of the interior and exterior effects of charity, see Carbone, *Ma la più grande di tutte è la carità*, 267–304.

217. *ST* II-II, q. 23, a. 1.

218. *ST* II-II, q. 23, a. 5, ad 2.

219. *ST* I-II, q. 28, a. 1.

220. Ibid., a. 2, s.c. See 1 Jn 4:16: "God is love, and he who abides in love abides in God, and God abides in him," and Jn 14:23. Mutual indwelling effects a transformation of the lover into the beloved, as Augustine notes. We become what we love: "You should rather possess the love of God, so that just as God is eternal, so you may remain in eternity: for as a person loves, so he becomes. Do you love the earth? You will be earth. Do you love God? What should I say? You will become a god? Do not say you heard this from me; let us listen to Scripture: 'I said, you are all gods and sons of the Most High' (Ps 82:6)." *In Epistolam Ioannis ad Parthos tractatus decem*, tract. 2, c. 2, par. 14 (PL 35:1997). Aquinas states that, to the extent that a person is not fully united with the God, charity causes an interior "wound of love." *ST* I-II, q. 28, a. 5.

5. Charity produces an "ecstasy" in which the loving human is brought outside of himself to his divine beloved.[221]
6. Charity excites a zeal in the lover, so that he desires to possess God more intensely, and to serve him more perfectly: and this zeal impels him to strive against whatever hinders his love.[222]
7. Charity melts the heart, softening and opening it to the presence of God, his beloved.[223]
8. Charity causes delight or *fruitio* to the extent that God is present to his soul.[224]
9. Charity strengthens, directs, and forms the other virtues.[225]
10. Perfect charity at least virtually causes every good act that a person performs.[226]
11. Charity causes spiritual joy in the soul, even amid sensory and emotional sufferings.[227]
12. Charity causes there to be peace between the individual and God, and it leads man to strive to extend that peace to his neighbor.[228]
13. Charity leads a person to exercise the virtue of mercy toward his neighbor in distress.[229]
14. Charity leads a person to do good to his neighbor, to whom he wills good.[230] In particular, charity leads a person to perform the spiritual and corporal works of mercy toward the needy.[231] Thus, charity leads a person to perform fraternal correction when prudence dictates such is appropriate.[232]

221. *ST* I-II, q. 28, a. 3.
222. Ibid., a. 4.
223. Ibid., a. 5.
224. Ibid.
225. *ST* II-II, q. 23, a. 8.
226. *ST* I-II, q. 28, a. 6.
227. *ST* II-II, q. 28, a. 3.
228. *ST* II-II, q. 29, a. 3, ad 2.
229. *ST* II-II, q. 30, a. 3.
230. *ST* II-II, q. 31, a. 4.
231. What are now called "spiritual and corporal works of mercy" were, for Aquinas, versions of almsgiving. See *ST* II-II, q. 32, a. 3.
232. *ST* II-II, q. 32, aa. 2–3.

15. By ordering a person and his affections to God, charity simplifies the moral life by ordering all other things in our life rightly.[233]

There are more effects of charity than these, not least the meritorious effects of grace working through charity in a person's good deeds. Merit will be discussed in the final chapter as a crucial feature of the upward spiral of personal perfection through habit development. Here we can note that the effects of charity seen above are the fruit of the love between the Trinity and the individual human. One can agree with Mansini's conclusion that "relative to all other friendships, charity is the architectonic friendship. Since it most surely brings us to our supernatural end in God and in company with all the saints, charity is *friendlier* than all other friendships."[234] Charity is "supereminently analogically friendship," a gift from Christ who, by making us his friends, initiates us into the eternal friendship in the Trinity.[235] As the principle by which man is immediately united to God, charity is therefore the greatest of the virtues and, in a way, the greatest of the habits.

## THE GIFTS OF THE HOLY SPIRIT

The goal of Christ was to communicate his life to us: he came so that we might be rescued from sin and death, and love his Father above all things, and act as he acted, so that he himself might be formed within us. He accomplishes this through the Holy Spirit, and especially through the Gifts of the Holy Spirit, which enable us to act in a truly divine manner. We can imitate the virtues of Christ—his love, his justice, his prudence—but how may we live the life of Christ? Augustine answers: by the Holy Spirit, who performs within the church, the mystical body of Christ, what a soul performs

233. Dunnington, *Addiction and Virtue*, 148.

234. Mansini, "Aristotle and Aquinas's Theology of Charity in the *Summa Theologiae*," 130.

235. Ibid. See Jn 15:14–15.

within a natural body.[236] Aquinas takes this teaching a step further and states that, by the Holy Spirit's Gifts, we co-perform the acts of God himself who uses us as freely cooperating instruments to accomplish His supernatural work.

Thomas's theology of the Gifts of the Holy Spirit is the culmination of his treatment of habits. Here Thomas relies and builds upon all of his previous discussions of habit, from innate habits to the infused theological virtues.[237] When Thomas's position on the Gifts is removed from these sources, it is more difficult to grasp why they are necessary for growth in holiness. But when seen within the ecosystem of man's diverse but harmonious habits, the Gifts of the Spirit not only are more understandable in themselves—they also illuminate the other habits.[238]

Aquinas begins his account by asking whether or not the Gifts of the Holy Spirit are distinct from other gifts of God. It could seem that the Spirit's Gifts are theological inventions, or at least indistinguishable from other graces and charisms. Among the gifts given by God is the Holy Spirit himself, whose Personhood is supremely the

236. See Augustine, *Sermon* 187 and 267.4. Quoted in Leo XIII, *Divinum Illud Munus*, Encyclical Letter, May 9, 1987, par. 6, and John Paul II, General Audience, July 8, 1998, par. 2; both available at www.vatican.va. See also Pius XII, *Mystici Corporis*, Encyclical Letter, June 29, 1943, par. 57; available at www.vatican.va.

237. I hold that in the *Summa Theologiae* Thomas did not change his position on the Gifts, but only articulated his understanding more precisely: his later thought marks an organic development and refinement of his earlier position. See Edward D. O'Connor, "Appendix 4: The Evolution of St Thomas's Thought on the Gifts," in *Summa Theologiae* (London: Blackfriars, 1974), 24:110–30, esp. 119. See also Bernhard Blankenhorn, *The Mystery of Union with God: Dionysian Mysticism in Albert the Great and Thomas Aquinas* (Washington, D.C.: The Catholic University of America Press, 2016), 270–73. In contrast, see James W. Stroud, "Thomas Aquinas' Exposition of the Gifts of the Holy Spirit: Developments in His Thought and Rival Interpretations" (PhD diss., The Catholic University of America, 2012), esp. chaps. 3–4, and John M. Meinert's *The Love of God Poured Out: Grace and the Holy Spirit in St. Thomas Aquinas* (Steubenville, Ohio: Emmaus Academic, 2018). My presentation has more in common with the accounts of Capreolus, Cajetan, John of St. Thomas, Santiago Ramirez, etc., than with rival versions, although I utilize especially Ramirez and Meinert below.

238. Here, unlike my account of the virtues above, I will not detail any natural analogies to the Gifts. The character of the Gifts entails that analogies drawn from nature would be less helpful than examples derived from the lives of the saints where we see the Gifts at work.

"Gift" of Father to the Son,[239] and whose mission is to be the supreme "Gift" to creation.[240] Furthermore, grace and the infused virtues are gifts attributed to the Holy Spirit in a special way. Charity in particular is "poured into our hearts" as participation in the procession and mission of the Holy Spirit.[241]

In response, Thomas explains that all of these graces are indeed gifts of the Holy Spirit, understood broadly. But the "Gifts" of the Holy Spirit, properly understood, are a distinct kind of gift from God. He distinguishes between the virtues and these "Gifts" by appealing to a difference in efficient causality, which affects the mode of operation. Based on a traditional interpretation of Isaiah 11:2–3, Thomas notes that these seven exist in us by "divine inspiration."[242] He explains: "Now inspiration signifies some exterior motion. For it must be understood that in man there is a twofold principle of movement, one that is interior, which is reason; but the other is exterior, which is God."[243] Santiago Ramirez explains that there are three possible modes for humans to act: in an animal way, in a human way, and in a divine way.[244] We can consider each in turn.

The first mode is beneath human nature; it can be called *bestial*, for it is the ordinary mode of animals that act solely according to instinct and acquired habits without the intervention of the deliberate intellect. Hence, an act of a human falls beneath the level of a human act if it does not proceed from deliberate choice, as when a man acts solely from the habit of natural instinct, or from nonvoluntary habits acquired in the womb or early childhood, without thinking about it

239. See *ST* I, q. 38, aa. 1–2.

240. See *ST* I, q. 43, a. 5, ad 1.

241. See Rom 5:5; *ST* II-II, q. 24, a. 2; I, q. 43, a. 5, ad 2; *Super Rom.*, c. 5, l. 1, n. 392.

242. *ST* I-II, q. 68, a. 1. See Is 11:2: "And the Spirit of the LORD shall rest upon him, the spirit of wisdom and understanding, the spirit of counsel and might, the spirit of knowledge and the fear of the LORD." The listing of seven Gifts is in the Vulgate but not the Septuagint.

243. *ST* I-II, q. 68, a. 1.

244. Jacobus M. Santiago Ramirez, *De Donis Spiritus Sancti Deque Vita Mystica: In II P. Summa Theologiae Divi Thomae Expositio*, ed. Victorino Rodriguez (Madrid: Instituto "Luis Vives" de Filosofia, 1974), 93–94.

in any way whatsoever. Acts proceeding from these principles do not operate in a human mode because they fall short of it. Ramirez notes that this bestial mode of action is rare, abnormal, and exists among relatively few people.[245]

The second mode is the common and ordinary, that is, in proportion to human nature. A fully-human act is one that proceeds from a person's deliberate choice. In that case, a person acts in a human mode. When his intellect is illumined solely by the light of natural reason, he acts in a human mode for a natural end. When his intellect is illumined by the light of faith and he directs himself to the triune God by charity, he acts in a human mode for a supernatural end. All virtues, therefore, whether acquired or infused, lie on this level—for a good human habit is by definition a perfection of a human faculty, which can operate only according to its own power. Given that God is the first mover of all acts, action in a human mode makes us "principal, secondary causes" in relation to God's primary motion.

The third mode of action is uncommon and extraordinary for it is above human nature: it exceeds the ordinary, human mode of virtues without destroying it. When God moves us through a Gift of the Holy Spirit, he acts as the principal proximate efficient cause of our act. When this happens, human action proceeds in a mode that exceeds human nature: "The Gifts exceed the common perfection of the virtues, not as to the *kind* of action … but as to the *mode* of acting, insofar as man is moved by a higher principle."[246] This supernatural mode is rare. It is divine insofar as it comes directly from an inspiration of God; it can be called heroic insofar as it inspires acts that greatly excel those of ordinary men.[247] But the heroic nature of some acts does not seem to distinguish gifts from virtues. Hence, we should take into account Aquinas's explanation:

245. Ibid., 93.

246. *ST* I-II, q. 68, a. 2, ad 1; emphasis added.

247. Ramirez, *De Donis Spiritus Sancti*, 94. Aquinas says: "The acts of the Gifts, which are above the human mode, are of blessed men." *Super Matt*, c. 5, l. 2: "Actus donorum, qui sunt supra humanum modum, sunt hominis beati."

> Whatever brings about operating well in a human mode is called a virtue. But whatever brings about operating above a human mode is called a Gift. Hence, the Philosopher places above common virtues some heroic virtues, reckoning that to know the invisible things of God is through a human mode: and this understanding pertains to the virtue of Faith; but to know those things clearly and in a super-human mode pertains to the Gift of Understanding.[248]

Aquinas's position here is clear: the characteristic and distinguishing mark of the Gifts of the Holy Spirit is that they dispose man to be moved in a supernatural mode, that is, in the way that God himself performs actions. Through the Gifts, God moves us directly and immediately as if we were extensions of himself by sanctifying grace.

The present interpretation is supported by Thomas's discussion of movers. He says, "It is manifest that whatever is moved must be proportionate to its mover, and the perfection of a moveable insofar as it is moveable is a disposition by which it is disposed to be well-moved by its mover."[249] From this, he argues that "human virtues perfect man insofar as it is natural for him to be moved by reason in his interior or exterior acts."[250] In other words, man acts according to nature when he is moved by reason; reason is a mover proportionate to his human nature. This natural mode of acting is the measure to which virtue can perfect man in his interior or exterior acts. However, man has a share in the divine nature through sanctifying, habitual grace. Therefore, he must have a principle of movement that is proportionate to that divine nature: "man needs higher perfections according to which he may be disposed to be moved more divinely [*divinius*]."[251] These perfections are the Gifts of the Holy Spirit.

Seeing how the Gifts are dispositions to be moved by the Holy Spirit, questions may arise: do the Gifts operate without human free-

248. *Super Gal.*, c. 5, l. 6.
249. *ST* I-II, q. 68, a. 1. For his discussion of "proportion," see *ST* I, q. 12, a 1, ad 4.
250. *ST* I-II, q. 68, a. 1.
251. Ibid.

dom? Is the height of the spiritual life to be passive? It may seem that Thomas would answer affirmatively, for he holds that the Gifts are dispositions *to be moved*, that they operate in a mode wholly inaccessible to a human mode. He argues that the Holy Spirit can be compared to an artist and humans to his handiwork, that the Holy Spirit is like a soul that moves its organs at will.[252] But, without further explanation, this understanding of the Gifts is in tension with his entire moral theology, which aims at explaining how man, made in the image of God, moves himself toward beatitude with God's help. It follows that, as Marilyn McCord Adams notes, the medieval doctrine of the Gifts of the Holy Spirit is rooted in a series of interrelated biblical and patristic "problems."[253] What concerns us particularly here is the Genuine Agency Problem, that is, how to reconcile divine and human agency in a non-Pelagian manner, in a way that preserves the primacy of God and the freedom of man to move himself.[254] As we will see, Aquinas resolves the Genuine Agency Problem by grounding his teaching on the Gifts on a deeper understanding of *habitus*.

We may recall that habits are necessary for the perfection of human acts: although an individual may command a discrete good act, action that is good and human proceeds according to a human mode proportionate to perfected (habituated) human nature. Robots are directed by rational programs, and a humanoid robot could potentially perform an exteriorly good act such as saving a drowning person. But a robot will never act in a human mode. Robotic acts cannot proceed from powers that have been perfected to be inclined toward the good apprehended by the senses, felt by the passions, estimated by the cogitative power, and grasped by reason. Only habituation, the product of deliberate choice, provides an agent with interior inclinations for right action. Furthermore, in the highest levels of habituation, an individual's intellect and will act as a united

252. See *ST* I-II, q. 68, a. 4, ad 1.

253. Marilyn McCord Adams, "Genuine Agency, Somehow Shared? The Holy Spirit and Other Gifts," in *Oxford Studies in Medieval Philosophy*, ed. Robert Pasnau (Oxford: Oxford University Press, 2013), 1:23–59.

254. Ibid., 24.

efficient cause that uses the instrumentality of the imagination to create creative and spontaneously good acts, as evidenced by an expert pianist's improvisations. Because of this, fully voluntary habits make actions that flow from them *more* voluntary, not less, because through these habits a person perfects his powers and acts more fully in accordance with his chosen good. Thus, human habits make a person act in a fully-human mode. As Thomas says in his discussion of the Gifts of the Holy Spirit, acquired *virtues* make humans act in a human mode, that is, according to human reason in proportion to human nature. For these reasons, Aquinas sees the Gifts of the Holy Spirit as infused habits, for through the Gifts "man is so acted upon by the Holy Spirit that he also acts, insofar as the act is of free choice."[255] As habits, the Gifts are perfections of the human person insofar as he is conformed to God by grace. They do not perfect human nature; that is the role of habitual grace. They do not perfect particular powers as such; that is the role of particular infused virtues. Rather, the Gifts perfect all of the powers of the soul together by making them docile to the Spirit's movements. Thomas develops this reasoning with the following comparison—Gifts of the Holy Spirit : all the powers of the soul :: moral virtues : appetitive power. Just as the moral virtues perfect man humanly by making the appetitive powers obedient to reason, so the Gifts of the Holy Spirit perfect man divinely by making the entire man docile to the Holy Spirit.[256] Hence, with respect to the *subject*, the virtues perfect particular faculties: justice exists as a perfection of the will, prudence the intellect, fortitude the irascible appetite, and temperance the concupiscible appetite. However, the Gifts exist in the higher part of the soul—the intellect and the will—and do not perfect faculties as do the intellectual or moral virtues, but instead render them supple to the shaping of the Spirit. Undoubtedly, when the Spirit moves the soul, the soul is thereby perfected, but the Gifts are not the perfections as such. Rather, they perfect the perfections of the virtues by

255. *ST* I-II, q. 68, a. 3, ad 2.
256. See *ST* I-II, q. 68, a. 4.

elevating the soul so that it can perform acts in manner higher than its faculties produce even with grace: "the Gifts perfect the virtues by elevating them above a human mode, as the Gift of Understanding perfects the virtue of faith."[257] From the perspective of agency one can say: just as reason perfects the appetites by subjecting them to itself and thereby developing the moral virtues, so the Holy Spirit perfects man by subjecting the entire man to the Spirit's own movements through the Gifts.

Thomas says that the Holy Spirit is the "principal mover" and men are like his "organs," similar to the way reason is the principal mover and the appetites its organs.[258] This is analogous to the "principal-instrument" relationship between man's rationality and his lower powers that we discussed earlier. Similar to the way human rationality in the natural sphere uses the instrumentality of the imagination or cogitative power to move the appetites and produce a creative act, so in the supernatural sphere, the Holy Spirit uses all the powers of the soul in order to move the person toward a creative divine act. The directives of the higher power enable the lower power to reach a greater potential than it could on its own: the natural cultivation of habit in this way can result in a Mozart; the supernatural infusion of habit (and man's cooperation with it) can result in an Aquinas. Habits of acquired virtue are the product of a man's art or self-shaping, and thus Aquinas says that the Gifts of the Holy Spirit are the product of the Spirit's "art" of shaping men by grace into the image of Christ so that they might act like him. This reveals that the Gifts of the Holy Spirit do not remove an individual's freedom; rather, they perfect his freedom. By means of the Gifts, man is enabled to act with all of the creative spontaneity and freedom of God himself, who is always good but never predictable in his goodness: the Spirit "blows" where he wills.[259] It follows that, though the Gifts are quasi-permanent dispositions *to be moved*, their trajectory is ac-

257. *De virtutibus*, q. 2, a. 2, ad 17.
258. *ST* I-II, q. 68, a. 4, ad 1.
259. Jn 3:8. See *Super Io.*, c. 3, l. 2, nn. 452–55.

tion—just as, on the human level, the moral virtues are dispositions of the appetites to be moved by reason for the sake of acting well. As infused habits, the Gifts of the Holy Spirit enable a human to be connaturally docile to the Holy Spirit who moves the individual to perform acts, including interior acts of contemplation, in a divine mode.

In the *Summa Theologiae,* Thomas prefers to describe the dynamic of the Gifts collectively as a "divine instinct" (*instinctus divinus*).[260] He states, "for those who are moved by divine instinct, it is not expedient that they be counseled according to human reason, but that they follow an interior instinct, because they are moved by a principle better than human reason."[261] On the natural level, instincts are more perfect than unconditioned reflexes such as pupil dilation, and more perfect than conditioned reflexes such as coughing. Natural instincts are innate habits or dispositions for movement that are activated by the impulse of direction provided by the estimative power. In animals, instincts are principles and causes of operations by which they are moved according to the mode of nature.[262] Instinctual behavior proceeds below the level of a human mode, but it remains intelligible, goal-directed, and the result of apprehension—for instincts are innate dispositions toward action that stem from the wisdom of God the creator.[263] By instinct, a sheep estimates that a wolf is dangerous.[264] Meanwhile, as discussed above, humans have a variety of instincts, including a "happiness instinct" that inclines the will to happiness; a "God instinct" that inclines the person to pay reverence to the divine; and so on. Hence, we have natural inclina-

260. For a good overview of Thomas's position, see Wojciech Giertych, "The New Law as a Rule for Acts" (STD diss., Pontifical University of Saint Thomas Aquinas, 1989), 238–50; and Servais Pinckaers, "Morality and the Movement of the Holy Spirit: Aquinas's Doctrine of *Instinctus*," in *The Pinckaers Reader*, 385–95. Although Aquinas says that the gifts operate *ad prompte obediendum Spiritus*, Edward D. O'Connor's translation of *instinctus* as "prompting" obscures the analogy between the natural and the supernatural levels. See his otherwise helpful "Appendix 5: *Instinctus* and *Inspiratio*," 131–41.

261. *ST* I-II, q. 68, a. 1.

262. See *ST* II-II, q. 95, a. 7.

263. See *ST* I-II, q. 40, a. 3.

264. See *ST* I-II, q. 12, a. 5.

tions toward specific actions that are in accordance with our nature.

If a person were to act solely according to his natural instincts, he would act in an *animal* mode, for such action is below his specific rational nature (even if the act is in accord with nature). When a person deliberately *chooses* to act in accordance with his human instincts, he acts in a *human* mode, which perfects and does not destroy his lower inclinations. But when a person acts according to the Gifts, which are instincts to be moved by God, he acts in a *divine* mode. Angelic operations help to clarify this Spirit-led movement. As purely spiritual creatures, angels do not move themselves with a step-by-step, plodding deliberation. Rather, they move themselves quasi-instantaneously by following an inclination that one might call a natural, rational instinct that follows from their intuitive judgment. In a similar but higher way, the Gifts of the Holy Spirit are inclinations according to the divine nature in which man participates by grace. Because action that exists in a divine mode can only come directly from God himself, the Gifts are habits that incline a person to be moved by God. Grace provides a second nature for humans, and the Gifts perfect all the powers of the soul by inclining them to a new kind of movement: that of the triune God.

Like natural instincts, divine instincts produce nonhuman action—but instead of being *infra*rational, the action produced is *super*rational, that is, in accordance with God's hidden counsels. Like natural instincts, divine instincts involve automaticity—but instead of working below the level of human volition, they work above it. A person who follows the divine instinct to act does not thereby abandon his rationality or his freedom, but instead allows it to be perfected by the Wisdom of God, which operates through him without the obstacles presented by imperfect human nature.[265] Finally, just as instincts help animals to perceive the goodness or evil in apprehended things, so divine instincts provide humans with a similar intuitive and connatural "feel" not only for sensory objects but even for

265. See Noble, *L'Amitié avec Dieu*, 215.

spiritual things.[266] Pinckaers insists that the *instinct of the Holy Spirit* "does not act in a sporadic way, through sudden inspirations, but in a constant way, supporting the enduring patience required by the practice and progress of virtues."[267] If my reading is correct, one may agree with Pinckaers that the Gifts are habitually present in the soul, but their operation may be more complex than he describes. The experience of the saints, those who have reached the heights of virtue in this life, suggests that the Gifts rarely if ever operate in a continual manner. Perfected virtue surely places no direct obstacles to the quasi-automatic movement of the Holy Spirit, but the Gifts seem to incline a person and provide predominant movements, for some in a nanosecond, and for others apparently for hours.

The extraordinary function of the Gifts of the Holy Spirit can be seen by comparing them with other supernatural gifts and virtues.[268] Some charismatic graces, such as prophecy or healing, are considered as gifts of the Spirit. However, these gifts are of lesser import for the soul who possesses them than what are more properly known as the Gifts of the Holy Spirit. Some actual graces enable a human to perform a supernatural act, but he can perform that act humanly or wickedly, for even sinners can receive these graces, as when Balaam the idolater prophesied about the Messiah.[269] In cases like this, Thomas says, the Holy Spirit gives a grace to a person in whom he does not

266. This truth gives rise to the doctrine of the "spiritual senses," which was explored much more directly and in depth by St. Bonaventure than Thomas. See the entries on "Bonaventure" by Gregory F. LaNave and "Thomas Aquinas" by Richard Cross in *The Spiritual Senses: Perceiving God in Western Christianity*, ed. Paul L. Gavrilyuk and Sarah Coakley (Cambridge: Cambridge University Press, 2011), 159–73 and 174–89, respectively.

267. Pinckaers, "Morality and the Movement of the Holy Spirit," 391.

268. In his commentary on 1 Corinthians, which exists only as a *reportatio* of Reginald of Piperno, Thomas treats various gifts of the Spirit in great detail: three lectures on 1 Cor 12, two lectures on relevant sections in 1 Cor 13, and six lectures on 1 Cor 14. For a discussion of this work and its textual difficulties, see Torrell, *Saint Thomas Aquinas: The Person and His Work*, 1:340; and Daniel A. Keating, "Aquinas on 1 and 2 Corinthians: The Sacraments and Their Ministers," in *Aquinas on Scripture: An Introduction to His Biblical Commentaries*, ed. Thomas G. Weinandy, Daniel A. Keating, and John Yocum (London: T and T Clark, 2005), 127–48, at 127–28 and 127–28nn1–3.

269. See *ST* II-II, q. 172, a. 6, ad 1.

dwell in order to manifest the truth of the Catholic faith that the sinner preaches.[270] Contrastingly, the proper Gifts of the Holy Spirit are united to grace and the theological virtues; they are possessed by the Christian and make him docile to the movements of the Spirit.

Compared to virtues, the Gifts of the Holy Spirit are more excellent according to their mode of action. But the theological virtues are superior insofar as they enable us to perform new, supernatural acts. Charity in particular is superior to all virtues and Gifts because it unites us with God as one who is known and loved. Because the Gifts do not enable us to perform just any new kinds of works, they are "regulated" by the theological virtues as the principles from which they derive.[271] However, the Gifts of the Holy Spirit are superior insofar as they perfect the entire person, "disposing all of the powers of the soul to be subordinated to divine motion."[272] By doing this, the Gifts enable man to perform actions in a supernatural mode. In other words, charity enables us to love God, but the Gifts enable us to love God in a divine way: by them, we can love the Father as Christ loved him, through the Spirit.

The necessity of the Gifts of the Holy Spirit is manifested by reason's role in human perfection. Reason informs the will in two ways: according to a human mode, and according to a divine mode. The human mode can be perfected in the natural sphere, when reason operates by knowing things that are within its purview; or it can be perfected in the supernatural sphere when it is informed by faith operating through charity. However, even when human reason is informed by the theological virtues, it remains imperfect because of its human mode of operation and because of other related limitations.[273] Stephen Long explains: "Human prudence is insufficient surely to govern man's practical life even when it is fortified by acquired and infused prudence, because these work in an essentially

270. See *Super I Cor.*, c. 12, l. 2.
271. *ST* I-II, q. 68, a. 8. See *ST* I-II, q. 68, a. 4, ad 3.
272. *ST* I-II, q. 68, a. 8.
273. See *ST* I-II, q. 68, a. 2, ad 3.

rational and discursive way, within the limits of our reason."[274] Long notes that ignorance will be always present even when other defects due to sin—such as folly and hardness of heart—are not. Hence, the Gifts of the Holy Spirit are necessary for making consistently virtuous decisions in this life: "Since man cannot, within the limits of human reason, grasp all the contingent singular circumstances that pertain to the perfection of action, only being directed by God through the Gift of counsel he can overcome this defect."[275] Thus, aside from cases such as infancy and insanity, when a person cannot use his intellect, a healthy and mature person cannot enter heaven unless he is moved and led by the Holy Spirit, because the theological virtues that are activated in a human mode do not suffice.[276]

Even in heaven, the Gifts are present within our souls. The acquired virtues, the infused virtues of faith and hope, and the sacraments all pass away in the next life. In contrast, Andrew Pinsent explains, the Gifts "are intrinsic to perfect human flourishing and not merely instruments to attain that flourishing."[277] Thomas alludes to this fuller flourishing with his observation that, even if man's reason should be perfected by the theological and moral virtues, he is not so perfected by them "as not to stand in continual need to be moved by a sort of superior instinct of the Holy Spirit."[278] John Meinert interprets this to mean that this divine *instinctus* is "[perpetually] necessary to act at all, to act well, and to counter the effects of fallen human nature," that is, "the Gifts are necessary for each operation of the theological virtues."[279] In my reading, the Gifts are not ab-

274. Stephen Long, "The Gifts of the Holy Spirit and Their Indispensability for the Christian Moral Life: Grace as Motus," *Nova et Vetera* (English edition) 11, no. 2 (2013): 357–73, at 367.

275. Ibid., 367.

276. See *ST* I-II, q. 68, a. 2.

277. Andrew Pinsent, *The Second-Person Perspective in Aquinas's Ethics: Virtues and Gifts* (London: Routledge, 2013), 34.

278. *ST* I-II, q. 68, a. 2, ad 2.

279. Meinert, *The Love of God Poured Out*, 113 and 120. Meinert equates the instinct of the Holy Spirit with the "common" *auxilium gratiae*, spoken of in *ST* I-II, q. 111, a. 2, which is necessary for man to will a good act directed toward the right supernatural end.

solutely necessary for the virtues to operate in a human mode, for a person can choose to make acts of faith, hope, charity, etc., without being moved by the instinct of the Holy Spirit.[280] However, the Gifts are necessary for the more perfect operation of the virtues in a divine mode, which contributes to the fullest flourishing that a person can experience. When Thomas says that Gifts are infused along with grace and the virtues, he indicates that they abide in the soul as long as man is in state of perfect grace, that is, forever in heaven.[281] This is because man needs to be moved by the instinct of the Spirit even in heaven. The full perfection of the human soul—which is to commune continually with God himself—requires that humans be moved in a mode that is proportionate to that divine end. Because man participates in the divine nature through grace, and obtains God through the theological virtues, he should also be moved in a divine way, which is the work of the Gifts: "the Gifts of the Holy Spirit perfect the human mind to follow the motion of the Holy Spirit, which especially will exist in heaven, when God 'will be all in all,' as it says in 1 Cor 15:28, and man will be entirely subject to God."[282]

Pinsent observes that it is easier to grasp the importance of the Gifts than the nature of their precise function.[283] We have seen their general function, which shows their relative necessity. We can better see their importance, and begin to glimpse their precise function, by considering their relation to Christ. An objection argues that the Gifts of the Holy Spirit belong uniquely to Christ: "it is proper to Christ that the gifts of the Spirit rest upon him."[284] In response, Aquinas replies that the Gifts are not like the hypostatic union, which unites the divine and human nature in one divine Person; rather, they are habits: qualities remaining in the soul that are difficult to remove.[285]

280. Meinert admits the reasonability of this solution in 121n227.
281. See *ST* I-II, q. 68, a. 3, s.c. and ad 1.
282. *ST* I-II, q. 68, a. 6.
283. See Pinsent, "The Gifts and Fruits of the Holy Spirit," 477.
284. *ST* I-II, q. 68, a. 3, obj. 1.
285. Ibid.

Consequently, they are "perfections of the powers of the soul insofar as they are naturally moved by the Holy Spirit."[286] This ability to be connaturally moved is not an active principle by which the creature can extend itself to what is beyond creation. Rather, it is an supernatural "obediential potency," a power that is passive with respect to divine agency.[287] The Gifts enabled Christ's humanity to operate in a divine mode, that is, according to the movement of the Spirit. Accordingly, insofar as through grace humans are conformed to Christ and participate in the divine nature, the Holy Spirit "always remains in the saints" through his Gifts.[288] Christ's exemplarity shows that, while the Gifts are a disposition to be *moved* by the Spirit, the Spirit moves us so that we may act in a divine way: after receiving the Spirit in a more intense way, Jesus went to the desert to contemplate and endure temptation, and then he began his public ministry. Likewise, the Gifts of the Spirit are directed toward enabling people to perform divine actions. In other words, through the Gifts, a person in state of grace is able to act in a Christ-like way, that is, to do works that are divine not only in their origin and their end, but also in their very manner. This is only possible through a series of divine habits: wisdom, understanding, knowledge, counsel, piety, fortitude, and fear of the Lord.[289]

286. *ST* III, q. 7, a. 5.

287. See *ST* III, q. 11, a. 1.

288. *ST* I-II, q. 68, a. 3, ad 1.

289. See *ST* I-II, q. 68, a. 4. For an analysis of each Gift's proper role, see Noble, *L'Amitié avec Dieu*, 210–40 and 316–38.

# PART 3

# Hacking Your Habits

# 9

## Elements of Habit Change

In 1869, Francis Galton, a Victorian gentleman, a Master Freemason and a half-cousin of Charles Darwin, penned a book that was meant to support his eugenicist theories. *Hereditary Genius* analyzed illustrious men of history and purported to prove that practice alone cannot substitute for irrepressible innate biological factors: training is important, but greatness is ultimately hereditary.[1] Over one hundred and twenty years later, Anders Ericsson and his colleagues questioned Galton's claims on empirical grounds. Their tests indicated that expert performance was primarily caused by high-level practice for a very long time.[2] Later, Malcolm Gladwell popularized these results as "The 10,000-Hour Rule": if you practice a skill for ten thousand hours, you will become an expert at it.[3] Critics later responded, arguing that individually-held traits ("differences") make a significant impact on the usefulness of practice.[4] The debate continues.[5]

1. Francis Galton, *Hereditary Genius: An Inquiry into Its Laws and Consequences* (London: Macmillan, 1869), 15, 39, and 318.

2. K. Anders Ericsson et al., "The Role of Deliberate Practice in the Acquisition of Expert Performance," *Psychological Review* 100, no. 3 (1993): 363–406.

3. Malcolm Gladwell, *Outliers: The Story of Success* (New York: Little, Brown and Company, 2008), 39–42, 47–50, etc.

4. David Z. Hambrick et al., "Accounting for Expert Performance: The Devil Is in the Details," *Intelligence* 45 (July 1, 2014): 112–14.

5. K. Anders Ericsson responds to negative reviewers (and to Gladwell) with his article, "Why Expert Performance Is Special and Cannot Be Extrapolated from Studies

One thing, however, is undeniable: right practice develops habits.

Most people turn to a book on habits to deal with bad habits and to gain better habits, rather than to learn theories of habituation. Romeo did not go to Friar Laurence for a discourse on the nature of love, but for advice regarding his beloved Juliet. Here I mean to offer practical help. Up to this point, I have almost entirely focused on what habits are in all their varied complexity. I have only gestured toward practical applications. In what follows, I mean to elaborate on principles for developing good habits and getting rid of bad ones. In other words, part 3 of this book is dedicated to discussing how to hack your habits.

In this chapter, I discuss the basic elements of habit-change, that is, central concepts and techniques one can implement to change habits. Because acquiring or developing fully human habits is a specifically human enterprise, it requires self-knowledge, as the first section discusses. Developing this theme, the second section addresses how simple and complex habits exist simultaneously within us and often vie for dominance. Having established the groundwork in which our habit development takes place, the third section treats well-established techniques for acquiring and developing habits, seen in light of Thomistic mnemonics and the habit loop. The last section explains how habits may be diminished or eradicated.

## HABITUAL SELF-KNOWLEDGE

The foundational habit for acquiring and developing fully voluntary habits is habitual self-knowledge. The inscription at Delphi, "know yourself," serves as a testimony to the centrality of self-knowledge for human life and action.[6] Self-knowledge in the sense I mean here is more than momentarily grasping a fact about oneself, a quick glimpse in the mirror that can easily be forgotten. Rather, this

---

of Performance in the General Population: A Response to Criticisms," *Intelligence* 45 (July 1, 2014): 81–103.

6. See Plato, *Protagoras* 343b.

knowledge abides in a person's soul lastingly, a habit subordinated to the virtue of truth that affects one's entire life. If actions speak louder than words, habits are the echo of our own voice.

One may distinguish three kinds of self-knowledge that lead to characteristic practices: a poetic habit, a philosophical-psychological habit, and a moral-theological habit. With self-knowledge as a poetic habit, a person comes to know himself chiefly for the purpose of creating art, such as Benvenuto Cellini's autobiography or Rembrandt's sundry self-portraits. Self-knowledge as a philosophical habit seeks to understand the self from the perspective of epistemology and metaphysics. Accounts of self-knowledge in the thought of Aristotle, Augustine, and Aquinas may be included under this rubric.[7] Various Thomists have covered concerns such as Aquinas's relation to Averroes's theory of mind[8] or the "subjective turn" of modernity, as signaled by figures such as Descartes, Kant, and Husserl.[9] Connected with philosophical inquiries is self-knowledge in psychology, which is in a neonatal state, only just distinguishing itself as a standalone subject of study rather than as dispersed through various established fields.[10] Psychological self-knowledge focuses on one's internal states, including feelings and desires, motives and actions, memory and prediction.[11] In its more practical mode, self-knowledge aims more at moral action than at speculative truths.

7. See chaps. 2, 5, and 6—respectively on Aristotle, Augustine, and Aquinas (and other scholastics)—in *Self-Knowledge: A History*, ed. Ursula Renz (New York: Oxford University Press, 2017).

8. See Cory, *Aquinas on Human Self-Knowledge*, and Richard T. Lambert, *Self Knowledge in Thomas Aquinas* (Bloomington, Ind.: AuthorHouse, 2007).

9. Robert Sokolowski provides a more phenomenological Thomistic approach. See his works *Phenomenology of the Human Person* (New York: Cambridge University Press, 2008) and *The God of Faith and Reason: Foundations of a Christian Theology* (Washington, D.C.: The Catholic University of America Press, 1995), chap. 8.

10. Timothy D. Wilson and Elizabeth W. Dunn, "Self-Knowledge: Its Limits, Value, and Potential for Improvement," *Annual Review of Psychology* 55 (2004): 493–518, at 494. For a summary of the latest research, see *Handbook of Self-Knowledge*, ed. Simine Vazire and Timothy D. Wilson (New York: The Guilford Press, 2012).

11. Timothy D. Wilson, "Know Thyself," *Perspectives on Psychological Science: A Journal of the Association for Psychological Science* 4, no. 4 (July 2009): 384–89.

In this present section, I am concerned with self-knowledge in the mode of a moral-theological habit. I will argue that self-knowledge as a moral exercise, when practiced with faith and charity, includes a theological exercise as well. Thomas's thought within the realm of moral theology helps us to see the importance of identifying which habits one possesses and to offer some suggestions for how to identify them correctly.

Self-knowledge, knowledge of God, and upright moral habits are inextricably intertwined. In Plato's dialogue *Charmides,* we find Critias insisting that self-knowledge is equivalent to the virtue of temperance.[12] Socrates characteristically dismantles this position, but the seed of the insight remains: to know oneself is fundamental to the practice of virtue, and virtue is impossible without self-knowledge. Aristotle in his *Nicomachean Ethics* develops this insight and argues that a person often comes to know himself through a friend who serves as mirror and collaborator. This mutual relation enables one to know oneself through the other, so that one sees oneself simultaneously as an object of consideration and as a thinking person and cause of action.[13] Scripture emphasizes the moral reality of self-knowledge, admonishing us: "Before judgment, examine yourself, and in the hour of visitation you will find forgiveness."[14]

Aquinas, for his part, argues that we cannot live well unless we know ourselves rightly. His account of various virtues reveals how he saw the habit of knowing oneself as crucial for the project of a good life. When one's self-knowledge is enlivened by charity, it is a part of habitual truthfulness toward oneself about oneself.[15] A precise knowledge of oneself is as necessary to one's growth in virtue as particular knowledge of the patient is necessary for a doctor

12. *Charmides* 164d–e. For a valuable discussion of Plato's treatment of the issue in various dialogues, see John I. Beare, "Self-Knowledge," *Mind* 5, no. 18 (April 1896): 227–35.

13. See Zena Hitz, "Aristotle on Self-Knowledge and Friendship," *Philosophers' Imprint* 11, no. 12 (2011): 1–28.

14. Sir 18:20.

15. See *ST* II-II, q. 109, a. 1, ad 3.

to heal.[16] A physician ought to possess a "medium" level of knowledge that includes both the general principles of healing along with a detailed understanding of the patient. If his knowledge lacks precision, then he cannot apply the general principles to a particular person—as new doctors often possess book-knowledge but lack much experience with patients. But a doctor's knowledge would be too particular if were detached from general knowledge—as when an experiment studies neurochemical processes without regard to their effect on health. All prudential action relies on a "medium" of self-knowledge, which is not so general as to be inapplicable to the particular, but not so narrow as to be disconnected from life as a whole. Effective self-knowledge is not a mere cool and detached observation of oneself; it is rather an understanding of oneself that stems from and leads to an ever-deepening encounter with reality. In other words, morally valuable self-knowledge includes attention to one's thoughts, words, deeds, and omissions with the intention of transforming them with the love of God. Knowledge of one's habits is crucial to moral uprightness, for as Charles Peirce rightly noted, habits bear, communicate, and perpetuate meaning—including the underlying meaning of one's own life.[17]

To gain and grow good habits, and to avoid and destroy bad ones, a person must properly diagnose them. Like actors who are always in costume on stage, people exhibit habits continually. Unfortunately, we are much better at deciphering the habits of others than our own. Aquinas notes that two kinds of knowledge are essential for knowing what habits we possess.[18] On the one hand, we need to know *what a particular habit is*. On the other hand, we need to know *whether or not we have a particular habit*. These forms of knowledge depend on each other, Thomas argues: "For the knowledge by

16. See *Sent. Ethic.*, lib. 3, l. 7, n. 11.

17. Peirce perhaps went too far in equating habits and information, but his position is worth considering. See the account in Terrance MacMullan, "The Flywheel of Society: Habit and Social Meliorism in the Pragmatist Tradition," in *A History of Habit* (ed. Sparrow and Hutchison), 234.

18. See *De veritate*, q. 10, a. 9.

which one knows that he possesses a habit presupposes the knowledge by which he knows what a habit is. For I cannot know that I possess chastity unless I know what chastity is."[19] Let us consider each in turn.

An objective of knowledge of habits takes a third-person perspective, considering habits as they are in themselves; this has largely been the focus of the book until now. The essence of a habit is revealed in its proper acts, for a habit is a principle of a particular kind of act.[20] Acts that are directed toward intelligible objects reveal the essence of the habits whence they come. For example, a chaste act is one whereby a person knowingly and volitionally preserves himself from illicit sexual pleasures. The habit of chastity is therefore one that produces acts whereby a person easily, quickly, delightedly, etc., preserves himself from illicit sexual pleasures.[21] The presupposition in Aquinas's example is that, in order to know what a habit is, one must be able to distinguish its proper act from other acts. To distinguish chaste acts from acts of kindness or courage, one must have a basic knowledge of chastity's general object (to preserve oneself from something) and its proper matter (illicit sexual pleasures). This sort of knowledge can be inculcated during childhood, as when a mother instructs her daughter how to dress and act modestly. The child need not know how to define "habit," "object," and "proper matter"; an implicit knowledge is sufficient to distinguish among types of acts. To act modestly, it is sufficient for one to be able to distinguish between modesty and immodesty. Hence, knowledge of a particular habit is accessible even to a person with a relatively limited intellect. In sum, to know one's habits, one needs a specula-

19. Ibid.

20. See *ST* I-II, q. 49, a. 3.

21. *De veritate*, q. 10, a. 9: "Habitus autem per essentiam suam est principium talis actus, unde si cognoscitur habitus prout est principium talis actus, cognoscitur de eo quid est; ut si sciam quod castitas est per quam quis se cohibet ab illicitis delectationibus in venereis existentibus, scio de castitate quid est." Chastity also has a positive sense, in that it is the proper self-giving of oneself to others by integrating one's sexuality according to the state of life—whether married, single, celibate, widowed, and so on.

tive knowledge of habits to some degree. One needs to know virtue and vice on a basic level in order to know whether or not they are present in the soul. Thomas's example indicates that "knowing what a habit is" involves knowledge in a very rudimentary form. It does not necessarily require extremely subtle or detailed speculation. This distinguishes morally necessary self-knowledge from other, more laboriously-obtained knowledge, such as quidditative knowledge of the soul or perceiving oneself in an intuitive act.[22] As Cory points out, it is quite difficult to achieve quidditative knowledge of the mind as a spiritual substance, but an attentive subject can know that he loves, knows, and chooses.[23] This leads us to the subjective side of habit-knowledge.

Once a person is able to distinguish among habits, he can next ask himself: does this particular habit exist in me? An answer might begin with a consideration of what inclinations one possesses according to one's "specific nature," that is, by belonging to the species *homo sapiens.* Chapter 1 of this book focused on this issue. Aquinas argues that the virtuous know themselves truly regarding their natures. They correctly reckon that their rational nature takes precedence over their emotions and body: "in this way, they reckon themselves to be what they are."[24] In contrast, he notes that the wicked "do not know themselves rightly," for they believe that their sensorial and bodily nature takes precedence.[25] For this reason, it seems that the virtuous have the best chance at recognizing what sort of inclinations they share in common with all other humans.

Next, one should consider the habits of one's own "individual nature": how one has been shaped by various inclinations, from

22. See Cory, *Aquinas on Human Self-Knowledge*, 92–114 and 174–98.

23. Ibid., 216: "Acquisition of quidditative self-knowledge, articulable in a true definition of the mind, demands considerable philosophical effort with high risk of error.... But when it comes to the *existence* of my mental acts or my mind or myself, matters are quite different. In thinking about something, I am certain of the reality of my act, and of my own reality as the one thinking."

24. *ST* II-II, q. 24, a. 7.

25. Ibid.

birth, upbringing, culture, along with freely acquired habits that stem from the individual as an agent of his own self-change. This was the topic of chapters 2 through 8. Self-knowledge in this regard "is necessary for the one who wills to become virtuous to attend to that to which his appetite is more naturally inclined to be moved," the *Doctor Humanitatis* says, "for different people are naturally more inclined to different things."[26] Aquinas continually argues that the vicious person does not have an accurate estimate of his own proclivities, abilities, strengths, weaknesses, and so on. In contrast, the virtuous man has true self-knowledge—a self-estimate in accord with reason—that accurately takes stock of his individual proclivities, abilities, strengths, weaknesses, and so on. Authentic humility rests in the knowledge of one's deficiencies, for this knowledge serves as a rule to moderate one's appetite for great things: a humble man avoids at aiming at things beyond his power.[27]

Knowing whether or not we have a particular habit is rather more difficult than we might expect. It might seem as if our habits are precisely the sort of thing we could easily know; as Thomas à Kempis observed, "wherever you go, you are burdened with yourself; and wherever you go, there you are."[28] But rarely do we know ourselves as we ought. For one thing, our memory is far more faulty than we reckon. Recollection of memories can be affected by many factors, including how we feel at the time of remembering, how we felt during the past event, by what we think we ought to remember, and by suggestions from third parties. Under such influences, we might misremember an element from the past or even imagine that a fictive episode is real. Perhaps surprisingly, research has shown that false memories are rather frequent, and we are sometimes as confident about them as we are about reality.[29]

26. *Sent. Ethic.*, lib. 2, l. 11, n. 6.

27. *ST* II-II, q. 161, a. 2.

28. Thomas à Kempis, *The Imitation of Christ: A New Reading of the 1441 Latin Autograph Manuscript*, trans. William C. Creasy (Macon, Ga.: Mercer University Press, 2007), Book II, c. 12 (49). Punctuation emended.

29. Elizabeth F. Loftus, "Memories of Things Unseen," *Current Directions in*

Even when memory functions well, the nature of one's soul makes habits difficult to discover directly. Aristotle notes: "To attain any knowledge about the soul is one of the most difficult things in the world."[30] There is an additional difficulty: habits have an existence that is between pure potential and actuality. Insofar as habits are less than perfect act, they fall short of being knowable in themselves.[31] Like our powers, fully human habits, which reside in the soul, only become manifest in the acts that they produce.[32] Dewey's observation is apt: habit "contains within itself a certain ordering or systematization of minor elements of action; which is projective, dynamic in quality, ready for overt manifestation; and which is operative in some subdued subordinate form even when not obviously dominating activity."[33] We cannot directly detect our habits, especially when they are operating in the background. Rather, we can infer their existence by recognizing acts that are produced by a stable, permanent, connatural disposition of the soul. In other words, we may come to recognize the presence of a habit by identifying acts that the habit properly produces.[34] Similar to acquiring objective knowledge *about* habits, knowledge of the existence of a habit proceeds from the exterior to the interior, beginning with objects toward which a person is directed, to acts he performs to reach those objects, to the power by which he performed the act. This can be schematized in the following way: obtained objects → acts → capacities *or* added capacities → habits.[35]

Aquinas is careful to distinguish between exterior acts and interior acts by which habits are known. Exterior acts that are directed

---

*Psychological Science* 13, no. 4 (August 1, 2004): 145–47. See Daniel M. Bernstein et al., "False Memories: The Role of Plausibility and Autobiographical Belief," chap. 6 in *Handbook of Imagination and Mental Simulation*, ed. K. Markman et al. (New York: Psychology Press, 2009), 89–102.

30. *De anima* I.1, 402a10.

31. *De veritate*, q. 10, a. 9, ad 3.

32. *ST* I, q. 87, a. 2, s.c.

33. Dewey, *Human Nature and Conduct*, 41.

34. *ST* I, q. 87, co.

35. See Pasnau, *Thomas Aquinas on Human Nature*, 336–47, esp. his schema on 340.

toward exterior objects of the senses can manifest the existence of habits of the body and the lower parts of the soul, as when the better functioning of the body indicates the return or increase of health, or when a Karate master demonstrates his lethal abilities in a fight, or when a person demonstrates his habitual anger through his frequent outbursts, violence, etc.[36] Exterior acts that are directed toward naturally intelligible objects can manifest intellectual habits, as when a professor displays his knowledge and understanding in a spontaneous question and answer session.[37] There are obvious parallels to this Thomistic method and using behaviorist diagnostic tools. [38] Behaviorist methods of observation and recording will take into account the habit loop and its various components. For example, resistance to change is one way to detect the power of habits in a person's life. Another indication of a habit's power is the preference one has for the habit behavior, which may be measured (1) by the behavior one performs in response to a stimulus, for example, the amount of laps a swimmer performs upon being "cued" by practice conditions; (2) by the pleasure one receives in performing the behavior which is the result of a habit's proper act, such as the delight a swimmer feels after doing laps in a pool;[39] (3) by the frequency with which one performs the behavior;[40] and (4) by how much a person persists in the behavior while in the presence of other stimuli that could activate other behaviors.[41] Results of neuroimaging may provide an-

36. See *De veritate*, q. 10, a. 9, ad s.c. 1.

37. See *De veritate*, q. 10, a. 9, ad s.c. 8.

38. David L. Watson and Roland G. Tharpe, *Self-Directed Behavior: Self-Modification for Personal Adjustment*, 10th ed. (Belmont, Calif.: Wadsworth Publishing, 2013), chap. 3. A further study might show how this process of self-knowledge in many ways resembles some complex recommendations for examining one's conscience, as in the classic Jesuit work, originally written in 1609: Alphonsus (Alonso) Rodriguez, *The Practice of Christian and Religious Perfection* (London: James Duffy and Sons, 1882), vol. 1, tr. 7.

39. See Nevin and Grace, "Behavioral Momentum and the Law of Effect," 83. Recall that Aristotle and Aquinas observe that habits naturally bring pleasure because they are connatural to us. See, e.g., *Sent. Ethic.*, lib. 7, l. 12, n. 10.

40. Hubbard, "Forms of Momentum Across Time," 63.

41. See Andrew R. Craig, "Extensions of Behavioral Momentum Theory to Conditions with Changing Reinforcer Rates" (PhD diss., Utah State University, 2017), 16.

cillary verification for the existence of habits. Evidence suggests that brain activity shifts in cortical and striatal regions when a person acquires habits.[42]

The will and its choices are also inaccessible to direct observation. As a spiritual power, the existence of the will is known through voluntary acts; and the existence of a voluntary act is manifested by various signs. A person who makes a voluntary act—even a purely interior act, such as to love another person—knows that he has acted, for one can act voluntarily only insofar as he acts with deliberate reason, which requires paying attention to the act he is performing with some intention. Thus, the character of the will may be indirectly revealed through its acts, for one may know the nature of an act of the will by considering what kind of habit would produce an act like that.[43] Nevertheless, the primary intention that forms a voluntary act is often complex and difficult to discover. Acts can have a nested set of ends-objects, only some of which may be clear to the agent himself. Exterior acts, or attempted acts, performed with the body are particularly opaque to easy categorization. Few exterior acts, if any, manifest the will's interior remote ends. The proximate end or object of an act of the will may be clear, as when a man murders another man. But the remote ends of the will may elude even the agent himself. The possibility of self-ignorance and self-deception lurks everywhere. Aquinas notes that a person may murder on account of adultery, and he may commit adultery for the sake of money.[44] There could be a further, more obscure, end to money acquisition. If a murdering adulterer were asked why he wanted the money—for which sake he murdered and committed adultery—he might not be able to articulate his reason. Perhaps he tells himself he wanted the money to help his needy grandmother, but in fact the murder-adultery-theft delights him with illusions of power. Man's

42. See Graybiel, "Habits, Rituals, and the Evaluative Brain," 363–65.

43. *ST* I, q. 87, a. 4.

44. For a helpful discussion on proximate and remote ends, see Joseph Pilsner, *The Specification of Human Actions in St Thomas Aquinas* (Oxford: Oxford University Press, 2006), 217–38.

deepest purposes often lie concealed from himself. Augustine attests: "That is the way I appear to myself; perhaps I am mistaken. For, there are those deplorable blind spots in which my capacity [for self-knowledge], which is within me, lies hidden to me.... For, what is in it, is often hidden, unless uncovered by experience."[45]

Habits of the will also elude us. The entirely spiritual nature of the will entails that another's intention is hidden from us, Aquinas argues: "For what a man does or thinks is manifested through his work, but by what intention he acts is entirely uncertain."[46] At times, a person's intentions can be manifested through the manner in which he accomplishes his act. If a wealthy businessman donates money easily, joyfully, skillfully, anonymously, with no direct benefit to himself, etc., then it is likely that he has developed the habit of generosity. But, like Augustine, the philanthropist might reasonably mistrust himself, especially if he previously had a habit of acting from selfish motives. Hence, even if some of the signs of a habit are present, a person can question his motives and wonder whether his heart is in the right place.

A further reason why we have trouble knowing our habits is that the causes of our habits are often hidden from us. Exterior actions and behaviors do not necessarily manifest a spiritual habit. Everyone knows hypocrisy may motivate a seemingly-holy act such as kneeling in a church or lighting a candle. The habit of faith is not known by mere external movements of the body.[47] A person can regularly speak about things of the faith without giving assent to the articles of faith. For similar reasons, habitual external acts of charity—such as almsgiving—are insufficient evidence that one loves God with charity, for exterior good acts can be produced by a natural love, whereas the primary act of charity is an interior act of the will.[48] Even interior introspection can fail to discover the causes of one's exteri-

45. *Confessions*, lib. 10, c. 32, n. 48 (306).
46. *Super Heb.*, c. 4, l. 2, n. 226.
47. *ST* I, q. 87, a. 2, ad 1.
48. *Quodlibet* VIII, q. 2, a. 2.

or habitual behaviors. An agent can know that he possesses faith by perceiving an interior act within his own heart, that is, through his interior act of belief and assent to the things of faith.[49] But without infused knowledge, one cannot have perfect knowledge regarding whether or not one is in a state of grace. One can recognize one's experience of the sweetness of grace within himself only to a certain extent: "insofar as one perceives within himself delight in God and a repugnance for worldly things, and insofar as man is not conscious of any mortal sin within him."[50] Spiritual delight *might* be a sign of a spiritual mode of action and the presence of a supernatural habit that produces an extraordinary act of loving God; but it might not. Such a sign is imperfect and typically nondefinitive. Experiences of sweetness, delight, or—on the contrary—repugnance are difficult to perceive and properly distinguish from similar natural emotions, deceptions from evil, or a mix of all of them.

The limits of self-knowledge solely in the light of our own reason lead us to seek help from others. Friends, counselors, coaches, psychologists, psychiatrists, physicians, and the occasional nosy neighbor all can play a role in how we come to know ourselves. But these persons, as helpful as they may be, operate on the plane of natural reason in the absence of infused knowledge. Because our souls are entirely spiritual, only God can infallibly discern our intentions: not even angels or demons can do this.[51] With remarkably strong language, Aquinas insists: "We must by necessity hold firmly that God has a most certain knowledge of all things that are knowable at any time or by any knower."[52] To truly plumb the depths of our person, we must turn to the higher source, the one who made us, to God himself. God knows himself, he knows the universe, and he knows us.

Contrasting with God's infinitely profound and unfathomably complete self-knowledge, Psalm 18:13 is a theological locus to de-

49. Ibid.

50. *ST* I-II, q. 112, a. 5.

51. *ST* I, q. 57, a. 4.

52. *De substantiis separatis*, c. 14, co.

scribe our self-blindness: "Who can understand sins? From my hidden ones cleanse me."[53] Augustine develops this insight, saying to God, "I stand in fear of my hidden parts, which Thy eyes perceive, though mine do not."[54] Aquinas notes: "certain sins can be hiding in me, which I do not know.... God reserves hidden things for His own judgment. But things which lie in our heart or are done in secret are hidden to ourselves."[55] Commenting on Psalm 18:13, the *Doctor Humanitatis* lists seven reasons why our sins and vices may be hidden from us.[56] Revelation, theology, and experience therefore demonstrate that "self-deception is a ubiquitous phenomenon."[57] This is an old problem for mankind. Before sin, Adam could easily know himself as a human distinct from beasts; after sin, he became a stranger to himself.[58]

Lost like Dante in the woods of passion, to come back to himself and understand his moral position in the universe, man needs an exterior assistance from one who sees all things rightly. We must turn to God if we desire self-knowledge in its profoundest sense. The Second Vatican Council, in *Gaudium et Spes*, acknowledged: "only in the mystery of the incarnate Word does the mystery of man take on light. For Adam, the first man, was a figure of Him Who was to come, namely Christ the Lord. Christ, the final Adam, by the revelation of the mys-

53. Ps 19:12 in the Hebrew.

54. *Confessions*, lib. 10, c. 37, n. 60.

55. *Super I Cor.*, c. 4, l. 1, nn. 194–95.

56. *Super Psalmo* 18, n. 8. *First*, faults cause spiritual blindness. *Second*, many sins make it difficult to single out one of them from the crowd. *Third*, some offenses are more "subtle" than others: blatant sins of commission are obvious, but sins of omission are more difficult to identify. *Fourth*, some an unknown or hidden root of sin may be at work, such as original sin, or sins that arise from secret desires. *Fifth*, some sins may be prompted by a bad influence or tempter: the sinner in this case does not know his own sin as well because the fault of the other is more apparent. *Sixth*, some sins are secret to the sinner because they stem from deception, "and this above all in prelates who knowingly dissimulate regarding the wickednesses of their subordinates." *Finally*, the origins of some sins are hidden, for some seem to be allowed by God's righteous judgment in offering less protection from temptation.

57. Floyd, "How to Cure Self-Deception," at 66.

58. Adam's knowledge before sin was very great (*ST* I-II, q. 34, a. 3). After sin, he suffered from the darkness of ignorance about many things (*ST* I-II, q. 85, a. 3).

tery of the Father and His love, fully reveals man to man himself and makes his supreme calling clear" (no. 22). The primary purpose of the incarnation was for the Son to reveal to the Father to us so that we might be saved by his grace. Secondarily and indirectly, Christ reveals us to ourselves by showing us how a perfect man lives and acts; and by showing what we imperfect, sinful men do and deserve. John Paul II explains that by the incarnation, the Word of God "came to bring full light to man": he enlightens the world, so that each may see himself, with the grace of Christ, as he truly is.[59] Knowing God and oneself, knowing ourselves as God knows us, is a process that begins in this life, can develop into a moral habit, and will end in the next life when all will be revealed. On judgment day, Aquinas says, "to each will be revealed his salvation or damnation, or rather, the accusation or defense of thoughts, which now are a testimony of conscience, will be represented to man on that day by divine power."[60] Until then, the prayer of the Psalmist may be ours even with respect to our hidden habits: "Search me, O God, and know my heart: try me and know my thoughts. See if there be any wicked way in me, and lead me in the way everlasting!"[61]

## KNOWING OUR SIMPLE AND COMPLEX HABITS

A careful examination of oneself and human nature in general will reveal that acts may be simple or complex depending on whether they have single ends or multiple ends linked together.[62] Disposi-

59. John Paul II, "Angelus Message," December 15, 1996, par. 2, available at www.catholicculture.org/culture/library/view.cfm?recnum=5701.

60. *Super Rom.*, c. 2, l. 3, n. 222. See also *Super I Cor.*, c. 4, l. 1, n. 196: "the Lord coming to judgment will illuminate what is now hidden in darkness, that is, will make clear and manifest the things done secretly in darkness. And He will make manifest the thoughts of the heart, that is, all the secrets of the heart."

61. Ps 139:23–24.

62. The chosen object specifies the act; and the end to which the object is directed provides further specification. Hence, a complex act is one that involves distinct objects or ends, or both, ordered to some further end that unifies them all: "the specific

tions and habits too may be simple or complex depending on their ends and objects.[63] Dunnington explains that a "simple habit" is one in which a single power or faculty is modified by a single habit.[64] As noted above, just as one can work backward from fruit to flower to identify a living branch of a tree, so by identifying the object of a behavior we can reason backward to identify the power that has been modified by a habit which is oriented toward its proper object. Hence, we have as many discrete dispositions as we have habituated powers and faculties: habits of imagination, habits of the cogitative power, habits of memory, habits of appetite (visceral and spiritual), and habits of the intellect. Habits by their nature as forms engage in some "material": habits of thought form judgments of propositions; habits of emotion form the passions. As related to reality outside of the person, habits also engage a multifaceted situation and its variants, often incorporating physical acts and objects into one's body space.[65] A single simple habit may allow for a multifaceted analysis insofar as it exists in relation to a specific context, as when a habitually angry person feels rage when incited by specific people at work committee meetings. The habit is "simple" in essence because it is a modification of the single irascible appetite.

As we move through life, simple habits tend to "combine and cohere to form habit groups."[66] One can call these groups "complex habits" or "coordinated habit groups" in which two or more habituated powers cooperate with each other to produce a habituated behavior for an end that unites them. For example, a father who drives

---

difference from the end [of the act] is more general; and the difference which is from the object which itself is ordered to that end, is specific with respect to its end" (*ST* I-II, q. 18, a. 7, co.). Thus, a tactical move by a regiment is specified by the further strategic end of the army as a whole. See *ST* I-II, q. 18, aa. 2 and 6; q. 19, aa. 1–2.

63. The analysis of habits according to ends and objects is more metaphysically precise than simply counting the steps (means) necessary to perform some behavior, as suggested in Barbara Mullan and Elizaveta Novoradovskaya, "Habit Mechanisms and Behavioural Complexity," in *The Psychology of Habit* (ed. Verplanken), 71–90.

64. Dunnington, *Addiction and Virtue*, 84.

65. See Casey, "Habitual Body and Memory in Merleau-Ponty" in *A History of Habit* (ed. Sparrow and Hutchinson), 215.

66. Dunnington, *Addiction and Virtue*, 84.

his family to Mass every Sunday will need habits of memory to recall the streets that lead to his destination; habits of the cogitative power to estimate dangers on the road; habituated patience during traffic jams; the habit of faith to keep in mind the reason why he is going to church; etc. Up to this point in this book, I have made efforts to distinguish among habits in order to elucidate their essential character and to undercover their particular causes. This has necessitated looking upon habits in their simple form. But dissection like this can kill while it distinguishes. By speaking about habits—including virtues and vices—singly, one could easily get the impression that habits only exist as discrete qualities that have a single kind of effect in our lives. It could seem as if the various virtues were like parallel tracks according to which our faculties operate reasonably but separately. A closer analysis shows that our habits interact with each other. Habituated powers exist within an organic whole person; they do not operate in isolation. Just as the skeleton does not operate on its own, but exists and operates with the entire person as a living system, neither does a single disposition or habit affect a person without reference to the whole.

Often we possess various inclinations and habits in different stages of perfection (or imperfection) in our body and soul. Earlier chapters detailed the various kinds of dispositions and habits. We have seen the physical foundations of natural dispositions such as instincts. Overviews of genetics, epigenetics, and other material causes such as nutrition helped us to see physical influences on individual inclinations as they arise from conception until birth. I also considered the nonvoluntary origins of dispositions that develop during infancy or early childhood. Then there are the myriads of influences that interact with a child's slowly flowering rationality and impress dispositions such as estimations of the cogitative sense. Finally, there are choices over time that can slowly shape a soul with virtue or vice. It is somewhat difficult to distinguish among various types of dispositions and habits in the abstract; it is more difficult to know which habits and dispositions exist within us at any particular time; and it is probably most difficult to know what causes are at work in any particular behavior. If a physical cause such as a mineral deficiency inclines a child toward anger and crying fits, it will probably remain unknown in the absence of a careful empirical study. On the other hand, if her upbringing is more at work, and underneath her dispositional sadness is a broken relationship with her father, that too might remain unknown without much experience and expert assistance. Even when habits are more clearly the result of our choices, we might not recall the series of small, seemingly insignificant choices that gradually forged our character.[67]

Juxtaposed dispositions and habits within ourselves—often at tension with each other, creating tension in our lives—help to explain an issue explored by Michael Sherwin, namely, the coexistence of infused virtues and the effects of acquired vice. Although a powerful grace of conversion helped Matt Talbot to become sober, he nevertheless experienced painful longings for alcohol, so painful that he would divest himself of money so as to prevent any relapse.[68] In a state of grace, Talbot undoubtedly possessed the infused cardinal virtues; but he still had to acquire the dispositions provided by the natural virtues in order to shape his faculties according to their natural ends. Examples such as this indicate that acquired and infused cardinal virtues coexist simultaneously in a soul in the state of grace. Acquired virtues are ordered to God *remotely,* for they fit into the structure of the universe, which is focused on God; they are ordered to God *indirectly,* for they directly or immediately focus a human on a good that is the last end in some respect but not the last end simply. Aquinas states: "In place of natural principles, God confers on us theological virtues, by which we are ordered to the supernatural end, as stated above. Hence, it is necessary that other divine *habitus,* which proportionally correspond to these theological virtues,

67. See John Henry Newman, Sermon no. 4, "Secret Faults," in *Parochial and Plain Sermons* (London: Longmans, Green, and Co., 1907), 1:41–56.

68. Michael Sherwin, "Infused Virtue and the Effects of Acquired Vice: A Test Case for the Thomistic Theory of the Infused Cardinal Virtues," *The Thomist* 73 (2009): 29–52, at 37.

should be caused in us, which are related to the theological virtues as the moral and intellectual virtues are related to the natural principles of the virtues."[69] In other words, the theological virtues serve as principles for the acts of the infused moral virtues, and this is analogous to the way natural law and synderesis provide the principles of action for acquired virtues. Aquinas is making the following comparison—theological virtues: infused moral virtues :: natural law/synderesis : acquired virtues.

Thomas clearly does not mean that theological virtues "take the place of" natural law and synderesis in the sense of supplanting them or substituting for them. Even after sin, natural law operates in man; it cannot be eradicated, for it is inextricably bound up with human nature. Instead, the theological virtues *play a role* for the infused moral virtues *similar* to what natural law/synderesis does for the acquired virtues. These are distinct species of perfections and ends. Good ends are compatible with one another. Infused cardinal virtues—infused prudence, infused justice, infused temperance, and so on—correspond to the acquired virtues and reside in the soul while remaining distinct from them. Certainly, all the formed virtues all exist together through prudence and charity. But there is more: the virtues and *all other habits* that a person possesses exist simultaneously, directing the person to good natural ends that are referable to the supreme final end, the Trinity.

Whereas acquired and infused virtues exist in harmony with each other, other habitual tendencies may shape the person while the virtues are being perfected. When attempting to develop a good habit or distinguish a bad one, it is important to know that before we begin to deliberate, habits and dispositions are already at work in us. Much of this book has provided a foundation for understanding which habits and dispositions may be operating within us, and in what ways, whether they arise from genetics, childhood experience, young adult choices, and so on. These dispositions affect our emotions and cogi-

69. *ST* I-II, q. 63, a. 3.

tative judgments; they incline us toward particular ends, sometimes without our knowing it. Frequently we do not become aware of their existence until they manifest contradictory tendencies and we seem to be at war with ourselves. William James notes that tensions can arise within an animal from various instincts that exist on a subrational level.[70] This is also the case for acquired habits, Dunnington observes: "Often, rational deliberation is only necessary when there is some conflict between [our] habits. Under normal circumstances, the habits of the agent enable the agent to act well or ill with ease, success, and consistency. However, when there is a conflict between habits, the habits do not thereby vanish. Rather, they vie for precedence as the agent struggles to navigate her situation."[71] A thousand examples might easily come to mind: a man's desire to be generous with the poor might conflict with early childhood lessons in frugality and self-sufficiency; a mother's worry for her children might be in tension with her trust in God's providence; and so on.

As with Matt Talbot, the effects of contending dispositions zoom into focus with cases of acquired continence and incontinence. Between the relatively stable and difficult-to-change characters of virtue and vice are the more malleable conditions of continence and incontinence. Here we find dispositions colliding, "negotiating and adjudicating their own increase and decrease, their making and unmaking."[72] Most dispositions derive from knowledge and judgments, whether deliberative or estimative, and they exist incarnationally in the person. Habits and dispositions can be characterized as embodied learning, memory in the flesh. Consequently, "the territory of incontinence is ... the territory in which knowledges collide: the abstract knowledges of deliberation confront the embodied knowl-

70. James, *The Principles of Psychology*, 2:393.

71. Dunnington, *Addiction and Virtue*, 80.

72. Ibid. According to Dunnington, the territory of continence and incontinence is where "habits" collide, fight, etc. But that seems to miss the point that virtue and vice are rooted habits, whereas continence and continence are not, which is why the latter are more flexible and easier to manage. However, his deeper insight remains, namely, that one's dispositions can war with one another in the field of one's body and soul.

edges of habit."[73] Other people only learn about their deeply-rooted habits, and their warring complex habits, when tragedy or trauma intervenes. Perhaps they "hit rock bottom" and finally see their addiction for what it is; or perhaps a martyr proves his heroic love for God in a singular act of sacrificial witness. But we need not, and ought not, rely on such soul-trying events.

Following Elijah Milgram,[74] Jean Porter describes a process of self-discovery that she calls a "practical induction." She notes that we are rarely fully aware of how our previous choices have shaped us: "we can, and we often do, discover what we really care about, respect, or love in and through processes of choice."[75] The inclination of the will itself in turn has an effect on the intellect, especially but not exclusively through the process of self-reflection. This is why we sometimes say, "I guess I didn't care about that after all" or "I can't believe I keep doing this. Why is this so important to me?" Porter describes the process this way:

> Prompted by a judgment that this or that desideratum is in some way good, the will determines itself towards a particular way of realizing its capabilities through a given choice, and then experience subsequently either confirms or calls into question the soundness of the initial judgment. The agent's experiences thus inform his sense of what the true good is, while his ongoing inclinations towards the good, thus understood, dispose him towards his activities which promote that overall good or at least do not undermine it.[76]

The interaction between habit and behavior therefore has a spiraling effect on the person, whereby choices deepen habits of thought, which incline a person more strongly toward particular choices and behaviors.

73. Ibid.

74. See Elijah Millgram, *Practical Induction* (Cambridge, Mass.: Harvard University Press, 1997), 43–66.

75. Jean Porter, "Why Are the Habits Necessary? An Inquiry into Aquinas's Moral Psychology," in *Oxford Studies in Medieval Philosophy*, ed. Robert Pasnau (Oxford: Oxford University Press, 2013), 1:113–35, at 129.

76. Porter, "Why Are the Habits Necessary?," 132.

Because habits and dispositions can lie beneath the surface of our attention, and their roots can lie even further buried in our past, their effect on our behavior can baffle ourselves. It is not at all uncommon for a person to be surprised at something he has done, especially if he worked hard to do the contrary: "I do not understand my own actions. For I do not do what I want, but I do the very thing I hate."[77] Only by digging more deeply into the soul can we discover the perplexing and seemingly paradoxical causes of Janus-like action, as when we upset a dear friend with a cruel insult. Often in cases such as these "we are confronted, not with reason struggling against appetite or emotion, but rather with free-floating reason struggling against reason as rooted in habits of the imagination and the cogitative estimation."[78] Most of our emotions have some *reason* underneath them, even if that reason does not stem from one's immediate deliberative choice. The reason may derive from a previous choice, or from the choice of another person who shaped our experience, or from the intelligibility embedded in natural law.

The presence of intentionality operating in one's life highlights how, in Julia Annas's view, the development of fully voluntary habits requires that one "give an account" of one's action, that is, to convey "reasons why what is done is done."[79] Annas, in comparing virtue to skill, distinguishes both from what she calls "routine."[80] A routine is performed through habituation, but without the agent's full cognitive attention, as when a commuter learns to drive home almost automatically. From a Thomistic perspective, one could call a routine a habit that is voluntary in origin—insofar as one originally made many decisions before establishing the habit—but partly vol-

77. Rom 7:15. Aquinas notes that a person might not understand what he does in two ways: in one way, he may understand in general that he should avoid sin, but he is overcome by a temptation "or by the inclination of a perverse habit"; in another way, a person in the state of grace might feel the first movements of a disordered desire, which he then impedes as soon as he is aware of it (*Super Rom.*, c. 7, l. 3, n. 563).

78. Dunnington, *Addiction and Virtue*, 81.

79. Annas, *Intelligent Virtue*, 20.

80. Ibid., 13.

untary in execution, for when deeply-rooted one's estimative powers are sufficient to perform the act unless something unusual arises: a driver needs to pay full attention to his drive home only when he confronts bad weather, an accident in the road, and so on. In contrast, skills and virtue are developed by giving attention to the object: one grows in skill and virtue only by becoming a learner, that is, through the virtue of *studiositas*. The person learning skill and virtue "needs to understand what she is doing, to achieve the ability to do it for herself, and to do it in a way that improves as she meets challenges as appropriate to her own life-situation."[81] Annas concludes: "This comes about when virtue is conveyed by the giving of reasons, in contrast with the nonrational picking up of a knack."[82]

Gregory Nazianzen well illustrates how some unthinkingly acquire habitual behaviors. In his funeral oration for his friend, Gregory distinguishes Basil's authentic virtues from his individual characteristics, such as "his paleness, his beard, the character of his gait, his deliberateness in speaking ... the quality of his garment, and the shape of his bed, and his mode of eating."[83] In Basil, these qualities were unstudied, natural, and spontaneous. But in his unthinking imitators, who sought the fame that he nonvoluntarily acquired, they were foolish repetitions. Aristotle and Aquinas point out that although a bumbling fool might accidentally create a work of art, virtuous action is more than an exterior result: it must stem from the perfection of the agent himself.[84] This is possible only if his action stems not from ignorance or happenstance, but from understanding.[85] The "intelligent" component is essential to virtue, Annas concludes. Aquinas explains: "Just as by previously known principles a person makes himself actually understand something

81. Ibid. Hence, depending on the intention of the agent, the automaticity incumbent on habit can create a mere routine or it can facilitate skill and virtue-acquisition.

82. Ibid.

83. Gregory of Nazianzen, *Funeral Oration* 43, quoted in John Henry Newman, *Historical Sketches* (London: Longmans, Green, and Co., 1906), 2:26.

84. See *Sent. Ethic.*, lib. 2, l. 4, n. 3.

85. Ibid., n. 4.

through discovery, so by acting according to the principles of practical reason, a person actually makes himself virtuous."[86] The result will be that, as a person develops virtue, she will also develop her understanding of the virtues themselves.[87] And as her understanding of courage, temperance, and honesty improves, she will act "in ways that embody increased understanding of [those virtues], and hence understanding of what [she is] doing."[88] With the knowledge, therefore, that a myriad of dispositions and habits exist within one's person, we can then begin the difficult work of utilizing particular techniques to carve out a new disposition in our souls, or to perfect the habit sculpture that is coming to be.

## TECHNIQUES FOR ACQUIRING AND DEVELOPING HABITS

Utilizing a specialized vocabulary for habit-change, Aquinas states that habits come to exist within us by "generation" and they go out of existence by "corruption." Once possessed, habits are augmented or reduced in two basic ways: either the habit is changed, or the person who possesses the habit is changed. Changing a habit *extensively* involves an increase or decrease of the scope of the habit with respect to some object. Changing the subject of a habit, the part of his person that possesses a habit, entails an increase or decrease of the *intensity* of the habit as he possesses it. Increasing a habit extensively is like piling more wood on a fire; increasing it intensively is similar to the fire growing hotter. These are related: although more wood on a fire may not increase its heat immediately, it provides the conditions for greater heat. In a similar way, increasing one's habits *extensively* does not necessarily increase them *intensively* but sets the stage for greater intensity. Similarly, to increase courage, one needs to exercise the virtue of courage itself—by performing more cou-

86. *Sent. Ethic.*, lib. 2, l. 4, n. 7.
87. See Annas, *Intelligent Virtue*, 38.
88. Ibid., 39.

rageous acts (increasing extension), or by making one's courageous acts more vehement (increasing intensity).[89]

Habit development is undoubtedly aided by a number of external causes, such as laws, societal customs, work conditions, climate, and abode. In his *Politics,* Aristotle discusses how many of these elements affect habit development or change, and in the latter books of the work he discusses specific societal practices that may aid the acquisition of virtue.[90] Aquinas touches upon similar themes in his *De regno*.[91] He speaks at length, for example, about how material prosperity and virtue will be furthered by a king's own virtue, in which he helps his people for their own good and not for the sake of private gain or glory.[92] Similarly, he argues that the internal structure of a city will better conduce to virtue if not every citizen sells goods. By focusing their lives on making money, an excess of trade could corrupt the hearts of citizens with greed and fraud.[93] Hence, one of the societal conditions for developing good habits is to have a balance of various professions, such as farmers, educators, lawyers, religious, along with merchants, and so on.[94]

Here I cannot discuss the large-scale contexts that may aid habit development, nor helps such as psychiatry, psychology, or pharmaceuticals. Instead, I will focus on general but flexible rules derived from the thought of Aquinas. The order a technique engenders in one's passions, intentions, and actions helps to make habit develop-

89. See *ST* I-II, q. 52, a. 2.

90. See the discussion in Leunissen, *From Natural Character to Moral Virtue in Aristotle,* 116–22. There we discover Aristotle's recommendations in *Politics* VII and VIII, among other places, for the establishment of particular laws, customs, education, games and play, and even music, to help establish the right habits in children and citizens within a city.

91. His own treatise *De regno,* "On Kingship," dedicated to the king of Cyprus, was often read and even conflated with Ptolemy of Lucca's *De regimine principum,* "On the Government of Princes," the student's completion of his master's work. See James M. Blythe, "Introduction," Ptolemy of Lucca, *On the Government of Rules: De Regimine Principum,* trans. James M. Blythe (Philadelphia: University of Pennsylvania Press, 1997), 1–7.

92. See, e.g., *De regno,* lib. 1, c. 4 and 8.

93. *De regno,* lib. 2, c. 3.

94. Rahmann and Rahmann, *The Neurobiological Basis of Memory and Behavior,* 223.

ment as effective as possible. These guidelines are largely compatible with a behaviorist method, though a caveat is in order. The necessity of grace entails that a mere technique will be insufficient for developing a deeply-rooted good habit, and for uprooting a vice.

In what follows, I will describe a framework to understand Aquinas's advice for developing a habit of mnemonics.[95] Aquinas's mnemonic techniques might seem out of place in his mighty *Summa* until one realizes that, in his view, excellent memory is in some way necessary for prudence. Instead of seeing memory cultivation exclusively as an adjunct to Aristotelian rhetoric, Thomas follows Albert the Great and Cicero in emphasizing the moral value of memory as that which makes experience, learning, and creativity available to prudence.[96] Thomas explains the need and possibility of cultivating memory: "Just as one possesses the aptitude for prudence from nature, but its completion exists from exercise or grace ... so memory not only arises from nature, but is also greatly possessed by art and industriousness."[97] Because memory serves a quasi-integral part of prudence, memory assists all of one's voluntary habits. Thus, habit might be called a stable and ready-to-perform memory of one's previous choices; and memory is a habit, namely, the developed capacity to recollect previous choices, learnings, experiences, and sense impressions.[98]

Aquinas's advice on developing the habit of memory serves as a

95. I will synthesize Aquinas's advice found in *ST* II-II, q. 49, a. 1, ad 2, and *Sent. De sensu*, tract. 2, l. 5, n. 13. Kevin White and Edward M. Macierowski provide a helpful analysis of the advice in their translation of Aquinas's *Commentaries on Aristotle's* On Sense and What is Sensed *and* On Memory and Recollection (Washington, D.C.: The Catholic University of America Press, 2005), 253–55n12.

96. See Carruthers, *The Book of Memory*, 81–88; Kimberly A. Rivers, *Preaching the Memory of Virtue and Vice: Memory, Images, and Preaching in the Late Middle Ages* (Turnhout: Brepols, 2010), 82–88; and *The Medieval Craft of Memory: An Anthology of Texts and Pictures*, ed. Mary Carruthers and Jan M. Ziolkowski (Philadelphia: University of Pennsylvania Press, 2004), 153–88. For a comprehensive bibliography on medieval mnemonics, see the translation by White and Macierowski of Aquinas's *Commentaries*, 256–57n9.

97. *ST* II-II, q. 49, a. 1, ad 2.

98. See *Sent. De sensu*, tract. 2, l. 3, n. 23; l. 2, n. 6.

paradigm for his advice regarding how to develop any habit. It can be accommodated within the now-familiar triad of elements of a habit loop: antecedents, behavior, and consequents. Each of these elements is essential for the analysis and preparation necessary to a "complete self-direction plan."[99] To paraphrase the advice of Duhigg, when planning on habit development, a person ought to verbalize his goal in this way: "When I see the CUE, I will do the ROUTINE to get the REWARD," specifying the cue, routine, and reward as desired. Here we may consider these elements according to the steps they represent in the habituation process, in line with figure 2 (above).[100]

### Step One: Behavior

The first step is as follows: *Identify the new behavior that you want to perform, and the habit that produces it.* Long-term goals are helpful motivators for habit development, but evidence suggests that focusing on the distant future may be less immediately effective than focusing on the necessary means to the goal.[101] A person should keep in mind very specific habitual behaviors and the situations in which they are to be performed.[102] Even in cases when the goal is not a specific behavior, but a product, skill, or state, reaching the goal will nevertheless necessitate eliminating or adding certain behaviors.[103] Whether the goal is to sing a song for a wedding reception or to develop the virtue of *eutrapelia,* you will need to subtract behaviors that distract or hinder you from acquiring your goal and you will need to add or augment behaviors that contribute to your goal.[104] This may necessitate "Habit Reversal Therapy," discussed at the end of this section.

99. Watson and Tharpe, *Self-Directed Behavior,* 151.

100. The following borrows heavily from Duhigg, *The Power of Habit,* 275–86 (diagram on 276).

101. Watson and Tharpe, *Self-Directed Behavior,* 36.

102. Ibid., 37–38.

103. Ibid., 41.

104. Ibid.

### Step Two: Consequents

The second step is as follows: *Identify the things that will give you a sense of reward for performing the behavior.* In Thomistic language, identify the material object or objects that bring a sense of enjoyment or fruition upon a successful completion of the act. As we saw in chapter 4, fruition is key for "sealing in" a voluntary habit, for it helps to give one a sense of well-being on account of completing the act, it attaches one's emotions and will more firmly to the behavior, and by these affirmations it intensifies the inclination to perform the act again. In behaviorist language, for self-regulation to be successful, one must arrange "reinforcement" for desired behaviors, that is, one must select a "reinforcer," a reward, to be delivered after, and only after, the desired response to a cue.[105] Unsurprisingly, studies show that a person will perform a habitual skill more quickly and accurately when a desired reward is at stake.[106] Above extrinsic rewards, however, intrinsic motivators—that is, rewards obtained within the performance of the act itself—are associated with stronger habits and habitual behavior.[107] Thus, people who enjoy running will hit the pavement more consistently than those who simply want to be fit; those who like playing the piano will tickle the ivories more often than children who are bribed to do so by their parent; etc.[108]

One might also consider punishments as possible consequences for performing an undesired behavior, or for not performing one's goal-behavior. Some punishments might include simply removing a reward or a pleasurable element from one's routine, or adding something that actively causes pain, such as verbally shaming oneself. Some punishments may help to deter undesirable behavior in a

105. Watson and Tharpe, *Self-Directed Behavior*, 233.

106. Marien et al., "Understanding the Formation of Human Habits," 61. For a discussion of motivation in stimulus-response habitual behavior, see 60–63.

107. Gardner and Lally, "Modelling Habit Formation and Its Determinates," 217.

108. Ibid.: "stronger positive affective responses to exercise fostered stronger physical activity habits."

single instance—the fear of hell, or the fear of confessing one's sins to a priest, has stopped many a person from sinning. But research indicates that self-punishment alone often is ineffective and can even worsen one's behavior because a person often rewards himself after punishing himself, and punishment by itself does not lead one to perform a behavior, it only teaches one to avoid punishment.[109] Therefore, one must focus on the good desired.

Aquinas offers one piece of advice in relation to consequents: *Make the desired object attractive by association.* In order to remember a particular thing, it is useful to associate the object to be remembered with something that more directly engages and rewards the senses, imagination, and passions. To do this, a person should tie the thing to be remembered to images that are fitting to his situation and desires, but that are not at all customary.[110] For example, to memorize a verse of scripture, one might imagine vivid characters moving about and doing striking or even silly things that illustrate the point of the verse: imagining a horrified, bleating goat in the backseat of Thelma and Louise's convertible as it flies over a cliff may help one remember Sirach 7:36: "In all you do, remember the end of your life, and then you will never sin." Such an image will be easier to remember than mere black-and-white words on a page, for the mind holds onto sensible things more strongly than to incorporeal things. Additionally, one's memory can become "desensitized" to particular inputs, as can any of the senses, so that what is familiar and frequent becomes less striking. Thus, the unusual is more easily remembered because change is often pleasing to the senses when it signals an undiscovered good.

To illustrate the nature of rewards as a motivator and reinforcer for habits, Duhigg argues that advertising often aims at developing a purchasing habit in the consumer by associating a product with something else that already rewards the senses, imagination, and even the passions. This helps consumers to remember a product and

109. See ibid., 263–64.
110. *ST* II-II, q. 49, a. 1, ad 2.

inclines them to buy it in order to facilitate an attractive habit. Claude Hopkins sold toothpaste to millions that did not (yet) brush their teeth by associating the product with beauty, and Procter & Gamble convinced consumers to purchase Febreze, an odor-removing spray, by associating the product with cleanliness.[111] Advertising in general leads the consumer to associate a product with feelings of pleasure, so that the consumer easily develops the habit of purchasing it. Such powerful means can be effective for virtue to a certain extent. Although virtue is good in itself, and its own reward, the beginner typically associates virtue with difficulty and pain, and therefore sees it as unattractive. To move a person to seek virtue, it is therefore insufficient to present virtue in general or a particular virtue as a goal worthy of pursuit. A person will not pursue those habits and develop them unless he sees them as good for himself in his present circumstances.

### Step Three: Antecedents

The third step is as follows: *Choose a cue within a stable performance context that will effectively initiate the desired behavior.* When developing a habit, a person must ensure that the cue is effectively associated and paired only with a chosen behavior.[112] Another term for antecedent/cue/trigger is "discriminative stimulus": it is a stimulus that an agent learns to discriminate from other stimuli that have no relation to a particular behavior.[113] Practically every habitual cue fits into one of the categories of location, time, emotional state, other people, or immediately preceding action. Hence, if a person is trying to discover the cue for eating excessively, he can ask himself about these five things when he feels the urge to act. The result of doing this for many days might look like the following:

111. See Duhigg, *The Power of Habit*, 31–59.
112. Gardner and Lally, "Modelling Habit Formation and Its Determinates," 208.
113. Watson and Tharpe, *Self-Directed Behavior*, 138.

- Where are you? (at home)
- What time is it? (late evening)
- What is your emotional state? (lonely, anxious)
- Who else is around? (no one)
- What action preceded the urge? (television show ended)

Aquinas observes that for gluttons who seek to eat sumptuously, the very sight or smell of food excites desire: a scrumptious treat is a cue to begin feasting.[114] Such is the case, psychologists explain, because the gourmand had become conditioned to respond to that sort of food as an antecedent to a rewarding behavior. In Thomistic language, a cue is an immediate efficient cause that initiates one's habitual act or chain of actions. Provided that the chosen behavior is not reinforced when the cue is absent, just about anything can become a cue to a behavior when the behavior is reinforced in the presence of the cue, or when the reward immediately follows the behavior.[115]

The presence of a "stable performance context" is key for a cue's effectiveness. The sight of a wolf behind glass might not trigger a sheep in a zoo, but it would do so in the context of an open field. Similarly, food is tempting to the gourmand only in the context of his lack of satiation, and a ringing bell will effectively call monks to prayer only in a context where they can hear and respond to it. The right context can thus support cue salience and stability, whereas the wrong context can do the opposite.[116] This is why a new context—like moving to a new city or getting a new job—can speed up habit acquisition or disrupt weaker habits.[117] Therefore, when we choose whatever will appropriately trigger a behavior that we hope will in-

114. *ST* II-II, q. 148, a. 4, ad 1.

115. Ibid. It bears repeating that, although the habit loop involves some automaticity in behavior, a person retains the power of choice for the various elements. If a person wants to establish a habit-behavior, he can choose to be moved by a particular cue, he can shape the initiated behavior, and he can assent to or reject the consequent reward.

116. Gardner and Lally, "Modelling Habit Formation and Its Determinates," 213–15.

117. Mazar and Wood, "Defining Habit in Psychology," 20.

stantiate a habit, we must also ensure that it exists within a context that will consistently promote behavioral performance.[118]

Step Four: Plans

The fourth step is as follows: *Devise a reasonable plan for shaping your desired habit loop.* The more specific your plan is, the more effective it will be, provided that enough flexibility is built into it to effectively handle contingencies that may arise.[119] Duhigg points out that we can develop habits well by choosing to follow this sort of instruction: "When I see the CUE, I will perform the ROUTINE in order to get the REWARD."[120] To make this decision effective, it is most helpful to practice "mental rehearsal," that is, to walk through the steps of the desired behavior in one's imagination with as much sensory detail as one can muster—including linking the precise cue to the desired behavior and the experience of a positive reward for the successful completion of the loop.[121] As stemming from free choice, these elements of one's chosen habituated behavior also partake in one's freedom. Over time, they come to play a role in one's moral character as one gradually shapes one's desired habits.

Aquinas advises two moves for memorizing material. This advice is patently congruent with more general counsel regarding how to make cues effective antecedent triggers for desired behavior. First, *organize the material well.* Thomas notes that the person who wants to retain something in his memory should arrange it in an orderly way through careful consideration.[122] Things that are disorganized, badly ordered, are more difficult to recollect.[123] Citing Aristotle and

118. Ibid., 19.

119. Marieke A. Adriaanse and Aukje Verhoeven, "Breaking Habits Using Implementation Intentions," in *The Psychology of Habit*, 169–88, at 178.

120. Duhigg, *The Power of Habit*, 285; text slightly altered.

121. Among the many studies of the effectiveness of using mental imagery and rehearsal, see Helen O'Shea and Aidan Moran, "Revisiting Imagery in Psychopathology: Why Mechanisms Are Important," *Frontiers in Psychiatry* 10 (2019): 457; and Stephanie J. Hanrahan, "Psychological Skills Training for Athletes with Disabilities," *Australian Psychologist* 50 (2015): 102–5.

122. *ST* II-II, q. 49, a. 1, ad 2.

123. *Sent. De sensu*, tract. 2, l. 5, n. 12.

Cicero, Aquinas notes that putting our memories in the context of a place can help us more easily move from one remembered thing to another.[124] It is said that the poet Simonides discovered the art of memory by associating particular memories with the images of physical places.[125] Such an orderly composition facilitates remembrance because it enables the agent to more easily move from one memory to another while engaging the imagination and intellect. For Simonides, orderliness gave rise to the mnemonic technique of the "memory palace," which involves placing in a particular place within one's imagination an image associated with the thing to be remembered.[126] For example, to recall the "armor of God" from Ephesians 6:10–17, one can place into one's memory palace a vivid, living figure of St. Paul in a church wearing and describing the various pieces of armor. Developing a habit likewise is greatly facilitated when the habit is properly ordered to its proximate and ultimate ends, as well as when the content of the habit is ordered in itself. Ordering various ends in relation to the final end is the work of prudence. Aquinas notes that "the formal principle of virtue ... is the good of reason,"[127] that is, a participation in reason through prudence, which orders the individual's passions and operations to his proper good.[128] Similar to the way that reason establishes locations within a memory palace to cue particular memories, so prudence will arrange habits so that one leads to another—as when one rises in the grades of charity and the steps of humility. Prudence will also order the parts of one's habits so a particular cue will engage a habit and initiate a desired behavior.

124. *ST* II-II, q. 49, a. 1, ad 2, referencing *De memoria et reminiscentia*, c. 2, 452a14–15. See also *Sent. De sensu*, tract. 2, l. 6, n. 6.

125. See Cicero, *De oratore* II, 86–87.

126. For a well-developed discussion and example of this technique, see Jonathan Spence's description in *The Memory Palace of Matteo Ricci* (New York: Viking, 1984).

127. *ST* I-II, q. 61, a. 1.

128. Ibid., a. 4: "quandam participationem rationis, per modum applicationis cuiusdam ad passiones vel operationes." Ibid., a. 1: "Ordinem enim rationis necesse est ponere circa passiones, considerata repugnantia ipsarum ad rationem."

### Step Five: Implementation

The fifth step is to put your plan into practice. Once the material to be remembered is well-organized, one ought to *begin at the beginning*.[129] Studies show that while a complex act "may shape the trajectory of habit formation," beginning with simple steps may allow habituation to proceed more quickly.[130] Furthermore, we want to start with that which comes first and proceed in order. Aquinas explains: "A consequent movement arises from a prior movement on account of practice ... therefore recollections are formed most quickly and best when one begins to meditate from the beginning of the whole matter, for according to the order by which the things follow each other, so are their motions in the soul are fashioned according to that order."[131] To illustrate: when we want to remember a verse from a poem, we begin to recite the first line and work through the whole thing in order.[132] In the language of habit loops, the first verse serves as an antecedent cue that helps trigger the behavior of remembering the series of connected verses. For other habitual behaviors, a cue may come in the form of a physical thing (e.g., seeing one's dress shoes may be a cue to get ready for Mass), an experience (e.g., hearing a bell reminds one to pray), or a situation. Accordingly, when we want to develop our habits, we ought to start with the cue best calculated to start the habit loop and lead to the behavior, fruition, and eventual end that we have in mind.

Mnemonic recall is a complex behavior that involves a series of necessary steps. The immediate goal of recollection is to remember in such a way that what one remembers is useful for prudential action: this constitutes the formal object of the act.[133] In order to successfully recall what we ought to remember in a given circumstance, Aquinas advises us to *frequently meditate in an orderly way on*

129. *Sent. De sensu*, tract. 2, l. 5, n. 13.

130. Gardner and Lally, "Modelling Habit Formation and Its Determinates," 215.

131. *Sent. De sensu*, tract. 2, l. 5, n. 11.

132. Ibid.

133. *ST* II-II, q. 49, a. 1, ad 3.

*the things to be remembered.* An ancient proverb captures part of the fundamental requirement for memorization: *repetitio mater memoriae est*—"repetition is the mother of memory." By itself, this proverb might give the impression that rote repetition is sufficient to establish a habit. But habits are most deeply rooted in us when they engage our entire person, especially our imagination, intellect, and will. Aquinas therefore prefers the more precise saying, *meditationes memoriam salvant,* "meditations preserve memories," that is, one ought to meditate upon the thing-to-be-remembered frequently, considering it from different angles, pondering it carefully, for doing so will root the object more deeply in our minds.[134] Studies support Aquinas's insight, showing that athletes who "meditate" on their desired athletic behavior and walk through it in their imagination—such as a golfer vividly imaging himself stepping up to a green, putting, and sinking the ball—are much more successful.[135] Aquinas says that his advice is effective because, in the words of Aristotle, "custom is a quasi-nature,"[136] such that our thoughts develop a habit of proceeding from one thing to another in a particular order that becomes like second nature to us.[137] By citing this crucial passage in Aristotle, one that is foundational for the understanding of habit in general, Aquinas underlines the connection between habit, repetition, and memory. Habit is like a memory of a particular faculty or power, and memory requires the careful repetition that creates a habit.

134. See *ST* II-II, q. 49, a. 1, ad 2, and *Sent. De sensu,* tract. 2, l. 3, n. 22: "Manifestum autem est quod ex frequenti actu memorandi habitus memorabilium confirmatur, sicut et quilibet habitus per similes actus, et multiplicata causa fortificatur effectus."

135. Magali Louis et al., "Effect of Imagined Movement Speed on Subsequent Motor Performance," *Journal of Motor Behavior* 40, no. 2 (March 1, 2008): 117–32. See Paul Holmes and Claire Calmels, "A Neuroscientific Review of Imagery and Observation Use in Sport," *Journal of Motor Behavior* 40, no. 5 (September 2008): 433–45; and Aidan Moran et al., "Re-Imagining Motor Imagery: Building Bridges between Cognitive Neuroscience and Sport Psychology," *British Journal of Psychology* 103, no. 2 (May 2012): 224–47.

136. See Aristotle, *On Memory and Reminiscence* II, 452a28.

137. See *ST* II-II, q. 49, a. 1, ad 2: "Meditationes memoriam salvant, quia, ut in eodem libro dicitur, consuetudo est quasi natura; unde quae multoties intelligimus cito reminiscimur, quasi naturali quodam ordine ab uno ad aliud procedentes." See also Aristotle, *Categories* 8b28–29a4; *Nicomachean Ethics* VII.10, 1152a29–33.

Right practice is crucial for acquiring habits. Arts, skills, and virtues, though distinct, share similar avenues of development based on right practice.[138] Just as people become skilled in practical arts by practicing their skills, so we acquire virtues by acting according to virtue: "Thus, people become builders by building, and harpists by playing the harp. Likewise, by doing just, or temperate, or courageous things, people become just, or temperate, or courageous."[139] But not all action is equal. Repetition performed negligently—that is, with less precision or energy than is within an agent's power—will lead to the destruction of a habit.[140] Every athlete knows that wrong practice can be worse than no practice. No practice only diminishes one's habituated powers whereas wrong practice can cause injury and thereby impede acting upon the skill: swinging a tennis racket repeatedly at the improper angle can lead to an irreparably torn rotator cuff.

Right practice and performance perfect one's powers: "men become good builders by building well repeatedly," and a master harpist is one who has mastered practicing and playing well.[141] It is the same with the virtues and vices. Whereas skill is an acquired excellence in a narrow area of life, virtue is perfective of an entire faculty and even of the person as a whole. Practice may be "right" as an act measured by its success in reaching its immediate object: shooting well means aiming properly and hitting one's target. However, practice is "right" because of the act's right life-goal. Shooting well means hitting one's target for the right reason, in such a way that conduces to the shooter's moral flourishing. Pinckaers highlights how discipline and steady application help a person to gradually acquire an "ability to execute works of his choice with perfection," whether as a Beethoven or a Shakespeare.[142] This ability "is based on natural dis-

138. *Nicomachean Ethics* II.1, 1103a31–b20.
139. *Sent. Ethic.*, lib. 2, l. 1, n. 6.
140. See *ST* I-II, q. 52, a. 3.
141. *Sent. Ethic.*, lib. 2, l. 1, n. 8.
142. Pinckaers, *The Sources of Christian Ethics*, 355.

positions and a talent developed and stabilized by means of regular, progressive exercises, or properly speaking, a *habitus*."[143]

Sherwin notes that there are five traits analogously present in both the acquisition of skills and the acquisition of virtues.[144] These are (1) a standard of excellence according to which an action is judged as successful or unsuccessful; (2) the internalization of the standard or rules which guide the structure of the activity, for example, the grammar of a language, the Ten Commandments, etc.; (3) trust in an expert, for beginners need to be guided by masters, who show the proper way to practice;[145] (4) the social context of learning, in which one's knowledge is tested and displayed; and (5) expertise as a freedom for excellence. Accordingly, good habits in the fullest sense are those that perfect the entire person, those in accord with right reason, those developed by right activity. Right practice aims to perform an action correctly as an action, and as directed toward the right object—as an archer desires to draw a bow, aim, and release an arrow rightly as a series of physical movements, and rightly so as to hit a chosen target—and to perform the action properly insofar as it suits him as a particular man. Right practice, then, is a result of good actions that produce good habits; and it produces good actions and thereby generates or reinforces good habits.

Finally, *pay attention and be fervent*. A person should apply solicitude (*sollicitudo*) and desire (*affectus*) to the things that he wants to remember, Thomas says, for the more a thing makes an impression on one's soul, the less he will forget it.[146] One should apply the mind "profoundly and intently" on the actions that lead to habituation, as well as upon the object to which we want to become habituated.[147] The virtue of *studiositas* is operative here, for *studium* "connotes the

143. Ibid.

144. Sherwin, "Virtue as Creative Freedom and Emotional Wisdom," 33.

145. *Sent. Ethic.*, lib. 2, l. 1, n. 8.

146. *ST* II-II, q. 49, a. 1, ad 2.

147. *Sent. De sensu*, tract. 2, l. 5, n. 13.

vehement application of the mind to something."[148] *Studiositas* moderates one's desire for knowledge, and insofar as the knowledge of prudence pertains to all the virtues, *studiositas* can likewise be applied to any good habit.[149] It follows that a person can build a habit up by devoting greater attention to it, and desiring it with greater intensity—two movements that correspond to solicitude and desire. Increasing one's desire includes inciting one's concupiscible appetite as well as one's will, for together they constitute an integrated human desire toward an apprehended good. When one's desire is intense, it can be called fervent. Hence, to acquire or develop a habit, one needs to pay attention to it and be fervent about it.

### HOW HABITS ARE DIMINISHED OR CORRUPTED

Newton's first law, seen in light of Thorndike's insights, indicates that a person will continue in his behavior with the same velocity unless some exterior force impedes or redirects him. That is, in the absence of a force sufficient to overcome his resistance to change, he will keep moving toward the end to which his behavior—whether considered as a single act, or as patterns of behaviors—tends. An equal and opposite force will stop the motion of an object entirely; friction will slow it down. In the case of merely physical objects, an exterior force is sufficient to change a thing's movement or trajectory. For human persons, however, exterior forces can only change a person's exterior movements, as a straitjacket can impede the use of one's hands. Situational friction can decelerate one's action, and gunk up one's work.[150] To change a person's interior disposition, some new force is needed.

Aquinas argues that habits are negatively affected by negligence,

148. *ST* II-II, q. 166, a. 1.

149. See ibid., a. 2, ad 1.

150. The analogy of situational friction was explored extensively by Karl von Clausewitz, *On War*, ed. and trans. Michael Howard and Peter Paret (Princeton, N.J.: Princeton University Press, 1989), esp. 119–21.

diminution, and corruption.[151] Modern parlance speaks of habit "extinction" to signify the cessation of habitual behaviors; it does not address whether or not the propensity remains. Because I am here focusing on causes, and less on effects, I will generally avoid speaking of habit extinction. *Neglecting* a habit involves ceasing from performing the act; this can be unintentional in the case of some forms of forgetfulness. *Ignoring* a habit means purposely neglecting to perform an act that flows from a habit; it involves self-restraint, and could entail the effort to forget the habit, its cue, its reward, or a combination of them. Aquinas argues that all habits can be diminished or even corrupted when a person simply ceases to perform their proper act.[152] The case for bodily habits is straightforward. By regular exercise, a person maintains the bodily habit of health, which forestalls unhealthiness; neglect of health removes obstacles to unhealthiness. But merely ceasing to perform habitual acts does not of itself diminish or corrupt intellectual habits; as forms that reside in the soul, these sorts of habits are not subject to destruction the way physical things are.[153] Neglect indirectly undermines these habits by removing or slowly dissolving obstacles to contrary kinds of habits that regular action previously kept at bay.[154] Aristotelian vocabulary uses terms such as reduction or *diminution* to name negative habit-change, the contrary of development or growth.[155]

*Corruption*, in scholastic language, is the contrary of generation; it can occur directly when one habit is replaced by another, or indirectly when the subject of the habit is corrupted and accordingly no

151. See *ST* I-II, q. 53.

152. Ibid., a. 3.

153. *ST* I-II, q. 53, a. 1.

154. Studies increasingly agree that by intellectual stimulation and physical exercise a person develops or preserves his brain-power and can possibly stave off dementia, whereas the lack of mental gymnastics weakens synapse use and thereby dissolves impediments to cerebral flabbiness. For a review of the literature, see Joyce Shaffer, "Neuroplasticity and Clinical Practice: Building Brain Power for Health," *Frontiers in Psychology* 7 (July 26, 2016): 1–12. See also Prashanthi Vemuri et al., "Cognitive Interventions in Alzheimer's and Parkinson's Diseases: Emerging Mechanisms and Role of Imaging," *Current Opinion in Neurology* 29, no. 4 (August 2016): 405–11.

155. See *ST* I-II, q. 52, a. 2, ad 1.

longer can maintain the habitual form.[156] Habits can be corrupted in two basic ways.[157] First, insofar as a habit's cause produces a contrary habit, that is, through the introduction of a contrary form into the subject, a habit can be directly corrupted. This corresponds to a complete loss of intensity because the habit has been lost, as the introduction of water extinguishes fire. Second, insofar as the subject of a habit is corrupted, so that the subject is less apt or entirely unfit for the habit, one can diminish or entirely corrupt a habit. This corresponds to a loss of extension and intensity in one's habits.

To explain the fundamental aspects of how habits are diminished or corrupted, Thomas outlines which kinds of habits can or cannot be changed, depending on the subjects in which the habits reside. For the sake of clarity, I will begin my analysis by considering the habits that cannot be corrupted. Then I will discuss how, by one's own actions, habits can be diminished or corrupted in modes that are somewhat parallel to the modes of increase discussed above.

Anyone who has developed bad habits may be encouraged by Thomas's firm position that some good dispositions *cannot* be corrupted in themselves. Contrary to Calvinistic theologies that posit a complete depravity of humanity on account of original and personal sin, Thomas holds that man's nature is not wholly corrupt, and so natural habitual dispositions of the intellect have a certain note of incorruptibility on account of their spiritual character. He states: "If there is a habit in the possible intellect caused immediately by the agent intellect, such a habit is incorruptible both *per se* and *per accidens*. Such are the habits of first principles, both speculative and practical, which no forgetfulness or deception can corrupt."[158] As we saw in our discussion of innate habits, synderesis is a "first natural habit" by which a person knows the first principles of right action.[159]

156. See *ST* I-II, q. 52, a. 1.

157. See *ST* I-II, q. 53, a. 1: "Secundum se dicitur aliqua forma corrumpi per contrarium suum, per accidens autem, per corruptionem sui subiecti. Si igitur fuerit aliquis habitus cuius subiectum est corruptibile, et cuius causa habet contrarium, utroque modo corrumpi poterit."

158. Ibid.

159. *ST* I, q. 79, a. 13.

Scholars have debated what counts as a first principle of the speculative and practical intellects.[160] The following, however, is clearly laid out by Thomas. In the speculative realm, the first principle is the principle of noncontradiction: something cannot be affirmed and denied in the same sense at the same time.[161] In the practical realm, first principles include (1) good is to be done and pursued, and evil is to be avoided[162] and (2) no one is to be harmed.[163] Related to the ineradicable nature of the practical and speculative first principles is the ineradicable nature of instincts. Thomas holds that humans possess many natural instincts. Because these innate habitual inclinations exist as a consequence of human nature, they cannot be eradicated in themselves as long as human nature itself persists, even if their operation is impeded in some way. Finally, Thomas follows Aristotle in holding that the habit of prudence cannot be eradicated directly and in itself by involuntary forgetfulness.[164] The reason for this is that a habit that resides in the reason alone can be forgotten, whereas prudence resides in the intellect while it perfects the appetitive faculty. Consequently, even when a person's memory fails, his appetites can virtually remain well-ordered through prudence so long as his right desires do not fail.[165]

In considering the ways in which habits can be diminished and corrupted, we first encounter *the introduction of bad habits contrary*

160. See David Klassen, "The Natural Law, the Virtues, and Consequences in the Ethical Theory of Saint Thomas Aquinas," *Lex Naturalis* 1 (2015): 23–50; Osborne, *Human Action in Thomas Aquinas, John Duns Scotus, and William of Ockham*, esp. 69–80; and R. A. Armstrong, *Primary and Secondary Precepts in Thomistic Natural Law Teaching* (The Hague: Martinus Nijhoff, 1966). Particularly helpful with respect to the present study is Mary Christine Ugobi-Onyemere, *The Knowledge of the First Principles in Saint Thomas Aquinas* (New York: Peter Lang, 2015), esp. chap. 4, "Habits of the First Principles," 185–264.

161. See *ST* I-II, q. 94, a. 2: "Primum principium indemonstrabile est quod non est simul affirmare et negare, quod fundatur supra rationem entis et non entis, et super hoc principio omnia alia fundantur."

162. See ibid.

163. *Sent. Ethic.*, lib. 6, l. 11, n. 3: "Primo quidem ex parte rationis, cui naturaliter indita sunt prima principia operabilium humanorum, puta nulli esse nocendum, et similia."

164. See *Nicomachean Ethics* VI.5, 1140b29. *ST* II-II, q. 47, q. 16.

165. See *Sent. Ethic.*, lib. 6, l. 4, n. 14.

*to good habits.* A habit is "corrupted" within a person directly when one habit replaces another, that is, when one form takes the place of its contrary.[166] The bodily habit of health is corrupted by sickness, a contrary form that also affects the subject of the habit (the body). Habits of the appetites, whether of the will or the irascible and concupiscible passions, are in some way caused by a judgment. Consequently, habits of the appetites can be corrupted by a faulty estimation of the cogitative power, or a faulty judgment of reason, which can introduce a form contrary to the habit into the appetite. Ignorance, passion, and deliberate choice may be culprits. For example, as discussed in chapter 6, the habit of charity, which resides in the will, can be corrupted when passion moves reason to judge that a particular mortal sin is to be performed rather than to be avoided.

Intellectual habits of knowledge, which reside in the possible intellect, can be corrupted in two ways: through a contrary idea that is more convincing than what was held previously, or through a process of reasoning that seems to demonstrate that the knowledge was false. For example, one's opinion about the reality of the moon landing, which resides in the soul as a habitual form, can be replaced by a conspiracy theory. Or one's opinion can be shown to be false through reasoning that shows its absurdity. Thomas says that intellectual virtues can be corrupted by sophistical reasoning and deception.[167] To overcome a habit that exists primarily in an incorruptible subject, that is, the intellect or will, one must attack the secondary "corruptible" subject—that is, overcome the mind through the sensory powers, or by harming bodily functions, by making one sleepy, distracting one's attention, inciting the passions, and so on. Habits of the appetitive part of the soul, including moral virtues or vices, can be corrupted by a judgment of reason that moves contrary to the habit, whether the judgment is on account of ignorance, passion, or choice.[168] Ignorance might lead a chaste person to believe that co-

166. *ST* I-II, q. 53, a. 1.
167. Ibid.
168. Ibid.

habitation is reasonable, thus leading to the generation of lust; passion might lead a person to judge that violence is acceptable whenever he is angry, thus undermining the virtues of justice and charity; choice may lead a person to judge that he prefers the pleasure of sin to the difficulty of virtue. Thus, Thomas concludes, "it is clear that false reason can corrupt the habit of true opinion or even of science."[169]

In general, the extinction of a behavior is inversely proportional to that behavior's momentum,[170] but the "corruption" of a habit is not as straightforward as one may initially think. If a person does not feel emotionally enthusiastic about performing some habitual behavior, or finds that his original reasons for so acting no longer pertain—and thus feels a loss of motivation—he will continue to perform the behavior until he makes some act contrary to the virtual intention the impels him to act. And that contrary act is only the beginning of despoiling oneself of the habit entirely: for subjects with deep-rooted habits, their intentions do not typically predict their actual behavior.[171]

Relapse is frequently a danger when one is trying to eliminate a bad habit. When old, undesired habitual behaviors are seemingly extinguished, the person might return to the behavior in three paradigmatic ways: reinstatement, renewal, and resurgence.[172] *Reinstatement*, the most common form of relapse, occurs when an original stimulus or reward is presented after the behavior disappears. After months of sobriety, a former heavy drinker might go to a party and, when presented with the smell of alcohol and other drinking-related triggers (certain friends, the sound of clinking glasses), he might feel intense cravings for his favorite beer and "reinstate" binge drinking. *Renewal* occurs when a behavior returns in its original context even though it may have been extinguished in another context. A violent

169. Ibid.

170. See Hubbard, "Forms of Momentum Across Time," 50.

171. Mazar and Wood, "Defining Habit in Psychology," 16 and 19.

172. Craig, "Extensions of Behavioral Momentum Theory," 42–44.

offender may learn to control his aggression in prison, only to renew such behavior once he is released on parole. *Resurgence* of a habitual behavior transpires when the rewards or reinforcement for a newly-learned behavior are withheld: the old habit raises its head again. For example, the former heavy drinker may return to his ways when he stops attending AA meetings; or the ex-con may again resort to violence when there is no immediate punishment to threaten him. Amid these forms of relapse, people in recovery from deeply engrained bad habits experience oscillations between "sobriety," or abstinence from the bad habit, and "falls" or relapse into the habitual behavior.[173]

Findings about habit-relapse corroborate the fact that the "corruption" of a habit, or extinction of a habitual behavior, does not necessitate that the habit itself is affected. The behavior may disappear while the habit itself remains; and the habit may remain even though another habit takes its place. For example, the introduction of a new idea does not eradicate a previous intellectual habit; it replaces it. One can retain certain reasons for a behavior and merely withhold assenting to the reasons in light of new facts and considerations. After learning about Einstein's theory of relativity, a physicist's original understanding of projectile movement does not necessarily disappear: the habit of thinking about moving bodies in Newtonian terms can remain even after he has seen the superiority of Einstein's explanation and mathematics. Likewise, a mother's single rash judgment of her son's behavior cannot immediately change her virtuous disposition of judging rightly into a vice of injustice. However, the rash judgment may induce actions that will lead to habits contrary to virtues of justice. To this extent, Thomas would agree with Duhigg's "Golden Rule of Habit Change": "A habit cannot be eradicated—it must, instead, be replaced."[174] Merely negating a habit is ineffective; planning to *not perform* some habitual behavior rarely works; dimin-

173. Inna Arnaudova et al., "Recovery Habits: A Habit Perspective on Recover from Substance Use Disorder," in *The Psychology of Habits*, 305–22, at 306.

174. Duhigg, *The Power of Habit*, 92.

ishing unwanted habits is less powerful than developing a new habit by performing a desired behavior.[175] "Just say no" and "I won't do it" are less effective than "Do this instead."

Duhigg's understanding of habit-change arose from empirical studies of habit reversal therapy (HRT), which suggests that deeply-rooted habits remain even after many years of recovery efforts—although extended habit-negligence predicts long-term stability in contrary habits.[176] HRT has been shown to be effective in a variety of situations.[177] Its effectiveness lies in successfully replacing old habits with new ones. By inculcating desirable habits that are contrary to our older, undesired habits, HRT reorders brain operations and repatterns synaptic connectivity, which underlie memory and processes of remembering.[178] HRT also emphasizes awareness training and competing-response training.[179] This means that HRT requires an engagement of the attention and intention, as well as engagement of the intellect and the will, so that one learns to have responses to stimuli that are contrary to one's undesired responses.

175. M. Adrianaase and A. Verhoeven, "Breaking Habits Using Implementation Intentions," in *The Psychology of Habit*, ed. B. Verplanken, 169–88 at 176–77.

176. This is a fundamental principle for Alcoholics Anonymous, verified by longitudinal studies. See John Francis Kelly, Molly Magill, and Robert Lauren Stout, "How Do People Recover from Alcohol Dependence? A Systematic Review of the Research on Mechanisms of Behavior Change in Alcoholics Anonymous," *Addiction Research & Theory* 17, no. 3 (January 1, 2009): 236–59. Also, Michael L. Dennis, Mark A. Foss, and Christy K. Scott, "An Eight-Year Perspective on the Relationship between the Duration of Abstinence and Other Aspects of Recovery," *Evaluation Review* 31, no. 6 (December 2007): 585–612.

177. See Neeladri Dutta and Andrea E. Cavanna, "The Effectiveness of Habit Reversal Therapy in the Treatment of Tourette Syndrome and Other Chronic Tic Disorders: A Systematic Review," *Functional Neurology* 28, no. 1 (June 3, 2013): 7–12; and Karina S. Bate et al., "The Efficacy of Habit Reversal Therapy for Tics, Habit Disorders, and Stuttering: A Meta-Analytic Review," *Clinical Psychology Review* 31, no. 5 (July 2011): 865–71.

178. Joshua D. Berke and Steven E. Hyman, "Addiction, Dopamine, and the Molecular Mechanisms of Memory," *Neuron* 25, no. 3 (March 1, 2000): 515–32.

179. See the seminal article, N. H. Azrin and R. G. Nunn, "Habit-Reversal," *Behaviour Research and Therapy* 11, no. 4 (November 1973): 619–28; and Douglas W. Woods and Raymond G. Miltenberger, "Habit Reversal: A Review of Applications and Variations," *Journal of Behavior Therapy and Experimental Psychiatry* 26, no. 2 (June 1, 1995): 123–31.

This is supported by a study among participants who successfully abstained from an addiction for two years: they reported that their most important "recovery habit" was "being rigorously honest."[180] In Thomistic language, HRT helps to "corrupt" undesired habits by impressing contrary forms within us. The method thus helps to restore the healthy state of the subject of good habits, namely, the soul.

Techniques of HRT are similar to those for establishing or developing new habits. Each step of the method focuses on different parts of the habit loop—the antecedent-cue, the behavior-routine, and the consequent-reward. (1) Identify the negative behavior to eliminate as well as a contrary habit to replace it. For example, defending a person's reputation instead of gossip. (2) Choose a reward to receive once the good behavior is performed. For example, one can silently affirm oneself after speaking well of another, or one can eat a small treat after avoiding gossip. Rewards should be doled out with care: research indicates that the more rewards a person receives during baseline conditions, the more likely a person will relapse when those rewards are absent.[181] (3) Isolate the cue and context that typically triggers the behavior, and work to resist performing the undesired behavior and instead responding with the desired behavior. Studies indicate that HRT is only effective to the extent that a person discovers the "critical cue" that initiates the undesired behavior.[182] It may therefore be necessary to undertake a fairly detailed self-study in order to see which triggers are most powerful, which behaviors are most desirable, and which rewards are most fitting. As much as possible, we should keep the same cue but work to establish a new routine. For example, a person could decide that, when watch-

180. Arnaudova et al., "Recovery Habits," 311 (Table 17.1).

181. Craig, "Extensions of Behavioral Momentum Theory," 45–46. This makes sense from a Thomistic perspective: change will be more lasting and effective when one's motivations and goals are addressed, rather than just an immediate reward for good behavior. Rewards alone may make a person dependent on some exterior force rather than an interior strength and directedness.

182. Adrianaase and Verhoeven, "Breaking Habits Using Implementation Intentions," 179.

ing TV at ten o'clock, instead of eating, he will sit in a particular chair and quietly meditate for five minutes. Over time, we will notice that though we do not receive precisely the same reward for the behavior, we experience a similar reward, or even something better—not least the reward of having changed our behavior for the better.

From concerted efforts as entailed by HRT, or even by neglect, habits can also *decrease by intensity*. One of the most effective forms of habit neglect is by removing oneself from the context or the cues, or both, that elicit habitual behaviors. Occasions that disrupt our behavioral patterns, called "habit discontinuities," include the beginning of a new year, a new job, residential relocation, a rite of initiation, serious illness, or the death of a loved one.[183] Such transitional moments can serve as pivot points for a new direction in life. They give us space to decide whether to adapt our habits to the new circumstances, or to delimit a habit's power in our lives by extinguishing a habitual behavior. But altering our environment is not always feasible or reasonable. Leaving one's job may eliminate anger triggers, but it may not be easy to find employment elsewhere, and at least some anger triggers are unavoidable, as our very thoughts may give rise to the unwanted feelings.[184] In that light, other forms of neglect may be necessary in order to diminish the intensity of undesired habits.

A habit will begin to diminish when a person recurrently performs its proper act less intensely than possible.[185] Thomas recognized that "some acts lessen the habits from which they proceed, as when they are done negligently."[186] Just as attention aids developing and strengthening a habit, so inattentiveness can do the opposite. Mind-wandering, inattentiveness, and frequent interruptions lower reading comprehension; they also lead to worse reading skills—in-

183. Bas Verplanken, "Cracks in the Wall: Habit Discontinuities as Vehicles for Behavior Change," in *The Psychology of Habit*, 189–205.

184. Adrianaase and Verhoeven, "Breaking Habits Using Implementation Intentions," 177.

185. See *ST* I-II, q. 52, a. 3.

186. *ST* I-II, q. 52, a. 3, s.c. See *Nicomachean Ethics* II.2, 1104a29.

cluding recall and comprehension—over time.[187] Similarly, if a musician does not play his instrument with focused attention, if he does not "put his heart" into his performances, then eventually his mastery will diminish. The same follows for the virtues: if a person repeatedly worships God distractedly and without his ordinary fervor, his charity will eventually cool.[188] A review of studies indicates that the costs of mind-wandering include decreased working memory, deficits in general intelligence—probably because the intellect relies on memory and attention—and even negative mood affect.[189] All these faculties are important for establishing and diminishing habits: memory, balanced emotions, intellectual attention, and volitional intention.[190] When they malfunction from attentional neglect, the likelihood of habit diminishment or "dishabituation" increases.[191]

Some inattention arises on account of "control-failure," that is, a failure to control one's intellectual attention. Scans show that the brain performs a ceaseless activity—evaluating sensory perceptions, sifting memories, etc.—even when the individual is resting, performing undemanding tasks, or even undergoes sensory deprivation.[192] Thus, mind-wandering is, in a way, an automatic, natural habit. Control-failure inattention is often initiated without the individual's awareness: it can be triggered by thought associations, sounds, slight changes in peripheral vision, and so on.[193] Another kind of inattention is more directly willed. Corroborating Aquinas's understanding of attention as an on-off toggle switch, the "global access hypothesis" suggests that we cannot have "global access" or di-

187. Benjamin W. Mooneyham and Jonathan W. Schooler, "The Costs and Benefits of Mind-Wandering: A Review," *Canadian Journal of Experimental Psychology* 67, no. 1 (March 2013): 11–18, at 12.

188. See *ST* II-II, q. 24, a. 6, s.c.

189. Mooneyham and Schooler, "The Costs and Benefits of Mind-Wandering: A Review," 13–14.

190. See Wayne Wu, "What is Conscious Attention?," *Philosophy and Phenomenology Research* 82, no. 1 (2011): 93–120.

191. Mooneyham and Schooler, "The Costs and Benefits of Mind-Wandering: A Review," 15.

192. Zedelius et al., "Mind Wandering: More than a Bad Habit," 367.

193. Ibid., 368.

rect attentiveness to all of our perceptions, feelings, fleeting insights, etc., simultaneously. Chosen inattention may be a way to toggle between tasks, letting less important processes rest while focusing on those more urgent or important, thus maximizing the efficiency of conscious thought, as when we ignore minor hunger pangs in order to complete an important task.[194] Or we might toggle from an attention-heavy task to a brief cognitively-easy task in order to allow the brain to process information, as when we sneak a quick glance around a room while trying to find the right work for a sentence. These sorts of intentional mind-wandering are less injurious to task performance, in part because they allow the mind and emotions to rest without derailing the primary action.[195]

Personality type and accompanying character traits can greatly affect both the content and the valence of inattention: anxious personalities report trouble focusing on account of "racing" thoughts, whereas those more open to new experience find that mind-wandering leads to greater creativity.[196] To diminish or eliminate a habit, though, choice makes the most difference. When a person focuses his attention on a habit, rejects it with his will, and begins to practice contrary behaviors, he slows the behavioral momentum of that habit and simultaneously reinforces his "character" mass that resists change in the direction of the habit. Remnants of the habit may remain on the physical or sensory levels—in the case of sin, such nonvoluntary inclinations to moral evil are called the "tinder" (*fomes*) that can be enflamed by an evil will.[197] Nevertheless, the force of choice, and the development of contrary habits, can serve to diminish the "mass" or intensity of the habit.

Habits can also *decrease in the number of objects* to which they extend. A nun might choose to pray for fewer people, or she might receive the Eucharist less often, and thereby cool her charity. As with

194. Ibid., 367.
195. Ibid., 369.
196. Ibid., 371.
197. *ST* I-II, q. 91, a. 6.

other kinds of habit diminishment, various factors can lead one to extend one's habit to fewer objects. When the chief factor is choice, then habit diminishment is voluntary: a man indirectly chooses to decrease his charity by performing fewer interior acts of charity. If circumstance intervenes contrary to a person's will, and he performs fewer exterior acts of a habit, then the habit is only affected if it is primarily physiological. If a person is put into a small, dark prison cell, his habit of good health may deteriorate. But if he does not make acts contrary to habits of virtue, then his virtues will habitually remain even if their exterior acts may be hindered—acts such as generously sharing material goods, or engaging in highly complex thought. The latent virtues could even virtually increase insofar as he exercises the theological virtues.

Perhaps most significantly, habits can be diminished or corrupted by *the corruption of the subject in which a habit resides,* that is, by reducing the extent to which a habit resides in a person. Thomas understood health, for example, as a habit that resides in the body as a whole, enabling it to function properly and help a person achieve his final end. From this perspective, sickness is a habit that directly corrupts health and indirectly corrupts it by weakening the body's aptness for the habit of health—which is possible because the body's materiality makes it a "corruptible subject."[198] Thus sickness is a disposition that introduces a new configuration to the body and weakens organic functioning. Any habit that primarily resides in the body is corruptible as such. In the case of subjects that are incorruptible by nature, such as the intellect and the will, their corresponding habits—such as science—can be diminished or corrupted *indirectly* through an attack on their corruptible secondary subject, namely, the sensory powers. The dispositions of one's imagination, memory, and cogitative power can be corrupted by introducing misleading images or sensory apprehensions into these faculties. Once in a subject, these misleading or irrelevant images or apprehensions can

198. See *ST* I-II, q. 53, a. 1.

then lead to a faulty judgment of reason and even incline a person to make a bad choice. If a disease such as Alzheimer's eradicates a person's memory, and such a person begins to perform bad exterior actions, then the inclinations of virtue as they shaped lower estimative judgments are also slowly eradicated.

Neuroscientists have studied and debated the nature of incorrect judgments for over a decade. In certain circumstances non-experts evaluate scientific reasoning positively when the scientific claims are accompanied by brain images,[199] especially when the images appear to be three-dimensional.[200] Across many sciences, the more irrelevant but reductive information included in a report, the more highly non-experts rated it.[201] In these ways, the rational judgment of people can be "corrupted," in the language of Aquinas, through striking images and simple explanations. The imaginations of the non-experts convinced them that what appeared to be rational was indeed so. One can easily extrapolate that these faulty judgments could easily become habits and affect actions negatively.

Finally, aside from complete extirpation, a habit can decrease its power when *the subject's capacity for the habit decreases*. The person no longer is as "apt" for the habit; in Aquinas's language, the subject of the habit has been "corrupted." When material is no longer apt for a form, the capacity for the exercise of that form is necessarily also diminished. This can happen voluntarily or nonvoluntarily.

A voluntary corruption of a subject of a habit is when a person chooses an action that harms or destroys the portion of his body in

199. N. J. Schweitzer, D. A. Baker, and Evan F. Risko, "Fooled by the Brain: Re-Examining the Influence of Neuroimages," *Cognition* 129, no. 3 (December 2013): 501–11.

200. Madeleine Keehner, Lisa Mayberry, and Martin H. Fischer, "Different Clues from Different Views: The Role of Image Format in Public Perceptions of Neuroimaging Results," *Psychonomic Bulletin & Review* 18, no. 2 (January 7, 2011): 422–28.

201. Deena Weisberg, Jordan Taylor, and Emily Hopkins, "Deconstructing the Seductive Allure of Neuroscience Explanations," *Judgment and Decision Making* (2015): 429–41. See Emily J. Hopkins, Deena Skolnick Weisberg, and Jordan C. V. Taylor, "The Seductive Allure Is a Reductive Allure: People Prefer Scientific Explanations That Contain Logically Irrelevant Reductive Information," *Cognition* 155 (October 2016): 67–76.

which the habit resides. For instance, a person could choose to lift barbells that are rather light when compared to his strength. In the long run, his muscles will deteriorate and his lifting power will be thereby diminished. Likewise, when a person introduces the habit of laziness into his life, his actions serve directly to corrupt the habit of health, and directly to corrupt the subjects in which health resides, that is, the rest of his body. His general musculature, digestion, etc., may deteriorate. Such physical deterioration entails a lower functional capacity—not merely functioning below prime level—if the laziness truly becomes habitual, he will lose his capacity for prime function, and his overall capacity will be lowered. He is diminished to a "new normal" that is less than before.

A nonvoluntary or involuntary corruption of a habit-capacity occurs when one's body deteriorates on account of circumstance, age, or another nonchosen factor. Health for a former professional basketball player is different from health when he was in his prime. An elderly person, or a person with brain trauma, may find that his body no longer responds to reason as it used to, making it more difficult to regulate his passions. Thus, he may experience what feels like a loss of acquired virtue. However, his infused virtues can remain and even increase in these situations. Because charity chiefly resides in the will, one's capacity for charity does not decrease even when the body decreases in strength. One's charity remains virtually and habitually in the soul unless one makes an act contrary to it. Therefore, a flourishing human life must not be content with asking: "How do I, as an autonomous will, overcome temptations and bad habits?" Rather, one must inquire: "How do I acquire and develop good habits that will last?"[202]

202. See MacMullan, "The Flywheel of Society: Habit and Social Meliorism in the Pragmatist Tradition," in *A History of Habit* (ed. Sparrow and Hutchinson), 244.

### SUMMARY OF ADVICE FOR ACQUIRING AND DEVELOPING HABITS

1. Identify the new behavior that you want to perform, and the habit that produces it.
2. Identify the things that will give you a sense of reward for performing the behavior.
3. Make the desired object attractive by association.
4. Choose a cue within a stable performance context that will effectively initiate the desired behavior.
5. Devise a reasonable plan for shaping your desired habit loop.
6. Organize the material well.
7. Put your plan into practice.
8. Begin at the beginning.
9. Frequently meditate on it in an orderly way.
10. Pay attention and be fervent.

# 10

# Forming Habits for Life

In the *Paradiso*, according to Dante's genius, St. Augustine is placed with Francis of Assisi and Bernard of Clairvaux, two saints who, in their exuberant expressions of charity, are surely his friends in heaven.[1] Like Francis, Augustine had a past that called for repentance; like Bernard, Augustine had a profound theological vision of love. Uniquely among nearly all saints, indeed all of humanity, Augustine's life, teaching, and self-reflection exemplify the power of habit. Without delving into his teaching here,[2] we can note that in the *Confessions* Augustine characterizes his life as a slow and difficult transformation from slavery to evil habit[3] to an authentic love of God through grace and divine habits: "The return to Thee is by way of humble devotion, and Thou dost cleanse us from evil habit," he says to his Savior.[4]

Taking a cue from the African Church Father's profound reflections, in this final chapter, I consider the habits that form us in life,

1. Dante, *The Paradiso*, trans. Robert Hollander and Jean Hollander (New York: Doubleday/Anchor, 2007), 32.35.

2. See Isabelle Bochet, "*Habitus* according to Augustine: Philosophical Tradition and Biblical Exegesis," and Kristell Trego, "*Habitus* or *Affectio*: The Will and Its Orientation in Augustine, Anselm, and Duns Scotus," in *The Ontology, Psychology, and Axiology of Habits* (ed. Faucher and Roques), 47–66 and 87–106, respectively.

3. Augustine, *Confessions*, lib. 6, c. 12, n. 22; c. 15, n. 25; lib. 8, c.11, n. 26; lib. 9, c. 12, n. 30.

4. Ibid., lib. 3, c. 8 (65–66).

and the sort of habits we should form in order to live well. Because supernatural habits are by far the most important and influential, I consider only them in this final chapter. The first three sections consider how to grow in faith, hope, and charity—infused habits that open the door and form all other habits. Fourth, I explain how, with grace, we can merit more habit acquisition and development. Finally, I discuss how friendship with the virtuous shapes us for good habits that can last through eternity.

## GROWTH IN FAITH

We have seen that, as helpful as the classic habit loop is as a diagnostic tool, it ignores the directionality of the habits. Absent is the end toward which individual habits, and habit loops in general, tend. In contrast, Thomas's teleological understanding of the world demonstrates that all habits are directed to a proper end. That end could be an object that serves as a reward for a particular good act, that is, some good for the sake of which the act is performed.[5] Insofar as the end of an act is grasped by reason, it serves to "form" the act by giving the act its ultimate purpose and character.[6] Even natural habits and nonvoluntary habits are directed toward some end. When the end of a habit is in conformity with human nature, the habit contributes to flourishing and benefits the individual considered as a whole, within his lifespan. Consequently, to fully understand habits, we must recognize not only some immediate consequent or reward that results from a habitual behavior and reinforces it; we must also posit a higher and more remote end toward which the habit loop as a whole tends (see figure 5, above).

We have already seen that grave sin blocks a person, along with each of his habits, from achieving his ultimate end. With the habit of faith enlivened by charity, however, a person and all of his habits are pointed to his supreme, ultimate end, which is God himself.

5. *ST* I-II, q. 18, aa. 1 and 5.
6. See *ST* I-II, q. 7, a. 4, ad 2.

As the "first thing in the spiritual life," that by which the soul lives in union with God, faith is the first of the infused virtues, the foundation to the house of virtue.[7] Hope is the bridge which we cross from this life to the next, and charity is the most perfect of the virtues, the source and summit of a life of good habits. In what follows, I will briefly discuss Thomas's advice regarding how to develop infused faith and in subsequent sections, I will delve more deeply into growth in hope and charity.

Jacob Wood insightfully notes that the intellect can be habituated in three degrees that parallel the increased habituation of the will to right reason.[8] First, there is a grasp of natural knowledge of the first principles of thought and action; this parallels "natural virtue" or temperamental inclinations toward particular goods. Second, acquired knowledge, gained through experience and deliberate consideration of things, parallels acquired virtue, which relies on prudence as a guide. Third, infused knowledge, as a participation in the rectitude of revealed divine rule, is paralleled by infused habits.[9] Aquinas seems to be indicating that the content itself is not infused, but the intellect participates in the rectitude of the "first rule" through an infused habit, namely, faith. Aquinas explains in later texts that all knowing of the truth is a participation in the eternal law,[10] but by grace the Holy Spirit is poured into the minds of men, which then participates in him in a particular way.[11] This is the way of faith, which is an imperfect participation of divine wisdom in this life,[12]

7. *Super Heb.*, c. 10, l. 4, n. 548: "Sicut per illud per quod primo unitur anima corpori, vivit corpus, ita per id per quod primo unitur Deus animae, vivit anima, hoc autem est fides, quia fides est primum in vita spirituali.... Si non credideritis, non permanebitis, sicut domus non permanet, destructo fundamento."

8. For references, see Wood, *To Stir a Restless Heart*, 154–55.

9. *Super Sent.*, lib. III, d. 23, q. 1, a. 1, co. By saying the third level of the intellect's habituation occurs when it "participat rectitudinem primae regulae in his quae intellectum agentem excedunt."

10. *ST* I-II, q. 93, a. 2. See Craig A. Boyd, "Participation Metaphysics, The 'Imago Dei', and the Natural Law in Aquinas' Ethics," *New Blackfriars* 88, no. 1015 (2007): 274–87.

11. *SCG* IV, c. 17, n. 22; c. 18, n. 8.

12. *De veritate*, q. 14, a. 1, ad 5.

but which becomes perfect participation in heavenly beatitude.[13]

"Lord, increase our faith."[14] This prayer to Christ helped Thomas prove that all habits can increase extensively or intensively, including infused faith.[15] Prevenient grace is operative in the first act of faith, for only actual grace, given to us without our willing it, can move the will to make an act of faith. This is properly understood as an initiative of the Holy Spirit.[16] After a person receives faith in baptism as a habitual principle, and he wills to believe with an act of faith, his habit of faith can be increased: "when man has a prompt will to believe, he loves the truth believed, and ponders over it, and if he is able to find reasons for his belief he embraces them."[17] Once faith is possessed, it may increase through time, as it did among the people of the Old Testament, progressing from imperfection to greater perfection, who were gradually assimilated to the form of divine revelation similar to the way that matter gradually receives a form.[18] Now that God has fully revealed himself in Christ, the faith of individuals has a naturally perfective trajectory. The act of faith proceeds from one's free choice: "believing is an act of the intellect assenting to divine truth from a command of the will moved by God through grace."[19] Extensively, faith grows when a person works to see more and more in the light of faith; this does not substantially change the habit of faith in itself, but only sheds illuminating truth upon more objects that are known. For example, a person can go beyond merely confessing the articles of faith—an act necessary, at times, for salvation[20]—and can gradually see his entire life in the light of faith, as Augustine did in his *Confessions*. Intensively, faith grows when the intellect's grasp of the faith is firmer and more certain, and also when

13. *De rationibus Fidei ad cantorem Antiochenum* (Leon. ed.), c. 9, co.
14. Lk 17:5.
15. *ST* I-II, q. 52, a. 1, s.c.
16. See *ST* II-II, q. 24, a. 3, ad 1.
17. *ST* II-II, q. 2, a. 10.
18. See *ST* II-II, q. 1, a. 7, ad 3.
19. *ST* II-II, q. 2, a, 9.
20. See *ST* II-II, q. 3, a. 2.

the will assents to truths of the faith more promptly, devoutly, or confidently.[21] Charity increases faith's intensity by moving the intellect to believe with greater and greater faith *unto* God, that is, to perform every act with a loving faith in accordance with the Catholic teaching.[22]

Reason is not opposed to faith, Aquinas insists. Rather, they are mutually enriching.[23] In certain cases, the exercise of reason serves as a stimulus for faith. Faith can be obscure for a person who possesses the virtue along with many errors regarding natural truths—which makes grasping supernatural truths more difficult. Overcoming these obstacles helps one live in the truth more fully. "Through science," that is, through a knowledge of things by their proper causes, "faith is brought forth and nourished through the mode of exterior persuasion, which is done by some science."[24] For example, a true understanding of the natural world, and human nature itself, can lead a man to know the existence of God as creator; this nourishes one's faith in the Trinity. The work of apologetics, which demonstrates the absurdity of objections to the faith, supports faith from without by removing obstacles to supernatural belief and showing the reasonableness in making an act of faith.[25] Infused faith adapts the mind to accept God as the first truth, and the further explanation of the content of faith comes through the church.[26] The faith has been faithfully transmitted in the Catholic church since the time of the apostles, taught through instructors so that the knowledge of faith could proceed from imperfection to perfection.[27]

21. See *ST* II-II, q. 5, a. 4.

22. See *Super Io.*, cap. 6, l. 3, n. 901: "Finis autem cum habeat rationem boni, est obiectum amoris; et ideo credere in Deum ut in finem, est proprium fidei formatae per caritatem."

23. See *ST* II-II, q. 2, a. 10.

24. *ST* II-II, q. 6, a. 1, ad 1: "Per scientiam gignitur fides et nutritur per modum exterioris persuasionis, quae fit ab aliqua scientia."

25. See *SCG* I, c. 2, nn. 2–4.

26. See *ST* II-II, q. 5, a. 3: "Unde quicumque non inhaeret, sicut infallibili et divinae regulae, doctrinae Ecclesiae, quae procedit ex veritate prima in Scripturis sacris manifestata, ille non habet habitum fidei, sed ea quae sunt fidei alio modo tenet quam per fidem."

27. *ST* II-II, q. 1, a. 7, ad 3.

"I believe; Lord, help my unbelief": Christ shows mercy in order that those who believe "might believe more firmly and robustly."[28] After faith has begun in a person's soul, the Holy Spirit's Gift of understanding develops the habit by enabling its possessor to more deeply penetrate the mysteries of God, and to bring the intellect to operate in a supernatural mode.[29] Good habits, especially purity and chastity, aid a deepening of the faith, because uncleanness of the flesh impedes spiritual contemplation.[30] The virtue of *studiositas*, which applies the mind's zealous attention to an object, plays a crucial role in the structuring of the mind within faith.[31] One's understanding of the mysteries can deepen, both on the natural level through study and on the supernatural through the Gift of the Holy Spirit, or through both working together.[32] Faith and understanding are mutually dependent and reciprocally perfective, for one cannot have faith in what one does not understand in some way, and one's understanding leads to a greater certainty of faith.[33] Thomas describes the dynamism of faith for a person in the state of grace: faith leads to charity, charity leads to contemplation, contemplation leads to study, and study leads to a greater firmness of the will in adhering to the truths of the faith.[34] The primary object of our contemplation and study, Thomas says, is the cross of Christ. Commenting on Hebrews 12:2, Aquinas says that Christ is the "perfecter of our faith" especially insofar as the cross is the remedy for every tribulation and the example of every virtue.[35]

28. *Super Io.*, c. 11, l. 3, n. 1502, quoting Mk 9:23.

29. See *ST* II-II, q. 8, a. 1.

30. *Super Evangelium S. Matthaei lectura* [hereafter *Super Mt.*], c. 5, l. 2, n. 435.

31. *ST* II-II, q. 166, a. 1. Just as an inordinate pursuit of worldly things can hinder the contemplation of divine things, and hinder the gift of prophecy, so it can hinder the perfection of faith in this life (see *ST* II-II, q. 172, a. 4).

32. See ibid., a. 4, ad 2.

33. See ibid., a. 8, ad 2.

34. See also *Super Heb.*, c. 12, l. 1, n. 557, in which Aquinas favorably quotes Augustine, *De Trinitate*, c. 10: "Contemplatio est merces fidei, cui mercedi per fidem corda mundantur."

35. *Super Heb.*, c. 12, l. 1, n. 667.

### GROWTH IN HOPE

Significantly for my analysis of faith, Duhigg argues that an indispensable element for developing new habits is what he calls "belief." He explains that real habit development is possible only if one believes that growth is possible. For recovering alcoholics, for instance, "belief was the ingredient that made a reworked habit loop into a permanent behavior.... for habits to permanently change, people must believe that change is feasible."[36] Duhigg then references William James's belief-theory, according to which faith can help to create a fact, or, in Duhigg's words, "If you believe you can change—if you make it a habit—the change becomes real. This is the real power of habit: the insight that your habits are what you choose them to be."[37] Such seems congruent with Albert Bandura's presentation of "self-efficacy," that is, the ability to be a cause for change in one's own life.[38] Bandura shows that self-efficacy, truly being a cause, is dependent on a person's "perceived self-efficacy," that is, "beliefs in one's capabilities to organize and execute the courses of action required to produce given attainments," the belief that one has the power to reach one's goals.[39] Aquinas would agree to some extent, for he says that belief underlies confidence, which is a mode of hoping with strong opinion.[40] Such a belief does not per se hold that habits are obtained quickly, easily, and unremittingly: only that obtaining them can truly happen when the conditions are right. Furthermore, one cannot develop habits without believing that they are possible to acquire, for choice only regards what is possible for us.[41] Hope goes beyond opinion, as it is primar-

36. *The Power of Habit*, 85 and 89.

37. Ibid., 273. See William James, "The Will to Believe," in *The Will to Believe: And Other Essays in Popular Philosophy* (London: Longmans, Green, and Co., 1912), 1–31.

38. See Albert Bandura, *Self-Efficacy: The Exercise of Control* (New York: W. H. Freeman and Company, 1997), 5–6.

39. Ibid., 3.

40. *ST* I-II, q. 40, a. 2, ad 2; II-II, q. 129, a. 6, ad 3.

41. See *ST* I-II, q. 13, a. 5.

ily a movement of the appetite to a good to be obtained, albeit a desire of hope based on a judgment about the obtainability of the good.[42] One aims at developing habits only because one has a reasonable hope that such development is achievable, for an agent only desires what he considers possible.[43] Indeed, progress in the spiritual life and the development of good habits is typically a slow and arduous path—but it can be traversed with God's help.[44]

Goals can be obtained in two ways: either by one's own power, or through the power of another.[45] Some skills and dispositions may be developed with our own concentrated, ordered effort. However, we have seen that it is impossible for people in the current state of the world to fully overcome the bad habits that are sins or obtain the perfect habits that are fully-formed virtues ordered to man's ultimate end. Although a person by his own effort may at times avoid single sins and even develop imperfect natural virtue, he can never entirely banish sin from his soul and continually love God above all things so perfectly that divine love perfects all of his acts. Therefore, a person cannot have a reasonable hope or belief that, solely with his own power, he can gain whatever habits he desires, or divest himself of habits he hates, or change his habits into whatever he wants them to be. A person needs grace and the infused good habits of moral and theological virtues, and the Gifts of the Holy Spirit, in order to truly hope that he can experience the fullness of flourishing. Only through supernatural help, above a mere self-initiated technique, can a person gain beatitude through his habits of holiness. We therefore turn to how one can increase natural and infused hope.

As a theological virtue, hope grows in ways that are analogous to the growth of hope as a natural passion. Thomas acknowledg-

42. See ibid., a. 2.

43. See *ST* I-II, q. 40, a. 1, ad 3.

44. Glenn, "A Comparison of the Thomistic and Scotistic Concepts of Hope," 32, notes that hope is best understood in light of man's progress toward his ultimate end, for "the principles of finality" integrate Thomas's moral system, and the virtue of hope is characterized as looking forward to man's supreme ultimate end.

45. Ibid., a. 2, ad 1.

es Aristotle's insight that hope abounds in youths and drunkards on account of their high spirits, and because they are heedless of dangers and defects in the world—whether because of lack of self-knowledge, lack of experience, or because of forgetfulness.[46] With Aristotle, he holds that experience can cause despair, as seen in the pessimism of older men who have frequently suffered and been defeated: they think something impossible what they once thought was possible.[47] Aquinas's understanding of habits enables him to go beyond Aristotle, however, and to recognize that experience can cause hope for two reasons. First, habituation facilitates action that was previously impossible for a person. Experience in this sense entails proper training, by which a person acquires the ability of doing something easily, quickly, and skillfully. The new habit-strength increases one's hope that one can obtain the desired object, for "no one fears to do that which he is confident of having learned well."[48] In other words, right practice leads to a good habit, which renders an action easier.[49] An experienced runner does not fear entering a race; an experienced speaker does not fear expostulating in front of a crowd. Alongside experience, anything that increases a person's power naturally augments hope and, for the same reason, diminishes fear.[50] This is why physical changes, such as a dilation of the heart, can increase hopeful feelings, for positive physical energy banishes feelings of fear.[51] Second, Thomas argues that experience can cause hope insofar as it demonstrates the possibility of something that earlier seemed impossible.[52] Success fosters hope. This is why a fearful, weak, or discouraged person would be well-advised to take a very small step toward his goal. By accomplishing a small step, he

46. See *ST* I-II, q. 40, a. 6; a. 5, ad 3; q. 45, a. 3, ad 2; Aristotle, *Rhetoric* I.12; *Nicomachean Ethics* III.8, 1117a14.

47. See *ST* I-II, q. 40, a. 5, co. and ad 2; Aristotle, *Rhetoric* II.13, 1390a4–5; *Nicomachean Ethics* III.8, 1117a10.

48. *ST* I-II, q. 40, a. 5.

49. Ibid., ad 1.

50. *ST* I-II, q. 42, a. 5, ad 1.

51. See *ST* I-II, q. 45, a. 3.

52. See *ST* I-II, q. 40, a. 5.

gains experience of his power and begins to hope that later, more difficult steps are possible for him.[53] More generally, Thomas says that hope is caused by anything that makes an individual estimate that something is possible for him—which is why both teaching and persuasion can make a person more hopeful.[54]

From the perspective of faith, we can see that the causes of natural hope and its increase apply *a fortiori* to the theological virtue of hope. Regarding habituation as a strengthening that increases hope, one can note that successes in doing good lead to a greater confidence that one can practice virtue even in difficult situations. This avoids the sin of presumption, for the infused virtues and the Gifts of the Holy Spirit constitute divinely-given power-boosts: with them, one does not rely on one's own power, but has confidence that what is impossible to human nature on its own is possible with God's grace.[55] As St. Paul says, "I can do all things through Him who strengthens me."[56] Trust in divine assistance therefore increases a man's hope and daring.[57]

Worldliness, attachment to the mundane goods, takes one's eye off of the prize of union with God, leads to distaste for spiritual goods, and ends in despair—loss of hope for gaining one's ultimate end.[58] In striking contrast, to suffer for the sake of Christ can *increase* a person's theological hope, unlike the way suffering for the sake of lesser things can lead to despair. Explaining Romans 5:3–4,

53. James Clear shows the great importance of small behaviors that, when compounded, can develop habits (*Atomic Habits*, 15–18); he recommends a "two minute rule": "when you start a new habit, it should take less than two minutes to do" (ibid., 162–67). The tiny scale of the behavior helps it to be easily accomplishable from the start, giving one an "easy win" that builds confidence in future success.

54. *ST* I-II, q. 40, a. 5.

55. See *ST* II-II, q. 21; Cessario, "The Theological Virtue of Hope," 240.

56. Phil 4:13. See *Super Epistolam ad Philipenses lectura* [hereafter *Super Philip.*], c. 4, l. 2, n. 174: "Cum dicit *omnia possum*, etc. ponit causam suae constantiae, dicens omnia possum, quasi dicat: non possem hos insultus sustinere, nisi manu Dei me confortante."

57. See *ST* I-II, q. 45, a. 3.

58. See David Elliot, "The Christian as *Homo Viator*: A Resource in Aquinas for Overcoming 'Worldly Sin and Sorrow,'" *Journal of the Society of Christian Ethics* 34, no. 2 (2014): 101–21.

"Suffering produces endurance, and endurance true hope," Aquinas says: "Hope in God becomes firmer the more one endures graver things for His Name. For by the sufferings which the saints of God endure for Christ, the hope of eternal life arises in them."[59] Additionally, because belief in the attainability of one's aim leads to hope, the success of others to whom we are tied through charity can increase our hope. The author of the Epistle to the Hebrews says that the reason for his confidence is God's promises and the past good works and the past moral victories of the saints.[60] Just as the young have greater hope because their energy is greater and they have suffered few evils, so the spiritual childhood of the saints, who trust in their heavenly Father, allows them to participate in Christ's victory and therefore have a spiritual "energy" and confidence in the future. Furthermore, similar to the way youths are heedless of present danger because of their focus on the present good, so those who are "youthful" in God are heedless of the dangers of this world on account of their hope for the ultimate good of eternal life.

Nature inclines us to hope for whatever good is proportionate to human nature and is within our individual power, but we cannot hope for a supernatural good without assurance that it is obtainable.[61] Whereas sin clouds our reason and makes us think that the supernatural is impossible, God provides promises, admonitions, and even commandments as ways to incite our hope and trust in him.[62] Thus, the hope inculcated by the Gospel is not a vain hope, but a sure hope, for it is founded on God's word and the victory of

59. *Super II Cor.*, c. 1, l. 3, n. 23.

60. Heb 11:33. See *Super Heb.*, c. 6, l. 3, n. 310; c. 11, l. 7, n. 633.

61. See *ST* II-II, q. 22, a. 1, ad 1.

62. Ibid., and co. Thomas argues that, if pagans did what was in their power with the aid of grace, God provided pagans with the means to believe and turn to him. See *Super Rom.*, c. 10, l. 3, n. 849: "Si qui tamen eorum fecissent quod in se est, dominus eis secundum suam misericordiam providisset, mittendo eis praedicatorem fidei." Thomas seems to agree with Augustine's famous statement in *De natura et gratia*, c. 43, n. 50: "God does not command the impossible, but gives His command as admonition to do what you can and to pray when you cannot."

God already accomplished in Christ and the saints.[63] "We hope and do not despair," Thomas explains, "because we have the same spirit of faith that the ancients had, because, although the times have changed, nevertheless, the Spirit and the Catholic faith is unchanged, except that they believed that Christ was to come and suffer, but we believe that he has come and suffered."[64] In this way, living faith bolsters hope, so that the more one's faith increases, the more one's hope can increase accordingly. The certitude of hope is manifested most at the time of death, for then it consists in the firm determination of the will to attain salvation with the help won by Christ's death and resurrection.[65] In this way, hope is an essential part in the *ars moriendi,* which, aided by the sacraments, helps one to die in the love and confidence of God.[66]

## GROWTH IN CHARITY

Charity's increase is a topic that Aquinas considered frequently and specifically, and not just sporadically and incidentally as with faith and hope. When Aquinas discusses the increase of charity, he argues that there are three grades (*gradus*) of the single virtue of charity distinguished according to the different actions that a man performs that are characteristic of each stage.[67] Accordingly, one finds the famous threefold division: (1) charity as it exists in beginners, which leads a person primarily to avoid sin and to resist his sinful inclinations; (2) charity as it exists in those making progress (*pro-*

63. See Col 1:5 and *Super Epistolam ad Colossenses lectura* [hereafter *Super Col.*], c. 1, l. 2, n. 13; 1 Cor 15:54–58 and *Super I Cor.*, c. 15, l. 9, nn. 1017, 1019, and 1022.

64. *Super II Cor.*, c. 4, l. 4, n. 141.

65. In making this point, Glenn notes that one's certitude is that God will offer help, although the promise of salvation is conditional ("A Comparison of the Thomistic and Scotistic Concepts of Hope," 37). She also notes that "the union with God produced by hope *is* the confidence we have in His helping power" (ibid., 41, citing *ST* II-II, q. 17, a. 6, ad 3).

66. See David Elliot, "The Theological Virtue of Hope and the Art of Dying," *Studies in Christian Ethics* 29, no. 3 (2016): 301–7.

67. *ST* II-II, q. 24, a. 9.

*ficientes*), who are chiefly occupied with progressing in virtue; and (3) charity as it exists in "the perfect" (*perfectos*), whose principal aim is to dwell in union with God and to experience fruition in him. To explain how charity develops according to these three stages, Aquinas applies the threefold schema to the image of fire gradually burning wood.[68] Parallel to this movement is how the Holy Spirit is given to Christians in each of these degrees for different purposes.[69]

In the first stage, when first coming into contact with a combustible thing, such as a piece of wet wood, fire expels "contrary dispositions" to itself. This can be described as a purgative action, for fire expels wetness from green wood; it is purifying because, by heating and drying wood, fire removes imperfections from the wood and transforms it more into fire's own hot and dry nature. On a natural level, reason is an agent that imposes a form upon the will. Reason does so by overcoming anything in the will that is contrary to the good-to-be-chosen, that is, reason shows how other goods should not take the place of the good-to-be-chosen. This corresponds to the first stage of charity in beginners, in which God's grace comes to a sinner from without and moves him to rid himself all that is not God, namely, whatever is disordered and sinful. Grace then moves interiorly in the sinner, who cooperates and confesses sin, corresponding to the act of fire expelling wetness from wood, which represents charity expelling the contrary forms and effects of sin. In this case, the Spirit is given to beginners as the principle of vivification, that is, in prevenient grace; then as the principle of charity in the "laver of regeneration," that is, in baptism[70]; and in the privilege of

68. *ST* I-II, q. 51, a. 3; II-II, q. 24, a. 10, s.c.; q. 27, a. 7. St. John of the Cross beautifully and insightfully develops the image of burning wood, showing how it illustrates spiritual purgation, enlightenment, and union with God. See *Dark Night of the Soul*, lib. 2, c. 10; c. 11, n. 1; *Living Flame of Love*, prol., nn. 3–4; stanza 1, nn. 3–4, 19, 22–23, 25, and 33; and *Ascent of Mt. Carmel*, lib. 1, c. 11, n. 6; lib. 2, c. 8.

69. See *Expositio super Isaiam ad litteram* [hereafter *Super Is.*], c. 44, n. 855.

70. See Ti 3:5: "Not by the works of justice which we have done, but according to his mercy, he saved us, by the laver of regeneration and renovation of the Holy Ghost." According to Aquinas, this verse refers to the sacrament of baptism, which makes a person a member of Christ, and confers sanctifying grace, the virtues, and the Gifts of the Holy Spirit. See *ST* III, q. 69, a. 4, s.c.

adoption as children of the Father.[71] Aquinas notes that "a powerful fire not only causes its substantial form to appear [in a combustible thing], but it also induces a powerful disposition [to burn]." Accordingly, because the Holy Spirit "is so powerful a mover, He so moves a person to love that He also causes the habit of charity."[72] Significantly, Aquinas notes that if charity is not attentively "nourished" or "fostered" in this stage, then it will be "corrupted" because the beginner will fall into mortal sin.[73] How charity is nourished will be addressed later on.

Next, fire impresses its likeness upon the wood.[74] As an agent, fire overcomes the passivity of the wood and actualizes its "burn-ability" by sharing with it the form of heat, so that the wood is transformed into fire. On the natural level, reason impresses the form of the good-to-be-chosen upon the will, so that in some way the will—and the whole person—is conformed to the good it chooses. This happens only gradually, for the appetitive power as a whole is inclined to various goods. To become habituated to a single thing, reason must form the will to grasp the object as suitable and thereby to choose it in many different times, places, and circumstances. Then the will comes to be attached to the thing in a quasi-natural way. A similar action occurs on the supernatural level, in which reason enlightened by faith so transforms the will, which itself is already aflame with charity, such that a person becomes more and more conformed to Christ by performing many acts of love. Thus, those who are more proficient in virtue experience its formative effects as they focus on progressing in virtue by augmenting charity.[75] Here, the Holy Spirit is given for the instruction of understanding, for the refreshment of the affections, and as a help in action.[76]

71. *Super Is.*, c. 44, n. 855.
72. *De virtutibus,* q. 2, a. 1, ad 2.
73. *ST* II-II, q. 24, a. 9.
74. *ST* I-II, q. 51, a. 3.
75. *ST* II-II, q. 24, a. 9, co. and ad 3.
76. *Super Is.*, c. 44, n. 855: "Datur spiritus … proficientibus ad instruendum intellectum, Ioh. 14: Paraclitus spiritus sanctus etc., ad reficiendum affectum, Eccli. 24: spiritus meus super mel etc., ad adiuvandum actum, Rom. 8: spiritus adiuvat infirmitatem etc."

Finally, in the perfect stage, fire so transforms the wood into itself that only fire remains and its heat radiates to everything around it with the tendency to transform all other flammable things into itself. Aquinas says that, having been transformed by charity, those who are "perfect" desire "to be dissolved and to be with Christ."[77] As a result of conformity to Christ, the saint manifests that he loves God above all things and most perfectly by performing acts of charity to his neighbor. Such is the stage of advanced virtue that has become perfected in a Christian.[78] As Aquinas notes: "For the power of fire is more perfect when it heats not only things that are near but also things that are distant. Likewise, charity is more perfect through which one is moved to loving and helping not only to neighbors, but also to strangers and enemies, not only in general but especially in particular."[79] For those with perfected charity, the Spirit is given as a certain benefit of liberty, a bond of unity, and a pledge of inheritance.[80] Indeed, "the properties of the Holy Spirit are in a spiritual man, just as the properties in fire are in burning wood."[81]

The threefold operation of "fire" fits with Aquinas's understanding of the grades of virtue and charity, as the following table shows.

It is important to note that even when charity exists in a perfect manner in the soul, it can still increase. Thomas goes so far as to say that it is of the *ratio* of charity in this life that it can be increased.[82] Charity can increase intensively, insofar as charity becomes more deeply rooted in the soul, which is an increase of fervor.[83] Aquinas describes this increase of charity as the subject participating in the form of charity in greater and greater degrees, which recalls the im-

77. *ST* II-II, q. 24, a. 9. This phrase is taken from the Vulgate version of Phil 1:23–24, "desiderium habens dissolvi et cum Christo esse."

78. *ST* II-II, q. 27, a. 8.

79. *De virtutibus*, q. 2, a. 8, co.

80. *Super Is.*, collationes c. 44: "Datur spiritus: . . . perfectis quasi beneficium libertatis, II Cor. 3: ubi spiritus domini etc., quasi vinculum unitatis, Eph. 4: solliciti servare etc., quasi pignus haereditatis, Eph. 1: signati estis et cetera."

81. *Super Io.*, c. 3, l. 4, n. 456.

82. *ST* II-II, q. 24, a. 4: "De ratione caritatis viae est ut possit augeri."

83. See ibid., ad 3.

Table 10-1. Grades of Virtue and Charity

| *Grades of virtue,* De virtutibus, *q. 5, a. 2* | *Kinds of virtue,* ST *I-II, q. 61, a. 5* | *Grades of charity,* ST *II-II, q. 24, a. 9* | *Development of habits (image of fire and wood) ST I-II, q. 51, a. 3, etc.* |
|---|---|---|---|
| [False virtue] | | | |
| Entirely imperfect virtue (good inclinations; natural virtues; innate temperaments) | | | |
| True but imperfect virtue (with prudence, but not charity) | "Social" (regulated by natural reason): check inordinate emotions | | |
| Perfect virtue (formed by charity) | Perfecting | Charity of beginners | Fire purges wood of wetness, dries and heats it |
| | | Charity of the proficient | Fire impresses its likeness on wood |
| | Perfect | Charity of the perfect | Wood is transformed entirely into fire and extends heat and light to others |
| | Exemplar (existing in God) | | |

age of fire gradually transforming the wood into itself as the flame grows hotter and hotter, consuming more and more of the wood.[84] Because charity is properly attributed to the Holy Spirit, one can understand the increase of charity as the process by which the soul more perfectly participates in the likeness of the Holy Spirit that is impressed upon it.[85] As a participation in the infinite, substantial, and personal love of God, charity according to its proper *ratio* is illimitably increasable.[86] On the part of God, the first cause of charity, the habit can always increase, for he is omnipotent. On the part of the human subject, there is also a limit to charity's potential increase,

84. See ibid., a. 5.
85. Ibid., a. 5, ad 3.
86. See ibid., a. 7.

for "as charity expands, it always super-abundantly expands the power for further growth."[87] In other words, "the capacity of a spiritual creature for charity is increased because through it the heart is enlarged."[88] This expansion is primarily the work of God, the surgeon who heals, strengthens, and expands the heart, and only secondarily the work of the individual who moves himself with the help of grace.

Though we may become friends of God in a single moment through the infusion of sanctification, we can deepen and improve our friendship with God throughout our lives. Lest we think that charity grows in merely in a passive way, Aquinas argues that to grow in charity, one must make more acts of charity: as a habit, charity must be exercised so that our earthly life becomes more and more a participation in the eternal life of heaven. Love begets love—the more one loves, the readier he is to love, and to love more fervently, and to advance in love.[89] However, not every act of charity immediately increases the habit. Imperfect or "remiss" acts of charity maintain the divine fire within us; they merely dispose the soul for a further increase of charity. Other acts dispose a person for the infusion of charity by removing obstacles to it. These include acting according to a pure heart, a good conscience, and an unfeigned faith.[90] But there are at least two ways in which charity may be increased: "The first is the separation of the heart from earthly things.... The second is firm patience in adversity."[91] Both acts facilitate opportunities to love God more than creatures, and thereby to more properly order our desires. We can consider these in turn.

Thomas's philosophy of attention undergirds his explanation of how the heart can be separated from earthly things. He notes that the will's intensity is proportional to the intellect's attention to an object, and that "the heart cannot be perfectly brought to diverse

87. Ibid., a. 7.
88. Ibid., a. 7, ad 2.
89. Ibid., a. 6. See also *ST* I-II, q. 52, aa. 2–3.
90. See *ST* II-II, q. 24, a. 2, ad 3.
91. *De decem praeceptis*, prol.

things."[92] As seen earlier, the mind can focus only on one thing at a time, such that the more a person focuses on one thing, the more he ignores other things.[93] Hence "the human heart is more intensely attracted to one thing in proportion as it is withdrawn from many things."[94] Consequently, whoever wishes to nourish charity should focus on diminishing his "cupidity," that is, his "love of acquiring or receiving temporal things."[95] To diminish one's cupidity is more than simply referring one's desire for creaturely goods to God. Referring all things to God is necessary for every act of charity. To *grow* in charity takes a further step, namely, drawing one's heart away from creatures as much as possible so that the heart can instead be drawn upward to divine things: "The more perfectly the human soul is directed to loving God, that much more will it be removed from affection for temporal things."[96] This helps us to more easily see that man must also be separated from himself in a certain way.

Because man is also a creature, in order to be perfect in charity, he must also "relinquish himself."[97] According to Thomas, God reveals that all of us are called to some manner of "salutary [self-]abnegation and charitable [self-]hatred."[98] One can recall the words of Christ, "If any one comes to me and does not hate . . . even his own life, he cannot be my disciple," and, "If any man would come after me, let him deny himself and take up his cross daily and follow me; for whoever would save his life will lose it; and whoever loses his life for my sake, he will save it."[99] Charity does not require everyone to abandon all temporal goods whatsoever, for different states of life and various professions call for various legitimate goods conducive

92. Ibid.

93. See Wu, *Attention*, 58; Aquinas, *Quodlibet* 7, q. 1, a. 2; and *ST* I, q. 85, a. 4, ad 4.

94. *De perfectione*, c. 6.

95. *De decem praeceptis*, prol.

96. *De perfectione*, c. 6.

97. Ibid., c. 10.

98. Ibid.

99. Lk 14:26 and 9:23–24. See also Mt 10:38–39; *Super Mt.*, c. 10, l. 2, nn. 889 and 890: "Hortatur dominus ut omni amori carnali praeponatur . . . Deus autem prae cunctis est diligendus . . . Deus enim ipsa bonitas est; ideo magis amandus."

to the fulfillment of duty and the right ordering of the world. But attachment to creatures can diminish love of the Savior. To the extent that one's own desires are imperfectly aligned with our ultimate end, or even contrary to the will of God, one must "hate" oneself and live in Christ. One must gradually purge from the soul all that is not God, or directed to God, so that one may live in accord with perfect charity. The work of purgation includes making satisfaction for sins.[100] In order to become more greatly *perfect* in charity, one must go further and, "on account of the intention of loving God, abandon what can be licitly used, so that through this he can more freely attend to God."[101] As St. Paul said: "For me to live is Christ, and to die is gain."[102] Thus, consecrated religious follow the counsels of poverty, chastity, and obedience in order to more perfectly intensify their love of God—which then spreads to love of neighbor.

With the martyrs in mind, Aquinas maintains that another factor for growing in charity is firm patience in adversity. He argues: "When we sustain weighty things for the one we love, love is not destroyed but rather grows."[103] Hence, "holy men, who sustained adversities for God, were more strengthened in His love, just as an artisan loves more the work into which he put more labor."[104] The martyrs perfectly fulfilled the perfection of charity, for they gave up

100. See *ST* III, q. 46, a. 6, ad 3. Daria Spezzano persuasively argues that Christ's charitable satisfaction for sins on the cross is both the objective cause of our satisfaction for sin, as well as our model: we ought to join him in atoning for our sins, for then we actively participate in ordering ourselves to God in the process of deification: "'Be Imitators of God' (Eph 5:1): Aquinas on Charity and Satisfaction," *Nova et vetera* (English edition) 15, no. 2 (2017): 615–51. Dante's *Divine Comedy* speaks eloquently of the need for satisfaction: *Purgatorio*, 6.37–39: "not demeaned or lessened is high justice / if in one instant love's bright fire achieves / what they who sojourn here must satisfy," trans. Jean Hollander and Robert Hollander (New York: Anchor Books, 2003), 121. See also *Purgatorio* 11.71; *Paradiso* 4.136 and 7.93–98.

101. *De perfectione*, c. 10.

102. Phil 1:21. See *Super Philip.*, c. 1, l. 3, n. 32: "Unde aliqui dicunt illud, ex quo moventur ad operandum, vitam suam, ut venatores venationem, et amici amicum. Sic ergo Christus est vita nostra, quoniam totum principium vitae nostrae et operationis est Christus."

103. *De decem praeceptis*, prol.

104. Ibid.

their exterior goods, and even their own lives, and were obedient to the providential will of God which allowed them to die for his sake. Accordingly, "the more afflictions the faithful sustained for God, that much more they were elevated to His love," similar to the way that Noah's ark floated higher the more the waters beneath it rose.[105]

Habit-growth is always in a positive direction: the more perfect a habit of virtue is, the more forcefully does it make the will tend toward the good of that virtue, and this is especially the case with charity.[106] For the Christian with charity, self-abnegation and drawing one's heart away from creatures in a properly ordered way is an act of love for the highest good, one that is nourished by the Eucharist. According to Aquinas, the Eucharist can be compared to the burning coal that touched the lips of the prophet Isaiah and transformed his soul, for the Eucharist arouses charity to act,[107] and through it "the soul is spiritually nourished, and in some way inebriated with the sweetness of the Divine goodness."[108] In his passion, Christ manifested his great love for us, the love of the Father, and he united us to God by winning grace for all of us. As the sacramental participation in the mystery of divine love, the Eucharist is called "the Sacrament of Charity" and "the bond of perfection."[109] The Eucharist constitutes a participation in Christ's greatest act of love for mankind. The fitting reception of Christ in the sacrament is therefore an unsurpassable way to grow in charity, grace, and all the other virtues that prepare a person for heaven.[110]

Seeing how receiving the sacraments can increase our charity and other virtues indicates the way in which charity particularly serves to further a feedback loop of habit development. The reason

105. Ibid.

106. *SCG* III, c. 138, n. 2.

107. *ST* III, q. 79, a. 4.

108. Ibid., a. 1, ad 2.

109. Ibid. See *ST* III, q. 75, a. 1.

110. Thus, in *ST* III, q. 80, Thomas argues that an unworthy reception of the Eucharist is a very grave fault (aa. 4–5), whereas a worthy reception is necessary for the salvation of adults (a. 11).

for this is that we can see growth in the infused virtues as "consequents" following acts that serve as means to increase them either extensively or intensively. But, as we have seen, charity is not only a consequence of faith; it is also the form of living faith, as well as the moving principle of all true and perfect virtue. Indeed, as has been said in a number of different ways, charity leads a person to exercise the corporal and spiritual works of mercy and thereby to extend the love of God to his neighbor. As the form of the virtues, charity thus constitutes the soul of every virtue and the motor of every virtuous act. It follows that charity strengthens all the other virtues and causes the increase of every virtue it forms as well as the good acts one performs by virtue. Charity is the formal cause of the other virtues, and therefore resides at the center of a Christian's habit loop, serving as an antecedent to good acts (both habitual and occasional), as a behavior itself insofar as loving is the proper act of charity, and as a consequent of good acts that it forms (recall figure 7, above). Furthermore, because charity directs all good acts to their proper end—and indeed unites a person to his proper end—it also helps to draw a person forward so that he makes more virtuous acts, and makes them more intensely, and thereby develops his good habits more securely as they speed toward their final goal in the flourishing of the individual as he is more perfected through union with God.

Although a person's capacity for charity at any given time is finite, "the capacity of a spiritual creature is augmented through charity, because through it his [spiritual] heart is enlarged."[111] That is, "when charity increases, it always super-increases the aptitude for further augmentation."[112] There is therefore no set limit to one's increase in charity.[113] Thus, in the view of Thomas, "charity is normally in perpetual growth."[114] Because it is the form of all the other virtues, growth in charity leads to eventual growth in the other virtues

111. *ST* II-II, q. 24, a. 7, ad 2.

112. *ST* II-II, q. 24, a. 7.

113. Ibid.

114. Jean-Pierre Torrell, *Saint Thomas Aquinas: Spiritual Master* (Washington, D.C.: The Catholic University of America Press, 2003), 2:353.

as well: and the growth of these good habits rooted in the soul leads to the spread of corresponding habitual behaviors. In this way, harmonious habits tend to strengthen and perpetuate each other. An essential aspect of charity's ability to act thus for good habits is that through union with grace, charitable acts merit further growth in charity along with many other graces and gifts, as we will see.

## MERIT'S INDISPENSABLE WORK IN DEVELOPING LONG-TERM GOOD HABITS

As we increasingly cooperate with how God "searches" our soul, the development of our good habits spirals upward increasingly closer to God himself, like Dante slowly winding his way up Mount Purgatory. A crucial aspect of our vertical-circular ascent in this life is merit. Like compound interest in one's investments, or amplified velocity, merit increases with time the closer one approaches the end. In contrast, *demerit* leads to a downward spiral of sin. As vice becomes more deeply rooted in the soul, the difficulties of uprooting it increase, and greater grace and effort are needed to establish goodness instead. In what follows, I will focus on merit's practical role in habituation to the good.[115]

In the *Summa Theologiae,* Aquinas discusses merit as an effect of cooperating grace, but I have delayed discussing it until now because the topic serves as the culmination of a theory of habit development. As a preliminary consideration for understanding merit, Thomas points out that habitual grace has a "double magnitude" or effect, as do all habits and forms.[116] The first is on the level of *esse,* which we have seen is sanctifying grace—habitual operating grace. The second is on the level of action: when habitual grace is put into

115. Here I particularly rely on Joseph P. Wawrykow, *God's Grace and Human Action: "Merit" in the Theology of Thomas Aquinas* (Notre Dame, Ind.: University of Notre Dame Press, 1996). See also Hyacinth Marie Cordell, "Meriting for Others: The Potentially Salvific and Co-redemptive Value of Human Action" (STL thesis, Pontifical Faculty of the Immaculate Conception, 2011); Noble, *L'Amitié avec Dieu,* 357–432.

116. *ST* I-II, q. 112, a. 4.

act, it is a cooperation with grace already present in the soul and therefore becomes a principle of works that merit goods.[117] Thomas equates merit with reward; both indicate being justly repaid for work performed.[118] Following Aristotle, Thomas holds that justice between persons indicates a sort of equality.[119] In the natural sphere, a person's good or evil actions toward his peers have a potential twofold merit: first, with respect to the individual to whom he has done good or harm; second, with respect to what retribution is owed him by all of society, for he has indirectly affected the common good through his actions.[120] In both ways, our actions acquire merit or demerit before God; graced actions which derive from our best habits are those which merit the most.[121] Indeed, they merit that their good habits should become more perfect and thereby they place the habit loop within a loop of grace. Let us explore how this works.

On the individual level, all of our actions relate to God, who is our true and proper last end.[122] On the communal level, as God is the most shareable good in existence. He is also the most common good;[123] his providence governs the entire common good of the universe, so that "it pertains to Him to repay for things done, for good or evil toward community."[124] It follows that "all that man is, and can do, and has, ought to be ordered to God, so that every act of man, whether good or evil, has the character of merit or demerit regarding God."[125] How man can demerit is clear; it is entirely on account of the disorder within his soul. Positive merit is more diffi-

117. See *ST* I-II, q. 111, a. 2: "Habitualis gratia . . . inquantum vero est principium operis meritorii, quod etiam ex libero arbitrio procedit, dicitur cooperans."

118. See *ST* I-II, q. 114, a. 1.

119. See Aristotle, *Nicomachean Ethics* V.6, 1134a25. The Greek philosopher is speaking about political justice among free men, but Aquinas extends the basic concept to all persons. See *ST* II-II, q. 57, aa. 1 and 10.

120. See *ST* I-II, q. 21, a. 3.

121. See *ST* I-II, q. 21, a. 4.

122. See *ST* I-II, q. 19, a. 10.

123. See *ST* I, q. 6, a. 4; q. 60, a. 5.

124. *ST* I-II, q. 21, a. 4.

125. Ibid., ad 3.

cult to explain, for there is a "maximum of inequality" between God and creatures.[126] Justice simply speaking does not exist between us and the Trinity, only justice according to a certain proportion, for we act by our own choice, similar to God's free action.[127] Absolutely speaking, therefore, we can do nothing to make God our debtor—to do so would subordinate God to a creature. Instead, God becomes a debtor to himself (*sibi ipsi*) according to "divine ordination."[128] This is the key to merit.

According to this plan of his wisdom, considered in general, "God ordained that human nature should attain the end of eternal life not by its own strength, but through the help of grace—and in this mode, an act can be meritorious of eternal life."[129] God's very providence and predestination provide for man's freedom, so that a person can freely choose to cooperate with God's plans. Thus, God's plan includes that people should be saved by actively participating in Christ's passion and death, so as to be resurrected with him.[130] We have seen how, through sanctifying grace, a person's soul becomes ordered to God, thus providing the active potency for a person to direct all his actions aright. Within God's providence, a person can move himself *while being moved by habitual grace* to accomplish a good action.[131]

According to the same divine providence, good actions merit rewards. On the one hand, this happens "first and principally from divine ordination … acts are said to merit that good to which man is divinely ordained."[132] Secondarily, it takes place "on the part of free choice."[133] More than other animals, man is the principle of his own actions and therefore he deserves a reward for the good he has

126. *ST* I-II, q. 114, a. 1.

127. Ibid.

128. *ST* I-II, q. 114, a. 1, ad 3.

129. Ibid., ad 1.

130. See *ST* III, qq. 1 and 46.

131. This is an example of God using a secondary cause in conjunction with his own act as primary cause. See *ST* I, q. 19, a. 5; q. 22, a. 3, ad 2; q. 23, a. 8.

132. *ST* I-II, q. 114, a. 4.

133. Ibid.

voluntarily performed. In his providence, God directs all things toward himself as their final end; God made man in his own image so that man might move himself toward God; God ordains to save all through Christ and only through Christ; God decrees that our salvation through Christ occurs through our use of free choice, and thus God also decides to elevate man's nature and action to participate in the redemptive act of Christ "in a way that respects and perfects our rational nature and freedom, so that we are able to come to our end voluntarily, lovingly, and joyfully with God."[134]

Within the framework of God's "divine ordination," there are at least four necessary conditions on the part of the agent for his act to be meritorious.[135] This can be seen in the acts Christ performed through his human nature. First, a meritorious act must be a fully voluntary good act: "merit cannot exist unless someone willingly does what he ought."[136] A person is rewarded only for a good work for which he is responsible. Christ's human acts were meritorious, for by the movement of his free choice, he directed himself to God.[137]

Second, a meritorious act must be an effect of habitual sanctifying grace. Supernatural merit only accrues to a supernatural act, and only habitual grace makes a meritorious act proportionate to its proper end, namely, eternal union with God in beatitude.[138] Habitual sanctifying grace conforms the soul to God, it produces an act that is a free human act, and it makes the act directed toward and fitting for complete union with God. Thus, to merit eternal kingship for himself and salvation for mankind, Christ possessed the "fullness" of sanctifying and actual grace, for through the hypostatic

134. *ST* I-II, q. 34, a. 3; q. 105, a. 4; II-II, q. 23, a. 2. See Cordell, "Meriting for Others," 65.

135. See Cordell, "Meriting for Others," 65–66. With alterations and additions, I substantially reproduce the list of what he calls "prerequisites" for an act of merit. This agrees with Noble, *L'Amitié avec Dieu*, 368–71.

136. *ST* I-II, q. 71, a. 5, ad 1; see q. 114, a. 4.

137. See *ST* III, q. 34, a. 3.

138. See *ST* III, q. 2, a. 11: "Opera meritoria hominis proprie ordinantur ad beatitudinem, quae est virtutis praemium et consistit in plena Dei fruitione."

union in the incarnation, the "principle of merit,"[139] Christ's soul "had the full power of performing all [graced] acts."[140]

Third, a meritorious act must be commanded by charity, for "the principle of merit consists in the power of charity."[141] The proper act of charity consists in the soul's self-motion toward a fruition of the divine good, which moves all the acts of the other virtues and directs them to that end, the proper end of a meritorious act.[142] Hence, the act of the infused habit of charity is the primary source of merit, and the acts of the other virtues obtain merit insofar as they are formed, commanded, and directed by charity to God as one's final end.[143]

Fourth, a meritorious act can only be performed by a person who is in the state of a "wayfarer," that is, one who is presently traveling on the way to beatitude in eternal life.[144] This is a consequence of the fact that "merit has the *ratio* of a means to an end,"[145] that is, merit is the means by which man, through his good acts, achieves the reward for a meritorious act, namely, eternal life and everything directed to that end.[146] It follows that, while Christ's acts were meritorious while he was on earth, "he is no longer in a state of meriting" now that he has ascended into heaven and is no longer a wayfarer.[147]

With the essentially Christological character of merit in mind, along with its relation to divine providence and its necessary conditions, we can now address the two modes of merit and their objects. The modes are derived from the source of a man's actions. Insofar as a good work proceeds from the grace of the Holy Spirit, it bears a

139. *ST* III, q. 2, a. 11, ad 2.

140. *ST* III, a. 7, a. 7, ad 1.

141. *ST* I-II, q. 114, a. 4.

142. See ibid.: "Motus autem humanae mentis ad fruitionem divini boni, est proprius actus caritatis, per quem omnes actus aliarum virtutum ordinantur in hunc finem, secundum quod aliae virtutes imperantur a caritate."

143. See *ST* I-II, q. 114, a. 4; q. 57, a. 1; II-II, q. 124, a. 2, ad 2.

144. See *ST* II-II, q. 26, a. 13; q. 83, a. 11, ad 5.

145. *ST* I, q. 62, a. 4: "Meritum habet rationem viae ad finem."

146. See *ST* I-II, q. 114, aa. 3 and 10 respectively.

147. *ST* III, q. 19, a. 3, ad 1: "[Christus] quia nunc non est viator, non est in statu merendi."

worth proportionate to the actions of God himself.[148] This is called "condign" merit, indicating an equality between the action's merit and its reward.[149] When the Holy Spirit initiates a good work as the principal agent, a human as a secondary agent can merit temporal goods, as well as divine goods such as an increase in grace, and even eternal life for himself once he is in a state of grace.[150] Thomas says that the holy patriarchs, by performing works of righteousness, merited salvation through faith in Christ's passion.[151] In contrast, insofar as a work proceeds from the man himself, it has a merit that is "congruous" or fitting and proportionate to a divine reward.[152] The nature of friendship entails that "one wants to fulfill the will of the other insofar it is for his good"; consequently, it is congruous that God should fulfill the will of his friend, especially when presented to him in prayer.[153] Furthermore, when a person voluntarily performs a good deed by using his divinely-gifted power well, it is fitting (*congruum*) that God should reward the agent and work more excellent things by his preeminently-excellent power.[154]

The greatness of merit's effects directly relates to the quality of one's charity and other virtuous acts.[155] Considered all together, condign and congruous merit signal the extraordinary power present in an act that proceeds from habitual grace. An increase in merit essentially entails utilizing divine help so as to gain more grace. Thomas argues that a person can congruously merit the first grace

148. In *ST* I-II, q. 70, a. 2, Thomas states that insofar as a work proceeds from man "according to a higher power, which is the power of the Holy Spirit, then man's operation is said to be a fruit of the Holy Spirit."

149. See *ST* I-II, q. 114, a. 1; and aa. 6 and 7, where Thomas says that condign merit is in virtue of the "divine motion of grace," and a. 6, ad 2, where he states that it is a matter of (strict) justice.

150. See *ST* I-II, q. 114, a. 10 (temporal goods), a. 8 (an increase in grace), and a. 3 (eternal life) respectively.

151. *ST* III, q. 49, a. 5, ad 1.

152. Ibid., a. 3.

153. *SCG* III, c. 95, n. 5.

154. *ST* I-II, q. 114, a. 6.

155. See *ST* I-II, q. 57, a. 1: "In actibus horum [i.e., virtutes] habituum potest esse meritum, si ex caritate fiant." See also q. 114, a. 4.

for another, and similarly merit graces necessary for one's own salvation—goods that are greater than anything in the natural sphere of the universe.[156] But these are *accidental* recompenses for our acts of charity compared with the *essential* recompense, which is union with God himself in beatitude.[157] The power of merit is truly unimaginable to natural reason.

There can be no doubt that the creation, the continuance, and the perfection of all things is a divine gift, an effect of God's free act of love. St. Paul expresses this truth with a rhetorical question: "What have you that you did not receive? If then you received it, why do you boast as if it were not a gift?"[158] Both natural and supernatural habits are from God as origin, preserved by God as sustainer, and are directed to God as supreme ultimate end. Just as an object with mass naturally increases in speed the closer it comes to its center of gravity, so a person who moves according to his good habits meritoriously "increases velocity" in the supernatural life, for merit brings us closer to God. Likewise, just as nonrational moving objects can keep their trajectory while being slowed by an exterior force, so a person continues toward God but with less speed if venial sin or lack of fervor impedes the natural effects of merit: "Every act of charity merits eternal life absolutely. But through subsequent sin, an impediment is placed in front of the preceding merit, so that the effect is not obtained, just as natural causes fail in their proper effects on account of a supervening impediment."[159] It follows that grace does not increase in a person merely whenever he wills it to increase. Rather, grace increases when, through his actions, a person removes impediments to it in his soul, and when he acts according to the grace he has received by performing acts of charity and acts commanded by charity in union with the movements of the Holy Spirit. Thus, Thomas says, "grace is not immediately increased, but

156. *ST* I-II, q. 114, a. 7, ad 2.
157. Noble, *L'Amitié avec Dieu*, 416–17.
158. 1 Cor 4:7.
159. *ST* I-II, q. 114, a. 7, ad 3.

in its own time, that is, when someone is sufficiently disposed for the increase of grace."[160]

I have noted four conditions of a meritorious act: (1) it must be freely made, (2) it must stem from sanctifying grace, (3) it must be commanded by charity, and (4) it must be performed in this life. These conditions point toward the fact that the root of meritorious action is God-likeness existing in us through divinely-given habits. The more we become transformed into the image of God in this life through our charity, enabled by grace, the more it is fitting that we experience the things of God now and in eternity. God intended that humans should have free choice and therefore the ability to develop the gifts we have received according to reason and by our own efforts enlivened by grace. According to his divine providence, God not only wills to give men gifts of supernatural habits by which their being is transformed by grace, their powers are elevated by infused virtues, and their acts are supernaturalized by the Holy Spirit. He also provides that, by using these gifts well, the human person should be made worthy to receive an intensification and extension of these gifts. This worthiness is what Thomas means by "merit." Once again, strict justice does not apply here: "No one can merit the love of God; but through our good works we can merit the effect of divine love, namely, the increase of grace and the transmission of divine goods."[161] That is, by acting in accord with an unmerited divine gift, man can then merit an increase in that gift and allied divine gifts by way of intensification and extension. This is "grace upon grace."[162] As Augustine said, our merits are the gifts of God, for he wants his gifts to be our merits.[163] Put more concretely, the more the Holy Spirit shapes us into living icons of Christ through his exterior and interior operations, and through our own actions that stem from good habits, the more we are made worthy to expe-

160. Ibid., a. 8, ad 3.

161. *Super Io.*, c. 10, l. 4, n. 1422. See *ST* I-II, q. 114, a. 1, ad 3.

162. Jn 1:16.

163. See *De gratia et libero arbitrio* 6, c. 15; *Sermon* 298.4–5.

rience what Christ experienced in his body and his soul. Accordingly, we can count the following as effects of grace operating through charity in a concrete good act:

1. Good acts proceeding from grace and charity, when sufficiently fervent, merit further grace and charity for the acting person.[164]
2. Good acts proceeding from grace and charity can condignly merit everlasting life for the one who possesses charity.[165]
3. Good acts proceeding from grace and charity can merit the purification and perfection of our habits.[166] This includes the grace of performing a good habitual act more perfectly, the grace of responding to cues and triggers more effectively, and the grace of greater fruition upon completing the good act.
4. Good acts proceeding from grace and charity can congruously merit grace for others.[167]
5. Good acts proceeding from grace and charity even merit temporal goods, which ought to be directed toward everlasting life in heaven.[168]

Merit therefore serves as a crucial aspect of the habit loop with charity as the motive force and God in himself as man's supreme final end, as illustrated below.

To understand how the charity-habit loop operates in concrete circumstances, we may consider two people who are slated for martyrdom. One has loved God throughout his life, and being habituated to enduring hardships for God, might go to his death readily and courageously, for, as Thomas says, "charity does not diminish the la-

164. *ST* I-II, q. 114, a. 8.
165. *ST* I-II, q. 114, aa. 3–4.
166. See Noble, *L'Amitié avec Dieu*, 389–98.
167. *ST* I-II, q. 114, a. 6.
168. Ibid., a. 10.

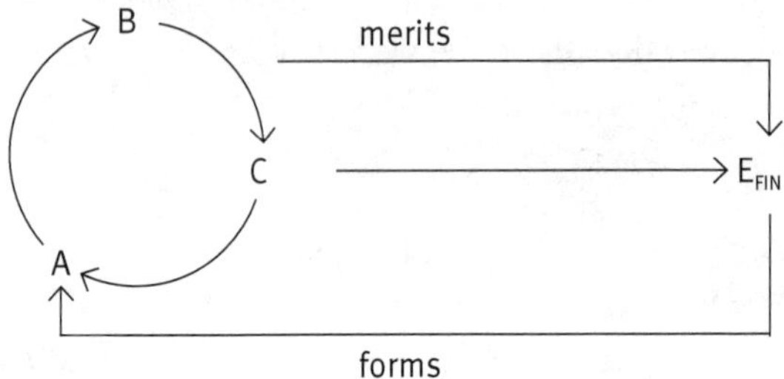


FIGURE 10. HABIT LOOP AND MERIT

bor, but rather makes us undertake the greatest works."[169] A great lover of God would gladly drink the chalice of suffering to its dregs. The other person, recently converted to the true faith, approaches the hangman with fear and trembling. His moral defects dispose him to be reluctant to do what is laborious and difficult. Aquinas argues that such reluctance diminishes merit and could lead God mercifully to allow the reluctant martyr to experience the consolations of charity so as to reduce his sufferings.[170] The first, having a greater "promptitude of the will" on account of greater charity, will be more disposed to receive God's love, and many other gifts, while the second, by the actual difficulty he endures, will be more disposed to make satisfaction for his sins.[171] In sum, the spiritual value of an act—and the grace that it can merit to receive—depends principally on the habit from which it proceeds. The more intense habit of charity gains greater merit, for it operates in a greater mode.

Suffering pertains to merit, but merit is not measured absolutely by the pain a person endures or the extent to which it is contrary to his will. If that were the case, then a selfish wimp would merit the most by suffering very light pain that was entirely against his will. In-

169. *ST* I-II, q. 114, a. 4, ad 2.

170. See ibid.: "Ex defectu ipsius operantis, unicuique enim est laboriosum et difficile quod non prompta voluntate facit. Et talis labor diminuit meritum, et a caritate tollitur."

171. *ST* I, q. 95, a. 4, ad 2.

stead, goodness is the measure of an action, not difficulty: "Therefore, it is not necessary that all difficulty is more meritorious, but only that which is more difficult such that it is also better,"[172] that is, better because of the kind of action that is produced, such as teaching the faith versus protecting one's property. Pain measures merit only when what we do or suffer is a sign of a more fervent charity: "Hence, the martyrs are commended the most insofar as they endured many things for the love of God that are contrary to the human will."[173] A work accomplished with more difficulty can be more meritorious, not because of the difficulty in itself, but because it elicits an act of greater virtue.[174] But the greatest act of virtue is charity. Therefore, to the extent that we accomplish difficult things for the sake of divine love, we thereby manifest the strength of our love, "just as the power of fire is greater the more it can set fire to less flammable material."[175] Love of enemies marvelously illustrates the greatness of one's charity, for the strength of a fire is proportionate to distance at which it can heat things: a stronger fire can heat things further away from it. In this regard, Thomas proposes a doctrine that may prove consoling to many: because sin weakens us, a greater reason for merit exists after Adam's Fall, and after our own—"for a small deed is more beyond the capacity of one who performs it with difficulty than a great deed is performed by one who does it without difficulty."[176] This is why the prodigal father welcomed back his wayward son with open arms; this is why parents praise even the slightest artistic efforts of their little children. God does not despise the efforts of those who try their best.

Christ calls the effects of meritorious action, particularly that of abandoning temporal things out of love for God and neighbor, a "hundredfold" reward. The reward includes temporal goods and relationships, temporal sufferings, and, ultimately, eternal beati-

172. *ST* II-II, q. 27, a. 8, ad 3.
173. *De perfectione*, c. 12.
174. See *ST* III, q, 49, a. 6, ad 1.
175. *ST* II-II, q. 27, a. 7.
176. *ST* I, q. 95, a. 4.

tude in union with the Trinity: "Truly, I say to you, there is no one who has left house or brothers or sisters or mother or father or children or lands, for my sake and for the gospel, who will not receive a hundredfold now in this time, houses and brothers and sisters and mothers and children and lands, with persecutions, and in the age to come eternal life."[177] In speaking of persecution as a consequence of charity, Christ overturns the Stoic-Kantian notion that the difficulty of an action is a measure of its moral quality. Christ is rather saying that *the higher the moral quality, the more suffering may result from it.* This is not to say that God punishes us on account of our good works. Rather, because purgation precedes perfection, the more one grows in perfection, the more he becomes worthy of the grace of being purified from sin. Good habits lead to better actions, and better acts lead to more perfect habits. The hotter the wet log becomes, the more disposed it is to release the moisture and take on the nature of fire. Once the log is blackened and dried, then it can begin to accept the form of fire and be transformed into a living flame. God, in his wisdom, knows that many temporal goods could be hindrances to our eternal good and our effectiveness on earth, so he often spares us from them. Even more, God knows that troubles are humbling to the good and reveal the transitory nature of this world and the lastingness of the world to come; even better, they can detach a person from this world so that he might be more firmly attached to God. To use an image derived from Christ, the vinedresser prunes the good branches so that they will bear more fruit.[178] Thomas explains:

> In a natural vine with many shoots, it could happen that it bears less fruit because the sap is diffused through all [the shoots]. And thus vinedressers purge [*purgant*] it of superfluous shoots. It is the same with humans. For when man is well-disposed and united to God, if his affections are inclined

177. Mk 10:30. See *Super Psalmo* 22, n. 1: "Et sufficienter pascit; unde dicit, nihil mihi deerit: scilicet de eo quod est necessarium ad salutem: et in temporalibus ... Tum in futuro omnem sufficientiam habebimus, quia nihil deerit nobis, quoniam habebimus Deum."

178. Jn 15:2.

to many things, his virtue is diminished and he is more ineffective in doing good. Hence God often removes such impediments and purges [*purgat*] him, that he might bear fruit well, sending trials and temptations, by which [man] is strengthened to do good.[179]

I spoke above of what can be called "active purgation," that is, a process by which we enact the virtue of penance to remove obstacles to virtue, Thomas speaks here of a passive purgation. God operates on man with passive purgations so that man might become more quickly habituated to the good. The latter is especially a sign of God's loving providence, for it is a sign that God sees good in the individual and wants to perfect him more quickly that he might be united to him more strongly and serve him more effectively. Thus, one author writes: "Could He have shown more clearly that the trials, renunciations, and sacrifices that God sometimes imposes upon the just are *veritable graces,* the *effects of merits* acquired, and destined to *help them acquire still more merits*?"[180] He continues: "We must ascend to this supernatural summit of grace to pass sound judgment on blessings and evils, and to grasp the real value of things."[181] God the Father allows the good to suffer so that they might merit salvific goods for themselves and others. When acted upon, this merit helps them to participate more fully in the fruitfulness of the cross, for we "are brought into immortal glory" through "being made conformable to the sufferings and death of Christ."[182] Through fidelity to the habits that God has implanted in us by nature and infused in us by grace, and by being open to the movements of the Holy Spirit in our souls and the circumstances in our lives, we can grow in union with the Father by being conformed to the mystery of his Son's life. In this way the saints, while living, merited to pray for us and bring

179. *Super Io.*, c. 15, l. 1, n. 1985.

180. Canon F. Cuttaz, *Our Life of Grace,* trans. Angeline Bouchard (Chicago: Fides, 1958), 279.

181. Ibid., 280.

182. *ST* III, q. 49, a. 3, ad 3.

us many graces from God.[183] In this way, the Virgin Mary merited grace that rendered her worthy and prepared to be the mother of God and thereby to share in Christ's redemption of the world.[184]

## THE ROLE OF FRIENDSHIP IN DEVELOPING HABITS

A great fault of many self-help books is to bamboozle readers with the false impression that, alone, you can gain whatever you need in life. Unreflective consumers of self-help books could be seduced by the semi-Pelagian suggestion that all you really need is willpower and some basic coaching to weave through the maze of life.[185] Many books on ethics and moral theology give a similar impression—even those that discuss the virtue theories of Aristotle and Aquinas—as if the development of one's moral excellence were a solitary affair, or, at most, a concern between the individual creature and his creator.

Aristotle was more realistic. Knowing that humans are naturally social creatures, he saw that friendship is so crucial to good habits that it is either a good habit—a virtue—or it consistently accompanies good habits.[186] In his *Nicomachean Ethics* he therefore devoted more space to friendship than to any particular virtue, and perhaps to any single topic other than virtue itself. Developing this trend, Aquinas argues that moral philosophy and theology ought to consider "all things necessary for human life, among which friendship is most necessary."[187] Accordingly, any examination of habit devel-

183. See *ST* II-II, q. 83, a. 11, ad 5.

184. See *ST* III, q. 2, a. 11, ad 3.

185. James Clear's *Atomic Habits* is somewhat of an exception. See chap. 17, "How an Accountability Partner Can Change Everything," 205–11.

186. *Nicomachean Ethics* VIII.1, 1155a1.

187. *Sent. Ethic.*, lib. 8, l. 1, n. 2. Here I will not address the extent to which Aquinas and Aristotle agree on the nature of friendship, as that has been investigated elsewhere. See, e.g., Mansini, "Aristotle and Aquinas's Theology of Charity in the *Summa Theologiae*" and Marko Fuchs, "Philia and Caritas: Some Aspects of Aquinas's Reception of Aristotle's Theory of Friendship," in *Aquinas and the Nicomachean Ethics* (ed. Hoffmann et al.), 203–19.

opment would be deficient if it overlooked the role of friendship. In chapter 8, I discussed charity's essential nature as the love of friendship for God, which is a form of the love of benevolence. Building on that previous exposition, my interest here is to see how friendship—especially friendship with God and the virtuous through charity—affects our habit development.

It may seem as if friendship is not in itself a virtue, just as natural faith, hope, and love are not complete virtues. The quality of those natural habits depends on their formal and material objects; likewise, it appears as if friendship is good only to the extent that the person befriended (material object) and the reasons for the friendship (formal object) are good. Even when a virtuous friendship with other humans encourages the practice of virtue, the relationship is *dispositive* to virtue, not per se *causative*. Perhaps surprisingly, Aquinas says that friendship stems from virtue, causes virtue, and is necessary for happiness. In this way, upright friendship as "a kind of virtue inasmuch as it is a chosen habit," and, at minimum, good moral habits are the proper causes of "true friendship."[188]

All friendship involves emotional attachment and partnership, Aristotle said: such that friends desire to be together, enjoy each other's company, do things together and share in each other's life as far as they can.[189] To eschew anthropomorphism, scientists have typically avoided attributing friendship to animals.[190] Nevertheless, there is evidence that many species possess non-kin relationships based on pleasure and utility.[191] "Affiliative behaviors" are apparent in higher animals, including play, mutual grooming, or simply having strong and consistent social associations, are correlated with

188. *Sent. Ethic.*, lib. 8, l. 1, n. 1: "amicitia autem est quaedam virtus, inquantum scilicet est habitus electivus . . . virtus est causa verae amicitiae."

189. *Nicomachean Ethics* IX.12, 1171b31–1172a6.

190. Jorg J. M. Massen et al., "Close Social Associations in Animals and Humans: Functions and Mechanisms of Friendship," *Behaviour* 147 (2010): 1379–1412, at 1379. With the breakdown of classic notions of friendship, this trend is weakening.

191. Lauren J. N. Brent et al., "The Neuroethology of Friendship," *Annals of the New York Academy of Sciences* 1316, no. 1 (May 2014): 1–17.

health benefits for macaque monkeys, hyenas, baboons, and humans as well.[192] Empirical studies corroborate that physical proximity and shared activity is a marker of friendship, manifested in how both apes and children spend more time nearer to their non-kin friendly relations.[193] Likewise, cooperation and reciprocity are key: apes literally scratch each other's backs, ravens preen one another, and humans exhibit positive physical touch in the form of pats, nudges, and hugs.[194] It follows that emotional engagement that leads to neurochemical and emotional attachment—which is bound up with pleasure—is somehow essential for friendship-like relationships.[195] Nevertheless, more is needed for authentic friendship.

Aristotle distinguishes between friendships of utility, friendships of pleasure, and friendships of virtue.[196] Friendships of utility are focused on love of what is useful: in these relationships, people desire useful goods for each other; friendships of pleasure focus on pleasure, especially that which is derived from the other or shared together.[197] Creatures in relationships centered solely on utility or pleasure do not love the other for what the other, but for what utility or pleasure he provides. Aristotle astutely observes that "friends" in these situations this are not focused on the good for the other, but what is good or pleasant for *themselves*.[198] The distinction between love of concupiscence and love of benevolence, which is equivalent to friendship—which we discussed regarding charity—helps make sense of Aristotle's threefold division of friendship based on the object loved in the relationship. Friendships of utility and pleasure are based on the love of concupiscence: they are focused on objects, not persons. They are ultimately selfish. In contrast, true friendship aims

192. Massen et al., "Close Social Associations," 1387–88.

193. References in ibid., 1382–83.

194. Ibid., 1383–84. For a thorough study of nonhumans, see Lee Alan Dugatkin, *Cooperation among Animals: An Evolutionary Perspective* (New York: Oxford University Press, 1997).

195. Carter, "Neuroendocrine Perspectives on Social Attachment and Love."

196. *Nicomachean Ethics* VIII.2–3, 1155b17–1156b24.

197. *Nicomachean Ethics* VIII.3, 1156a10–18.

198. Ibid.

not at whatever is pleasant or useful, but at what is morally good.[199]

We have seen that nonvoluntary and partly voluntary habits do not rise to the level of fully human habits; in a similar way, merely emotional friendship (whether useful or pleasant) does not rise to the level of true friendship properly speaking. On the subjective side, this is because emotional relationships may not possess the rational foundation necessary for fully human habits. As the result of many free choices made with respect to another, friendship is a habit of the soul: a stable, abiding quality directed toward action and measured by nature.[200] On the objective side, emotionally friendly relationships, however much they may ape friendship, do not possess the essence of friendship. There may be nonhuman animal relationships similar to friendships of pleasure and of utility, but missing is a direct analogue to what Aristotle calls friendship properly speaking, namely, the friendship of virtue.[201] Authentic friendship is the perfection of voluntary love, which is based on a deliberate choice to will the authentic good for the other.[202] The nature of benevolent love just is

199. *Nicomachean Ethics* VIII.3, 1156b7. In *De amicitia*, Cicero remarks that virtue is the basis of true friendship (6.20, 8.27–28, etc.); utility is not sought as the aim of true friendship, but it naturally flowers from it (27.100).

200. *Sent. Ethic.*, lib. 8, l. 5, n. 9. Commenting on Aristotle's observations, Aquinas realistically notes that perfect friendships—between virtuous persons who also provide utility and pleasure in a stable, long-lasting way; who are in close contact, have the same tastes, and share the same sorrows and joys—are exceedingly rare. One does not have the energy to love many people with a superabundant love; even those who please each other find it difficult to do so continually in many different occasions; circumstances may intervene to separate the friends; etc. Furthermore, although virtue has an attractiveness on its own, and friends who are mutually virtuous will appreciate their friend's virtue, it is erroneous to think that virtuous people never disagree or always find such relationships satisfying. One's imperfect character or the effects of virtue itself may be emotionally painful, as when one friend corrects another. See *Sent. Ethic.*, lib. 8, l. 6; lib. 9, l. 4.

201. *Nicomachean Ethics* VIII.3, 1156a7. The classic triple division is admirably presented in Lorraine Smith Pangle, *Aristotle and the Philosophy of Friendship* (Cambridge: Cambridge University Press, 2008), chap. 2. Howard J. Curzzer argues that despite up to seventy-two different varieties described by Aristotle, only "character" or virtuous friendships fit the definition: see *Aristotle and the Virtues* (New York: Oxford University Press, 2012), chap. 12, "Varieties of Friendship."

202. See Daniel Schwartz, *Aquinas on Friendship* (New York: Oxford University Press, 2012), 2–3.

willing good toward another. Because virtue is the perfection of humans, a perfection of nature, virtue also is the measure of all human things.[203] To will another virtue is simply to will the best good for that person, for his own sake, because virtue perfects the soul interiorly. It follows that virtuous friends love each other for the sake of the other, which is nothing other than loving each other with the highest form of benevolent love, and because friendship is a habit, this love exists in each permanently.[204] Accordingly, friendships which have less of the *ratio* of friendship, that is, are based on utility or pleasure but not virtue, are naturally less permanent.[205] Animals can find pleasure through each other, and can use each other, but only humans can care for each to the extent that they desire to help their friend develop good habits and become morally excellent.[206] Although Fido can be *friendly*, the furry fellow cannot really be man's best friend.

In authentic friendships, good persons will the good for each other, for the other's sake.[207] "Perfect friendship" is between good men who are alike in virtue and are focused on moral excellence: "for they wish well alike to each other *qua* good, and they are good in themselves."[208] Practical and speculative reason play an important role here, Cicero insists: true friendship is inseparable from such intellectual virtues as good-faith and fidelity to the truth, which enables friends to discuss all things and make good decisions together.[209] Such friendship can be described as *virtuous* for it is possessed by those who also possess good habits of virtue; *perfect* because it is

203. *Sent. Ethic.*, lib. 9, l. 4, n. 7.

204. Ibid., l. 1, n. 5.

205. *Sent. Ethic.*, lib. 8, l. 6, n. 16.

206. In the *Eudemian Ethics* VII.2, 1236b1, Aristotle speaks about the analogous nature of friendship and then makes this observation: "The primary friendship, that of good [virtuous] men ... is peculiar to man, for he alone perceives another's choice. But the other friendships are found also among the brutes where utility is in some degree present, both between tame animals and men, and between animals themselves." See also, Cicero, *De amicitia* 8.27 and 21.81: he states the loving impulses of animals may be clearly seen, and they even bear "some resemblance" to human love.

207. *ST* I, q. 20, a. 1, ad 3. See *Nicomachean Ethics* VIII.3, 1156b7.

208. *Nicomachean Ethics* VIII.3, 1156b9.

209. *De amicitia* 5.19, 18.65 (*fides* and *fidelitatem*); 24.89–90 (*veritas*); 6.22 (discussion); 25.91 (giving advice). See Gruber-Miller, "Exploring Relationships," 91.

the highest form of friendship and it perfects those who have it; and *complete* because it lasts through time, because each friend gets what he gives in the friendship, especially growth in moral goodness, and because it is both useful and pleasant and thus encompasses the incomplete and imperfect relationships that serve to prepare a person for authentic friendships.[210]

One effect of this sort of friendship-love is *exstasis*, being carried from oneself in order to help one's friend enjoy the good that one also enjoys: "In the love of friendship, the affection of someone goes out from himself simply, for he wills the good to his friend and works for it, taking care and providing for him, for his friend's sake."[211] Friendship does not leave utility and pleasure behind; rather, it possesses them in a more perfect way.[212] Good people who love each other are often the most "useful": in desiring another's good, they attentively consider what would truly be useful and ultimately good for the other, and they strive to make that good come to fruition.[213] In addition, friends who are good are pleasant "without qualification," for whatever is good is attractive and enjoyable as such.[214] Here we can note that the effects of the habit loop are particularly prominent with friendship. All that was said about *frui*—actional fruition—is especially true for friends. The pleasure of their company, and their delightful attitude, helps to confirm, strengthen, and increase virtuous inclinations within us. As every athlete knows, the presence of a friend will more deeply stamp us with habits we acquire through practice; and they will engrave their own habits within our souls, for we come to think like our friends, to desire similar things, and to behave like them.

210. *Nicomachean Ethics* VIII.5, 1157b25 (virtuous); VII.3, 1156b6 (perfect); VIII.4, 1156b33–35 (complete).

211. *ST* I-II, q. 28, a. 3.

212. *Sent. Ethic.*, lib. 8, l. 3, n. 17.

213. Aquinas remarks that it is characteristic of a friend to give more than to receive; and it is better for a person to be good to friends rather than strangers, because friends call forth greater and more pleasurable generosity. Consequently, a virtuous person "needs friends whom he can benefit" (*Sent. Ethic.*, lib. 9, l. 10, n. 5).

214. *Nicomachean Ethics* VIII.3, 1156b14.

Especially significant for this study, in authentic friendships, friends will that each other have the best habits, and they work to help each other achieve those habits. That is, good friends are most useful for developing virtue, and because habits are acquired through regular practice, they encourage us to perform works of virtue, and help us to accomplish them. Virtuous friendship is particularly noteworthy in disposing man for grace and charity. Just as natural science opens man's mind to the truth and natural hope opens him to possibilities of good, so virtuous friendship perfects man's ability to love in relationships. None of the natural practices—knowledge, hope, or friendship—are in and of themselves simply virtuous, but they *dispose* a person to the infusion of grace and charity by removing obstacles to the working of the supernatural. Aquinas states that "although charity is a divine gift, nevertheless, for receiving it, a disposition on our part is required."[215] One of these dispositions is friendship that is virtuous on the natural plane, for "every friend necessarily should have an habitual disposition to do the things pertaining to friendship as well as the function itself of friendship," and virtue is that which pertains most to good friendship, while the function of good friendship is, above all, to further virtue.[216] Accordingly, the stable habit of natural, good friendship disposes a person for the more perfect friendship which stems from sanctifying grace and infused charity.

Friendship with God and God's friends directly and invariably leads to virtue, and itself is virtuous, because it is good to love God in himself, and an exchange of love between God and man always leads to goodness.[217] According to the order of being, God is eminently knowable and loveable in himself, being truth and goodness in itself. But the order of knowing operates slowly: it comes only after we acquire certain good habits, and we only know through our senses, which are weakened by the effects of sin. To love God above all things is in accordance with nature absolutely speaking,[218] for

215. *De decem praeceptis*, prol.
216. *Sent. Ethic.*, lib. 8, l. 7, n. 4.
217. See *ST* II-II, q. 23, a. 3, ad 1.
218. See *ST* I, q. 109, a. 3.

God is "supremely loveable in Himself."[219] Consequently, all appetites are focused on God in a general way, even from the very beginning; but not all people love God immediately and as a friend. We must learn to walk the path of divine love by walking the way of virtuous creaturely love. Aquinas states: "From the things that it knows, the soul learns to love the unknown, not that the things it knows are the reason for loving what it does not, as in the mode of formal, final, or efficient cause, but that through it [i.e., natural love] man is disposed to loving what is unknown."[220] Given that our neighbor is the first person we encounter, he is thus the first loveable object to call for our love.[221] Here "neighbor" means human persons with whom we are associated—ordinarily and above all, our father and mother, family, and close friends. The better we understand creatures truly, and the more we love our friends rightly, the more we are disposed to love God and all creation with charity.[222] By practicing virtuous friendship with our neighbors, we open ourselves to friendship with God the Father, in Christ, through the Holy Spirit.

Aquinas insists that the love of God is not a mere passion, a positive feeling toward God; nor is it a single act of loving God, say in gratitude for a favor received. It is a stable, abiding habit. Once charity is infused into the soul, the cycle of habit formation quickens its revolutions, and the virtue perfects our other habits with ever greater velocity. Unlike falling objects, which increase speed until they reach terminal velocity, charity can move a person toward God ever more quickly because there is no upward limit to its powerful effects on earth. By its own inner dynamism, the virtue of charity acts in a friendly manner toward others and in doing so builds up friendship. Wishing someone well is insufficient for friendship.[223] Sports spectators may have benevolent desires toward a particular team or contestant, and wish that they could win the game. But, Aqui-

219. *ST* II-II, q. 24, a. 2, ad 2.
220. *ST* II-II, q. 27, a. 3, ad 1.
221. See *ST* II-II, q. 26, a. 2, ad 1.
222. See *ST* II-II, q. 26, a. 2.
223. *Sent. Ethic.*, lib. 9, l. 5, n. 4.

nas points out, superficial well-wishing does not bring about another's success. Nevertheless, benevolence serves as a necessary beginning from which friendship can develop.[224] From that foundation, a true friend then goes to *will* and to *do* what is good for the sake of his friend.[225] The chief outward acts or effects of charity outlined by Aquinas are beneficence, alms deeds, and fraternal correction.[226] These acts are not focused on merely helping another person to material sufficiency; their ultimate goal is to build up friendship in Christ, so that together both persons flourish spiritually. For this reason, fraternal correction is considered as an act of charity; it manifests one's care for a friend's soul and the common good, which is the soil of upright friendships.[227] In a similar way, contrary to those who believe that benefactors think they can "buy" their way into heaven by almsgiving, Aquinas replies: "He who gives alms [virtuously] does not intend to buy something spiritual through something material, for he knows that spiritual things infinitely surpass material things; rather, he intends to merit spiritual things through the love of charity."[228] Friends who intensely care for each other, Aquinas notes, manifest their care in zeal, a quasi-virtue that works to remove obstacles and to oppose whatever is opposed to the good of one's friend.[229] As Mother Teresa of Calcutta would often say, the work of the Missionaries of Charity is not that of an NGO or mere social workers: it is *charity* indeed, meant to bring all—benefactors, religious sisters, the destitute—closer to God.

The life and work of Mother Teresa, a canonized saint, illustrate the important role of the saints in habit formation: they serve as exemplars of the good habits that we develop.[230] Nicholas Austin

224. Ibid., n. 5.
225. *Sent. Ethic.*, lib. 9, l. 4, n. 2.
226. *ST* II-II, qq. 31–33.
227. *ST* II-II, q. 33, a. 1.
228. *ST* II-II, q. 32, a. 4, ad 2.
229. *ST* I-II, q. 28, a. 4.
230. Undoubtedly acquaintanceships and friendships of utility or pleasure with those who are vicious increase one's propensity to sin and vice. That topic deserves its own separate treatment.

notes that an exemplar cause may be understood as an idea "according to which something is formed" or "after whose likeness something is made."[231] Exemplary causality is radically distinct from efficient causality: a person comes to be formed by an exemplar, not by enduring some serendipitous event, but by voluntarily imitating the exemplar. Unlike the way a person is "formed" by nonvoluntary and partly voluntary habitual dispositions, exemplary causes are those that form us because we allow—and actively choose—them to form us. An exemplar instantiates an idea, not by existing separately in the world of ideas in the strong Platonic sense, but insofar as its own essence exists in a more perfect mode that may be grasped by another. The exemplar forms an agent by *in*forming the agent in some way, thereby *con*forming the agent to itself. The way to develop mastery is by imitating a master. Artists, for example, learn their craft by informing themselves about the works of the great masters and then by initially conforming themselves to the beautiful forms, structures, images, that the masters created. In the realm of morals, the virtuous man is the measure of upright action. Aristotle writes, "each state of character has its own ideas of the noble and the pleasant, and perhaps the good man differs from others most by seeing the truth in each class of things, being as it were the norm and measure of them."[232] In this way, what delights a virtuous person indicates what is truly good, for "those things are agreeable to the habit of virtue that are in fact good because the habit of moral virtue is defined by what is in accord with right reason," which entails that the virtuous person is "as it were the norm and measure of all that is to be done."[233] Aquinas beautifully comments that a virtuous person

231. Austin, *Aquinas on Virtue*, 77. See Aquinas, *De veritate*, q. 3, a. 1.

232. *Nicomachean Ethics* III.4, 1113a35.

233. *Sent. Ethic.*, lib. 3, l. 10, n. 7. He notes in lib. 10, l. 8, n. 13, that just as a healthy person can truly recognize what is sweet, as his taste is not damaged by sickness, so the virtuous man has correct judgment about what is good. Indeed, "virtue is the measure by which all human things should be judged, and a man is good inasmuch as he is virtuous; it follows that real pleasures are those which are seen as such by the virtuous, and genuinely delightful things are those which the virtuous man enjoys." See ibid., lib. 9, l. 4, n. 7.

delights in the actions of those who are both virtuous as well as their friends: his friend's virtuous actions make him especially happy, because it is a sign of the goodness of his friend, a goodness directly desired by friendship. In addition, a virtuous person is delighted with his friend's virtuous action, inasmuch as he seeks to study and imitate that good man who is his friend.[234]

Exemplar causality is tightly woven into the fabric of Aquinas's thought, and it is extended throughout his moral tapestry. As we saw at the beginning of this work, the medieval friar organizes his *Summa Theologiae* on a principle of exemplarity: God is the principle of his actions and the exemplar of all that is good (*ST* I); humans, made in the image of God, are principles of our actions (*ST* II); Christ, as God and man, is the principle and exemplar of how our acts are to become God-like (*ST* III).[235] Christ is the "primordial exemplar" of all goodness, and especially of all spiritual graces with which spiritual creatures are illuminated.[236] Hence, Christ "possesses exemplarily in himself the splendors of all the saints."[237] The saints, in their own way, are supreme examples of acquiring and developing Christ-like habits. Their diverse individuality leads to splendorous varieties in natural habits, in degrees of charity, and in expressions of infused virtues and Gifts of the Holy Spirit. Undoubtedly, on account of the imperfection of the current state of the world, "[the full] clarity of the saints is hidden from us in this life, just as is the darkness of the wicked."[238] Nevertheless, God works so that these paragons of virtue can shine like "cities on a hill" and be seen by many, so that they may guide us to our homeland in heaven.[239]

234. *Sent. Ethic.*, lib. 9, l. 10, n. 12.

235. See *ST* I-II, prol.

236. *Super I Cor.*, c. 11, l. 1, n. 583.

237. Ibid.

238. *Expositio super Iob ad litteram* [hereafter *Super Iob*], c. 20, l. 2 (Leon. ed., 304–6).

239. See Mt 5:14. Aquinas states that the "city" consists in the holy lives of the apostles strengthened by virtues (*Super Mt.*, c. 5, l. 5, n. 459). Friendship should flourish not just between individuals, but within a larger group, a "societate sanctorum" which is perfected in the next life. *Super Heb.*, c. 12, l. 4, n. 706: "In the glory of heaven there are two things that most powerfully gladden the good, namely, the fruition of deity and the common life

In considering the reasons why the Book of Job was written, Thomas explained the lofty role the saints play for us in our struggle to gain good habits and dissolve bad ones. He writes:

> God not only orders the lives of the just for their own good but also renders them visible for others. Now onlookers are not affected by it in the same way, for the good profit from having their example, whereas the evil if they are not corrected so that they are made good by their example, revolt against the lives of the saints they saw, either when they are tortured by envy or attempt to pervert the lives through false judgments.... Thus God wills that the lives of the just should be considered not only by the elect for their progress in salvation, but even by the wicked for the increase of their damnation, because from the lives of the saints the damnable perversity of the impious is manifested.[240]

Just as a person would be at fault if he purposely avoided medicine that he needed for his health, so intentionally to ignore the example of the saints is a culpable fault. According to Thomas, this fault is described in Jeremiah 6:16, "Thus says the LORD: 'Stand by the roads, and look, and ask for the ancient paths, where the good way is; and walk in it, and find rest for your souls.' But they said, 'We will not walk in it.'" Aquinas comments: "He establishes the fault, namely, disobedience towards the precept of imitating the saints."[241] Therefore, it is morally imperative for us to be shaped by the example of the saints; to develop the best habits, we must become habituated to imitating the virtuous.

To the extent that we ought to follow—and even obey—their examples, a "mentor dynamic" exists between us and Christ and his clear reflections, the saints.[242] But the saints are not only examples and mentors. They may be like stars in the sky that guide us to our heavenly homeland, but they are also friends who love us and offer

---

of the saints, for there is no joyful possession of good without a companion." See *Super Sent.*, lib. 4, d. 46, q. 1, a. 3, co.; *ST* II-II, q. 85, a. 3, ad 1; III, q. 80, a. 4.

240. *Super Iob*, c. 1, l. 2 (Leon. ed., 469–73).

241. *Super Ieremiam*, c. 6, l. 8.

242. Our need for expert mentors to guide us is explained in Robert Greene's *Mastery* (New York: Viking, 2012), 93–121.

us companionship and help along the way. "No longer do I call you servants, for the servant does not know what his master is doing; but I have called you friends," Christ said to his apostles.[243] Aquinas explains: a friend is "a guardian of the other's soul" such that "servitude is opposed to friendship," for servitude is a relation based on fear, whereas friendship is between free persons who freely choose to share their good with each other out of love.[244] Even now in heaven, the saints are our friends. Their charity impels them to share with us, through their intercession, the splendorous love, joy, peace, and grace they currently enjoy. As "cooperators of God" in conformity with divine providence, the saints exercise their charity and "greatly help their neighbors."[245] In this way, the saints serve as exemplar causes and models of good habits, and they also serve to strengthen good habits within us as secondary causes cooperating with the primary cause of our sanctification. The saints therefore show us that one of the best ways to develop good habits is to make friends with those who already enjoy them. Surely it is no coincidence that many saints were friends with each other: Christ and his apostles; Paul and Barnabas; Basil and Gregory; Perpetua and Felicity; Patrick and Brigid; Ignatius Loyola and Francis Xavier; and many, many others. By way of synthesis, Dante's journey through the *Divine Comedy* provides one of the most brilliant illustrations of how friendship helps us to develop and perfect good habits. The entire journey from the Inferno through Purgatory to Paradise is contextualized by friends helping Dante along the way, in a cycle of assistance, starting with the Virgin Mary, the "gracious lady," who summoned St. Lucy, the "enemy of every cruelty."[246] St. Lucy in turn called upon the beloved Beatrice, who called upon Virgil to assist Dante, "my friend, who is

243. Jn 5:15.

244. *Super Io.*, c. 15, l. 3, nn. 2011, 2014–15.

245. *Super Sent.*, lib. 4, d. 45, q. 3, a. 1, co. and ad 3. Also: "God wills that what the saints see Him to will should be fulfilled through the prayers of the saints" (a. 3, ad 5).

246. Dante, *The Inferno,* trans. Robert Hollander and Jean Hollander (New York: Doubleday, 2000), 2.94 and 2.100.

no friend of Fortune," as a poet-mentor.[247] Virgil then brings Dante through Hell, where bad acts and habits are punished, to Beatrice, who conducts him to St. Lucy; the saint introduces him to Purgatory, where he experiences the joyful yet painful perfection of habits, until he reaches the end of his journey and discovers the "Virgin Mother" who is a "noonday torch of charity," who sits amidst the Trinity and "the Love that moves the sun and all the other stars" with an eternal, circular motion.[248]

247. Ibid., 2.61.
248. Dante, *Paradiso*, 33.1, 33.10, and 33.145.

CONCLUSION

# The Habitual Readiness to Flourish

Having in hand his book, *The Principles of Psychology,* opened to the chapter on habits, William James penned the following inscription: "Sow an action, and you reap a habit; sow a habit and you reap a character; sow a character and you reap a destiny."[1] James's observation terrifically encapsulates the power of acquired habits. Above dispositions, skills, and intellectual virtues, human habits encompass the whole person, especially one's volition for a final end, and are therefore either good or evil. When good, habits are perfections measured according to the ends established by nature[2] or by supernature when infused by grace.[3] With habitual self-knowledge, a person will have some knowledge of what he is, what he ought to be, and the gap between the two. What a person needs, in addition to this knowledge, is the habitual readiness to flourish. Thomas Aquinas posits that human perfection requires habituation, and habituation requires change—but not just any change or "alterna-

1. Cited and discussed in cited earlier, p. 423n17 MacMullan, "The Flywheel of Society: Habit and Social Meliorism in the Pragmatist Tradition," in *A History of Habit* (ed. Sparrow and Hutchinson), 229–53, at 235.

2. See Aristotle, *Physics* VII.3, 246b27–29; version β quoted in Leunissen, *From Natural Character to Moral Virtue in Aristotle,* 112.

3. *ST* I-II, q. 55, aa. 1 and 4.

tion"; fully human habits are not neutral changes.[4] Human perfection requires deep change on a personal level, such that an individual becomes a "new" creature through the second nature provided by new habits. This is especially true in the supernatural realm, in which a person ought to put aside his previous life willingly in order to be gradually transformed by cooperating with sanctifying grace. In this way, we are more perfect in charity as children of God, ready to bear spiritual fruit.[5]

Dietrich von Hildebrand insightfully notes that the "willingness to change" is necessary for perfection.[6] Aquinas would agree, with this qualification: a *particular kind of change* is necessary, namely, change in the direction of our proper ends. A "readiness" to change is also necessary, because a state of perfection is achieved not by a mere wish for some good, nor by a momentary intention, but by an abiding and stable preparedness for whatever leads to or constitutes perfection. This stable state is a "habitual readiness," similar to the state of a healthy plant that is always ready to absorb necessary nutrients or grow or bear fruit when the conditions are right. Flourishing and bearing fruit is the subjective final end of a creature, the end toward which other ends are ordered as their perfection. Thus, a Thomistic view would prefer the term "habitual readiness to flourish" as a richer and more precise concept to supplement the notion of "readiness to change." Von Hildebrand's insight that this trait is a "high virtue" helps us see that it consists in a meta-habit that underlies all other habit development, for it is a habitual readiness to develop habits as needed.[7] In this way, a habitual readiness to flourish can be considered as the moral correlate to a habitual intellectual attitude of openness to truth, one that keeps a person's mind open to learning in any realm that he encounters.

Obstacles to good habit development can be ranked according to

4. See Leunissen, *From Natural Character to Moral Virtue in Aristotle*, 111–15.

5. See *ST* II-II, q. 24, a. 9.

6. Dietrich von Hildebrand, *Transformation in Christ* (New York: Longmans Green and Co., 1948), chap. 1.

7. Ibid., 23.

their susceptibility to change: material-individual nature is impossible to change without mutilation or self-destruction; fully-developed habits are very difficult to change, especially without grace; finally, mere acquired dispositions are easiest to change. As Aristotle states, it is easier to cure incontinence that derives from habituation than incontinence that is somehow innate, which would arise from one's material composition;[8] and human habits are more difficult to change than mere acquired dispositions, for habits are a sort of second nature that are rooted in one's choice whereas mere acquired dispositions are less rooted in the will or not at all. Rigidly clinging to dispositions that are innate, or to chosen nonvirtuous habits, or to acquired dispositions, constitutes, at base, a rejection of a habitual readiness to change in the direction of flourishing. Positive habit development aims at generating a lasting and perfective "second nature" that replaces the imperfect and unstable dispositions one has from birth, from poor choice, or from unordered exterior influences.[9] Even if one is born with inclinations toward the good, these too need to be changed, that is, perfected through habit. Innate seeds of virtue bear no moral advantage unless they are cultivated through good action, for "habit has the power to change these natural traits for the better or the worse."[10]

A limiting belief that stems from habits and dispositions is the conviction that these traits cannot change because they are natural to the individual. Habits and dispositions cause feelings, behaviors, and experiences that we associate with our identity. Often our inclinations feel natural, inseparable from the rest of our life. We then erroneously equate what is secondary with what is primary in ourselves. We conclude that these traits are *identical* with our very nature; we come to identify ourselves with them, and we label ourselves by them. "I am lazy," one person might say; "I am just attracted to that sort of person; that's the way I am," another might insist. But

8. *Nicomachean Ethics* VIII.10, 1152a28–32.

9. See Leunissen, *From Natural Character to Moral Virtue in Aristotle*, 117.

10. Ibid., 105, referencing Aristotle, *Politics* VII.13, 1332a35-b11.

our nature is what we are, and it is unchangeable.[11] To change what we are would make us into entirely different persons, and no one wants to change what he is essentially, for that would mean annihilation, and no one would prefer non-existence to existence.[12] This leads to the limiting belief that these habitual traits cannot change, for we do not attempt the impossible nor try to change the unchangeable.

To respond to this limiting belief, we may recall that habits are "principles of human acts," as Aquinas holds, but they exist as *secondary* principles, that is, modifications of the *primary* principles of movement: the natural powers of a person, especially one's soul.[13] Whatever causes movement in a primary way is that which is unmoved—it is the primary reality. In an individual, the primary reality and first cause is the essence of a thing, our form, our soul, which enacts our specific nature.[14] Habits, then, are accidents added to the substance of a person. In the words of Dunnington, habits are "*qualifications* of the self, and therefore must never be identified with the self."[15] Undeniably, some of our deep-seated inclinations can seem to be nature when, in reality, they are not natural but have been inculcated through nonvoluntary causes. Ancient Germanic tribes could have easily defended their thieving on the grounds that it was "natural" to them.[16] Such a defense would be flawed. Aquinas agrees that secondary precepts of the natural law "can be erased from the human heart, either by evil persuasions ... or by depraved customs and corrupt habits, as among some men theft was not considered sinful, and vices contrary to nature, as the Apostle states (*Rom.* 1:32)."[17] Once the emotions, mind, and will lose good habits and dispositions in certain matters, and instead are formed with evil hab-

11. Aristotle, *Nicomachean Ethics* V.7, 1134b25.

12. See Augustine, *On the Free Choice of the Will*, trans. Thomas Williams (Indianapolis, Ind.: Hackett, 1993), lib. III, sections 6–8 (83–87).

13. *ST* I-II, q. 49, prol.

14. Aristotle, *Physics* II.7, 198b1–4.

15. Dunnington, *Addiction and Virtue*, 183.

16. See *ST* I-II, q. 94, a. 4.

17. *ST* I-II, q. 94, a. 6.

its and dispositions in the same matters, a person comes to instinctively judge to be good what is, in reality, evil.[18] However, precisely because this "perversion" is contrary to the objective good of the person, it should be corrected.[19] The fact that it can be corrected means that it is not "natural" in the deepest meaning of the term. Indeed, changing one's disordered dispositions and habits may be difficult—but change is possible with grace.

To overcome the limiting false belief that our habits are aspects of our unchangeable nature, we must overcome our desire to avoid knowing our defects. Put more positively, to acquire a greater readiness to flourish we must more willingly accept the truth—about ourselves, about our nature, about our dispositions and habits. Intentional in genesis, fully voluntary habits also manifest intention. In the words of a philosopher of neuroscience, "insofar as we act from habit, then our actions are transparently revealing—that is to say, they are exposing. To be exposed is to be understood. And to be understood … is to be found out."[20] Habit is not only a window through which others can peer into our souls; it is also a mirror which reveals us to ourselves, if we are willing to look into it. What we do on account of habit reveals who we have made ourselves to be, for, even when they are seemingly spontaneous and automatic, "habitual modes of thought and behavior are themselves frequently expressions of intelligence and understanding."[21] The image of God becomes visible in the virtuous person, and the touch of evil is made manifest in a man with vice.

Related to the limiting belief described above is the limiting desire to avoid the difficulty involved in flourishing. Thomas helps us to realistically predict that eliminating old habits and acquiring new ones, or developing habits that are barely nascent, will chafe us. Because habits are like nature to us, they also give us pleasure,

18. See *ST* I-II, a. 94, a. 5, ad 1.
19. Ibid.
20. Noë, *Out of Our Heads*, 117.
21. Ibid., 119.

for what is connatural gives us pleasure as being suited to us and satisfying of deeply felt desire.[22] The more deeply rooted a habit is, the more it holds us as a second nature, the more it will pain us to change it—the more we will experience the loss of the habit as a sort of death to ourselves. Because habits are sources of stability and self-chosen identity, a person can experience a disturbing *instability* and perhaps even a sense of a loss-of-self when striving to replace one near-and-dear habit with another. Because habits are long-lasting, they are replaced only after much time and effort. They exact physical and emotional energy from the individual intent on changing them and they drain his patience and perseverance as he strives to achieve his habit-goal. Thus, to change our bad habits will almost necessarily entail suffering. Even when grace inundates our soul and we possess the infused virtues as active principles, the effects of disordered habits may remain within us for many seasons, much as tree that was uprooted in a storm may, when replanted, retain some crookedness while being bent back straight. A continuing inclination toward vice will reduce the feeling of ease and pleasure in exercising some particular virtue: instead of experiencing the smoothness of "flow," we may find ourselves for a while acting rightly in fits and starts.[23] Discouragement may darken our doorsteps: by the time we are more fully aware of ourselves and we want to develop good habits, we are already burdened by habits—from individual nature, childhood, choice, etc.—and these will not be easy to reshape.

Indeed, the habits we need to change the most are precisely those to which we cling most closely. Dunnington's description of devotion to addiction can be reformulated with respect to any disordered and deeply-rooted vicious habit, such as violence, avarice, sexual deviancy, or gluttony:

> Connatural evil habits show us that devotion to one consuming end and dependence on one overriding good can lead, and usually does lead, to

22. See *ST* I-II, q. 31, a. 1, ad 1.

23. *De virtutibus*, a. 10, ad 15; see *ST* I-II, q. 65, a. 3, ad 2.

> self-deception. For such devotion and dependence are almost always an attempt to bestow an order and integrity on our lives in such a way that we must ignore or deny the fundamental disorder and disunity of the self. Devotion to a disordered habit then becomes a strategy of control, a mode of fashioning oneself a self and structuring an identity, which is fundamentally dishonest because it is not in accord with our nature, and only God is ultimately in control of our lives. The habituation of vice is seductive because, by means of a connatural disorder, it promises to address the disorder and disunity of the self without requiring that we relinquish control over our own lives.... Thus the order and unity that we achieve in such a case is always illusory and requires that we deceive ourselves about who we are.[24]

We typically do not want to eradicate our (bad) habits, nor even adjust our littlest habitual behaviors, nor even admit their existence—for to do so would be like rebreaking a bone that, once broken, healed crookedly. Even worse, it would mean that we no longer identify ourselves with the limp that we have taken as the defining characteristic of our life.

If we do not desire to change our habits, how can we come to change our desire? If we misunderstand ourselves and reality so much that we mistake corruption for flourishing, and flourishing for death, how can we ever come to have the habitual readiness for authentic flourishing, which constitutes the foundation of all habit development? As a first move, we might recall that the soul moves itself: although it cannot change *what* it is, it can change *how* it is—it can gain new qualities that allow it to live in a new way. The soul can acquire good, perfective habits, and these are the beginning of virtue. Things that exist "by nature," such as the soul, have within themselves "a principle of motion [i.e., of change] and of stationariness [i.e., cessation of change]."[25] A characteristic of a natural entity is to change under its own impetus, as it were. Human nature remains the primary intrinsic principle that moves a person to live and act in accordance with reason, which is proper to each of us.[26] Even

24. See Dunnington, *Addiction and Virtue*, 176; substantially revised.
25. Aristotle, *Physics* II.1, 192b14.
26. Ibid., 192b20–23.

when a soul realizes that it cannot fully achieve its natural goodness on its own power, on account of the debilitating effects of vice, despair should be banished. God can move the soul to move itself freely by grace so that the individual truly flourishes, achieving the natural and supernatural good in accordance with his nature as a human and as an adopted child of God. Aquinas's reading of St. Paul gives some directions on this point. In his Epistle to the Ephesians, St. Paul taught that to be "renewed" and to "put on a new man" (*novum hominem*), you must first "put off your old man" (*veterem hominem*), "which belongs to your former way of life and is corrupt through deceitful lusts."[27]

Aquinas explains that the "old man" involves exterior and interior realities. The man enslaved to sin has grown "old" in sin, no longer possessing the "newness" of grace: his soul bears the character of sinfulness and he uses his body as a tool for sinning.[28] In other words, connatural bad habits constitute an "old" nature that needs to be renewed, not only through a change in exterior behavior, but especially through the acquisition and development of perfective interior habits. How does one "put off" the "old man" of connatural but disordered habits? According to Aquinas, St. Paul indicates that the "cause of renewal is the Holy Spirit," while simultaneously "the first principle of newness and renewal is Christ."[29] We might also add that God the Father, together with the Holy Spirit and Jesus Christ, is the cause of our spiritual and behavioral regeneration, for, in the words of St. Paul, "God has sent the Spirit of His Son into [our] hearts, crying, 'Abba, Father.'"[30] Aquinas explains that this cry, "Abba, Father," is not a loud and audible shout, but rather an exclamation of fervent affection that expresses our desire for union with

27. Eph 4:23, 24, 22, referencing the Vulgate.

28. *Super Eph.*, c. 4, l. 7, n. 240.

29. Ibid., nn. 243 and 245: "Dicit autem causam renovationis esse spiritum sanctum, qui habitat in mente nostra.... Quod sicut uniuscuiusque rei primum vetustatis principium fuit Adam, per quem peccatum in omnes intravit, ita principium primum novitatis et renovationis Christus est."

30. Gal 4:6.

the God who made us new creatures by adopting us as his sons and daughters.[31] Here, then, we find the root of how we are to come to desire a change of our most intransigent disordered habits: we cry out to God the Father for the grace of deep change, for "we are enflamed through our affections by the warmth of the Holy Spirit to desire God."[32] Through the spiritual adoption that takes place in baptism, we are given the gift of habitual sanctifying grace, which offers us union with the Trinity along with the principles by which we may be conformed to Christ in our behavior, namely, the infused virtues and the Gifts of the Holy Spirit. As for our own active contribution to habit development, St. Paul tells Christians: "put to death . . . what is earthly in you."[33] He specifies what we ought to slay within ourselves: habits, words, and deeds.[34] He targets evil habits, that is vices, including impurity, passion, evil desire, anger, wrath, and malice. As for evil words, he mentions slander, foul talk, and lying to one another. Finally, for deeds, he specifies fornication. "Put them all away," St. Paul commands, for they comprise the "old man with its practices," whereas our life is "hid with Christ in God."[35]

If putting away these evil habits and habitual behaviors seems impossible to us, Aquinas advises that we seek God's grace in prayer, as exemplified in Psalm 50 (51). There the Psalmist prays that sin be removed as well as sin's effects, namely, "pollution of the soul and disordered affect."[36] The prayer, "create a clean heart in me, O God," can be the prayer of everyone who desires to overcome a disfiguring habit that feels like second nature, for we ask that something be created "out of nothing," namely, a new second nature of grace.[37]

31. *Super Gal.*, c. 4, l. 3, n. 215.

32. Ibid.

33. Col 3:5. See *Super Col.*, c. 3, l. 1, n. 145: "In tantum ergo morimur culpae, inquantum vivificamur per gratiam."

34. For the following, see Col 3:5, 8, 9.

35. Col 3:9, 3. Aquinas notes that our life is hid with Christ in God because "he is the author of our life, and our life consists in knowing and loving him" (*Super Col.*, c. 3, l. 1, n. 143).

36. *Super Psalmo* 50, n. 6.

37. Ibid.

Christ's promise, "ask and you will receive, seek and you will find," is a promise that God will give us what we need most, and what truly benefits us, namely, Christ who is the source of our renewal and flourishing.[38] Thus we see that the habit of habit-change can be characterized as "readiness to change" or a "habitual readiness to flourish." This habit, especially when activated by grace, will incline a person to desire to change, and, trusting in God's goodness, we may have a sure hope that God will accomplish all necessary change with our cooperation: "He who began a good work in you will bring it to completion at the day of Jesus Christ."[39]

38. *Super Mt.*, c. 7, l. 1., n. 642, referencing Mt 7:7–9: "Ask, and it will be given you; seek, and you will find; knock, and it will be opened to you. For every one who asks receives, and he who seeks finds, and to him who knocks it will be opened. Or what man of you, if his son asks him for bread, will give him a stone?"

39. Phil 1:6. Aquinas comments that Paul's promise here is against the Pelagian heresy, which claims that the principle of every good work is from ourselves although its completion is from God. This is not true, Aquinas insists, for the principle of every good work within us is from God, the first mover of all. See *Super Philip.*, c. 1, l. 1, n. 12.

APPENDIX 1

# Habits Summary

Table A1-1. Habits Summary

| *Category of Habit* | | *Kind of Habit* | *Name* | *Example* |
|---|---|---|---|---|
| Supernatural entitative habit of grace | Supernatural operative habits | Divine: infused by God, activated by God moving man freely | Gifts of the Holy Spirit | Fear of the Lord, wisdom, understanding, counsel, knowledge, piety, fortitude (see Is 11:1–2) |
| | Supernatural operative habits | Divine: caused/ infused by God, activated by man | Theological virtues | Faith, hope, charity; infused cardinal virtues |
| Natural operative habits | | Human: caused by the individual | Acquired virtues (and vices): *habitus* | Prudence, temperance, fortitude, justice |

| *Category of Habit* | | *Kind of Habit* | *Name* | *Example* |
|---|---|---|---|---|
| Natural entitative habits | Subhuman: caused by genetics, physical composition | Imperfectly human: caused by experience | Acquired, nonvolitional habits | Post-traumatic stress disorder, speech accents acquired in childhood |
| | Subhuman: caused by the nature of the thing | Individual dispositions | Basic temperaments (sanguine, phlegmatic, choleric, melancholic) | |
| | | General human disposition; human instincts | Synderesis: natural habit toward pursuing good, avoiding evil; "God instinct"; "sharing" and "political" instincts | |
| Nominal habits | | Subhuman: a quality caused by something extrinsic to the individual | Exterior habit | A nun's habit (religious clothing) |

APPENDIX 2

# Thomistic Habit Loop

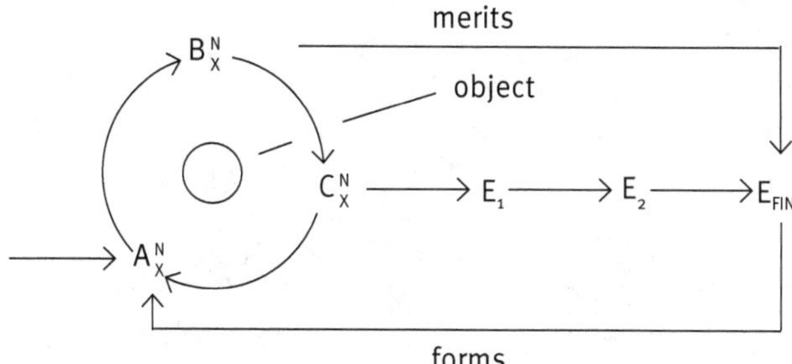


FIGURE A2-1. THOMISTIC HABIT LOOP

$A^X_N$: Antecedents: Interior (N), interior antecedents to a human behavior, especially habits and thoughts; Exterior (X), events and things that serve as stimuli or triggers antecedent to human behavior.

$B^N_X$: Behaviors: Interior (N), that is, all of the movements of perception, intellection and willing, and passions leading up to command; Exterior (X), *usus* properly speaking, the activation of motor powers.

$C^N_X$: Consequents: Interior (N), one's interior response, especially *fruition*, to one's behavior and interaction with one's environment; Exterior (X), that which changes in the world outside of the agent as a consequence of the agent's behavior.

O: material and formal object of the act

$E_1$, $E_2$: Proximate ends toward which the behavior is aimed.

$E_{FIN}$: The final end toward which the behavior (and person) is aimed.

# Selected Bibliography


#### THOMAS AQUINAS: LATIN TEXTS AND ENGLISH TRANSLATIONS

*Opera Omnia.* Parma: Typis Petri Fiaccadori, 1858–63.

*Opera omnia.* Rome: Marietti, 1926–65.

*Opera omnia, iussu Leonis XIII P. M. edita.* Rome: Commissio Leonina, 1882–.

*Scriptum super libros Sententiarum magistri Petri Lombardi.* 4 vols. Edited by R. P. Mandonnet and R. P. Maria Fabianus Moos. Paris: Lethielleux, 1929–47.

*Summa theologiae.* Rome: Editiones Paulinae, 1955.


All in-text translations are my own. The list below contains texts of Aquinas with the full Latin title, the Latin edition used in brackets, which provides section, paragraph, or line numbers when absent from the *Corpus Thomisticum*; also, any published English translation (ET) that I consulted. In-text citations of line numbers from the Leonine edition are denoted: (Leon. ed., ##).


*Collationes in decem praeceptis.* J.-P. Torrell, "Les 'Collationes in decem praeceptis' de saint Thomas d'Aquin. Édition critique avec introduction et notes." In Jean-Pierre Torrell, *Researches Thomasiennes: Études revues et augmentées*, 65–117. Bibliothèque Thomiste 52. Paris: J. Vrin, 2000.

*Commentaria in octo libros Physicorum Aristotelis.* [Leonine]

*Compendium theologiae ad fratrem Raynaldum.* [Leonine] (ET) *Compendium of Theology.* Translated by Cyril Vollert. St. Louis, Mo.: Herder, 1947.

*De ente et essentia.* [Leonine]

*De motu cordis ad magistrum Philippum de Castro Caeli.* [Leonine]

*De operationibus occultis naturae ad quendam militem ultramontanum.* [Leonine]

*De perfectione spiritualis vitae.* [Leonine] (ET) *The Religious State, the Episcopate and the Priestly Office.* Translated by John Procter. St. Louis, Mo.: Herder, 1902.

*De rationibus Fidei ad cantorem Antiochenum.* [Leonine]

*Expositio libri Boetii De ebdomadibus.* [Leonine]

*Expositio Posteriorum Analyticorum.* [Leonine]
*Expositio super Iob ad litteram.* [Leonine]
*Expositio super Isaiam ad litteram.* [Leonine]
*In duodecim libros Metaphysicorum Aristotelis expositio.* [Marietti]
*In librum Beati Dionysii De divinis nominibus expositio.* [Marietti]
*In psalmos Davidis expositio.* [Fiaccadori, Busa]
*In Symbolum Apostolorum, scilicet "Credo in Deum" expositio.* [Marietti]
*Liber de sortibus ad dominum Iacobum de Tonengo.* [Leonine]
*Liber de veritate catholicae Fidei contra errores infidelium seu Summa contra Gentiles.* [Marietti] (ET) *On the Truth of the Christian Faith.* Book I, translated by Anton C. Pegis; Volume/Book II, translated by James F. Anderson; Volume/Book III, Parts I and II translated by Vernon J. Bourke, 1956; Volume/Book IV, translated by Charles J. O'Neil, 1957. New York: Image, 1955–57.
*Quaestiones de quolibet.* [Leonine]
*Quaestiones disputate de malo.* [Leonine] (ET) *On Evil.* Edited by Brian Davies. Translated by Richard Regan. Oxford: Oxford University Press, 2003.
*Quaestiones disputate de potentia.* [Marietti]
*Quaestiones disputate de veritate.* [Leonine] (ET) *Truth.* Translated by Robert W. Mulligan, James V. McGlynn, and Robert W. Schmidt. 3 vols. Chicago: Henry Regnery, 1952–54.
*Quaestiones disputate de virtutibus.* [Marietti]
*Scriptum super libros Sententiarum magistri Petri Lombardi.* [Mand / Moos]
*Sentencia De sensu.* [Leonine]
*Sentencia libri De anima.* [Leonine] (ET) *The Soul.* Translated by John Patrick Rowan. St. Louis, Mo.: Herder, 1949.
*Sententia libri Ethicorum.* [Leonine] (ET) *Commentary on the Nicomachean Ethics.* Translated by C. I. Litzinger. Chicago: Henry Regnery, 1964.
*Summa theologiae.* [St. Paul] (ET) *Summa Theologica.* Translated by Fathers of the English Dominican Province. New York: Benziger, 1947.
*Super Boetium De Trinitate.* [Leonine]
*Super Epistolam ad Colossenses lectura.* [Marietti]
*Super Epistolam ad Ephesios lectura.* [Marietti] (ET) *Commentary on St. Paul's Epistle to the Ephesians.* Translated by Matthew L. Lamb. Albany, N.Y.: Magi Books, 1966.
*Super Epistolam ad Galatas lectura.* [Marietti] (ET) *Commentary on St. Paul's Epistle to the Galatians.* Translated by Fabian R. Larcher. Albany, N.Y.: Magi Books, 1966.
*Super Epistolam ad Hebraeos lectura.* [Marietti] (ET) *Commentary on the Epistle to the Hebrews.*
*Super Epistolam ad Philipenses lectura.* [Marietti]
*Super Epistolam ad Romanos lectura.* [Marietti]
*Super Evangelium S. Ioannis lectura.* [Marietti] (ET) *Commentary on the Gospel of*

*John*. Chapters 1–7 translated by James A. Weisheipl; chapters 8–21 translated by Fabian R. Larcher. Albany, N.Y.: Magi Books, 1998.

*Super Evangelium S. Matthaei lectura*. [Marietti]

*Super primam, secundam Epistolam ad Corinthios lectura*. [Marietti]

## SELECTED SCIENTIFIC BIBLIOGRAPHY

This section includes some of the more significant works of empirical science quoted in the text. Because this book synthesizes a large number of studies, for sake of space I do not quote any scientific articles below, and I omit references to much scientific literature; citations may be found in the body of the text. Furthermore, eschewing conventions of modern scientific literature, I choose to quote only one representative study though many others studies may support my conclusions.

Allport, Alan. "Attention and Control: Have We Been Asking the Wrong Questions? A Critical Review of Twenty-five Years." In *Attention and Performance XIV (Silver Jubilee Volume): Synergies in Experimental Psychology, Artificial Intelligence, and Cognitive Neuroscience*, edited by David E. Meyer and Sylvan Kornblum. Cambridge, Mass.: MIT Press, 1992.

American Psychiatric Association. *Diagnostic and Statistical Manual of Mental Disorders*. Fifth edition [*DSM-5*]. Washington, D.C.: American Psychiatric Association, 2013.

Anderson, Michael L. *After Phrenology: Neural Reuse and the Interactive Brain*. Cambridge, Mass.: MIT Press, 2015.

Anokhin, Peter K. *Biology and Neurophysiology of the Conditioned Reflex and Its Role in Adaptive Behavior*. Translated and edited by Samuel A. Corson. New York: Pergamon, 1974.

Asma, Stephen T. *On Monsters: An Unnatural History of Our Worst Fears*. Oxford: Oxford University Press, 2011.

Baer, John, James C. Kaufman, and Roy F. Baumeister, eds. *Are We Free? Psychology and Free Will*. Oxford: Oxford University Press, 2008.

Bandura, Albert. *Self-Efficacy: The Exercise of Control*. New York: Worth Publishers, 1997.

Barrows, Edward M. *Animal Behavior Desk Reference: A Dictionary of Animal Behavior, Ecology, and Evolution*. Third Edition. Boca Raton, Fla.: CRC Press, 2011.

Bauer, Isabelle M., and Roy F. Baumeister. "Self-Regulatory Strength." In *Handbook of Self-Regulation: Research, Theory, and Applications*, edited by Kathleen D. Vohs and Roy F. Baumeister. Second edition. London: The Guilford Press, 2013.

Bennett, M. R., and P. M. S. Hacker. *Philosophical Foundations of Neuroscience*. Malden, Mass.: Wiley-Blackwell, 2003.

Bentall, Richard P., and Aaron T. Beck. *Madness Explained: Psychosis and Human Nature*. London: Penguin, 2004.

Brooker, Robert J. *Genetics: Analysis and Principles*. Fourth edition. New York: McGraw Hill, 2012.

Bunge, Mario. *Causality and Modern Science*. Third revised edition. New York: Dover, 2011.

Carey, Nessa. *Junk DNA: A Journey Through the Dark Matter of the Genome*. New York: Columbia University Press, 2015.

Clark, W. R., and M. Grunstein. *Are We Hardwired? The Role of Genes in Human Behavior*. Oxford: Oxford University Press, 2000.

Corballis, Michael. *The Wandering Mind: What the Brain Does When You're Not Looking*. Chicago: University of Chicago Press, 2015.

Costa, Paul T., Jr., and Robert R. McCrae. "A Theoretical Context for Adult Temperament." In *Temperament in Context*, edited by Theodore D. Wachs and Geldolph A. Kohnstamm. Mahwah, N.J.: Lawrence Erlbaum Associates, 2001.

Coutlee, Christopher G., and Scott A. Huettel. "Rules, Rewards, and Responsibility: A Reinforcement Learning Approach to Action Control." In *Moral Psychology Volume 4: Free Will and Moral Responsibility*, edited by Walter Sinnott-Armstrong. Cambridge, Mass.: MIT Press, 2014.

Csikszentmihalyi, Mihaly. *Flow: The Psychology of Optimal Experience*. New York: Harper and Row, 1990.

Damasio, Anthony. *Descartes' Error: Emotion, Reason, and the Human Brain*. London: Penguin Books, 2005.

Dennett, Daniel. *Consciousness Explained*. Boston: Little, Brown, 1991.

Doidge, Norman. *The Brain That Changes Itself: Stories of Personal Triumph from the Frontiers of Brain Science*. London: Penguin, 2008.

Duhigg, Charles. *The Power of Habit: Why We Do What We Do, and How to Change*. London: Random House, 2013.

Eichenbaum, Howard, and Neal J. Cohen. *From Conditioning to Conscious Recollection: Memory Systems of the Brain*. New York: Oxford University Press, 2004.

Eliot, Lise. *What's Going on in There? How the Brain and Mind Develop in the First Five Years of Life*. New York: Bantam, 2000.

Eysenck, Michael W., and Mark T. Keane. *Cognitive Psychology: A Student's Handbook*. Seventh edition. New York: Psychology Press, 2015.

Fanu, James Le. *Why Us? How Science Rediscovered the Mystery of Ourselves*. London: HarperPress, 2010.

Garrett, Bob L. *Brain and Behavior: An Introduction to Biological Psychology*. Fourth edition. Los Angeles: SAGE Publications, 2014.

Gazzaniga, Michael. *The Mind's Past*. Berkeley, Calif.: University of California Press, 1998.

Glannon, Walter. *Brain, Body, and Mind: Neuroethics with a Human Face*. Oxford: Oxford University Press, 2013.

Glick, Thomas F., Steven Livesey, and Faith Wallis. *Medieval Science, Technology, and Medicine: An Encyclopedia*. London: Routledge, 2014.

Gluck, Mark A., Eduardo Mercado, and Catherine Myers. *Learning and Memory: From Brain to Behavior, International Edition*. Second edition. New York: Worth Publishers, 2013.

Gracia, Jorge J. E. *Individuality: An Essay on the Foundations of Metaphysics*. Albany: The State University of New York Press, 1988.

Haig, Brian D. *Investigating the Psychological World: Scientific Method in the Behavioral Sciences*. Cambridge, Mass.: MIT Press, 2014.

Hall, John E., and Arthur C. Guyton. *Guyton and Hall Textbook of Medical Physiology*. Thirteenth edition. Philadelphia: Saunders, 2015.

Hartwell, Leland. *Genetics: From Genes to Genomes*. Fourth edition. New York: McGraw Hill, 2011.

Hebb, D. O. *The Organization of Behavior: A Neuropsychological Theory*. Mahwah, N.J.: Lawrence Erlbaum Associates, 2002.

Henriques, Gregg. *A New Unified Theory of Psychology*. New York: Springer Science and Business Media, 2011.

Higgins, E. Tory. *Beyond Pleasure and Pain: How Motivation Works*. New York: Oxford University Press, 2014.

Hoffmann, Peter M. *Life's Ratchet*. New York: Basic Books, 2012.

Hofman, M. A., G. J. Boer, E. J. W. Van Someren, J. Verhaagen, D. F. Swaab, and A. J. G. D. Holtmaat, eds. *Plasticity in the Adult Brain: From Genes to Neurotherapy*. Boston: Elsevier, 2002.

Jablonka, Eva. *Evolution in Four Dimensions: Genetic, Epigenetic, Behavioral, and Symbolic Variation in the History of Life*. Revised edition. Cambridge, Mass.: Bradford, 2014.

James, William. *The Principles of Psychology*. 2 vols. New York: Henry Holt and Company, 1890.

John, Oliver P., Richard W. Robins, and Lawrence A. Pervin. *Handbook of Personality: Theory and Research*. London: The Guilford Press, 2010.

Joseph, Jay. *The Gene Illusion: Genetic Research in Psychiatry and Psychology Under the Microscope*. New York: Algora Publishing, 2004.

———. *The Missing Gene: Psychiatry, Heredity, and the Fruitless Search for Genes*. New York: Algora Publishing, 2006.

———. *The Trouble with Twin Studies: A Reassessment of Twin Research in the Social and Behavioral Sciences*. New York: Routledge, 2016.

Kagan, Jerome. *Galen's Prophecy: Temperament In Human Nature*. New York: Westview Press, 1997.

Kagan, Jerome, and Nancy C. Snidman. *The Long Shadow of Temperament*. Cambridge, Mass.: Belknap Press of Harvard University Press, 2004.

Kandel, Eric R., et al., eds. *Principles of Neural Science.* Fifth edition. New York: McGraw-Hill Education/Medical, 2012.

Kane, Robert. *The Oxford Handbook of Free Will.* Second edition. New York: Oxford University Press, 2011.

Kalter, Harold. *Teratology in the Twentieth Century Plus Ten.* New York: Springer Science and Media, 2010.

Kelly, Edward F., Adam Crabtree, and Paul Marshall. *Beyond Physicalism: Toward Reconciliation of Science and Spirituality.* Lanham, Md.: Rowman and Littlefield, 2015.

Kincaid, Harold, and Jacqueline A. Sullivan. *Classifying Psychopathology: Mental Kinds and Natural Kinds.* Cambridge, Mass.: MIT Press, 2014.

Leary, Mark R., and Rick H. Hoyle. *Handbook of Individual Differences in Social Behavior.* New York: Guilford Publications, 2013.

Leroi, Armand Marie. *Mutants: On the Form, Varieties and Errors of the Human Body.* London: Harper Perennial, 2005.

———. *The Lagoon: How Aristotle Invented Science.* London: Bloomsbury Circus, 2014.

Linden, David. *The Biology of Psychological Disorders.* New York: Palgrave Macmillan, 2011.

Little, Bertis. *Drugs and Pregnancy: A Handbook.* Boca Raton, Fla.: CRC Press, 2006.

Maltby, John, Liz Day, and Ann Macaskill. *Personality, Individual Differences and Intelligence.* Third edition. London: Pearson, 2013.

Miller, Christian B. *Character and Moral Psychology.* Oxford: Oxford University Press, 2014.

Moore, David S. *The Developing Genome: An Introduction to Behavioral Epigenetics.* Oxford: Oxford University Press, 2015.

Morasch, Katherine C., et al. "The Development of Cognitive Control from Infancy Through Childhood." In *The Oxford Handbook of Cognitive Psychology,* edited by Daniel Reisberg. Oxford: Oxford University Press, 2013.

Mullins, Andrew. "An Investigation into The Neural Substrates of Virtue to Determine the Key Place of Virtues in Human Moral Development." PhD diss., University of Notre Dame Australia, 2012.

Noback, Charles R., et al. *The Human Nervous System: Structure and Function.* New York: Springer Science and Business Media, 2005.

Noble, H.-D. *L'Amitié avec Dieu: essais sur la vie spirituelle d'après saint Thomas d'Aquin.* Paris: Desclée de Brouwer, 1932.

Noë, Alva. *Out of Our Heads: Why You Are Not Your Brain, and Other Lessons from the Biology of Consciousness.* New York: Hill and Wang, 2010.

Ochsner, Kevin, and Stephen M. Kosslyn. *The Oxford Handbook of Cognitive Neuroscience,* vol. 1: *Core Topics.* New York: Oxford University Press, 2013.

Panksepp, Jaak, and Lucy Biven. *The Archaeology of the Mind: Neuroevolutionary Origins of Human Emotions.* New York: W. W. Norton and Company, 2012.

Parrington, John. *The Deeper Genome: Why There Is More to the Human Genome than Meets the Eye.* Oxford: Oxford University Press, 2015.

Pavlov, Ivan P. *Conditioned Reflexes: An Investigation of the Physiological Activity of the Cerebral Cortex.* Mineola, N.Y.: Dover, 2003.

Pawlik, Kurt, and Mark R. Rosenzweig. *The International Handbook of Psychology.* London: SAGE, 2000.

Peterson, Christopher. *A Primer in Positive Psychology.* New York: Oxford University Press, 2006.

Peterson, Christopher, and Martin Seligman. *Character Strengths and Virtues: A Handbook and Classification.* Washington, D.C. / New York: American Psychological Association / Oxford University Press, 2004.

Porges, Stephen. *The Polyvagal Theory: Neurophysiological Foundations of Emotions, Attachment, Communication, and Self-Regulation.* New York: W. W. Norton and Company, 2011.

Rahmann, Hinrich, and Mathilde Rahmann. *The Neurobiological Basis of Memory and Behavior.* New York: Springer Science and Business Media, 2012.

Raine, Adrian. *The Anatomy of Violence: The Biological Roots of Crime.* New York: Vintage, 2014.

Rothschild, Babette. *The Body Remembers: The Psychophysiology of Trauma and Trauma Treatment.* New York: W. W. Norton and Company, 2000.

Rubin, Gretchen. *Better Than Before: Mastering the Habits of Our Everyday Lives.* New York: Crown, 2015.

Schacter, Daniel L., and Endel Tulving. *Memory Systems 1994.* Cambridge, Mass.: MIT Press, 1994.

Schwartz, Jeffrey M., and Rebecca Gladding. *You Are Not Your Brain: The 4-Step Solution for Changing Bad Habits, Ending Unhealthy Thinking, and Taking Control of Your Life.* New York: Penguin Books, 2011.

Seligman, Martin E. P. *Flourish: A Visionary New Understanding of Happiness and Well-Being.* New York: Atria Books, 2012.

Shettleworth, Sara J. *Cognition, Evolution, and Behavior.* Second edition. Oxford: Oxford University Press, 2009.

Siraisi, Nancy G. *Medieval and Early Renaissance Medicine: An Introduction to Knowledge and Practice.* Chicago: University of Chicago Press, 2009.

Strelau, Jan. *Temperament: A Psychological Perspective.* New York: Springer Science and Business Media, 1998.

Tallis, Raymond. *Aping Mankind.* Durham: Acumen, 2011.

Uttal, William R. *Mind and Brain: A Critical Appraisal of Cognitive Neuroscience.* Cambridge, Mass.: MIT Press, 2014.

Varela, Charles R. "Biological Structure and Embodied Human Agency: The Problem of Instinctivism." *Journal for the Theory of Social Behavior* 33, no. 1 (2003): 95–122.

Verplanken, Bas, ed. *The Psychology of Habit: Theory, Mechanisms, Change, and Contexts.* New York: Springer, 2018.

Vingerhoets, Ad. *Why Only Humans Weep: Unravelling the Mysteries of Tears*. Oxford: Oxford University Press, 2013.

Vohs, Kathleen D., and Roy F. Baumeister, eds. *Handbook of Self-Regulation: Research, Theory, and Applications*. Second edition. London: The Guilford Press, 2013.

Wachs, Theodore D., Robert R. McCrae, and Geldolph A. Kohnstamm. *Temperament in Context*. New York: Psychology Press, 2001.

Wickens, Andrew. *Introduction to Biopsychology*. Third edition. Essex: Pearson, 2009.

Wu, Wayne. *Attention*. London: Routledge, 2014.

Zeligs, Jenifer A. *Animal Training 101: The Complete and Practical Guide to the Art and Science of Behavior Modification*. Minneapolis, Minn.: Mill City Press, 2014.

## SELECTED PHILOSOPHICAL, THEOLOGICAL, AND OTHER SECONDARY SOURCES

This section includes some of the more significant philosophical, theological, and other secondary sources quoted in the text. Because this book synthesizes a large number of studies, for the sake of space I quote only a few articles below.

Adams, Robert Merrihew. *A Theory of Virtue: Excellence in Being for the Good*. Oxford: Oxford University Press, 2009.

Adler, Mortimer J. *The Difference of Man and the Difference It Makes*. New York: Fordham University Press, 1993.

Aertsen, Jan. *Nature and Creature: Thomas Aquinas's Way of Thought*. New York: Brill, 1988.

Agazzi, Evandro. "Some Epistemological Remarks: Unity of the Referent, Diversity of the Attributes, Specificity of the Scientific Approaches." In *Moral Behavior and Free Will: A Neurobiological and Philosophical Approach*, edited by Juan José Sanguineti et al. Vatican City: IF Press, 2011.

Amerini, Fabrizio. *Aquinas on the Beginning and End of Human Life*. Translated by Mark Henninger. Cambridge, Mass.: Harvard University Press, 2013.

Annas, Julia. *Intelligent Virtue*. Oxford: Oxford University Press, 2011.

Aristotle. *The Complete Works of Aristotle: The Revised Oxford Translation*. 2 vols. Edited by Jonathan Barnes. Princeton, N.J.: Princeton University Press, 1984.

Ashley, Benedict M. *The Way Toward Wisdom: An Interdisciplinary and Intercultural Introduction to Metaphysics*. Notre Dame, Ind.: University of Notre Dame Press, 2009.

Augustine of Hippo. *The Confessions*. Translated by Vernon J. Bourke. Washington, D.C.: The Catholic University of America Press, 1953.

Austin, Nicholas Owen. "Thomas Aquinas on the Four Causes of Temperance." PhD diss., Boston College, 2010.

Bacon, Francis. *New Organon*. Edited by Lisa Jardine and Michael Silverthorne. Cambridge: Cambridge University Press, 2003.

Baumann, Gabriel. "La surnaturalisation des actes humains par la grâce: L'enracinement ontologique des vertus morales infuses chez S. Thomas." STD diss., University of Fribourg, Switzerland, 2008.

Blankenhorn, Bernhard. *The Mystery of Union with God*. Washington, D.C.: The Catholic University of America Press, 2015.

Bourke, Vernon J. "The Role of Habitus in the Thomistic Metaphysics of Potency and Act." In *Essays in Thomism*, edited by Robert E. Brennan. New York: Sheed and Ward, 1942.

———. "The Background of Aquinas' Synderesis Principle." In *Graceful Reason*, edited by Lloyd P. Gerson. Toronto: PIMS, 1983.

Brennan, Robert Edward. *General Psychology: A Study of Man Based on St. Thomas Aquinas*. New York: Macmillan, 1952.

Budziszewski, J. *Commentary on Thomas Aquinas' Treatise on Law*. Cambridge: Cambridge University Press, 2014.

Bullet, Gabriel. *Vertus morales infuses et vertus morales acquises selon saint Thomas d'Aquin*. Fribourg: Editions universitaires de Fribourg, 1958.

Burnyeat, Myles F. "Aristotle on Learning to be Good." In *Essays on Aristotle's Ethics*, edited by Amelie Rorty. Los Angeles: University of California Press, 1980.

Butera, Giuseppe. "On Reason's Control of the Passions in Aquinas's Theory of Temperance." PhD diss., The Catholic University of America, 2001.

Carruthers, Mary. *The Craft of Thought: Meditation, Rhetoric, and the Making of Images, 400–1200*. Cambridge: Cambridge University Press, 2000.

———. *The Book of Memory: A Study of Memory in Medieval Culture*. Second edition. Cambridge: Cambridge University Press, 2008.

Cates, Diana Fritz. *Aquinas on the Emotions: A Religious-Ethical Inquiry*. Washington, D.C.: Georgetown University Press, 2010.

Cessario, Romanus. *Introduction to Moral Theology*. Washington, D.C.: The Catholic University of America Press, 2001.

———. *The Moral Virtues and Theological Ethics*. Second edition. Notre Dame, Ind.: University of Notre Dame Press, 2008.

Chase, Michael. "The Medieval Posterity of Simplicius' Commentary on the Categories: Thomas Aquinas and Al-Farabi." In *Medieval Commentaries on Aristotle's Categories*, edited by L. A. Newton. Leiden: Brill, 2008.

Churchland, Paul M. *Matter and Consciousness: A Contemporary Introduction to the Philosophy of Mind*. Second edition. Cambridge, Mass.: MIT Press, 1988.

———. *Neurophilosophy at Work*. Cambridge: Cambridge University Press, 2007.

Clark, Patrick M. *Perfection in Death: The Christological Dimension of Courage in Aquinas*. Washington, D.C.: The Catholic University America Press, 2015.

Clarke, William Norris. *The Creative Retrieval of Saint Thomas Aquinas: Essays in*

*Thomistic Philosophy, New and Old*. New York: Fordham University Press, 2009.

Cole, Basil. *Music and Morals: A Theological Appraisal of the Moral and Psychological Effects of Music*. New York: Alba House, 1993.

Corbin, Michel. *Le Chemin de la Thèologie chez Thomas D'Aquin*. Paris: Beauchesne, 1974.

Cordell, Hyacinth Marie. "Meriting for Others: The Potentially Salvific and Co-redemptive Value of Human Action." STL thesis, Pontifical Faculty of the Immaculate Conception, 2011.

Cory, Therese Scarpelli. *Aquinas on Human Self-Knowledge*. New York: Cambridge University Press, 2013.

Cottingham, John. "Cartesian Dualism: Theology, Metaphysics, and Science." In *The Cambridge Companion to Descartes*, edited by John Cottingham. Cambridge: Cambridge University Press, 1992.

Cunningham, Francis L. B. *The Indwelling of the Trinity: A Historico-Doctrinal Study of the Theory of St. Thomas Aquinas*. Dubuque, Iowa: The Priory Press, 1955.

Dauphinais, Michael, Barry David, and Matthew Levering. *Aquinas the Augustinian*. Washington, D.C.: The Catholic University of America Press, 2007.

Davies, Brian. *The Thought of Thomas Aquinas*. Oxford: Clarendon Press, 1992.

———. *Thomas Aquinas's Summa Theologiae: A Guide and Commentary*. Oxford: Oxford University Press, 2014.

Davies, Brian, and Eleonore Stump, eds. *The Oxford Handbook of Aquinas*. Oxford: Oxford University Press, 2014.

de Biran, Maine. *Influence de l'habitude sur la faculté de penser*. Paris: Chez Henrichs, 1802.

Decosimo, David. *Ethics as a Work of Charity: Thomas Aquinas and Pagan Virtue*. Stanford, Calif.: Stanford University Press, 2014.

Deferrari, Roy J. *A Latin-English Dictionary of St. Thomas Aquinas*. Washington, D.C.: The Catholic University of America Press, 1949.

De Haan, Daniel. "Thomistic Hylomorphism, Self-Determination, Neuroplasticity, and Grace: The Case of Addiction." *Proceedings of the American Catholic Philosophical Association* 85 (2012): 99–120.

———. "Moral Perception and the Function of the *Vis Cogitativa* in Thomas Aquinas's Doctrine of the Antecedent and Consequent Passions." *Documenti e studi sulla tradizione filosofica medievale* 25 (2014): 289–330.

———. "Perception and the *Vis Cogitativa*: A Thomistic Analysis of Aspectual, Actional, and Affectional Percepts." *American Catholic Philosophical Quarterly* 88, no. 3 (2014): 397–437.

———. "*Delectatio, gaudium, fruitio*: Three Kinds of Pleasure for Three Kinds of Knowledge in Thomas Aquinas." *Quaestio* 15 (2015): 543–52.

Dobson, Melanie L. *Health as a Virtue: Thomas Aquinas and the Practice of Habits of Health*. Eugene, Ore.: Pickwick, 2014.

Doig, James. *Aquinas's Philosophical Commentary on the "Ethics": A Historical Perspective.* Dordrecht: Kluwer, 2001.

Dougherty, M. V. *Aquinas's Disputed Questions on Evil: A Critical Guide.* Cambridge: Cambridge University Press, 2015.

Duckworth, Angela. *Grit: The Power of Passion and Perseverance.* New York: Scribner, 2016.

Dunnington, Kent. *Addiction and Virtue: Beyond the Models of Disease and Choice.* Downers Grove, Ill.: IVP Academic, 2011.

Eikeland, Olav. *The Ways of Aristotle: Aristotelian Phrónêsis, Aristotelian Philosophy of Dialogue, and Action Research.* New York: Peter Lang, 2008.

Elders, Leo. *The Philosophical Theology of St. Thomas Aquinas.* New York: Brill, 1990.

Emery, Gilles. "Trinity and Truth." In his *Trinity, Church, and the Human Person: Thomistic Essays.* Naples, Fla.: Ave Maria University, 2007.

———. "Trinitarian Theology as Spiritual Exercise in Augustine and Aquinas." In *Aquinas the Augustinian*, edited by Michael Dauphinais, Barry David, and Matthew Levering. Washington, D.C.: The Catholic University of America Press, 2007.

———. *The Trinitarian Theology of St. Thomas Aquinas.* New York: Oxford University Press, 2010.

Emery, Gilles, and Matthew Levering, eds. *Aristotle in Aquinas's Theology.* New York: Oxford University Press, 2015.

Faucher, Nicholas and Magali Roques, eds. *The Ontology, Psychology, and Axiology of Habits* (Habitus) *in Medieval Philosophy.* New York: Springer, 2018.

Floyd, Shawn. "Aquinas on Temperance." *The Modern Schoolman* 77, no. 1 (1999): 35–48.

Gallagher, David. "Thomas Aquinas on the Will as Rational Appetite." *Journal of the History of Philosophy* 29 (1991): 559–84.

———. "Person and Ethics in Thomas Aquinas." *Acta Philosophica* 4 (1995): 51–71.

Garrigou-Lagrange, Reginald. *The Three Ages of the Spiritual Life.* Translated by Sr. M. Timothea Doyle. St. Louis, Mo.: Herder, 1947.

———. *Reality: A Synthesis of Thomistic Thought.* Translated by Patrick Cummins. St. Louis, Mo.: Herder, 1950.

———. *Beatitude: A Commentary on St. Thomas' Theological Summa Ia IIa, qq. 1–54.* Translated by Patrick Cummins. St. Louis, Mo.: Herder, 1956.

Gavrilyuk, Paul L., and Sarah Coakley. *The Spiritual Senses: Perceiving God in Western Christianity.* Cambridge: Cambridge University Press, 2011.

Gherovici, Patricia. *Please Select Your Gender: From the Invention of Hysteria to the Democratizing of Transgenderism.* New York: Routledge, 2010.

Giertych, Wojciech. "Theological Ethics or Moral Theology?" In *Camminare nella Luce: Prospettive della teologia morale a partire da Veritatis splendor*, edited by L. Melina and J. Noriega. Rome: Lateran University Press, 2004.

———. "La pienezza della speranza Cristiana ne vuoto della modernità. Nicola Gori a colloquio con il teologo della Casa Pontificia sull'enciclica Spe Salvi." *L'Osservatore Romano* (December 31, 2007): 8.

———. "Virtue and Addiction." *Nova et Vetera* (English edition) 13, no. 3 (2015): 201–37.

Gilby, Thomas. *Poetic Experience*. New York: Sheed and Ward, 1934.

Gracia, Jorge J. E. *Individuality: An Essay on the Foundations of Metaphysics*. Albany: The State University of New York Press, 1988.

Harris, Murray J. *The Second Epistle to the Corinthians: A Commentary on the Greek Text*. University Park: Pennsylvania State University Press, 2005.

Harris, Sam. *The Moral Landscape*. New York: Random House, 2011.

Hendriks, Lambert. *Choosing from Love: The Concept of "Electio" in the Structure of the Human Act According to Thomas Aquinas*. Siena: Edizioni Cantagalli, 2010.

Hibbs, Thomas. *Virtue's Splendor: Wisdom, Prudence, and the Human Good*. New York: Fordham University Press, 2001.

Hoffmann, Tobias, Jörn Müller, and Matthias Perkams, eds. *Aquinas and the Nicomachean Ethics*. New York: Cambridge University Press, 2013.

Jansen, Katherine Ludwig. *The Making of the Magdalen: Preaching and Popular Devotion in the Later Middle Ages*. Princeton, N.J.: Princeton University Press, 2001.

Jaworski, William. *Philosophy of Mind: A Comprehensive Introduction*. Malden, Mass.: Wiley-Blackwell, 2011.

Jensen, Steven J. "Venial Sin and the Ultimate End." In *Aquinas's Disputed Questions on Evil: A Critical Guide*, edited by M. V. Dougherty. Cambridge: Cambridge University Press, 2016.

John Paul II. *Fides et Ratio*. Encyclical Letter. September 14, 1998. Available at www.vatican.va.

———. *Veritatis Splendor*. Encyclical Letter. August 6, 1993. Available at www.vatican.va.

Journet, Charles. *The Meaning of Evil*. Translated by Michael Barry. London: Geoffrey Chapman, 1963.

Kaczor, Christopher. "Thomas Aquinas's *Commentary on the Ethics*: Merely an Interpretation?" *American Catholic Philosophical Quarterly* 78, no. 3 (2004): 353–78.

Kahm, Nicholas. *Aquinas on Emotion's Participation in Reason*. Washington, D.C.: The Catholic University of America Press, 2019.

Keating, Daniel A. "Aquinas on 1 and 2 Corinthians: The Sacraments and Their Ministers." In *Aquinas on Scripture: An Introduction to His Biblical Commentaries*, edited by Thomas G. Weinandy, Daniel A. Keating, and John Yocum. London: T and T Clark, 2005.

Kemp, Kenneth W. "Just-War Theory and the Casuistry of Prima Facie Duties." PhD diss., University of Notre Dame, 1984.

Kerr, Fergus. *After Aquinas: Versions of Thomism*. Oxford: Blackwell, 2002.

Kim, Andrew. "Progress in the Good: A Defense of the Thomistic Unity Thesis." *Journal of Moral Theology* 3, no. 1 (2014): 147–74.

Klubertanz, George. *Habit and Virtue*. New York: Meredith, 1965.

Knobel, Angela. "Ends and Virtues." *Journal of Moral Theology* 3, no. 1 (2014): 105–17.

Knuuttila, Simo. *Emotions in Ancient and Medieval Philosophy*. Oxford: Clarendon Press, 2004.

Kraut, Richard. "Aristotle on Becoming Good: Habituation, Reflection, and Perception." In *The Oxford Handbook of Aristotle*, edited by Christopher Shields. Oxford: Oxford University Press, 2012.

Kretzmann, Norman, and Eleonore Stump, eds. *The Cambridge Companion to Aquinas*. Cambridge: Cambridge University Press, 1993.

Kwasniewski, Peter A. "The Ecstasy of Love in Thomas Aquinas." PhD diss., The Catholic University of America, 2002.

Levering, Matthew, and Michael Dauphinais. *Reading Romans with St. Thomas Aquinas*. Washington, D.C.: The Catholic University of America Press, 2012.

Lombardo, Nicholas E. *The Logic of Desire: Aquinas on Emotion*. Washington, D.C.: The Catholic University of America Press, 2010.

Long, Steven A. "Speculative Foundations of Moral Theology and the Causality of Grace." *Studies in Christian Ethics* 23, no. 4 (2010): 397–414.

———. "The Gifts of the Holy Spirit and Their Indispensability for the Christian Moral Life: Grace as Motus." *Nova et Vetera* (English edition) 11, no. 2 (2013): 357–73.

Luijten, Eric. *Sacramental Forgiveness as a Gift of God: Thomas Aquinas on the Sacrament of Penance*. Leuven: Peeters, 2003.

Mansini, Guy. "Aristotle and Aquinas's Theology of Charity in the Summa Theologiae." In *Aristotle in Aquinas's Theology*, edited by Gilles Emery and Matthew Levering. New York: Oxford University Press, 2015.

Marshall, Bruce. "Beatus vir: Aquinas, Romans 4, and the Role of 'Reckoning' in Justification." In *Reading Romans with Aquinas*, edited by Michael Dauphinais and Matthew Levering. Washington, D.C.: The Catholic University of America Press, 2012.

Martínez, Alejandro Néstor García, Mario Šilar, and José M. Torralba. *Natural Law: Historical, Systematic and Juridical Approaches*. Newcastle upon Tyne: Cambridge Scholars Publishing, 2009.

Mattison, William C. "Can Christians Possess the Acquired Cardinal Virtues?" *Theological Studies* 72 (2011): 558–85.

McCabe, Herbert. *God Matters*. London: A and C Black, 2005.

———. *God and Evil: In the Theology of St Thomas Aquinas*. London; New York: Bloomsbury Academic, 2010.

McCord Adams, Marilyn. "Genuine Agency, Somehow Shared? The Holy Spirit and Other Gifts." In *Oxford Studies in Medieval Philosophy*, vol. 1, edited by Robert Pasnau. Oxford: Oxford University Press, 2013.

McCormick, Patrick T. *Sin as Addiction*. New York: Paulist Press, 1989.

McGinnis, John. *Great Medieval Thinkers: Avicenna*. Oxford: Oxford University Press, 2010.

Merleau-Ponty, Maurice. *The Phenomenology of Perception*. Translated by Colin Smith. London: Routledge, 2002.

Merriell, Donald Juvenal, and The Pontifical Institute of Mediaeval Studies. *To the Image of the Trinity: A Study in the Development of Aquinas' Teaching*. Toronto: PIMS, 1990.

Miller, Joshua F. "On Whether Or Not Merleau-Ponty's Phenomenology of Lived Body Experience Can Enrich St. Thomas Aquinas's Integral Anthropology." PhD diss., Duquesne University, 2009.

Miner, Robert. *Thomas Aquinas on the Passions: A Study of Summa Theologiae, 1a2ae 22–48*. Cambridge: Cambridge University Press, 2011.

Newman, John Henry. *Historical Sketches*, vol. 2. London: Longmans, Green, and Co., 1906.

Osborne, Thomas M. *Human Action in Thomas Aquinas, John Duns Scotus, and William of Ockham*. Washington, D.C.: The Catholic University of America Press, 2014.

Pasnau, Robert. *Thomas Aquinas on Human Nature: A Philosophical Study of Summa Theologiae, 1a 75–89*. Cambridge: Cambridge University Press, 2008.

———, ed. *Oxford Studies in Medieval Philosophy*, vol. 1. Oxford: Oxford University Press, 2013.

Pieper, Josef. *The Four Cardinal Virtues*. Translated by Richard and Clara Winston. New York: Harcourt, Brace and World, 1965.

Pinckaers, Servais. "La structure de l'acte humain suivant S. Thomas." *Revue Thomiste* 55 (1955): 393–412.

———. "La vertu est tout autre chose qu'une habitude." *Nouvelle Revue Theologique* 82 (1960): 387–403. Translated as "Virtue Is Not a Habit" by Bernard Gilligan, *Cross Currents* 12 (1962): 65–81.

———. *The Sources of Christian Ethics*. Third edition. Translated by Mary Thomas Noble. Washington, D.C.: The Catholic University of America Press, 1995.

———. *The Pinckaers Reader: Renewing Thomistic Moral Theology*. Washington, D.C.: The Catholic University of America Press, 2005.

Pinsent, Andrew. *The Second-Person Perspective in Aquinas's Ethics: Virtues and Gifts*. London: Routledge, 2013.

Plato. *Complete Works*. Edited by John Cooper. Indianapolis, Ind.: Hackett, 1997.

Pope, Stephen J. *The Ethics of Aquinas*. Washington, D.C.: Georgetown University Press, 2002.

Porter, Jean. "Why Are the Habits Necessary? An Inquiry into Aquinas's Moral Psychology." In *Oxford Studies in Medieval Philosophy*, vol. 1. Edited by Robert Pasnau. Oxford: Oxford University Press, 2013.

Ramirez, Santiago Jacobus M. *Opera Omnia*. Edited by Victorino Rodriguez. Madrid: Instituto "Luis Vives" de Filosofia, 1972–73.

Ravaisson, Félix. *Of Habit*. Translated by Clare Carlisle and Mark Sinclair. London: Continuum, 2008.

Rivers, Kimberly A. *Preaching the Memory of Virtue and Vice: Memory, Images, and Preaching in the Late Middle Ages*. Turnhout: Brepols, 2010.

Rubenstein, Eric M. "Nominalism and the Disappearance of Individuation." *Logical Analysis and History of Philosophy* 5 (2002): 193–204.

Ryken, Leland, et al., eds. *The Dictionary of Biblical Imagery*. Downers Grove, Ill.: InterVarsity Press, 1998.

Scheeben, Matthias J. *A Manual of Catholic Theology: Based on Scheeben's 'Dogmatik'*, vol. 1. Edited by Joseph Wilhelm and Thomas B. Scannell. Cincinnati, Ohio: Benzinger, 1909.

———. *Nature and Grace*. Translated by Cyril Vollert. St. Louis, Mo.: Herder, 1954.

———. *The Glories of Divine Grace*. Rockford, Ill.: TAN Books, 2001.

Sherwin, Michael S. *By Knowledge & By Love: Charity and Knowledge in the Moral Theology of St. Thomas Aquinas*. Washington, D.C.: The Catholic University of America Press, 2005.

———. "Infused Virtue and the Effects of Acquired Vice: A Test Case for the Thomistic Theory of the Infused Cardinal Virtues." *The Thomist* 73 (2009): 29–52.

Simon, Yves. *The Definition of Moral Virtue*. Edited by Vukan Kuic. New York: Fordham University Press, 1986.

Simplicius. *On Aristotle, Categories 7–8*. Translated and edited by Barrie Fleet. London: A and C Black, 2014.

Simpson, J. A., and E. S. C. Weiner. *The Oxford English Dictionary*. Oxford: Oxford University Press, 1989.

Siwek, Paul. *The Philosophy of Evil*. New York: Ronald Press, 1950.

Skrzypczak, Edmund Robert. "Actual, Virtual, and Habitual Intention in St. Thomas Aquinas." Master's thesis, Loyola University Chicago, 1958. Available at http://ecommons.luc.edu/luc_theses/1701.

Smith, Lucy. "Temperance and the Modern Temper: Aristotle and Aquinas Revisited." In *Temperance Revisited: A Call for Restraint in Contemporary Australia*, edited by Phillip Elias. Sydney: Warrange College, 2009.

Smith, Vincent Edward. *The General Science of Nature*. Milwaukee, Wis.: Bruce Publishing Co., 1958.

Song, Miri. *Choosing Ethnic Identity*. Cambridge: Polity, 2003.

Sorabji, Richard. *Emotion and Peace of Mind: From Stoic Agitation to Christian Temptation*. Oxford: Oxford University Press, 2003.

Sparrow, Tom, and Adam Hutchinson, eds. *A History of Habit: From Aristotle to Bourdieu*. New York: Lexington Books, 2013.

Spezzano, Daria. *The Glory of God's Grace: Deification According to St. Thomas Aquinas*. Ave Maria, Fla.: Sapientia Press, 2015.

Stagnitta, Antonino. *Le Abitudini: "volàno" e perdizione dei popoli.* Naples: Editrice Domenicana Italiana, 2005.

Staudt, R. Jared. "Substantial Union with God in Matthias Scheeben." *Nova et Vetera* (English edition) 11, no. 2 (2013): 515–36.

Stern, David S. *Essays on Hegel's Philosophy of Subjective Spirit: Imaginative Transformation and Ethical Action in Literature.* Albany: The State University of New York Press, 2013.

Swanton, Christine. *Virtue Ethics: A Pluralistic View.* Oxford: Oxford University Press, 2005.

Sweeney, Eileen C. "Aquinas on the Seven Deadly Sins: Tradition and Innovation." In *Sin in Medieval and Early Modern Culture: The Tradition of the Seven Deadly Sins,* edited by Richard G. Newhauser and Susan Janet Ridyard. Rochester, N.Y.: Boydell and Brewer, 2012.

Taylor, Thomas, *Works of Aristotle Translated from the Greek with Copious Elucidations from the Best of His Greek Commentators,* vol. 1. London: Robert Wilkes, 1812.

Thero, Daniel P. *Understanding Moral Weakness.* New York: Rodopi, 2006.

Thompson, Evan. *Mind in Life.* Cambridge, Mass.: Belknap Press, 2007.

Titus, Craig Steven. *Resilience and the Virtue of Fortitude: Aquinas in Dialogue with the Psychosocial Sciences.* Washington, D.C.: The Catholic University of America Press, 2006.

———. "The Christian Difference of Habitus in Virtuous Acts, Dispositions, and Norms." *Edification* 6, no. 1 (2012): 38–42.

Torrell, Jean-Pierre. *Aquinas's "Summa": Background, Structure, and Reception.* Washington, D.C.: The Catholic University of America Press, 2005.

———. *Saint Thomas Aquinas: Person and His Work,* vol. 1. Revised edition. Washington, D.C.: The Catholic University of America Press, 2005.

Velde, Rudi Te. *Participation and Substantiality in Thomas Aquinas.* New York: Brill, 1995.

———. *Aquinas on God: The "Divine Science" of the Summa Theologiae.* Burlington, Vt.: Ashgate, 2006.

Wallace, William A. *The Role of Demonstration in Moral Science.* Washington, D.C.: The Thomist Press, 1962.

Wawrykow, Joseph P. *God's Grace and Human Action: "Merit" in the Theology of Thomas Aquinas.* Notre Dame, Ind.: University of Notre Dame Press, 1996.

Wegner, Daniel M. *The Illusion of Conscious Will.* Cambridge, Mass.: MIT Press, 2002.

Weinandy, Thomas Gerard, Daniel A. Keating, and John Yocum. *Aquinas on Scripture: An Introduction to His Biblical Commentaries.* London: A and C Black, 2005.

Westberg, Daniel. *Right Practical Reason: Aristotle, Action, and Prudence in Aquinas.* Oxford: Clarendon Press, 1994.

Wiley, Tatha. *Original Sin: Origins, Developments, Contemporary Meanings*. New York: Paulist Press, 2002.

Wippel, John F. *The Metaphysical Thought of Thomas Aquinas: From Finite Being to Uncreated Being*. Washington, D.C.: The Catholic University of America Press, 2000.

———. "Thomas Aquinas on Our Knowledge of God and the Axiom That Every Agent Produces Something Like Itself." In his *Metaphysical Themes in Thomas Aquinas II*. Washington, D.C.: The Catholic University of America Press, 2007.

# Index of Names

Kielhofner, Gary, 329n19, 329n21

# Subject Index

ALSO IN THE
THOMISTIC RESSOURCEMENT SERIES

Series Editors: Matthew Levering
Thomas Joseph White, OP

*Reading Job with St. Thomas Aquinas*
Edited by Matthew Levering, Piotr Roszak, and Jörgen Vijgen

*To Stir a Restless Heart*
*Thomas Aquinas and Henri de Lubac on Nature, Grace, and the Desire for God*
Jacob W. Wood

*Aquinas on Transubstantiation*
*The Real Presence of Christ in the Eucharist*
Reinhard Hütter

*Bound for Beatitude*
*A Thomistic Study in Eschatology and Ethics*
Reinhard Hütter

*Analogy after Aquinas*
*Logical Problems, Thomistic Answers*
Domenic D'Ettore

*The Metaphysical Foundations of Love*
*Aquinas on Participation, Unity, and Union*
Anthony T. Flood

*The Cleansing of the Heart*
*The Sacraments as Instrumental Causes in the Thomistic Tradition*
Reginald M. Lynch, OP

*Habits and Holiness: Ethics, Theology, and Biopsychology* was designed in
Arno and composed by Kachergis Book Design of Pittsboro, North Carolina.
It was printed on 60-pound Natural Eggshell Cream and bound by
McNaughton & Gunn of Saline, Michigan.